D0048639

THE**GREEN**GUIDE
French Riviera

Sanary-sur-Mer © G. Labriet / Photononstop

MICHELIN

THEGREENGUIDE **FRENCH RIVIERA**

Editorial Director	Cynthia Clayton Ochterbeck
Editorial Manager	Gwen Cannon
Contributing Writers	Judy Edelhoff, Françoise Klingen, Tony Marsden, Anne McDowall
Production Manager	Natasha G. George
Cartography	Peter Wrenn
Photo Researcher	Nicole D. Jordan
Interior Design	Chris Bell
Layout	Nicole D. Jordan, Natasha G. George
Cover Design	Chris Bell, Christelle Le Déan
Cover Layout	Michelin Travel Partner, Natasha G. George

Contact Us

Michelin Travel and Lifestyle North America
One Parkway South
Greenville, SC 29615
USA
travel.lifestyle@us.michelin.com
www.michelintravel.com

Michelin Travel Partner
Hannay House
39 Clarendon Road
Watford, Herts WD17 1JA
UK
&01923 205240
travelpubsales@uk.michelin.com
www.ViaMichelin.com

Special Sales

For information regarding bulk sales,
customized editions and premium sales,
please contact us at:
travel.lifestyle@us.michelin.com
www.michelintravel.com

HOW TO USE THIS GUIDE

PLANNING YOUR TRIP

The blue-tabbed PLANNING YOUR TRIP section at the front of the guide gives you **ideas for your trip** and **practical information** to help you organise it. You'll find tours, practical information, a host of outdoor activities, a calendar of events, information on shopping, sightseeing, kids' activities and more.

INTRODUCTION

The orange-tabbed INTRODUCTION section explores the French Riviera's **Nature** and geology. The **History** section spans 1500 BC through the Revolution to the present. The **Art and Culture** section covers architecture, art, literature and music, while the **Region Today** delves into modern-day French Riviera.

DISCOVERING

The green-tabbed DISCOVERING section describes Principal Sights by region, featuring the most interesting local **Sights**, **Walking Tours**, nearby **Excursions**, and detailed **Driving Tours**. Admission prices shown are normally for a single adult.

ADDRESSES

We've selected the best hotels, restaurants, cafés, shops, nightlife and entertainment to fit all budgets. See the Legend on the cover flap for an explanation of the price categories. See the back of the guide for an index of where to find hotels and restaurants.

Sidebars

Throughout the guide you will find blue, peach and green-colored text boxes with lively anecdotes, detailed history and background information.

😊 A Bit of Advice 😊

Green advice boxes found in this guide contain practical tips and handy information relevant to your visit or to a sight in the Discovering section.

STAR RATINGS★★★

Michelin has given star ratings for more than 100 years. If you're pressed for time, we recommend you visit the ★★★, or ★★ sights first:

★★★   **Highly recommended**
★★   **Recommended**
★   **Interesting**

MAPS

- Principal Sights map.
- Regional maps.
- Maps for major cities and villages.
- Local tour maps.

All maps in this guide are oriented north, unless otherwise indicated by a directional arrow. The term "Local Map" refers to a map within the chapter or Tourism Region. A complete list of the maps found in the guide appears at the back of this book.

©Romain Cintract/Hemis/Photolibrary

© Camille Moirenc / hemis.fr

PLANNING YOUR TRIP

INTRODUCTION TO THE FRENCH RIVIERA

CONTENTS

© Peter Adams / age fotostock

DISCOVERING THE FRENCH RIVIERA

Welcome to the French Riviera

The French Riviera, or la Côte d'Azur, stretches along the Mediterranean coast in southeastern France between the Italian border and the Rhône Valley. It's an amazingly diverse region of sunny beaches and prestigious ports, as well as dramatic mountain peaks and medieval hilltowns perched atop secluded escarpments and headlands. Aside from its natural beauty, visitors will also discover a rich artistic, cultural and architectural heritage from Roman times and the Middle Ages through the Belle Époque to the present day.

Îles des Embiez

©Camille Moirenc/Hemis/Photoshot

TOULON & AROUND (pp98–125)

The oft-overlooked city of Toulon at the western edge of the French Riviera is well worth a stop for its historic harbour, naval museum and restored old town. The surrounding villages produce some of the finest wines and olive oils in the south, while the region's coastal paths and isolated beaches offer a sunny retreat from the summer crowds, especially around the Îles des Embiez.

HYÈRES, THE GOLDEN ISLANDS AND THE MASSIF DES MAURES (pp126–169)

For those who dream of unspoiled islands, sandy beaches and chic resorts, this Eden-like stretch of the Riviera won't disappoint. The natural beauty of the Maures Massif and the Golden Islands has been fiercely protected from over-development. And even after the summer crowds of St-Tropez and Hyères have disappeared, the Provençal-style fishing villages, tropical parks and gardens, eccentric villas and Belle Époque palaces make for pleasant sightseeing.

Cotignac

S. Sauvignier/MICHELIN

INLAND PROVENCE (pp170–195)

Far from the showy splendour and busloads of tourists found at the coastal resorts, the villages, valleys and prehistoric monuments of Inland Provence are given to peaceful exploration. The 12C Abbaye du Thoronet is worth a detour of its own, while wine connoisseurs won't want to miss the organic vineyards around Brignoles. Aups and Cotignac remain two of the most charming spots in the region, along with the cave dwellings of Villecroze.

Île de Porquerolles

©Luca Chiartano/Dreamstime.com

Esterel Massif viewed from Fréjus

©Guillaume Besnard/Fotolia.com

FRÉJUS & THE ESTEREL MASSIF *(pp196–225)*

The most Provençal area of the French Riviera is known for its pristine forests and red rock hills of the Massif de l'Esterel. The lively twinned towns of Fréjus and St-Raphaël attract visitors who prefer a more discreet resort experience at its beaches. History *aficionados* won't want to miss the impressive Gallo-Roman remains found in and around Fréjus or the archaeology museum in St-Raphaël.

CANNES & THE GRASSE REGION *(pp226–292)*

Don't forget to pack your swim suit and sunglasses. The most popular beaches on the French Riviera are found in the dynamic resort towns of Cannes, Antibes and Juan-les-Pins. Farther inland the hills are home to the world-famous perfume-making town of Grasse and its surrounding perched villages. The fashionable palace hotels and private yachts are a surprising contrast to the Provençal-style villages with their shady squares and ancient churches, making the region an ideal place to experience both worlds. And if you're interested in exploring the area's exceptional artistic heritage, don't miss the cutting-edge galleries and museums of Mougins, Vallauris and Antibes.

NICE, THE RIVIERA & MONACO *(pp293–357)*

This glamorous stretch of the Riviera features the glittering Principality of Monaco, with its Belle Époque casino and oceanographic institute; the bustling city of Nice, known for its colourful Carnival parades, old town market, and world-class art collections; and Menton, with its exotic gardens and Cocteau museum. While driving between them on the scenic corniche roads, visitors will find more tranquil coastal paths along Cap Ferrat and Cap d'Ail, as well as amazing views from the perched villages of Èze and Ste-Agnès, Europe's highest coastal village.

THE PRE-ALPS OF NICE *(pp358–397)*

The most dramatic landscape on the French Riviera is found in the hinterlands above Nice, where the sunny Mediterranean meets the snow-covered Alps. The rocky peaks and deep river valleys attract hikers, rock climbers, rafters and mountain bikers in summer, as well as skiers in winter. The Mercantour National Park, which shares a border with Italy, offers glimpses of rare flora and fauna, as well as prehistoric engravings in the Vallée des Merveilles. Sturdy shoes and reliable maps are a must.

Rock cliffs of La Colmiane

©Michel Megret/Robert Harding

Promenade des Anglais and Hôtel Negresco, Nice
©Romain Cintract/Hemis/Photolibrary

Michelin Driving Tours

1 VAR COASTLINE AND THE GOLDEN ISLANDS

Round trip of 146mi/235km
starting from Toulon

The city of Toulon should be visited in the local tradition, in other words at a leisurely pace, taking time to explore the intricate streets shaded by centuries-old plane trees. After dropping by the lively marché Lafayette and choosing a few fresh vegetables and mouthwatering local treats, set out to discover "the most beautiful harbour" on the Riviera, passing by Pointe du Fort Balaguier and Cap Sicié. Nestled between land and sea, Sanary and Bandol, and their islands of Bendor and Embiez, will seduce you with their heavenly setting. Farther on, the perched villages of Le Castellet, Beausset and Evenos compose the perfect picture of Provençal bliss. Next, admire the harbour from atop Mont Faron. Continue to the bird sanctuary at La Londe for an escape to the tropics. Treat yourself to a stay on the gorgeous islands of Port-Cros and Porquerolles; the underwater sightseeing trail offers incomparable views of the sea's fauna and flora for divers and snorkellers. A tour of the Mine de Cap-Garonne at Le Pradet is the perfect way to round off your outing.

2 LE HAUT VAR

Round trip of 152mi/245km
starting from Draguignan

This itinerary will take you across the upper stretches of the Var Valley, with its rolling wooded countryside dotted with old abbeys and remarkable sites: Tourtour nestling on the crest of a hill overlooking olive groves; Cotignac perched precariously on a cliff; Villecroze and Seillans enhanced by hardened volcanic ash rock formations; Entrecasteaux, whose château is graced by gardens attributed to Le Nôtre. You'll be surprised by the diversity of the villages and towns you encounter. Some clearly enjoy perpetuating local tradition while others promote a more dynamic artisan culture. Don't miss the colourful markets offering truffles, goat's cheese or olives, depending on the season, and the restaurants, where you will be served tasty regional cuisine pleasantly seasoned with aromatic herbs.

3 LE MASSIF DES MAURES

Round trip of 171mi/275km
starting from Fréjus

Far away from the coast and its bustling crowd, this tour will take you through refreshingly cool forests of cork oak and the pretty Gratteloup arboretum, where eucalyptus, chestnut, maple, cedar and juniper trees exude their intoxicating aroma. Visit the superb Domaine du Rayol, laid out at the turn of the 20C, and discover regional arts and crafts: the cork industry in Gonfaron; *marrons glacés* in Collobrières; pipe-making and carpet weaving in Cogolin. The hill villages of Ramatuelle, Grimaud and Gassin command **panoramic views** of the coast, as do the Moulins de Paillas. Before taking a swim in one of the many sheltered rocky inlets, you may want to settle on the terrace of the Sénéquier in St-Tropez alongside the rich and famous or you may prefer to browse among the market stalls in the old port in the hope of chancing upon a fake Picasso.

4 MASSIF DE L'ESTEREL AND THE FAYENCE REGION

Round trip of 177mi/285km
starting from Cannes

Whatever the season, this itinerary will prove an enchanting experience on many counts: the rich, luxuriant vegetation, the chirping of the cicadas, the delicately fragrant mimosa blossoms, the warm embrace of the sun and the red rock of the Esterel heights. Running between La Napoule and Agay, the Corniche d'Or offers stunning **views** of the sea.

You'll find it hard to resist the charms of St-Raphaël, a lively seaside resort, and Fréjus, with its exceptional Roman and military heritage, not to mention Fréjus-Plage, which boasts the longest sandy beach on the Riviera. Farther inland, the Fayence area will introduce you to a host of perched villages huddled on mountain slopes, dominated by vestiges of their medieval citadels: Caillan, Fayence, Tourrettes, Seillan, Tanneron and Auribeau-sur-Siagne.

5 FRAGRANCES AND COLOURS OF THE PRE-ALPS

*Round trip of 134mi/215km
starting from Grasse*
The Pre-Alps of Provence, extending to the foot of the Alpine range and cut across by steep ravines, offer a delightful combination of colours and fragrances, where the heady smells of olive and cypress trees vie with the more subtle scent of rose, jasmin, oleander and violet. Grasse's reputation is built on flowers, so don't miss the International Museum of Perfume and the different *parfumeries* explaining the secrets of the trade. The entrance to the Gorges du Loup is the perfect place to stop and admire the hill village of Gourdon, jealously guarding its abyss, and the Caussols Plateau, a curiously barren stretch of land riddled with chasms. After observing the geological formations in the caves of St-Vallier and St-Cézaire, continue to St-Paul-de-Vence, a typical medieval village known for its crafts and world-class art gallery, and to the delightful hamlet of Tourrettes-sur-Loup, where terraced violet fields have been cultivated from generation to generation. The Baou of St-Jeannet dominating the Var River is a sheer rocky cliff popular among seasoned climbers. Lastly, the coastal road stretching between Cagnes-sur-Mer and Antibes offers pretty **views** of the Baie des Anges and access to a number of contemporary art museums.

6 ARRIÈRE-PAYS NIÇOIS

*Round trip of 168mi/270km
starting from Nice*
This driving tour will provide you with a fascinating selection of natural sites and architectural riches: quaint perched villages, chapels decorated by famous painters or unknown artists from the Middle Ages, steep cliffs overlooking gorges echoing with the swirling of crystal-clear waters and lush forests rustling with the sounds of local fauna.

Running alongside the lower Var Valley, bordered to the west by the Baou of St Jeannet, approach the heights to the rear of Nice, dominated by Mont Chauve. After driving through Aspremont, Levens and Duranus, take an hour or two to admire the breathtaking Vésubie Gorges. From there, brace yourself for the long series of steep hairpin bends leading up to the Madone d'Utelle sanctuary, a popular place of pilgrimage, and the nearby belvedere commanding a splendid **panorama** of the Alpes-Maritimes and the Mediterranean. Proceeding upstream along the Vésubie River towards Col de Turini, gateway to the vast Forêt de Turini, stop at Bollène-Vésubie, precariously nestling on a mountain slope.

On reaching L'Authion, go round to Pointe des Trois-Communes and feast your eyes on the sweeping landscape. Continue towards the Gorges of Piaon. After the curious Notre-Dame-de-la-Menour Chapel, with its two-storey Renaissance façade, head for Sospel, springing from its verdant setting, and visit its fortified bridge and imposing Maginot Line fort. Drive through several passes before rejoining Lucéram Valley, famed for its heritage museums and religious artworks. Finally, three belvederes, each home to a small village, Berre, Falicon and Tourrettes, will complete your tour of the Nice hinterland.

7 THE CORNICHES OF THE RIVIERA

Round trip of 155.5mi/250km starting from Nice.

If you have seen Hitchcock's thriller *To Catch a Thief,* then you will know that it is advisable to hug the road winding its way between Nice and Monte Carlo as closely as possible. This route, which features a series of vertiginous viewpoints, goes past some of the prettiest spots on the Côte d'Azur. Set out from Villefranche, famous not only for its Chapelle St-Pierre decorated by Jean Cocteau, but also for its pretty harbour and succulent seafood dishes. Follow the Grande Corniche up to Roquebrune, with forays downhill to Beaulieu (Villa Kérylos), St-Jean-Cap-Ferrat (Villa Rothschild and Villa Santo Sospir) and Èze, the muse of philosopher Frédéric Nietzsche, clinging to its rocky spur, where a tour of artists' workshops can be pleasantly rounded off by a visit to the Jardin Exotique.

Enjoy the **view** from the Vistaero before descending towards Roquebrune with its medieval castle and venerable olive tree believed to be more than 1,000 years old.

After Menton and the Cocteau Museum, the road will take you through the perched villages of Ste-Agnès, Europe's highest coastal village, Peille and Peillon, where steep alleyways *(calades)* lead to chapels adorned with fine frescoes.

When and Where to Go

WHEN TO GO
SEASONS

The **tourist season** on the French Riviera lasts virtually all year round. **Winter months** are characterised by a mild, sunny climate and are ideal for those seeking to avoid the peak tourist season. However, some hotels, restaurants and attractions are closed between November and February. **Spring** and **autumn** can sometimes bring heavy rainfall and the infamous *mistral* wind, but neither overshadows the magnificent display of flora in full bloom at these times.

Summer is of course the best season for swimming and working up a suntan, not to mention taking part in the energetic nightlife. Traffic on the coast is, however, always very congested during this period; it can also be difficult to find accommodation, so it's advisable to book well in advance, particularly in August.

WEATHER FORECASTS

Cost is 1.35€ a call + 0.34€/min for:
Recorded report

♦ for the Alpes-Maritimes:
   ℘08 99 71 02 06
♦ for the Var: ℘08 99 71 02 83
♦ for conditions at sea:
   ℘08 99 71 08 08
♦ for the mountains (snow, avalanches):
   ℘08 92 68 10 20

Online weather reports
♦ www.meteo.fr

Road conditions
♦ www.bison-fute.equipement. gouv.fr
♦ www.autoroutes.fr (highways)
   ℘08 92 68 10 77
♦ www.viamichelin.com (itineraries and weather updates)

WHAT TO PACK

As little as possible! Try to pack everything into one suitcase and a tote bag. Porter help may be in short supply, while new purchases will add to the original weight. Take an extra tote bag for packing new purchases, shopping at the market, carrying a picnic, etc. Be sure luggage is clearly labelled and old travel tags removed. Do not pack medication in checked luggage, but keep it in your carry-on.

Tourist Information Centres – The **Michelin Guide France** gives the addresses and telephone numbers of the Tourist Information Centres *(Syndicats d'Initiative and offices de tourisme)* to be found in most large towns and tourist resorts. They can supply large-scale town maps, and information on local entertainment, accommodation, sports and sightseeing.

WHERE TO GO
WEEKEND BREAKS

Two itineraries for those who want to spend a long weekend in the Riviera:

NICE

Day 1	Visit the seafront and the Vieille Ville in the morning, then Cimiez and a museum or gallery.
Day 2	Spend the morning in **Monaco★★★**, then drive up to **Èze ★★** and or along to **Cap Ferrat★★** via the corniche roads.
Day 3	Drive up to the **Gorges de la Vésubie★★★**, with a detour to the **Madone d'Utelle Panorama★★★** for **views** across the whole of the Alps-Maritimes region, returning via **Sospel★**.

CANNES

Day 1	Visit the Marché, Le Suquet and the port in the morning, with lunch, sunbathing and shopping on the Croisette.
Day 2	Drive to **Antibes★★** via the **Cap★** to stroll around the **Old Town★**, followed by a tour of **St-Paul-de-Vence★★**, returning via **Grasse★** and **Mougins★**.
Day 3	Drive along the **Corniche de l'Esterel★★★** to **St-Raphaël★**, then visit the Roman remains at **Fréjus★**.

ONE-WEEK ITINERARY

For a seven-day visit, make Nice your base for the first three days. Visit the Old Town and its world-class museums, then the towns along the Corniche roads from Villefranche up to Menton for the best **views**, including an evening in Monte Carlo.

Head west to Antibes and Cannes for the next three days, with time for a trip to the Île des Lérins, an afternoon at the beaches of Juan-les-Pins and a drive up the Loup Valley to St-Paul-de-Vence or Gourdon.

Use the last day to drive the scenic Corniche de l'Esterel, with a detour to St-Tropez if the traffic isn't too bad, or to Le Thoronet to escape the heat and crowds.

View of the Massif de l'Esterel

J. Malburet/MICHELIN

Promenade des Anglais, Nice

B. Pérrousse/MICHELIN

TWO-WEEK ITINERARY

Two weeks on the French Riviera will allow you time to explore each area in-depth, to enjoy the many opportunities for watersports or hiking, or to visit the museums or explore the ancient churches off-season. To the one-week itinerary add a day in the hinterlands of Nice, hiking in the Mercantour to see the Vallée des Merveilles or rafting down the Roya Valley. Add an extra day for shopping in the artisan villages of Èze, Vence or Valbonne, or the fashionable boutiques of Monaco or Cannes. The remaining two days can be spent diving in the Îles de Porquerolles or hiking along the nature trails at Port-Cros, with a guided tour of the historic naval harbour at Toulon and a drive up to Mont Faron for exceptional **panoramic views**.

THEMED TOURS
FOREST PARKS

All along the Alpes-Maritimes coast there are islands of greenery *(parcs forestiers départementaux)* provided for walkers of all abilities.
- **Parc de la Grande-Corniche** in Èze (access from Col d'Èze on the Grande Corniche)
- **Parc de Vaugrenier** (access by RN 7 between Antibes and Marina Baie des Anges)

- **Parc de la Vallée de la Brague** (at the eastern end of Biot village)
- **Parc du San Peyre** (from La Napoule towards A 8 motorway and a left turn onto Route du Cimetière), a former look-out post (alt. 430ft/131m), which offers a superb **panorama** of Cannes Bay
- **Parc de la Pointe de l'Aiguille** (car park on D 6098 at the edge of Théoule).
- **Route Historique des Hauts-Lieux de Provence** – A circuit from St-Maximin-la-Ste-Baume via Draguignan and Les Arcs to Fréjus returning along the coast to Toulon, organised by the Office de Tourisme, pl. du Général-De-Gaulle, Les Arcs-sur-Argens, ℘04 94 73 37 30.
- **Route des Côtes de Provence**

SCENIC VIEWS
Riviera Caves

The limestone region of the Pays Grassois (especially the Caussols Plateau) features many interesting geological features dating from different periods – the caves *(grottes)* at St-Cézaire (&*see GRASSE*), the gigantic limestone crevices such as the original caves consisting of a succession of natural dams *(gours)* including the Grotte de Baume Obscure (&*see ST-VALLIER-DE-THIEY*).

The **Grottes de Villecroze** near Draguignan (☞see VILLECROZE) are formed of tufa (hardened volcanic ash). Other caves, which are accessible with adequate equipment and some technical knowledge, belong in the caving category (☞see p23). People with no caving experience can get an idea of the activity in the first section (about 39ft/12m) of the **Embut de Caussols** (embut is the Provençal word for swallowhole).

Military Fortifications of the Alpes-Maritimes

The strategic significance of the frontier zone in the southeast was developed in 1880 by Sérés de Rivières. The project was completed and improved in 1929 by its integration into the Maginot Line, which defended the eastern frontier from Dunkirk to Menton. It offers a fascinating insight into military architecture in the 19C and 20C. Some of the buildings have been disarmed, restored and are accessible to visitors:

- **Fort de Ste-Agnès** (☞see MENTON)
- **Fort du Barbonnet** (☞see Forêt de TURINI)
- **Fort Suchet (19C)**, the only one that can be visited (☞see Forêt de TURINI)
- **Fort St-Roch** (☞see SOSPEL)

Other forts make pleasant destinations for walks with fine **views**.

☺ Visitors should bear in mind that although the buildings of the Maginot Line appear to be in good condition, they may conceal indoor wells or dangerous passages. Some properties are private, as they have been acquired by individuals.

In the highly strategic sector of L'Authion, near Col de Turini (☞see Forêt de TURINI), several structures designed by Sérés de Rivières have survived and can be reached by the loop road encircling the massif:

- Fort des Mille-Fourches
- La Forca
- Redoute des 3 Communes (1897), the first building constructed using reinforced concrete.

From Mont Chauve d'Aspremont (☞see NICE) there is a brilliant **view** of the whole coast under clear skies. On the summit (2,802ft/854m) is a Sérés de Rivières fort with a monumental southern façade, typical of the period; it is occupied by the Service des Télécommunications.

Mont Chauve de Tourette is visible farther north, capped by a fort from a similar period.

The section near Col de Tende, which was Italian from 1860 to 1947, is an impressive example of the Italian defence system. The central fort is set on top of the col and approached by the narrow road, which branches off by the entrance to the road tunnel. The interior (☺difficult access) was self-sufficient in supplies.

On the Track of Macaron

The old rail bed of one of the dismantled sections of the pinecone train (train des pignes), which linked Toulon to St-Raphaël from early in the 20C to 1950, is open to walkers. Although the track and stations have mostly disappeared, works of art and some stations (Carqueiranne) have survived.

The tunnels are often used by walkers as short cuts, providing unusual and surprising glimpses of the Maures coast.

Beware Snakes!

Avoid moving rocks, and wear sturdy walking boots when hiking through scrubland. If you are bitten, go straight to the nearest hospital; do not attempt to remove the poison yourself. To ward off a snake, simply stamp your feet or make a loud noise.

What to See and Do

OUTDOOR FUN
BOAT TRIPS

There are regular ferries to the Île de Bendor, Îles des Embiez, Îles d'Hyères and Îles de Lérins, and also boat trips from the following resorts:

Bandol
- Port d'embarquement Îles des Embiez, Île de Bendor, Toulon via Cap Sicié, Gare Maritime, Cassis and the Calanque d'En-Vau via La Ciotat– whole day to the Château d'If and Îles du Frioul.

Cannes
- Îles de Lérins

Le Lavandou and Cavalaire
- Île du Levant and Îles d'Hyères

Menton
- La Riviera, Monaco

Nice
- La Riviera, Monaco, Corse

Ste-Maxime
- Les Issambres, Port-Grimaud (navettes), Baie des Cannebiers

St-Raphaël
- St-Tropez *(shuttles)*, Îles de Lérins, Fréjus, St-Aygulf, St-Tropez

St-Tropez
- Îles d'Hyères, Ste-Maxime (shuttles), Les Issambres (shuttles), Port-Grimaud (shuttles), Baie des Cannebiers

Toulon
- La Seyne-sur-Mer, Les Sablettes, Tamaris, St-Mandrier *(shuttles)* and bay of Toulon, Îles d'Hyères Port-Cros, Île Ste-Marguerite, Calanques du massif de l'Esterel

SAILING

Most of the seaside resorts on the French Riviera, from Les Lecques to Menton, have well-equipped marinas, making this coast arguably the best in France for sailing. Although nearly every port has moorings with good facilities, the enthusiasm for sailing is such that enormous marinas have been constructed with extensive services to satisfy even the most exacting yachtsman. Ports providing over 1,000 berths are Bandol, Toulon, Hyères (Port-St-Pierre), La Londe (Port Miramar), Le Lavandou, St-Raphaël (Ste-Lucia), Cannes (Pierre Canto and the Vieux Port), St-Laurent-du-Var and Antibes (Port-Vauban), which is the largest to date.

Another great place for sailing and other watersports is Mandelieu-La-Napoule, which has six ports *(www.mandelieu.com)*.

There are sailing clubs which provide lessons in most resorts; during the summer it is possible to hire craft with or without a crew.

Further information is available from each port authority and from the **Fédération française de voile** (*17 rue Henri-Bocquillon, 75015 Paris; ℘01 40 60 37 00; www.ffvoile.fr*).

SCUBA DIVING

There are many clubs providing scuba diving lessons. The main centres are Bendor (Centre Padi is one of the largest in Europe), Le Pradet (Garonne beach), Giens (La Tour Fondue), Sanary, Cavalaire, Ramatuelle (L'Escalet), St-Tropez, Ste-Maxime, St-Raphaël, Mandelieu-La-Napoule, Cannes and Villefranche.

A brochure listing all the local clubs is available from the **Maison du tourisme du Golfe de St-Tropez** in Gassin (*℘04 94 55 22 00; www.golfe-saint-tropez-information.com*).

Excursions to explore Mediterranean flora and fauna are provided by the Domaine du Rayol (*℘04 98 04 44 00; www.domainedurayol.org*) and the Parc National de Port-Cros (*www.portcrosparcnational.fr*).

Cannes marina

© Monika Lewandowska/iStockphoto.com

The **Fédération française d'études et de sports sous-marins (FFESSM)** *(24 Quai de Rive-Neuve, 13284 Marseille Cedex 07; ℘04 91 33 99 31; www.ffessm.fr)* is an umbrella organisation, comprising 100 local clubs, which publishes a comprehensive yearbook covering all underwater activities in France. Information is also available from the **Comité régional Côte d'Azur de la FFESSM** *(875 chemin des charrettes, 83390 Cuers; ℘04 94 00 40 71; www.ffessmcotedazur.fr).*

Maritime archaeology

The coves of the Maures and the Esterel on the Var coast and the clear water around the Îles d'Hyères invite you to discover the charm of the Mediterranean *(La Grande Bleue)* and the silent underwater world.

Over the centuries, the volume of marine traffic has turned the seabed into a museum of shipwrecks – about 100 ships and upwards of 20 aircraft have sunk along this coast. Most of them are lying in more than 65ft/20m of water, accessible only to experienced divers who are members of specialist clubs. Other wrecks, lying in more shallow waters, can easily be visited by amateurs. Information about underwater centres near such wrecks

is available from the Fédération des Sports Sous-marins in Marseille.

The wrecks of the Provençal coast and their history are described in *Naufrages en Provence* by J-P Joncheray.

UNDERWATER FISHING

The abundance of creeks along the coast should satisfy all demands. The sport of fishing is strictly regulated; the essential regional regulations are given below.

Underwater fishing is forbidden in certain areas of the coastline from early November to the beginning of March. It is essential to check with the local maritime authorities: **Direction départementale des affaires maritimes du Var** *(244 avenue de l'Infanterie-de-Marine, 83000 Toulon; ℘04 94 46 92 00)* and **Direction départementale des affaires maritimes Alpes-Maritimes** *(22 Quai Lunel, 06303 Nice; ℘04 92 00 41 50).* Some areas are out of bounds to fishing all year round such as the south coast of St-Mandrier Peninsula, part of Porquerolles Island, Port-Cros Island and its neighbouring islets. There are underwater nature reserves, marked by buoys, near Golfe-Juan, Beaulieu and Roquebrune-Cap-Martin. Note that Villefranche harbour is a protected area.

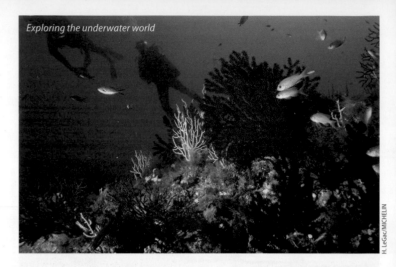

Exploring the underwater world

H. LeGac/MICHELIN

Underwater anglers must comply with general fishing regulations and bear in mind that in the Mediterranean Sea:

- it is illegal to catch or fish for grouper and oysters (for mother-of-pearl)

- it is illegal to fish for sea urchins from 1 May to 30 September

- it is illegal to pursue or catch marine mammals (dolphins, porpoises), even without intending to kill them

- the minimum size of catch is 4.7in/12cm (except for sardines, anchovies), 7.1in/18cm for crayfish

- whatever the circumstances, it is illegal to be in possession of both diving equipment and an underwater gun

Underwater safety

Enthusiasm for exploring the superb underwater landscape of the Riviera should not blind amateur divers to the need to observe certain regulations:

- never go diving alone, nor after eating a heavy meal, nor after drinking alcohol or fizzy drinks, or when tired

- avoid shipping lanes and areas used by windsurfers

- when signalling for help, make it known that it is a diving accident so that the rescuers can prepare a decompression chamber, which is the only effective aid in the case of diving accidents, even minor ones.

SEA FISHING

In Sanary, in the Cogolin Marina and in Ste-Maxime visitors may hire out boats and professional fishermen for sea fishing trips or join a sea fishing party (usually in summer from 6am to 10am). Contact the local tourist offices for more information.

OTHER SEASIDE ACTIVITIES

The long stretches of the Var coast, consisting of beaches where the *mistral* blows, have become some of the most popular locations in the Mediterranean for those who enjoy riding the waves on a **sail board** (windsurfing) or a **funboard**. Almanarre beach on the west side of the Giens peninsula has become a mecca for funboarders and has played host to the World Championships. More technical skill is required on other beaches such as Six-Fours-les-Plages and the two sides of Cap Nègre. For a different view of their favourite beaches, holidaymakers can indulge in a spot of **parascending**: flying over the water below a parachute towed by a motorboat.

The aim is to stay in the air for as along as possible and as high as possible. Instruction in this sport is available on nearly all the organised beaches, where there is enough wind.

Jet-skiing is practiced on certain stretches of coast, which have been carefully chosen and are not accessible from the land. Although offering a guaranteed adrenalin rush, it is, however, strictly regulated:

- machines must be 164yd/ 150m apart
- machines may operate only during the day
- machines may operate between 328yd/300m outside the channels and up to 1 nautical mile
- pilots must hold a proficiency certificate.

Most of the large resorts offer jet-ski rentals by the hour or the half day. It is also possible to hire sea canoes in Salins d'Hyères and certain resorts on the Var coast. Motor vessels are forbidden within 328yd/300m of the shore (except in the access channels) and must not exceed 5 knots in certain restricted areas (Îles d'Hyères, Îles de Lérins and Villefranche harbour). Elsewhere the top speed is 10 knots.

COASTAL WALKS

Before the late 20C building boom, the famous Customs Path ran all along the Riviera coast; some particularly picturesque sections still survive and have been developed by the Coastal Conservation Service (*Conservatoire du Littoral*).

There are several signed country footpaths along the Var coast, of which about 10, from Bandol to St-Aygulph, are described in a topo-guide published by the **Fédération française de la randonnée pédestre** (*www.ffrandonnee.fr*). The name of the topo-guide is " Le Var… à pied ".

It proposes 24 walks and hikes. The reference number for this guide is D083.

HIKING

A network of waymarked paths covers the region described in this guide. **GR (Grande Randonnée) paths**, which are fully open only from the end of June to early October, are for experienced hikers accustomed to mountain conditions.

- **GR 5:** the oldest and most majestic, which terminates in Nice after crossing Europe; the last section from Nice to St-Dalmas-Valdeblore passes through Aspremont, Levens, the Vésubie gorge and Madone d'Utelle.
- **GR 52:** from St-Dalmas-Valdeblore to Menton via Le Boréon, La Vallée des Merveilles, Turini Forest, Sospel.
- **GR52A:** among the peaks in the eastern part of the Parc National du Mercantour beyond the Col de Tende.

Other paths, open all year, for walkers of all levels of competence:

- **GR 4:** from Grasse via Gréolières and Entrevaux to the Verdon Gorge.
- **GR 51:** nicknamed "the Mediterranean balcony", from

Jet skis

© Rocky Reston/Bandu/Dreamstime.com

Castellar (east of Menton) to Col de la Cadière (Esterel) providing **panoramic views** of the coast from the first ridge.

- **GR 510:** entirely in the Alpes-Maritimes region, from Breil-sur-Roya via Sospel, Villars-sur-Var, Puget-Rostand, Roquestéron, St-Auban and Escragnolles to St-Cézaire-sur-Siagne, discovering another valley dotted with hill villages at each stage of the 10-day hike.
- **GR 9:** from Signes through the Massif des Maures to St-Pons-les-Mûres.
- **GR 99:** from Toulon through the Brignolais country to the Verdon Gorge.
- **GR 90:** the shortest, from Le Lavandou through the Massif des Maures to Notre-Dame-des-Anges, where it meets the GR 9.

Topo-guides for the **Grandes Randonnées** (long hikes) and **Petites Randonnées** (short hikes) are published by the Fédération Française de la Randonnée Pédestre – *Comité National des Sentiers de Grande Randonnée, 64 rue du Dessous-des-Berges, 75013 Paris;* ℘*01 44 89 93 93; www.ffrandonnee.fr.* Alternatively, contact the **Comité départemental de randonnée pédestre des Alpes-Maritimes**, Maison des associations – *49 avenue de Nice 06800, Cagnes-sur-Mer;* ℘*04 93 20 74 73, www.cdrp06.org* or the **Comité départementale de randonnée pédestre du Var**, L'Hélianthe, *rue Emile-Ollivier, La Rode, 83000 Toulon;* ℘*04 94 42 15 01; http://var.ffrandonnee.fr.* The Conseil Général des Alpes-Maritimes publishes three free hiking guides *(Haut Pays, Moyen Pays, Pays Côtier)* as part of its **RandOxygène** series covering various altitudes and coastal paths. They are available by calling ℘04 97 18 79 16 or visiting www.randoxygene.org. They can also be found in tourist offices of the Alpes-Maritimes.

NATURE PARKS

Wildlife – Parc National du Mercantour

Mercantour National Park was created in 1979 and covers an area of 169,267 acres/68,500ha in the Alpes-Maritimes and Alpes-de-Haute-Provence *départements* (encompassing 22 and 6 *communes* respectively).

Until 1947, the park was a hunting ground for Italian kings and extended over both sides of the Alps; it has been twinned since 1987 with the Italian Argentera Nature Park, with which it shares a 20.5mi/33km border.

These two organisations are in charge of introducing and monitoring animal species across this protected region. In this way, ibexes which have wintered in the Argentera arrive to spend the summer months in the Mercantour, while wild sheep *(mouflons)* do the opposite.

The Mercantour is a high, mountainous park, with terraces from 1,640–10,312ft/500–3,143m in altitude, offering breathtaking **views** of natural amphitheatres, glacial valleys and deep gorges.

It contains a rich variety of flora; over 2,000 species have been counted there, including **Saxifraga florulenta**, one of the park's emblems. All types of vegetation are present, from olive trees to rhododendrons and gentians, making for a splendid display of colour in the spring.

Fauna includes some chamois, ibexes and mouflons, various deer and smaller mammals such as hares, ermines and marmots. Feathered members of this community include black grouse, ptarmigans and birds of prey. The reintroduction of the bearded vulture was successfully achieved in the summer of 1993. For the first time in France since 1942, wolves have returned from Italy of their own accord to live in the park.

The 373mi/600km of footpaths laid out within the park's boundaries enable tourists to discover the park on foot. These include the **GR5** and the **GR52A** ⚲, or the Mercantour

Ibex, Parc National du Mercantour

© jm/ Fotolia.com

panoramic footpath, which crosses the Vallée des Merveilles, as well as footpaths at L'Authion, Le Boréon and Madone de Fenestre.

This guide describes the regions of the Vésubie and Merveilles valleys, the Authion Massif and Turini Forest. ⊕*Mountain bikes are not allowed in the central area of the park.*

OTHER PARKS

The old royal hunting ground of the Sardinian monarchy extended until the Second World War over the two slopes of the Mercantour and the Marguareis. Since then the Italian section has been administered as a nature reserve with an active policy dedicated to the conservation of species and habitats. Two large natural parks have been created: **Parco delle Alpi Marittime**, the largest, and **Alta Valle Pesio**, farther east. Together with the Parc du Mercantour, they have conducted a campaign for the reintroduction of endangered species – the bearded vulture and the ibex. In the **Parco delle Alpi Marittime**, there are many "royal" botanical paths easily accessible to hikers from the French side of the border by the frontier passes – Col de la Lombarde and Col de Tende. From the latter pass two paths *(each about 3hr)* follow the peaks towards

Rocca dell'Abisso (9,039ft/2,755m – west) and Cima di Pepino (7,661ft/2,335m – east).

The Alta Valle Pesio park, in the Marguareis, is the wildest and least easy to reach from France. Hikers should branch into the northeast route from Limone-Piemonte or go up the valley from Savone.

The Vermenagna Valley, which extends from Col de Tende to the Cuneo Plain, still reveals its strong Provençal roots; Provençal spectacles *(Roumiage de Provenço)* are held in the Grana Valley in July. The district's specialities include a famous cheese, Castelmagno, and handmade cutlery, such as the Vernantino pocket knife.

Parco delle Alpi Marittime
Piazza Regina Elena, 30
12010 Valdieri (CN)
☎+39 0171/97397
www.parcoalpimarittime.it

Parco Naturale Regionale del Marguareis
Via Sta Anne 34 – 12013 Chiusa Pesia (CN) ☎+39 0171/734021
www.vallepesio.it/vedi/13,
parco-naturale-del-marguareis/1

Tourist office Limone-Piemonte
Via Roma (CN) ☎+39 0171/925281,
www.limonepiemonte.it/turistico

GOLF

There are dozens of golf courses spread across the region, many of them open to non-members. The most attractive courses lie along the western coast of the Riviera.

♦ **Fédération française de golf (FFG)** – 68 rue Anatole-France, 92300 Levallois-Perret, ℘01 41 49 77 00. www.ffgolf.org.

♦ **Comité départemental du Var** – Maison départementale des sports L'Hélianthe, La Rode rue Émile-Ollivier 83000, Toulon, ℘04 94 03 78 08. www.cd83golf.com.

♦ **Section départementale des Alpes-Maritimes** – Maison régionale des sports, Esterel Gallery, BP 211, 809 bis blvd. des Écureuils, 06210 Mandelieu, ℘04 92 97 46 96. www.cdgolf06.com.

HORSE RIDING

♦ **Comité National de tourisme équestre** Parc équestre, 41600 Lamotte-Beuvron, ℘02 54 94 46 80. www.tourisme-equestre.fr or www.ffe.com.
This service produces an annual guide (in French) called "Cheval Nature".

♦ **Comité régional de tourisme équestre Côte d'Azur**
Immeuble "Bricorama", 2 rte de Nice, 06650 Le Rouret, ℘04 92 97 46 77. http://cheval.d.azur.crte.free.fr.

Exploring the Border on Horseback
This is an original way of exploring the Massif du Mercantour.
There is a waymarked route on the **Franco Italian Natural Spaces Equestrian Itinerary** (*Itinéraire Équestre des Espaces Naturels Franco-Italiens – Itinerario Equestre degli Spazi Naturali Franco-Italiani*) from St-Martin-Vésubie through the Italian parks – Parco delle Alpi Marittime and Parco Naturale Regionale del Marguareis – to Certosa di Pesio; there are 10 staging posts with facilities for riders and their mounts.
Practical information is available from the Parc du Mercantour and the Parco delle Alpi Marittime information offices (*see Hiking p19*).
The Parc du Mercantour publishes a brochure containing various bridle routes and staging posts in the Parco delle Alpi Marittime and the Mercantour highlands.

WINTER SPORTS

It is only a short distance (*less than 2hr by car*) from the coast to a range of winter sports stations such as:

♦ Colmiane-Valdeblore
♦ Boréon-St-Martin-Vésubie
♦ Turini-Camp d'Argent
♦ Gréolières-les-Neiges
♦ L'Audibergue

There are cross-country skiing runs near la haute Roya – La Brigue (alt. 2,953ft/900m) and Tende-Val Casterino (alt. 4,921ft/1,500m). The proximity of the Italian ski resort, Limone-Piemonte, which can be reached by rail, means that many types of snow sport are available. Visit www.randoxygene.org for details of RandoNeige itineraries published by the Conseil Général des Alpes-Maritimes.

MOUNTAINEERING

Mountaineers can choose from a wide variety of different terrains, from the Pre-Alps of Nice to the rockfaces of the Verdon Gorge. Guided excursions in rock-climbing, mountaineering, rambling, downhill skiing and cross-country skiing are organised by:

♦ **Club alpin français – Section du Var**
Caserne Lamer, 95 rue Montebello, 83000 Toulon ℘04 94 62 19 16 www.clubalpintoulon.org

- **Club alpin français – Section des Alpes-Maritimes**
  14 avenue Mirabeau, 06000 Nice
  ℘04 93 62 72 21
  www.cafnice.org

- **Association des guides et accompagnateurs des Alpes Méridionales**
  26 avenue Corniglion-Molinier, 06450 Roquebillière
  ℘04 93 03 51 60
  www.vesubian.com
  Place du Marché, 06450 St-Martin-Vésubie
  ℘04 93 03 31 32
  www.guidescapade.com

- **Altitude 06**
  71 Blvd. de la Rocade, 06250 Mougins
  ℘06 09 55 80 67
  www.altitude06.com

VIA FERRATA

A combination of climbing, mountaineering and hiking, via ferrata is practiced across a handful of sites in the region such as some of the following:

At Col de la Colmiane, the **baus de la Frema** course (*see ST-MARTIN-VÉSUBIE*) provides a great introduction, while more experienced enthusiasts will enjoy the Baus (2 246m/7368ft), with **views** of the Massif de Mercantour.

At **Lantosque**, the via ferrata passes through a rocky jungle of vegetation and down the narrow Canyon du Riou and up the Gorges de la Vésubie (*see VALLÉE DE LA VÉSUBIE*).

The "Comtes de Lascaris" circuit includes two sites: **Tende** and **Peille** (*see below*).

La Ciappéa at **La Brigue** is a particularly demanding course overhanging deep caves.

Lastly, the **via souterrata** in Caille, at the foot of the Audibergue, near Grasse, offers a circuit including two sinkholes.

The Conseil général des Alpes-Maritimes produces a guide called "**Randoxygène**" available from tourist offices and www.randoxygene.org.

CAVING

The Var has many original sites. The Siou Blanc Plateau includes chasms and potholes for amateurs. Among these is the deepest pothole in the region (1,148ft/350m). The Grotte de Mouret, near Draguignan, is useful for practice.

Massif du Marguareis

©De Agostini/Photoshot

In the Alpes-Maritimes, both the Pays Grassois and the Caussols Plateau offer many opportunities for seasoned cavers. The legendary Massif du Marguareis (northeast of Tende), the site of the exploits of the potholer Michel Siffre in the 1960s, is still a paradise for the experienced caver. This immense chalky plateau is peppered with sinkholes and vertiginous rockfaces overhanging the Italian slopes, and contains deep chasms (more than 2,953ft/900m). Information available from:

- **Comité départemental de spéléologie du Var**
  L'Hélianthe, rue Émile-Ollivier
  La Rode, 83000 Toulon
  ℰ04 94 31 29 43
  www.cdspeleo83.fr

- **Comité départemental de spéléologie des Alpes-Maritimes**
  Maison régionale des sports,
  Immeuble Esterel Gallery
  809 blvd. des Ecureuils
  06210 Mandelieu
  ℰ04 92 97 46 85
  http://cds06.ffspeleo.fr

- Speleology divisions of the **Club alpin français** in Nice or Toulon.

WATERSPORTS
Canoeing
Some of the rivers in the Alpes-Maritimes can be explored by canoe throughout the year but the best time is in spring. In any season beware of sudden floods caused by heavy rain upstream. The most attractive stretches of river are to be found just inside the boundaries of the Mercantour or near St-Martin-Vésubie. Shooting rapids excursions through gorges accompanied by experts are organised by the Toulon division of the Club Alpin Français. Those offering the best services are awarded the title **Point-Canoë-Nature** by the **Fédération française de canoë-kayak** *(87 Quai de la Marne, 94340 Joinville-le-Pont Cedex; ℰ01 45 11 08 50; www.ffcanoe.asso.fr)*.
Comité régional de canoë-kayak de la région PACA – 50 ave. du 11-novembre, 06600 Antibes ℰ04 93 34 08 65, www.canoe-paca.fr.

Canyoning
The most attractive stretches of water in the Alpes-Maritimes for this activity, which combines rock-climbing, potholing and swimming in running water, are to be found within the Parc du Mercantour and in St-Martin-Vésubie. There are also two exceptional sites in the valley of the

Canyoning, Verdon Gorges

© Philippe Crochet/Photononstop

Canoeing on Lac de Saint-Croix, Verdon

© Jan Mineal/iStockphoto.com

Haute-Roya near Saorge – **La Maglia** (through caves) and **La Bendola** (two days in the water). Canyoning is strictly forbidden in the central part of the Parc du Mercantour.

Between St-Martin-Vésubie and its confluence with the Var, the **River Vésubie** offers a variety of canyons – Duranus, L'Imberguet, La Bollène and Gourgas, which is technically demanding.

The **Estéron**, an eastern tributary of the Var, provides classic stretches in exceptional settings between Roquestéron and St-Auban.

The network of rivers in the Var provides many opportunities for canyoning, with 11 authorised sites of varying difficulty suitable for all levels of competence. The **Destel Gorge**, between **Caramy** and **Carcès**, the lower stretches of the **Jabron** (downstream of **Trigance**) and the **Pennafort Gorge** are suitable for beginners. Seillans-la-Cascade, the Nartuby and the Destéou in the Maures demand greater skill. At all times of the year there is a risk of sudden increases in the volume of water following a storm upstream and a sudden release of retained water. Canyoning trips with guides are organised by the Toulon branch of the Club Alpin Français.

The **"Clues et Canyons" guide** published by the Conseil Général des Alpes-Maritimes *(www.randoxygene. org)*, available from tourist offices throughout the Alpes-Maritimes, is essential reading.

Lakes

The largest lake in the Estérel, **Lac de St-Cassien** (430ha/1 062 acres) not only supplies electricity and water to the eastern Var and water for fire-fighting aircraft, but also has a nature reserve at the west end with a reed-bed, where more than 150 species of wintering migratory seabird have been recorded.

There are facilities for windsurfing and pedalo – tuition at the base and equipment for hire from the open air cafés along the sometimes steep banks; motorised vessels are forbidden.

◆ **Base nautique de St-Cassien**
Lieu-dit " Biançon
83440 Montauroux le Lac
☏04 94 39 88 64

The **Lac de Carcès** (247 acres/100ha) is a reservoir formed by a dam and fed by the River Argens. There is a pleasant wooded road along the eastern bank; the opposite bank, more rural, is much-used by fishermen. Canoeing in kayaks is permitted.

Pushing Pedals from Sea to Sea

EuroVelo is a venture funded by the European Union and 23 national coordination centers. Visit **www.eurovelo.org** to discover the 15 cycling routes that will trace 43,495mi/70,000km throughout Europe when complete. Routes include Moscow to Galway, Ireland, and another from northern Norway to the tip of Sicily. The Mediterranean route follows the coastline from Cadiz, Spain, to Athens, via the French Riviera and Monaco.

Game Fishing

Local and national fishing regulations apply to fishing in lakes (Carcès and St Cassien) and in rivers (Gapeau, Réal Martin, Argens, Roya, Bévéra, etc.). It is also advisable to join the Association de Pêche et de Pisciculture in the area in question by paying the annual fees appropriate to the form of fishing practised and then by buying a daily permit from an authorised vendor. Trout fishing is permitted from the 2nd Saturday in March to the 3rd Sunday in September; pike fishing is allowed only between 31 January and 15 April. Fishing for common grayling in the Siagne is banned year round. Up-to-date information available from:

- **Fédération du Var pour la pêche et la protection du milieu aquatique**
  rue des Déportés
  Immeuble Foch
  83170 Brignoles
  ✆ 04 94 69 05 56
  www.fedepechevar.com

- **Fédération des Alpes-Maritimes pour la pêche et la protection du milieu aquatique**
  455 promenade des Anglais, "Le Quadra", 06299 Nice Cedex 3
  ✆ 04 93 72 06 04
  www.peche-cote-azur.com

- **Fédération nationale de la pêche en France et de la protection du milieu aquatique**
  17 rue Bergère, 75009 Paris
  ✆ 01 48 24 96 00,
  www.unpf.fr (this website provides information about fishing regulations).

CYCLING AND MOUNTAIN BIKING

The diversity of the inland terrain and the network of cycle tracks along the coast and in the massifs of the Esterel and the Maures make mountain biking a popular sport in this region. Many organisations, hotels and clubs hire out mountain bikes and provide details of local cycle tracks. Lists of suppliers are also available from local tourist offices.

Main Railway Stations

Antibes, Bandol, Cagnes-sur-Mer, Cannes, Hyères, Juan-les-Pins and St-Raphaël hire out various types of bicycle, which can be returned to a different station.

Information for Cyclists

The regulations concerning admission to the Parc du Mercantour apply also to cyclists. The Conseil Général des Alpes-Maritimes publishes the **Rando VTT** guide containing 30 routes across the region (available at www.rando xygene.org).

The **Comité départemental du tourisme du Var** publishes a leaflet covering more than 20 signed routes for cyclists, including:

- Roof of the Var (*Le Toit du Var*) (43mi/71km)
- Bauxite Road (*La Route de la Bauxite*) (50mi/80.5km)
- North face of the Maures (*L'Ubac des Maures*) (50mi/82.5km)
- Maures chestnut woods (*Les Châtaigneraies des Maures*) (56mi/93km)

- **Comité départemental de cyclotourisme des Alpes-Maritimes:** 2 Blvd. Settimelli Lazare, 06230 Villefranche-sur-Mer
  ℰ04 93 01 81 85
  www.cyclotourisme06-ffct.org

- **Comité départemental de cyclotourisme du Var:**
  L'Hélianthe, La Rode
  Rue Émile-Ollivier,
  83000 Toulon
  ℰ06 63 85 02 52
  www.cyclotourisme83-ffct.org

- **Fédération française de cyclotourisme:** 12 rue Louis-Bertrand, 94207 Ivry-sur-Seine Cedex.
  ℰ01 56 20 88 88
  www.ffct.org

AERIAL SPORTS

Hang-gliding, parachuting and ultra-light craft
There are about 20 suitable sites for parachuting, hang-gliding *(vol libre)* and ultra-light craft *(planeur ultra léger motorisé)*.

- **Envol de Provence:** 239 chemin de St-Clair, 83870 Signes
  ℰ04 94 90 86 13 or 06 07 28 93 41
  www.envol-parapente.com

- **Fédération française de vol libre:** 4 rue de Suisse,
  06000 Nice
  ℰ04 93 88 62 89
  www.ffvl.fr

- **Fédération française de d'ULM (Planeur Ultra-Léger Motorisé):**
  96bis rue Marc-Sangnier,
  94704 Maisons-Alfort Cedex
  ℰ01 49 8174 43
  www.ffplum.com

Gliding
The main gliding centre, which is run by the **Association aéronautique Provence-Côte d'Azur**, is near Fayence, where aerological conditions are exceptional. It has become the leading gliding centre in Europe and has contributed to the rapid development of glider aerobatics. Each year champions from all over the world demonstrate their skill at the *open de france de planeur.*

- **Association aéronautique Provence-Côte d'Azur**
  83440 Fayence
  ℰ04 94 76 00 68.
  www.aapca.net.

ACTIVITIES FOR KIDS 👥
For a change from the beach, on cloudy days there are many attractions all along the riviera, including leisure pools and animal parks. In this guide, sights of particular interest to children are indicated with a kids symbol (👥). Some attractions offer discount fees for children.

LEISURE POOLS

- **Niagara Parc aquatique**
  Route du Canadel, 83310 La Môle
  ℰ04 94 55 70 84
  www.parcniagara.com
- **Marineland**
  RN7, 06600 Antibes
  ℰ08 92 42 62 26
  www.marineland.fr
- **Aqualand Fréjus**
  Quartier le Capou
  RN98, 83600 Fréjus
  ℰ04 94 51 82 51
  www.aqualand.fr
- **Aqualand St-Cyr-sur-Mer**
  ZAC des Pradeaux
  559 Chemin Départemental,
  83270 St-Cyr-sur-Mer
  ℰ04 94 32 08 32
  www.aqualand.fr

ANIMAL PARKS

- **Sanary-Bandol** – Zoo
- **Toulon** – Zoo du Mont-Faron
- **La Londe-les-Maures** –
  Jardin Zoologique Tropical
  (see HYÈRES)
- **Gonfaron** – Village des Tortues
  (see Massif des MAURES)
- **Fréjus** – Zoo

- **Antibes** – La Petite Ferme, le Golf Adventureland and Marineland
- **Monaco** – Jardin Animalier

SPAS AND WELLNESS

Spas and wellness facilities are found across the region, including: **Antibes** (fitness), **Bandol** (thalassotherapy), **Hyères** (fitness), **St-Raphaël** ("thalasports"), **Fréjus** (thalassotherapy), **Île des Embiez** (balneotherapy).

- **France Thalasso** – ℘06 66 85 64 50. www.france-thalasso.com.
- The tiny resort of **Berthemont-les-Bains** (℘see *VALLÉE DE LA VÉSUBIE*), treats respiratory and articular disorders (06450 Roquebillière ℘04 93 03 47 00, www.valvital.fr).
- **Conseil national des exploitants thermaux** – 1 rue Cels, 75014 Paris, ℘01 53 91 05 77, www.france-thermale.org.

SHOPPING

Most of the larger shops are open Mondays to Saturdays from 9am to 6.30 or 7.30pm, and some chain stores now open on Sundays in Nice. Smaller, individual shops may close during the lunch hour. Food shops – grocers, wine merchants and bakeries – are generally open from 8am to 6.30 or 7.30pm; some open on Sunday mornings. Many food shops close between noon and 2pm and on Mondays. Bakery and pastry shops sometimes close on Wednesdays. Hypermarkets usually open until 9pm or later. Those travelling to the USA cannot import plant products or fresh food, including fruit, cheeses and nuts. It is acceptable to carry tinned products or preserves.

RECOVERING VALUE ADDED TAX

There is a Value Added Tax in France (TVA) of 19.6% on almost every purchase (some foods and books are subject to a lower rate). However, non-European visitors who spend more than 175€ in any one participating store can get the VAT amount refunded. Usually, you fill out a form at the store, showing your passport. Upon leaving the country, you submit all forms to customs for approval (they may want to see the goods, so if possible, don't pack them in checked luggage). The refund is usually paid directly into your bank or credit card account, or it can be sent by mail. Big department stores catering to tourists provide special services to help you; be

Market day in Lorgues

D. Pazery/ MICHELIN

sure to mention that you plan to seek a refund before you pay for goods (no refund is possible for tax on services). If you are visiting two or more countries within the European Union, you submit the forms only on departure from the last EU country. The refund is worthwhile for those visitors who would like to buy fashion, furniture or other fairly expensive items, but remember, the minimum amount must be spent in a single shop (though not necessarily on a single day).

PROVENÇAL MARKETS

Provençal markets, fragrant with thyme, tarragon, lavender and garlic, are part of the traditional image of the South of France.

A list of traditional craft markets where the products of the Var region are sold is published annually by the **Chambre des métiers et de l'artisanat des Alpes-Maritimes** *(Service promotion export, Département stratégie et développement des entreprises, 110 ave. de Verdun, 06700 St-Laurent-du-Var, ✆04 93 14, 24 49, www.cm-alpesmaritimes.fr).*

As a rule, during the summer season stalls selling fruit and vegetables and craftwork can be found in even the smallest villages. They typically open at about 8am or 9am, and finish at lunchtime or about 1pm.

The most picturesque and lively markets of the Var and the days on which they are held are listed in the table opposite.

CRAFTS AND SOUVENIRS

In high season many villages and resorts organise courses on local arts and crafts – painting on porcelain in Le Cannet, weaving and woodwork in the Cannes district and regional cuisine in St-Martin-Vésubie. Certain villages are designated "Ville et Métiers d'Art" such as Biot, Cagnes-sur-Mer, Fréjus, Ollioules and Vallauris. For more information on these, call ✆01 48 88 26 56 or visit www.vma.asso.fr.

MARKETS www.jours-de-marche.fr	
Aups	Wednesday, Saturday
Bargemon	Thursday
Le Beausset	Friday
Bormes-les-Mimosas	Tuesday, Wednesday
Brignoles	Wednesday
Callas	Tuesday, Saturday
Cogolin	Wednesday, Saturday
La Croix-Valmer	Sunday
Draguignan	Monday, Wednesday, Saturday
Fayence	Tuesday, Thursday
Fréjus	Tuesday, Wednesday, Friday, Saturday
La Garde	Tuesday, Friday Saturday
Grimaud	Thursday
Hyères	Tuesday, 3rd Thursday/month, Saturday
Le Lavandou	Thursday, Sunday
Lorgues	Tuesday
Le Luc	Friday
Ramatuelle	Thursday, Sunday
St-Tropez	Tuesday, Saturday
Ste-Maxime	Monday, Thursday
Toulon	daily
Tourtour	Wednesday, Saturday
Trans-en-Provence	Sunday
Villecroze	Thursday

REGIONAL SPECIALITIES

The main areas where craftwork and local produce can be bought by visitors from the producers are shown on the map – Specialities & Vineyards (&see pp66–67).

Biot glasses

S. Sauvignier/ MICHELIN

Further information on specialist products:

Sweets

Confiserie Florian des Gorges du Loup, Le Pont-du-Loup, 06140 Tourrettes-sur-Loup. 𝒫04 93 59 32 91. www.confiserieflorian.com. You will also find nougat in Roquebrune-sur-Argens and honey in Bandol, Cotignac or the Massif du Tanneron.

♦ **Marrons glacés and preserved chestnuts**
Confiserie Azuréenne, blvd. Général- Koenig, 83610 Collobrières.
𝒫04 94 48 07 20.
www.confiserieazureenne.com.

Glassware

Verrerie de Biot in Biot, where it is possible to watch master glassblowers at work.

Perfume

Scents for the home or body are made in Grasse, Èze and Gourdon.

Ceramics

Biot, Vallauris, and Salernes (⟲see AUPS) specialise in pottery as well as ceramics.

Liqueur de Lérina

This drink is made on the Îles de Lérins, by the monks of the Abbaye St-Honorat.

Leather

The *sandale tropézienne* is the model that has been made by the same company since 1927 (⟲see ST-TROPEZ).

WINE TASTING

Wine Cooperative Cellars

The **Côte de Provence wine road** wends its way through the vineyards; wine cellars open for tastings are usually indicated on roadside signs (look for *dégustation*). To organise tours and tastings of particular wines, contact these organisations:

♦ **Vins de Bandol**
Maison des Vins du Bandol, Pl. Lucien-Artaud, 83150 Bandol
𝒫*04 94 29 45 03.*
www.maisondesvins-bandol.com.

♦ **Coteaux-varois**
Maison des vins coteaux varois en Provence (inside the Abbaye Royale de la Celle) Pl. de la Mairie, 83170 La Celle. 𝒫*04 94 69 33 18. www. vinsdeprovence.com.* The coteaux varois AOC is spread out over 28 communes around Brignoles, and Sainte-Baume to Bessillons.

Santon Fairs in the Var

Clay figures *(santons)* became popular during the French Revolution, when many churches were closed. A craftsman in Marseille decided to market these figurines so that people could set up Nativity scenes at home. The term comes from the Provençal *santoun*, meaning "little saint". Originally, these statuettes were confined to religious or biblical themes, but they have come to represent traditional aspects of the region (arts, crafts, folklore, animals).

- **Côtes-de-Provence**
  Maison des vins des Côtes-de-Provence, RN 7, 83460 Les Arcs-sur-Argens. &04 94 99 50 20.
  www.cotes-de-provence.com.
  This is the most popular wine of the Provence-Alpes-Côte d'Azur region. There are three vineyards on Île de Porquerolles producing an AOC *(Appellation d'Origine Contrôlée)* Côte-de-Provence wine. All offer wine tasting sessions:
- Domaine de l'Île, the oldest
- Domaine Perzinsky
- Domaine Courtade.

Other Côte-de-Provence wines are made in Les Arcs, Draguignan (organic wine), Fréjus, Gassin *(&see RAMATUELLE)*, Le Luc (organic wine) and Lorgues. This Maison des Vins also offers classes on wine tasting.

Vallauris pottery

S. Sauvignier/ MICHELIN

- **Vins de Bellet**
  Clos St Vincent
  Collet des Fourniers - Saint Roman de Bellet, 06200 Nice
  &04 92 15 12 69
  www.vinsdebellet.com
  Vin de Bellet is produced on the hillsides behind Nice around St-Romain-de-Bellet; it is on sale in the cellars, which are open to the public; further information from the Nice tourist office.

- **Domaine de Lauzade**
  Rte de Toulon (RD 97),
  83340 Le Luc en Provence
  &04 94 60 72 51
  www.lauzade.com
  Tastings of Provençal wines Mon–Sat morning.

- **La Cave de Mougins**
  50 avenue Jean-Charles Mallet,
  06250 Mougins &04 92 28 06 11
  Oenologie courses and wine tasting.

Wine Courses

Although most vineyards offer wine tasting sessions, only a few have professional courses, where you can learn more about local wines. Try the addresses below or contact your local *Maison des vins* for more details:

- **Maison des vins des Côtes-de-Provence** – RN 7, 83460 Les Arcs-sur-Argens. &04 94 99 50 10. www.vinsdeprovence.com.
- **Domaine de Lauzade** – rte de Toulon, 83340 Le Luc. &04 94 60 72 51. www.lauzade.com. Daily tasting sessions of Provençal wines.

COOKING CLASSES

The Comité Régional du Tourisme Provence-Alpes-Côte d'Azur *(www.decouverte-paca.fr)* provides information on cooking classes throughout the region and publishes an annual brochure on local gastronomy, *Terre de Saveurs.*

- **Lenôtre Cannes**
  63 rue d'Antibes, 06400 Cannes.
  &04 97 06 67 67. *www.lenotre.fr.*
  Classes for children, teens and adults on everything from pastries to perfectly prepared vegetables.

SIGHTSEEING
TOURIST TRAINS

The single-track main railway line between Nice and Cuneo (Italy) crosses the old County of Nice, passing through Peille, L'Escarène, Sospel, Breil-sur-Roya, Fontan-Saorge, St-Dalmas-de-Tende, Tende, Vievola and finally, Limone in Italy. The track was built from 1920 onwards and incorporates some spectacular engineering feats as it twists and turns through the tortuous mountain landscapes. The **views** are particularly wonderful between L'Escarène and Sospel and between Breil and Tende along the rugged gorges of the River Roya. On the Italian side of the border, the line descends less steeply down to Cuneo through the charming Vermegnagna Valley. The frequent service enables skiers to reach the Massif du Mercantour and spend the day skiing in the Italian winter sports resort of Limone-Piemonte. There are at least four daily return services to and from Nice-Ville station, but check the schedule carefully, download from the website. For information: ℘08 91 70 30 00 (0.23€/min); www.ter-sncf.com/paca/fr.

The **Train des Merveilles** is a scenic tourist train between Nice and Tende-Castérino that runs daily June–September through Sospel, Peille, Breil-sur-Roya and La Brigue. The winter service, known as the **Train des Neiges**, runs weekends January–March. For information, **SNCF** – ℘08 91 70 30 00 (0.23€/min); www.ter-sncf.com/ paca.

Association Développement touristique Roya-Bévéra – ℘04 93 04 92 05 or www.royabevera.com.

Chemins de Fer de Provence
The famous **Train des Pignes** (pine-cone train) is named after the pine cones which were once used as fuel to stoke the engines. It runs between Nice and Digne-les-Bains (93mi/151km) passing through Puget-Théniers, Entrevaux, Annot and St-André-les-Alpes. The single track was constructed from 1890 to 1911 and comprises 60 remarkable feats of engineering – metal bridges, viaducts, tunnels (one of which is 2.3mi/3.5km long). It is a relic of a vast regional network which once served the whole inland area from Toulon to Draguignan. The journey, 2hr by train, 3hr by omnibus, passes through five valleys often difficult to reach by car. All year round it is possible to take the train to Lac de Castillon, the Verdon Gorges and the winter sports stations in the Alpes-Maritimes *département*. From Plan-du-Var there is a service to the walking country in the Vésubie Valley. In summer the Alpazur service runs from Nice as far as Grenoble and there is a tourist steam train on the Puget-Théniers section. There are wayside halts at which walkers can leave or rejoin the train at the beginning and end of a day's hike. Information **Chemins de Fer de Provence**: Gare de Nice, 4 bis rue Alfred-Binet, 06000 Nice. ℘04 97 03 80 80. www.trainprovence.com. Also: Gare de Digne, avenue P.-Sémard, 04000 Digne-les-Bains. ℘04 92 31 01 58. www.trainprovence.com.

FROM THE AIR

Several companies organise aerial sightseeing (*see previous AERIAL SPORTS for hang-gliding, para-gliding*):

♦ **Fédération française de vol à voile** – 29 rue de Sèvres, 75006 Paris.
℘01 45 44 04 78.
www.ffvv.org.

For helicopter sightseeing and transfers:

♦ **Héli Air Monaco** – Héliport de Monaco, 98000 Monaco.
℘377 92 050 050 50 (reservations)
www.heliairmonaco.com

♦ **Héli Sécurité** – Héliport de Grimaud Saint-Tropez, BP 10-161 83310 Grimaud.
℘04 94 55 59 99
www.helicopter-saint-tropez.com.

BOOKS

*Travels through France and Italy –
Tobias Smollett (1766).*

Seasoned grumbler, Tobias
Smollett wrote this travel journal
on his journey through France
and Italy, complaining bitterly
about the service, inns and people
at every stop... except Nice. Not
surprisingly, there is now a rue
Smollett, just off place Garibaldi.

Les Misérables – Victor Hugo (1862). An
historic look at the slave-galley
days of Toulon from the point of
view of the convict Jean Valjean,
who spent 19 years in the Bagne of
Toulon for stealing bread to feed
his starving family.

*Tender is the Night – F. Scott Fitzgerald
(1934).* Inspired by the Boston art
collectors Gerald and Sara Murphy,
as well as by his own wife, Zelda,
Fitzgerald's classic story of
Americans adrift on the French
Riviera describes the slow demise
of Dick Diver, a psychiatrist, who
marries his patient, Nicole.

The Rock Pool – Cyril Connolly (1936).
Originally rejected by publishers in
England on grounds of obscenity,
this book examines the decadent
side of the expatriate community
in Juan-les-Pins and Antibes.

*Bonjour Tristesse (Hello Sadness) –
Françoise Sagan (1954).* A classic of
French literature, the heroine,
Cécile, is a precocious 17-year-old
(the author's age when she wrote
the story), who grapples with her
widowed father's second marriage
and her own coming-
of-age on the Esterel Coast.

Letters from Colette – Colette. (1980).
The letters of this renowned
French author document the
change in St-Tropez from a
secluded, peaceful fishing
village, where artists and writers
would retreat to a glitzy tourism
destination.

Voices in the Garden – Dirk Bogarde (1981).
The British actor, who resided in
Grasse for many years during the
latter part of his life, wrote this
fascinating novel about a middle-
aged couple living on the Riviera,
whose life is irrevocably changed
after meeting a young English
tourist and his girlfriend and
offering them hospitality in their
sumptuous villa.

*The Garden of Eden – Ernest Hemingway
(1986).* This story, published after
the author died, unfolds on the
Riviera and involves a young
writer, his glamorous wife and the
pressures of a destructive love
triangle.

*Maigret on the Riviera – Georges
Simenon (1988).* Only mildly distracted
by the balmy weather and lush
vegetation, the famous, pipe-
smoking Inspector Jules Maigret
must discover how an inoffensive,
down-at-heel Australian came to
be murdered in this idyllic setting.

Perfume – Patrick Süskind (1989). A
dramatic thriller set in the 18C
perfume-making industry of
Grasse.

*Artists and their Museums on the
Riviera – Barbara Freed, Alan Halpern;
Harry Abrams (1998).*

A useful paperback guide for
exploring the art museums in the
region, placing the artists and
their work in context.

*Art-Sites France: Contemporary Art &
Architecture Handbook – Sidra Stich
(1999).* Invaluable for those interested
in contemporary artwork, this
book covers the whole of France
with detailed descriptions of
galleries, museums, film and video
centres, specialised bookstores,
sculpture parks and many
architectural sites.

*Once Upon a Time: The Story of Princess
Grace, Prince Rainier and Their Family –
J. Randy Taraborrelli (2003).*

A biography of the Monégasque
Royal family, which starts with the
history of the principality vis-à-vis
the life of Grace Kelly and finally,
Monaco today.

FILMS

Max in Monaco (1913).
A silent comedy, featuring Max Linder, is set in the Principality of Monaco.

Fleur d'Amour (1927).
Maurice Vandal portrays the formerly "hot" district of "Chicago" in Toulon.

À Propos de Nice (1929).
Jean Vigo's classic focused on the contrast between holidaymakers loafing around on the beach in Nice and the working-class districts.

César (1936).
The colourful pre-war setting of Toulon appears in this locally-made Marcel Pagnol film with Provençal actor Raimu (see COGOLIN).

Les Visiteurs du Soir (1942).
Tourrettes-sur-Loup was the Medieval setting for Marcel Carné's period drama.

Les Démons de l'Aube (1945).
Yves Allégret's film set in the Var is about the Provençal landings in the Second World War.

To Catch a Thief (1955).
The impressive drops of the Grande Corniche provided a marvellous backdrop (before urban development changed the look of Monaco) in this thriller by Alfred Hitchcock starring Cary Grant and Grace Kelly.

And God Created Woman (1956).
Roger Vadim launched both Brigitte Bardot and St-Tropez with this provocative film.

The Collector (1967).
Eric Rohmer's love triangle takes place in a vacation villa in St-Tropez.

Le Gendarme de St-Tropez (1964).
The absurd side of the glitzy St-Tropez lifestyle is shown in six episodes of this celebrated comedy detective series.

Monte Carlo or Bust! (1969).
A comedy set in 1920s Monte Carlo, starring Tony Curtis, Dudley Moore, Peter Cook and Eric Sykes.

La Nuit Àméricaine (1973).
Partly filmed at the Studios de la Victorine, François Truffaut's movie used several locations, including Nice and the Vésubie Valley.

Herbie Goes to Monte Carlo (1977).
The comic adventures of the *Love Bug* throughout the world had to include an episode in Monaco, starring Dean Jones.

La Cage aux Folles (1978).
The original version of this comedy is set within a transvestite club in St-Tropez.

Festival in Cannes (2002).
An insider look at the movie industry from the international film festival in Cannes by Ron Silver.

Ocean's Twelve (2004).
The Monte Carlo Casino is the high-stakes setting for this drama starring George Clooney, Brad Pitt, Matt Damon, Julia Roberts, Catherine Zeta-Jones and Vincent Cassel.

Heartbreaker (2010).
Alex breaks up relationships for a living. Hired by a father unhappy at his daughter's impending wedding, he scours the luxurious hot spots of Monaco bent on seduction. Starring Vanessa Paradis and Romain Duris.

Kiss and Tell (2010).
A woman on holiday in the South of France meets her ideal man and has a shot-gun wedding. Once back home, their idyllic life takes a turn for the worst.

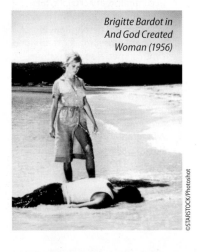

Brigitte Bardot in And God Created Woman (1956)

©STARSTOCK/Photoshot

Calendar of Events

FÊTES, FESTIVALS & SPORTING EVENTS

JANUARY

Barjols – Festival of St Marcel, celebrated since 1350 (Sunday closest to Jan 17).

Bormes-les-Mimosas – Mimosalia mimosa festival.

Valbonne – Festival of St Blaise Grape and Olive Festival (last weekend).

Monaco – International Circus Festival (mid-Jan). *www.montecarlofestival.mc*

Monaco and hinterlands – Monte Carlo Rally (end of the month).

Monaco (La Condamine) – Festival of St Dévote. A torchlight procession, symbolic burning of a boat and fireworks to honour the patron saint (Jan 27).

FEBRUARY

Menton – Lemon Festival (3 weeks around Shrove Tuesday).

Villefranche-sur-Mer – Flowered Naval Parade (Shrove Monday).

Nice – Carnival and Flower Festival (2 weeks around Shrove Tuesday). *www.nicecarnaval.com*

MARCH

Golfe-Juan – Reenactment of Napoleon's landing (first weekend).

Gonfaron – Donkey festival procession and blessing (last weekend).

Nice (Cimiez) – Fête des coucourdons: dried and painted gourds (end of the month).

Nice – Arrival of the Paris–Nice Cycling Race.

APRIL

Roquebrune-Cap-Martin – Evening Procession of the Entombment of Christ. Reenacted annually since the time of the White Penitents, with snail-shell candles and symbols of the Passion carried by costumed participants.

Vence – Provençal Folklore Festival. A joyous village festival commemorating their resistance to the Huguenot siege during the Wars of Religion of 1592.

Fréjus – Bravade St-François: costumed military procession to honour St-Francis-de-Paul, who saved the town from the Plague (third Sunday after Easter).

Monaco – Printemps des arts. Spring Arts Festival celebrating the latest in theatre, dance and music: *www.printempsdesarts.com*

Mouans-Sartoux – Honey Festival (last Sunday).

MAY

Cannes – International Film Festival. *www.festival-cannes.com*

Fréjus – Bravade St-François (third Sunday after Easter)

Grasse – Rose Festival: market, concerts and rose competition *www.ville-grasse.fr/exporose*

La Garde-Freinet – Fête de la Transhumance: moving of sheep and cattle to traditional pastures.

Monaco – Formula One Grand Prix *www.formula1.com*

Nice (Cimiez) – Fête des Mai. Oldest folk festival in Nice, with dancing and picnics in the Cimiez gardens (Sundays and holidays).

Lemon Festival, Menton

©Sean Nel/Bigstockphoto.com

Parade at Nice Carnival

© southmind/Fotolia.com

Grimaud – Wool Festival (Ascension Day): sheep shearing contests, market and village feast.

LATE MAY TO MID-JULY
Toulon – and surroundings – Summer Music Festival

JUNE
St-Tropez – Bravade des Espagnols: Colourful Provençal festival and procession to honour the town's patron saint since the 15C (mid- June).

JULY
Cannes (Le Suquet) – Nuits musicales du Suquet: musical evenings featuring famous virtuosos and young talent (second fortnight). ℘04 92 99 33 83.
Antibes – Fêtes de Notre-Dame de Bon-Port: includes procession of barefoot seamen carrying gilded statue of Notre-Dame de la Garoupe from Antibes cathedral to the chapel in La Garoupe.
Vence – Fête de la Conque. Traditional music festival (first weekend) with concerts and a village-wide country-style buffet: http://pagesperso-orange.fr/locepon

Tende – Feast of St Eligius, patron saint of muleteers (second weekend).
Sospel – Les Baroquiales festival of baroque art (first fortnight). ℘04 93 04 15 80.
Thoronet (Abbaye) – Medieval music festival (second fortnight). ℘04 94 60 10 94 http://musique-medievale.fr
Îles des Embiez – Les Voix du Gaou: salsa, rock, soul, reggae, Raï, etc. www.voixdugaou.com.
Juan-les-Pins – World Jazz Festival. (around the second week) ℘04 97 23 11 10.
Nice – Nice Jazz Festival. Albert Ier garden and Théâtre de Verdure (first fortnight). ℘08 92 70 74 07. www.nicejazzfestival.fr
Ramatuelle – Classical Music Festival (second fortnight). ℘04 98 12 64 00.
Toulon – Jazz Festival (second fortnight). ℘04 94 09 71 00. www.jazzatoulon.com

JULY–AUGUST

Thoronet (Abbaye) – Rencontres de musique médiévale: medieval and Traditional Music Festival. *www.musique-medievale.fr*

Cotignac – Festival de théâtre du Rocher: open-air cinema festival (evenings). *www.lestoilesdusud.fr*

St-Tropez – Festival des nuits du château de la Moutte: evenings of music, dance and theatre at the Château de la Moutte. *www.lesnuitsduchateaudelamoutte.com*

Vence – Les Nuits du Sud: world music festival.

JULY–OCTOBER

Vallauris – Biennial International Festival of Ceramic Art (even years).

AUGUST

BarJols – **Foire du cuir**: leatherwork Fair

Entrecasteaux – Chamber Music Festival (mid August).

Fréjus – Fête du raisin: grape festival (beginning of month). Celebration of the first grapes harvested, with tastings and traditional dancing, followed by a special mass.

Grasse – Fête du jasmin: jasmine festival (first weekend). Flowered float parade and fireworks. *www.ville-grasse.fr/jasminade*

Hyères – Festival'Hyères: music festival on the beachfront.

Menton – Festival de musique de chambre: chamber music festival during which concerts are held in front of the Basilique St-Michel.

Nice – Musicalia (grassy amphitheatre): free world music concerts.

Roquebrune-Cap-Martin – Passion Procession through the old village streets (on August 5).

Vallauris – Fête de la poterie: pottery festival (second Sunday).

Ramatuelle – Theatre Festival *www.festivalderamatuelle.com*

SEPTEMBER

Cannes – Régates royales: royal regattas (last week). *www.regatesroyales.com*

Fayence – Aoïlis festival.

Many villages – Fête de la St-Michel Michaelmas celebrations (September 29th).

Throughout France – Journées du Patrimoine (Heritage Days): yearly, for two consecutive days, many buildings of historical, political or cultural interest that are usually closed to the public, are exceptionally open to the public.

OCTOBER

Collobrières – Fête de la châtaigne: Chestnut Festival (last three Sundays). Local produce market, activities for children and chestnut products to celebrate the harvest.

Fréjus – Roc'Azur: mountain biking races (beginning of the month).

Gonfaron – Chestnut Festival. Grilled chestnuts and a market of local products made from *chataignes* (chestnuts).

La Garde-Freinet – Fête de la châtaigne: Chestnut Festival (3rd and 4th Sundays).

Ollioules – Fête de l'olivier: Olive Festival (first weekend).

Roquebrune-sur-Argens – Fête du miel: Honey Festival (first weekend).

Royal Regattas, Cannes

©Serge Villa/Dreamstime.com

St-Tropez – Les Voiles de St-Tropez sailing race (beginning of October).

NOVEMBER
Cannes – International dance festival (last week on odd years).
Monaco – Monaco's National Day (19th).
Taradeau – New wine festival (third Sunday).

DECEMBER
Bandol – Wine Festival (first Sunday).
Lucéram – Pastorale des bergers: Shepherds' Christmas Offering and Provençal Mass.
Vallée de la Roya – Santon Festival, with Nativity scenes. (mid-Dec to mid-Jan).

Know Before You Go

USEFUL WEBSITES
www.ambafrance-us.org
The French Embassy in the USA has a website providing basic information (geography, demographics, history), a news digest and business-related information. It offers special pages for children, and pages devoted to culture, language study and travel, as well as links to other selected French sites (regions, cities, ministries).

www.fngi.fr
The website of the Federation of Licenced Tour Guides and Interpreters, which boasts a membership of more than 800 guides working in 35 languages.

www.francekeys.com
This website has a regional map of France, temperature information and a selection of events plus other practical information for visiting France.

http://france.meteofrance.com
Check the weather forecast in advance of your trip. Temperatures given by region, the coast and the mountains. In French language.

http://france.usembassy.gov
The official website of the United States' Embassy in France.

www.gov.uk/government/world/france
The official website of the United Kingdom's Embassy in France.

http://int.rendezvousenfrance.com
The website of Atout France (France tourist development agency) is packed with practical information and tips for those travelling to France (available in both English and French).

VIRTUAL RIVIERA
Here are a few selected websites devoted to the French Riviera (Côte d'Azur):

www.beyond.fr
Provence and Beyond is a website in English with lots of links, information on places, sports, history, accommodation and more; practical and comprehensive.

www.provenceweb.fr
Provence on the Web includes an online magazine with featured villages, upcoming events, recipes and touring suggestions (thematic tours, bike tours and others).

www.rivieratimes.com
The online edition for the monthly English newspaper *The Riviera Times* includes the latest news, classified ads.

http://riviera.angloinfo.com
AngloINFO is a popular website for the English-speaking expatriate

community along the Côte d'Azur. It includes a directory of local businesses and organisations, particularly those run by or catering for English speakers, plus lively community Forums.

www.riviera-reporter.com
This is the website for the monthly printed English magazine *Riviera Reporter*. It has archived articles that are helpful for both visitors and English-speaking locals on the Riviera.

TOURIST OFFICES
Public information hotline "**France on Call**": ℘(514) 288-1904.

INTERNATIONAL

Australia – New Zealand
- **Sydney**
  French Tourist Bureau
  Level 13, 25 Bligh Street,
  Sydney, New South Wales 2000
  ℘(02) 9231 5244

Canada
- **Montreal**
  1800 Avenue McGill College,
  Bureau 1010,
  Montreal PQ H3A 3J6
  ℘(514) 288-2026

Great Britain and Ireland
- **London**
  LIncoln House, 300 High Holborn,
  London WC1 V7JH
  ℘00 (44) 207 061 66 00

South Africa
  C/O Air France - Village Walk Office
  Tower Blg
  3rd Floor - Cnr Maud and
  Rivonia Road
  Sandton, South Africa
  ℘00 (27) 11 523 82 92

United States
- **East Coast**
  825 Third Avenue,
  New York, NY 10022
  ℘ 00 (1) 212 838 7800

- **West Coast**
  9454 Wilshire Boulevard,
  Suite 210,
  Beverly Hills, CA 90212
  ℘00 (1) 310 271 6665

LOCAL/REGIONAL
Visitors may also contact local tourist offices for more detailed information and to receive brochures and maps. The addresses and telephone numbers of tourist offices for individual towns in this guide are located in that town's description after the symbol 🗓.

Below, the addresses are given for tourist offices of the *départements* and *régions* covered in this guide.

- **Comité régional du tourisme de Provence-Alpes-Côte d'Azur**
  Maison de la Région
  61 La Canebière
  13231 Marseille, Cedex 01
  ℘04 91 56 47 00
  www.tourismepaca.fr

- **Comité régional du tourisme Côte d'Azur**
  455 Promenade des Anglais,
  Bâtiment Horizon
  CS 53126, 06203 Nice Cedex 1
  ℘04 93 37 78 78
  www.cotedazur-tourisme.com

- **Var Tourisme - Agence de développement touristique**
  1 Boulevard de Strasbourg,
  BP 5127 83093 Toulon Cedex
  ℘04 94 18 59 60
  www.visitvar.fr

- **Direction du tourisme et des Congrès de la Principauté de Monaco**
  2A Boulevard des Moulins,
  Monte Carlo, MC 98030
  Monaco Cedex
  ℘377 92 16 61 16
  www.visitmonaco.com

- **Parc national du Mercantour**
  23 rue d'Italie, CS 51316
  06006 Nice Cedex 1
  ✆04 93 16 78 88
  www.mercantour.eu

- **Parc national de Port-Cros**
  Allée du Castel Ste-Claire,
  BP 70220 83406 Hyères Cedex
  ✆04 94 12 82 30
  www.portcrosparcnational.fr

- **Réseau national des destinations départementales**
  74-76 rue de Bercy, 75012 Paris
  ✆01 44 11 10 20
  www.rn2d.net

DUTY-FREE ALLOWANCES	
Spirits (whisky, gin, vodka, etc.)	2.6gal/10l
Fortified wines (vermouth, port, etc.)	5.2gal/20l
Wine (not more than 60 sparkling)	23.7gal/90l
Beer	29gal/110l
Cigarettes	800
Cigarillos	400
Cigars	200
Smoking Tobacco	2.2lb/1kg

Tourist Information Centres

The **Michelin Guide France** gives the addresses and telephone numbers of the Tourist Information Centres (*Syndicats d'Initiative or Offices de tourisme*) to be found in most large towns and many tourist resorts. They can supply large-scale town plans, timetables and information on local entertainment, accommodation, sports and sightseeing.

INTERNATIONAL VISITORS
DOCUMENTS
Passport

Nationals of countries within the European Union entering France need only a national identity card (a passport for UK nationals). Nationals of other countries must be in possession of a valid national **passport**. In case of loss or theft, report to your embassy or consulate and the local police.

Visa

No **entry visa** is required for Canadian, US or Australian citizens travelling as tourists and staying for up to 90 days, except for students planning to study in France. If you think you may need a visa, apply to your local French Consulate. US citizens are advised to consult www.travel.state.gov for entry requirements, security and other information including contact numbers of US embassies and consulates. In an emergency call the **Overseas Citizens Services hotline**: ✆1-888-407-4747 *(inside the US)*, ✆1-202-501-4444 *(outside the US)*.

CUSTOMS

In the UK, **HM Revenue & Customs** *(www.hmrc.gov.uk)* provides information about customs and duty-free allowances (click on the "Individuals & employees" section/"More topics"). **US citizens** should view *Tips for Traveling Abroad* online *(http://travel.state.gov/travel/ tips/tips_1232.html)* for general information on visa requirements, customs regulations, medical care, etc. There are no customs formalities for holidaymakers bringing their caravans into France for a stay of less than six months. No customs document is necessary for pleasure boats and outboard motors for a stay of less than six months but the registration certificate should be kept on board. Americans can bring home, tax-free, up to US$ 800 worth of goods (limited quantities of alcohol and tobacco products); Canadians up to CND$ 750; Australians up to AUS$ 900 and New Zealanders up to NZ$ 700. Persons living in a member state of the European Union are not restricted with regard to purchasing goods for private use.

EMBASSIES AND CONSULATES IN FRANCE

Australia	Embassy	4 rue Jean-Rey, 75724 Paris Cedex 15 ℘01 40 59 33 00. www.france.embassy.gov.au
Canada	Embassy	35 avenue Montaigne, 75008 Paris ℘01 44 43 29 00. www.international.gc.ca
Ireland	Embassy	12 avenue Foch, 75116 Paris ℘01 44 17 67 00. www.embassyofireland.fr
New Zealand	Embassy	7 ter rue Léonard-de-Vinci, 75116 Paris ℘01 45 01 43 43. www.nzembassy.com/france
South Africa	Embassy	59 quai d'Orsay, 75343 Paris Cedex 07 ℘01 53 59 23 23. www.afriquesud.net
UK	Embassy	35 rue du Faubourg St-Honoré, 75383 Paris Cedex 08 ℘01 44 51 31 00. http://.ukinfrance.fco.gov.uk/en
	Consulate-General	16 rue d'Anjou, 75008 Paris ℘01 44 51 31 00
	Consulate	24 avenue du Prado, 13006 Marseille ℘04 91 15 72 10
USA	Embassy	2 avenue Gabriel, 75382 Paris Cedex 08 ℘01 43 12 22 22. http://france.usembassy.gov
	Consulate-General	pl. Varian-Fry, 13006 Marseille ℘04 91 54 92 00. http://marseille.usconsulate.gov

HEALTH

First aid, medical advice and chemists' night service are provided by chemists/drugstores (pharmacie), identified by the green cross sign. Since the recipient of medical treatment in French hospitals or clinics must pay the bill, it is advisable to take out comprehensive insurance coverage. Nationals of non-EU countries should check with their insurance companies about policy limitations. Reimbursement can then be negotiated with the insurance company according to the policy held. All prescription drugs should be clearly labelled and it is recommended you carry a copy of the prescription. **British and Irish citizens**, if they are not already in possession of an **EHIC** (European Health Insurance Card), should apply for one before travelling. The card entitles UK residents to free or reduced-cost medical treatment. Apply at UK post offices call: ℘0845 606 2030 (automated EHIC application service) or visit www.ehic.org.uk. You pay upfront but can reclaim most of the money (see website for details). **Americans** concerned about travel and health may contact the International Association for Medical Assistance to Travelers, which can also provide details of English-speaking doctors in different parts of France: ℘(716) 754-4883. www.iamat.org. The **Hôpital Américain de Paris (American Hospital of Paris)** is open 24hr for emergencies as well as consultations, with English speaking staff (63 Blvd. Victor-Hugo, 92200 Neuilly-sur-Seine; ℘01 46 41 25 25; www.american-hospital.org). The hospital is accredited by major insurance companies. The **Institut hospitalier franco-britannique (British Hospital)** is just outside Paris in Levallois-Perret (3 rue Barbès and at 4 rue Kléber - for emergencies; ℘1 47 59 59 59; www.ihfb.org/fr). This facility is registered as a charity in the UK and provides English-speaking medical staff to the British community in France.

ACCESSIBILITY

The sights described in this guide that are easily accessible to people of reduced mobility are indicated by the symbol ♿. Many of France's historic buildings, including musems and hotels, have limited or no wheelchair access. Older hotels tend to lack lifts (elevators). Tourism for All UK (*℘0845 124 9971; www.tourismforall.org.uk*) publishes some handy information about accessibility, which is also available from French disability organisations such as **Association des Paralysés de France** (*17 blvd Auguste-Blanqui, 75013 Paris; ℘01 40 78 69 00;*

www.apf.asso.fr). Useful information on transport, holidaymaking and sports associations for the disabled is available from French-language website: www.handicap.fr. In the UK, www.radar.org.uk is a good source of info and support and US website www.access-able.com provides information for mature travellers or those with special needs, including lists of experienced travel agents and useful Internet links.
The **Michelin Guide France** indicates hotels and campsites with facilities suitable for travellers with physical disabilities.

Getting There and Getting Around

BY PLANE

The French domestic network operates frequent services from Paris (Charles-de-Gaulle and Orly airports), covering the whole country. The main holiday destinations in the south of France are Nice, Marseille, Toulon and Monaco.
Air France is the leading airline for domestic flights but there are also flights available on the European carrier, **easyJet**.
Direct flights from the UK can be booked with **easyJet**, **British Airways**, **British Midland** and **Ryanair**. There are transfer buses to town terminals and to rail stations. The **RER-B** regional rail links to the centre of Paris from both Roissy and Orly. There are also package tour flights with a rail or coach link-up. Information, brochures and timetables are available from airlines and travel agents.

- **easyJet**
  ℘0820 420 315 (0.12€/min)
  from France
  www.easyjet.com
- **British Airways**
  ℘0844 493 0787 *from England*
  ℘0825 825 040 (0.15€/min)
  from France
  www.britishairways.com
- **Air France**
  ℘3654 (0.34€/min) *from France*
  www.airfrance.com
- **Ryanair**
  ℘0892 562 150 (0.34€min)
  from France
  www.ryanair.com
- **Aéroports de Paris**
  ℘3950 (0.34€/min) *from France*
  or 33 1 70 36 39 50 *from abroad*
- **Aéroport international de Nice-Côte d'Azur**
  ℘0820 423 333 (0.12€ TTC/min) *from France* or 00 33 4 89 88 98 28 *from abroad*
  www.nice.aeroport.fr
- **Aéroport international de Toulon-Hyères**
  ℘0825 01 83 87 (0.15€ TTC/min). www.toulon-hyeres.aeroport.fr

BY SEA
FROM THE UK OR IRELAND

There are numerous **cross-Channel services** from the United Kingdom and Ireland. To choose the most suitable route between your port of arrival and your destination use the **Michelin Tourist and Motoring Atlas France**, **Michelin map 726** (which gives travel times and mileages) or **Michelin Local maps** from the 1:200 000 series.

BY TRAIN/RAIL

Eurostar runs via the Channel Tunnel between London St Pancras and Paris in 3hr *(bookings and information ℘08432 186 186 in the UK; ℘44 1233 617 575 from outside the UK; www.eurostar.com.* In Lille and Paris it links to the high-speed rail network **(TGV)**, which covers most of the country and has been extended to the South of France. *For details call ℘3635 (0.34€/min) from France; www. tgv.com.* The main towns served by the TGV network are Lyon, Avignon, Valence, Montpellier, Aix-en-Provence and Marseille. As far as the Riviera is concerned, there are trains leaving daily from Paris-Gare de Lyon for Nice station, running roughly between 8am and 10.30pm (night train). The fastest schedule takes 5hr.

Eurail *(www.eurail.com)* offers travel passes that may be purchased by residents of countries outside the European Union. In the US, contact your travel agent.

☺ Practical Information ☺

The French railway company SNCF operates a telephone information, reservation and prepayment service in English from 7am to 10pm (French time). In France call ℘08 36 35 35 39 *(when calling from outside France, drop the initial 0).*

P&O Ferries	In the UK: ℘08716 645 645. In France: ℘0820 900 061 (0.15€/min) www.poferries.com
DFDS Seaways	In the UK: ℘0871 574 7235 Outside the UK: ℘+44 208 127 8303 www.norfolkline-ferries.co.uk
Brittany Ferries	In the UK: ℘0871 244 0744 In France: ℘0825 828 828 (0.15€/min) In Ireland: ℘021 4277 801 www.brittany-ferries.com
Irish Ferries	In the UK: ℘08717 300 400 In Ireland: ℘0818 300 400 In France: ℘01 70 72 03 26 In the US and Canada: www.irishferries.com
My Ferry Link	In the UK: ℘0844 2482 In France: ℘0811 654 765 www.seafrance.com

☺*Tickets must be validated (composter) by using the orange automatic date-stamping machines at the platform entrance (☺failure to do so may result in a fine).* **Eurailpass**, **Flexipass** and **Saverpass** are travel passes that may be purchased by residents of countries outside the European Union. In the US, contact your travel agent or **Rail Europe** *(44 South Broadway, White Plains, NY 10601; ℘1-800-622-8600; ww.ralleurope.com).* If you are a European resident, you can buy an individual country pass if you are not a resident of the country you are buying it for. Information on schedules can be obtained on websites for these agencies and the **SNCF**, respectively: www.raileurope.com, www.voyages-sncf.com. At the SNCF site, you can book ahead, pay with a credit card, and receive your ticket in the mail at home free of charge (seven days minimum before leaving in the case of foreign countries, four days for France).

TGV Méditerranée

France's southern high-speed rail link makes Provence within three hours of Paris and six of London. The streamlined blue and silver train reaches Marseille after a mere 3hr, leaving from Paris. The 12-year campaign to complete the route followed by the TGV Méditerranée was fraught with difficulties. Besides the opposition shown by local residents, there were a number of geographical, architectural and ecological constraints. Considerable care was taken to preserve the natural environment and to avoid disturbing protected species. Moreover, new bridges and viaducts had to be built with local stone in order to blend in with the surrounding landscape. Indeed, on the journey from Valence to Marseille you will see no fewer than 23 bridges! Today the line carries thousands of passengers every day.

The line travels from Paris–Lyon-Saint Exupéry Airport, Paris–Valence, Paris–Avignon, Paris–Aix-en-Provence, Paris–Marseille, Paris–**Toulon**, Paris–**Hyères**, Paris–**Fréjus**, Paris–**Nice**, Paris–Nîmes, Paris–Montpellier, Paris–Béziers and Paris–Perpignan.

The trains provide a very good service to passengers: more legroom, a central luggage rack, an area set aside for bicycles, family and disabled facilities, telephone booths, plug sockets for European 2-pin plugs (first class), a wide range of light snacks or meals and even a free newspaper with your breakfast in first class.

DISCOUNTS

There are numerous **discounts** available when you purchase your tickets in France, from 25–50 percent below the regular rate. These discounts include those for using senior cards and youth cards (the nominative cards with a photograph must be purchased beforehand), and lower rates for 2–9 people travelling together (no card required, advance purchase necessary). A limited number of discount seats are available in peak travel times, but the best discounts are available during off-peak periods. For more information on the following **TER lines**, visit the website of the SNCF "réseau régional TER Provence - Alpes - Côte d'azur"at www.ter-sncf.com/Regions/Paca/fr. The website has an interactive map of the lines that cross the PACA region. You can make up your own itinerary and get train schedules along that itinerary.

- **Line no 1**
  Marseille, Toulon, Hyères
- **Line no 2**
  Marseille, Toulon,
  Les Arcs Draguignan
- **Line no 3**
  Les Arcs Draguignan,
  St-Raphaël, Cannes, Nice
- **Line no 4**
  Mandelieu, Cannes, Nice,
  Ventimiglia (Italy)
- **Line no 5**
  Nice, Breil-sur-Roya, Cueno (Italy)
- **Line no 6**
  Marseille, Toulon, Nice,
  Ventimiglia (Italy)
- **Grasse,Cannes via Le Bosquet**
  Grasse, Le Bosquet, Cannes

Valid June to December, the **Pass Isabelle Famille** applies to families only (2 adults plus 2 children under 16) and allows, for one day only, an unlimited number of train trips on the TER lines of the Alpes-Maritimes.

BY COACH/BUS

- **Eurolines UK**
  ℰ44 871 781 8178.
  www.eurolines.co.uk.
- **Eurolines France**
  ℰ0892 89 90 91
  (0.34€/min) *from France*.
  www.eurolines.fr.

- **www.eurolines.com**
  The international website with information about travelling all over Europe by coach (bus).

BY CAR

The area covered in this guide is easily reached by main motorways and national routes. **Michelin map 726** indicates the main itineraries, as well as alternative routes for avoiding heavy traffic during busy holiday periods, and gives estimated travel times. The latest Michelin route-planning service is available on the Internet: **www.viamichelin.com**. Travellers can calculate a precise route using such options as shortest route, route avoiding toll roads, Michelin-recommended route, as well as gain access to tourist information (hotels, restaurants, attractions). The service is available on a pay-per-route basis or by subscription. Roads are very busy during holiday periods (particularly weekends in July and August) and to avoid traffic congestion it is advisable to follow the recommended secondary routes (signposted as *Bison Futé – itinéraires bis*). The motorway network includes rest areas *(aires d'autoroute)* and petrol/gas stations, usually with restaurant and shopping malls attached, about every 25mi/40km, so that long-distance drivers have no excuse not to stop for a rest every now and then.

DOCUMENTS

Driving licence

For British drivers unaccustomed to driving on the right, extra care will be needed. Road signs generally use easy-to-understand international visual symbols instead of words. When driving in France, EU nationals must have their own valid **national driving licence**. Travellers from other EU countries and North America can drive in France with a valid national or home-state **driving licence**. An **international driving licence** is useful because the information on it appears in nine languages (keep in mind that traffic officers are empowered to fine motorists). A permit is available (US $15 plus shipping and handling fees) from the **National Automobile Club** *(373 Vintage Park Dr., Suite E Foster City, CA 9440; ✆650-294-7000; www.nationalautoclub.com)* or contact your local branch of the **American Automobile Association** *(www.aaa.com)*. All drivers must also have with them the vehicle's **registration papers** and a current **insurance certificate**.

The originals of all documents are required. Copies are not acceptable.

INSURANCE

Many motoring organisations offer accident insurance and breakdown service schemes for members. Check with your current insurance company regarding coverage while abroad. If you plan to hire a car using your credit card, check with the company, which may automatically provide liability insurance (and thus save you having to pay the cost for optimum coverage).

ROAD REGULATIONS

The minimum driving age is 18. Traffic drives on the right. All passengers must wear **seat belts**. Children under the age of 10 must ride in the back seat. Headlights must be switched on in poor visibility and at night; use side-lights only when the vehicle is stationary. In the case of a **breakdown**, a red warning triangle or hazard warning lights are obligatory, as well as a luminous jacket. In the absence of stop signs at intersections, cars must **yield to the right**. Traffic on main roads outside built-up areas (priority indicated by a yellow diamond sign) and on roundabouts has right of way. Vehicles must stop when the lights turn red at road junctions and may filter to the right only when indicated by an amber arrow. The regulations on **drinking and driving** (limited to 0.50g/l) and **speeding** are strictly enforced, usually by an on-the-spot fine.

RENTAL CARS – RESERVATIONS IN FRANCE		
Avis	✆ 08 21 23 07 60 (France)	www.avis.com
Europcar	✆ 08 25 35 83 58 (France)	www.europcar.com
Budget France	✆ 08 25 00 35 64 (France)	www.budget.com
Hertz France	✆ 08 25 86 18 61 (France)	www.hertz.com
SIXT	✆ 08 20 00 74 98 (France)	www.e-sixt.com
CITER	✆ 08 25 16 12 20 (France)	www.citer.fr

Speed Limits

Although liable to modification, these are as follows:

- Toll motorways (autoroutes) 80mph/130kph (68mph/110kph when raining);
- Dual carriageways and motorways without tolls 68mph/110kph (62mph/100kph when raining);
- Other roads 56mph/90kph (50mph/80kph when raining) and in towns 31mph/50kph;
- Outside lane on motorways during daylight, on level ground and with good visibility – minimum speed limit of 50mph/80kph.

Parking Regulations

In town there are zones where parking is either restricted or subject to a fee; tickets should be obtained from the ticket machines (horodateurs) and displayed inside the windscreen on the driver's side; failure to do so may result in a fine or towing.

Tolls

In France, most motorway sections are subject to a toll (péage). You can pay in cash or with a credit card (Visa, MasterCard).

CAR RENTAL

There are car rental agencies at airports, railway stations and in large towns. Drivers must be over 21; between ages 21–25, drivers are required to pay an extra daily fee;

some companies allow drivers under 23 only if the reservation has been made through a travel agent. It is relatively expensive to hire a car in France; Americans in particular will notice the difference.

MOTORHOME RENTAL

Motorhomes Worldwide offers fully equipped camper vans for hire: ✆ 61 3 8781 1100; www.motorhomesworldwide.com. Also try www.aviscaraway.com and www.motorhome-hire-france.com.

PETROL/GASOLINE

French service stations dispense:
- sans plomb 98 (super unleaded 98)
- sans plomb 95 (super unleaded 95)
- diesel/gazole (diesel)
- GPL (LPG).

For US citizens: gasoline is more expensive in France than in the USA. Prices are listed on signboards on the motorways; it is usually cheaper to fill up after leaving the motorway; check hypermarkets on the outskirts of town. You can pay at the pump using credit/debit cards.

MENU READER

La Carte	The Menu
ENTRÉES	**STARTERS**
Crudités	Raw vegetable salad
Terrine de lapin	Rabbit terrine (pâté)
Frisée aux lardons	Curly lettuce with bacon bits
Escargots	Snails
Cuisses de grenouille	Frog's legs
Salade au crottin	Goat cheese on a bed of lettuce
PLATS (VIANDES)	**MAIN COURSES (MEAT)**
Bavette à l'échalote	Sirloin with shallots
Faux filet au poivre	Sirloin with pepper sauce
Côtes d'agneau	Lamb chops
Filet mignon de porc	Pork filet
Blanquette de veau	Veal in cream sauce
Nos viandes sont garnies	Our meat dishes are served with vegetables
PLATS (POISSONS, VOILAILLE)	**MAIN COURSES (FISH, FOWL)**
Filets de sole	Sole fillets
Dorade aux herbes	Sea bream with herbs
Saumon grillé	Grilled salmon
Coq au vin	Chicken in red wine sauce
Poulet de Bresse rôti	Free-range roast chicken from the Bresse
Omelette aux morilles	Wild-mushroom omelette
PLATEAU DE FROMAGES	**SELECTION OF CHEESES**
DESSERTS	**DESSERTS**
Tarte aux pommes	Apple pie
Crème caramel	Cooled baked custard with caramel sauce
Sorbet: trois parfums	Sorbet: three flavours
BOISSONS	**BEVERAGES**
Bière	Beer
Eau minérale (gazeuse)	(Sparkling) mineral water
Une carafe d'eau	Tap water (no charge)
Vin rouge, vin blanc, rosé	Red wine, white wine, rosé
Jus de fruit	Fruit juice
MENU ENFANT	**CHILDREN'S MENU**
Jambon	Ham
Steak haché	Ground beef
Frites	French fried potatoes

Where to Stay and Eat

WHERE TO STAY
FINDING A HOTEL

Turn to the **Addresses** within individual sight listings for descriptions and prices of typical places to stay **(Stay)** with local flair. The key on the front cover flap of the guide explains the symbols and abbreviations used in these sections. The French Riviera offers a wide array of accommodation options, from simple bed and breakfasts (known as *gîtes* or *chambres d'hôte*) in charming villages to palatial hotels overlooking the Mediterranean.

Prices tend to rise in proximity to the beaches and in the larger cities such as Nice, Cannes, Toulon and Monte Carlo, while some of the best deals can be found in the smaller perched villages and quiet country inns in the hinterlands.

For an even greater selection, use the **Michelin Guide France**, with its famously reliable star-rating system and hundreds of establishments all over France.

Book ahead! The French Riviera is a very popular holiday destination. The **Fédération nationale des comités départementaux de tourisme** (RN2D) (74-76 rue de Bercy, 75012 Paris; ℘01 44 11 10 20, www.destination-france.net) is a booking service that has offices in some French *départements*: contact tourism offices for further information.

The **Fédération Internationale des Logis** (℘01 45 84 70 00; www.logishotels.com) publishes each year a guide that can be ordered online at www.logishotels.com/commande guide/commandeGuide.ph).

Relais & Châteaux is a collection of luxury hotels throughout the world: within France: ℘0825 825 180; within the UK: ℘00 800 2000 00 02; within the US: ℘1 800 735 2478; www.relaischateaux.com.

Economy Chain Hotels

If you need a place to stop en route, chain hotels can be useful, as they are relatively inexpensive and generally located near the main road. While breakfast is available, there may not be a restaurant; rooms are usually small, with a television and bathroom. Central reservation numbers:

- **Akena** ℘01 69 84 85 17 www.hotels-akena.com
- **B&B** ℘0 892 782 929 (0.34€/min) www.hotel-bb.com
- **Etap Hotel** ℘0892 688 900 www.etaphotel.com
- **Hotel F1** ℘0892 685 685 (0.34€/min) www.hotelf1.com
- **Campanile** ℘0 892 230 591 (0.34€/min) www.campanile.com
- **Etap** ℘0892 688 900 www.etaphotel.com
- **Ibis** ℘0892 686 686 (0.34€/min) www.ibis.com. Now includes: **Ibis Budget** (formerly Etap Hotel) ℘0 892 688 900 (0.34€/min) – http://ibisbudgethotel.ibis.com **Ibis Styles** (formerly All Seasons) http://ibisstyleshotel.ibis.com

COTTAGES, BED & BREAKFASTS

The **Maison des Gîtes de France et du Tourisme Vert** is an information service on self-catering accommodation on the French Riviera (and the rest of France). *Gîtes* usually take the form of a cottage or apartment decorated in the local style, where visitors can make themselves at home, or bed and breakfast accommodation (*chambres d'hôtes*), which consists of a room and breakfast at a reasonable price. Contact the Gîtes de France office in Paris (℘01 49 70 75 75; www.gites-de-france.com) or the **Fédération des Stations Vertes de Vacances et des Villages de Neige** (BP 71698, 21016 Dijon Cedex; ℘03 80 54 10 50; www.stationverte.com). Local tourist offices may have lists of available properties and local bed and breakfast establishments.

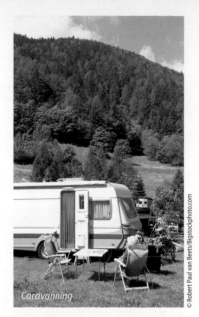

Caravanning

HOSTELS, CAMPING

To obtain a **Hostelling International card** (there is no age requirement, and a senior card is available, too), contact HI in your own country for information and membership applications (US ☎ 1 301 495 1240; UK ☎ 01629 592 700; Australia ☎ 61 2 9283 7195).

There is a booking service online (www.hihostels.com), which you may use to reserve rooms as far as six months in advance.

There are two main youth hostel (auberges de jeunesse) associations in France, the **Ligue Française pour les Auberges de Jeunesse** (67 rue Vergniaud, bâtiment K, 75013 Paris; ☎ 01 44 16 78 78; www.auberges-de-jeunesse.com) and the **Fédération Unie des Auberges de Jeunesse** (27 rue Pajol, 75018 Paris; ☎ 01 44 89 87 27; www.fuaj.org). The Féderation's informative website provides an online booking service.

The French Riviera has numerous officially graded **campsites** with varying standards of facilities. The area is popular with campers in the summer months, so it is wise to book in advance.

WHERE TO EAT

A selection of places to eat (**Eat**) in the different locations covered in this guide can be found in the **Addresses** appearing in the *Discovering The French Riviera* section. The key on the front cover flap of the book explains the symbols and abbreviations used in the Addresses. We have highlighted an array of eating places primarily for their atmosphere, location and regional delicacies. Prices indicate the average cost of a starter, main dish and dessert for one person. Use the red-cover **Michelin Guide France**, with its well-known star-rating system and hundreds of establishments throughout France, for an even greater choice. If you would like to experience a meal in a highly rated restaurant from **The Michelin Guide**, be sure to book ahead.

A number of associations aim to promote good-quality, often local and independent businesses throughout France. **Sites remarquables du goût** (www.sitesremarquablesdugout.com) organise activities such as walks and cookery courses and their logo will help you identify a restaurant that contributes to the preservation of local or artisan products and customs. **Bistrot des Pays** (www.bistrotdepays.com) are open all year and located in villages of fewer than 2,000 inhabitants, making a vital contribution to local economies and the social life of rural communities. In the countryside, restaurants usually serve lunch between noon and 2pm and dinner between 7.30 and 10pm. It is not always easy to find something in between those two mealtimes, as the "non-stop" restaurant is still a rarity in the provinces. However, a hungry traveller can usually get a sandwich (often a filled baguette) in a café, and ordinary hot dishes may be available in a brasserie. Throughout France, the culture leans more towards sitting and eating than grabbing a sandwich on the go, so plan ahead.

Useful Words and Phrases

Sights

	Translation
Abbey	Abbaye
Belfry	Beffroi
Bridge	Pont
Castle	Château
Cemetery	Cimetière
Chapel	Chapelle
Church	Église
Cloisters	Cloître
Convent	Couvent
Courtyard	Cour
Fountain	Fontaine
Garden	Jardin
Gateway	Porte
Hall	Halle
House	Maison
Lock (Canal)	Écluse
Market	Marché
Monastery	Monastère
Museum	Musée
Park	Parc
Port/harbour	Port
Quay	Quai
Ramparts	Remparts
Square	Place
Statue	Statue
Street	Rue
Tower	Tour
Town Hall	Mairie
Windmill	Moulin

On the Road

	Translation
Car Park	Parking
Driving Licence	Permis de conduire
East	Est
Garage (For Repairs)	Garage
Left	Gauche
Motorway/Highway	Autoroute
North	Nord
Parking Meter	Horodateur
Petrol/Gas	Essence
Petrol/Gas Station	Station essence
Right	Droite
South	Sud
Toll	Péage
Traffic Lights	Feu tricolore
Tyre	Pneu
West	Ouest
Wheel Clamp	Sabot
Zebra Crossing	Passage clouté

Shopping

	Translation
Baker's	Boulangerie
Bank	Banque
Big	Grand
Butcher's	Boucherie
Chemist's	Pharmacie
Closed	Fermé
Cough Mixture	Sirop pour la toux
Cough Sweets	Cachets pour la gorge
Entrance	Entrée
Exit	Sortie
Fishmonger's	Poissonnerie
Grocer's	Épicerie
Newsagent, Bookshop	Librairie
Open	Ouvert
Post Office	Poste
Pull	Tirer
Push	Pousser
Shop	Magasin
Small	Petit
Stamps	Timbres

Common Words

	Translation
Hello/Good Morning	Bonjour
Goodbye	Au revoir
Excuse Me	Excusez-moi
Please	S'il vous plaît
Thank You	Merci
Yes/No	Oui/Non
I Am Sorry	Pardon
How	Comment
Why	Pourquoi
When	Quand
Today	Aujourd'hui
Tomorrow	Demain
Yesterday	Hier

© Robert Paul van Beets/Bigstockphoto.com

Basic Information

BUSINESS HOURS

Many museums are closed Monday or Tuesday. Shop hours are usually Monday to Saturday 10am to 6pm. In smaller towns, shops may also close for lunch and off-season. Churches, especially in secluded areas or small villages, are often only opened for services or on request.

DISCOUNTS

Significant discounts are available for senior citizens, students, under 25-year-olds, teachers and groups for public transportation, museums and monuments plus some leisure activities such as films (at certain times of day). Bring student or senior cards with you, and bring along some extra passport-size photos for discount travel cards.

The **World Youth Student & Educational (WYSE) Travel Confederation** (www.wysetc. org), global administrator of the International Student and Teacher Identity Cards, is an association of student travel organisations around the world. WYSE Travel Confederation members collectively negotiate benefits with airlines, governments and providers of other goods and services for the student community, both in their own country and around the world. The non-profit association sells international ID cards for students and youngsters under the age of 25 (who may get discounts on museum entrances, for example).

The WYSE Travel Confederation is active in a network of international education and work exchange programmes. The corporate headquarters address is:

- Herengracht 479,
  1017 BS Amsterdam,
  The Netherlands
  ℰ 31 20 421 28 00
  Fax 31 20 421 28 10.

ELECTRICITY

The electric current is 220 Volts/50Hz. Circular two-pin plugs are the rule. Adapters and converters (for hairdryers, for example) are best bought before you leave home. If you have a rechargeable device, read the instructions carefully. Sometimes these items only require a plug adapter; in other cases you must use a voltage converter.

EMERGENCIES

EMERGENCY NUMBERS
Police: ℰ 17
SAMU (Paramedics): ℰ 15
Fire (Pompiers): ℰ 18

INTERNET ACCESS

Internet access is often easiest to find in hotels in larger towns such as Nice, Monaco, Cannes and Antibes, where WiFi has become standard (often free). These towns have many wireless hotspots in cafés, bars and libraries, as well as a few Internet cafés for those travelling without a computer. The villages and mountain valleys inland have less reliable access; always call hotels or local tourist offices to confirm in advance. You can look online to find the nearest Internet café.

☺ Museum Passes ☺

The Comité Régional du Tourisme Riviera Côte d'Azur has three different museum passes available: City of Nice Pass (municipal museums), Museums of Menton pass (eight sights in and around Menton), and the French Riviera Museum Pass, which offers unlimited free priority access to museums, monuments and gardens on the Riviera from Fréjus to Menton. For more information contact any of the tourist offices within the region, or visit **www.guideriviera.com**.

MAIL/POST

Main post offices open Monday to Friday 8am to 7pm, Saturday 8am to noon. Smaller branch post offices generally close at lunchtime between noon and 2pm, and at 4pm.

Postage via airmail:

- **UK:** letter (20g) 0.80€
- **North America:** letter (20g) 0.95€
- **Australia, NZ:** letter (20g) 0.95€

The website www.laposte.fr has a convenient tool to calculate how much it will cost to send a letter from France anywhere in the world, depending on its weight.

Stamps are also available from news agents and *bureaux de tabac*. Stamp collectors should ask for *timbres de collection* in any post office.

MEDIA

With a large Anglophone expatriate population living on the Côte d'Azur year-round in addition to the seasonal tourists, there are several news sources available in English.

NEWSPAPERS

Local print media in English include the bi-monthly *Riviera Reporter* magazine, the monthly *Riviera Times* newspaper, and the *Var Village Voice*. Newsstands in major towns carry the daily editions of the *International Herald Tribune*, the *Financial Times* and the London *Times* the day they are printed. Other newspapers often arrive on the Riviera a day later.

RADIO

Riviera Radio

Feeling pangs for your native language? Desperately seeking an English-speaking doctor or nanny? Looking for rented accommodation? Riviera Radio is the answer to all your problems. The only 100 percent English-speaking radio in the area, it broadcasts on FM *(106.5 FM in Monaco; ℰ00 377 97 97 94 80 from France; http://rivieraradio.radio.mc)* and covers the stretch of coastline running

between St-Tropez and the Italian resort of San Remo. This Monaco-based radio station provides useful tips for tourists and residents alike, and presents a great many regular programmes: business and financial news, local traffic and weather reports, guide to English-speaking films in VO *(Version Originale)*, job offers, updated news bulletins in conjunction with the BBC World Service, calendar of major fairs and conferences, etc. One of Riviera Radio's most popular features is their weekday morning Community Chest *(9.20am)*, when listeners call in to buy or sell miscellaneous items.

TELEVISION

French channels Canal+ and Arte often air American and British programmes in their original language; however most English-speaking residents and hotels subscribe to satellite for channels such as BBC and CNN.

MONEY
CURRENCY

There are no restrictions on the amount of currency visitors can take into France. Visitors carrying a lot of cash are advised to complete a currency declaration form on arrival because there are restrictions on currency export.

Notes and coins

Since January 2002, the **euro** is the official currency of France and other participating EU Member States. One euro is divided into 100 cents, or *centimes*.

BANKS

Banks are generally open from 9am to noon and 2pm to 4pm while branches are closed either on Monday or Saturday. Banks close early on the day before a bank holiday. A passport is necessary as identification when cashing traveller's cheques in banks. Commission charges vary and hotels usually charge more than banks for cashing cheques. One of the most economical ways to access your

American Express ☏ 01 47 77 72 00

Visa ☏ 08 36 69 08 80

MasterCard ☏ 0 800 90 13 87

Inter-bank emergency ☏ 0 892 705 705

1 January	New Year's Day (*Jour de l'An*)
Monday after Easter Sunday	Easter Day Monday (*Pâques*)
1 May	Labour Day (*Fête du Travail*)
8 May	VE Day (*Fête de la Victoire*)
Thursday 40 days after Easter	Ascension Day (*Ascension*)
7th Sunday after Easter	Whit Sunday and Monday (*Pentecôte*)
14 July	France's Nationale Day (*Fête de la Bastille*)
15 August	Assumption (*Assomption*)
1 November	All Saint's Day (*Toussaint*)
11 November	Armistice Day (*Jour du Souvenir*))
25 December	Christmas Day (*Noël*)

money in France is to use **ATM** to get cash directly from your bank account or using your credit cards to get cash advances (but be aware that your bank will charge you for this service). Be sure to remember your 4-digit PIN: you will need it to use cash dispensers and to pay with your card in most shops, restaurants, etc. Code pads are numeric; use a telephone pad to translate a letter code into numbers. PINs have four digits in France; enquire with the issuing company or bank if the code you usually use is longer. Visa is the most widely accepted credit card, followed by MasterCard; other cards, credit and debit (Maestro, Plus, Cirrus, etc.) are also accepted in some cash machines. American Express is not widely accepted in France, more often only in premium establishments. Most places post signs indicating the cards they accept; if you don't see such a sign and want to pay with a card, ask before ordering or making a selection. Cards are widely accepted in shops, hypermarkets, hotels and restaurants, at tollbooths and in petrol stations. If your card is lost or stolen in France, call one of the following 24-hour hotlines:
You must report any loss or theft of credit cards or traveller's cheques to the local police, who will issue you with a certificate (useful proof to show the issuing company).

PUBLIC HOLIDAYS
See the box for a list of major public holidays in France. There are other religious and national festivals days, and a number of local saints' days, etc. On all these days, museums and other monuments may be closed or may vary their hours of admission. In addition to the usual school holidays at Christmas and in the spring and summer, there are long mid-term breaks (10 days to a fortnight) in February and early November.

SMOKING
Smoking is banned inside all public spaces, including hotel rooms, bars, and clubs, since January 2008. It is still permitted on outdoor café terraces and in specially-built *fumoirs*.

TELEPHONES
PUBLIC TELEPHONES
Most public phones in France use pre-paid phone cards (*télécartes*), rather than coins. Some telephone booths accept credit cards (Visa, MasterCard/Eurocard). *Télécartes* (50 or 120 units) can be bought in post offices, branches of France Télécom, *bureaux de tabac* (cafés that sell cigarettes) and newsagents and may be used to make calls in France and abroad. Calls can be received at phone boxes where the blue bell sign is shown; the phone will not ring, so keep your eye on the small digital screen.

INTERNATIONAL DIALLING CODES (00 + code)			
Australia	☏61	**New Zealand**	☏64
Canada	☏1	**United Kingdom**	☏44
Ireland	☏353	**United States**	☏1

NATIONAL CALLS

French telephone numbers have ten digits. Paris and Paris region numbers begin with 01; 02 in northwest France; 03 in northeast France; 04 in southeast France and Corsica; 05 in southwest France.

INTERNATIONAL CALLS

To call France from abroad, dial the country code (33) + 9-digit number (omit the initial 0). When calling abroad from France dial 00, then dial the country code followed by the area code (*see box below*), minus the first 0, and number of your correspondent.

International information:
US, Canada, UK, Australia: 118 700
International operator:
00 33 12 + country code
Local directory assistance: 118

TO USE YOUR PERSONAL CALLING CARD	
AT&T	☏0-800 99 00 11
Sprint	☏0-800 99 00 87
Verizon	☏0-800 99 00 19
Canada Direct	☏0-800 99 00 16

MOBILE/CELL PHONES

In France these have numbers that begin with 06 and 07. Two-watt (lighter, shorter reach) and eight-watt models are on the market, using the Orange, Bouygues Télécom or SFR networks. *Mobicartes* are prepaid phone cards that fit into mobile units. Mobile phone rentals (delivery or airport pickup provided):
World Cellular Rentals:
www.worldcr.com

TIME

France is one hour ahead of Greenwich Mean Time (GMT). Even though the Prime Meridian (0°) passes through Spain and France, both countries use the mean solar time of 15 degrees east (Central European Time) rather than 0 degrees (GMT). Paris is 6hrs ahead of New York City.

WHEN IT IS NOON IN FRANCE, IT IS	
3am	in Los Angeles
6am	in New York
11am	in Dublin
11am	in London
7pm	in Perth
9pm	in Sydney
11pm	in Auckland

In France "am" and "pm" are not used but the 24-hour clock is widely applied.

TIPPING

Since a service charge is automatically included in the price of meals and accommodation in France, any additional tipping is up to the visitor, generally small change, and generally not more than 5 percent. Hairdressers are usually tipped 10–15 percent. As a rule, prices for hotels and restaurants as well as for other goods and services are significantly less expensive in the French regions than in Paris.

Restaurants usually charge for meals in two ways: a *forfait* or *menu*, that is a fixed price menu with two to three courses, sometimes a small pitcher of wine, all for a set price, or *à la carte*, the more expensive way, with each course ordered separately.

Cafés have very different prices, depending on where they are located. The price of a drink or a coffee is cheaper if you stand at the counter *(comptoir)* than if you sit down *(salle)* and sometimes it is even more expensive if you sit outdoors *(terrace)*. In some big cities, prices go up after 10pm in the evening.

CONVERSION TABLES

Weights and Measures

1 kilogram (kg) 6.35 kilograms 0.45 kilograms	**2.2 pounds (lb)** 14 pounds 16 ounces (oz)	**2.2 pounds** 1 stone (st) 16 ounces	*To convert kilograms to pounds, multiply by 2.2*
1 metric ton (tn)	**1.1 tons**	**1.1 tons**	
1 litre (l) 3.79 litres 4.55 litres	**2.11 pints (pt)** 1 gallon (gal) 1.20 gallon	**1.76 pints** 0.83 gallon 1 gallon	*To convert litres to gallons, multiply by 0.26 (US) or 0.22 (UK)*
1 hectare (ha) **1 sq kilometre (km²)**	**2.47 acres** 0.38 sq. miles (sq mi)	**2.47 acres** 0.38 sq. miles	*To convert hectares to acres, multiply by 2.4*
1 centimetre (cm) **1 metre (m)**	**0.39 inches (in)** 3.28 feet (ft) or 39.37 inches or 1.09 yards (yd)	**0.39 inches**	*To convert metres to feet, multiply by 3.28; for kilometres to miles, multiply by 0.6*
1 kilometre (km)	**0.62 miles (mi)**	**0.62 miles**	

Clothing

Women					Men			
	○	▥	⌗			○	▥	⌗
Shoes	35	4	2½		**Shoes**	40	7½	7
	36	5	3½			41	8½	8
	37	6	4½			42	9½	9
	38	7	5½			43	10½	10
	39	8	6½			44	11½	11
	40	9	7½			45	12½	12
	41	10	8½			46	13½	13
Dresses & suits	36	6	8		**Suits**	46	36	36
	38	8	10			48	38	38
	40	10	12			50	40	40
	42	12	14			52	42	42
	44	14	16			54	44	44
	46	16	18			56	46	48
Blouses & sweaters	36	6	30		**Shirts**	37	14½	14½
	38	8	32			38	15	15
	40	10	34			39	15½	15½
	42	12	36			40	15¾	15¾
	44	14	38			41	16	16
	46	16	40			42	16½	16½

Sizes often vary depending on the designer. These equivalents are given for guidance only.

Speed

KPH	10	30	50	70	80	90	100	110	120	130
MPH	6	19	31	43	50	56	62	68	75	81

Temperature

Celsius (°C)	0°	5°	10°	15°	20°	25°	30°	40°	60°	80°	100°
Fahrenheit (°F)	32°	41°	50°	59°	68°	77°	86°	104°	140°	176°	212°

To convert Celsius into Fahrenheit, multiply °C by 9, divide by 5, and add 32.
To convert Fahrenheit into Celsius, subtract 32 from °F, multiply by 5, and divide by 9.
NB: Conversion factors on this page are approximate.

Antibes
© Camille Moirenc / hemis.fr

The Region Today

LIFE ON THE RIVIERA
THE COAST

A Holiday Destination – Visitors seeking fashionable and elegant resorts can choose between the hustle and bustle of Cannes and Monte Carlo or the quieter and more discreet setting of Hyères, Beaulieu, Menton, Cap Ferrat or Cap Martin. Those longing for the rush of a big city with all its amusements will undoubtedly turn to Nice. Lively St-Tropez attracts a large number of summer visitors, while anyone seeking a little solitude should head for the isolated rocky inlets along the coast. Wherever you stay, the Riviera offers a full range of hotels for every budget.

Architectural styles vary widely on the Riviera, although small country houses built in Provençal rustic style, with pink or ochre-coloured façades and overhanging red-tiled roofs, definitely set the tone. Most towns and villages, and many former grand houses maintain exotic gardens that are a pleasure to visit all year round. Many magnificent parks offer fine **views** from their terraces, where the unique light and colour of the Mediterranean come to life.

The coast is heavily built-up, particularly towards the east, and some towns are even erected over the water, such as the lake town of Port-Grimaud, the Cogolin Marina, the marine city of Port-la-Galère and Fontvieille in Monaco.

Ambitious construction projects, some of them totally out of proportion, have sprung up on all sides; a great number of private properties have appeared at the water's edge, although the public has right of access all along the coast. Anyone looking for deserted coastlines should head west to the Hyères region.

Ports and Fishing – The naval port of Toulon is in a league of its own on its popular recreational coast. Cannes, Monaco and Antibes are long-established pleasure boat ports: beautiful yachts with polished wood and gleaming steelwork lie at anchor in their bays or are moored along the quaysides.

Fishing on the Riviera is confined to the coast and as the catch is insufficient for the area, it has to be supplemented by shipments from the Atlantic.

Rather than large fishing ports, the coast is dotted with small harbours. Bandol, St-Tropez, St-Raphaël and Villefranche-sur-Mer have adapted to the demands of tourists and equipped themselves with moorings for pleasure boats.

The Nice region has modernised the fishing industry and increased the number of boats in use by resorting to large running nets known as *lamparos* and *seinches* and constructing fish canneries.

The Markets – Most of the coastal towns have their own open-air markets where, to the colourful banks of flowers, fresh produce and stalls of gleaming fish, are added the noisy bustle and the warmth of the local accents of buyers and sellers, creating a true Côte d'Azur scene.

INLAND

The interior reveals the last vestiges of what was once a rough and precarious way of life: valleys and hill slopes terraced with stone walls retaining small strips of soil for growing cereals or two or three rows of vines and a few olive and almond trees.

The *garrigue*, where small flocks of sheep and goats are put to graze, form a sharp contrast with the fertile valleys and irrigated plains of the lowlands and the coast, where cereals, early vegetables and flowers are harvested and vines and fruit trees flourish. The lonely villages clinging to solitary ridges and small farms lying abandoned among their terraced walls bear little resemblance to the market towns of the plains, spread along the main roads, or to the farms *(mas)* scattered in the midst of large cultivated areas.

At the centre of most villages is a small square *(cours)* shaded by plane trees round a fountain and much-frequented cafés. Many villages seem unoccupied, but very often shutters remain closed to keep out the heat and insects.

21ST CENTURY

While the museums, old town markets, quaint perched villages and sandy beaches keep the continuous influx of tourists occupied for most of the year, the Riviera economy doesn't solely depend on tourism, an industry vulnerable to international politics and economic slumps. Nice, Monaco and Cannes have invested heavily to become important business travel destinations, hosting conferences and trade shows year round, and Toulon continues to develop its thriving port, while technology and research centres have been booming throughout the region.

The French Riviera will always preserve and promote its colourful history and natural beauty, but in the 21C it has shrugged off its sleepy resort reputation to embrace a dynamic and international identity.

POPULATION

The population of the French Riviera was just 200,000 in 1860, growing to about one million residents today, with a 3 percent growth rate since 1990, more than twice the national average. Over 90 percent of this population is concentrated in the coastal cities of Menton, Nice, Antibes, Cannes, Hyères, Fréjus and Toulon. International residents make up 12 percent of the population, with half of them coming from the European Union and almost 45 percent from North Africa.

LIFESTYLE

The French Riviera lifestyle is perfectly summed up as *Art de Vivre*, or the Art of Living. Everything from the lush Mediterranean landscape to the sun-drenched Provençal cuisine contributes to the overall sense of people living the good life and taking the time to enjoy it. The region runs at the leisurely pace typical of Latin countries, where afternoon siestas and Sunday boules games around the village square with a glass of chilled rosé or pastis are still very much commonplace.

RELIGION

Like much of France, Catholicism is the most widespread religion on the French Riviera, with Catholic churches, chapels, abbeys and monasteries found throughout the region. Other religions, including Judaism, Islam, and Christian faiths such Protestantism and Russian Orthodoxy are also represented here, often with architecturally fascinating places of worship, thanks to the large international communities from North Africa, Russia, northern Europe and the Middle East.

LOCAL GOVERNMENT

The French Riviera is made up of 316 *communes* (town, village or city) and two administrative *départements* (the Var and the Alpes-Maritimes), within the larger Provence-Alpes-Côte-d'Azur (PACA) region. This guide covers the Riviera from Bandol to Menton, including the mountainous inland regions of the Provençal Tableland, the Pre-Alps of Grasse and the high country north of Nice. Also included in this guide is Monaco, a small principality on the Riviera surrounded by the Alpes-Maritimes. Michelin Green Guides *Provence* and *French Alps* describe adjacent regions.

Since the early 1980s, the government of the French Republic has decentralised its legislative authority so that each *commune*, *département* and *région* now has its own locally elected council and mayor or president.

Nice is the *prefecture*, or administrative capital, for the Alpes-Maritimes, while Toulon is the *préfecture* for the Var. Since 2008, both Nice and Toulon elected mayors from the Union for a Popular Movement (UMP), the party of former President Nicolas Sarkozy.

INDUSTRY

Economic activities in the French Riviera have evolved significantly over the centuries, from shipping and fishing to farming and wine-making. The first major shift happened in the 18C with the arrival of the first tourists. Since the 1970s, the region has evolved into a region focused on technology, science, and international business.

TOURISM

The French Riviera is second only to Paris in tourism. It represents almost 10 percent of French tourist activity (€ 5 billion in spending), with more than 11 million overnight visitors, ranging from 60,000 to 600,000 present on the Rivieria at any one time, around 50 percent of them from outside France. A third of all tourists stay in Nice. One in 5 visitors is a business traveller, and today the region is home to the largest concentration of conference and trade show facilities in Europe. In addition to an attractive setting and enviable climate, the region is ultimately successful because of its highly developed infrastructure and accommodation for all budgets. The pleasure ports of the French Riviera are the largest in Europe, hosting 50 percent of the world's yachts and cruise ships each year.

CRAFTS

Many craftworkers have moved into the old inland villages, which they have often restored with care, producing traditional objects using age-old methods.

Biot – The production of large **earthenware jars** in Biot goes back to the days of the Phoenicians. In the Middle Ages Biot was an important centre for ceramics; it was not until the 19C that it was eclipsed by Vallauris. Several modern workshops specialise in traditional earthenware jars, pottery, ornamental stoneware and metalwork.

Since 1956, Biot has owed a growing international reputation to its glass craftsmanship. By visiting a glass workshop, you can see how the various pieces are made using early techniques. Exhibits include carafes, bottles, glasses, small oil lamps and traditional Provençal jugs with long spouts (*calères, ponons*) for drinking without touching the vessel with the lips.

Vallauris – Ceramics from Vallauris enjoy a worldwide reputation. In 1947, **Pablo Picasso** came to work in a studio in the town, attracting a crowd of followers. Nowadays it is difficult to distinguish between the mass-produced pot and the handmade article.

Many of the potters – whether they use old methods (wood firing) or new techniques – produce attractive work, including glazed kitchenware (tureens, bowls, jugs), handsome stoneware, various glazed and unglazed articles and clay pipes. Besides pottery, other interesting activities have been introduced, including the production of hand-crafted puppets, furniture and decorative sculpture made from olive wood, colourful painted chests and cupboards, fine hand-woven linen and furnishings.

Tourrettes-sur-Loup – Tourrettes has been revived by its crafts industry. It was an important weaving town in the Middle Ages. After the Second World War, it renewed its connection with this craft, becoming a renowned centre for hand-woven fabrics. The weavers produce very high-quality goods in small quantities.

Several of the workshops in the winding streets offer a varied range of cloth: reproductions of old Provençal fabrics, colourful textiles for the high fashion market or furnishings, and hand-woven ties.

Tourrettes is home to a number of potters using a Mexican process to make earthenware sheep, as well as to engravers working in vivid enamels, and painters and sculptors using olive wood.

AGRICULTURE

Cut Flowers – Alphonse Karr (*see ST-RAPHAËL*), a political refugee living in Nice before the annexation, is generally credited with founding the flower trade on the Riviera. With the help of an associate, Karr began growing flowers in large quantities and had the idea of sending bunches of fresh violets and small packets of mixed seed to Paris. From these modest beginnings the trade in cut flowers and mimosa developed considerably, owing to irrigation and hothouses.

Hill Villages

The Riviera's first inhabitants built their strongholds on isolated hills. Many old villages can still be seen perched like an eagle's nest on hilltops or set on the flank of a hill; some are practically deserted, while others have been restored, such as the villages of Gourdon, Èze, Utelle and Peille. For centuries the peasants built their villages in this way, at a distance from their lands and water supplies, and surrounded them with ramparts.

This precaution proved to be a wise one against the Saracen pirates and mercenaries, who stalked the area from the Middle Ages through to the 18C. Greater security, better communications and the development of farming techniques in the 19C ended this isolation. Villages began to expand in the plains, sometimes doubling in size, and country dwellers were able to live on the land they cultivated and build their houses there.

These secluded villages are picturesque to visit. Built with stones from the hillsides, they seem to blend in with the countryside. The winding streets and alleyways *(calades)*, which are steeply sloped and only to be traversed on foot, are paved with flagstones or cobbles, intersected by tortuous stairways and crossed overhead by vaults and arches. Sometimes arcades follow one another at ground level, affording the passer-by shelter from the sun and rain.

The houses, roofed with curved clay tiles, have high narrow fronts, worn by the centuries. They buttress each other and often surround a church or château, which dominates the village. Old nail-studded doors, wrought-iron hinges and bronze knockers still adorn the more prosperous residences.

Some of these villages, now inhabited by craftworkers and artists, are still enclosed by ramparts, with a fortified gate as the main entrance.

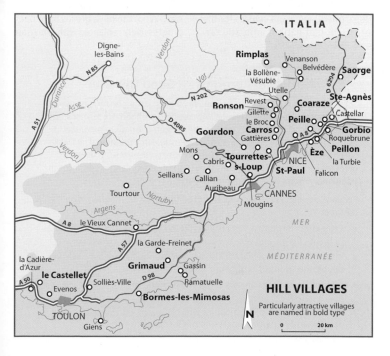

HILL VILLAGES

Particularly attractive villages are named in bold type

0   20 km

Flowers and Scented Plants of the Grasse Region – The two main flower crops of this area are roses and jasmine. The May tea-rose is the same as that grown in the east but the Mediterranean variety has a fine scent. Jasmine is of the large flowering variety, which has been grafted onto *jasmine officinalis*. It is a particularly costly and delicate plant, which flowers from the end of July to the first winter frosts.

The orange blossom used for perfume is obtained from the bitter fruit tree, known as the Seville orange *(bigaradier)*. Orange-flower water is made from direct distillation. The cherry laurel, eucalyptus and cypress are distilled both for their essence and for *eau de toilette*. Mimosa is used for the production of essence by extraction.

Sweet basil, clary (sage), tarragon, melissa or balm mint, verbena, mignonette, peppermint and geranium all yield products used in perfumery, confectionery and pharmaceuticals. Scented plants include wild lavender, aspic, thyme, rosemary, and sage.

Le Bar-sur-Loup, Golfe-Juan, Le Cannet and Vallauris, as well as Seillans (Var department) are major centres for the production of natural aromatic raw materials, although Grasse is number one in this domain.

This luxury industry, which caters mostly to the export market, is supplemented by the synthetic perfume industry. The French perfume industry's exports exceed €5.9 billion, the most important customers being the United States, Japan, Germany and the United Kingdom.

First Vegetables – After North Africa, Spain and Italy, the region of Toulon and Hyères provides the first seasonal vegetables and fruit. The Var is noted for cherries from Solliès-Pont and peaches from the region around Fréjus.

Olive Trees and Oils – Traditionally the northernmost place where olive trees (the symbol of Southern agriculture) are grown is also the limit of the Midi or South of France.

Production of olive oil in the region accounts for more than two-thirds of that of the whole country, and is spread throughout the Var, around Draguignan and Brignoles, and in the Bévéra and Roya valleys. Following the frosts of 1956, when nearly a quarter of the olive trees died, the olive groves have been progressively replanted with two more

How to Recognise a Good Olive Oil

The essential characteristic of virgin olive oil is its extraction by a mechanical process from the first cold pressing without being refined. Six further steps are necessary before the oil is ready to be marketed: grading *(calibrage)* and washing in cold water *(lavage)*, crushing *(broyage)* in a traditional mill, after which the resulting paste is pressed on fibre mats *(scourtins)*. The oil thus obtained is purified by centrifuge (or by natural settling and decanting if the traditional process is followed throughout).

Regulations define several categories of oil that must be mentioned on the label:

♦ Extra-virgin oil *(huile vierge extra)*, which is easily digested, has the most nutrients, flavour and very low acidity (less than 1 percent)

♦ Virgin oil *(huile vierge)*, which also has a very good flavour but can have double the acidity of extra-virgin oil

♦ Olive oil *(huile d'olive)* blends virgin and refined oils with limited acidity (less than 1 percent)

♦ Refined oil *(huile d'olive lampante)*, which is mixed with virgin oil as its acidity (nearly 4 percent) makes it unfit for consumption.

Bouillabaise

S. Sauvignier/MICHELIN

hardy species: the **aglandau** and the **verdale**. There are many other varieties, with flavours that vary according to the soil and date of harvest.

Traditionally, several varieties are grown in one olive grove. Harvest begins the end of August, depending on the area; table olives are picked by hand, while those destined for milling are shaken off the tree and collected in nets.

Around Nice, shaking *(gaulage)* is always used. Olives from Nyons *(tanches)* are the only ones to be designated AOC *(Appellation d'origine contrôlée* – of guaranteed quality).

The **belgentiéroise** olive, harvested at the end of August, can be eaten within the month; the **grossane** is a fleshy black, salted olive; the **salonenque** is a green variety also known as *olive des Baux*. The **cailletier**, or little Nice olive, is stored in brine for six months before being eaten. All of these olives can be eaten as an apéritif or made into oil.

SHIPPING

Toulon is the largest commercial shipping port in the French Riviera and one of the leading commercial shipping ports in the Mediterranean. It is the primary port for shipments of cargo and passengers to Corsica. It's immense harbour is also home to the largest naval base in France.

There is a smaller commercial shipping port in Nice, although regional shipping activity consists mainly of cruise ships, ferries and pleasure yachts.

FISHING

Most of the fishing in the French Riviera is done on a small *artisanale* scale for local consumption, as it has for centuries. Despite its relatively small contribution to the region's economy, the fishing industry nevertheless touches many coastal communities, where the activity has been an important way of life for the locals for many generations.

TECHNOLOGY

The high-tech industry has grown significantly since the 1970s, encouraged by the establishment of science parks such as **Sophia-Antipolis**, near Valbonne. Today, information technology and telecommunication represent €4.2million in annual revenue, and biotechnology and chemical research (cosmetics, scents, flavourings) account for another €2.1million annually. Aerospace research and development have also grown in importance, both in the public and private sectors, while Toulon invests in naval technology tied to national defence.

FOOD AND DRINK

The main features of Provençal cooking are using garlic and frying in oil (preferably olive oil). Garlic has inspired many poets, who have called it the "Provençal truffle", the "divine condiment" and even "man's friend"! Olive oil is used wherever butter would be used farther north. "A fish lives in water and dies in oil" according to a local proverb.

Bouillabaisse – The most celebrated of Provençal dishes, classic *bouillabaisse* consists of the "three fishes": scorpion fish *(rascasse)*, red gurnet and conger eel. Several other kinds of fish and shellfish are usually added: it is essential that the fish be freshly caught and cooked in good-quality olive oil. The seasoning is just as important: salt, pepper, onion, tomato, saffron, garlic, thyme, bay leaves, sage, fennel and orange peel. Sometimes a glass of white wine or brandy gives the final flavour to the broth, which is poured onto thick slices of bread.

Aïoli – *Aïoli* – a mayonnaise made with olive oil, strongly flavoured with crushed garlic – is another Provençal speciality. Comparing the northern variety of mayonnaise with *aïoli*, Frédéric Mistral, a 19C writer and defender of Provençal culture, dismissed it as insipid "jam". *Aïoli* is served with fish, *hors-d'œuvres*, or with *bourride* (a soup of angler fish, bass and whiting, etc.), among many other dishes.

Fish – One of the Mediterranean's tastiest fish is the red mullet *(rouget)*, which the famous gastronome, Brillat-Savarin, called the "woodcock of the sea", probably because gourmets cook it without first scaling or cleaning it. The *loup* (local name for bass) grilled with fennel or vine shoots is another delicious dish. *Brandade de morue* is a purée of pounded cod mixed with olive oil, some garlic cloves and truffle slices.

Aromatic herbs – Considered with garlic and olive oil to be one of the basics of Southern cooking, aromatic herbs, cultivated or growing naturally on sunny hillsides, perfume gardens or found in markets, form an essential part of local cuisine. Known as *herbes de Provence,* the mixture includes **savory** *(sarriette)*, used to flavour goats' and ewes' milk cheeses; **thyme** *(thym)* cooked with most vegetables and also grilled meat; **basil** *(basilic);* **sage** *(sauge)*, **wild thyme** *(serpolet)*; **rosemary** *(romarin)*, which is good for the digestion; **tarragon**

(estragon); **juniper** *(genièvre),* used to flavour game; **marjoram** *(marjolaine);* and **fennel** *(fenouil).* It is used in many dishes and can, according to taste, be a main constituent or just a trace.

Thirteen desserts – Provençal tradition presents diners at Christmas with 13 desserts (representing Christ and the 12 Apostles): raisins, dried figs, walnuts, hazelnuts, almonds, grapes on the vine, apples, pears, black nougat (made with honey), *fougasse* (a sort of savoury brioche), prunes stuffed with almond paste, melons stored in straw, and dry cakes flavoured with orange blossom. At Epiphany, a **galette des rois** is served in the form of a brioche filled with almond paste and topped with a paper crown, which goes to whoever finds the china figurine in their slice.

Wines – Vines have been cultivated in Provence since Antiquity.
Rosé wines, their glowing colour achieved by a special process using particular varieties of black grapes, are increasingly popular; pleasant and fruity to the palate, they go well with any dish. **White wines** are generally dry in character but have a good bouquet and are an excellent accompaniment to shellfish and Mediterranean fish.
There is a wide variety of full-flavoured **red wines**: full-bodied or subtle and delicate depending on whether they come from Bandol or the southern slopes of the Maures or, on the other hand, from the Argens Valley or St-Tropez.
The most popular wines are from the region of Bandol, Ollioules, Pierrefeu Cuers, Taradeau and La Croix-Valmer, from the Niçois area and particularly the wines of Bellet, La Gaude, St-Jeannet and Menton (*see PLANNING YOUR TRIP: Wine Tasting*).

SPECIALITIES FROM NICE

Niçois cuisine, a lively expression of the character of Nice, is inspired by the cooking of Provence and Liguria in Italy.
The narrow streets of Old Nice, clustered at the foot of the castle hill, overflow with opportunities to try the best-

known specialities as well as seasonal variations. Two well-known examples are **onion tart** *(pissaladière)*, garnished with a thick anchovy sauce *(pissala)* and black Nice olives, and **salade niçoise**, a tasty combination of local tomatoes, cut into four, lettuce leaves, radishes, green and red peppers, spring onions, hard-boiled eggs and Nice olives, garnished with anchovy fillets and basil leaves then moistened with olive oil. As a tasty snack, try the large chickpea flour pancake *(socca)*, divided into portions and accompanied by a small glass of local wine *(pointu)*; it is sold around place St-François.

At lunchtime recharge your batteries for more sightseeing with a round sandwich (*pan bagnat* or soaked bread) containing tuna, tomatoes, lettuce, onions, anchovies and olives, moistened with olive oil and flavoured with garlic. Salad, soup or omelette may accompany a marinade of young fish *(poutina)*, which are caught with the permission of the local authorities between Antibes and Menton in February. During the rest of the year, gourmets may console themselves with a **fish soup** *(soupe aux poissons de roche)*, which also contains little crabs *(favouilles)*.

The evening menu may be enlivened by a slice of **suckling pig** *(porchetta)* stuffed with herbs and its own offal, served with a mixed salad *(salade de mesclun* in the local dialect) composed of 14 types of young salad plant picked in the area. The dishes on offer in the tiny village restaurants inland include stuffed courgette or squash blossoms *(fleurs de courgette farcies)*; a vegetable stew *(ratatouille)* made of tomatoes, aubergine or eggplant *(aubergines)*, peppers and courgettes (zucchinis) gently cooked in oil and water; shell-shaped pasta *(gnocchi)* made of wheat and potato flour and served with a thick meat sauce *(daube)*; deep-fried pastry parcels *(barbajouan* – Uncle John) filled with rice, squash, garlic, onion and cheese; a stockfish dish known as **estocaficada** (&see right). The convivial family dish, known as **soupe au pistou**, is a vegetable soup to which is added

Pissaladière

©Tips Images

an unctuous concoction of basil, garlic, tomatoes and olive oil.

For dessert there is a sweet tart *(tourte de blettes)* garnished with chopped chard leaves, pine kernels and currants. Halfway through Lent the pastry cooks' windows display small sweet pastry cushions known as **ganses**. A cake flavoured with orange-flower water *(fougasse)* is sold all year round; in Monaco it is decorated with aniseed in the national colours of red and white. Resist the midday heat with a glass of crushed ice flavoured with mint *(gratta queca)*.

Estocaficada – This is the local version of the stockfish of Marseille, known to old hands as "estocafic". To fillets of stockfish (dried cod), flaked with a fork and lightly browned, are added peeled and de-seeded tomatoes, the tripe of the stockfish cut into strips, chopped olives and bouquets of herbs, including fennel, marjoram, parsley, thyme, bay and savory. The dish is braised for three to four hours and generously laced with brandy *(la brande)*. When the liquor has reduced to a level which only the vigilance of the cook can determine, a good measure of stock is added to the pot.

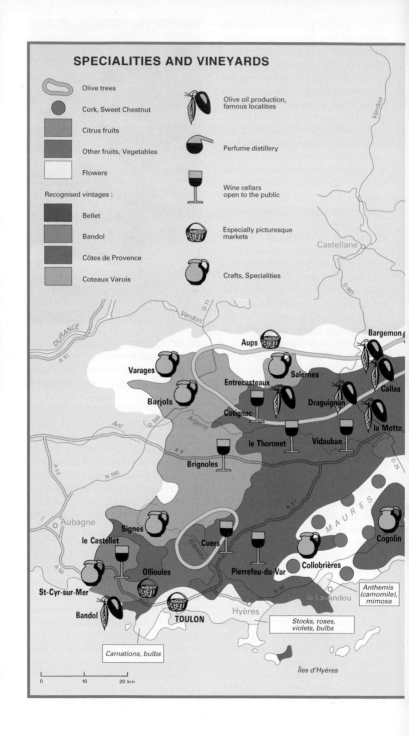

SPECIALITIES AND VINEYARDS

Olive trees

Cork, Sweet Chestnut

Citrus fruits

Other fruits, Vegetables

Flowers

Recognised vintages :

Bellet

Bandol

Côtes de Provence

Coteaux Varois

Olive oil production, famous localities

Perfume distillery

Wine cellars open to the public

Especially picturesque markets

Crafts, Specialities

Castellane

Verdon

DURANCE

A 51

Verdon

D 11

Bargemon

Aups

Varages

Salernes

Callas

Entrecasteaux

Barjols

Draguignan

Cotignac

la Motte

le Thoronet

Vidauban

Brignoles

D 25

Arc

D 560

Argens

A 8

N 560

A 52

MAURES

Aubagne

Signes

Cogolin

le Castellet

Cuers

Gapeau

Collobrières

Ollioules

Pierrefeu-du-Var

A 57

St-Cyr-sur-Mer

Anthemis (camomile), mimosa

A 50

le Lavandou

Bandol

Hyères

Stocks, roses, violets, bulbs

TOULON

N 98

Carnations, bulbs

Îles d'Hyères

0   10   20 km

ITALIA

Tende

PARC NATIONAL DU MERCANTOUR

St-Martin-Vésubie

Breil-sur-Roya

Sospel

Castillon

Menton

MONTE-CARLO
MONACO

Tourrettes-sur-Loup

le Bar-sur-Loup

Vence

Biot

Carnations, roses, anthemis (camomile), exotic flowers

NICE

Grasse

Opio

**Flowers for perfume :
Jasmin, roses, violets, orange blossom**

Mougins

Antibes

Fayence

Vallauris

CANNES

Nursery

Mandelieu-la-Napoule

Roquebrune-sur-Argens

ESTEREL

Fréjus

Mimosa

MÉDITERRANÉE

Roses

MER

les Issambres

Ste-Maxime

St-Tropez

Ramatuelle

Barjols	*Leather*
Biot	*Glass*
Castillon (A.-M.)	*Crafts, specialities*
Cogolin	*Pottery, pipes, carpets, cork*
Collobrières	*Sweets (chestnuts)*
Fayence	*Pottery*
Mandelieu-la-Napoule	*Glass*
Roquebrune-sur-Argens	*Sweets (nougat), Santons*
Salernes	*Pottery, floor tiles*
Signes	*Sweets (nougat)*
St-Cyr-sur-Mer	*Santons*
Ste-Maxime	*Wood carvings*
Tourrettes-sur-Loup	*Sweets (candied fruit)*
Vallauris	*Ceramics*
Varages	*Ceramics*

History

Events in italics indicate milestones in history.

BC

1500	Engravings in the Vallée des Merveilles.
900	The Ligurians occupy the Mediterranean seaboard.
600	Founding of Massalia (Marseille) by the Phocaeans. They bring olive, fig, nut, cherry trees, the cultivated vine; they substitute money for barter.
5–4C	The Greek settlers in Marseille introduce trading posts: Hyères, St-Tropez, Antibes, Nice and Monaco. The Celts invade Provence, mingling with the Ligurians.

GALLO-ROMAN PROVENCE

122	The Romans intervene to protect Marseille from the Celts, whom they defeat in 124.
102	Marius defeats the Teutons from Germania, near Aix.
58–51	Conquest of Gaul by Julius Caesar.
49	Julius Caesar founds Fréjus.
6	Building of the Alpine Trophy at La Turbie.

AD

1, 2 and 3C	Roman civilisation in evidence in some coastal towns (Fréjus, Cimiez, Antibes); the Via Aurelia (Ventimiglia-Brignoles-Aix) is the country's main highway.
313	*Constantine grants Christians freedom of worship by the Edict of Milan.*
4, 5C	In 410 St-Honorat establishes a monastery on the Îles de Lérins. Christianity takes root in the coastal towns, then inland.

5, 6C	Vandals, Visigoths, Burgundians, Ostrogoths and Franks invade Provence in turn.
496	*Clovis, King of the Franks, defeats the Alemanni from Germania at Tolbiac.*
800	*Charlemagne is crowned Emperor of the West.*

PROVENCE UP TO THE "REUNION"

843	*Treaty of Verdun* regulates the division of Charlemagne's Empire between the three sons of Louis the Debonair. Provence is restored to Lothair (one of Charlemagne's grandsons) at the same time as Burgundy and Lorraine.
855	Provence is made a kingdom by Lothair for his son, Charles.
884	The Saracens capture the Maures.
962	*Restoration of the Western Empire as the Holy Roman Empire under Otto I.*
974	William "The Liberator", Count of Arles, drives out the Saracens.
10, 11C	Provence, after passing from hand to hand, is finally made part of the Holy Roman Empire. Despite this, the counts of Provence enjoy effective independence. The towns are freed and proclaim their autonomy.
12C	The comté de Provence passes to the comtes de Toulouse, then to the counts of Barcelona. The counts maintain an elaborate court at Aix.
1226	*Accession of St Louis.*
1246	Charles of Anjou, brother of St Louis, marries the daughter of the Count of Barcelona and becomes comte de Provence.

The Wars of Religion – 1562–98

This name given is to a 36-year-long crisis marked by complex political and religious conflicts. During the latter half of the 16C, the French monarchy was in poor shape to withstand the looming hegemony of Spain, with political life in chaos and the national debt reaching incredible dimensions. The firm stand on religion taken by Spain and Italy on the one hand and by Protestant countries on the other was missing in the France of Catherine de' Medici's regency, where both parties jostled for favour, and a policy of appeasement prevailed.

The nobility took advantage of the situation, seeking to bolster their power base in the provinces and under cover of religion, to grasp the reins of government. The Catholic League was formed by the Guise and Montmorency families, supported by Spain and opposed by the Bourbon, Condé and Coligny factions, Huguenots all, with English backing.

Though historians distinguish eight wars separated by periods of peace or relative tranquillity, the troubles were continuous: in the country, there were endless assassinations, persecutions and general lawlessness, and the royal court was split by intrigue and *volte-faces*. Actual warfare, threatened ever since the Amboise Conspiracy, began at Wassy in 1562, following a massacre of Protestants. The battles of Dreux, Nîmes, Chartres, Longjumeau, Jarnac, Montcontour, St-Lô, Valognes, Coutras, Arques, and Ivry followed in bloody succession. The Peace of St-Germain in 1570 demonstrated a general desire for reconciliation, but only two years later came the St Bartholomew's Day Massacre.

The States General were convened at Blois at the request of the supporters of the League, who were opposed to the centralisation of power in royal hands. Fearful of the power enjoyed by Henri duc de Guise, head of the Catholic League and the kingdom's best military commander, King Henri III had him assassinated in the château de Blois one cold morning in December 1588, only to be cut down himself by a fanatical monk the following year. The assassination left the succession open for the Huguenot Henri de Navarre, the future Henri IV. By formally adopting the Catholic faith in 1593 and promulgating the Edict of Nantes in 1598, this able ruler succeeded in rallying all loyal Frenchmen to his standard, putting at least a temporary end to the long-drawn-out crisis.

1254	Landing of St Louis at Hyères on return from the seventh Crusade.
1295	Charles II establishes the village and port of Villefranche.
1308	Overlordship of Monaco is bought from the Genoese by a member of the Grimaldi family.
1343–82	Queen Jeanne becomes comtesse de Provence. Plague decimates the population.
1388	Nice hands itself over to the comte de Savoie.
1419	Nice is officially ceded to the duc de Savoie.
1434	René of Anjou, "Good King René", becomes comte de Provence. He sets up court in Aix and helps revive the economy of the region.
1481	Charles of Maine, nephew of René of Anjou, bequeaths Provence (except Nice, which belongs to Savoie) to Louis XI.
1486	Reunion of Provence with France ratified by the "Estates" of Provence (assembly of representatives of the three orders); Provence attached to the Kingdom "as one principal to another".

1489	The independence of Monaco is recognised by regional powers, Provence and the comté de Nice, both of whom attempt to increase the population with favourable immigration incentives.

PROVENCE AFTER THE "REUNION"

1501	Establishment of Parliament at Aix (Parliament of Provence), sovereign court of justice, which later claims certain political prerogatives.
1515	*Accession of François I.*
1524	During the wars between François I (1515–45) and Emperor Charles V, Provence is invaded by Imperial forces.
1536	Invasion of Provence by Emperor Charles V.
1539	Edict of Villers-Cotterêts decrees French as the language for all administrative laws in Provence.
1543	Nice besieged by French and Turkish troops.

1562–98	*Wars of Religion. Promulgation of the Edict of Nantes.* Henri IV builds the first military port in Toulon.
1622	Louis XIII visits Provence.
1639	Richelieu establishes the French Royal Navy, with the a fleet in Toulon.
1643–1715	*Reign of Louis XIV.*
1691	Nice taken by the French.
1696	France returns Nice to Savoie.
1707	Invasion of Provence by Prince Eugene of Savoie.
1718	Comté de Nice becomes part of the newly created Kingdom of Sardinia.
1720	The great plague decimates the population of Provence.
1746	Austro-Sardinian offensive is broken at Antibes. Austrian War of Succession.
1787	Reunion of the "Estates" of Provence.
1789	*The French Revolution.*

REVOLUTION–EMPIRE

1790	Provence divided into three *départements*: Bouches-du-Rhône, Var, Basses-Alpes. Wealthy French aristocrats buy property in Nice.

The French Revolution

The French Revolution, which opened up the continent of Europe to democratic ideas, was the culmination of a long crisis that had paralysed the Ancien Régime.

Hastened along by the teachings of Enlightenment philosophers as much as the inability of a still essentially feudal system to adapt itself to new social realities, the Revolution broke out following disastrous financial mismanagement and the emptying of the state's coffers. In 1789, the commoners created the National Assembly, stormed the Bastille prison, abolished artistocratic and church privileges (night of 4 July) and proclaimed the Rights of Man. The royal family tried to flee in 1791 and after being captured, they were tried as traitors and guillotined in 1793.

The main events unfolded in Paris, but their repercussions were felt throughout France and Europe. In 1792, the French Revolutionary Army captured Nice, which had been under Sardinian rule (to whom it would return 1814–60). In 1793, a counter-revolution broke out in several southern cities, including Toulon, where Royalists handed the city to an Anglo-Spanish fleet. The Revolutionary Army laid siege to Toulon for four months, ultimately driving the British out under the command of the young artillery commander Napoleon Bonaparte, who was then promoted to Brigadier General.

19C print depicting the Siege of Toulon in 1793

1793	Siege of Toulon, in which Bonaparte distinguishes himself. Nice is reunited with France.
1799	On 9 October, Bonaparte lands at St-Raphaël on his return from Egypt.
1804	*Coronation of Napoleon.* The Riviera economy suffers from his Continental Blockade. Completion of the **Grande Corniche** from Nice to Menton.
1814	*Abdication of Napoleon at Fontainebleau, 6 April.* Embarkation of Napoleon at St-Raphaël, 28 April, for the Island of Elba. The comté de Nice is restored to the King of Sardinia.
1815	Landing of Napoleon at Golfe-Juan, 1 March. He reaches Paris in record time by crossing the Alps. *Battle of Waterloo, 18 June.*

19TH CENTURY
THE DEVELOPMENT OF THE FRENCH RIVIERA

In the 19C, the French Riviera was slowly transformed from the isolated, impoverished and somewhat unwelcoming corridor between Provence and Italy into a chic resort destination. Early travel guides by Tobias Smollett *(Travels through France and Italy)* and Stephen Liégeard (*La Côte d'Azur*) offered glowing descriptions of flowering gardens and sparkling blue seas, but the popularity of the region really took off after the British Lord Brougham and Queen Victoria began visiting on a regular basis for the curative climate. Aristocrats and royal courts from Europe and Russia were first to build their palaces along the coast in Cannes, Nice and Monaco, where the casino was booming. The arrival of the railway in 1864 brought the affluent bourgeoisie and famous artists, many of whom shocked locals by sunbathing and swimming in the Mediterranean. By the turn of the century the French Riviera was an internationally renowned resort for the rich and famous.

1830	*Accession of Louis-Philippe.*
1832	The duchesse de Berry lands at Marseille, hoping to raise Provence in favour of a legitimist restoration.
1834	Ex-Chancellor Lord Brougham "discovers" Cannes.
1852-1870	*Reign of Napoleon III.*
1860	Comté de Nice restored to France.
1865	Roquebrune and Menton, who declared their independence from Monaco in 1848, become part of France.
1865	The railway links Marseille to Nice, reaching Monaco in 1868.
1878	Opening of the Monte Carlo Casino. Development of the

American troops landing East of Toulon, August 1944

© Popperfoto/Getty Images

winter tourist season of
the Riviera.

1887 The journalist Stephen
Liégeard coins the phrase,
"Côte d'Azur", or Azure Coast.

late 19C Artists such as Paul Signac
establish the St-Tropez
School of Painting.

20TH CENTURY
THE SUMMER SEASON DEBUTS

In the late 19C and early 20C, most of
the tourism on the French Riviera was
still reserved for the winter months. Ski
resorts began appearing in the snowy
mountains above Nice as early as 1909.
The summer season, popularised by
American artists and writers, officially
launched in 1931, when hotels and
resorts remained open throughout
the year, and Coco Chanel made sunbathing fashionable. In France, the first
paid vacations made the French Riviera
accessible for the average worker.

After WWII, the French Riviera's infrastructure grew exponentially, with
high-speed trains, highways and an
international airport opening up the
region to the mass tourism that the
region enjoys to this day.

1911 First Monte Carlo Rally

1914–18 Many village populations
depleted by the First
World War.

1920 Moyenne Corniche built.

1931 Resorts open in summer.

1940 The Italians occupy Menton.

1942 The Germans invade the Free
Zone. The scuttling of the
French Fleet in Toulon harbour.

1944 Liberation of Provence.

ALLIED LANDING
IN PROVENCE (1944)

Operation "Dragoon" – "Dragoon"
(Allied invasion of southern France) was
an extension of Operation "Overlord",
which had liberated Normandy three
months earlier. At a critical moment
in the battle of Normandy, the Allies
landed on the coast of Provence, which
was fortified by the Germans under the
name "Südwall". The American 7th Army
under Gen. **Alexander Patch** made an
amphibious landing on 15 August. The
French Ist Army (composed mostly of
African soldiers) followed 16 August.

**"Nancy a le torticolis" (Nancy has a
stiff neck)** – This laconic message, broad-
cast by the BBC the evening of 14 August
to announce the landings in Provence,
raised the hopes of the Resistance groups
that had been on alert since the projected landings reported on 6 June 1944.
Between June and August, the dropping
of arms by parachute was stepped up,
notably in the *pouvadous* (dry and stony
moors); these arms were destined for
the Maquis (Resistance) in the Maures,
the Alps, Bessillon and Ste-Baume. In the
early hours of 15 August, airborne Anglo-
American troops were dropped around
Le Muy to take control of the strategic
communications route, RN 7. The village
of **La Motte** became the first Provençal
village to be liberated. At the same time,
French commandos from Africa landed
at Cap Nègre and Esquillon Point, while
American Special Forces attacked the Îles
d'Hyères. Thus protected, the main army,

assembled on 2,000 ships, including 250 warships, landed at 8am on the beaches of Cavalaire, St-Tropez, Le Dramont and the Esterel. Despite a rapid advance, the two sectors were still separated at the end of the day by pockets of German resistance at St-Raphaël and Fréjus, which fell only the following day. On 16 August the French B Army under General De Lattre landed at Cavalaire Bay and in the gulf of St-Tropez and, having relieved the Americans, attacked the defences of Toulon.

General Montsabert outflanked the town to the north to fall on Marseille. After the fall of Hyères and Solliès, Toulon was reached on 23 August, but fighting continued until 28 August with the surrender of the St-Mandrier peninsula. On the same day, after five days of fighting, Marseille was liberated.

To the east, the Americans of the First Special Force advanced to the Alpes-Maritimes to back up the Resistance forces and drive the Germans back into the Italian Alps: Nice fell on 30 August and Menton on 6 September. In the hinterland, the Massif de l'Authion, transformed into an entrenched camp by the Germans, was the site of hard fighting for 8 months. L'Authion was overcome on 13 April 1945, Saorge on 18 April, but Tende was liberated only on 5 May, three days before the General Armistice.

Provence had been liberated in less than 15 days. The Allies pursued the Germans, who retreated up the Rhône Valley; the 1st French Army under De Lattre effected a link-up with the 2nd Amoured Division under Leclerc in Côte d'Or south of Châtillon-sur-Seine.

1946 First International Film Festival in Cannes.

Since 1946 Development of the summer tourist trade on the Riviera.

1947 Upper valley of the Roya incorporated into France.

1960–63 Modern art flourishes in the region with the New Realism and the School of Nice artists.

1970 International technology park opens at Sophia Antipolis, near Valbonne.

1980 The Provençal Motorway (A 8) links the Rhône and Italian networks.

1989 Law passed to strengthen measures against forest fires.

1989 The **TGV** (*train à grande vitesse* – high-speed train) arrives on the Riviera.

August 1994 Celebration of the 50th anniversary of the Liberation of Provence.

21ST CENTURY

2000 The naval base at the Toulon Arsenal becomes home to the French nuclear-powered aircraft carrier, the *Charles De Gaulle*.

2001 The *TGV Méditerranée* is inaugurated, reducing the Paris–Marseille trip to three hours.

2005 Prince Albert succeeds his father, Prince Ranier III, who died after ruling the Principality of Monaco for 57 years.

2007 Construction completed on the first line of the Nice tramway.

2009 Planning begins for the new LGV PACA high-speed train linking Marseille to Nice, by 2020.

2011 Launch of Auto Bleue, the world's first large-scale self-service electric hire car service in Nice.

2012 Socialist Party candidate François Hollande defeats incumbent Nicolas Sarkizy for French presidency. French chef Alain Ducasse invites 240 other top international chefs for a gastronomic summit on Mediterranean cuisine.

2013 High-profile jewellery thefts in Cannes make headlines.

2014 Chauvet Pont-d'Arc, the oldest known decorated cave in the world, plans to open a replica cave, at a projected cost of 43 million euros.

Art and Culture

ABC OF ARCHITECTURE

Roman Era

LA TURBIE – The Alpine Trophy (1stC BC)

This monument was erected in homage to Augustus' victory in the Alps. Damaged and despoiled over the years, it was finally restored by the architect Formigé in the 1930s.

Frieze in the Doric order: alternating metopes (plain panels) and triglyphs (slightly raised blocks of 3 vertical bands, separated by V-shaped grooves)

Peristyle

Commemorative inscription

Plinth: visible projecting base of the wall.

Blind arcading

Circular tower built in the feudal period

Column shaft

Pedestal: base of a column or a statue

Trophy: sculpted composition of arms and armour

Early Christian Era

FRÉJUS – Interior of the baptistery (5C)

This is one of the few edifices from the Early Christian Era visible in the region. Some parts date from the Roman Era. An early 20C restoration restored the building to its former appearance.

Semicircular arch

Masonry course alternating brick and stone

Corinthian capital

Wrought iron gate (18C)

Baptismal font

Cupola (partly reconstructed during restoration works)

Embrasure: enlargement of the opening for the bay at the inside face of the wall

Arcading: series of small arcades

Springer: stone block supporting the curve of the arch

Monolithic column

Base: foot of the column

Terra cotta basin for washing the feet of the faithful

R. Corbel

Religious architecture

LE THORONET – Ground plan of the abbey church (11C)

Because it did not serve a parish, the church in Thoronet does not have a central doorway. The rounded east end is typical of the region of Provence, in contrast to the flat chevet usually preferred by the Cistercian order.

Bay: transverse section of the nave between two pillars

Side aisles

Nave   Transept

Pilaster

Transept chapel

Apse: the eastern end of a church behind the main altar (interior). Compare to **chevet** (exterior)

Chancel, generally facing east

Transept crossing or arm of the transept

Cross-section of a Romanesque Provençal church

The right and left-hand sides of the drawing show two main variations of this type of church.

Transverse arch: placed under the vault to reinforce it

High window

Half-barrel arch

Side aisle

Pilaster

Nave

Broken barrel arch

Rampant arch: the impost on one side is higher than that on the other

Grooved **colonnette**

Impost: The a moulding on which an arch without capitals rests

GRASSE – Doorway of the Chapelle de l'Oratoire (14C)

The Gothic doorway and windows of this chapel were recovered from the old Franciscan church. In 1851, they were moved to this chapel, set on a hill in the old town centre.

Broken barrel arch

Quatrefoil

Flamboyant ornamentation: the flame-like shapes give this style its name

Lintel

Jamb shaft with a capital and base, bearing the arch above

Arch: a curved construction which spans an opening; a series of arches forms the archivolt

Open-work tympanum

Coussinet: this overhanging stone reduces the load of the lintel on the jamb shaft

Trefoil arch decorative motif

Upright post or **bearing shaft**

R. Corbel

NICE – Cathédrale Sainte-Réparate (17C)

Sainte-Réparate was originally a chapel, built in the 13C. The current Baroque façade and ground plan are the work of the local architect Jean-André Guilbert.

Crown

Candelabrum: an ornamental torch-shaped spike on top of a tower, chimney, etc

Curved pediment

Pilaster or attached pier: rectangular support projecting partially from a wall

Composite capital: with details from both Ionic and Corinthian Orders

Scroll

Triangular pediment

Moulding

Statue in a niche

Table: a vertical slab

Entablature: the projecting crown is made up of the architrave (lowest member), frieze and cornice

Modillions: horizontal bracket or console supporting the corona under the cornice

LES ARCS – Altar screen of the Sainte-Roseline chapel (early 16C)

Baroque altar screens in Nice and the surrounding region are mostly made of coloured marbles and stucco; gilded wood is more common on the other side of the Var.

Attic: a small story built above the wall cornice and crowning the building

Rinceau: an ornamental band of undulant and recurring plant motifs

Twisted column with a flower garland

Altar table

Console with scrolling

Angel

Shell-shaped niche

High-relief sculpture

Predella: the bottom tier of the altarpiece

Cherub: an angel represented by a child's head with wings

Antependium: a decorative panel suspended over the front of the altar

R. Corbel

Traditional architecture

SAINT-TROPEZ – Houses on the harbour

The houses typically found in a village on the Riviera, known in France as the Côte d'Azur, are narrow and high, packed together along the waterfront or the winding streets of a hillside town; they are enlivened by colourful façades.

Louvered shutters: the slats filter out the sun and let in the air

Shade

Canvas awning

Balcony

Curved tiles

Chimney cap: crowning termination

Dormer cheek: the side of a dormer

Modern **dormer window**

Roof with **two slopes**

Tile creasing: two courses of tiles project beyond both faces of the wall to throw off rainwater

LE VIEUX-CANNET – Campanile

Campaniles appeared in the 16C, atop bell towers or belfries. Of various sizes, some are quite elaborate.

Metal frame withstands wind

Masonry course: the height of the regular rows is variable

Ressaut (projecting part)

Weather vane

Cross atop the **gable**

LORGUES – Fontaine de la Noix (1771)

Each town or village has one or more fountains, whether a simple spigot or a sculpted, dated monument.

Pin-and-ball

Blazon or **coat of arms**

Fish

Console: supporting bracket

Basin

R. Corbel

77

Seaside architecture

HYÈRES – Villa Tunisienne (1884)

Seaside architecture of the 19C was inspired by Moorish culture. Chapoulart, the architect who designed the Villa Mauresque in Hyères, built this variation on the theme for himself, with a patio. Previously, it was also known as the "Algerian Villa".

Crenellations: made of crenels (notches) and merlons

Rosette: round pattern with a floral motif

Projecting pointed arch

Denticulated merlons

Interlace

Ceramic ornamentation

Multifoil arch

Meshrebeeya: lattice screen

Fore part of the building, projecting from the façade and as high as the main building

Balustrade: railing with balusters

MONTE-CARLO – Game room in the casino (late 19C)

Monte-Carlo grew up around the casino, which typifies the eclectic style of seaside architecture at the end of the 19C. The luxurious decoration inside echoes the elaborate ornamentation on the outside.

Sun

Winged cartouche: framing a decorative embellishment

Framework: a set of iron stays to support and protect the glass roof

Pine cone ornament

Rocaille ornamentation combining forms based on water-worn rocks, plants and shells, made in **stucco** (a fine plaster mixed with marble dust)

Shell

Grooved Ionic column

Bull's eye

Cabling: embellishing the grooves on the lower third of the column

Basket-handle arch

Gaming tables

Chandelier

R. Corbel

Military architecture

ANTIBES – Fort Carré (16C)

The ramparts of Antibes were demolished in 1895. All that remains is this fort, completed in 1585; the bastion design is a precursor of the star bastion defensive system developed by Vauban in the century following.

Straight stair: a steep stairway built against a fortification

Old St-Laurent tower (first fort)

Governor's lodge

Bastion: pentagonal projection from the fortified wall

Chapel

Second **fortified wall**

Sentry box

Watchpath

Curtain wall between two bastions

Cavalier: raised portion of the fortress for commanding adjacent defences or for the placement of weapons

Cannon carriage fitting

Batter slope: the inclined plane on the outer surface of the wall

Contemporary architecture

SOPHIA ANTIPOLIS – Commercial building (1978)

The buildings in the Valbonne business park were constructed beginning in 1970. They have been designed to fit into the natural shape of the landscape. Some are equipped to use solar energy.

Roof terrace

Glass wall

Pole

Balcony terrace

Solid railing or parapet

Band of windows

French window

Terrace garden

Open-work railing

R. Corbel

HISTORY OF ARCHITECTURE

The Riviera enjoys an incredibly rich art and architectural heritage, dating from Antiquity right up to the present day. Whether you're exploring the alleyways of picturesque perched villages or strolling along the coast, you'll find every major architectural movement reflected in this region.

GALLO-ROMAN REMAINS

Provence and particularly the Riviera have enjoyed a high level of prosperity since Roman times. As later generations took the materials used by the Romans to construct their own new buildings, only a few fragments of this ancient civilisation have survived. Despite this fact, in the districts of Fayence, Fréjus and St-Raphaël, Roman canals are still being used to carry water to this day.

The Roman ruins at Cimiez (*see NICE*) are extensive and consist of one of the best preserved bath complexes in southern Europe. Fréjus (*see FRÉJUS*) still boasts an impressive restored arena and fascinating traces of a Roman harbour.

The Alpine Trophy at La Turbie (*see LA TURBIE*) is of special interest; it is one of the few such Roman trophies still in existence. Buildings from the Merovingian and Carolingian periods include the baptistery at Fréjus and the chapels of Notre-Dame-de-Pépiole and La Trinité at St-Honorat de Lérins.

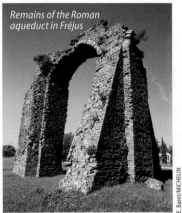

Remains of the Roman aqueduct in Fréjus

E. Baret/MICHELIN

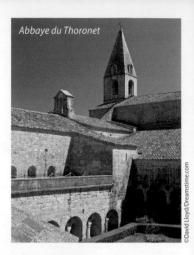

Abbaye du Thoronet

©David Lloyd/Dreamstime.com

ROMANESQUE PERIOD

In the 12C an architectural renaissance in Provence led to the construction of dozens of churches. The Romanesque style here is more eclectic than innovative, resulting not in large buildings, such as those in Burgundy, but in rather unpretentious churches, remarkable for the bonding of their evenly-cut stones with fine mortar work.

The churches are plain outside, with austere façades broken only by powerful buttresses. The square belfry and the east end are sometimes decorated with applied blind arcades, known as **Lombard bands**, evidence of a northern Italian influence.

On entering, the visitor is struck by the simplicity and austerity of the interior, which often consists of a single nave and a shallow transept. If aisles form part of the plan, the apse ends in a semicircle flanked by two apsidal chapels.

The interesting abbey of Le Thoronet (*see Le THORONET*) contains a church of the Cistercian Order with the wide transept and bare appearance characteristic of the churches built by the Benedictines. In contrast, however, the roof of broken barrel vaulting and the semicircular apse show the influence of local craftsmen.

GOTHIC TO BAROQUE

There are few Gothic buildings in the region. Provençal Gothic is a transitional style that depends heavily on Romanesque traditions. The best examples of this style can be found in the powerful groined vaulting in Grasse and the remarkable cloisters at Fréjus.

In the 15C, Good King René brought numerous Italian craftsmen to Provence. But although Provençal painting was influenced by the Renaissance, the architecture remained largely unaffected.

Most churches in the comté de Nice are based on Romanesque, Piedmontese, Genoese models. Façades are adorned with pediments, niches and statues; inside, the architectural lines are often concealed by highly ornate altarpieces, panelling and baldaquin. The façade of the Lascaris palace (1648–80) and the colossal order (upright structural members spanning over two storeys) of the former Sénat de Nice, are a display of wealth and power, as are the regular lines and porticoes of place Garibaldi (1782–92), which structures the extension of the city along the road to Turin.

MODERN PERIOD

The 19C showed little originality, and Baroque continued to be favoured for new constructions and restorations. The Romanesque-Byzantine style was employed in the church of Notre-Dame-de-la-Victoire-de-Lépante, St-Raphaël, the neo-Gothic style on the west front of the church at Cimiez and the neo-Romanesque style for Monaco's cathedral. Slightly later, the Casino in Monte Carlo and the Hôtel Negresco in Nice were designed in an ostentatious style borrowed from the Belle Epoque (c 1900). Examples of 20C works include the church of Ste-Jeanne-d'Arc in Nice, the country church of St-Martin-de-Peille and the Chapelle du Rosaire des Dominicaines in Vence (also known as the Chapelle Matisse). The Fondation Maeght in St-Paul, the Musée Marc-Chagall in Nice and the striking property development of the Baie des Anges Marina in Villeneuve-Loubet or Port-Grimaud are other fine examples of modern architecture.

Baroque-style house (1890), Place l'Île-de-Beauté, Nice

E. Baret/MICHELIN

ART
PAINTING
Primitives

From the middle of the 15C to the middle of the 16C, a school of painting, at first purely Gothic, then influenced by the Italian Renaissance, flourished in the comté de Nice. It is best known through the works of **Louis Bréa** and **Durandi**. Bréa has been described as the "Provençal Fra Angelico", praise justified by the sincerity and sobriety of his brushwork and his gift for stressing the humanity of his subjects. However, his simplicity is a far cry from the mysticism of Fra Angelico, and his colours and dull tones lack the sparkle of the great Italian genius.

These Provençal artists worked mainly for the Penitent brotherhoods, which explains why their paintings are scattered in many churches and pilgrim chapels. They can be seen in Nice (where Bréa's brother Antoine and nephew François are represented), Gréolières, Antibes, Fréjus, Grasse and Monaco.

During the same period, the humblest churches of the comté de Nice were decorated with the most striking mural paintings. There are still fine examples in Coaraze, Venanson, Lucéram, Saorge and Notre-Dame-des-Fontaines, where Renaissance Primitive **Giovanni Canavesio**, working beside **Jean Baleison**, created Gothic-inspired works of exceptional quality.

The Classical Period

The 17C and 18C were marked by the work of the Parrocles, the Van Loos, Joseph Vernet and Hubert Robert. It is **Fragonard**, however, who is the pride of Provence. Rakish scenes were his favourites; he painted them with great enthusiasm and exquisite style. He often used the light-filled landscapes and flowering gardens around his native town of Grasse as a background to his jubilant party scenes.

Modern Painting

At the end of the 19C, numerous artists, representing the main trends in modern painting, were fascinated by the radiant light of the Mediterranean South of France.

Impressionism

The return of **Cézanne** to Provence (1881) was followed by many Impressionists such as **Berthe Morisot** (Nice), **Monet** (Antibes) and **Renoir** (Cagnes),

Love Letter *(c. 1770)*
by Jean-Honoré Fragonard

©Imagestate/Tips Images

who sought to portray the subtle effects of light on Mediterranean landscapes. Monet's works marked the first appearance of the Riviera in painting: "I fence and wrestle with the sun" (letter from Monet to Rodin, January 1888). They mark a turning point in his career

Amphorae

From ancient times, the Provençal coasts have been plied by merchant ships, often of imposing size (more than 98ft/30m long) and heavily laden (up to 8,000 amphorae, or two-handled jars). The problems of manoeuvring these heavy boats with oar, sail, plus a lack of knowledge of the reefs, led to innumerable shipwrecks. The wrecks salvaged with their cargoes of amphorae bear witness to the busy commercial exchanges among the regions producing these goods and consumers in urban centres. Navigation took place between April and September, when the weather conditions were most favourable. Foodstuffs such as wine, oil and fish were also transported.

The cargo on these boats was arranged at right angles to the keel; the pointed ends of the amphorae were wedged in place by the branches of trees, and the empty spaces between their necks were filled with the next row, thus assuring the whole cargo was stable. Some holds contained up to four levels of amphorae. Some fascinating examples are on display on the Ile Ste-Marguerite.

⚅ Regulations concerning underwater archaeological finds:

⚅ All cultural goods from the sea (amphorae, etc.) found on public property belong to the State. Therefore, anyone diving who finds any archaeological remains must leave them in place and untouched.

⚅ In the event of objects being brought up by chance (e.g. in nets), it is forbidden to dispose of them and the find should be reported to the nearest Affaires Maritimes within 48hr. Offenders are dealt with in the High Courts.

⚅ Lastly, as a small consolation, divers who have declared a find of a wreck or archaeological remains could benefit from a reward fixed by the government.

and starting with his "series", he subsequently devoted himself to variations of light on the same subject. Renoir spent the last years of his life in Cagnes, painting flowers and fruits, landscapes and the people of the South.

Impressionism gave birth to a new school, **Pointillism**, a method of painting created by **Seurat**, which consisted of dividing shades into tiny dots of pure colour, distributed so as to intensify the effect of light.

Paul Signac, Seurat's disciple, established himself in St-Tropez in 1898 and many of his friends followed him, namely Manguin, Bonnard and Matisse.

Fauvism

Matisse and Dufy, who had settled in Nice, reacted against Impressionism and through their use of pure and brilliant colours, juxtaposed in simplified forms and perspectives, tried to express not just the fleeting sensation evoked by the spectacle of nature but the very thoughts and emotions of the artist.

Contemporary Movements

Picasso, co-founder with Braque of Cubism – an art concerned above all with form – was in his turn seduced by the Riviera and lived in Vallauris in 1946, then in Cannes and finally in Mougins. **Braque** spent his last years painting

Pierre Puget (1620–94)

This native of Marseille was one of the greatest French sculptors of the 17C. He began by carving the prows of ships and later developed huge carved poops. During a journey in Italy, he developed his many talents by working as a pupil of Pietro da Cortona.

After the fall of his patron Fouquet, Puget established himself away from Versailles and was appointed director of Toulon harbour by Colbert, who thought well of him. Jealousy and conspiracy soon brought him into disgrace, so he threw himself into the embellishment of Toulon. His best-known works are the atlantes supporting the balcony of Toulon Town Hall and the *Milo of Croton*, which is exhibited in the Louvre in Paris. Puget's Baroque style could express power, movement and pathos.

in Le Cannet, while **Fernand Léger**, another Cubist painter, lived in Biot. **Dunoyer de Segonzac** was tireless in his portrayal of St-Tropez. **Chagall** found the light and flowers of Vence a marvellous stimulus to his multicoloured dreams.

©Photo Scala, Florence/Musee de l'Annonciade

Detail of Port St-Tropez *by Paul Signac*

Pablo Picasso in his studio at Vallauris in 1957

©Underwood & Underwood/Corbis

Other artists, such as **Kandinsky** in La Napoule, **Cocteau** in Menton, **Van Dongen** in Cannes, **Magnelli** in Grasse and **Nicolas de Staël** in Antibes, although not spending much time in the region, nevertheless left an indelible impression. At the same time in Nice in the 1960s a group of artists including **Arman**, **César**, Dufrêne, Hains, **Klein**, Raysse, Rotella, Spoerri, Tinguely and Villeglé formed the **Nouveau Réalisme** movement, later by Niki de Saint Phalle, Deschamps and Christo. They were reacting against **Abstraction**, which was the prevailing artistic trend after the war, and experimented with new approaches to reality, making use of objects found in the modern industrial and consumer world. Alongside these innovators were the members of the **Nice School**, who each sought their own vision (**Ben**, Bernar Venet, Sacha Sosno); and **Bernard Pagès** and **Claude Viallat**, who, closely linked to the theories of Conceptual Art, led to the creation of the Support-Surface movement in the 1970s (for more on contemporary movements *see NICE – Musée d'Art Moderne et d'Art Contemporain*).

LITERATURE

The region's fine climate and natural beauty, which so appealed to artists throughout the centuries, have also worked their magic on writers and poets from around the world. Tobias Smollett, whose *Travels Through Italy and France*

was published in 1766, was an early visitor, who helped put the Riviera on the literary map. In the second half of the 19C, the area acquired its second name when French author Stephen Liégeard published his guide to the Provençal coast called *La Côte d'Azur*.

By now, the tide of visiting authors had become a flood. Some came for the sake of their health, others to escape unhappy marriages or persecution, or heavy taxes, and still more for the way of life. These literary refugees include some of the art's greatest names: D.H. Lawrence, James Joyce, Vladimir Nabokov, Berthold Brecht, Katherine Mansfield, W.B. Yeats, Graham Greene, Anthony Burgess, W. Somerset Maugham, Aldous Huxley, H.G. Wells, Ernest Hemingway, F. Scott Fitzgerald, Dorothy Parker and James Thurber.

For some, the Riviera provided a comfortable place in which to write about distant lands and the list of titles written along this stretch of coastline is vast. Others, such as F. Scott Fitzgerald in his tragic *Tender is the Night* (1934), were inspired by the people and landscapes they found there.

Not all the writers who flocked to the Riviera were foreign, however. Jean Cocteau arrived on the Côte d'Azur at a young age, spending much of his life around Menton, while Colette lived in St-Tropez for 10 years in the 1920s and 1930s.

CINEMA

The Riviera's association with moving pictures is almost as long as the history of film itself. In 1895, the pioneering brothers Auguste and Louis Lumière shot several of their first works in and around their summer residence, the Villa du Clos des Plages in La Ciotat, including *L'Arrivée d'un Train en Gare de La Ciotat* (The Arrival of a Train at La Ciotat Station), which so alarmed early audiences. The seaside town's cinematic credentials don't stop there; the Eden Theatre, which opened soon after, is the world's oldest-surviving movie theatre. During the early decades of the 20C, the "seventh art" put down firm roots in the Riviera, with stars and directors alike lured by the light, the climate and the way of life. The Victorine, the area's first film studio, opened in Nice in 1919, around the same time as Hollywood was setting up shop. Its acquisition, six years later, by Hollywood director Rex Ingram established it as the focus of the burgeoning European film industry.

The launch of an international film festival in Cannes in 1946, originally planned for 1939, served to confirm the Riviera's place in the cinematic universe and heralded a "golden era" for film-making in the region. The following decades produced US and French classics such as Alfred Hitchcock's *To Catch A Thief* (1956) starring Cary Grant and Grace Kelly, while Roger Vadim's *Et Dieu... créa la femme* of the same year catapulted both Brigitte Bardot and the fishing port of St-Tropez into the limelight.

Since the 1970s, increasing competition from other parts of Europe – particularly after the fall of Communism in eastern Europe from the late 1980s – has helped to create a more challenging era. However, the industry's leading lights still flock to Cannes each May for the festival; more than 300 of them have added their handprint and signature to the Pavement of the Stars in front of the Palais des Festivals since its inception in 1985. Nice's Victorine studio still attracts international as well as local stars.

MUSIC

Though eclipsed by a starrier literary and cinematic heritage, the Riviera has a musical tradition, too. The *gaboulet-tambourin*, a cross between a flute and a tambourine thought to date from the 13C, is an intrinsic element of the local traditional songs and dances, in particular the *farandole*. On the classical side, Nice's Opera opened in 1776, and hosted many of the south's most famous concerts; the lyric society of Nice was founded in the 19C, and still organises private concerts as well as weekly open-air free concerts in the Albert 1er garden.

Cannes Film Festival

In 1939, Jean Zay, the French Minister of Fine Arts, founded the International Film Festival at Cannes, which was chosen for its sunny climate.

The inauguration, planned for September, was cancelled when the Second World War broke out. The real launch of the festival took place on 20 September 1946 in the former Casino Municipal near the Old Port; the festival returned to this site 40 years later at the time of the inauguration of the Nouveau Palais des Festivals in 1983. In 1949 the festival moved to the Palais de la Croisette (demolished in 1988). In spite of its suspension in 1948 and 1950 for financial reasons and an interruption in May 1968, the fame of the festival has grown over the years, with a star-studded jury presided over by celebrities.

During the 10 days of the event, several competitions take place: the *Selection Officielle* (competing for the prestigious **Palme d'Or**); *Hors-Compétition* (not in competition); *Semaine de la Critique* (critics' picks); *Quinzaine des Réalisateurs* (film directors' programme); *Caméra d'Or* (first films); *Un Certain Regard* (independent productions). The great media interest generated by the festival offers a unique springboard for the films screened at the event, including both mainstream and fringe productions.

Nature

TOPOGRAPHY
A LANDSCAPE OF CONTRASTS
Coastline

Extending from Bandol to Menton, the Riviera landscape is extremely varied (*see The Coast p89*). The sheltered inlets between the red rock promontories of the Esterel differ markedly from the great sweeping bays and flat shores which gently punctuate the coastline; while elsewhere on the coast, such as at Cap Sicié, mountains plunge steeply into the sea, sheer as a wall.

Relief

Inland, the countryside is just as varied. The fertile plains and foothills of Provence are covered by typically Mediterranean vegetation dotted with barren, rugged heights like those to the north of Toulon. The mountain masses of the Maures, which rise to no more than 2,600ft/800m, are crisscrossed by valleys and ravines and covered with fine forests of cork oak and chestnut; the Esterel massif is dominated by the outline of Mont Vinaigre and the peaks of Pic de l'Ours and Pic du Cap Roux. The country behind Cannes and Nice is one of undulating hills stretching to the Pre-Alps of Grasse, where gorges have been cut into the plateaux and the mountain chains are split by rifts *(clues)*, particularly in Haute-Provence.

Behind the Riviera the peaks of the Pre-Alps of Nice rise to more than 6,560ft/2,000m, while farther to the north and northeast the true Alpine heights tower over the Italian border.

Climate

The winter months are relatively warm on the Nice coast (the average temperatures for January in Nice are max 55°F/13°C; min 39°F/4°C), although the icy air of the ski slopes is less than two hours away by car; in summer the coast is fairly hot in contrast to the exhilarating coolness of the mountain resorts.

Vegetation

The forest of Turini, with its centuries-old beeches and firs, has a northern feel; the woods of the Maures and the Esterel are more typically southern, carpeted with their cork oaks and pines, periodically ravaged by forest fires. The wild scrub and underbrush of the mountain *maquis* contrast starkly with the orderly rows of the orange and lemon groves of the plains; in many western areas, lavender and thyme grow wild in vast cultivated fields of flowers; in the pre-Alps of Nice, the palm trees, agaves and cacti of the coast merge into the firs and larches of the highlands.

Baie de Briande, St-Tropez Peninsula

E. Baret/MICHELIN

Activity

The coastline is extremely busy in summer, with the busiest roads, largest towns and best-equipped resorts concentrated there. Inland, however, there is peace and quiet, even complete solitude, with sleepy towns and old villages perched like eagles' nests high up on the hillsides.

Economy

Nice is the coast's tourist capital and the centre of a thriving high-tech industry. The busy flower trade and the production of perfume exist side by side with new research centres dealing with oceanography and data processing.

Land of the Sun

The region is united, of course, by one common factor – the Mediterranean climate. Here, the sun shines almost continually (2,725 hours annually in Nice compared to 1,465 hours in London).

Except in high summer, outlines are sharpened and natural features acquire an architectural aspect in the clear air. The shining blue of the sea and sky blends with the green of the forests, the silver-grey of the olive trees, the red porphyry rock and the white limestone.

TERRAIN

Provence was formed from two mountain systems: one very old – the Maures and the Esterel – the other much younger – the Provençal Pyrenean ranges and the Pre-Alps.

The Maures

This crystalline mountain mass spreads from the River Gapeau in the west to the Argens Valley in the east, and from the sea in the south to a long depression in the north, beyond which are the limestone peaks of the Pre-Alps. Long low parallel ranges, covered with fine forests which have not escaped recent forest fires, make up the Maures Massif; the highest point is La Sauvette (556ft/779m).

The Esterel

Separated from the Maures by the lower Argens Valley, the Esterel, has also been eroded by time and therefore lies at a low altitude. Its highest peak is Mont Vinaigre at 2,027ft/618m. The deep ravines cut into its sides and its jagged crests dispel any impression of mere hills. The Esterel, like the Maures, was once entirely covered with forests of pine and cork oak but these have been periodically ravaged by forest fires.

Shrubs and bushes grow beneath the trees (tree heathers, arbutus, lentisks and lavender), while scrub (maquis) covers the open ground. In spring the red and white flowers of the cistus, yellow mimosa and broom, and white heather and myrtle form a brilliant floral patchwork.

Provençal Ranges

These short limestone chains, arid and rugged, rise to heights of 1,200–3,500ft/400–1,150m. Of Pyrenean origin with a highly complex structure, they do not have the continuity of those of Alpine origin such as the Southern Pre-Alps. The most southerly peaks, just north of Toulon, are the Gros Cerveau (1,407ft/429m), which is bisected by the Ollioules gorges, Mont Faron (1,778ft/542m), which dominates the town; and Le Coudon; Montagne de la Loube rises 17.4mi/28km to the north. Between the ranges are fertile valleys, where the traditional crops of cereals, vines and olives are cultivated.

Maritime Alps and Mercantour

To the northeast, the horizon is dominated by a vast mountainous mass (alt. 4,922–9,515ft/1,500–2,900m), which is dissected by the upper valleys of the Var, Tinée, Vésubie and Roya. On the Italian border these mountains meet the great crystalline massif, Le Mercantour, the peaks of which exceed 9,842.5ft/3,000m.

Pre-Alps

This region contains a large part of the Southern Pre-Alps. Between the River Verdon and River Var the **Pre-Alps of**

River Loup

J. Malburet/MICHELIN

Grasse are formed by a series of parallel east-west chains, with altitudes varying between 3,609–5,249ft/1,100–1,600m, which are frequently indented by wild and narrow rifts *(clues)*.

The **Pre-Alps of Nice** rise from the coast in tiers to a height of 3,281ft/1,000m, affording a wide variety of **views** inland from Nice and Menton. These ranges, which are Alpine in origin, run north-south before abruptly changing direction to finish up parallel with the coast.

Provençal Tableland

From Canjuers plateau to the Vence pass, the Pre-Alps are rimmed with a tableland of undulating limestone plateaus, similar to the *causses*, through which water penetrates into rifts that feed resurgent streams like the Siagne. The gorge carved out by the River Loup is very picturesque.

Below lies a **depression** or "lowland", where the towns of Vence, Grasse and Draguignan are situated. Beyond the River Argens, the depression extends east down the river to Fréjus and west towards Brignoles; the main axis, however, is southwest to Toulon to the northern slopes of the Maures and Le Luc basin.

RIVERS

Mediterranean rivers are really torrents and their volume, which varies considerably from a mere trickle to a gushing flood, is governed by melting snow, rainfall and evaporation, depending on the season.

The lack of rain and the intense evaporation of the summer months reduce the rivers to dribbles of water along their stony beds.

In spring and autumn the rains fall suddenly and violently, and even the smallest streams are immediately filled with rushing water.

The flow of the Argens varies from 60–132,000gal/3–600m^3 a second and that of the Var from 17–5,000m^3/3,790 to over a million gallons. At the height of its spate the Var is more than half a mile wide and the stain of its muddy waters can be seen in the sea as far away as Villefranche on the far side of Nice.

The water level of rivers in limestone regions is always very uneven. Rains seep into the ground through numerous fissures to reappear often a considerable distance away as large springs gushing out from the sides of valleys. Some of the springs rise in riverbeds, such as the gushers *(foux)*, which cause the River Argens to flood. Most of the rivers with torrential rates of flow transport material but the River Argens is the only one to have built up an alluvial plain comparable to those of the Languedoc coast. All the torrential rivers have created beautiful valleys, deep gorges (the Loup and the Siagne gorges) or rifts (*clues* – the Clue de Gréolières), which are among the attractions of inland Provence.

CAVES AND CHASMS

In contrast to the region's deeply dissected green valleys, such as the gorges of the Loup and the Siagne, the Caussols plateau (*see ST-VALLIER-DE-THIEY*) rolls away to the far horizon, stony and deserted, a typical karst relief. The dryness of the soil is due to the calcareous nature of the rock, which absorbs rain like a sponge.

Water Infiltration

Rainwater, charged with carbonic acid, dissolves the carbonate of lime found in the limestone. Depressions, which are usually circular in shape and small in size, known as **cloups** or **sotchs**, are then formed. The dissolution of the limestone rocks, containing large quantities of salt or gypsum, produces a rich soil particularly suitable for growing crops; when the *cloups* increase in size they form large, closed depressions known as **dolines**. Where rainwater infiltrates deeply through the countless fissures in the plateau, the hollowing out and dissolution of the calcareous layer produces wells or natural chasms, which are called **avens**. Little by little, the chasms grow, lengthen and branch off, communicating with each other and enlarging into caves.

Le Boréon in the upper valley of Vésubie

E. Baret/MICHELIN

Underground Rivers

The infiltrating waters finally produce underground galleries and collect to form a more or less swiftly flowing river. The river widens its course and often changes level, to fall in cascades. Where the rivers run slowly, they form lakes above natural dams known as **gours**, which are raised layer by layer by deposits of carbonate of lime. The dissolution of the limestone also continues above water-level in these subterranean galleries: blocks of stone fall from the roof and domes form, the upper parts pointing towards the surface of the earth. When the roof of the dome wears thin it may cave in, disclosing the cavity from above and opening the chasm.

THE COAST

The mainly rocky coastline reflects the different types of mountain and plateau to be found inland, emerging as cliffs and rocks where they meet the sea.

The Toulon Coast

This highly indented section of the coast provides well-sheltered harbours, Bandol and Sanary bays and the outstanding port of Toulon.
The stretches of almost vertical cliffs are interrupted by some fine beaches.

Development of a resurgent spring

The Maures Coast

Between Hyères and St-Raphaël, the Maures Massif meets the sea and the coastal scenery offers charming sites and enchanting **views**.

The Giens Peninsula, formerly an island, is now joined to the mainland by two sandy isthmuses. Nearby are the Hyères islands, densely covered with vegetation, and the Fréjus plain, once a wide bay but now filled by alluvial deposits brought down by the Argens. Characteristic also of this particular section of the coast are great promontories such as Cap Bénat and the St-Tropez Peninsula, narrow tongues of land such as Cap Nègre and Cap des Sardinaux, and wide bays like the Bormes harbour and the gulf of St-Tropez.

The Esterel Coast

The red porphyry rocks of the Esterel Massif, steep and rugged, form a striking contrast with the blue of the sea. Along this stretch of coast the mountains thrust great promontories into the sea, between inlets *(calanques)* and small bays. Offshore, the surface of the sea is scattered with thousands of rocks and small, green moss-covered islets, while submerged reefs can be seen beneath the clear water. The Corniche d'Or *(see MASSIF DE L'ESTEREL)* is internationally reputed for its breathtaking scenery, superb viewpoints and resorts.

The Antibes Coast

Once again the vista changes between Cannes and Nice. The shore is no longer eaten away by the sea; it is flat and opens into wide bays. On this smooth, unbroken coast, the Cap d'Antibes peninsula is the sole promontory.

The Riviera Proper

From Nice to Menton the Alps plunge abruptly into the sea. Here, the coastline forms a natural terrace, facing the Mediterranean but isolated from its hinterland. Cap Ferrat and Cap Martin are the two main promontories along this stretch of coast. The term Riviera, which has already passed into the language of geography, is applied to this type of coastline. A triple roadway has been cut over the steep slopes, lined with villas and terraced gardens.

THE MEDITERRANEAN SEA

The Mediterranean is Europe's bluest sea. The shade – cobalt blue to artists – comes from the clarity of the water. Visitors soon realise that the colour often changes depending on the nature of the sky, the light, the seabed and the depth of water so that at times the "blue Mediterranean" is opal or a warm grey.

The Water

The temperature of the water, governed on the surface by the sun's heat, is constant (55.4°F/13°C) from 650–13,000ft/200–4,000m downwards, whereas in the Atlantic it drops from 57.2–35°F/14–2°C. This is an important factor in the climate, for the sea cools the air in summer and warms it in winter. Rapid evaporation makes the water noticeably more salty than that of the Atlantic. The waves are small, short and choppy; storms come and go quickly.

The Tides

Tides are almost non-existent (about 10in/25cm). Sometimes when the wind is very strong the tide may reach as much as 3ft/1m. These levels are markedly different from the tides of the Atlantic or from the tides of 40–50ft/13–15m round Mont-St-Michel, off the Normandy coast. This relative tidal stability has resulted in the Mediterranean being chosen as the base level for all French altitudes.

The Provençal coastline drops sharply into water that becomes relatively deep a short distance from the shore. Between Nice and Cap Ferrat soundings indicate a depth of 3,281ft/1,000m about half a mile out.

THE SEASONS

A Superb Climate

Crowds come flocking in summer and the tourist season lasts almost the whole year.

The Côte d'Azur is one of the most inviting names in the world! Properly speaking, the name Riviera applies to the French coast between Nice and Menton and to the Italian coast between Ventimiglia and Genoa. English visitors, at first for health reasons but later more and more in search of pleasure, have been attracted to the Riviera (especially Nice) since the 18C. The Côte d'Azur (Bandol to Menton) has now become widely known as the French Riviera.

Winter

The proverbial mildness of the French Riviera is due to a number of factors: a low latitude, the presence of the sea, which moderates temperature variations, a wholly southern aspect, and the screen of hills and mountains, which protects it from cold winds. The average temperature for January in Nice is 46°F/8°C. Icy winds blow from the east and from the southeast bringing rain. Fog and sea-mists appear only on the coast in the height of summer and harsh winters with ice and snow are rare.

The thermometer may rise to 72°F/22°C, but at sunset and during the night the temperature drops suddenly and considerably. There is little rainfall; it is the dew that keeps the vegetation fresh. The hinterland is cold and often snow-covered but the air is limpid and the sun brilliant – an ideal climate for winter sports.

Spring

Short but violent showers are characteristic of springtime on the Riviera, when the flowers are at their best and a joy to behold. The only drawback is the *mistral*, which blows most frequently at this season, especially west of Toulon. The mountains, however, act as a buffer and the wind is never so intense as it can be in western Provence and the Rhône Valley.

The Romans made a dreaded god of this fearsome wind. It comes from the northwest in cold gusts; after several days this powerful blast of clean air has purified everything and the windswept sky is bluer than ever.

Summer

The coast offers an average temperature of 79°F/26°C throughout July and August. The heat, however, is bearable because it is tempered by the fresh breeze that blows during the daytime. This is not the season for flowers: overwhelmed by drought, the vegetation seems to fall into slumber.

The hinterland offers a wide variety of places to stay at varying altitudes up to 5,905ft/1,800m; the higher one climbs the more invigorating the air.

Autumn

There are plenty of perfect days during the Mediterranean autumn, punctuated by violent storms after which the sun reappears, brilliant and warm. In the whole year, there is an average of only 86 days of rain in Nice (150 in London), but the quantity of water which falls is higher (34in/863mm in Nice against under 24in/609mm in London).

FLORA AND FAUNA

Plants and trees do not grow in the same way on the Riviera as they do farther north. New shoots appear, as they do elsewhere, in the spring but a second growth begins in the autumn and continues throughout most of the winter. The dormant period is during the summer when the hot, dry climate favours only those plants that are especially adapted to resist drought. These have long tap roots, glossy leaves which reduce transpiration, bulbs acting as reservoirs of moisture and perfumes which they release to form a kind of protective vapour.

TREES

Olive Trees

2,500 years ago, the Greeks brought olive trees to Provence, where they grow equally well in limestone or sandy soils. The olive has been called the immortal tree for, grafted or wild, it will always grow from the same stock. Those grown from cuttings die relatively young, at about 300 years old. Along the coast, the trees reach gigantic dimensions, attaining 65.6ft/20m in height, their

Umbrella pines of Porquerolles

S. Sauvignier/ MICHELIN

domes of silver foliage 65.6ft/20m in circumference and trunks 13ft/4m round the base. The olive tree, which has more than 60 varieties, is found up to an altitude of 1,968.5ft/600m and marks the limit of the Mediterranean climate. It grows mainly on valley floors and on hillsides. The trees begin to bear fruit between their sixth and twelfth year and are in full yield at 20 or 25; the olives are harvested every two years. Olive groves are numerous in the areas around Draguignan, Sospel and at Breil, in the Roya Valley.

Oak Trees

The oaks native to the Mediterranean region are evergreen. Durmast and holm oaks grow in chalky soil at altitudes below 2,624.5ft/800m. As scrub-oaks, they are a characteristic feature of the *garrigue* (rocky, limestone moors). In its fully developed state the holm oak is a tree with a short, thick-set trunk covered in grey-black bark and with a dense, rounded crown. The cork oak is distinguished by its large dark-coloured acorns and its rough bark. Every eight to twelve years the thick cork bark is stripped off to expose a reddish brown trunk.

Pine Trees

The three types of pine to be found in the Mediterranean region have unmistakable silhouettes.

The maritime pine, which grows only on limestone soil, has dark, blue-tinged green needles and deep red bark.

The **umbrella pine** is typically Mediterranean and owes its name to the easily recognisable outline. It is often found growing alone.

The **Aleppo pine** is a Mediterranean species that thrives on chalky soil along the coast; it has a twisted, grey trunk and lighter, less dense, foliage.

Other Provençal Trees – The smooth-trunked **plane tree** and the **lotus tree** shade the courtyards, streets and squares and also line the roads.

The dark silhouette of the coniferous, evergreen **cypress** is a common feature of the countryside; planted in rows, the pyramidal cypress forms an effective windbreak.

The common **almond tree**, a member of the Rosaceae, is widespread in Provence and blossoms early. The robust **chestnut** flourishes in the Maures Massif. Certain mountain species of **fir** and **larch** are to be found in the Alps; the forest of Turini is a fine fir-growing region.

Exotic Trees

In parks and gardens and along the roads stand magnificent **eucalyptus trees**. This hardy specimen is particularly suited to the climate. In winter another Australian import, **mimosa**, covers the slopes of the Tanneron Massif with a yellow mantle.

The greatest concentration of **palm trees** is to be found in the Hyères district. Two types most common to the Riviera are the date palm, with its smooth, tall trunk sweeping upwards, and the Canary palm, which is much shorter and has a rough, scaly trunk.

Orange and **lemon groves** flourish on the coastal stretches between Cannes and Antibes, and Monaco and Menton.

BUSHES AND SHRUBS

The **kermes oak** is a bushy evergreen shrub, which rarely grows more than 3.3ft/1m in height. Its name comes from the kermes, an insect halfway between a cochineal fly and a flea, which lives throughout its existence attached to stems of the oak.

The **lentisk** is an evergreen shrub with paired leaves on either side of the main stem and no terminal leaf. The fruit is a small globular berry, which turns from red to black when mature.

The **pistachio** is a deciduous shrub which can grow to a height of 13–16.4ft/ 4–5m. Leaves grow in groups of five to eleven, one of which is terminal. The fruit is a very small berry, red at first, ripening to brown.

The **Mediterranean thistle** is a perennial, which attains a height of 3.3ft/1m. Its irregular pointed leaves are bright green on top and covered with white down on the underside.

The Garrigue

Some of the limestone areas are so stony (Vence pass road and D 955 from Draguignan to Montferrat) that even thorns (kermes oak, gorse and thistle) and aromatic plants (thyme, lavender and rosemary) can survive only here and there in between the bare rocks; this is the *garrigue*.

Lavandin

Lavandin is a hybrid plant resulting from the cross of true lavender with spike lavender. Its flowers may be blue, like true lavender or grey, like aspic. The plants are used for landscaping but they also produce oil of an excellent quality. In France, lavandin has been grown in Provence on a large scale for many years. Thanks to its camphoraceous smell with strong eucalyptus overtones, it is often used to scent soaps and detergents.

The Maquis

Scrub *(maquis)* thrives on sandy soil and forms a thick carpet of greenery, which is often impenetrable. In May and June when the cistus is in flower it is a marvellous spectacle, especially in the coverts of the Esterel.

SUCCULENTS

Some varieties of succulent are African in character: Barbary figs, agaves, cacti and aloes grow in open ground. Ficoids, with large pink and white flowers, cling to ancient walls. The **aloe** has thick and fleshy leaves, from which a bitter juice is extracted for medicinal use.

The **Barbary fig** is an unusual plant from Central America, which grows in arid soil in hot climates; its broad, thick, fleshy leaves bristle with spines. The Moroccans call it the Christian fig; it is also known as the "prickly pear".

For a wider knowledge of exotic flora, take a stroll in:

- *Jardin Exotique in Monaco*
- *Jardin de la Villa Thuret in Cap d'Antibes (👁 see ANTIBES)*
- *Several botanic gardens in Menton*
- *Domaine du Rayol (including Val Rameh 👁 see p352)*
- *Jardin Olbius Riquier in Hyères.*

FOREST FIRES

From time immemorial the scourge of the Provençal woodland, especially in the Maures and the Esterel, has been the

The Three Musketeers of the "Silent World"

In August 1937, two young divers with homemade equipment based on recycled tubes attempted to beat a harpooning record. In the absence of any substantial booty, J.Y. Cousteau and P. Taillez found that their dive in the midst of shoals of grouper and bass revealed the potential of underwater exploration.

A third leading harpoonist, J. Dumas, soon joined them and the hunt for pictures superseded the hunt for sea-bass. In the autumn of 1943, Dumas, experimenting with an aqualung, dived to a depth of 203ft/62m and was affected by nitrogen narcosis (rapture of the deep). After the Second World War, the underwater explorers' odyssey was immortalised on film and their craft, *Calypso*, was seen all around the world.

forest fire, which causes more damage by man than deforestation, now carefully monitored, and destruction by goats, which live on the tender young shoots. During the summer the dried-up plants of the underbrush, pine needles, resins exuded by leaves and twigs are all highly combustible and sometimes catch fire spontaneously. Once started, a fire may spread to the pines with disastrous results in a strong wind. Great walls of flame, sometimes 6mi/10km in length and 100ft/30m high, spread at speeds of 2–3mi/5–6km per hour. When the fire has passed, nothing remains standing except the blackened skeletons of trees, while a thick layer of white ash covers the ground.

The Riviera still bears the scars of the particularly severe forest fires that raged during the summer of 2003, fuelled by the worst drought and heatwave in 15 years, and it will be many years before regeneration of its natural habitat is complete.

Preventive measures include the removal of undergrowth near residential areas, the creation of fire-breaks and the appointment of fire-watchers and patrols. Active intervention is provided by the fire brigade and the airborne water carriers based in Marignane. In the event of a major fire risk, the ALARME plan enables access roads to private homes to be cleared for firefighters and limits the movements of walkers.

For information on the closures in forests, there is a recorded message service (✆04 98 10 55 41 or 04 94 47 35 45) for the use of hikers.

MEDITERRANEAN MARINE LIFE

Life in the Mediterranean Sea resembles a house full of animal tenants with astonishing characteristics, living

Cacti in the Jardin Exotique, Eze

© Sergio Pitamitz/age fotostock

one above the other. During an under water dive, the following species may be observed.

Brown Grouper

Depending on its age and size, the grouper is first female, then male. It changes sex at about nine years old when it weighs 22lb/10kg. Since the fish can live for about 50 years, it spends most of its life as a male.

The young female grouper lives on rocky seabeds in shallow water (less than 33ft/10m deep), which makes it an easy prey for underwater hunters and other predators. As it reaches adult-hood, it makes its home in holes in the rocks at a depth of at least 164ft/50m, where it lives as a formidable carnivore at the extremity of the marine food chain. It may eventually reach a length of 4ft/1.2m and weigh 66–88lb/30–40kg. This fish, which had become very rare in the Mediterranean, has benefited from a 5-year moratorium prohibiting the catching of groupers.

The Parc Naturel de Port-Cros is now designated to protect the grouper within an area around the island.

Jellyfish

Jellyfish, which appear seasonally in coastal waters, sometimes cause prob-lems for holidaymakers. The most com-mon species, **pelagia**, can sting with its mouth, tentacles and umbrella. Its poison, which is intended to immobilise prey, is powerful enough to cause red-ness and burning of the skin. The popu-lation of pelagia follows a 12-year cycle, depending on climatic conditions, and their arrival is usually preceded by a very dry spring. Another species of jellyfish, the Portuguese Man-of-War, has long tentacles (up to 33ft/10m), which are invisible to swimmers and have a very powerful sting. They are fortunately rare in the Mediterranean.

Posidonia

This flowering plant, which has bunches of long, dark-green leaves, plays an essential role in the Mediterranean environment. Its rhizomes grow slowly,

Pelagia noctiluca

©Planctonvideo/Dreamstime.com

thus allowing it to fix the sediments from the coast and create a habitat rich in oxygen and favourable to many ani-mal species. When the posidonia dies, these animal species either die out or migrate.

A dive into the colourful world of the posidonia provides the possibility of seeing many amazing species. The **sea cucumber**, also known as holothurian, is the dustbin of the sandy seabed and lives only in the posidonia. The **sea-slug**, found all over the Mediterranean, is a white mollusc with brown spots, which contrasts with the red sponges. The **striped weever fish** lives on the seabed near the posidonia, buried in the sand with just its head visible. It has an extremely poisonous dorsal fin, the sting of which can be serious. The **sea-horse** likes to hide near its relative, the **pipe-fish**, whose amazing threadlike form, with trumpet-shaped mouth, mimics the leaves of the posidonia, among which it lives.

In the last few decades harbour works and construction along the coast have caused much sedimentation and the resultant pollution is endangering the fragile habitat. A genetically altered strain of algae, the non-toxic **taxifolia**, has spread rapidly along the French Riviera since 1989. It is feared the spread of this alga, created to decorate aquariums, may be harmful to the posidonia, as well as other marine life in the Mediterranean.

TOULON AND AROUND

The city of Toulon and its surrounding villages on the western fringes of the French Riviera are often overlooked by travellers passing through on their way to Provence. But this dynamic region has done much to restore its image over the past decade, offering pleasant surprises throughout the year to curious visitors who take the time to explore its mountain views, charming seaside resorts and historic naval harbour.

Highlights

1 Visit the famous harbour of **Toulon**, home of the French Navy since the 16C (p103)
2 Take in the spectacular views from the top of **Mont Faron** (p111)
3 Try your hand at wine-tasting in the prestigious Bandol Vineyards (p117)
4 Explore the Gallo-Roman villa at the **Musée de Tauroentum** (p118)
5 Snorkel in the blue waters off the **Îles des Embiez** (p122)

Largest Naval Base in France

As the third largest city in the Provence-Alpes-Côte-d'Azur region (after Nice to the east and Marseilles to the west), Toulon and its immense harbour have sustained the local economy since the Middle Ages.

Aside from being one of the leading commercial shipping ports in the Mediterranean, Toulon once served as a defensive port for Provence, a departure point for maritime exploration, a renowned centre for shipbuilding and fishing, and today houses France's largest naval base. While traditionally not considered a tourist destination, the city has restored much of its old town and the public areas of the port used for local sightseeing cruises.

Resort Towns

Although the arrival of the railway in the mid-1800s ended much of the maritime passenger traffic, it ushered in a new era of seasonal tourism that would rejuvenate sleepy fishing villages such as Bandol, Six-Fours-les-Plages and Île des Embiez. Not just popular with French tourists seeking vacation homes, it was also a magnet for writers, filmmakers and artists such as Thomas Mann, Katherine Mansfield, Aldous Huxley and Marcel Pagnol.

Marine explorers Philippe Tailliez, Jacques-Yves Cousteau and Frédéric Dumas perfected their scuba-diving equipment in the waters off Bandol, Sanary and Embiez.

Today these resorts are carefully monitored to protect the local flora and fauna, botanical coastal trails and thriving marine preserves.

Toulon naval harbour

D. Pazery/ MICHELIN

Bandol vineyards in Le Castellet with a view to the perched village

©David Noble/Pictures Colour Library

The Mountains

Toulon and its neighbouring coastal towns are dominated by the towering Mont Faron, Le Gros Cerveau and Mont Caume. A network of steep, winding roads allow you to explore these rocky peaks where you can enjoy panoramic **views** over Toulon and the entire Mediterranean. If you prefer to avoid the vertiginous drive, take the cable car from Toulon to the top of Mont Faron, where you'll find a monument commemorating the 1944 Allied landings in Provence. One of the more charming perched villages in this area is Le Castelet, which offers **views** over the Bandol vineyards from its historic ramparts.

The Climate

Toulon has the warmest temperatures in metropolitan France, averaging 8.8°C/48°F in winter, although the *mistral* winds make it seem cooler when they blow with their legendary ferocity. Sunny days predominate, with short but heavy rainfall in early spring and late autumn. Its relatively mild climate and sheltered resorts make the city a popular destination year round. This climate is also the secret behind one of the most prestigious Côte de Provence appellations, the strong red wines of Bandol, which can be tasted in many of the region's cellars and wine shops.

Toulon★

Var

Dominated by the majestic peak of Mont Faron, France's largest naval port sits in one of the Mediterranean's most beautiful natural harbours. Although cruise ships and military freighters have long since replaced the galleys of yesteryear, it is still possible to explore Toulon's nautical heritage in the narrow alleyways of the old town and the bustling quaysides of its historic port.

A BIT OF HISTORY
Mediterranean stronghold

Settled by Ligurian and Celtic tribes, Toulon came under Roman authority in 120BC. Annexed by France in 1481, it grew rapidly after Henri IV ordered the building of its first arsenal in 1595. The port was fortified and expanded by Louis XIV in the late 17C.

Age of the Galleys

One of the attractions for travellers of the 17C and 18C was to visit the galleys moored in the old port. The triangular sails and masts of these vessels were decorated by craftsmen from the arsenal. Galley slaves were used to power the ships. Four men were needed to pull each of the 25 or 26 oars. They were criminals of various ilk, Turkish slaves, political and religious prisoners, and "volunteers" driven by extreme poverty, who stayed with their oars at all times, even to eat and sleep.

In 1748, the system of galley slaves was abandoned and the oarsmen became forced labourers, building ships and maintaining the harbour. This penal colony, the Bagne de Toulon, is described in detail by Victor Hugo in his novel *Les Misérables*. At its peak the colony held nearly 4,000 convicts. The Bagne de Toulon closed in 1874.

Bonaparte's First Feat of Arms

On 27 August 1793, Royalists handed Toulon over to an Anglo-Spanish fleet. A Republican army was sent to Toulon, with its artillery under the command of

▶ **Population:** 167,816.

🚗 **Michelin Map:** 340 K7; local map pp104–105.

ℹ **Info:** 12 pl. Louis-Blanc, Le Port. ℘04 94 18 53 00. www.toulontourisme.com.

▶ **Location:** The Old Town is located on the Old Port, or Vieille Darse, bounded to the east by Cours Lafayette, to the west by rue Anatole-France and to the north by rue Landrin. The greater Toulon area includes the towns surrounding the harbours as well as the Bay of Lazaret formed by the peninsula of the Presqu'île de St-Mandrier. The Old Town is accessible to pedestrians only.

🅿 **Parking:** The largest parking areas are located on Place d'Armes, Place de la Liberté/Palais Liberté, and at the Centre Mayol.

👁 **Don't Miss:** The most appealing areas of Toulon are the winding streets of the Old Town and the old port around the Arsenal and Quai Cronstadt. If you have access to a car, don't miss the **views** from the top of Mont Faron.

🕐 **Timing:** Plan on a half day for the walking tours, more if you plan to do some shopping along the Rues d'Alger, Jean-Jaurès, Hoche and Place Victor-Hugo. The afternoon can include a boat tour of the harbour and Presqu'île de St-Mandrier, then driving excursions up to Mont Faron.

👪 **Kids:** Children fascinated by model-making will find plenty to keep them occupied in Toulon's arsenal and naval museums.

Toulon and Mont Faron

© Helen Shorey/iStockphoto.com

an obscure junior captain called Bonaparte. A battery was installed facing the British fort, called "little Gibraltar", but was subjected to such terrible fire that the gunners faltered. The young Corsican set the example; he laid the guns and manned the sponge-rod, and soon had enough fearless volunteers. "Little Gibraltar" fell on 17 December. The foreign fleet withdrew after burning the French ships, the arsenal and the provision depots.

Second World War

In November 1942, in response to the Allied Landings in North Africa, Hitler decided to invade the French free zone. To prevent French ships falling into the hands of the enemy, the French admiralty decided to scupper the entire fleet on 27 November. On 19 August 1944, four days after the Allied Landing on the Maures beaches, French troops attacked the Toulon defences, a plan of which had been smuggled out in 1942 by sailors in the Resistance. The city was liberated on 26 August.

Post-war

Up to 1939 Toulon had been too dependent on the naval dockyard and isolated geographically. After the war, efforts were made to diversify its economy: the Arsenal's production was broadened and the port's commercial trade was developed alongside a number of new industries. The construction of holiday homes in the region sustained the building trade after the post-war reconstruction boom, while road improvements made the town more accessible.

WALKING TOUR

As you stroll through the town, keep an eye out for the distinctive painted walls (rue du Noyer, rue Micholet, ave. Franklin Roosevelt) that illustrate the life and times of the town.

Toulon Purple

In Roman times Toulon was famed as a producer of imperial purple dye. The dye was obtained by steeping the colour glands of pointed conches (genus *Murex*), which proliferate along the coast, in salt solution brought to boiling point in lead vats 10 days prior to the dyeing process. The purple obtained was used to dye silk and woollen materials. This sumptuous colour was initially reserved for emperors but later its use spread, although the imperial treasury maintained a monopoly over its manufacture. The foundations of the old Toulon dye-works were uncovered during reconstruction work on the arsenal.

PRACTICAL INFORMATION

Aéroport International de Toulon-Hyères – *blvd de la Marine* – *83400 Hyères* – *📞08 25 01 83 87 (0.15 €/min)* – *www.toulon-hyeres.aeroport.fr.*
Located 14mi/23km from Toulon, this airport is served by a regular 40-min bus service (Réseau Mistral 102) from Toulon coach station. Allow 20 min by car. Air France operates six daily flights to Paris-Orly; Ryanair flies to Liverpool twice a week (Mon and Fri) and London Stansted on Wed, Fri and Sun; CityJet flies twice-weekly to London City.

Guided tours of the city
Themed guided tours in English *(2hr)* starting from the tourist office are a great opportunity to discover the old town of Toulon. *Reservations required: 📞04 94 18 53 00.*

Train Touristique: Departs (Mar–Oct) from the Carré du Port for a tour with commentary in English *(50min)* of the Old Town, the beaches at Mourillon and the Tour Royale. *📞06 20 77 44 43. www.traintoulon.com. 🚋5€ (child 3€).*

TRANSPORT

Pedestrian area: The historic centre of Toulon bordered by rue Anatole-France, avenue de la République, avenue de Besagne and boulevard de Strasbourg is closed to traffic.

Buses: The RMTT *(📞04 94 03 87 03, www.reseaumistral.com)* provides an efficient bus service covering Toulon and its outskirts. Maps, timetables and tickets can be obtained from "bar tabacs" and newsstands across the city.

Boat shuttle service: *SITCAT/RMTT on Quai Cronstadt or 720 ave. du Colonel-Picot. 📞04 94 03 87 03.* Part of the local transport system, several daily "navettes" operate to and from La Seyne-sur-Mer, Tamaris and St-Mandrier-sur-Mer.

Pass Téléphérique: This day pass is good for the entire Réseau Mistral bus and boat network and the téléphérique on Mont Faron. *🚋6.60€ (child 4.60€).*

1 FROM THE STATION TO THE ARSENAL

Place de la Liberté
Lying at the heart of modern Toulon, with a monumental Fontaine de la Fédération erected in 1889 to cele-brate the centenary of the Republic, this square is home to the superb Grand Hôtel (1870), the city's last remaining Belle Epoque building. On either side of the square, boulevard Strasbourg and avenue du Général-Leclerc form the city's main thoroughfare. The Opéra Municipal (1862) was a gathering point for Toulon's high society before the Second World War. Today, this neighbourhood's cafés and cabarets give it a festive atmosphere.

Place Victor-Hugo
Farther along the boulevard, take a moment to admire the Théâtre de Toulon. Designed by the architect of the Paris Opéra, Charles Garnier, it is one of France's finest regional theatres. Walk around the theatre to best appreciate its restored façade overlooking Place Victor-Hugo and its lively pavement cafés.

▷ Take rue Jean-Jaurès and turn left on rue Anatole France.

Place d'Armes
Originally called the Champ de Bataille, this square was commissioned by Louis XIV's Finance Minister Jean-Baptiste Colbert for the king to take the salute. Formerly sporting a bandstand, cafés and restaurants, it soon became a popular meeting place for the bourgeoisie and officers leaving on a tour of duty. Today, it is a popular venue for open-air concerts.

Corderie
To the south of place d'Armes. 🔒 Military property, closed to the public.
Designed by Louis XIV's military architect Vauban to house the naval rope fac-

tory (*corderie*), this 350yd/320m building now houses the navy's administrative offices. The ornately carved **door★** (1689), depicting allegories of Law and Might came from a former Jesuit college and was added in 1976.

▶ Continue on rue Anatole France.

▲▲ Musée de la Marine★
♿*Pl. Monsenergue.* 🕐*Open daily Jul–Aug 10am–6pm; Sept–Dec and Feb–Jun Wed–Mon 10am–6pm.* 🎧*Audio guide in English 4€.* 🕐*Closed 1 Jan, 1 May, 25 Dec.* 🎟5.50€ *(under 26 years no charge).* ☎*04 94 02 02 01. www.musee-marine.fr.*

This recently restored and modernised museum (2011) is entered through the 18C **porte de l'Arsenal**. Decorated with trophies and flanked by four columns, it supports a pediment surmounted by representations of Mars (left) and Minerva (right). The collection is divided into two parts, starting on the ground floor with the history of the royal arsenal.

The displays include large-scale models of a frigate, *La Sultane*, and an 18C vessel, the *Duquesne*, fine paintings, drawings and other exhibits recalling Toulon's seafaring history and its prison. The second section explores the Mediterranean's maritime history, from 18C galleys to 20C battleships.

Arsenal Maritime
Covering 240ha/595acres and employing around 6,300 civilians, the modern arsenal mainly maintains the Mediterranean fleet: frigates, carriers, sloops, subs and minesweepers. Some of the dry docks are 17C. The Darse Vieille is now a marina and the departure point for passengers heading to the Iles d'Hyères, Corsica and Sardinia.

② A MILITARY PAST

The Port★
The old port (Darse Vieille or Darse Henri-IV) was begun in 1589 and extended by two breakwaters on the south side in 1610.

At that time there was no royal fleet; when the king required ships, he leased them from lords and captains, who had them built, armed and equipped. It was Cardinal Richelieu, chief minister to Louis XIII, who created a military arsenal to build and repair warships from 1631. Under Louis XIV the port proved too small and Vauban had the new port (Darse Neuve) excavated between 1680 and 1700. To accommodate further growth, an annex was built in 1836 at Mourillon, and two harbours added under Napoleon III at Castigneau and Missiessy.

Quai Cronstadt
Lined with shops and cafés, this rather unharmonious wall of tall modern buildings forms a screen between the old port and the old town. The only reminders of the past are the famous **atlantes★** by Pierre Puget on the old town hall balcony.

Boat Tour of the Rade★
Bateliers de la Côte d'Azur, landing on Quai Cronstadt, beside the Préfecture Maritime. 🎧*Commentated tours (1hr); check website for departure times.* 🎟*10€. Reservations* ☎*04 94 93 07 56. www.bateliersdelacotedazur.com.*

Guided tours range from 30-min crossings (Porquerolles) to one-day cruises (La Croisière), although the one-hour "Rade de Toulon" tour is by far the most popular. Kicking off with a tour of the French fleet, including aircraft carriers, minesweepers, anti-submarine and missile-launcher frigates and the slender, dark contours of a nuclear submarine, it continues along the Tamaris coastline with its mussel beds and two forts, Balaguier and Ayguillette, before returning via Lazaret Bay, along the St-Mandrier Peninsula and the long sea wall, affording excellent **views★** over Toulon.

▶ At the roundabout Gen. Bonaparte, follow the ave. de la Tour-Royale.

WHERE TO STAY

Amirauté (New Hôtel de l')...................... ①	Little Palace (Hôtel)............................ ④
Bonaparte (Hôtel)................................... ②	Trois Dauphins (Hôtel Les)................... ⑤
Corniche (Hôtel La)................................ ③	Val Hôtel... ⑥

G ⚓ **CORNICHE DU MONT FARON**

Victoire

Av. de la Victoire

Rue Rebufat

Fraize

Louvois

Bd

CONSEIL
GÉNÉRAL

Rue

Impasse

IMMACULÉE
CONCEPTION

1

SALLE
OMEGA ZENITH

R. Grandual

R. Delpech

ESPACE CULTUREL
DES LICES

Commandant

CENTRAL

Bd

de

Tessé

Nicolas

Bd de la Démocratie

Ch. de la Loubière

R.

Victor

Colbert

Clappier

Pl. du Souvenir
français

Av. Vert coteau

Bd
Pastoureau

de

Strasbourg

Pl. Noël
Blache

Bd

Raynouard

2

**Pl. Victor-
Hugo**

R. Berthelot

Av. Cdt Marchand

TUNNEL NORD

R. Philippe Lebon

**Place des
Trois-Dauphins**

CITÉ
ADMINISTRATIVE

**Fontaine des
Trois-Dauphins**

Pl.
Puget

R. P. Landrin

Clemenceau

Rond-Point
Bir Hakeim

Av. F. Cuzin

NICE, HYÈRES A 57

VIEILLE VILLE
**Pl. du
Globe**

Pl. de la
Visitation

Bernard

SQUARE DU
PRÉS. KENNEDY

R. d'Alger

R. A.
Daudet

Av. A. Juin

6

**Mⁿ de la
Photographie**

Ste-Marie

Pl. A.
Vallée

R. des Riaux

R. Garibaldi

**Musée du
Vieux Toulon**

I. S. E. M.

ST-
PIEX

Pl.
Raimu

R. F.
Brunetière

R. F. de
Pressensé

**Porte
d'Italie**

Roosevelt

Poincaré

Pl.
Gambetta

R. H.
Seillon

Cours

R. du Murier

CENTRE MAYOL

LA RODE

Atlantes

la

Cronstadt

Pl. Louis
Blanc

Av. de Bessagne

3

**St-François-
de-Paule**

République

PALAIS
DES
CONGRÈS

STADE MAYOL

Franklin

Bd Paul Bert

es d'Hyères
a Seyne
amaris
es Sablettes
t-Mandrier

Q. de
la Sinse

Rond-Point
de la 9ᵉᵐᵉ D.I.C.

Jaujard

Le Bellegou

GARE
MARITIME

Rond-Pont
Bonaparte

Place
Pasteur

Rue Amiral

Av.
de l'Infanterie
de Marine

S.N.C.M.

G **TOUR ROYALE** ⚓ ③③ H

WHERE TO EAT

Al Dente.. ①

Gros Ventre (Le).. ③

Daniel et Julia
"Restaurant du Rivage" (Chez)...................... ②

Pascalou (Le).. ④

Atlantes by Puget on the old town hall, Quai Cronstadt

Tour Royale

Ave. de la Tour-Royale. ⏱*Open Jul–Oct Wed, Sat, Sun 9am–noon, 2pm–6pm.* ⏱*Closed Nov–Jun and public holidays.* ☎*04 94 23 07 88.*
The Grosse Tour or Mitre Tower was built by Louis XII in the early 16C for defensive purposes (its walls are 23ft/7m thick at the base) before mainly serving as a prison. Don't miss the **panorama★** of Toulon and Mont Faron from the battlements.

③ OLD TOWN★

The ancient heart of Toulon is a colourful maze of streets. Many of its charming façades and fountains have been restored as part of a major renovation project begun in 1985.

▷ Enter pl. de l'Amiral-Senès, then turn right onto rue Notre-Dame.

Église St-Louis

rue Louis-Jourdan.
This church is a fine example of Neoclassical architecture, built in the late 18C in the form of a Greek temple.

▷ Continue on rue Vezzani.

An 18C reproduction of a ship's prow, which seems to sprout out of a wall, is a tribute to the city's shipbuilders.

▷ Take rue Pomet on the right.

The curious fountain on Place du Globe evokes the Bagne of Toulon.

Maison de la Photographie

Pl. du Globe, rue Nicolas-Laugier. ⏱*Open Tue–Sat noon–6pm.* ⊘*No charge.* ☎*04 94 93 07 59.*
Housed in a former public bath house, the Musée de la Photographie hosts six temporary exhibitions a year.

▷ Take rue du Noyer, just off pl. Raimu. On the right is a mural painting on rue Micholet. Return to rue de la Glacière and turn left, then follow rue Andrieux.

Fontaine des Trois-Dauphins

Lined with café terraces, this shady square features a curious fountain wrapped in a cloak of moss, ferns, a fig tree, a medlar and an oleander, topped by three intertwined dolphins sculpted in 1780 by two local artists.

▷ Go down rue Hoche.

Rue d'Alger

This modernized pedestrian precinct is the main commercial street leading to the old port, Darse Vieille.

▶ Turn left onto rue Seillon, then follow rue de la Fraternité.

Église St-François-de-Paule
Pl. Louis-Blanc. ☎04 94 92 28 91.
This small church was built in 1744 by the Recollects. Its double-arched façade and Genoan bell tower identify it with the Nice Baroque style.

▶ Return to the square and turn right down the first street.

Rue Méridienne and place à l'Huile (the site of the old olive oil market) lead to place de la Poissonnerie, which for several centuries played host to the fish market, demolished in 1988.

▶ Go up rue Pressensé, then take rue des Boucheries.

Cathédrale Ste-Marie
🕐*Open daily 9am–noon, 2pm–6pm.*
Constructed in the 11C and restored in the 12C, the cathedral was extended and given a Classical façade in the 17C and a bell tower in 1740.
The rather dark interior mixes Romanesque and Gothic style, with works by Puget and Van Loo.

▶ Continue to Cours Lafayette.

Cours Lafayette
A colourful, bustling vegetable and flower **market** is held here every Tuesday to Sunday.

Musée du Vieux Toulon
🕐*Open Tue–Sat 2pm–5.45pm.*
🕐*Closed public holidays. ☜No charge.*
☎04 94 62 11 07.
This museum, housed in a former 17C episcopal palace, has two galleries displaying maps, engravings and paintings that recall the history of the city since the Middle Ages. Don't miss the large collection of firebacks salvaged from houses destroyed in bombing raids of 1943-44. The exhibit also features ceramics, statuettes and costumes.

▶ Leave Old Town by rue Garibaldi.

Porte d'Italie
This bastioned gate, built in 1790 on the site of ancient fortifications, is the only remnant of the defences that once surrounded Toulon.

SIGHTS
Musée d'Art
113 blvd. du M.-Leclerc.
🕐*Open Tue–Sun noon–6pm.*
🕐*Closed public holidays.*
☜No charge. ☎04 94 36 33 30.
Housed in the left wing of a Renaissance-style building, the museum displays works by 19C artists, including a large number of Provençal painters such as the Toulon landscapist Vincent Courdouan. Flemish, Dutch, Italian and French Schools (16C–18C) are all represented in the collections. The museum also has an eclectic contemporary art collection.

The adjacent **Jardin Alexandre I** is home to many attractive trees, including magnolias, palms and cedars. Don't miss the *Fontaine du Buveur* (Drinker's Fountain) by Hercule.

Hotel des Arts – Centre méditerranéen des arts
236 blvd. du M.-Leclerc. 🕐*Open Tue–Sun 11am–6pm.* 🕐*Closed public holidays. ☜No charge. ☎04 94 91 69 18. www.hdatoulon.fr.*
This arts centre offers five temporary exhibitions exploring the visual arts on two floors, alongside a collection of 160 contemporary artworks (paintings and photos) by more than 30 artists.

ADDITIONAL SIGHTS
Musée d'Histoire naturelle de Toulon et du Var
737 chemin du Jonquet, parc Mark Burnett (northwest of the city).
♿🕐*Open Tue–Sun 9am–6pm.*
🕐*Closed public holidays.*
☜No charge. ☎04 83 95 44 20. www.museum-toulon.org.
The former neighbor of the Museum of Art located in Old Town moved to this new, larger space in 2011. The natural history museum features exhibits on the zoology, paleontology and botany of the

Toulon and Var region. Highlights of the permanent collection are the mineralogy collection and taxidermied animals, mostly birds. Two thematic exhibits are mounted each year.

Plage du Mourillon

○ *East along the Frédéric-Mistral coast, between the Fort Saint-Louis and the sailing center. Facilities include a restaurant, toilets and a free car park.*
Toulon's large artificial beach has four coves (sand, pebbles and a mix of both) protected by sea walls and a gently sloping shoreline for easy bathing.

Plage des anses Méjean et Magaud

○ *From Mourillon, follow the signs for La Garde-Le Pradet.*
On the outskirts of La Garde, the sea walk explores two natural sandy coves: Magaud *(left)* and Méjean *(right)* ❧ *90min round trip.* From Fort Saint-Louis via Cap Brun, the **sentier des douaniers** winds its way to Méjean cove, offering stunning **views** of the natural harbour along the way.

EXCURSIONS

○ Take blvd. Ste-Anne and follow signs (Téléphérique du Mont Faron) to the cable-car station in ave. Perrichi. During peak times, it is possible to park below the station on the left.

Mont Faron★★★

The limestone massif of Mont Faron *(alt 1,916ft /584m)*, bordered by deep valleys, dominates the city of Toulon. It is a pleasant drive in summer over pine-clad slopes, providing good **views★** of Toulon, the harbours, the St-Mandrier and Cap Sicié peninsulas.

Téléphérique du Mont Faron★

○*Open Feb–Nov. Check the website for opening times and admission price.* ℘*04 94 92 68 25. www.telepherique-faron.com.*
The cable-car ride *(6min)* offers fine **views★** out over the town, the harbour and the limestone cliffs around Toulon.

To the left the remains of many small forts can be seen. A pleasant **view** can also be enjoyed from the Mont Faron access road, about 33ft/10m on the left.

Musée-Mémorial du Débarquement en Provence★

Top of Mont Faron. ⬤🕐*Open Jul–mid-Sept daily 10am–1pm, 2pm–5.30pm; late Sept–Jun Tue–Sun 10am–1pm, 2pm–4.30pm.* 🕐*Closed 1 Jan, 1 May, 25 Dec.* ⬤*3.80€.* ℘*04 94 88 08 09.*
Housed in the Beaumont Tower, to the left of the road, this memorial commemorates the liberation of southeast France by the Allies in August 1944.
An exhibit explores the Liberation and includes accounts by British, American, Canadian, French and German eye-witnesses, dioramas of the liberation of Toulon and Marseille, and a 15min documentary featuring archive footage. From the terrace *(accessible during tours of the museum)*, there is a magnificent **panorama★★★** *(three viewing panels)* of Toulon, the harbours, and the islands and mountains around Toulon.

👥 Zoo du Faron

75-76 Route du Faron, Mont Faron. ⬤🕐*Open Feb–Apr daily 10am–5:30pm; May–Jun daily and Sept 10am–6pm; Jul–Aug daily 10am–6.30pm; Oct–Jan daily 10am–5pm.* 🕐*Closed 1 Jan and in inclement weather.* ⬤*9€ (child 4-10 years 5.50€).* ℘*04 94 34 72 33. www.zoo-toulon.com.*
This zoo specialises in breeding endangered animals such as snow panthers and ocelots. There are also lions, tigers, bears and monkeys.

La Garde

○ *5.5mi/9km via D 29 to the east towards La Valette.*
Now part of the industrial suburbs of Toulon, La Garde plays host to the **Musée Jean-Aicard-Paulin-Bertrand**, once home to the author of *Maurin des Maures*, where he was visited by friends including the painter Paulin Bertrand (1852–1940). A reconstruction of Bertrand's studio and some of his works

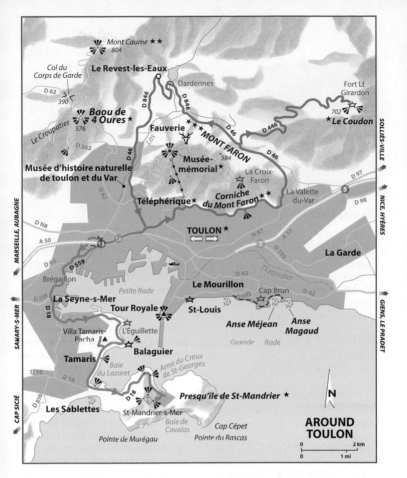

AROUND
TOULON

are on display. An exhibit of pottery by **Clément Massier** (late 19C–early 20C) occupies the ground floor *(705 ave. du 8 Mai 1945; 1hr30min guided tour Tue–Sat noon–6pm; last entry 30min before closing; no charge. 04 94 14 33 78).*

Solliès-Ville

9mi/15km northeast – 1.5hr.
From Toulon take A 57 motorway. Follow directions to La Farlède and then D 67 to Solliès-Ville. Parc du Château de Solliès-Pont (opposite Post Office). 04 94 28 92 35. www. tourismevalleedugapeau.fr.
Pass through Solliès-Pont, a busy market town in a region famous for its cherry orchards and fig trees, before reaching the old town of Solliès-Ville overlooking

the rich Gapeau Plain. On **Esplanade de la Montjoie**, the ruined castle of the Forbins, lords of Solliès, commands a beautiful **view★** of the Gapeau Valley and Massif des Maures. The **church**, a former chapter house, houses a high altar made from a 15C ciborium and a walnut wood organ case from 1499.

Maison Jean-Aicard

Open Tue–Sat 10am–noon, 2pm–5.30pm. Closed public holidays. No charge; 04 94 33 72 02. www.solliesville.fr.
This second house lived in by Jean Aicard (1848–1921) now holds a small museum featuring furniture and paintings by famous artists, with fine **views** of Massif des Maures from the top floor.

Fort Balaguier, Toulon

© Guy DOYEN/Fotolia.com

🚗 DRIVING TOURS

The roads in these tours serve military installations; traffic is permitted up to the entrance, but access to places indicated by notices is forbidden.

1 TOUR OF THE HARBOURS★★

10.5mi/17km/south. Allow 1hr.

▶ Leave Toulon by highway A 50, then D 559 and turn left towards La Seyne.

La Seyne-sur-Mer

Built beside the bay that bears its name, La Seyne has a port for fishing boats and pleasure craft but is essentially an industrial town that depended on the naval shipyards for its livelihood. A small bay, bordered by the forts of Éguillette and Balaguier, offers excellent **views** over Toulon, Le Faron and Le Coudon.

Fort Balaguier Naval Museum

🕐*Open Tue–Sun Jul–Aug 10am–noon, 3pm–7pm; Sept–Jun 10am–noon, 2pm–6pm.* 🕐*Closed public holidays.* 🎫*3€ (under 18, 2€).* 📞*04 94 94 84 72.* The fort was recaptured from the English in 1793 by the young Napoleon. Set up in the fort's rooms, which have 13ft/4m-thick walls, a naval museum displays a collection of model ships and memorabilia from the Napoleonic era. The 17C chapel contains objects from Toulon's galleys and naval prisons: registers, chains and works of art made by the prisoners. The terrace overlooking the fort's garden and its aviary, affords a remarkable **view★** of the coastline from Toulon to the Île du Levant.

Tamaris

The author George Sand wrote several of her novels in this shaded resort on the hillside.

Unusual Military Career of the St-Mandrier Peninsula

From September 1943 to August 1944, La Croix aux Signaux hill was a secret German naval base where midget submarines were assembled before being transported through a tunnel to Cavalas beach. On the same site in 1929, the Marine Nationale Française buried two enormous gun turrets (14m/46ft deep) each holding two 340 guns, 17m/56ft long, covering a sector from Le Lavandou to La Ciotat. Shelling preparations for the landing in Provence in 1944 brought an end to development of this base. It was from the rifle range at St-Mandrier that the first French liquid-powered rocket was launched in March 1945, inaugurating the European space race.

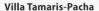

Villa Tamaris-Pacha

Ave. de la Grande Maison. ♿ 🕐*Open Tue–Sun 2pm–6.30pm.* 🕐*Closed public holidays.* ✍*No charge.* ☏*04 94 06 84 00. www.villatamaris.fr.*

In the mid-19C, architect Marius Michel, a native of Sanary, built lighthouses for the Ottoman Empire, and helped create the modern port of Istanbul. He was building his wife this palace, inspired by Florentine villas in Tamaris, but she was killed in 1893, and all work ceased. Unoccupied for a century, the palace now houses a cultural institution.

Les Sablettes

This long, wide beach of fine sand looks out to the open sea. Take the road along the narrow sandy isthmus, which links the peninsula to the land mass, for fine **views** of Toulon and the mountains.

Presqu'île de St-Mandrier★

The road round the peninsula offers a **view**★ of the whole harbour and Toulon before skirting Le Creux St-Georges, home to an aeronaval base and training centre for marine engineers as well as the fishing and leisure port of **St-Mandrier-sur-Mer**. A right-hand turn at the entrance to the town climbs steeply to a small cemetery offering a **panorama**★★ of Toulon.

② CORNICHE DU MONT FARON★★

25mi/40km. Allow 2hr.

▷ To reach the Corniche du Mont Faron, take Pont de Ste-Anne, ave. de la Victoire and blvd. Ste-Anne (left).

The drive along the **Corniche Marius-Escartefigue** and the slopes of Mont Faron provides views of Toulon. The **view**★ of the harbours includes the Petite Rade between *(west)* Le Mourillon and La Seyne backed by the cliffs of Cap Sicie, and the Grande Rade, partially enclosed *(south)* by the St-Mandrier Peninsula and its low narrow isthmus and *(east)* by Cap Carqueiranne, Giens Bay and Giens Peninsula.

▷ At the end of the corniche turn left down ave. Canaillette, which leads to D 46, then right down the narrow, steeply sloping D 446.

Le Coudon★

Alt 2,303ft/702m.

At the start of the climb, you can see Mont Coudon in its entirety, La Crau and the surrounding plain. The road crosses a pine forest and several olive groves before opening onto scrubland dotted with evergreen oaks. The **view**★ expands until you reach Fort Lieutenant-Girardon, from which the entire coast from the Giens Peninsula to the former island of Gaou near Le Brusc is visible.

▷ Return to D 46 and turn right. After 1.5mi/2.5km, the D 846 crosses a dam to Le Revest-les-Eaux.

Le Revest-les-Eaux

This delightful village with a 17C church at the foot of Mont Caume is overlooked by a "Saracen tower". Its late-16C château, with two pepperpot turrets, now houses a café-bar. The church dates from the same period.

▷ Return to Toulon through the Las Valley (D 846) between the mountains of Faron and Croupatier.

③ BAOU DE QUATRE OURES★

7mi/11km northwest. Allow 1hr.

▷ From Toulon take ave. St-Roch, rue Dr-Fontan, ave. Général-Gouraud and then left on ave. des Routes; on pl. Macé turn right onto D 62 (ave. Clovis), then left onto D 262.

Continue 2mi /3km to a platform offering a magnificent **view**★★ of Toulon.

▷ The narrow road to the top (2.5mi /4km) crosses a firing range (open to traffic).

At the top there is a fine **panorama**★★ of the coast from Cap Bénat to La Ciotat and inland from Ste-Baume to the Maures.

ADDRESSES

🛏 STAY

Hôtel Little Palace – *6-8 rue Berthelot.* ✆*04 94 92 26 62. www.hotel-littlepalace.com. 23 rooms.* �*9€.* This charming and simple hotel, decorated in warm earth tones, is known for its copious breakfast buffet.

Hôtel Bonaparte – *16 rue Anatole-France.* ✆*04 94 93 07 51. www.hotel bonaparte.com. 22 rooms.* ⊐*8.50€.* This Provençal-style hotel in the centre of town has small but well-appointed rooms. Air-conditioned top floor.

Les Trois Dauphins – *9 Pl. des 3 Dauphins.* ✆*04 94 92 65 79. 15 rooms.* ⊐*9€.* The windows of this hotel look onto a tiny square. The smallish rooms have been tastefully appointed and decorated in cheerful shades.

Val'Hôtel – *Ave. René-Cassin, La Valette. Take exit 5 off the A 57, follow signs to ZI de Toulon-la-Valette.* ✆*04 94 08 38 08. www.monalisahotels.com. 47 rooms.* ⊐*8€. Restaurant* ⊜. This hotel offers several advantages: a lush garden setting; large, colourful rooms with balcony or terrace and inexpensive weekend rates. A bit close to the motorway exit.

New Hôtel de l'Amirauté – *4 rue Adolphe-Guiol.* ✆*04 94 22 19 67. www.new-hotel.com. 58 rooms.* ⊐*10€.* ♿ Located in the centre of town, the hotel is reminiscent of the large luxury liners of bygone times in its decor. Rooms are functional, efficiently soundproofed.

Chambre d'hôte La Lézardière – *Les Allées des Tamaris, La Seyne-sur-Mer.* ✆*04 94 63 26 06. http://villalalezardiere.fr. 5 rooms.* ⊐. In lovely grounds in a well-to-do neighbourhood, this 1890 villa exudes the Oriental charm beloved by architect Marius Michel. Rooms are individually decorated. Swimming pool, spa, and a boat for rental.

La Corniche – *17 littoral Frédéric-Mistral.* ✆*04 94 41 35 12. www.bestwestern-hotelcorniche.com. 28 rooms.* ⊐*14€. Restaurant* ⊜⊜. Close to Port St-Louis, this Best Western property sits just steps from the beaches at Mourillon, offering views of the sea. It's perfect for those looking for a seaside holiday atmosphere.

🍴 EAT

Al Dente – *30 rue Gimelli.* ✆*04 94 93 02 50. Closed Sat, Sun lunch.* The main reason for coming here is the remarkable choice of pasta dishes and Italian specialities. Additional menus offer highly affordable prices.

Chez Mimi – *Square Léon Vérane.* ✆*04 94 24 97 42. Closed Mon and Jul.* This warm and friendly family restaurant serves couscous and other North African dishes in a simple dining room decorated with traditional Tunisian paintings.

La Coupole – *290 rue Jean-Jaurès.* ✆*04 94 10 20 40. Set menu 13.50€.* On a small, centrally located street, this trendy bistro is housed in a former cinema. In its understated but welcoming interior, La Coupole serves good "bistro-nomique" fare in generous portions.

Le Gros Ventre – *279 Littoral Frédéric Mistral.* ✆*04 94 42 15 42. www.legrosventre.net. Closed Sat lunch, Thu, Fri.* This family-run establishment serves the day's catch and grilled meats, as well as fine wines from their cellar, in an elegant setting just off Le Mourillon beach.

Le Pascalou – *3 Pl. à l'Huile.* ✆*04 94 62 87 02. Closed Mon.* In a tiny square, this lunchtime restaurant, adjoining the fish market of the same name, prepares the catch of the day.

Le St-Pierre – Chez Marcel – *47 rue de la Citadelle, Six-Fours-les-Plages.* ✆*04 94 34 02 52. www.lesaintpierre.fr. Closed Mon, Jan, and Sun eve Sept–Jun.* ♿ Located close to the port, this former fisherman's house offers a choice of fish dishes bursting with regional flavours for patrons to savour in a dining room filled with light.

Chez Daniel and Julia "Restaurant du Rivage" – *La Seyne-sur-Mer, 2.5mi /4km south of La Seyne by rte. de St-Mandrier and country lane.* ♿ ✆*04 94 94 85 13. Closed Nov, Sun eve, Mon Sept–Jun (except public holidays).* A small rocky inlet is the ideal setting for this seafood restaurant that knows the true meaning of Provençal life. The freshly caught fish offered to diners comes straight from the sea or the big fish tank set up on the premises.

ON THE TOWN

Café-Théâtre de la Porte d'Italie – *Pl. Armand-Vallée. ℰ04 94 92 99 75. Check the programme of events. Closed Jul–Aug.* This café-théâtre presents clarinet and jazz concerts, stand-up comedy and pantomime shows.

Opéra Toulon – *blvd. de Strasbourg. Tue–Sat 9:30am–12:30 pm, 3pm–6pm. Closed Aug. ℰ04 94 92 58 59. www. operadetoulon.fr.* Built in 1862, the Opéra Toulon is ranked second largest in France on account of its seating capacity and remarkable acoustics.

CAFÉS

La Cade à Dédé – *17 rue Charles-Poncy. ℰ04 94 89 32 32. Daily 8.30am–12.30pm Closed Mon and 3 wks in Jan.* You need to be an early bird to see Dédé at his stove preparing his daily *cade*, Toulon's traditional chickpea flour pancake.

Chichi Fregi – *8 rue Vincent-Courdouan, next to the cours Lafayette. ℰ06 09 18 83 27. Jul–Aug Tue–Sat 9am–12.30pm; Sept–Jun Tue–Sat 9am–6pm.* This friendly snack bar sells traditional Toulon fare, including *chichi fregi*, doughnuts fried in olive oil and flavoured with orange-flower water, and *fougasse*, which is olive flat bread.

CULINARY SPECIALITIES

The natives of Toulon particularly enjoy *l'escabèche de sardine, la cade* (a flat cake made from chickpeas, similar to *socca* in Nice), *la pompe à l'huile* (a hard cake, oiled and flavoured with orange water) and the famous sweet doughnut *(chichifregi)*, which can be bought from the stalls in the Lafayette market.

SHOPPING

The best place to go shopping is the area around rue Jean-Jaurès, rue Hoche, place Victor-Hugo and rue d'Alger. Rue Lamalgue (near the Port St-Louis) has a good range of gourmet stores.

Provençal Market – *Tue–Sun mornings.* Cour Lafayette (city centre), the Marché du Pont du Las (west) and the Marché du Mourillon (east, and close to the beaches).

Le Caillou du Faron – *82 rue Alézard. ℰ04 94 62 89 49. Tue–Sat 9.30am–12.30pm, 2.30pm–6.30pm.* This well-known

chocolate-maker has had the bright idea of reinterpreting chocolate versions of delights called sailor hats, grains of sand and Toulon cannon balls.

Moulin à huile du Partegal – *159 chemin des Laures, La Farlède. ℰ04 94 48 48 85. www.moulindupartegal.com. Tue, Thu, Sat 10am–noon, 3pm–6pm. Fri 3pm–6pm. Closed mid-Jan–early Feb.* Reservation and payment required for group visits. Located amid an 800-tree olive grove on a site dating from the 14C, this olive oil mill uses traditional production methods. Tours by expert millers.

EVENTS

Bacchus, Fête des Vins et de la Gastronomie – *ℰ04 94 91 56 87. www.bacchus-fete.com.* Wine and gastronomy festival staged in the Place d'Armes late July–early August. Wine tasting, courses and musical entertainment.

Toulon Music Festival – *ℰ04 94 93 55 45. www.festivalmusiquetoulon.com.* This classical music festival is divided into two seasons: a "summer festival" from mid-June to mid-July and a "festival classics" season from mid-October to mid-May. Venues across the region.

Toulon Jazz Festival – *ℰ04 94 09 71 00. www.jazzatoulon.com.* Ten-day jazz festival (sometimes longer) in July. Free evening concerts across Toulon.

Festival de Noël – Christmas festivities throughout the month of December, including a Nativity scene, crafts market and ice skating.

Festival du Cirque contemporain – Street performances, courses and introductions to circus acts under the big top in La Seyne-sur-Mer in January/ February.

Fête de la Mer et des Pêcheurs – A sea and fishing festival held in the port of La Seyne-sur-Mer the last weekend in June/ first weekend in July.

Summer aïoli festivals – Solliès-Toucas celebrates this traditional Mediterranean dish of fish, garlic mayonnaise and vegetables with a giant aïoli in mid-July, followed by an aïoli festival in Solliès-Ville held in late June–early July.

Bandol★

Var

Bandol is a pleasant resort nestling in an attractive bay, sheltered from the north winds by high wooded slopes. Home to one of the most famous vineyards in the south, it is also a paradise for watersports enthusiasts.

RESORT LIFE
The Marina
Enjoy the bracing sea air with a walk along the **Allée Jean-Moulin★** and Allée Alfred-Vivien, both bordered by pines, palms and flower beds.

The Beaches
This seaside resort has four sandy beaches: the east-facing Lido, the well-sheltered Rènecros facing west, and the Centrale and Casino beaches facing due south.

The rest of the coast (*towards ST-CYR-SUR-MER*) offers smaller beaches alternating with rocky areas.

Chemin de la Corniche skirts the little peninsula with Bendor Island lying off shore, affording a fine **view** of the coast from Cap de l'Aigle to Cap Sicié.

SIGHTS
Église St-François-de-Sales
Opposite the port of Bandol.
Built in stages (the main nave between 1746 and 1748, and the two side chapels in 1773), this church is adorned with 19C **Neoclassical frescoes** by Siro Orsi, the decorator of the Milan opera house. The west nave houses a **statue** of Notre-Dame de Grâce in olive wood

> **Population:** 8,647.
> **Michelin Map:** 340 J7.
> **Info:** Allée Alfred-Vivien. 04 94 29 41 35. www.bandol.fr.
> **Location:** Accessible by the A50, the resort town of Bandol lies 18km/11mi west of Toulon.
> **Timing:** Allow a full day for a stroll around the port, visits to the exotic gardens and zoo, and a drive through the perched villages. An excursion to Bendor Island takes about 45 minutes, or a half day for a swim at the beach.
> **Kids:** The zoo and exotic gardens are particularly child-friendly.

by students of Pierre Puget. A statue of Saint Vincent de Saragosse, patron saint of wine-growers, watches over the east nave.

ZOA Parc Animalier and Exotique Sanary-Bandol
2mi/3km north-east towards A 50. At the roundabout leading to the motorway, go down the access road on the right. After 550yd/500m, turn right (sign "Zoo-Jardin Exotique"). Open May–Sept daily 9.30am–7pm (6pm Oct & Feb–Apr); Nov–Jan Wed, Sat, Sun 9.30am–5:30pm. 9€ (child 3-10 years 6€). Last admission 1hr before closing. 04 94 29 40 38. www.zoosanary.com.
In these shaded tropical and Mediterranean gardens, cacti, agaves, orchids and other plants are grown to remarkable sizes. Hundreds of rare plants are also on-site.

The zoo is home to animals from all over the world, such as monkeys, coatis, lemurs, peccaries, deer, ponies, miniature goats and llamas. You can also observe colourful parrots, peacocks, pink flamingoes and cranes.

Bandol AOC
Beyond the villas scattered in groves of pine and mimosa behind the seafront lie fields of flowers and vineyards that produce Bandol, the best-known of the Côtes-de-Provence wines. Ask at the tourist office for the brochure detailing Bandol vineyard tours.

Île de Bendor

Boat trips (◷ *depart Bandol every 30min in season, 7min duration;* ⊜ *11€ round trip;* ℘ *04 94 05 90 90; www.bendor.com)* to the island make a pleasant summer excursion. The island offers fine beaches, a harbour, and a Provençal village with craft shops.

Named for the famous maker of *pastis* (anise-flavored liqueur), the **Espace Culturel Paul-Ricard** hosts a **Wine Exposition** (◷ *open Jul–Aug Tue–Thu 1pm–6pm;* ⊜ *no charge;* ℘ *04 94 05 15 61; www.euvs.org).* Set up in a large hall decorated with frescoes, it covers the production of wine, aperitifs and liqueurs in 51 different countries, with some 8,000 bottles on display.

🚗 DRIVING TOUR

PERCHED VILLAGES★

Round trip of 29mi/55km. Allow a half day.

▷ From Bandol take D 559 northeast; go left on D 559B towards Le Beausset. Pass under the railway bridge.

Just after Le Beausset (where you should be sure to stop on market days: Friday and Saturday), turn right on N8 towards Toulon. The narrow road winds its way through olive groves, orchards and vineyards.

Chapelle Notre-Dame-du-Beausset-Vieux

Leave the car below the chapel. ◷ *Call for hours. Guided tours on request.* ℘ *04 94 98 61 53.*

This stark Provençal Romanesque chapel, with barrel vaulting in the nave and cul-de-four vaulting in the apse, has been restored by volunteers.

The Virgin and Child in the choir comes from Pierre Puget's studio. In the left niche a group of 400-year-old clay figures called **santons** (*see box p30)* illustrates the Flight to Egypt. Some of the votive offerings *(side aisle)* date back to the 18C. From the terrace above the chapel a sweeping **panorama★** takes in Le Castellet, Ste-Baume, Gros Cerveau and the coast from Bandol westwards to La Ciotat.

▷ Return to N 8 and continue north towards Aubagne.

Circuit du Castellet Paul-Ricard

2760 rte. des Hauts du Camp. ℘ *04 94 98 36 66. www.circuitpaulricard.com.*

ZOA Parc Animalier and Exotique Sanary-Bandol

© Christelle-Fotolia.com

This track (3.7mi/6km long) was officially opened in 1970 for the first Grand Prix de France, won by Jackie Stewart.

Since then, many international F1 and F3 drivers, such as Alain Prost in 1976, have competed on the circuit.

Although the racing season peaks in April and May, the track offers a full calendar of events.

▶ On leaving the circuit, turn right down the D N8 towards Aubagne. At Camp-du-Castellet crossroads, turn left on D 26, then left again on D 226.

Le Castellet★

Nestled on a wooded hill dominating the vineyards, this stronghold has well-preserved ramparts, a restored 12C church and a castle, parts of which date to the 11C. From beyond the gate on Place de la Mairie, a fine **view** opens inland towards Ste-Baume. Many houses were built in the 17C and 18C. There are art and craft workshops.

▶ Leave Le Castellet going downhill towards D 66.

La Cadière-d'Azur

This very old hill town produces Bandol wine. Some of its former defences are still standing. The 13C **Peï gate**, in front of the town hall, leads to a maze of picturesque old streets. From the eastern end of the village there is a **view ★** inland over Le Castellet to Ste-Baume.

▶ Follow D66 to St-Cyr-sur-Mer and then the D 559 back to Bandol.

ADDRESSES

🛏️STAY

🍴 **Golf Hôtel** – *10 Corniche Bonaparte, on Rénecros Beach by blvd. Louis-Lumière. ℰ04 94 29 45 83. www.golfhotel.fr. Closed mid-Nov–Feb. 24 rooms.* 🅿️. *10€. Restaurant* 🍽️. This seaside hotel is complete with deckchairs and a beach restaurant in summer. Most of the cosy rooms look to the sea; some are fronted by a small balcony. Dinner served only in July and August.

🍽️ **Auberge La Cauquière** – *7 Puits d'Isnard, Le Beausset. ℰ04 94 98 42 75. www.lacauquiere.com. 10 rooms.* 🅿️ *6.50€. Restaurant* 🍽️ *(closed Sun eve, Mon off-season).* A charming inn with a garden and swimming pool in the centre of Le Bausset, only 10 minutes by car from the beaches and Route des Vins de Bandol. Rooms are arranged around a cosy courtyard.

Chambre d'Hôte Les Cancades – *1195 Chemin de la Fontaine de Cinq-Sous, Le Beausset. 2mi/3km E of Le Castellet, take Chemin de la Fontaine de Cinq-Sous (across from Casino supermarket). ℘04 94 98 76 93. www.les-cancades.com. 4 rooms.* A steep, narrow path leads to the wooded, residential area and this charming Provençal mas. The handsomely furnished rooms, park, swimming pool and summer kitchen are all blissfully quiet and relaxing.

EAT

Snack Bar Le Souco – *9 rue de la Poste, Le Castellet. ℘04 94 32 67 94.* This café-restaurant frequented by the locals is open year-round. Terraces at the front and back.

L'Oasis – *15 rue des Écoles. ℘04 94 29 41 69. www.oasisbandol.com. Closed Dec, Sun eve off-season.* Delightful dining room painted in warm Mediterranean tones. In summer, enjoy the charming terrace looking out onto the garden. Smallish but impeccably-kept rooms are available for overnight stays.

Le Clocher – *1 rue de la Paroisse. ℘04 94 32 47 65. www.leclocher.fr. Closed Sun eve, Wed.* In an ancient stone house at the foot of the church belltower in Vieux Bandol, this tiny restaurant serves typical regional dishes of the Midi. Small terrace is located on the street.

ON THE TOWN

Tchin Tchin – *11 Allée Jean-Moulin. ℘04 94 29 41 04. www.tchintchin.fr. Mon–Fri 8am–1am, Sat–Sun 8am–3am.* This prestigious bar saw its golden age in the 1970s, when it attracted many celebrities from the entertainment world, namely Jacques Brel and Richard Antony, who coined the name of the club. A good selection of cocktails and regular jazz concerts.

Casino de Bandol – *2 Pl. Lucien-Artaud. ℘04 94 29 31 31. www.partouche.com. Jul–Aug daily 11am–4am; Sept–Jun Mon–Fri 11am–3am, Sat–Sun 11am–4am.* Not only does this casino have 130 slot machines, a traditional gaming room and a piano bar, it's also a popular place in the region for its nightclub and special events.

SHOPPING

Le Beausset Market – *℘04 94 98 55 76 .* Fri and Sun 8.30am–noon in the centre of town: fresh produce, gourmet specialities, flowers, local crafts and clothing.

Le Tonneau de Bacchus – *296 ave. du 11-Novembre. ℘04 94 29 01 01. www.tonneau-de-bacchus.com. 9.30am–12.30pm, 4pm–8pm. Closed Sun afternoon.* This cellar offers a wide selection of wines from France and especially the Bandol area. Regular oenology courses and themed evenings. Fine gastronomic specialities from Provence.

Domaine de Souviou – *Earl Olivier Pascal, Le Beausset. ℘04 94 90 57 63. www.domaine-souviou.fr. Easter–Sept daily 9.30am–noon, 3pm–7pm; Oct–Easter Mon–Sat, 9:30am–noon, 2pm–6pm.* Producer and seller of both wine and olive oil. Tastings and tours of the ancient farm available.

Moulin de St-Côme – *D266 between St-Cyr and Bandol, Quartier St-Côme, La Cadière-d'Azur. ℘04 94 90 11 51. www.moulindestcome.com. Mon–Sat, 9am–noon, 2.30–7pm (winter 2pm–6pm).* Free visit to the mill and olive oil tastings. The boutique has olive oils from France, soaps, perfumes, pottery, fabrics and Provençal specialities.

OUTDOOR ACTIVITIES

Bandol offers a wide range of watersports and a diving centre.

Aquascope – *Quai de Gaulle, Bandol port. ℘04 94 32 51 41. http://altantide1.com. Closed mid-Nov–Mar. Tours (35min)* on a glass-bottom boat for underwater observation of marine flora and fauna.

EVENTS

Fête du Millésime – *℘04 94 90 29 59. www.vinsdebandol.com.* A wine and gourmet food festival in the port on the first Sunday in December.

Printemps des Potiers – *℘04 94 63 04 64. www.leprintempsdespotiers.com.* Pottery displays and markets. Mid-April.

Circuit du Castellet Paul-Ricard – *2760 rte. des Hauts du Camp. ℘04 94 98 36 66. www.circuitpaulricard.com.* Car races held every April. Other events offered pre-and post-racing season.

Saint-Cyr-sur-Mer

Var

Situated between Marseille and Toulon, Saint-Cyr-sur-Mer marks the starting point of the French Riviera with its long, fine sandy beaches bordering fertile plains of grapevines and olive trees. Popular for its mild climate, it is home to the only surviving Roman villa on the Mediterranean coast.

▶ **Population:** 11,797.
♿ **Michelin Map:** 340 J6.
ℹ **Info:** Pl. de l'Appel-du-18-Juin. ✆04 94 26 73 73. www.saintcyrsurmer.com.
▶ **Location:** Located 3.7mi/6km northwest of Bandol. A long avenue of residential buildings leads to the coast, with the Port des Lecques to the west, and Port de la Madrague to the east.

SIGHTS
Beaches
Follow blvd. de la Plage south to the Chemin du Littoral.

The semicircular bay boasts 1mi/2km of sandy beaches, from the narrow shoreline at Les Lecques to the wide beaches of **La Madrague** of the south. To the west *(10min by car)*, the **Calanque du Port-d'Alon**, surrounded by a pine forest, is more secluded.

Musée de Tauroentum★
131 Rte. de La Madrague, towards Port de Lecques. ⏱Open Apr–Nov Wed–Mon 3pm–7pm; Oct–May Fri–Sun 3pm–6pm. Closed 1 Jan, 1 May, 25 Dec. ⌂3€. ✆04 94 26 30 46.

The museum is built around the foundations of the only **coastal Roman villa** in the region. Remains include wreathed columns with Corinthian capitals from the villa's peristyle and a granite column from a pergola that adorned the seafront.

The museum contains three 1C black and white **mosaics**, along with fragments of frescoes and amphorae, tools and jewellery. A 1C **dolium**, which could hold 400 gallons/1,500 l of wine or olive oil, a monolithic **sarcophagus**, and France's only **house tomb** stand in front of the museum.

Centre d'Art Sébastien
12 blvd. Jean-Jaurès. ⏱Open Jun–Sept Wed–Mon 3pm–7pm; Oct–May Wed–Mon 9am–noon, 2pm–6pm. ⏱Closed 1 Jan, 25 Dec. ⌂1€. ✆04 94 26 19 20.

Set up in a former factory in 1993, this arts centre hosts temporary exhibits and a permanent collection of works by the artist **Sébastien** (1909–90), a friend of Picasso, Matisse and Cocteau.

EXCURSION
Coastal Path
▶ *Take D 87 from St-Cyr along the coast to La Madrague. The path starts at Pointe Grenier.*

🚶 *3mi/4.5km to port d'Alon (yellow trail markers) or 3.7mi/6km to Bandol. The walk is not difficult, but wear sturdy shoes and bring drinking water.*

☺ *Keep a close eye on children: dangerous cliff drops and a railway line.* This coastal path from La Madrague to Bandol offers hikers a commanding **view** of the sea. At the peak of Pointe Grenier are a chapel and a Napoleon III **military battery**. On the inland side, admire the vineyards and spot local species of violet and mushrooms.

Vineyard Path
Leave your car at the car park next to the Aigues Marines residences and the hamlet of La Madrague. Return down rue Abbé-Dol to the bus stop (the walk starts from the path opposite). Ask for more details from the tourist office.

Diving at Saint-Cyr-sur-Mer

©Mirko Zanni/WaterF/age Fotostock

🚶 *1.2mi/2km – about 1hr.*
From La Madrague to Port-d'Alon
(information panels).

Walk down the steps into the under-growth at the foot of the Bastide and Nartette vineyards. Continue to the orchid meadow. Pass along an **area of dunes** surrounded by sparse woodland to the gateway of the Nartette estate before rejoining the road. The path continues on the other side through an olive grove and leads to the "**immortal tree**". Follow the fencing on the right and enter the undergrowth. When you reach a chain, turn right along the path leading to the **Table des Cultures Traditionnelles**. Walk back along the path in the opposite direction.

Underwater Discovery Tour

Around 2hr. Diving suit, flippers, masks and snorkel supplied. Reservations required. 🕐 *Jun–Sept 9.30am and 2pm.* 👓 *18€ (child 15€).* 📞 *04 94 88 06 15.* Discover the marine world, its fauna and flora, around Port-d'Alon.

ADDRESSES

🛏 STAY

🍴 **Le Petit Nice** – *11 allée Docteur Seillon, Les Lecques.* 📞 *04 94 32 00 64. www.hotelpetitnice.com. Closed mid-Nov–mid-Mar. 31 rooms.* 🅿. 🛏 *8.50€. Restaurant* 🍴. Beautiful garden. Small rooms with contemporary decor; annexe rooms are simpler but more spacious. The restaurant's bay windows open onto the swimming pool and greenery.

🍴 **Grand Hôtel Les Lecques** – *24 ave. du Port, Les Lecques.* ♿🅿 📞 *04 94 26 23 01. www.grand-hotel-les-lecques.com. 60 rooms.* 🛏. *Restaurant* 🍴. The paths cutting across the grounds are bordered with palms, pine trees and morning glory, an appealing setting for the 19C mansion. Cheerful rooms appointed in Provençal tradition. Outdoor pool.

🍴 **Hôtel Dolce Frégate** – *rte. de Bandol.* 📞 *04 94 29 39 39. www.dolcefregate.com.* 🅿. *133 rooms.* 🛏 *22€.* This hotel-leisure complex, conference centre and 27-hole golf course is set amid lush vineyards. The Provençal interior is soothing and simple. Restaurant **Le Mas des Vignes** (🍴) enjoys a panoramic terrace. La Restanque Club House is ideal for less formal dining.

SHOPPING

Markets – Traditional market on Sunday mornings; regional specialities at La Madrague Port (Mon and Thu mornings), Place Gabriel Péri (Tue and Fri mornings) and Les Lecques (Wed and Sat mornings).

SPORT AND LEISURE

Port de la Madrague – *Port authority.* 📞 *04 94 26 39 81.* 400 moorings, including 37 set aside for tourist traffic.

Golf de Dolce Frégate – *D 559, route de Bandol.* 📞 *04 94 29 38 00. www.fregate. dolce.com.* An 18-hole, world-class course and a 9-hole course offer views of the sea.

👥 **Aqualand** – *ZAC des Pradeaux.* 📞 *04 94 32 08 32. www.aqualand.fr. Jul–Aug daily 10am–7pm; Jun + first wk Sept 10am–6pm.* 👓 *25€ (child 18.50€).* Waterpark with slides, wave pool and swimming pools.

Lecques Aquanaut Centre – *Nouveau Port des Lecques.* 📞 *04 94 26 35 35. www.lecques-aquanaut.fr.* Diving club.

Sanary-sur-Mer★

Var

This charming resort, a vision of pink and white, is lively year-round. A little fishing port is bordered by palm trees and a bay with fine beaches well-protected from the Mistral winds by the wooded hills. Exiled German intellectuals and writers, including Berthold Brecht and Thomas Mann, made their home here in the 1930s.

▶ **Population:** 18,023.
⏾ **Michelin Map:** 340 J7; local map p121.
🛈 **Info:** 1 quai du Levant. ℘04 94 74 01 04. www.sanarysurmer.com.
◗ **Location:** 3mi/5km SE of Bandol; 8mi/13km west of Toulon.

SIGHTS
Chapelle Notre-Dame-de-Pitié
Access via blvd. Courbet.
The 16C chapel on a hillock west of the town is decorated with votive offerings, mostly naive paintings. Outside a **view★** of Sanary Bay can be obtained.

Tour Romane
Port. ◗Open daily 10am–12.30pm, 3pm–6.30pm. ⬤No charge. ℘04 94 74 01 04. www.scuba-museum.com
This 13C watchtower (70.5ft/21.5m tall), encased within Hôtel de la Tour, houses a museum dedicated to F. Dumas, a pioneer of deep-sea diving. The collection includes vintage tools for underwater hunting and diving, and objects from ancient shipwrecks in Sanary Bay.

🚗 DRIVING TOURS

1 GROS CERVEAU★★
8mi /13km. Allow about 1.5hr.

◗ From Sanary take ave. Europe-Unie, at Ollioules turn left onto D 20.

The drive begins through terraced gardens and vineyards, with **views** over the inner harbour of Toulon, gradually extending southeast over Toulon and Cap Sicié Peninsula.
Farther on, the **view★** is stunning, starting with the Grès de Ste-Anne (enormous rocks honeycombed with caves), on the right, Beausset Plain, the Ste-Baume Massif, the Évenos hills, the Ollioules Gorge and the sweeping coastline.

◗ 5mi/8km after Ollioules pull into the layby (where you can also do a U-turn, if necessary).

Walk through scrubland along a winding path to the top of Gros Cerveau. At the foot of the small fort (alt. 1,453ft/443m), take in the **view★★** of the coast from the Giens Peninsula to Île Verte, south of La Ciotat.

2 MONT CAUME★★
14.3mi/23km northeast. Allow 2hr.

◗ Leave Sanary on ave. de l'Europe-Unie going east on D 11 to Ollioules.

Ollioules
This flower-growing town is dominated by a 13C castle skirted by historic arcaded houses and a Provençal Romanesque church.

◗ Beyond Ollioules turn left onto D N8 and through the gorge.

Gorges d'Ollioules★
Admired by Victor Hugo, this arid and sinuous gorge was formed by the Reppe, which flows into Sanary Bay. Higher up on the left are the Grès de Ste-Anne, a curious mass of eroded sandstone rocks.

◗ In Ste-Anne-d'Évenos, turn right onto D 462. Turn right towards Évenos and park near a cross set in a rock.

Sanary-sur-Mer harbour

© Wadey James/Apa Publications

Évenos★

🏃 *15min round trip.*

The village is a jumble of grey basalt stone houses, now restored, clinging to the steep rocky slopes beneath the ruins of a 16C castle. Its keep stands on the edge of a volcano whose lava slag is still visible. A platform affords **views** of Destel, Ollioules Gorge, Gros Cerveau and Sainte Baume on the horizon.

▶ Continue east along D 62 turning left at Col du Corps-de-Garde onto D 662.

Mont Caume

Mont Caume rises to a height of 2,628ft/801m, and its steep approach road offers fine view-points. Once you reach the top, there is a magnificent **pano-rama★★** of the coast.

③ PRESQU'ÎLE DU CAP SICIÉ★

Round trip of the peninsula 15.5mi /25km. Allow 2hr.

▶ From Sanary take ave. d'Estienne-d'Orves towards Six-Fours-les-Plages. The road skirts Bonnegrâce beach. Turn right at the foot of Cap Nègre.

👪 Parc de la Méditerranée

Corniche de la Coudoulière. ⏰*Open Jul–Aug Wed–Sun 9am–noon, 2pm–6pm.* 📞*04 94 25 53 84.* ⊘*No charge.*

This public park is filled with exotic spe-cies for plant lovers and play areas for children.

The top of **Cap Nègre** affords a **view** over Sanary Bay. The 19C **battery** houses a military history centre.

AROUND SANARY

Le Brusc

Le Brusc is a fishing village and resort; ferries to **Île des Embiez** (*see below*) leave from the port.

Petit Gaou

The rocky promontory, once an island, resembles a Breton seascape, offering good **views** of the coast.

Grand Gaou

Accessed via a pedestrian bridge, this island was designated a nature preserve in 2000 and enjoys a wild aspect. It is crossed by a botanical path and has designated areas for picnics.

▶ Return to Le Brusc and take D 16 on the right; turn off to the left at Roche-Blanche.

The road runs parallel to the coast about 0.6mi/1km inland, but gives glimpses of La Ciotat, Bandol and Sanary. At the crossroads there is a **view★★** of the Toulon harbour, Cap Cépet, the Giens Peninsula and the Îles d'Hyères.

▶ Turn right; park at the radio station. No access to cars mid-Jun to mid-Sept.

Chapelle Notre-Dame-du-Mai★★

Behind radio station. ○*Oct–Apr first Sat and first and third Sun of the month 2pm–6pm. May daily 9am–noon, 2.30pm–6pm.*
The chapel sits at the highest point of Cap Sicié (1,043ft/318m). Perched over a dizzying drop, it affords a **panorama★★** of the coast from the Îles d'Hyères to the calanques east of Marseilles.

▶ Make a U-turn; at the crossroads continue straight ahead.

The narrow road cuts through the **forêt de Janas,** planted with conifers, before rejoining D 16 on the left.

Six-Fours-les-Plages

see SIX-FOURS-LES-PLAGES.

▶ Return to Sanary on D 559.

EXCURSION
ÎLES DES EMBIEZ★

The largest of the five islands (95ha/235 acres), Île de la Tour Fondue, is known as Les Embiez. The second largest island is Grand Gaou. Île du Grand Rouveau has an automated lighthouse, and Petit Rouveau is a bird sanctuary. The smallest island is Petit Gaou.

Access to the Island – *Société Paul Ricard.* ℰ*04 94 10 65 20. www.les-embiez. com.* ∞*9€ winter/11€ summer round trip (child 7€/9€).* 13 to 24 crossings per day *(8min)* from Le Brusc at Six-Fours.

♁♁ Aquascope – *Île des Embiez, Brusc, Six-Fours-les-Plages.* ○*Open Jul–Aug 9am–6pm; Apr–Jun and Sept 2.30pm–5pm.* ○*Closed public holidays.* ⟵ *Guided tours (30min).* ∞*16€ (child 9€).* ℰ*04 94 34 17 85.* Observe underwater life through the transparent hull of a boat.

♁♁ Aquavision – *Île des Embiez, Quai St-Pierre, Six-Fours-les-Plages.* ○*Open Apr–Jun and Sept Wed–Sun 2.15pm. Jul–Aug 10.30am, 11.45am, 2.15pm, 3.30pm, 4.45pm.* ∞*16€ (child 9€).* ℰ*06 62 11 72 89. www.littoral-bleu.com.* Passengers enjoy a 40min tour of the port and sealife in a glass-bottom boat.

Visit

Separated from the Port du Brusc by a lagoon and surrounded by rich fishing banks, the Île des Embiez is highly popular with anglers and divers. Boasting statues, kitsch houses, an oceanographic museum, creeks and beaches, this island, which belongs to the Fondation Paul-Ricard (*see BANDOL*) is ideal for a day-long excursion.

♁♁ Institut Océanographique Paul-Ricard★

Aquarium Museum ○*Open Mon–Fri 10am–12.30pm, 1.30pm–5pm. Sat 2pm–5pm.* ○*Closed 1 Jan, 24 , 26, 30, & 31 Dec.* ∞*4.50€ (child 2€).* ℰ*04 94 34 02 49. www.institut-paul-ricard.org.*
An old naval gun site on the St-Pierre promontory houses an oceanographic institute that performs research on marine biology, fish farming and sea pollution. The **museum** has 30 sea-water **aquariums** and 100 species of aquatic animal.

Beaches

The coast is lined with a succession of sandy coves and rocky headlands. Dorée and Gorguette beaches lie between Sanary and Bandol; Cousse Bay is home to Beaucours pebble beach; Portissol beach is nestled in the bay of the same name, and Bonnegrâce beach lies between Sanary and Six-Fours.

TOUR OF ÎLE DES EMBIEZ

The island is reserved for walkers and cyclists. A small tourist train also makes regular runs in season (*see below*).

Coastal Path★

4.3mi/7km. Maps of the island are available from the Six-Fours tourist office or the island's information point (peak season).

Allow 90min on foot to tour the island's fine gravel beaches, rugged coastline with coves, salt marshes, scrubland, umbrella pine woods, flower gardens and vineyards.

♣ Little Train

Operates Apr–Oct. Times are posted at the info point; about 10 departures a day depending on boat service. 7€ (6–18 yrs 4€). 06 88 69 76 78. The train offers a 40min discovery tour of the former salt marshes, the Japanese garden and vineyards.

Les Terres

Start at the **chapelle Ste-Cécile**, with its stained-glass windows celebrating Paul Ricard's passions (a rose, an anchor and a guitar). Statues, low-reliefs and colonnades in the style of ancient Greece scattered among the island's gardens pay tribute to Ricard's interest in Mediterranean culture. To the south, don't miss Ricard's last resting place at the foot of the **Tour du Coucoussan**.

The Marina

Dominated by the ruins of the Château de Sabran, this busy, high-tech marina plays host to some 750 boats a year, mostly sailboats.

ADDRESSES

🛏 STAY

Chambre d'Hôte Villa Lou Gardian – *646 rte. de Bandol.* 04 94 88 05 73. 4 rooms. Despite being near a main road, this B&B has minimally decorated rooms that are comparatively quiet. Large garden, pool, tennis court and a table d'hôte set up in the summer patio.

Le Cabanon – *Plage de Portissol.* 04 94 74 64 17. 5 rooms. Providing exceptional views of the sea, this small hotel sports a contemporary decor. Its air-conditioned rooms boast private balconies and the beach at their doorstep. Open year-round, its restaurant () serves inspired Mediterranean dishes.

🍴 EAT

Chez Mico – *18 rue Barthélémy-de-Don.* 04 94 74 16 73. www.pizzeria-sanary. com. Closed Mon–Tue off-season; Jul–Aug no lunch Tue and Fri. A local institution for more than 35 years, this restaurant is known for its Italian staples, including pizzas, served in a dining room decorated with old cooking utensils, travel souvenirs and carnival masks.

Restaurant du Théâtre – *8 impasse de l'Enclos, near the theatre.* 04 94 88 04 16. Closed Sun eve., Mon. Take a few steps down and enter this U-shaped restaurant appointed with rustic furnishings. Your attention will soon be caught by the sight of mouthwatering salmon, meats, prawns and skewered game roasting in the open fireplace.

ENTERTAINMENT

Centre National de Création et de Diffusion Culturelles – *Chateauvallon.* 04 94 22 02 02. www.chateauvallon.com. Closed Sun. Indoor and open-air theatres offer a diverse programme of drama, music, dance, circus and arts shows throughout the year.

CALENDAR

St-Pierre et de la Lavande – Festival of the sea, last weekend in June.

Fête de la St-Nazaire – Late August, with Provençal games.

Six-Fours-les-Plages

Var

Sandy beaches, a wild coastline and an ancient abandoned village make Six-Fours ideal to explore on foot.

OLD SIX-FOURS

▶ *Access via ave. du Maréchal-Juin; turn left onto a narrow road.*

Fort de Six-Fours★

From the platform (alt. 689ft/210m) at the entrance to the 19C fort (⊶ *closed to the public*), a **panorama**★ extends from east to west over Toulon harbour and coastline.

Collégiale St-Pierre

⊙*Open Wed–Mon 9am–12pm, 2pm–6pm.*

At the foot of the fortress stands the church of the now-abandoned village of old Six-Fours. The monks of Montmajour and St-Victor established the priory and chapel in the 11C. Don't miss the polyptych by **Louis Bréa**.

Coastal Trails

To follow this by road, *see Driving Tour* ③*Cap Siciéa in SANARY-SUR-MER.*
The first of the two hikes here is easy (3.7mi/6km), the second more difficult (6mi/10km).

🚶 *1.5hr. Start at Bonnegrâce beach.*
The path runs along the beaches through low, thorny vegetation and over the **Cap Négre** to the fishing port of **Le Brusc**.

🚶 *4hr. Start from Le Brusc.*
From the roundabout, climb the Chemin de Gardiole—and via the Chemin de la Lèque—ascend the Haute-Lecques. The tarred path ends after the chemin des Gargadoux. This part of the coastal trail is called the Corniche Merveilleuse. Climb to the **Chapel Notre-Dame-de-Mai** (⚲ *see p 122).* The trail continues to Cap Sicié's Fabrégas beach.

▶ **Population:** 34,325.
ⓘ **Michelin Map:** 340 K7; region map p99.
🔖 **Info:** Promenade Général-de-Gaulle. ℘04 94 07 02 21. www.six-fours-les-plages.com.
▶ **Location:** The *commune* of Six-Fours-les-Plages encompasses 125 hamlets and districts around the central town of Reynier.

ADDRESSES

🏠 STAY

⊜⊜ **Hôtel du Parc** – *112 rue Marius-Bondil, Le Brusc. ℘04 94 34 00 15. www.locanna.com. Closed 3 weeks in Jan. 18 rooms. ⊇8€.* This hotel is located just 218yds/200m from the port of Le Brusc and its beaches. Situated within a large house, the hotel has a dining room overlooking the back garden.

🍽 EAT

⊜⊜ **Lou Figuier**– *43 rue Marius-Bondil, Le Brusc. ℘04 94 34 00 29. www.loufiguier. com. Closed Thu eve til Sun afternoon off-season.* Located in an alley behind the port, this small family-owned kitchen prepares evening meals and sometimes lunch. Provencal specialities include blue sardines with garlic as well as squid.

SPORT AND LEISURE

Hiking and Cycling

The massif du Cap Sicié has five hiking trails *(about 2hr each)* and five circular bike trails (6mi/10km to 15mi/25km).

Watersports

Six-Fours/Les Embiez has been awarded the "station nautique" label for its range of watersports facilities.

EVENTS

Fête de la Bouillabaisse – Held in June, this festival celebrates the local dish *bouillabaisse* (tastings and other activities).

Le Pradet
Var

This charming resort nestled beneath the Massif de la Colle Noire has a good selection of small, easily accessible beaches tucked between rocky outcrops. Its minerology museum and botanical trail make this a pleasant excursion from Toulon.

▶ **Population:** 10,603.
✦ **Michelin Map:** 340 L7; region map p90.
▣ **Info:** Pl. Général-de-Gaulle. ☏04 94 21 71 69. www.lepradet-tourisme.fr.
◗ **Location:** Pradet sits on the eastern edge of Toulon, at the foot of the Colline de Paradis and Mont des Oiseaux, on D559.

RESORT LIFE
Beaches
La Garonne Bay is punctuated by remarkable **creeks**. Some are accessible by car, but the best way to explore them is to take the coastal walking path.

Parks and Gardens
Bordering the tourist office, **Cravéro park** is renowned for its palm groves and shady, wooded pet village with parrots, goats and other animals. Also in the park, the Cravéro Le Camus gallery, housed in a former rose pergola, holds regular contemporary art exhibits (◔open Sat–Thu 3pm–6pm; Fri 10am–noon, 3pm–6pm; ☏ 04 94 08 69 79). The centrally-located **Bois de Courbebaisse** is home to a 12acre/5ha botanical garden. Be sure to see the Moorish pavilion.

Coastal Footpath★
◗ 4.2mi/7km. Allow 3 to 4hr.
🚶 ☏04 94 05 35 26. The winding path is very steep in places. Sheer steps cut from the rock give access to the beaches.
Following a fire that swept through the **Colle-Noire** massif in 2005, some changes have been made to the path network. To the west, the steep slope above **Pin de Galle** beach offers magnificent **views** over Toulon harbour. The numerous cabins in the pine wood add to the bucolic charm of the setting. The shaded path joins the road through the park before descending steeply to **Monaco Beach**. At the end of this beach, part of which is used by naturists, the path begins beyond a low wall and climbs a cliff covered by superb *maquis* vegetation.
A little farther on there is a lovely **view★** of the inlets along the coast. A well-marked path leads down to **Les Bonnettes beach** at the foot of a remarkable rocky inlet. A former path linking this beach to La Garonne beach is closed due to fire damage, as is the path between the Pas des Gardéens and La Mine. In season there is a lifeguards' post and an open-air café here. Walk to **Oursinières** along the road. Beyond the port a footpath to the right leaves the road to Le Pradet. It leads past **panoramic** viewpoints on the cliffs to **Bau Rouge**.

SIGHT
👥 Musée de la Mine de Cap-Garonne★
In Le Pradet take D86 south towards Plage de la Garonne. After the beach, take the road that climbs to the left, signposted "La Mine".
♿👣Guided tours (75min) 2pm–5pm.
◔Closed first 2 weeks Jan, 25 Dec.
⬞6.50€ (child 4€). ☏04 94 08 32 46. www.mine-capgaronne.fr.
Wearing a hardhat, visitors get to explore the old copper ore mines worked here since the 16C. The mines closed in 1917, when a reduction in the ore's copper content made it unprofitable.
The tour focuses on the redeveloped part of the galleries and, through several reconstructions and presentations, illustrates the long-standing evolution of working methods and the daily lives of miners at Cap Garonne.
At the end of the tour, in the **great hall★**, you can discover the various colours of copper ore at tables with magnifying glasses.

HYÈRES, THE GOLDEN ISLANDS

When most people think of the French Riviera, they imagine sunbathing on secluded beaches, discovering local crafts in the cobblestone streets of historic villages and partying in glitzy clubs surrounded by celebrities. That's exactly what visitors to the "Golden Islands" of Hyères and the Maures Massif will find. This part of the Mediterranean coastline is an Eden-like paradise of unspoiled islands and sandy beaches framed by forested mountains. Chic resorts full of luxury yachts share a decidedly Provençal spirit with tiny perched villages that haven't changed in centuries. And while humans have made their mark with their lush gardens, Belle Époque mansions, imported palm trees and ancient forts, the natural beauty of the region has been carefully protected from the unchecked development plaguing less fortunate corners of the Côte d'Azur.

Highlights

1 Hire a boat for the day to visit the **"Golden Islands,"** a world away from the glitz of the French Riviera (p137)

2 Snorkel along the underwater nature trail at the **Île de Port-Cros** (p140)

3 Drive through the scenic forested hills along the **Corniches des Maures** (p147)

4 Escape the crowds of St-Tropez with a coastal hike around the **St-Tropez Peninsula** (p162)

5 Enjoy panoramic views from the 11C ramparts of the perched village of **Grimaud** (p166)

The Green *Département*

The residents of the "Golden Islands" (Îles d'Or, in French) and Maures Massif take the protection and preservation of their environment very seriously. Situated at the heart of the Var *département*, where 62 percent of land remains undeveloped, this area is the second-greenest place in France.

Maritime pines, cork oaks, chestnut trees and maquis scrub make up most of the Maures Massif flora, thriving on the ancient geological formations that form its rocky peaks.

Forest fires are a constant threat. After the partial devastation of the Maures Massif during the heatwave of 2003, the authorities have cracked down on barbecuing and smoking along forest trails.

Aerial view of Petit Langoustier, Île de Porquerolles

D. Pazery/ MICHELIN

Environmental Preservation

By far the greatest threat to the local environment is property development. Much of the land, coastline and even the waters around the "Golden Islands", named for the glow given off by **mica and quartz rock** when it catches the sun, has now been placed under the protection of the French National Park of Port-Cros. Île de Port-Cros is the only 100 percent car-free island along this stretch of coastline, and its clear waters and underwater nature trail are popular with divers. The Golden Islands are also a haven for endangered fauna, with sanctuaries for tropical birds, fish and even the threatened Hermann tortoise.

Clean and Accessible Coastline

Coastal hiking trails, known as the *"sentier littoral"*, have their own special protection agency, the Conservatoire du Littoral. Not only does it keep the coastline clean, the agency also makes sure the area stays open to the public. Since 1976 any new properties built on the beach have to leave a 9.8ft/3m path closest to the water for hikers to use. This law covers more than 125mi/200km of the Var coastline, including the scenic St-Tropez peninsula. While there are many sandy, family-friendly beaches such as Le Lavandou, Ste-Maxime and Pampelonne, much of the coastline consists of rocky inlets perfect for fishing or finding a bit of privacy away from the crowds.

From Pirates to Artists

Like most of the French Riviera, the Golden Islands of Hyères were a haven for pirates until they were hounded out of the region in the 17C by Louis XIV, who replaced their lairs with military forts, many of which still dot the coastline today. The early perched villages and monasteries were often given their lands and allowed to cultivate them tax-free in return for keeping an eye out for invaders.

The arrival of the railroad in the mid-1800s attracted the likes of Queen Victoria and other wealthy Anglophone travellers hoping for a little winter sun.

Cap Lardier, St-Tropez Peninsula

J. Malburet/MICHELIN

The chic crowds eventually moved eastward to Cannes and Nice, leaving this area to the writers, artists and filmmakers such as Colette, Anaïs Nin, Matisse, Jean Cocteau, Paul Signac and Roger Vadim, whose 1956 film, *"And God Created Woman"* starring his then wife, Brigitte Bardot, launched St-Tropez into the limelight it still enjoys today.

Local Industry

Tourism is the principal industry in this region, with more than 25 percent of properties used as second homes for holidaymakers. Flowers, fruit, and grapes for Côte de Provence wines are also produced here, along with natural cork from cork oak trees. Before becoming part of the nature reserve in 1995, the marshland ponds of the Giens Peninsula were used to harvest some 30,000 tons of sea salt each year.

Although the Var *département* is named after the river that runs through the Côte d'Azur region, administrative juggling after the French Revolution redrew the boundaries, and the river no longer flows through the administrative division that bears its name.

AIX-EN-PROVENCE

TOULON

A   **B**

1

2

3

Lac de Carcès

Caramy

Argens

D N7

D N7

D 43

Issole

Corany

A 8

D 97

A 57

Aille

D N7

D 97

D N7

3

D 97

Gonfaron

D 75

D 75

▲ Village de tortues

N.-D.-des-Anges

La Sauvette · 780

780 ✝ 535

Col des Fourches

d e s

Col de Taillude · 411

D 39

Pierrefeu

Collobrières

D 41

D 14

D 24 ✕

Monastère de la Verne

D 97

A 57

Réal Martin

Réal Collobrier

de

414

Forêt des Maures

D 98

D 14

Col de Babaou

Forêt

M a s s i f

Maravenne

Arboretum Col de Gratteloup

192

Pierre d'Avenon

· 443

D 41

Aiguebelle St-Clair

Réal Martin

D 12

Pensard

Col de Caguo-Ven

229

Forêt du Dom

Le Fenouillet

Gapeau

Jardin Zoologique Tropical ♲

A 570

○ La Londe-les-Maures

D 98

Bormes-les-Mimosas

🚗 **Le Lavandou**

A 57

Hyères

D 559

Plage de la Favière

Cap Bénat

Salins des Pesquiers

Hyères-Plage ○

Rade d'Hyères

Cap de Brégançon ☆

Cap Blanc

Et⁹ des Pesquiers

Giens ○

☆ La Tour Fondue

Presqu'île de Giens

ÎLES D'HYÈRES

Île de Bagaud

N

ÎLE DE PORT-CROS

ÎLE DE PORQUEROLLES

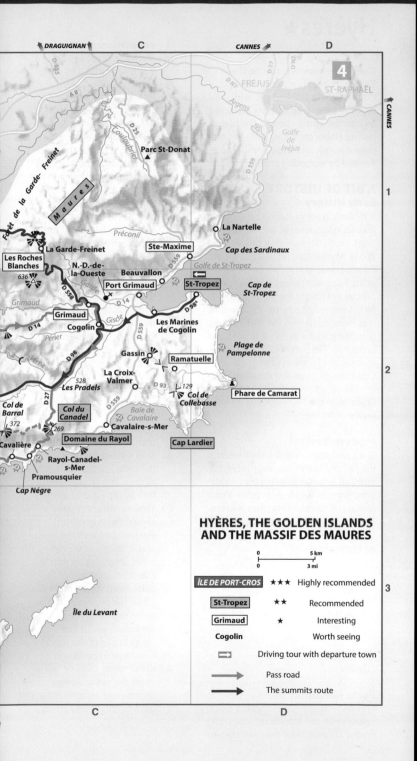

Hyères★

Var

The southernmost resort on the Riviera, Hyères is also the oldest. Popular in the 18C and 19C with wealthy English aristocrats attracted by its mild winter climate, the town boasts elaborate villas, Belle Époque palace hotels and wide avenues flanked by magnificent palm trees.

A BIT OF HISTORY
Early History

A Hellenic trading station called Olbia was founded here in the 4C, trading skins, coral, oil, wine and salt. Around 200 BC, the Romans set up a galley port, Pomponiana, next to the Greek settlement. The name Hyères appeared in an official document for the first time in 963. A nunnery, St-Pierre-d'Almanarre, was founded here in the Middle Ages, coinciding with a period of growth and prosperity. The port of L'Aygade (subsequently silted up) was used as a base by Crusaders; St Louis disembarked there in 1254 on returning from the Seventh Crusade. In the 17C Hyères declined in favour of Toulon.

Modern Revival

The town became a well-known resort in the 19C, particularly among the English, Irish and Americans, laying the foundations for the beach resorts we know today. The surrounding plain is extensively cultivated to produce early fruit (strawberries and peaches), vegetables and wine grapes.

 WALKING TOUR

1 OLD TOWN
Allow 1.5hr.

▶ Leave from pl. Georges-Clemenceau.

Porte Massillon

This late-13C gate, inset with a clock, opens onto rue Massillon, a bustling shopping street. Once the town's richest

▶ **Population:** 55,007.

🚲 **Michelin Map:** 340 L7; local maps p131 and p132.

🚏 **Info:** Rotonde du Park Hôtel, ave. de Belgique, Hyères. ℘04 94 01 84 50. www.hyeres-tourisme.com.

▶ **Location:** Greater Hyères is divided in two by the Voie Rapide (Olbia motorway, or N 98 trunk road), with the old quarters on the slope to the north, and airport, beaches and harbour to the south.Hyères and the Giens Peninsula operate several bus lines (bus station on pl. Joffre, ℘08 25 00 06 50), serving mostly the beaches (Almanarre and Ayguade). Links to the Îles d'Or by boat.

🅿 **Parking:** No charge for parking in the harbour or on place Louis-Versin. Pay car parks (some underground) can be found outside the Casino, in the Olbia shopping mall and in the Denis gardens on place du Maréchal-Joffre.

👁 **Don't Miss:** A tour of the Belle Époque villas in the summer, arranged through the tourist office.

🕐 **Timing:** An entire day should be reserved for Hyères. Start with the scenic streets of the old town, shopping on the rue Massillon and tours of the palm-lined streets and 19C villas. The afternoon can be spent exploring the Giens peninsula, with a few hours at one of the sunny beaches and ports.

👪 **Kids:** Young children will enjoy the zoo at Jardins Olbius-Riquier, while older ones might prefer karting.

street, it features numerous elaborate Renaissance doorways.

Place Massillon, home to a daily market, is dominated by a 12C tower, **Tour des Templiers** (also known as Tour St-Blaise), the last remnant of a Knights Templar commandery, which now houses temporary art exhibitions (◷open Apr–Oct Wed–Sun 10am–noon, 4pm–7pm; Nov–Mar Wed–Sun 10am–noon, 2pm–5pm; ◌no charge; ℘04 94 35 22 36).

◔ From pl. Massillon take the steps to rue Ste-Catherine and pl. St-Paul.

Place St-Paul

From this terraced square, once the site of the cloisters of the Collégiale St-Paul, there is a fine **view★** (viewing table) over the peninsula.

Ancienne Collégiale St-Paul

The Romanesque bell tower of this former collegiate church dates back to the 12C. A monumental stairway and a fine Renaissance door lead to a narthex (formerly the nave of the Romanesque church) covered with votive offerings, some dating from the 17C.

Old Streets

Porte St-Paul (gateway) near the collegiate church is incorporated into a handsome **Renaissance house** with a turret at one corner.

Pass beneath and follow rue St-Paul to rue Ste-Claire, where the **porte des Princes** frames the chevet and bell tower of the Collégiale St-Paul.

Retrace your steps to rue de Paradis (to the right of the Renaissance house), where there is a fine **Romanesque house** (no 6), which has been restored.

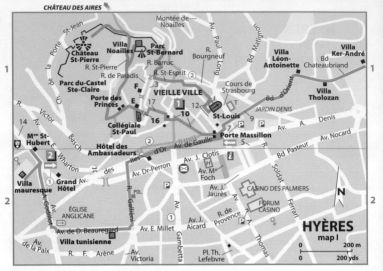

▶ Continue down rue du Four Cauvin, right into rue Saint Bernard and down rue Barruc. Enter parc St-Bernard.

Villa Noailles

Montée de Noailles. ◀•*Guided tours on request.* ○*Open Jul–Sept Wed–Mon 2pm–7pm, (Fri 4pm–10pm); Oct–Jun Wed –Sun 1pm–6pm (Fri 3pm–8pm).* ✎*No charge.* ✆*04 98 08 01 98. www.villanoailles-hyeres.com.*

In 1923 the Vicomte de Noailles and his wife Marie-Laure, wealthy patrons of the arts, commissioned this winter villa from the French architect **Robert Mallet-Stevens**. With its covered swimming pool and 60 or so rooms, it was one of the first modern homes on the Riviera and quickly became a favourite rendezvous for avant-garde artists in the 1920s (Picasso, Giacometti, Cocteau, Man Ray and Dalí).

The city restored the villa in 1986. The Cubist garden was designed by Gabriel Guévrékian. Today temporary exhibitions are held on the first floor. The villa also hosts the International Fashion and Photography Festival in April, and the Design Parade in July and August.

Parc St-Bernard (Jardin de Noailles)

Next to the Villa de Noailles.

The park encloses the castle ruins (⬆*see Château des Aires below*) and has a variety of Mediterranean flora. The terraces command a sweeping **view**★ of the Maures *(to left)*, as well as the old town, St Paul's abbey, the Giens peninsula, and the islands.

▶ Exit the villa to the west and walk north along the rue St-Pierre.

Château des Aires

The castle ruins can also be reached by car along Montée de Noailles (car park). The ruins are quite extensive, with sections of wall, square and round towers (13C–15C), and a crenellated keep. The panoramic **views**★ from the northern side are particularly stunning.

▶ Return to rue St-Pierre, taking a left down the small rue du Puit St-Pierre onto rue Barbuc. Continue down rue Saint-Esprit and rue Bourgneuf. Before the bottom of the street, take a right to pl. Bourgneuf, then left onto rue St-Louis.

Église St-Louis
Pl. de la République. ✆*04 94 00 55 50.*
This is the former church of the Cordeliers convent. The façade with three doors surmounted by a rose window brings to mind the Italian Romanesque style. It's a fine example of the transition from Romanesque to Provençal Gothic.

② THE 19C TOWN
By car or on foot.

Between 1850 and 1880, dozens of luxurious hotels and villas were built to accommodate the town's wealthy winter tourists. Its famous visitors include Queen Victoria, the novelist RL Stevenson, Victor Hugo and Maupassant.

"Godillot" District
This is the unofficial name of the western part of the town centre developed by **Alexis Godillot**, supplier to the Second Empire, who commissioned the **maison St-Hubert** *(70 ave. des Îles-d'Or)*.

▶ Go down ave. Godillot and turn left on ave. de Beauregard.

At the other end of the street from the Anglican St Paul's Church stands the **Villa Tunisienne** in Moorish style, once home to Godillot's architect, Chapoulart. Turn left down rue Gallieni, where you'll find the ex-Hôtel des Palmiers (1884).

On avenue des Îles-d'Or, the entrance to **Hôtel des Ambassadeurs** is flanked by four caryatids mounted on plinths.

▶ At pl. Georges Clemenceau, follow the rue Dr-de-Seignoret, then blvd d'Orient.

Quartier Chateaubriand
The Classical-style villas in the Quartier d'Orient, developed from 1850, have a touch of fantasy.
On boulevard Chateaubriand and boulevard d'Orient, admire the villas Léon-Antoinette, **Tholozan**, La Favorite and Villa Ker-André.

OTHER SIGHTS
Walks and Tours
The **tourist office** offers free guides to the medieval town and the region's forests, forts, coastal paths, gardens and parks. Fee-based **guided tours** led by qualified guides are also available by reservation.

Parc du Château Ste-Claire
Ave. Edith-Wharton. 🕐 *Open summer 8am–7pm; rest of the year 8am–5pm.* 🚫*No charge.*
A fine villa built in 1850 by Colonel Voutier, the man who discovered the *Venus de Milo,* sits in the middle of these pleasant gardens filled with exotic plants.

♟♟ Jardins Olbius-Riquier
Ave. Ambroise-Thomas. 🕐*Open daily 7.30am–6pm; summer until 8pm.* 🚫*No charge.*
These extensive gardens (16 acres/6.5ha) have a rich variety of tropical plants, palms and cacti. In the **greenhouse** the more fragile species can be seen.

A Touch of Exoticism

Hyères is famous for its palm trees. The cultivation of palms began around 1867 and reached its peak in the 1930s. There are no fewer than 10 varieties of Hyères palms, many of which have been exported as far as Saudi Arabia. In Hyères itself, strollers can enjoy the exotic charm of the palms in avenue Godillot, one of the most attractive streets in France, and in three public gardens: the Casino gardens, Roy gardens and Denis gardens. Discover a complete range of existing species in the fine Olbius-Risquier gardens.

Tour Fondue, Gien peninsula

S. Sauvignier/ MICHELIN

The grounds include a small **zoo** with a few rare animals, a little train, pony rides and roundabouts of interest to children.

Chapelle Notre-Dame-de-Consolation

Access from Hyères on the D 559, direction Carqueiranne, to the top of Colline de Costebelle. 𝄞*04 94 57 75 93.* There has been a sanctuary on the top of Costebelle hill since the 11C. The pre-

sent chapel was built in 1955. A huge coloured sculpture of Our Lady against the cross by Lambert-Rucki forms the bell tower's vertical axis.

The stark interior is enhanced by the monumental blue and gold **stained-glass windows★**.

The neighbouring promenade gives a **view★** of the Hyères and Toulon harbour.

Olbia Archaeological Site

Access from Hyères on the D 559, direction Carqueiranne, located at the northernmost point of L'Almanarre.

A fortified village and maritime market port in the 4C BC, Olbia was a stopping point on the Greek trading routes. It is one of the few sites of its kind still existing on the Mediterranean coast.

BEACHES

Hyères has 12.4mi/20km of beaches under lifeguard supervision in the summer, except those on the Giens Peninsula.

L'Almanarre

This long sandy beach near the site of the ancient town of Olbia is popular with windsurfers. The salt road *(Route du Sel; accessible only in summer)* leads along the peninsula, passing a vast salt-marsh (988 acres/400ha) and the Étang des Pesquiers.

Hyères-Plage

Fringed by a small forest of umbrella pines, the Hippodrome, La Capte and La Bergerie beaches, which run up to Giens, are lapped by shallow waters (200ft/60m along the shore). Boats leave from the **port** for the Îles d'Hyères.

Ayguade-le Ceinturon

This is the old port of Hyères, from which St Louis disembarked on his return from the Seventh Crusade. It is now a pleasant resort area with two sandy beaches, one on the boulevard du Front-de-Mer and the other on avenue des Girelles.

Les Salins

The salt marshes were replaced by a beach many years ago. This site is sometimes called Port-Pothuaud after the fishing village.

🚗 DRIVING TOUR

GIENS PENINSULA★★

Guided tours of the salt marshes can be booked at Hyères Tourist Office.

The Giens Peninsula was produced by an extremely rare natural phenomenon called **tombolo**. Favourable maritime currents and the mouths of two rivers straddling the former island of Giens created a double isthmus of sand and pebbles on the rocky seabed.

The parallel bars enclose a lagoon, the **Étang des Pesquiers** (🕐*open Apr–Sept for supervised ornithological visits;* ℘*04 94 12 79 52)* that provides an ideal habitat for water fowl. Up to 1,500 flamingos migrate here in mid-September.

The castle ruins in the small seaside resort village of **Giens** form a mound from which there is a magnificent **panorama★★**. To the south lies the port of Niel surrounded by a pine wood.

🔾 Drive east to La Tour Fondue.

Tour Fondue

Built around 1634 then remodelled, the tower crowns a rocky promontory and once controlled the Petite Passe narrows, along with two other forts (⚬ *closed to the public)* on the isles of Grand and Petit Ribaud. Boats sail to the Île de Porquerolles from here. The **view** of the islands and peninsula is lovely.

Peninsula Hike

🔾 *11mi/18km. Allow 5hr.*

The partly signed route links the port of La Madrague to La Badine beach via a mountainous and pine-forested coastline of hidden beaches and inlets.

EXCURSION
Sommet du Fenouillet

🔾 *4km/2.5mi. From Hyères take ave. de Toulon, turn right onto the road signed "Fenouillet".* 🔾 *30min round trip.*

From the neo-Gothic **chapel**, follow the path to Le Fenouillet, the highest point of the Maurettes (955ft/291m) that provides a good **panorama★** of the Hyères and Toulon harbour and surrounding mountains.

ADDRESSES

🏠 STAY

🛏 **Hôtel Port Hélène** – *D 559, at L'Almanarre.* ℘*04 94 57 72 01. www.hotel-port-helene.fr. 15 rooms.* 🍽*10€.* This inviting hotel fronted by a pink façade is lost among umbrella pines and palms. The rooms are well-kept, with balconies offering views of the sea.

🛏🛏 **Hôtel Les Orangers** – *64 ave. des Îles-d'Or.* ℘*04 94 00 55 11. www.orangers-hotel.com. 16 rooms.* 🍽*7€. Closed Jan.*This charming, comfortable and cosy hotel is set in the medieval part of Hyères.

🛏🛏 **Hôtel Les Voiliers** – *ave. du Dr-Robin, port St-Pierre.* ℘*04 94 38 39 24. www.yachtclubhyeres.fr. 37 rooms.* 🍽*7.50€.* Decorated with a nautical theme, this hotel on the port has reasonably priced doubles and more expensive rooms with harbour views.

🛏🛏 **Hôtel Le Soleil** – *4 rue Neuve.* ℘*04 94 65 16 26. www.hotel-du-soleil.fr. 20 rooms.* 🍽*7€.* This old house in the upper part of the old town, near the Noailles villa, has lots of character. The rooms are small, but clean.

🛏🛏🛏 **Hôtel l'Europe** – *45 ave. Édith-Cavell.* ℘*04 94 00 67 77. www.hotel-europe-hyeres.com. 40 rooms.* 🍽*10€.*🔾 This restored 19C mansion close to the train station has bright guest rooms.

🛏🛏🛏🛏 **Chambre d'hôte La Buanderie** – *36 ave. des Colibris, le Mont des Oiseaux, Hyères, 2.5mi/4km south of Almanarre.* ℘*04 04 94 38 30 98. www.la-buanderie.com. 3 rooms.* 🔾🍽*.* On a hillside overlooking the sea, this bed and breakfast is tastefully decorated with minimal fuss. The pool has a teak deck for sunbathing.

Hôtel BOR – *3 allée Émile Gérard.* ℘*04 94 58 02 73. www.hotel-bor. com. 20 rooms.* ⬜*15€.* Situated near the port, this small, high-style hotel is sleek and streamlined within and without. It edges the beach and offers good views of the islands from bedroom balconies. Giant chairs and ottomans invite relaxation. On Thursday evenings in summer, enjoy live jazz in the restaurant *(serving breakfast and lunch only)* along with your cocktail and nibbles.

❡/ EAT

L'Abri-Cotier – *pl. J-P Daviddi, Plage de l'Ayguade.* ℘*04 94 66 42 58. Closed Wed and Oct–Mar.* Set in a beach cabana, this cheerful eatery serves Mediterranean dishes. Try the flank steak with goat cheese and pesto.

Le Poisson Rouge – *Port du Niel, Giens Peninsula.* ℘*04 94 58 92 33. www. restaurantlepoissonrouge.com. Closed Mon, Mar Tue–Thu eve., early Oct.* This seafood restaurant is housed in an enchanting stone building. Shaded by olive trees, the terrace overlooks Port Niel.

La Colombe – *663 route de Toulon, 1.5mi/2.5km, in La Bayorre.* ℘*04 94 35 35 16. www.restaurantlacolombe.com Closed Sat lunch, Mon, Sun eve off-season; Jul–Aug Tue and Sat lunch and Mon.* Carefully prepared local cuisine is served in this traditional Provençal house. A spacious, sunny terrace and friendly service.

La Maison des Saveurs – *18 ave. Jean-Jaurès, Carqueiranne (town centre).* ℘*04 94 58 62 33. www.maisondessaveurs.fr. Closed Wed off-season; Jul–Aug Wed lunch.* This cosy, central restaurant decorated in Provençal tradition has a lovely terrace shaded by a plane tree as well as an affordable menu.

Les Jardins de Bacchus – *32 ave. Gambetta.* ℘*04 94 65 77 63. www. bacchushyeres.com. Closed Sun–Mon.* This eatery in the town centre serves regional wines and local meals in a renovated and modern-style dining area or on the summer terrace.

Joy – *24 rue de Limans.* ℘*04 94 20 84 98. Closed 2 weeks Nov and Jan; Sun eve–Mon off-season; Mar Wed lunch.* Limited lunch menu, fuller menu in the evening. A quiet location in a pedestrianised street, an elegant setting, and contemporary cuisine make this restaurant, run by a Dutch couple, a popular choice.

SHOPPING

Pastor – *86 ave. Gambetta.* ℘*04 94 01 46 46. Closed Mon.* One of the most popular bakeries in Hyères, with olive fougasses, lavender bread in summer and sorbet in amazing flavours.

Markets

Farmers' – Tue mornings on pl. de la République and Sat mornings along ave. Gambetta.

Organic – Tue, Thu and Sat mornings in pl. Vicomtesse de Noailles.

Antiques – Every first Sun of the month in pl. Clémenceau and pl. République.

SPORT AND LEISURE

Hyères has been awarded the *station nautique* label for its watersports facilities. Info from the tourist office or *www.france-nautisme.com*.

Diving – The area's many diving clubs include those in La Londe and Hyères; Porquerolles Plongée in Porquerolles; Sun Plongée in Port-Cros and Levant-Plongée in Le Levant.

Hyères-Port Saint-Pierre – ℘*04 94 12 54 40 (Hyères).* ℘*04 94 58 02 30 (La Capte, 125 moorings),* ℘*04 94 66 33 98 (l'Ayguade, 500 moorings). www.ville-hyeres.fr.* Marinas with 1,350 moorings, 120 of which are for temporary stays.

Casino – *Casino des Palmiers, ave. Ambroise-Thomas.* ℘*04 94 12 80 80. www.partouche-casino-hyeres.com. Daily 10am-4pm.* Some 170 slot machines, roulette, blackjack and nightclub.

CALENDAR

International Fashion and Photography Festival – Held at the end of May through Jun at Villa Noailles *(see p. 132).* Exhibitions of recognized and lesser-known photographers at several city locations.

Jazz under the Palms – Jazz concerts are held in July in pl. République and pl. Clémenceau and Parc Olbius Riquier.

Festival 'Hyères – A week of rock and other concerts is scheduled at the end of July and early August.

Design Parade – This event is held in July and August at the Villa Noailles. The festival attracts many well-known designers to Hyères. It hosts an international competition open to young designers and, during the festival, mounts an exhibition of the work of the designers selected.

Îles d'Hyères★★★

Var

These popular islands off Hyères harbour are just a short boat trip from the coast. Le Levant, Port-Cros and Porquerolles are also known as the **Îles d'Or** (Islands of Gold) because of the golden reflections cast by their mica shale rocks in certain lights. They offer many beautiful scenic walking trails, sandy beaches and verdant hills.

A BIT OF HISTORY
A Land of Asylum

The islands were a haven of peace and prosperity for its Greek and Roman settlers. However, from the Middle Ages the islands came under repeated attack by pirates until François I placed Port-Cros and Le Levant under the protection (and rule) of the Marquis des Îles d'Or, provided that he kept them under cultivation.

Despite exemption from taxes, the islands lacked manpower until a right of asylum was established, granting criminals immunity if they remained there. Jailbirds swarmed ashore, where they turned to piracy, even attempting the capture of one of the king's ships from Toulon. Only under Louis XIV did the last of these dubious characters leave the area.

⚙ **Michelin Map:** 340 M/N7/8; local maps p139 and p140.

🏢 **Info:** Bureau d'Information, Porquerolles. ℘04 94 58 33 76. www.porquerolles. com. Maison du Parc National de Port-Cros, exit village towards the lighthouse. ℘04 94 58 07 24. www.portcros parcnational.fr.

◗ **Location:** The three islands of the Îles d'Hyères are accessible by ferry boat. Île de Porquerolles, the largest, is close to the Giens peninsula. The best way to get around is by bike. Port-Cros, smaller and more mountainous, is a nature reserve; bicycles are not allowed. To the east is Le Levant, occupied primarily by a naval base and private nudist beaches. No matter which island you visit, be sure to take along plenty of drinking water.

👥 **Kids:** A bike ride on Île de Porquerolles and, for children who swim, a snorkelling trip to the underwater trail at Port-Cros. A glass-bottom boat makes trips from Giens to Porquerolles (⚙*see Addresses*).

Mexico-sur-Mer

For 60 years Porquerolles was the private property of a single family. In 1911, a Belgian engineer, F. Joseph Fournier, having made his fortune in Mexico, decided to give the island as a wedding gift to his young bride. Once settled on the island with his family and an army of gardeners, he attempted to re-create the atmosphere of a Latin American hacienda by importing exotic plants. He began with the cultivation of several exotic fruits, then unknown in France – pineapples and kumquats – before adding species such as the bellombra, with its massive roots. The 445 acres/180ha of vines originally planted have been reduced by half but continue to produce a reputable rosé. This was the first vineyard to gain the AOC Côtes de Provence *appellation*.

GETTING THERE

The islands are accessible from several ports, with many companies offering half- or full-day excursions or links. Be sure not to miss the last boat back to the mainland!

From La Tour Fondue (Giens Peninsula) – *TLV (Transports Littoral Varois), Port de La Tour Fondue.* ℘*04 94 58 21 81. www.tlv-tvm.com.* Regular daily service to Porquerolles. Circuits of Porquerolles and Port-Cros available weekdays Jul–Aug.

From Hyères – *TLV, Port Saint-Pierre.* ℘*04 94 57 44 07. www.tlv-tvm.com. 1 to 4 departures per day depending on the season.* Trips to Port-Cros (1hr), Le Levant (1.5hrs); circuit of Port-Cros and Le Levant available Jul–Aug.

From Le Lavandou, Cavalaire – *Vedettes des Îles d'Or.* ℘*04 94 71 01 02. www.vedettesilesdor.fr. Check website for schedule.* Departures for Port-Cros, Le Levant, Porquerolles, and St-Tropez.

A FEW GUIDELINES

Fire – During periods of major fire risk, the ALARME plan comes into force (announced before embarkation); it means that access is limited to the beaches, the coastal path and the villages. A recorded message is available by phone from 7pm the evening before: ℘*04 98 10 55 41.*

Rules – At Porquerolles and Port-Cros, it is forbidden to smoke, make fires, camp, pick the plants or flowers, leave the marked paths, litter or walk pets (outside the village); at Port-Cros it is forbidden to use bicycles, collect seashells, or fish.

Water – There are few or no places to find water on the island (but it can be purchased in the village shops), so bring plenty of your own and be sure to fill up before going on long hikes.

A British Coup

In 1793, after the capture of Toulon by French Revolutionaries (*see TOULON*), British and Spanish squadrons anchored off the Îles d'Hyères.

The commander of Fort Ste-Agathe at Porquerolles, forgotten on his island by the French authorities, had only the vaguest idea of what was happening on the mainland.

The British admiral invited him on board his flagship and the commander went unsuspectingly. While the whisky was circulating, British sailors landed, surprised the garrison and destroyed the fort (it was rebuilt in 1810). The ships then raised anchor taking with them, as their prisoner, the crestfallen commander.

Allied Landing

During World War II, on the night of 14 to 15 August 1944, American troops landed on the islands of Port-Cros and Levant. Their mission was to eradicate the German batteries threatening the Allied Landing.

ISLANDS TOURS

ÎLE DE PORQUEROLLES★★★

Porquerolles measures 4.3mi/7km long by 2mi/3km, and was called Protè (First) by the Greek settlers who came to live along its shores. The best way to explore the island is by bicycle *(hired in the village)*. The north coast has sandy beaches bordered by pine trees, heather and scented myrtle; the south coast is steep and rugged with one or two inlets that are easily accessible. There are few inhabitants inland, where you'll find vineyards, pine and eucalyptus woods and thick Mediterranean vegetation.

The Village

The small village of Porquerolles, which lies at the end of a minute port now used as a harbour for pleasure boats, has given its name to the whole island. The village was built by the military in the mid-19C. It consists of a main square, a humble church containing a Stations of the Cross carved by a soldier with his penknife, and a few fishermen's

ÎLE DE PORQUEROLLES

cottages, as well as more recently constructed hotels and private houses.

Fort Ste-Agathe

⏱ *Open May–Sept: call for hours.* ⊕ *4€.* ☎ *04 94 00 65 41.*

This fort occupies a strategic position on a mound overlooking the port. Its walls in the shape of a trapezium are surmounted by a massive corner tower, all that remains of the original structure built by François I in 1532. It was rebuilt in 1810 (after being burnt down by the English in 1793) to meet new military requirements.

The round tower is constructed on a massive scale, with walls 13ft /4m thick, 66ft/20m in diameter and 49ft/15m high; here the Parc de Port-Cros has exhibits on the history and maritime archaeology of the islands and Hyères harbour. The large circular room has a 20ft/6m high ceiling with a magnificent timber frame. From the terrace on top of the tower, with its five embrasures for large-bore cannon, a magnificent **view**★ of the beaches of Courtade and Notre Dame to the east, and the wooded massifs to the west unfolds.

▶ On exiting the village of Porquerolles, follow the route du Phare, then turn right at Les Oliviers crossroads to the Hameau Agricole.

Conservatoire Botanique National Méditerranéen

⏱ *Open Mar–mid-Oct daily 10am–12.30pm, 1.30pm–5pm.* ⊕ *No charge.* ☎ *04 94 12 30 32.*

Since 1985 most of the island has been managed by the National Park of Port-Cros, which owns the land. Created in 1979, the conservatoire was set up for botanical research and to preserve the Mediterranean basin's flora. The educational displays are informative.

Walks on Porquerolles
Lighthouse Walk★★

🚶 *1.5hr round trip.*

This walk to the lighthouse *(phare)* is a "must" even for tourists with only a few hours to spend on the island. The **lighthouse** (⊶ *closed to the public*) stands on the most southerly point of the island; its beam reaches 34mi /54km. A **panorama**★★ extends over most of the island.

Beach Walk★★

🚶 *2hr round trip.*

This pleasant walk along sandy paths, in the shade of pine trees, starts from Fort Ste-Agathe *(bear left)* and skirts the Plage de la Courtade. After Pointe du Lequin, the path dips towards the sea, revealing **Plage Notre-Dame**, a beautiful sandy beach bordered by pine

Plage Notre-Dame, Îles de Porquerolles

© Taylor Richard/Sime/Photononstop

trees. The **signal station** (sémaphore), Plage d'Argent, **Pointe du Grand Langoustier** and **Cap des Mèdes** all make worthwhile destinations.

ÎLE DE PORT-CROS★★★

Rising higher above the sea than its neighbours, Port-Cros is hillier, more rugged; its lush vegetation is unrivalled on the coast. The island measures 2.5mi/4km long by 1.5mi/2.5km wide and its highest point, Mont Vinaigre, reaches 679ft/194m. Port-Cros, together

with Île de Bagaud and neighbouring islets, has been designated a **Parc National,** covering 2.7sq mi/700ha on land and 7sq mi/1 800ha at sea.

A few fishermen's cottages, a huddle of shops and a small church adorn the bay area's village, which is commanded by Fort du Moulin (aka the "Château").

▶ The principal walks are signed at the quayside; variations are shown by a broken line in red on the map below.

🐾 Walks on Port-Cros
Plage de la Palud★
🚶 1.5hr round trip.

Climb up to the castle for a **view** of the neighbouring Île de Bagaud. A **botanical path** with Mediterranean specimens winds its way along La Palud Cove before reaching the beach. It passes by **Fort de l'Estissac** (⏰open Jun–Sept; ✆no charge; 📞04 94 01 40 72), which houses marine environment displays.

👥 Sentier sous-marin★
⏰Open mid-Jun–mid-Sept. Guided tours by park attendants (except in bad weather). ✆No charge. 📞04 94 01 40 70. A preliminary visit to the **Maison du Parc National**, which sells encapsulated aquaguides, is recommended. If you're diving alone, bring a mask, snorkel and flippers.

This underwater observation point, no deeper than 33ft/10m, is located between the little island of Rascas and La Palud beach, marked by yellow buoys. Here, anyone who can swim (diving is not necessary, but snorkelling is) can observe a great variety of typical Mediterranean species that live at this depth. Numbered buoys mark the best viewpoints.

▷ Return to the village, passing between the forts of L'Éminence and L'Estissac.

Vallon de la Solitude★
🚶 2hr round trip (marked path).

This is the ideal walk for visitors spending an entire day on the island. At the beginning of the valley stands the Manoir d'Hélène – a manor house converted into a hotel – named after the heroine in Melchior de Vogüé's novel Jean d'Agrève, which is set on Port-Cros. The path is in deep shade for almost all its length. Once within sight of Fort de la Vigie, start back along the cliff walk (Route des Crêtes), offering **views** of the sea.

▷ At Mont Vinaigre bear right into the Vallon de la Fausse Monnaie (Valley of False Currency).

Biodiversity on the Islands

Scientists and marine enthusiasts identified 410 groupers in 2002, along with numerous other species, including barracuda, leerfish, sargo bream and large sea bream. The harbour is carpeted with one of the most beautiful Posidonia seagrass beds in the region. This flowering plant is a home to over 70 species of fish. Protected land fauna includes the little-known Mediterranean puffin.

Port-Man★
6mi/10km. 🚶 4hr round trip (marked paths).

This pleasant excursion along a shaded and nearly level path affords a **view** of Île du Levant at the end of the Col de Port-Man, then winds its way to the **Baie de Port-Man**, a sheltered green bay.

▷ Return via Pointe de la Galère, Plateau de la Marma and Plage de la Palud.

ÎLE DU LEVANT
The island consists of a rocky spine 5mi/8km long but only 1,300yd/1,200m wide, skirted by vertical cliffs inaccessible except at two points: the Avis and Estable calanques. Disembark at the Aiguade landing and follow the path to Héliopolis. The Lérins monks used the island as their garden and granary. Today 90 percent of the island is occupied by the French navy (access is forbidden).

Héliopolis
In the western part of the island, the village of Héliopolis and the Grottes area (private property) are home to one of the oldest nudist camps in Europe, opened in 1931.

In season local clubs organise diving activities, and these are open to the general public.

ADDRESSES

🏠 STAY

🍽️🍽️🍽️ **Villa Sainte Anne** – *See EAT below.*

🍽️🍽️🍽️ **L'Auberge des Glycines** – *22 Pl. d'Armes, Porquerolles. ℘04 94 58 30 36. www.auberge-glycines.com. Closed 1 Jan. 11 rooms, half-board.* 🍴 *Restaurant* 🍽️🍽️🍽️. This adorable villa with lavender-blue shutters has rooms overlooking a shaded patio or the village square. The restaurant serves Provençal cooking.

🍽️🍽️🍽️🍽️ **Le Manoir** – *Port-Cros. ℘04 94 05 90 52. Closed early Oct–Apr. 22 rooms, half-board.* 🍴 *Restaurant* 🍽️🍽️🍽️🍽️. This charming 1830s hotel occupies an exceptional garden setting near the port. Rooms are comfortably furnished. Swimming pool.

🍽️🍽️🍽️🍽️ **Mas du Langoustier** – *West of the port, Porquerolles. ℘04 94 58 30 09. www.langoustier.com. Closed Oct–mid-Apr. 50 rooms, half-board.* 🍴. *Restaurant* 🍽️🍽️🍽️🍽️. At this chic hôtel-restaurant, the quality and service are worth the high price. Guest rooms are elegantly appointed and have a marble bathroom; some have private terrace. The **dining room** overlooks the sea and the Fort du Langoustier. The cuisine is gourmet Mediterranean and French.

🍽️ EAT

île de Porquerolles
Convenience Store – *pl. d'Armes. Closed afternoons off season.*

🍽️🍽️ **Villa Sainte Anne** – *pl. d'Armes. ℘04 98 04 63 00. www.sainteanne.com.* 🍴. *Closed Nov–25 Dec, Jan–Feb.* This restaurant near the church has a shady terrace and cuisine based around the catch of the day. Real Provençal

atmosphere and great people-watching. 25 rooms available 🍽️🍽️.

🍽️🍽️🍽️🍽️ **Mas du Langoustier** – *See STAY opposite column.*

ÎLE DE PORT-CROS
🍽️🍽️ **Sun Bistrot** – *At the port. ℘04 94 05 90 16. Closed Nov–Dec.* Brasserie and snack bar frequented by students from the diving school, selling pizzas, salads, fish and patés.

ÎLE DE LEVANT
Héliopolis – Apart from the floating snack boats at the port, this village is the only place to eat.

SPORT AND LEISURE

Diving – The great depths and the lack of strong currents around the islands and in the Baie de Carqueiranne provide ideal conditions for diving and underwater photography of the many shipwrecks. Diving clubs in Hyères and La Londe include: *Sun Plongée (℘04 94 05 90 16. www.sun-plongee.com)* in Port-Cros and *Porquerolles Plongée (℘04 98 04 62 22. www.porquerolles-plongee.com)* in Porquerolles.

👥 **Marabel Aquascope** – *Île de Port-Cros. ℘06 08 26 91 99.* 👁️*15€ (4–12 years, 10€). Closed Nov–Mar.* Guided tours *(30min)* in a boat specially designed to observe underwater life. Departures every 40min. Only 10 seats.

👥 **TLV** – *Port de la Tour-Fondue, Giens. ℘04 94 58 95 14. www.tlv-tvm.com. 6 departures per day –* 👁️*17€ (children 4–10 15.30€).* Glass-bottomed boat tours of the underwater flora and fauna *(35min)*.

Île de Levant – *www.iledulevant.com.fr.* The accessible areas of the island are in the west and north; in the north a channel is reserved for watersports and an area set aside for windsurfing. *🏖️The main beaches, reached by the coast path on each side of the landing-stages, are for naturists (nudist) only.*

LOCAL WINES

Domaine de la Courtade – *Porquerolles. ℘04 94 58 31 44. www.lacourtade.com. Closed Sat–Sun, 1 Jan, 25 Dec.* This reputable vineyard can be reached after a pleasant 15min walk. Call ahead if you would like to purchase wine.
Domaine Perzinsky – *Porquerolles. ℘04 94 58 34 32. Closed mid-Nov–Easter.* Created in 1989, this vineyard is the closest to the village. Tastings and tours available.

Half Board

The lodging prices on these islands are high, but the accommodation rate described as "half board" means that breakfast and one other meal (usually dinner) are included in the per diem rate. In some cases, taxes and service charges are also included.

Bormes-les-Mimosas★

Var

Bormes-les-Mimosas stands in an enchanting **setting**★ near the sea at the foot of the Forêt du Dom. Scented by colourful oleander, camomile, eucalyptus and mimosa, the winding, sloping streets of the old village lead down to a modern marina and beaches.

▶ **Population:** 7,051.
◉ **Michelin Map:** 340 N7.
▯ **Info:** Pl. Gambetta. ☎04 94 01 38 38. www.bormesles mimosas.com.
▷ **Location:** The beaches of this Var village stretch 10.5mi/17km from Le Lavandou to the bay of Brégançon: La Favière, Gaou Bay, Cabasson and Léoube. The Massif des Maures flanks the village.

 WALKING TOUR

HISTORIC STREETS★

The streets below the church have retained their traditional Provençal character. Many steep alleyways tumble down from the castle, the steepest known as "neck-breaker" *(Rompi-Cuo)*.

Place St-François

The terrace fronting the 16C **Chapelle St-François** affords a **view** of Bormes harbour and Cap Bénat. The round tower seen at the far end is an old windmill.

Église St-Trophyme

▷ *218 yd/200m from the Hôtel de Ville.*
The sundial on the façade of this 18C Romanesque-style church bears a Latin inscription: *Ab Hora Diei ad Horam Dei* (from the time of day to the time of God).

Château

Follow the *Parcours Fleuri*, a flower-lined walk round the partially restored castle (13–14C). The terrace provides a fine **view**★ over Bormes, the harbour, Cap Bénat and the islands of Port-Cros.

SIGHTS
Musée Arts et Histoire

65 rue Carnot. ⊙*Open Tue–Sun Jun–Sept 10am–noon, 3pm–6.30pm; Oct–May 10am–noon, 2pm–5.30pm.* ⊙*Closed Sun afternoon, Wed morning and 1 Jan, 1 May, 25 Dec.* ⊗*No charge.* ☎*04 94 71 56 60.*
This local history museum has exhibits about the village's past. It also features several regional paintings, including landscapes by **Jean-Charles Cazin** (1841–1901).

View of Bormes-les-Mimosas

© Gerth Roland/age fotostock

143

Latin American Ties

Two inhabitants of Bormes-les-Mimosas played an important part in the Wars of Independence in Latin America in the 19C: **Hippolyte Mourdeille** (1758–1807) lost his life chasing the Spaniards out of Montevideo; **Hippolyte Bouchard** (1780–1837) organised the Argentinian navy. Today Bormes honours their achievements by celebrating Argentina's National Independence Day (9 July).

EXCURSION
Cap de Brégançon

At the eastern end of Hyères harbour, the 16C **Fort de Brégançon** (☞ *closed to the public*) sits on a small island linked to Cap Bénat by a footbridge. Abandoned in the early 18C, then restored under the young General Bonaparte, in 1968 it became the summer retreat of French presidents.

The coast from Lavandou to Brégançon cove is lined with 11mi/17km of **beaches**. From Lavendou, take the wooden walkway to the marina and beach at **La Favière**, just beyond the Gouron headland. Continue on the **coastal trail**, then west to the beaches of Cap Bénat, Cabasson, Pellegrin and Estagnol (👝*charge for admission*).

ADDRESSES

👜 STAY

👝🍴 **Le Grand Hôtel** – *167 rte. du Baguier, exit north of Bormes, towards Collobrières.* 📞*04 94 71 23 72. www.augrandhotel.com. Closed Nov–Jan.* ♿ 🅿 *42 rooms.* 🍽*7.50€. Restaurant* 👝. For a whiff of Victoriana, check in at this hillside grand hotel built in 1903. Rooms vary in size; most have a balcony overlooking the sea.

👝👝🍴🍴 **Hôtel Les Palmiers** – *chemin du Petit-Fort, 5mi/8km south of Bormes.* 📞*04 94 64 81 94. www.hotel-palmiers.com. Closed 10 Nov–1 Feb.* 🅿 *17 rooms, half-board only in summer.* 🍽*14€. Restaurant* 👝🍴. Lying in a residential district halfway between the beach and

Brégançon Fort, this hotel is a haven of peace. Most of the rooms have large balconies. The dining room opens out onto a flowered terrace.

🍴/EAT

👝🍴 **L'Imprévu** – *Ave. de la Grande-Bastide, Le Lavandou.* 📞*04 94 15 27 18. Closed Oct.* As it's hard to find a restaurant at affordable prices around here, this fairly inexpensive pizzeria is a good choice. Seating is available on the large terrace, very pleasant on a summer's evening, and so, naturally, it's much in demand by locals and holidaymakers.

👝🍴 **Pâtes et Pâtes** – *1 rue Toesca.* 📞*04 94 64 85 75. Closed lunch Jul–Aug, Oct–Jan, and rest of the year Wed eve and Thu.* One of the best value places to eat in Bormes, with some great Italian specialities, and plenty of pasta, of course. Small, shady terrace.

👝💰💰 **Lou Portaou** – *rue Cubert-des-Poètes.* 📞*04 94 64 86 37. www.louportaou.fr. Closed mid-Nov–mid Dec. See website for days open.* This former 12C lookout-post has plenty of charm and character. A medieval style and personalized decor adorn two small vaulted dining rooms. Traditional dishes revisited.

SHOPPING

Markets – Wednesday mornings in the old village, Saturdays at La Favière (in summer) and on Tuesday mornings at Pin-de-Bormes, plus "Sauto Coupo" last weekend in Sept in Pin-de-Bormes.

TOURS

Guided Tour – *Apr–Sept.* 👝*Tickets 5€.* A 90min walking tour of the old town's architecture *(Thu 5pm)* and flora *(Tue 5pm)*. Sign up at the tourist office.

Brochures – Pick up a map of the old village at the tourist office, along with brochures of walking and car tours.

CALENDAR

Mimosalia – *Last weekend in January.* Open market for show plants.

Corso – *End of February.* Bormes celebrates Mardi Gras with a Corso parade with floats through the village.

Foire aux Santons – *First weekend in December.* Display and sale of the Provençal figurines called *santons.*

Le Lavandou★

Var

This genteel resort sheltered by the Cap Bénat was once the biggest fishing port in the Var. Its marina and beaches are now very popular with families.

THE TOWN

The main square, **place Ernest-Reyer**, has **views** of the islands of Le Levant and Port-Cros. **Boulevard de-Lattre-de-Tassigny** is a pleasant promenade along the beach, offering **views** of the port and the coast eastwards to Cap Lardier. There are lively **markets** on place du Marché and avenue du Président-Vincent-Auriol on Thursdays and in Cavalière on Mondays *(Jun to Sept)*.

The Village

Park in the village (parking discs on sale at town hall or tourist office).
Arrive early to admire the *pescadous* returning to port with their daily trawl of sea bass and John Dory. Next, explore the covered market close to the quayside before strolling through this typical Provençal village.

Thirteen Fountains Walk

Map available from the tourist office.
This walk explores the historic fountains of Le Lavandou, including the **Fontaine des Trois-Dauphins,** which bears the town's arms (three dolphins and a lion), a **drinking fountain** near the boules court on quai Gabriel Péri, the **public laundry fountains** on place de Mado and place du Lou-Lavandou, and the historic tiled St-Louis **wall fountain**.

Gardens

There are three small gardens in the town centre: the **Jardin du Cadran** on rue des Pierres-Précieuses with its giant palm tree and lavender plants, the aromatic **Jardin du Grand Bleu** which boasts a huge jacaranda from the American tropics and honeysuckle from China, and the more secluded **Grand Jardin**, avenue de la Grande-Bastide, which blooms with bright yellow mimosa in late winter.

▶ **Population:** 5,780.
Michelin Map: 340 N7.
Info: Quai Gabriel-Péri. ℘04 94 00 40 50. Cavalière: La Rotonde, ave. du Golf. ℘04 94 05 80 50. www.ot-lelavandou.fr.
Location: Le Lavandou sits on the Corniche des Maures (*see Massif des MAURES*), southeast of Bormes-les-Mimosas. The centre of town overlooks the port, while most hotels are situated near the beaches to the southwest.

Artists' Walk

1.5mi/2.5km, 1hr walk or 90min guided tour. Contact the tourist office.
This walk follows in the footsteps of Neo-Impressionist painters and writers **Henri-Edmond Cross**, **Théo van**

The Song of Summer

The image of the Mediterranean is invariably associated with the song of the cicada, together with the game of boules *(pétanque)* and a siesta under the pine trees.
The song of the cicada is stimulated by a combination of particular conditions – the temperature must be at least 77ºF/25°C in the shade, and there should not be too much noise. A tiny change – such as a cloud passing in front of the sun or the wind rustling in the trees – is enough to upset the insect. Only the male cicada sings, since the noise is a mating call to females. The dawn serenade is produced when the insect contracts two rigid plates – cymbals – on its abdomen, which vibrate at 500 times a second. The sound is amplified by a ventral cavity full of air that acts as a resonance chamber. When the female has located the sound using ears on her abdomen, she joins her suitor in the tree.

Rysselberghe and **Paul Signac**, who lived in St-Clair between 1892 and 1926. Panels depicting works by the artists are featured along the route.

BEACHES

All beaches are sand. Supervised by lifeguards, they are equipped with warning flags and information panels. Standards of comfort, hygiene and sporting facilities vary from beach to beach. More adventurous types will head to St-Clair for windsurfing and La Fossette for canoeing. Naked sunbathing is permitted on Plage du Rossignol and the beach in Le Layet is a naturist beach.

BOAT TRIPS
Îles d'Hyères★★★
Allow one day. (For maps and description see ÎLES d'HYÈRES).

ADDRESSES

🛏 STAY

🛌 **Hôtel Les Alcyons** – *ave. des Trois Dauphins in Aiguebelle, 3mi/ 4.5km east of Le Lavandou.* ☎04 94 05 84 18. *www.hotellesalcyons.com . Closed mid-Oct-Apr. 24 rooms.* 🅿 ⊒7€. At the foot of the Maures Massif, barely 20min from the beach, this friendly hotel is perfect for swimming and hiking. Each room has a balcony and air-conditioning.

🛌🛌 **Roc Hôtel** – *rue des Dryades in St-Clair, 1mi/2km east of Le Lavandou.* ☎04 94 01 33 66. *www.roc-hotel.com. Closed mid-Oct-Mar. 29 rooms.* 🅿 ⊒10€. This beachfront hotel is housed in a modern ochre-coloured building. Most rooms have sea views.

🍴 EAT

🍽 **Chez Zète** – *41 ave. du Général-de-Gaulle.* ☎04 94 71 09 11. *Closed Dec, Mon, and Sun evening (except Jul–Aug).* In Le Lavandou's main shopping street, this family business draws large crowds year round with succulent Provençal cooking and a shaded terrace.

🍽🍽 **Hélios Plage** – *In Aiguebelle, ave. du Général-Bouvet, then take the footbridge.* ☎04 94 71 49 79. *Closed mid-Nov–Mar*

and eves except Tue Jul–Aug. 🍽. If you want to lounge around on the sand and enjoy views of Le Levant Island, try this charming cabin with white and blue woodwork, and choose among a salad, the chef's special or a tasty dish of pasta.

SHOPPING

Domaine de l'Anglade – *ave. Vincent-Auriol.* ☎04 94 71 10 89. *www.domaine delanglade.fr. Call for hours or check website.* This attractive and central vineyard produces red, white and rosé wine, wine for apéritifs and vinegar. Tasting sessions and shop.

Markets – Thursday morning *(all year)* on ave. Prés-Vincent-Auriol and Monday morning *(Jun–Sept)* in Cavalière. Flea market: all day Sundays *(all year)* in Cavalière.

OUTDOOR THEATRE

Grassy Amphitheatre – *Cinéma Plein Air, Ave. du Grand-Jardin.* ☎04 94 00 41 71. *Open Jul–Aug. Call for the programme of events.* This outdoor theatre puts on summer plays and concerts.

SPORT AND LEISURE

École de Voile de Cavalière – *ave. du Cap-Nègre.* ☎04 94 05 86 78. *www. ecolevoilelavandou.com. Open Apr–Oct daily 9am–6pm.* This club gives sailing lessons and rents various sailing boats (catamaran, dinghy, Optimist) and windsurfing boards.

👥 **Seascope** – *Gare Maritime.* ☎04 94 71 01 02. *www.vedettesilesdor.fr.* ⊜13€ *(children 4-12 years 9.50€).* The Seascope's transparent hull affords wonderful views of the sea depths, marine flora and many Mediterranean fish species.

CIP du Lavandou – *Le Lavandou Port, Quai des Îles-d'Or.* ☎04 94 71 54 57. *www.cip-lavandou.fr.* Local diving club with a friendly atmosphere.

Lavandou Scuba Diving School – *New Port, underneath the restaurant Le Barracuda.* ☎04 94 71 83 65. *www.lavandou-plongee.com.* Lessons for beginners and experienced divers and various other services (equipment hire, shipwreck tours, exploring sites around Port-Cros, etc.). *Call to reserve.*

Massif des Maures★★

Var

The emerald forests of the Massif des Maures stretch along the coastline from Hyères to St-Raphaël and up into the Gapeau and Argens river valleys. A drive along the **Corniche des Maures** reveals glimpses of the cobalt blue sea against rocky inlets, contrasting with the wilder landscape of the inland hills.

A BIT OF HISTORY

Les Maures, from the Provençal "Leï Mauro", meaning "black mountain" (a reference to its dark rocks and dense forests), is the most heavily wooded area in the Var, with 371,000 acres/150,000ha of forest. Its schist rock provides ideal growing conditions for cork oaks, which supplied the region with its main source of revenue from the 17C to 19C. The vogue for sea-bathing brought this magnificent coast back to life in the 20C and provided it with a new source of income. On 15 August 1944 the Allied armies landed on the Maures beaches before liberating the south of France.

🚗 DRIVING TOUR

CORNICHES DES MAURES★★
From Le Lavandou to St-Tropez on D 559.

Le Lavandou★
🚶*see Le LAVANDOU.*

St-Clair
This small resort lies a short distance from the main road and has a large, beautiful beach.

Aiguebelle
This peaceful seaside resort is nestled in a small pine-fringed cove.

Cavalière
Cavalière has a fine **view** over Cap Nègre, a beach sheltered from the *mistral,* and excellent watersports facilities.

- 🚽 **Michelin Map:** 340 M/P5/7 or 528 folds 47 to 49.
- 🚹 **Info:** Several tourist offices cover this region: contact Var Tourisme to locate the nearest one. ℘04 94 18 59 60. www.visitvar.fr.
- ▷ **Location:** The Maures is made up of four parallel chains of geographical relief, two along the coast (including the Îles d'Hyères) and two inland (La Verne and La Sauvette), separated by the River Grimaud and the River Collobrières.
- 👥 **Kids:** Exotic birds in Jardin Zoologique Tropical.
- 👁 **Don't Miss:** Guided nature hikes through the Massif.
- 🕐 **Timing:** Set aside 1–2hr for a guided nature hike. Allow one day for a drive along the Maures corniche. Other tours require half a day or longer.

Pramousquier
This modest resort offers a sheltered beach of fine sand and attractive villas. The road leaves the shore to wind through pines and gardens.

Canadel-sur-Mer
Lying at the base of the last foothills of the Pradels range and flanked by superb pine woods, Canadel has one of the most sheltered beaches on the Maures coast. The **Allied Landings** in Provence were launched here at midnight on 14 August 1944.

Cavalaire-sur-Mer
This perfect holiday destination has a sand beach, scuba diving and a marina with 1,200 moorings. Just beyond are the beaches of Le Rayol (🚶*see Domaine du RAYOL*).

GENERAL ADVICE ABOUT VISITING THE MASSIF

Cars – Roads belonging to the DFCI (Défense Forestière Contre l'Incendie – forest fire-fighters) are closed to public traffic. They count as private roads; an open barrier does not indicate that access is permitted. Parking in front of these barriers is prohibited, and cars should be parked well to the side of narrow roads to allow the passage of emergency vehicles. Pedestrian access is always possible.

Fire Risk – Fires are prohibited at all times, and smoking is not permitted Mar–Oct. During periods of high fire risk, the ALARME plan is put into action and certain public roads (classed as major fire risks) may be closed to vehicles. Offenders are liable for heavy fines.

Walkers are strongly advised to avoid such areas for reasons of safety. To check for closures, call ℰ04 98 10 55 41.

Camping – Camping is prohibited in the massif and within 656ft/200m of any of the forests.

Animals – Do not disturb wild animals. Pets must be kept on a leash.

Plants and chestnuts – Do not stray from marked paths or pick plants or fruit, in particular chestnuts, as you may be requested to pay a fine.

Litter – Use the rubbish bins provided or take any rubbish with you.

La Croix-Valmer

Surrounded by 741 acres/300ha of protected countryside, this village boasts 4mi/6km of beaches; it has been a winter retreat and spa since the early 1900s. Today it is known for its reputable Côtes de Provence wines. According to legend, Constantine saw a cross in the sky here with the words, *In hoc signo vinces* ("in this sign you will conquer"), a prediction of his forthcoming victory and succession as Roman Emperor. A stone cross erected on the pass commemorates the story and gives the village its name.

ST-TROPEZ TO FRÉJUS★★

On the opposite side of the peninsula, the Massif des Maures slopes gently towards the sea. On the sunny coast along the D 559, the seaside resorts of St-Tropez, Fréjus and others have fine beaches (⛺see Driving Tour ③).

Beauvallon

Well shaded by pine trees and cork oaks, the village of Beauvallon lies on the north shore of St-Tropez Bay, between Port Grimaud and Ste-Maxime.

View from Col du Canadel

© F. Guiziou/hemis.fr

Ste-Maxime★
see STE-MAXIME.
Circling the Cap Sardinaux, the rugged coastline between **La Nartelle** and **St-Aygulf** is broken up by rocky inlets *(calanques)* with small beaches.

Les Issambres
Along with Val d'Esquières, San Peïre and Les Calanques, this pretty resort is part of an extensive tourist development. Popular with bathers for its 5mi/8km of sand beaches and creeks, it boasts a small port offering local boat trips.

St-Aygulf
Shaded by woods of pine, eucalyptus, holm oak and cork oak, this resort has one of the biggest fine sand beaches on the Riviera, with **views** over Les Issambres and Fréjus Bay. The dunes are currently being restored: walkers are asked to tread carefully. Follow the chemin des Douaniers to access four **calanques** (rocky inlets). St-Aygulf also has a small sheltered marina.

⌖ DRIVING TOURS

① MAURES COUNTRY
44mi /70km leaving from Hyères.
Allow 1 day. See map pp128–129.

▷ Leave Hyères northeast on N 98.

After crossing the Gapeau, the road hugs the salt marshes as it passes through the Hyères plain, affording good **views** of Cap Bénat and Port-Cros.

♣♦ Jardin Zoologique Tropical
583 rte. de St-Honoré, La Londe-las-Maures. Open Jun–Sept daily 9.30am –7pm; Oct and Feb–May daily 2pm–6pm; Nov–Jan Wed, Sat, Sun, public holidays 2pm–5pm. 9€ (child 4.50€). 04 94 35 02 15. www.zootropical.com.
Filled with palms and exotic plants from Australia, Mexico and Asia, this nature park in La Londe is home to tropical birds of all sizes and colours from every continent, many of them in danger of extinction.

▷ D 98 to La Môle, then D 27 towards Le Rayol and right into Col Canadel.

Col du Canadel★★
Alt 876ft/267m.
From here a **view★★** of Canadel, Pramousquier beach, Cap Nègre, the Bormes harbour and Cap Bénat is obtained.
⊠ *Park your car on the col and follow the forest track on the right to the Col de Caguo-Ven.*
This is a picturesque route providing magnificent **views★** of the Maures Massif and to the south, the coast and the Îles d'Hyères. Vieux-Sauvaire is reached after one hour's walk *(restaurant open in season)*, after which the path goes back down to Col de Barral (1,220ft/372m). If you're feeling fit, walk another two hours to reach Col de Caguo-Ven.

▷ Continue along D 27 then turn left onto N 98, towards La Môle, then straight to Dom Forest.

Forêt Domaniale du Dom★
This state forest, composed mainly of pines, cork oaks and chestnuts, covers the Les Pradels and La Verne ranges. Novelist Jean Aicard (1848–1921) set his work *Maurin des Maures* in this area.

Arboretum de Gratteloup
⊡ *Car park beside the D 98, by the Maison Forestière.* Open daily. No charge. 04 97 71 06 07.
This arboretum (7.4 acres/3ha), created in 1935, contains mostly Mediterranean species (cypress, pines, juniper, yoke elms and hop hornbeams) and an area specifically devoted to chestnut trees.

▷ At Col de Gratteloup, take D 41 and head for Bormes-les-Mimosas.

Col de Caguo-Ven
Alt 778ft/239m.
From the pass, there is a **view** of the Hyères and Bormes ports and the Île de Porquerolles.
⊠ *At the peak, take the forest trail towards Col de Barral and Col du Canadel.*

Guided Nature Hikes

The 10 communes of the Massif des Maures organise hikes of 1–2.5hr with different themes (flora and fauna, forest life, cultural heritage, evening walks, etc.). The calendar of walks is available from the Comité Départemental du Tourisme du Var *(www.visitvar.fr)*. Get information and register at the following tourist offices: Bormes-les-Mimosas ℘04 94 01 38 38; Hyères ℘04 94 01 84 50; La Londe-les-Maures ℘04 94 01 53 10; Le Muy ℘04 94 45 12 79; Le Pradet ℘04 94 21 71 69; Pierrefeu-du-Var ℘04 94 28 27 30; Ramatuelle ℘04 98 12 64 00; Roquebrune-sur-Argens ℘04 94 19 89 89.

After 45 minutes, you will arrive at the giant boulders of **Pierre d'Avenon** *(alt 1,450ft/443m)*, where the circular **view**★ encompasses the whole Maures coastline from Cap Lardier to Hyères, the port of Le Lavandou and Bormes.

▶ Return to Hyères via Le Pin then D 559.

② PASS ROAD★★
67mi/109km leaving from Le Lavandou. Allow one day. 🕐See map pp128–129.

This beautiful, circular tour along very hilly, but quiet roads, goes over at least seven passes *(cols)* and penetrates deep into the heart of the massif.

▶ From Le Lavandou take D 559 west to Le Pin and turn right onto D 41.

The road winds uphill, with a fine **view** ahead of Bormes and its castle.

Bormes-les-Mimosas★
🕐*see BORMES-LES-MIMOSAS.*

▶ Continue on D 41 to Col de Caguo-Ven. Continue downhill to Col de Gratteloup *(alt 656ft/199m)*.

The road passes over wooded slopes of cork oak and chestnut, cuts through deep valleys *(east)* and offers glimpses of the sea and the mountains around Toulon *(west)*.

▶ Continue along D 41.

Col de Babaou★
Alt 1,362ft/414m.

This pass offers a stunning **view**★ of the Hyères salt marshes, the Giens peninsula and the Îles d'Hyères. Beyond it rise the tallest of the Maures summits, wooded by magnificent chestnuts and cork oaks.

▶ Turn right onto D 14.

Collobrières
The picturesque houses of this shaded town overlook the river swirling beneath an old humpback bridge. The local specialities are *marrons glacés* (candied chestnuts) and other delicacies made with chestnuts.

▶ Continue east on D 14. After 3.7mi/6km turn right at La Croix d'Anselme.

After 2mi/4km a narrow road leads to the ruins of the former Carthusian monastery of La Verne lying in a majestic forest setting.

Monastère de la Verne★★
🕐*Open Wed–Mon Sept–Dec, Feb–May 11am–5pm; Jun, Jul, Aug until 6pm.*
🕐*Closed Jan and religious holidays.*
☞6€. ℘04 94 48 08 00.
The monastery was founded in 1170 on an isolated wooded slope in the Maures. Rebuilt several times, it survived until it was abandoned by the monks during the Revolution. Since 1983 it has been occupied by the Order of Bethlehem. The central **porch** is built from blue-green serpentine stone. Two annulated columns flank the doorway, surmounted by a triangular pediment resting on two pilasters.

Enter through the **gatehouse** (*to the left of the building*), now a display area for products made by the monks, before exploring the buildings where **guests** were once received. A window at the end of the barn, where the grain was stored, overlooks the monks' cells and the Romanesque church. A staircase leads down to the bakery and a vast oven, where bread was baked for 45 people. Take the spiral staircase to the **chapelle d'adoration**, the ramparts, and the remains of the small **17C cloister** before entering the restored Romanesque church. From the window of the side chapel, admire the **great cloisters** complete with 100yds/90m of galleries covered by surbased groin vaulting. On the ground floor, don't miss the **oil mill** and **vaulted storeroom**.

▷ Return to D 14 and proceed east.

After **Col de Taillude** the road looks across La Verne Valley to the ruins of the charter house crowning the opposite slope and then, after passing high above the hamlet of Capelude, makes its way into the upper valley of the Le Périer stream. From the centre of the valley, there is a **view** of the Grimaud Plain and St-Tropez Bay.

The road turns sharply into the **Valley of the Giscle** (or the Grimaud rivulet) from which Grimaud can be spotted in the distance.

Grimaud★
see GRIMAUD.

▷ From Grimaud take D 558 south, crossing the Grimaud Plain.

Cogolin
see COGOLIN.

▷ N 98 follows the Môle Valley upstream. 5.1mi/8km from Cogolin, just before La Môle, the winding D 27 strays from the valley to cut across the coastal range. Go back to Le Lavandou by the coast road.

③ FROM ST-TROPEZ TO ST-AYGULF
20mi/30km. Allow half a day not including tours of St-Tropez and St-Raphaël. See map pp128–129.

St-Tropez ★★
see ST-TROPEZ.

▷ Leave St-Tropez to the southwest on D 98A. After 4km/2.5mi turn right.

Port-Grimaud ★
see GRIMAUD.

▷ Return to D 559, which skirts the north shore of the bay overlooking St-Tropez. Follow D 559 to St-Aygulf.

St-Aygulf
see p149.

Beyond St-Aygulf the **view** sweeps over the lower Argens Plain. The splendid rocks of the Montagnes de Roquebrune stand out from the Maures Massif. Turning towards the Esterel range, you can see the Dramont Signal with the peak of Cap Roux looming in the background.

④ SUMMITS ROUTE★
74.5mi/120km. Allow one day. See map pp128–129.

Round trip starting from St-Tropez
This excursion passes through wooded countryside to the lower slopes of the twin peaks of Notre-Dame-des-Anges and La Sauvette.

▷ Leave St-Tropez to the southwest on D 98A along the bay of St-Tropez. At La Foux turn left onto D 98 to Cogolin.

Cogolin
see COGOLI.

▷ Stay on N 98 towards Môle Valley.

Shortly before the village of **La Môle** stands a château (*right*) with two pepperpot turrets. **Antoine de Saint-Exupéry** (1900–44), aviator and writer, lived here as a child (👆see Massif de l'Esterel). Vineyards give way to the forest-covered slopes of **Dom Forest★**.

▶ Continue along D 98. At Col de Gratteloup turn right onto D 41, up to Collobrières, then after La Rivière turn right onto D 14. After 2mi/3km to the east of Collobrières, turn left onto D 39.

The road winds through wooded countryside overlooking a steep-sided stream and affords the occasional glimpse of La Sauvette peak to the right. Shortly before **Col des Fourches**, the road to the left leads to the Notre-Dame-des-Anges Hermitage, pinpointed by the television relay mast.

Notre-Dame-des-Anges
Restored in the 19C, the priory near the summit (2,559ft/780m) stands in an attractive setting amid schist rocks and chestnut trees.
Beyond the screen of trees surrounding the chapel, there is a remarkable **view★** (north) of the Argens depression backed by the Alps, (west) Ste-Baume, (south) over the Maures to the sea,

the Iles d'Hyères, the Giens Peninsula and Toulon.

▶ Return to Col des Fourches and turn left towards Gonfaron.

The road passes by **La Sauvette** (2,556ft/779m), the highest point in the Massif des Maures, before descending to Le Luc Plain.

Gonfaron
Set within the Massif des Maures, this village is still an active centre for cork production. At the north edge rises an isolated hill, crowned by a chapel dedicated to St Quinis.

👥 Village des Tortues de Gonfaron
In Gonfaron turn right onto D 75 for 1mi/2km. The best times to visit are 11am or 4pm. ♿ⓒOpen Mar–Oct 9am–7pm; Nov–Feb 9am–6pm. ☞8€, children 6€ (Dec–Feb 5€, children 3€) ✆04 94 78 26 41. www.villagetortues.com.
The village is a breeding centre for the Hermann tortoise species (Testudo hermanni hermanni), a million-year-old herbivorous species threatened

Hermann Tortoise, Gonfaron

© softattitude/Fotolia.com

Hermann's Tortoise

This tortoise, the only species native to France, appeared in Mediterranean Europe about one million years ago. It lives in the scrub (maquis), which provides its food – oak leaves, fruit and molluscs. After hibernating in a tree stump until about June, the female lays her eggs in a nest which she immediately abandons. If they survive the first two months of life, as well as predatory badgers, the baby tortoises can look forward to a life of 60 to 100 years.

Falling victim to man-made alterations in its habitat and unregulated collecting, the tortoises now survive only in Corsica and in the Massif des Maures, where a tortoise village has been established to protect the species.

Cork Oak

The cork oak is an evergreen that requires heat and humidity. It grows near the sea up to a height of 1,640ft /500m and has proved particularly resistent to fire. It is easy to spot on account of its large blackish acorns and scored bark.

Bark is gathered *(démasclage)* for the first time when the tree is 25 years old and is known as the male bark. Subsequent harvests, which take place in July and August when the sap is rising, occur every nine or 10 years, which is the time it takes for a new layer of cork to form, known as the female bark. Female bark is highly prized by industry (manufacture of corkboard at Le Muy) and craftsmen (boards, ornamental objects and materials for ceramicists).

By the mid-1960s the Maures area was producing 5,000t of cork yearly, supplying 100 or so local firms. In 1994 the foresters of the Var department produced 500t of cork. Nowadays, the cork is mostly exported to Sardinia.

S. Sauvignier/MICHELIN

with extinction. This tortoise can live up to 100 years. Mating takes place in April, May and September, egg-laying in mid-May and hatching in early September.

The village is also home to France's freshwater turtle and the common or European tortoise *(Testudo graeca)*. Don't miss the hot house and museum.

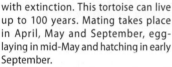 Continue east on D 75 then onto D 558 towards La Garde-Freinet.

La Garde-Freinet

www.lagardefreinet-tourisme.com.
Strategically placed between the Argens Valley and St-Tropez Bay, the quiet village of La Garde-Freinet is a flourishing crafts centre surrounded by scenic cork oak and chestnut forests.

Owing to its strategic location, La Garde-Freinet suffered more than a century of occupation by the Saracens. In local tradition the name Saracen is applied collectively to the Moors, Arabs, Turks and Berbers, who harassed the country from the 8C to the 18C. After being defeated by Charles Martel at Poitiers in 732, the Arabs drifted down into Provence. Although driven back several times, they managed to hold on to the region around La Garde-Freinet. On the height that dominates the pre-

sent village they built a fortress from which they pillaged inland Provence. In 973 Count William, the Liberator, managed to expel them.

In contrast to the damage they caused, the Saracens taught the Provençal people how to use the bark of the cork oak and how to extract resin from pine trees. They also introduced flat house tile and the tambourine.

La Garde-Freinet makes a perfect base for a day of hiking, biking or horseback riding. The tourist office has marked out a route through the steep, winding streets of this perched village *(1hr)* with arrows and an accompanying map. *Suitable footwear is a must.*

A Provençal market is held on place Neuve *(Sun and Wed mornings).*

Ruins of Fort Freinet

1hr round trip. 0.6mi /1km.
Take the road south towards Grimaud. Just before leaving the village after the boules court, turn right up a steep road towards La Croix. Park on the side of the road and follow the arrow painted on a rock: this path is not suitable for the elderly or children. Map available from the tourist office.

There is a good **view** of Le Luc Plain and the first Alpine foothills. A path leads to a mission cross (Croix des Maures), then climbs steeply to the ruins of a fortress and the foundations of a fortified village (12C–16C) with a chapel, cistern, oven and seigniorial lodgings.

▶ Return to your car and follow the forest track on foot for 3mi/5km until you reach the sign for Roches Blanches.

Panorama des Roches Blanches★
Alt. 2,093ft/638m. At this spot *(for access, walk round the barrier)*, a view extends of *(left)* La Garde-Freinet Forest and the River Argens valley *(right)* across to the north Maures and *(straight ahead)* St-Tropez Bay.

▶ Take D 558 south.

The road passes cork oak and chestnut-covered slopes with glimpses of the bay and peninsula of St-Tropez.

Grimaud★
see GRIMAUD.

▶ Return to St-Tropez by D 14, D 98 and D 98A at La Foux.

ADDRESSES

⌂ STAY

Chambre d'Hôte Le Mas des Oliviers – *chemin les Ferrières, Puget-Ville, 2.5km/1.5mi by N 97 Route de Cuers.* ℘04 94 48 30 89. www.chambre-d-hote-le-mas-des-oliviers.com. 3 rooms. ⌑ P ⊐ Meal ◷◷◷. This charming Provençal *mas* seems lost among vineyards and olive groves. Large, carefully kept and air-conditioned rooms are decorated in Mediterranean style. Sauna, fitness room, pool. Horse riding and cycling nearby.

Chambre d'hôte Cante Cigalo – *Rond-point de Sylvabelle, Rte. de Gigaro, La Croix Valmer.* ℘06 80 21 05 85. www.cantecigalo.com. Closed Aug and 20 Oct–Easter. 5 rooms. P ⊐. The rooms open off a long outdoor gallery, which also serves as a terrace. Decor combines comfort and good taste; the Moroccan tiles in the bathrooms and objects from far-off lands add a little exotic touch. Pleasant wooded grounds and a swimming pool.

⊰/ EAT

Restaurant des Maures – *19 blvd. Lazare-Carnot, Collobrières.* ℘04 94 48 07 10. www.hoteldesmaures.fr. This village inn enjoys a well-deserved reputation among its regular clientele on account of its excellent value for money and warm welcome. In summer meals are served on the terrace beneath the plane trees. 10 guest rooms (◷⊐5€).

Les Alizés – *Promenade de la Mer, Cavalaire-sur-Mer.* ℘04 94 64 09 32. www.alizescavalaire.com. A lively atmosphere and the undeniable charisma of the owners are the main assets of this modern hotel and restaurant offering sea views. Family cooking with an emphasis on fish and homemade desserts. 18 guest rooms (◷◷◷◷⊐).

Chante-Mer – *43 Pl. Ottaviani, Les Issambres.* ℘04 94 96 93 23. www.chantemer.com. Closed Mon and Tue afternoon. Far from the tourist bustle, this friendly establishment offers a traditional menu. The dining room features white tablecloths and walls and chairs of light-coloured wood. In summer, the covered terrace out front is pleasant.

SHOPPING

Confiserie Azuréenne – *Blvd. Koenig, Collobrières.* ℘04 94 48 07 20. www.confiserieazureenne.com. This confectioner's shop is entirely devoted to chestnuts. It makes and sells *marrons glacés*, chestnut jam, sweet chestnut purée, etc. Visitors can also be shown around the factory museum.

MARKET
Marché in La Croix Valmer *(Sunday morning)*.

SPORT AND LEISURE
Smash Club – *ave. du Golf, Cavalière.* ℘04 95 05 84 31. Daily Jul–Aug 8am–2am; Apr–Jun and Sept–Oct 9am–9pm; Nov–Mar 2.30pm–7pm. This sports centre has six tennis courts, golf practice range, a weight room and archery gallery. Tennis tournaments and badminton, beach-volley, football and boules competitions are organised during the summer season. The latest feature is an "Indiana River" course.

Domaine du Rayol★★

Var

Le Rayol is in one of the most beautiful spots on the Var coastline. Forming an amphitheatre of wooded slopes carpeted with cork oaks, mimosas and pines, it started life as an exclusive seaside resort in the early 20C, when European industrialist and bankers built holiday seaside resorts amid the lush virgin landscape. The beach at Rayol-Canadel-sur-Mer *(2km/1mi west via D 599)*, a sheltered cove bordered by pines, is one of the most breathtaking in the region.

SIGHTS
The Domaine★★

Ave. des Belges. ○*Open Jul–Aug daily 9.30am–7.30pm; rest of the year daily 9.30am–6.30pm.* ☞*10€.* ℘*04 98 01 44 00. www.domainedurayol.org.*

These "Gardens of the Mediterranean" cover 49.5acres/20ha of protected land. The first exotic gardens on the site were commissioned by a Parisian banker named Courmes, who had a house built on the estate in 1910. After the stock market crash of 1929, the estate fell into disrepair, and it wasn't until the aeronautics engineer Henri Potez, who took refuge on the coast in 1940, renovated the property, that the garden returned to its former glory. He had a belvedere built with a circular pergola, linked to the coast by a magnificent flight of steps.

After several more decades of neglect, in 1989 the Conservatoire du Littoral acquired the entire estate to preserve some of the last wild shores of the Corniche des Maures. The landscape gardener Gilles Clément was then brought in to create a patchwork of gardens planted with rare and exceptional species found growing in Mediterranean climates around the world, including dragon trees from the Canary Islands, agaves from Central America and rare honey palms from Chile.

⚓ **Michelin Map:** 340 N7.

ℹ **Info:** Pl. Michel-Goy, Le Rayol-Canadel-sur-Mer. ℘ 04 94 05 65 69. www.lerayolcanadel.fr.

◗ **Location:** Coming from St-Tropez, the road into the Domaine branches left at the entrance of the village of Rayol-Canadel-sur-Mer.

Domaine du Rayol

D. Pazery/ MICHELIN

Posidonia – the Lungs of the Mediterranean

This flowering plant, which looks like bunches of long green leaves, is an essential element of marine life in the Mediterranean, where it grows in sandy seabeds on narrow coastal fringes.

Posidonia plays the same role as a forest: it provides a habitat for animal and plant species, produces oxygen and stabilises the seabed.

It is now threatened with damage and extinction from unpurified sewage discharge, uprooting by boat mooring, building along the coast and by the invasion of another species *(Caulerpa taxifolia)*.

The estate's many winding paths offer glimpses of the turquoise sea and the pine-carpeted headland. Both the farm and beach house feature educational displays.

Sentier Marin★

Open Jul–Aug. Guided underwater tours of Mediterranean flora and fauna. Allow 2hr (45min in the water). Daily Jun–Sept, reservation required. 18€ (children 14€). All equipment supplied.
A trip from the Domaine's little beach offers an unusual view of marine life in the Mediterranean. This tour, accompanied by guides from the Conservatoire, is preceded by an introduction to the species most likely to be seen, their description and the best place to look for them among the posidonia.

ADDRESSES

CAFÉ

Le Café des Jardiniers – *Open noon-6pm. 04 98 04 44 00.* The Domaine's on-site café serves seasonal dishes and homemade desserts with a selection of hot and cold drinks. The grocery sells Fair Trade products and regional items such as vinegar, preserves and cordials.

CALENDAR

Concerts – In the summer season, evening concerts are held at the Domaine du Rayol, with an opportunity to stroll through the illuminated gardens during the interval. *Reservation required 04 94 05 63 07.*

Themed visits and workshops – Discover everything from the secrets of aromatherapy to edible plants and waterless gardens.

Ramatuelle★

Var

Set on a slope among vineyards and scrubland, this village of pink houses with red-tile roofs typifies the architecture of old Provençal hill towns. It's a mix of narrow winding streets, vaulted arches and dwellings huddled against an ancient town wall.

VISIT
The Village

Despite its isolated location, in the 10C, the village fell to the Saracens who had otherwise made their lair in La Garde-Freinet *(Rahmatu'llah means "divine providence" in Arabic)*. During the Wars of Religion in 1592, having opted to side with the Catholic League, Ramatuelle was once again placed under siege and almost entirely destroyed. Many door lintels mention the year in which the village was rebuilt (1620), including that on the entrance to the Romanesque **church**. The church contains two 17C Baroque altarpieces of magnificent gilded wood. At the bottom of the village, on rue du Moulin-Roux, you'll find the **prisons**

- ▸ **Population:** 2,271.
- **Michelin Map:** 340 O6.
- **Info:** Pl. de l'Ormeau. 04 94 12 64 00. www.ramatuelle-tourisme.
- ▶ **Location:** Ramatuelle lies 7mi/11km east of La Croix-Valmer (*see Massif des MAURES*) and south of St-Tropez on the D 93.
- **P** **Parking:** There are parking areas around the church, the cemetery and the Town Hall *(Mairie)*.

built under Napoleon III (late 1800s) often wrongly attributed to the Saracens because of its Moorish style.
The central square, place de l'Ormeau, hosts restaurants, cafés and a Provençal market *(Thu and Sun)*.

Monument to the Resistance
Opposite the cemetery stands a memorial to the members of the Special Services who died during the Second World War. The submarines that stayed in contact with the members of the Resistance

during the Occupation used to wait offshore by the Roche-Escudelier.

EXCURSIONS
Moulins de Paillas
▶ *2mi/3km to the north of Ramatuelle.*
At an altitude of 1,066ft/325m, these three ruined olive mills *(one restored,* ◷*open Mar–mid-Oct; enquire at tourist office for hours;* ⊜*no charge;* ℘*04 98 12 64 00)* were active until the 19C. Don't miss the **panorama★★** over the Esterel, Massif des Maures coast, the Pradels range *(southwest)* and the Sauvette chain *(northwest).*

Gassin
▶ *3mi/5km north of Ramatuelle.*
This village, at an altitude of 656ft/201m, retains its Provençal character and is especially lively on market day *(Sun).* The **Terrasse des Barri,** planted with lotus trees, provides a **view★** of St-Tropez Bay, the Îles d'Hyères, Cavalaire Bay and on clear days, the Alps to the east.

ADDRESSES

⌂ STAY
⊜⊜⊜ **Chambre d'hôte Leï Souco** – *Route des Plages, le Plan district.* ℘*04 94 79 80 22. www.leisouco.com. 5 rooms. Closed mid-Oct–Mar.* ▣ . ⤴. ⌷ Nestled amid vineyards and olive trees, this peaceful mas offers charming rooms decorated with Salernes earthenware; some are air-conditioned. The family room sleeps four. Each room has a private terrace.

Cogolin

Var

This typical Provençal village along St-Tropez Bay lies at the foot of an ancient tower. A wine-growing centre, Cogolin is also known for its artisan crafts and hand-made pipes.

WALKING TOUR
The top of the village, with its alleyways and small squares joined by vaulted passageways, has kept its medieval character. Local craft workers produce **briar pipes** made from heather roots, reeds for musical instruments and even carpets.

▶ From the tourist office, pass the Hôtel de Ville, and turn left onto rue du 11-Novembre 1918.

Église St-Sauveur-St-Étienne
Dating back to the 11C, the church is entered through a Renaissance serpentine portal.
A side chapel contains an altarpiece by Hurlupin (1540) depicting St-Antony. On exiting the church, don't miss the fountain in Place Abbé-Toti.

▶ **Population:** 11,066.
◔ **Michelin Map:** 340 O6; local map: *see Massif des MAURES.*
ℹ **Info:** Pl. de la République. ℘04 94 55 01 10. www.cogolin-provence.com.
▶ **Location:** Located south of Grimaud on the D 558 and west of St-Tropez on the N 98 (beware of seasonal traffic jams).
♣♣ **Kids:** The rooster museum is filled with animal models.
◔ **Timing:** Allow 2hr to soak up the charm of Cogolin.

Rue Nationale
This street is lined with Renaissance doorways, some dating from the 12C; the bourgeois building at no 46 is the 17C Château Sellier (*⌂see Sights*). Continue to place Bellevue and the **Chapelle St-Roch**, decorated with contemporary artworks. Farther up the hill, via Montée Aloes, the **clock tower** (14C) is the only remaining trace of the fortified castle.

Pine Nuts

Pine nuts, also called *pignons*, are delicately flavoured seeds taken from the cones of the stone pine. Their presence in Provençal cooking is by no means recent: the Romans are believed to have used them to make wine and mustard. Today, pine nuts are a common feature of Mediterranean cuisine. In savoury dishes, they add texture to green vegetables and lend a crunchy consistency to stuffings. They are also used in pastries, preferably toasted, notably in delicious almond tarts known as *amandines*.

SIGHTS

Musée Sellier

46 rue Nationale. ◷*Open Tue–Sat Jun–Sept 10am–1pm, 3pm–6.30pm; Oct–May 10am–12.30pm, 2.30pm–5.30pm.* ⬡*No charge.* ✆*04 94 54 63 28.*
This château houses arts exhibits, the **Rooster Museum** (the town's symbol), and the **Knights Templar Museum**, with documents and uniforms illustrating the history of the religious order.

Espace Raimu

18 ave. G. Clémenceau. ◷*Open Wed–Mon 10am–noon, 3pm–6pm (Jul–Aug 10am–noon, 4pm–7pm). Closed Sun morning, mid-to end Nov, 2nd week Jan.* ⬡*4€.* ✆*04 94 54 18 00. www.musee-raimu.com.*
Housed on the ground floor of the town's cinema, this exhibit explores the life of film actor **Jules Muraire**, aka Raimu, through his letters, posters and costumes.

Coastal Cogolin

▶*3mi /5km northeast by D 98 and D 98A. Regular shuttle bus in summer.*
Near Cogolin lies a fine sand beach and a marina with 1,500 moorings. The more secluded **Port-Cogolin** has 150 moorings.

ADDRESSES

🛏 STAY

⬡⬡⬡ **Le Coq'Hôtel** – *pl. de la Mairie.* ✆*04 94 54 13 71. www.coqhotel.com. Closed Jan. 24 rooms.* 🅿️ ⬡*9€. Restaurant* ⬡⬡. The hotel's mascot is the rooster, whose emblem can be found on the façade and perched inside the lounge. Lively colours adorn the eclectically furnished rooms. Double-glazed windows overlook the square; other rooms face the inner courtyard.

🍴 EAT

⬡⬡ **Côté Jardin** – *rue Pasteur, facing pl. du Marché, aka pl. des Boules; also by the passage at 1 rue Gambetta.* ♿ ✆*04 94 54 10 36. Closed Oct–Mar.* This open-air restaurant in the heart of Cogolin serves grilled meats, sandwiches, snacks and ice cream in a leafy garden.

SHOPPING

Provençal Market – Lively market Wed and Sat, and in Jul–Aug also Fri night.

Fabrique de M. Rigotti – *Zone Industrielle, 5 rue François-Arago.* ✆*04 94 54 62 05. www.rigotti-reeds.com. Closed Aug and public holidays.* Rigotti *(guided tours)* produces and sells locally-made reeds and parts for musical instruments.

Cogolin Pipes – *Maison Courrieu, 58 ave. G.-Clémenceau.* ✆*04 94 54 63 82. www.courrieupipes.fr.* Briar roots from the nearby Maures Forest have been providing the raw material for pipes in Cogolin for over 200 years. Discover manufacturing techniques and finished products.

Manufacture de Tapis de Cogolin – *6 blvd. Louis-Blanc (off ave. G.-Clemenceau). Exhibit open Mon–Fri 9am–noon, 2pm–5.30pm. Closed 1 Jan, 2 weeks Aug, 25 Dec.* ✆*04 94 55 70 65. www.tapis-cogolin.com.* Armenian refugee weavers established the Cogolin carpet factory in 1928. A special tour explores hand-weaving using low-warp looms and hand-tufting.

St-Tropez★★

Var

A magnet for celebrities, artists, musicians and their admirers, famed St-Tropez enjoys an enviable location on the southern shore of arguably the most beautiful bay on the Riviera. The little port's mix of modern luxury yachts and scruffy but colourful Provençal facades clustered around an ancient citadel never seems to go out of fashion.

A BIT OF HISTORY
The Legend of St Tropez

The town is named after the Christian centurion **Torpetius** (Torpès), who was beheaded by the Emperor Nero. His body was cast adrift in a boat with a cockerel and a dog, who were meant to devour his remains. Instead it arrived ashore intact where St-Tropez stands.

Republic of St-Tropez (15C–17C)

In 1470 the Grand Seneschal of Provence accepted the offer of a Genoese gentleman, Raffaele de Garezzio, to settle with 60 Genoese families in St-Tropez, which had been destroyed by war at the end of the 14C. De Garezzio rebuilt the town and its defences, and St-Tropez grew into a sort of small, prosperous republic administered by the heads of these families and later, by elected consuls.

Judge Suffren (18C)

Among the St-Tropézian navigators who contributed to the rise of the town and the defence of France in the 17C, the most famous is **Pierre-Andre de Suffren** (1729–88). A judge under the Knights of Malta, he became a captain in the Royal Navy (his statue can be seen on the quayside). He was sent to the Indies, where he won several victories against the British.

The Bravades

Two *bravades* or "acts of defiance" take place every year. The first, a simple religious procession in honour of Saint Tropez, has been held in the town since the end of the 15C. On 16 and 17 May, a

> **Population:** 5,612.
> **Michelin Map:** 340 O6; local maps p160 and p163.
> **Info:** Quai Jean-Jaurès. ℘0892 68 48 28. www.ot-saint-tropez.com.
> **Location:** Unless you arrive by yacht, access is slow and frustrating, with infamous summer traffic jams on the only road to the town (D 98a) in July and August; try to get there early in the morning, or stay on the less crowded southeastern coasts of the St-Tropez Peninsula.
> **Parking:** Parking in the village, even in parking garages, is difficult. The map designates free covered and paying parking areas on the peninsula.

gilded wooden statue of Saint Tropez is carried through the festive town decked out in red and white (the colours of the corsairs). The second *bravade* celebrates the victory of the St-Tropez militia which, on 15 June 1637, fended off 22 Spanish galleys attempting to take the town by surprise.

Intellectual Haven

When the writer **Maupassant** sailed into St-Tropez on his yacht in 1887, it was a charming little village unknown to tourists. A decade later, the painter **Paul Signac** was blown into the port during a storm. He was so impressed, he invited his artist friends to join him, including **Matisse**, who spent several months here, immortalising the town in a number of major works.

A campaign to rebuild the war-damaged port led by the writer **Collette** in the 1950s revived its fortunes, attracting a new generation of visitors, including Errol Flynn, Anaïs Nin and **Jean Cocteau**. The arrival of film star Brigitte Bardot in 1956 finally sealed St-Tropez's reputation as a playground for the rich and famous.

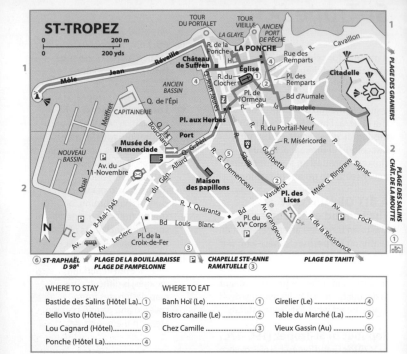

ST-TROPEZ

WHERE TO STAY	WHERE TO EAT	
Bastide des Salins (Hôtel La).. ①	Banh Hoï (Le) .... ①	Girelier (Le) .... ④
Bello Visto (Hôtel) .... ②	Bistro canaille (Le) .... ②	Table du Marché (La) ....⑤
Lou Cagnard (Hôtel) .... ③	Chez Camille .... ③	Vieux Gassin (Au) ....⑥
Ponche (Hôtel La) .... ④		

RESORT LIFE
The Port★★

Lined with luxury yachts, the port is the centre of life in cosmopolitan St-Tropez The old pink and yellow houses of the waterfront and neighbouring streets have been converted to cafés and pastry shops, cabarets and restaurants, pricey boutiques, galleries and antique shops.

The Beaches

St-Tropez' 6mi/10km of beaches have fine sand and charming rocky coves. The nearest is **Bouillabaisse Beach** (perfect for windsurfing when the *mistral* is blowing). To the east of town lies **Les Graniers Beach** *(access from rue Cavaillon)*. Farther east round the headland stretches **Les Salins Beach** *(via ave. Foch)*. But by far the most appealing and the most fashionable are the **Pampelonne Beaches** *(many are private)*, well sheltered from the *mistral* winds. Reached by a **coastal path** that skirts the entire peninsula, **Les Cannebiers Bay** affords glimpses of the superb villas of the rich and famous.

WALKING TOUR

Môle Jean-Réveille
The **panorama★** from the top of the jetty includes St-Tropez, Ste-Maxime, the Esterel and in fine weather, the Alps.

La Ponche Quarter
Tucked between the port and the citadel, this district is the oldest and most charming of St-Tropez, where fishermen and artists used to live.

◖ Turn right at the seaward end of quai Jean-Jaurès onto pl. Hôtel-de-Ville.

On the left stands a massive tower, all that remains of the 16C **Château de Suffren**, the residence of the lords of St-Tropez.

◖ Turn left beyond the Hôtel de Ville to reach La Glayel cove.

Rue de la Ponche leads through the old gateway to a beach overlooked by the

Vieille Tour *(old tower)*, where fishing boats anchor.

◗ Follow the street to the adorable pl.des Remparts, then to blvd. d'Aumale.

Citadelle★
The citadel stands on a hillock at the east end of town. The hexagonal keep with three round towers was built in the 16C. A fortified wall was added in the 17C (◷*open Apr–Sept 10am–6.30pm, Oct–Mar 10am–12.30pm, 1.30pm–5.30pm; ⊚2.50€, Jun–Sept 5.50€; ℘04 94 97 59 43)*. The ramparts command a fine **view★** of St-Tropez to the Maures.

◗ Retrace your steps to rue d'Aumale, then to pl. de l'Ormeau.

Notre-Dame-de-l'Assomption
Rue du Cdt Guichard.
◷*Open 9.30am–noon.*
Built in the Italian Baroque style in the early 19C, this church has a finely carved woodwork interior. To the left of the high altar, a bust of St Tropez is surrounded by several old blunderbusses that are set off during the May bravade.

◗ From rue du Clocher, turn left on rue Commerçants and right on rue Marché.

The charming **Place aux Herbes** is the backdrop to a small morning market. Walk past the lively fish stalls underneath Porte de la Poissonnerie and proceed to Quai Jean-Jaurès.

◗ Leaving the port, take rue Laugier, then rue Gambetta.

These two lively shopping streets are lined with famous store brands.

Place des Lices is a popular meeting place with cafés, a Provençal market and leafy plane trees.

SIGHTS
L'Annonciade, Musée de St-Tropez★★
Pl. Grammont. ◷*Open Dec–Oct 10am–noon, 2pm–6pm, Wed–Mon.* ◷*Closed 1 Jan, 1 May, Ascension, 25 Dec.* ⊚*5€.* ℘*04 94 17 84 10.*
The chapel of Our Lady of the Annunciation, built in 1510 and deconsecrated during the Revolution, was split into two levels and opened as a museum in 1937, with artworks dating from 1890 onwards. The collection includes works by **Pointillists** Paul Signac, H-E Cross, Théo van Rysselberghe, Maximilien Luce and Picabia; **Fauvists** Matisse, Braque, Manguin, Vlaminck, Kees Van Dongen and Dufy; and painters from the **Nabis** school, including Bonnard, Vuillard and Félix Vallotton. **Expressionist** painters are represented by Rouault, Chabaud, Utrillo and Valadon.

♣♣ Maison des Papillons (Musée Dany-Lartigue)
9 rue Étienne-Berny. ◷*Open Wed, Fri–Sat 10am–12.30pm and 2.30pm–6pm, Tue and Thu 10am–12.30pm only.* ⊚*3€ (children under 10 free).* ℘*04 94 97 63 45.*

La Nioulargue Sailing Festival

First held in 1981, this major European meeting of vintage boats, which takes place every year in October, now attracts more than 250 competitors.

The race starts at the Tour du Portalet, skirts the shallows marked by the Nioulargue (sea nest, in Provençal) buoy and returns to the harbour. The skilful dances performed by ketches (recognisable by the small mast at the stern) and schooners (with the small mast in the bows) call on the sailors to anticipate each manœuvre. The stress at the foot of the main mast can be as much as 500t, so the entrants need brawn as well as brains. Watch the race from a boat shuttle service in the bay (℘*see Addresses p165*), or share the rental of a small boat. A more peaceful view of the scene is possible from the citadel. Binoculars are a must.

History of the Cap Lardier Estate

In Edwardian times a vineyard occupied the site of the present development and the Mas de Gigaro. In the early 1970s, a banking institution purchased the estate, together with a few plots of land around Brouis beach, with the intent of building a marina. The residents rallied against this plan and the Conservatoire du Littoral bought the estate in 1976, guaranteeing the preservation of this stretch of coastline.

Customs Officers' Footpath – This footpath, which follows 124mi/200km of the Var coastline, dates from the First Empire (early 19C). It was commissioned by Fouché when he was Minister of Police and was intended to help armed customs officers protect the coast against smugglers. Since 1976 the path has been restored, and all private properties adjoining the shore are obliged to allow a pathway (at least 10ft/3m wide) across their land.

This charming Provençal house is the former home of painter and entomologist Dany Lartigue, son of the photographer J.-H. Lartigue. It houses a collection of 4,500 butterflies – all the diurnal species existing in France, caught by the artist himself – as well as a donation of exotic butterflies.

EXCURSIONS
Chapelle Ste-Anne
▷ 0.7mi/1km. Exit St-Tropez to the south and take ave. Paul Roussel, then route de Ste-Anne. ◐Open during Bravades (17–18 May), 26 July and 15 Aug only.
Standing on a volcanic peak in the towering shadow of a cypress tree, this attractive Provençal chapel (1620) is a place of pilgrimage for seafarers and bravadeurs. It affords a view★ of St-Tropez Bay, the Maures and the start of the southern Alps in the distance.

Ramatuelle★
⌖See RAMATUELLE.

🅷 HIKING TOURS
Presqu'île de St-Tropez★★
🅷 Wear good walking shoes and avoid the hottest times of the day.
Although in high season tourism takes over St-Tropez, the surrounding country presents a traditional landscape of vineyards, cypress trees and immaculate farmhouses (mas) shaded by umbrella pines. The **St-Tropez Peninsula** consists of the rocky headlands of Cap Camarat, Cap Taillat and Cap Lardier, the long ribbon of fine sand at Pampelonne Bay, the beaches of Gigaro, Briande and Escalet, and countless creeks for secluded bathing.

St-Tropez to Tahiti Beach
🅷 Allow 3hr.
The path, with **views** of the foothills of the Maures and red rocks of the Esterel, leaves from Graniers Beach at the west end of the harbour. After running along the Rabiou Point and Cap de St-Tropez, the path wends its way to Les Salins beach, where refreshments are available in open-air cafés (guingettes) in summer. The path then rounds Cap Pinet and ends at Tahiti beach in Pampelonne Bay.

Tahiti Beach to Cap Camarat
🅷 Allow 2hr.
The path parallels the long sandy stretch of Pampelonne Beach (3mi/5km) to Bonne-Terrasse Point. At Bonne-Terrasse Bay, the path climbs the rocks through thick vegetation. Near Rocher des Portes, a path (right) leads to Camarat lighthouse.

▷ From Ramatuelle take D 93 east to the "Route du Phare" and beyond the Tournels camp site.

Phare de Camarat★
This **lighthouse**, commissioned in 1831, was converted to electricity after the World War II and automated in 1977. At 425.8ft/129.8m tall, it is one of the highest above sea level in France, with a 37mi/60km range.

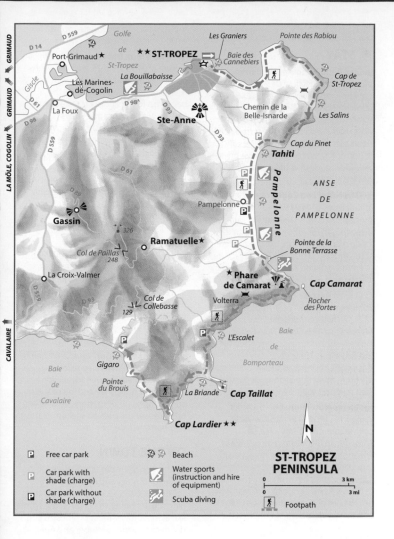

ST-TROPEZ
PENINSULA

▣	Free car park
▣	Car park with shade (charge)
▣	Car park without shade (charge)
🏖 🏖	Beach
🏄	Water sports (instruction and hire of equipment)
🤿	Scuba diving
🚶	Footpath

0   3 km
0   3 mi

From the summit **views★★** extend over the whole peninsula.

Cap Camarat to Cap Taillat
😊*No refreshments, except in L'Escalet.*
🚶 *Allow 2hr.*
After skirting Rocher des Portes, the path leads to L'Escalet beach over isolated, accessible coves that are ideal for sunbathing. The **views** of the **Château de Volterra** (⭕ *closed to the public)* are rewarding. The path ends at Cap Taillat.

⬛ You can rejoin the road from the customs shed at the L'Escalet car park.

The path cuts across the base of the headland through scrubland and oak forests. **Cap Taillat** is a *tombolo* sand bar connecting the reef to the coast.

🚶 Cap Taillat to Gigaro via Cap Lardier
Allow 2hr.
The path runs through the protected **Cap Lardier★★** with **views** of Briande Bay. Return to Gigaro from Briande Beach by the inland path *(route DFCI).*

ADDRESSES

🏨 STAY

Bello Visto – *pl. des Barrys (pl. deï-Barri), Gassin. ℰ04 94 56 17 30. www.bello-visto.eu. 9 rooms. ⛄☐8€. Restaurant.* A small family-run hotel and restaurant at the top of Gassin. Most rooms, along with the terrace, offer **views** over the Massif des Maures and St-Tropez Bay, but only two have private bath. Dining room with fireplace and Provençal cuisine.

Hôtel Lou Cagnard – *18 ave. Paul-Roussel. ℰ04 94 97 04 24. www.hotel-lou-cagnard.com. Closed late Oct–Jan. ℗. 19 rooms. ☐11€.* Enjoy breakfast in the shade of a mulberry tree in the garden of this Provençal house, just off Place des Lices. At night you'll be lulled to sleep by the chirping of cicadas.

Bastide des Salins – *2.5mi/4km southeast of St-Tropez. ℰ04 94 97 24 57. www.bastidedessalins.com. ℗. 14 rooms. ☐18€. Closed Nov–Feb.* This old Provençal house is surrounded by extensive leafy grounds. Barely 5min from Place des Lices and yet totally isolated, the hotel offers large rooms decorated in the Provençal spirit. Swimming pool.

Hôtel Ponche – *5 rue des Remparts. ℰ04 94 97 02 53. www.la ponche.com. Closed Nov– Feb. ℗. 17 rooms. ☐19€. Restaurant.* The rooms of this upscale hotel occupy four village houses formerly belonging to fishermen; the blue one was a favourite of actress Romy Schneider's. Great views, bright hues and considerate service make a stay here a must.

🍴 EAT

Bistro Canaille – *16 rue des Remparts. ℰ04 94 97 40 96. Closed Mon–Fri in winter.* Bistro fare and Canaille's relaxed ambience in this small square attract a youngish clientele. Early evenings the place becomes a wine bar with tapas.

La Table du Marché – *38 rue Georges-Clémenceau. ℰ04 94 97 85 20. www.christophe-leroy.com.* This temple of gastronomy located near Place des Lices is open all hours of the day. In addition to the restaurant offering traditional French cuisine, La Table du Marché also sells homemade pastries: croissants, cakes and the legendary "gendarme de St-Tropez" –

mouthwatering chocolate mousse filled with vanilla crème brûlée.

Au Vieux Gassin – *pl. deï-Barri, Gassin. ℰ04 94 56 14 26. www.au-vieux-gassin-var.fr. Closed mid-Oct–mid-Mar.* A little hilltop village serves as the backdrop for this popular restaurant. A terrace with **panoramic views** is partially enclosed and heated in cooler weather, taking over a little corner of the charming place deï Barri. The regional menu has a few "exotic" specialities.

Le Banh Hoï – *12 rue Petit St-Jean. ℰ04 94 97 36 29. Closed early Oct–early Apr.* Low lighting, black lacquer walls and Asian artworks decorate this restaurant specialising in Thai and Vietnamese cuisine.

Chez Camille – *Bonne Terrasse quarter, Ramatuelle. ℰ04 98 12 68 98. www.chezcamille.fr. Closed Fri lunch, Tue and early Oct–early Apr.* This family-run restaurant on the waterfront has served *bouillabaisse* (spicy fish stew) and grilled fish since 1913. Ask about the boat shuttle service.

Le Girelier – *quai Jean-Jaurès. ℰ04 94 97 03 87. www.legirelier.fr. Closed Nov–mid-Mar.* A harbourside fishermen's hut which converted into a stylish, contemporary dining room, Le Girelier prepares simply cooked shellfish platters and bouillabaisse.

ON THE TOWN

In summer, St-Tropez is the place for the rich and wealthy and is given over to sailing, sunbathing, entertainment and nightlife. However, in winter it looks more like a ghost town. Most businesses close down between November and April, when the swinging bars, restaurants and hotels become completely deserted.

Bar du Château de la Messardière – *route de Tahiti. ℰ04 94 56 76 00. www.messardiere.com. Closed Nov–mid-Apr.* This bar belongs to one of the Riviera's most prestigious hotels, housed in a former 18C private residence. The ambience in the piano bar is hushed and cosy. The terrace commands great **views** of St-Tropez Bay.

Bar Sube – *15 quai de Suffren. ℰ04 94 97 30 04.* This bar is one of the most beautiful night spots in the city. Model boats decorate the interior, where leather armchairs and a fireplace make for a cordial and comfortable atmosphere. Small tables installed on the balcony offer prime **views** of the old port.

SHOPPING

MARKETS AND FAIRS

Place des Lices – Held Tuesdays and Saturdays.

Foire de la Ste-Anne – Fair in Place des Lices, every 26 July.

SHOPPING STREETS

The most lively shopping streets are **rue Clémenceau, rue Gambetta** and **rue Allard**, offering an impressive selection of local arts and crafts: pottery, glassware, and other merchandise.

STORES

Les Sandales Tropéziennes – *16 rue Georges Clémenceau. ℘04 94 97 19 55. www.rondini.fr.* The Rondini house has been crafting natural leather St-Tropez sandals since 1927.

Le Petit Village – *La Foux roundabout, near the shopping centre just outside Gassin. ℘04 94 56 40 17. www.maviqne.com. Closed Sun.* Just off the busy La Foux, this showroom brings together wines from eight prestigious vineyards on the St-Tropez peninsula, including the famous Château de Pampelonne vineyard. Free tastings and many regional products for sale.

FOR YOUR SWEET TOOTH

La Tarte Tropézienne – *pl. des Lices. ℘04 94 97 04 69. www.la-tarte-tropezienne.com.* It was in this pâtisserie that the famous *tarte tropézienne (see photo above)* saw the light of day, invented in 1955 by Polish baker Alexandre Micka: it's a round, delightfully moist brioche cake flavoured with orange blossom, filled with custard and sprinkled with crystallised sugar.

Sénéquier – *pl aux Herbes. ℘04 94 97 00 90. www.senequier.com.* The pavement terrace and red chairs of this tea room are famous throughout the world, or so say the locals. Renowned personalities such as Colette, Jean Marais and Errol Flynn would come here for a cup of delicately fragrant tea, an iced coffee, a delicious ice cream or a few squares of homemade nougat.

Tarte Tropézienne

S. Sauvignier/ MICHELIN

SPORT AND LEISURE

Octopus Club – *Capitainerie du port. ℘04 94 56 68 71. www.octopus-plongee. assoc.fr. Closed Dec–Mar.* Scuba diving lessons and excursions for all levels in the blue waters around St-Tropez.

Maison du Tourisme du Golfe de St-Tropez – *Carrefour de la Foux, Gassin. ℘04 94 55 22 00. www.st-tropez-lesmaures.com.* This tourist office issues a list of all the companies based in St-Tropez Bay who specialise in deep-sea diving. Or see the website.

TRANSPORT

Les Bateaux Verts – *14 quai Léon Condroyer, Ste-Maxime. ℘04 94 49 29 39. www.bateauxverts.com.*

Return trip from St-Tropez to Ste Maxime (20min) 12€.

Return Trip from Ste Maxime to Baie des Canoubiers (45min) 13.40€.

Return Trip from St Tropez to Baie des Canoubiers 9€.

Grimaud★

Var

A warren of narrow cobbled streets, shady squares and flights of stone steps running up to the ruins of a medieval castle, the perched village of Grimaud has retained its traditional Provençal character. In contrast, the modern Port-Grimaud, built in the 1960s, although not to everyone's taste, is a lively and bustling summer destination.

▶ **Population:** 4,181.
⚘ **Michelin Map:** 340 O6.
🅸 **Info:** Blvd. des Aliziers. ℘04 94 55 43 83. www.grimaud-provence.com
◖ **Location:** The old town is 6mi/10km west of St-Tropez on the N 98A, then D 61.
🅿 **Parking:** In high season it's best to leave your car near the cemetery *(Parking du Château)*, on the north side of town near the Pont des Fées.

 WALKING TOUR

OLD TOWN★
Allow 1hr.

◖ Tour marked by arrows. A map with commentary is available from the tourist office.

The Ancient Grimaldi Feifdom

This large perched village owes its name to **Gibelin de Grimaldi**, who received it as a gift in the 10C from the Count of Provence for helping to expel the Saracens from Provence.

Start at the **Eglise St-Michel**, a small Romanesque church (12–13C) with a 16C bell tower, 18C sacristy and restored 19C frescoes *(lighting time switch on left on entering)*, before exploring the imposing ruins of the nearby 11C **castle**. Home to the powerful comtes de Provence and the Cossa and Castellane families, it was originally surrounded by a triple-walled enclosure protected by four three-storey corner towers. The towers were demolished in 1655, but the castle still boasts a stretch of 23ft/7m-high crenellated ramparts. One medieval tower survives to the north. The two southern towers date from the 17C, when the fortifications were rebuilt. From the upper ramparts

Castle at Grimaud

© Olivier Simon/Var Tourisme

there are fine **views★** of the Maures, St-Tropez Bay and, in the foreground, the restored olive mill of Grimaud.

Head east to the 15C-18C **Chapelle des Pénitents**, which houses the relics of St. Theodore, then join the Route Départementale *(county road)*, where you'll find the **Musée d'Art et Traditions Populaires** (◷*open Mon–Sat 10am–12.30pm, 2.30pm–6pm;* ◷*closed public holidays;* ⊜*no charge;* ℘*04 94 43 39 29*). Housed in a 17C olive mill, this folk museum explores the history of the village in the 19C through a series of archival photographs. A collection of tools illustrates the village's traditional activities, such as cork-making, silkworm breeding and wine-growing. A farmer's residence filled with household objects, garments and headdresses offers a glimpse of pre-industrial agricultural life.

▶ Pass by the tourist office and walk towards pl. Neuve.

A **fountain** here commemorates the installation of running water in Grimaud in 1886. Head towards the church along the **rue des Templiers**, where a 15C Maison des Templiers still stands. Once home to a garrison of Knights Templars, it has an impressive façade of basalt arcades and a serpentine doorway.

EXCURSION
Port-Grimaud★
▶ Follow signs for Port-Grimaud (north) 3mi/5km to the car park outside the port complex.

Designed in 1966 by the architect **François Spoerry** (1912–99), Port-Grimaud is a luxury housing complex designed to look like a fortified Mediterranean fishing village, complete with a fully-equipped marina and a fine sand beach. Public transport is available in passenger barges *(coches d'eau)*.

The ecumenical church of **St-Francis of Assisi** is modern, though inspired by the Provençal Romanesque style. The stained-glass windows are by Vasarely. The tower affords a **view★** of Port-Grimaud, St-Tropez Bay and Maures Massif.

ADDRESSES

🏠 STAY

⊜⊜⊜ **Chambre d'Hôte La Toscane** – *route départementale, Villa la Toscane, 2.5mi/4km from Grimaud Village.* ℘*04 94 43 24 11. www.la-toscane.com. 4 rooms.* ⊞. ⊒. The rooms of this Tuscan-style villa are cheerfully decorated with Provençal furnishings and tiled floors. Nice garden and swimming pool.

⊜⊜⊜⊜ **La Bastide de l'Avelan** – *Robert quarter, 1mi/2km from Grimaud Village by the D 94.* ℘*04 94 43 25 79. www.bastideavelan.com. 4 rooms.* ⊞. ⊒. Simple but charming rooms in a typical Provençal house, all facing the gardens and swimming pool.

🍽 EAT

⊜⊜ **L'Écurie de la Marquise** – *3 rue Gacharel.* ℘*04 94 81 59 04. Closed Tue eve and Wed Oct–May.* Located on a small pedestrian street in the old town, this unpretentious restaurant has a rustic decor and tasty Provençal cuisine.

⊜⊜⊜ **La Cousteline** – *1.5mi/2.5km southeast on D 14.* ℘*04 94 43 29 47. www.restaurantlacousteline.fr.* This converted farmhouse set in lush vegetation has a cosy country atmosphere and a market-fresh menu that changes with the seasons.

GUIDED TOURS

👥 **Petit Train Touristique** – *Apr–mid-Oct.* ℘*04 94 97 22 85.* ⊜*6€.* This train makes a circle between Grimaud *(place Neuve)* and Port-Grimaud *(main entry to Port-Grimaud Nord, near the coach park).*

CALENDAR

Markets – Thursdays in Place Vieille in Grimaud. Thursdays, Sundays in Port-Grimaud.

Fête du Moulin – A celebration held in June.

Les Grimaldines – ℘*04 94 55 43 83. www.les-grimaldines.com.* This festival of World Music is held from mid-July to mid-August (Tuesday eves).

Sainte-Maxime★

Var

Less glamorous than its neighbour St-Tropez, this small family resort has a tastefully restored old town, fishing harbour, well-appointed marina and fine sand beaches.

▶ **Population:** 13,739.
⑥ **Michelin Map:** 340 O6.
🖪 **Info:** 1 promenade Simon-Lorière. ℘04 94 55 75 55. www.sainte-maxime.com.
◗ **Location:** Sainte-Maxime sits on the edge of the Massif des Maures and 8.7mi/14km across the bay from St-Tropez on the N 98.

VISIT
Seafront and Beaches

Running from the port to the Préconil bridge, **Promenade Simon-Lorière**, shaded by umbrella pines and palm trees, commands **views** of St-Tropez.

Not far from place du 15-Août-1944, a **stele** commemorates the Allied landings in 1944. Running below the promenade, **Casino beach**, one of the 6.5mi/10km of fine sand beaches in Ste-Maxime, is flanked by La Croisette *(east)* and La Madrague *(west)* beaches. For more secluded sunbathing, try **La Nartelle**, Eléphants, or La Garonnette beyond Sardinaux Point.

Tour Carrée des Dames
Pl Aliziers.

This 16C square defensive tower houses the **Musée des Traditions Locales** (◐*open Wed–Sun 10am–noon, 3pm–6pm, Jul 7pm); closed Feb;* ⊜*2.30€)* devoted to local folklore and traditions.

Church

This church (1672) has a Baroque interior decorated with a green and ochre marble altar. Note the 15C choir stalls.

EXCURSION
Parc St-Donat
6mi/10km. Allow 1hr.

◗ From Ste-Maxime take blvd. Georges-Clemenceau, D 25 north.

A leisure park has been laid out in the woods between Col de Gratteloup and St-Donat Chapel. The main attraction is the **Musée du Phonographe et de la Musique Mécanique** (&◐*open May–Sept Wed–Sun 10am–noon, 4pm–6pm;* ⊜*3€; 1hr guided tour on request;* ℘*04 94 96 50 52)* housing an astonishing collection of 350 musical instruments and sound recording machines.

Port at Sainte-Maxime

© Olivier Simon/Var Tourisme

ADDRESSES

🏨 STAY

Le Chardon Bleu – *29 rue de Verdun.* *☎04 94 55 52 22. www.aubergeduchardon bleu.fr. 23 rooms. �8€.* Conveniently situated at the heart of the resort, barely 150 yards from the sea, this hotel offers air-conditioned rooms, most with a small balcony. Two rooms have a large terrace.

Hotellerie de la Poste – *11 blvd. F.-Mistral. ☎04 94 96 18 33. www.hotelleriedusoleil.com. Closed 6-27 Dec. 28 rooms. �9€.* Situated opposite the post office, but not far from the beach, this hotel offers brightly painted bedrooms with a Cuban-inspired decor. Quieter rooms are in the rear. Small terrace and swimming pool.

🍴 EAT

Chez Sophie – *4 pl. des Sarrasins. ☎04 94 96 71 00. Closed Nov–Dec.* This inviting restaurant epitomises the Provençal spirit: colourful decoration, wooden furnishings, terrace shaded by a plane tree, menu inspired by regional cuisine. The dishes and tasty homemade desserts are served by charming locals.

La Maison Bleue – *48 rue Paul Bert. ☎04 94 96 51 92. Closed Nov–Dec.* This Provençal house is entirely dedicated to pasta and its history: early advertising posters and enamelled plaques adorn the ochre walls of this restaurant, whose terrace is pleasantly shaded by plane trees.

ON THE TOWN

Café de France – *pl. Victor-Hugo. ☎04 94 96 18 16. www.lecafedefrance.fr.* A whiff of the past permeates this brasserie, opened in 1852 when Ste-Maxime was a fishing village. Old-time photographs and an ancient mirror evoke this bygone era. The big terrace sheltered by plane trees faces the marina. Fresh oysters in season.

Bar de l'Amarante Golf Plaza – *ave. Célestin. ☎04 94 56 66 66. www. golf-plaza.fr. From 6pm. Closed Feb.* This prestigious hotel bar is set against a backdrop of cork oaks and Mediterranean scrubland, overlooking Ste-Maxime and St-Tropez Bay. Golf course, fitness club and large-scale game of chess.

SHOPPING

Markets – *☎04 94 55 75 55. Summer: daily 8am–1pm, 4pm–8pm; winter : Tue–Sun 8am–1pm.*

Lively **covered market** in pl. du Marché every morning except Mon in winter.

Open market Fri morning in pl. Jean Mermoz.

Regional products available Thu morning in pl. des Sarrazins.

Artisans market mid-Jun–mid-Sept 5pm–11pm in the town centre's pedestrianised streets.

OUTDOOR PERFORMANCES

Théâtre de la Mer – *promenade Simon Lorière. ☎04 94 55 75 55. www.ste-maxime.com. Closed Oct–May.* Every summer this open-air theatre stages concerts of classical music and contemporary pop, folk dance and firework displays. Obtain details from the tourist office.

SPORT AND LEISURE

Héli Sécurité – *Quartier Perrat, Z.A. Grimaud. ☎04 94 55 59 99. www.helicopter-saint-tropez.com.* This company offers recreational flights in helicopters and shuttle services between airports or resorts.

Club Nautique de Sainte Maxime – *21 blvd. Jean-Moulin. ☎04 94 96 07 80. www.club-nautique-sainte-maxime.fr Open school holidays.* During the school holidays, this watersports club organises sailing courses that are available to the public.

Golf de Sainte-Maxime – *rte. du Débarquement. ☎04 94 55 02 02. www.bluegreen.com/saintemaxime.* Here you will find a superb, undulating golf course laid out over the heights of Ste-Maxime, dominating St-Tropez Bay. The bar has a terrace facing the sea.

Les Bateaux Verts – *14 quai Léon-Condroyer. ☎04 94 49 29 39. www.bateauxverts.com.* This company offers coastal excursions from Easter to October, such as tours of the St-Tropez Bay, the inlets of the Esterel, and Îles d'Hyères.

INLAND PROVENCE

Despite its historic towns and villages, lush green vineyards, dense pine forests and plunging cliffs, the *arrière pays* or "hinterland" of Provence manages to keep well below the tourist radar. Ideally explored at a leisurely pace, this region is filled with historic gems, from prehistoric funeral monuments and cave villages to towering ramparts and clock towers. Renowned for its olives, truffles and world-famous organic wines, it is also the perfect place to embark on a culinary adventure or two. Tucked away in millennial forests, perched on rocky peaks, hidden in deep valleys or simply located on fertile plains, these towns and villages offer a welcome respite from the crowded coastal cities of the French Riviera.

Highlights

1 Taste the local wines in and around **Brignoles** (p172)

2 Take part in the colourful *Fête de St-Marcel* in **Barjols** (p176)

3 Take a tour of the cave dwellings in **Villecroze** (p178)

4 Listen to medieval music at **Abbaye du Thoronet** (p183)

5 Visit the perched village of **Châteaudouble** (p192)

Villages of Character

Since 1999 an exclusive group of villages in eight French regions, including the Var, have been awarded the "Villages de Caractère" label. To qualify for this label, a village must have a harmonious blend of historic architecture, fewer than 3,500 residents, and at least one registered monument or sight. In the Var *département*, Aups and Cotignac are two of the eight villages that have been awarded this prestigious designation and are well worth a detour.

Historic Riches

There are more than 70 megaliths in this region, making it one of the richest sites for prehistoric treasures in the country. One of the most famous is in Lorgues, where visitors can see the Peyrcervier Dolmen, a type of megalithic tomb resembling a stone table.

Gallo-Roman ruins can be found in many villages, including vestiges of the Roman road from Spain to Italy in Draguignan, the Gayole Tombstone in Brignoles and artefacts from the Bouverie caves, now on display in the Musée du Patrimoine in Roquebrune-sur-Argens.

The towns and villages of Inland Provence have been marked by history at every turn, from the Middle Ages and the Ancien Régime to the Third Republic and the Second World War.

Local Economy

Dotted with ancient stone mills, Inland Provence has been producing wine and olive oil since Roman times. Today Brignoles lies at the heart of its rapidly growing organic wine-growing industry. A stop-off at one of the region's dozens of vineyards is now a must for wine lovers. Pottery, faïence and terra-cotta Santon dolls are produced in the region, while Aups is famous as the Black Truffle capital of Provence.

Tourism, however, is not so prevalent in this part of the French Riviera, despite its ideal location between the sea and the Gorges de Verdon, its Roman remains, the cave dwellings at Villecroze, and plentiful vineyards.

INLAND PROVENCE

★★ Recommended
★ Interesting
Other sight described in this guide

Le Thoronet
Cotignac
Aups

Driving tour with departure town
Pays brignolais
Vallon Sourn
Les plateaux du Haut Var
Le Haut Var
Gorges de Châteaudouble

Brignoles

Var

The narrow, winding streets of old Brignoles sit on the northern side of a low hill crowned by a venerable crenulated castle that once belonged to the counts of Provence. Lying on a rich, fertile plain, this market town is renowned for its peaches, honey, olives, oil and wine.

▶ **Population:** 14,963.
◔ **Michelin Map:** 340 L5.
🛈 **Info:** Office de Tourisme. La Provence Verte, carrefour de l'Europe. ✆ 04 94 72 04 21. www.la-provence-verte.net.
🅿 **Parking:** Large car park at place des Augustins.

VISIT

Head south of place Carami and stroll through the medieval streets to the church of St-Sauveur and the 12C castle, the birthplace of several counts of Provence. Walk along the covered rue du Grand-Escalier, rue du St-Esprit and rue des Lanciers with its twin-windowed **Romanesque house**.

Église St-Sauveur

This church has a fine Romanesque doorway (12C) flanked by ionic columns leading to a Provençal Gothic style nave. The south chapel contains a **Descent from the Cross** by Barthélemy Parrocel, who died at Brignoles in 1660.

Musée du Pays Brignolais

Place des Comtes de Provence.
◔*Open Apr–Sept Wed–Sat 9am–noon, 2.30pm–6pm, Sun and public holidays 9am–noon, 3pm–6pm; Oct–Mar Wed–Sat and public holidays 10am–noon, 2.30pm–5pm.* ◔*Closed 1 Jan, 1 May, 11 Nov, 25 Dec.* ◔*4€.* ✆*04 94 69 45 18. www.museebrignolais.com.*

Dominated by a large tower, this regional museum is housed in the former **palace of the Counts of Provence** (partly 12C).

The highlight of the exhibition is the **La Gayole sarcophagus★** (2C), thought to be the oldest surviving Christian monument from Ancient Gaul. Featuring iconography marked by the Greco-Roman polytheist tradition (a fisherman, an anchor, a shepherd herding a ewe, trees in the celestial garden and a personified sun), it illustrates the transition from pagan to Christian iconography.

Don't miss the reconstruction of an 18C Provençal kitchen and a cement boat by Joseph Lambot, the inventor of reinforced concrete.

Musée du Pays Brignolais

© Camille Moirenc/hemis/Photoshot

ST-MAXIMIN TAVERNES AUPS

Châteauvert
D 554
Vallon Sourn
D 45
Correns Montfort-s-Argens Carcès
D 22
Argens Cascades Le Thoronet ★★
D 45
D 562 Lac de Carcès
539 Pays
Le Val St-Vincent 395
461 Caramy
A 8 Cabasse brignolais ★
35
D N7 A 8
D 405 BRIGNOLES D N7
D 5 Flassans-s-Issole
Abbaye 455 D 13
de la Celle D N7
830 636 N
Montagne de la Loube ★ Besse-s-Issole
443 Issole
La Roquebrussanne D 15

BRIGNOLES AREA

0   4 km
0   2 mi

TOULON TOULON, HYÈRES

AIX-EN-PROVENCE, TOURVES — DRAGUIGNAN — ST-RAPHAËL

EXCURSION
Abbaye royale de La Celle
◗ *Leave Brignoles by the D 554 going south and turn right on the D 405.*
Guided tours available.
04 94 59 19 05.

This Benedictine convent was home to 100 cloistered nuns in 1268. From the 14C, a decline in morals (many of the nuns lived openly with their lovers) led to the transfer of the order to Aix en Provence in 1658. Sold after the Revolution, the abbey was used as a farm, then turned into a luxury hotel.

The minster, cloisters, chapter house and refectory are all open to visitors. The Romanesque abbey church featuring a cul-de-four nave contains an astonishingly realistic early-14C Christ.

👥 Little Train
◗ *Gare de Carnoules, 19mi/31km SE of Brignoles by D 43, D 15 and D 13.*
◷*Operates May–Oct (call or check website for hours).* ⊜*8.50€ (4–10 years 5€).* ✆ *06 07 98 03 09. www.attcv.fr.*
Hop onboard the *Picasso* (1955) railcar and admire the countryside between Carnoules and Brignoles via St-

Anastasie-sur-Issole, Besse-sur-Issole, Forcalquier and La Celle.

🚗 DRIVING TOUR

1 BRIGNOLES COUNTRY★
35mi/56km Allow 3hr. ◔*See local map above.*

◗ Leave Brignoles north on the D 554.

Le Val
Lying beside the Roman Via Aurelia, Le Val's narrow houses are clustered around the 18C wrought-iron **tour de l'horloge** (clock tower). The Romanesque church is decorated with 18C **frescoes**. Near the entrance to Le Val, the **Hôtel des Vins** sports **murals** on the façade and a carving on the stage backdrop wall by **Le Couëdic**, one of Salvadore Dalí's pupils.

👥 Musée du Santon
♿ ◷*Open Mon–Fri 8.30am–12.30pm, 1.30pm–6.30pm; enquire for weekends and public holidays.* ◷*Closed 1 Jan, 1 May, 25 Dec.* ⊜*2€ (6–12 years 1€).*

Brignoles Wine Valley

On either side of the Via Aurelia, the ancient Roman road that once linked Fréjus to Aix, lies the Brignoles wine valley. This fertile clay and limestone plateau stretching from Brignoles to Sainte-Baume boasts 3,953 acres/1,600 ha of vineyard producing an annual 1.5 million gallons/60,000 hl of mostly organic red (40 percent), rosé (55 percent) and white (5 percent) wine. The region's vineyards were awarded the AOC Coteaux Varois label in 1993; most welcome individual visitors. Maison des Vins des Coteaux Varois in La Celle (*04 94 69 33 18*) organises regular exhibits and tasting sessions.

The long, vaulted room of the former communal bread-oven (12C) is now home to santon figurines from Provence and elsewhere, in all sorts of different materials. There's also an animated Provençal Nativity scene.

Musée d'Art Sacré

North of the village. Open Mon, Tue, Thu, Fri 9am–noon, 1pm–5pm. Closed public holidays. 2€, tickets from Reception Desk, pl. du 4 Septembre. *04 94 37 02 22.*
Located in a 16C Pénitents Noirs chapel, this religious art collection features 17C embroidered sacerdotal garments, votive offerings and statues.

Musée du Jouet Ancien

*Chemin des Tanneries, southeast of the village. Enquire about hours. Guided tour (20min) on request. *04 94 37 02 21.*
This museum has a fine collection of antique toys, figurines, several military uniforms and dioramas of Napoleon's most famous battles.

Take the D 562 northeast to Carcès.

Carcès

The town produces oil and honey and has extensive wine cellars. The colourful ceramic tiles on the buildings of Carcès afford protection against the strong east winds.

Head towards Cabasse on the D 13 along the banks of the Carami.

Carami Falls

2.5hr. Park at the bridge and follow the signed trail 5mi/8km to a tiered waterfall (22ft/7m per tier).

Continue along the D 13.

Lac de Carcès

The pine-clad shores of this lake, created in 1936, are a favourite haunt of fishermen (*swimming not allowed*).

Continue on D 13 and turn left onto D 79 for the Abbaye du Thoronet.

Abbaye du Thoronet★★

see Abbaye du THORONET.

Return to D 13 and turn left towards Cabasse along the Issole Valley.

Cabasse

Situated on the Côtes de Provence wine route, Cabasse is dotted with dolmens and Gallo-Roman ruins. The 16C **Église St-Pons** has a **high altar★** in Spanish Renaissance style (1543). Gallo-Roman milestones stand near a 2C funerary inscription set in the outside wall.

Proceed along D 13, then turn right onto D N7 back to Brignoles.

2 VALLON SOURN

*Round trip 25mi/39km. Allow about 1hr.
See local map.*

Take D 554 north to Le Val. Turn right onto D 562, then left onto D 22.

Montfort-sur-Argens

A former Templar commandery, this walled village is dominated by the ruins of a forbidding **feudal castle** featuring two square towers, mullioned windows and a 15C spiral staircase. Grapes and peaches fill the surrounding fields.

▶ Return to the crossroads and turn right onto D 45, following the Argens.

Correns
Straddling the River Argens, this village has a castle and keep with interesting gargoyles. Renowned for its organic **white wine**, Correns hosts an annual organic and natural produce festival *(third weekend Aug; contact the tourist office for details ℘04 94 37 21 31).*

Vallon Sourn
The steep cliffs of this valley (*sourn* means sombre in Provençal) are honeycombed with caves that served as a refuge during the Wars of Religion. It is now an ideal spot to walk, swim or hire a canoe. The cliffs are also popular with rock-climbers.

▶ In Châteauvert turn left onto D 554 to return to Brignoles.

③ MONTAGNE DE LA LOUBE★
8.7mi/14km southwest. Allow 3hr, including hike. ♿See local map.

▶ Take D 554 south. Turn right onto D 405; turn left onto D 5. Park on left 0.6mi/1km before La Roquebrussanne.

Montagne de la Loube★
2hr on foot round trip.
🚶The narrow road skirts a formation of eroded dolomitic rocks, some of which resemble animals and human beings.

▶ Climb the final steps to the telecommunications mast.

From the summit (2,723ft/830m) is an interesting **panorama★**. The farmland is hemmed by barren ridges and the bauxite mines tear red gashes in the green quilt of pine and oak.

▶ Return to Brignoles by D 5 and N 7.

ADDRESSES

🛏 STAY

⊜⊜ **Hôtel La Cabro d'Or** – *5 ave. Giraud-Florentin. ℘04 94 04 50 26. www.lacabrod-or.com. 5 rooms. Restaurant⊜⊜.* Close to the town centre, this small, unpretentious hotel housed in a renovated 19C hospice boasts a Provençal restaurant.

⊜⊜⊜ **Chambre d'Hôte Château de Vins** – *Vins-sur-Caramy, 6mi/9.5km from Brignoles on D 24, rte du Thoronet. ℘04 94 72 50 40. www.chateaudevins.com. Closed Nov–Apr. 🍽. 5 rooms.* Listed 16C castle with four turrets and austere, imposing rooms.

⊜⊜⊜ **Chambre d'Hôte La Cordeline** – *14 rue des Cordeliers. ℘04 94 59 18 66. www.lacordeline.com. Reservation required. 4 rooms. Restaurant ⊜⊜ by reservation only.* Handsome 17C mansion providing accommodation in tastefully furnished rooms with fully equipped bathrooms and small salon.

🍴 EAT

⊜ **La Remise** – *4 ave. de la Libération, Besse-sur-Issole, 9mi/15km southeast of Brignoles on N 7 towards Le Luc and right on D 13. ℘04 94 59 66 93. Closed Sun evening Sept–Jun; 3 weeks in Jan; 2 weeks in Nov.* Small, unpretentious establishment located in the centre of the village. The white walled decor has a simple, minimalist feel. Outside is a shaded courtyard. Simple fare with a Mediterranean touch.

SHOPPING

Open-Air Markets – Wed pl. Caramy. Sat pl. Général de Gaulle, pl. du 8 Mai.
Maison des Vins Coteaux Varois – *Abbaye de La Celle, La Celle. ℘04 94 69 33 18. Mon–Fri and Sun afternoons (winter closed Sun).* Housed in a part of the 12C abbey, this shop stocks wines from 80 regional producers.

EVENTS

Agricultural Fair – Wines from Provence and the Var, as well as honey, olives and olive oil. 10 days in April. www.foiredebrignoles.fr
Foires à la Saucisse au Val – Sausage festival first weekend Sept. ℘04 94 72 04 21.

Barjols

Var

The village of 30 fountains, Barjols is surrounded by a natural amphitheatre of lush green hills irrigated by dozens of waterfalls. Once a major centre for earthenware and leather tanning, the village is still home to dozens of workshops.

▶ **Population:** 2,963.
- **Michelin Map:** 340 L4.
- **Info:** Office de Tourisme de Barjols, boulevard Grisolle. ℘04 94 77 20 01. www.ot-barjols.provenceverte.fr.
- **Location:** Barjols is located in the Var, 13.6mi/22km north of Brignoles, off the D 554.
- **Parking:** West of the village near the tourist office.

WALKING TOUR

OLD TOWN

Maps of the 30-fountain tour are available from the tourist office.
Old Barjols contains 12 wash houses and 30 **fountains**. Start with the fountain near the town hall, known locally as the *Champignon,* formed from a moss-covered mushroom-shaped limestone deposit.

A magnificent **plane tree** (circumference 39ft/12m), said to be the largest in Provence, dominates the town hall square. In the lower town, the **Pontevès Mansion**, named after an old Provençal family, sports a Renaissance doorway.

Collegiate church

Ave. de la République.
The original 11C Romanesque structure was rebuilt in the 16C with a Gothic nave. Note the 16C organ case, choir panelling and carved misericords. A 12C font stands to the right of the entrance. Stained-glass windows (19C) in the choir are by the painter **Van Loo**.

Réal★

Clinging to the hillside, north of the church, Réal has been inhabited since the 12C by tanners, who used three levels of partially troglodyte (16C–17C) basins for tanning their hides.

EXCURSIONS

Source d'Argens

9mi/15km to the southwest.

▶ From Barjols take D 560.

Vallon de Font-Taillade

The road plunges into a green valley of forests and vineyards, following a winding stream.

▶ 547yd/500m after Brue-Auriac a path to the left leads to a chapel.

Chapelle Notre-Dame

Next to a graveyard stands an abandoned Romanesque chapel built from local red stone. Its pleasant façade topped by a wall-belfry with twin windows is obscured by undergrowth.

▶ Return to D 560 and turn left. Stop in front of the bridge after 2mi/3km.

Source d'Argens

🚶 On the right of the road a path leads through the bushes to a spring which feeds the River Argens.

DRIVING TOUR

PLATEAUX DU HAUT VAR

32mi/52km. Half a day.

▶ Leave Barjols just before the public pool, following a small road northwest towards Varages.

Varages

This village has been producing faience since 1695. Many of the workshops organise regular visits. Contact the tourist office for times and dates.

Festival of St Marcel

On 17 January 1350, a group of pious citizens were removing the relics of St Marcel (a 5C bishop) from the abandoned abbey of Montmeyan when they came across a group of villagers. These villagers were washing tripe to commemorate a siege they had survived, thanks to the presence of an ox within their village walls. Every year since then, on the Sunday nearest to 17 January, St Marcel's bust is carried in procession throughout the town. Every three years, an ox is decorated before the patron saint of Barjols, blessed and led round the town on its way to the abattoir. After High Mass on the following day, the procession winds its way to the place de la Rougière, where the ox is roasted on a spit. At the end of a Provençal-style celebration with flutes, tambourines, music and dancing, the roasted ox is distributed to the crowd (&see CALENDAR OF EVENTS).

Musée des Faïences

12 pl. de la Libération. ©Open Jul–Aug *Tue 3pm–7pm, Wed–Sun 10am–noon, 3pm–7pm; Sept–Jun Wed–Sun 2pm–5pm (until 6pm Jun & Sept).* ©Closed Jan. ≈2.50€. ℘04 94 77 60 39. www.musee-faience-varages.fr Once the residence of a Napoleonic general, this museum explores the history of faience in Varages from the late 17C.

Church

Built in Provençal Gothic style, the 17C church has a bell tower covered in glazed multicoloured tiles. Inside, the altar of St Claude, patron saint of faience-makers, is decorated with medallions.

▶ Take D 554 north from Varages.

La Verdière

This hillside village is dominated by a church and an abandoned 10C **castle**.

▶ East of La Verdière take D 30 towards Montmeyan.

Montmeyan

This medieval perched village dominates the mouth of Verdon Gorge. There is a fine **view** from the southern entrance to the village. The **belvedere** beyond the Tour Charlemagne, once part of the 14C castle, affords more views.

▶ D13, then D 71 to Tavernes.

Tavernes

Set amid olive groves and vineyards, this typical Provençal village boasts a square belfry with an 18C wrought-iron campanile and ruined medieval walls. *2hr.* At the top of the village sits **Notre-Dame-de-Bellevue** (1642).

▶ The D 554 back to Barjols crosses then runs along a charming brook called the Ruisseau des Écrevisses.

ADDRESSES

STAY

⊜⊜ **Hôtel Le Pont d'Or** – *rue Eugène, Payan, rte. de St-Maximin.* ℘04 94 77 05 23. Closed early Dec–mid-Jan. 12 rooms. ⊊8.50€. Restaurant ⊜⊜. Each cosy room in this fomer coaching inn is decorated in a modern style. Provençal cuisine.

EAT

⊜⊜ **Le Resto des Petits Boudin** – *pl. Capit.-Vincens.* ℘04 94 77 29 87. Closed Nov–mid-Jan, Wed low season. Typical, homemade dishes with a regional twist are served in a modern dining room or on the shady terrace.

SHOPPING

Market – Sunday morning; Varages: Monday and Thursday.

Local arts – Traditional artisans can be found in the old tannery to the east of the town.

Aups

Var

Shaded by magnificent plane trees, the squares and historic alleyways of Aups burst into a riot of colour on market days when stalls of olives, truffles, thyme, honey and wine line the streets.

▶ **Population:** 2,029.
Michelin Map: 340 M4.
Info: Pl. F.-Mistral. ℰ04 94 84 00 69. www.aups-tourisme.com.
▶ **Location:** Aups sits at the foot of the Espiguières hills, bordered to the northwest by the highlands of Haute-Provence with the Massif des Maures dominating the horizon to the south.
Parking: Parking can be found just off avenue Verdun, near the tourist office.

 WALKING TOUR

OLD TOWN

A detailed walking tour map is available at the tourist office.

Heading north from the tourist office, explore the **Collégiale St-Pancrace** on place du Géneral-de-Gaulle. Originally built between 1489 and 1503, this Provençal Gothic collegiate church was severely damaged during the Wars of Religion. Entered through a Renaissance doorway, the church houses some interesting 15C–18C gold- and silver-ware. Continue north along rue G.-Péri to place L. Gauthier, with its 82ft/25m-high **clock tower**, built in the 16C as a lookout before serving as a prison. Walk down rue des Aires past an ornate rock balcony (crowned by a Latin motto, "I aspire to heaven") to the **Porte des Aires**, flanked by 12C and 16C ramparts. Skirt along the avenue Victor Maria and left into place Mar. Joffre, where the **Saracen Tower** rises in the

Black Gold of the Haut Var

The truffle (called *rabasse* in Provence) is a fungus that grows on the secretions seeping out of diseased oak trees. There are two categories of truffle: the white and the black, which are recognisable by their distinctive smell. They are harvested from November to February by dogs or by sows that take two years to train. The largest truffle market in the Var takes place in Aups every Thursday during the gathering season.

south. Formerly protected by a drawbridge, this was once the town's main gate. Next, head north onto avenue Albert 1er to the **Musée Simon-Segal** (*open Jun–mid-Sept Wed–Mon 10am–noon, 4pm–7pm; no charge; ℰ04 94 70 01 95*). This modern art museum contains 280 paintings, including 175 from the Paris School.

 DRIVING TOUR

LE HAUT VAR★

33mi/53km. Allow about 5hr.

▶ *From Aups take D 77 east.*

After Château de la Beaume, bear left on D 51 through **Tourtour★** (*see TOURTOUR*), passing olive trees, pines and vineyards on the way to Villecroze.

Villecroze

Surrounded by vineyards, orchards and olive groves, Villecroze lies in the wooded foothills of the Provençal plateau. Once squeezed into a ring of ramparts, the medieval village lingers on in the 15C **clock tower** and the surprising **rue des Arcades**. The 18C Romanesque church and wall belfry are worth a detour.

The **Parc Municipal** (*open 8.30am–8.30pm; entrance via route d'Aups, then* *a right-hand turn leading to a car park)* sports a waterfall that cascades 130ft/40m down the cliff face to form a stream in an oasis of greenery beside a rose garden. A marked path leads to the **caves**. The lords of Villecroze turned these caves into dwellings in the 16C. The tour includes several small chambers pierced by mullioned windows. The **Belvédère de Villecroze** affords a circular **panorama** of Tourtour, Villecroze, Salernes and the Maures.

◯ From Villecroze continue along the D 51, then turn right onto D 560.

Salernes

Salernes is known for the manufacture of hexagonal terra-cotta Provençal floor tiles known as **tomettes** and pottery. The church, set among 17C houses, boasts a belfry at both ends. The open-air market takes place every Wednesday and Sunday.

🚶 A fold-out map of walking and mountain biking trails is available from the tourist office in Salernes. (*🛈Pl. G.-Péri; 📞04 94 70 69 02; www.ville-salernes.fr).*

Terra Rossa, Maison de la céramique architecturale

◯*Open Jun–Sept Mon–Fri 10am–1pm, 3pm–7pm, Sat–Sun 10am–7pm; Apr–May, Oct–Nov Mon 3pm–6pm, Wed Sat 10am 1pm, 3pm–6pm, Sun 10am–6pm. ∞€3. 📞 04 98 10 43 90. www.terrarossasalernes.over-bloq.fr.* Housed in a former factory, this museum explores the production of *tomettes* in the early 20C.

◯ Take D 31 south by Bresque Valley.

Entrecasteaux

ℹ*See ENTRECASTEAUX.*

◯ Take D 31 south. Turn right on D 50.

Cotignac

ℹ*See COTIGNAC.*

◯ Take D 22 north.

Cascade de Sillans★

Before the village turn right onto a signed path. 🚶 *30min round trip.* The Bresque River cascades over a 138ft/42m drop into an emerald pool.

Sillans-la-Cascade

Perched on La Bresque, this village is surrounded by woodland and boasts ancient ramparts and picturesque streets. The 18C château (◯*open Mar–Dec Wed–Sun; ∞no charge)* hosts regular art and artisan exhibitions.

◯ Continue on D 22 to return to Aups.

ADDRESSES

🍴 EAT

⊜⊜ **Des Gourmets** – *5 rue Voltaire. 📞04 94 70 14 97. Closed late Jun–early Jul, 2 weeks in Nov, Mon, Sun evening except Jul–Aug.* Located next to the biggest truffle market in the Var, this family eatery serves traditional Provençal cuisine in cheerful rustic surroundings.

SHOPPING

Specialities – Here, the famous truffle reigns supreme and can be found in many dishes. The area is also known for its production of honey and goat's cheese made in the Upper Var Valley.

Moulin à Huile Gervasoni – *91 montée des Moulins. 📞04 94 70 04 66. Closed Oct–Mar.* This 18C olive mill still manufactures and sells olive oil alongside other regional specialities such as tapenade, Provençal fabrics and olive wood.

Markets – Aups: Wednesday and Saturday morning on place Frédéric-Mistral. Truffle market on Thu *(Dec–mid-Mar).* Evening artisan market *(Jul–Aug).*

SPORT AND LEISURE

Office du tourisme de Salernes – *📞04 94 70 69 02. www.ville-salernes.fr.* Salernes is surrounded mountains that are crisscrossed by hiking and bike trails. Hunting (boar) and fishing are also extremely popular in the area.

Tourtour★

Var

Set in a cool, wooded region, this village, flanked on either side by ancient castles, occupies a dominant position on a ridge affording views over the Varois Plain.

▶ **Population:** 533.
⚬ **Michelin Map:** 340 M4.
▯ **Info:** Château communal, ave. des Ormeaux, ℘04 94 70 59 47. www.tourtour.org.
◖ **Location:** Located southeast of Aups at the foothills of the Pre-Alps, facing the Varois plain.

WALKING TOUR

OLD VILLAGE★

Linked by vaulted passageways, the sloping streets of this village converge on a central square lined with restaurants and cafés shaded by two venerable olive trees.

Head out of the square to the **clock tower** *(tour de l'horloge)* and the old mill, which now houses the Fossil Museum *(⚬ see Sights below)*.

To the left of the museum, a restored 12C castle now houses an art and antiques gallery. Continue up the street, past a charming wash house on the right, to a two-storey medieval tower, the **Tour Grimaldi**.

On the other side of the central square, the town hall occupies the former **Château des Raphelis**, a solid 16C building with pepperpot towers.

Église St-Denis

This 11C church, standing on the southeastern edge of the ridge, was extensively modified in the 20C.

Viewpoint

From the church esplanade there is a wide **panorama★** *(viewing table)* over the Argens and Nartuby valleys, extending *(east)* to the Maures and *(west)* to Ste-Baume, Ste-Victoire mountain and the Luberon.

SIGHTS
▲▲ Musée des Fossiles

rue des Moulins. ⚬⚬*Open Jul–Aug Wed–Mon 11am–12.30pm, 3.30pm–7pm; Sept–Jun enquire at tourist office.* ⚬*No charge.* ⚬*Guided tours (1hr30min) by request* ⚬*3.50€.* ℘*04 94 70 59 47. www.tourtour.org.*

This museum contains local fossils, including dinosaur eggs, reptilian teeth and ammonites. Ammonites are fossilised molluscs in spiral shells that were in abundance in the region 130 million years ago.

Moulin à Huile

rue des Moulins. ⚬⚬*Open Jun–Sept daily 11am–12.30pm, 3.30pm–7pm. Mill operates Dec–Jan.* ⚬*No charge.* ⚬*Guided tours (1hr30min) on request* ⚬*3.50€.* ℘*04 94 70 59 47. www.tourtour.org.*

This communal oil mill has been in service since the 17C. It has three presses producing 1,100 gallons/5,000 litres of oil every autumn. During the summer, the mill houses exhibitions of paintings.

ADDRESSES

⚲ STAY

⚬⚬⚬ **Auberge St-Pierre** – *2mi/3km east of Tourtour on the D 51 and secondary road.* ℘*04 94 50 00 50. www.aubergesaintpierre.com . Closed mid-Oct–Easter.* ▯*16 rooms.* ⚬*11.50€. Restaurant*⚬⚬⚬ *closed lunch except Sun and public holidays.* Nature lovers will enjoy this hotel hidden within the vast grounds of a Provençal estate. The rooms are calm, bright and handsomely furnished. Pool, tennis, fitness room and Jacuzzi.

SHOPPING
MARKETS

Wednesday and Saturday mornings.

Entrecasteaux

Var

Built on the slopes of a hill overlooking the banks of the River Bresque, this village prides itself on its public gardens designed by Le Nôtre. The streets are shaded by 100-year-old plane trees.

VISIT

The town's narrow streets wind around an old **fortified church** with a buttress spanning the road. From the church esplanade, head down to the Pont St-Pierre and the wash house (*lavoir*), where you'll see the château's round ice house. Go around the back through the ancient entrance gate, cross the formal gardens and exit by the pretty horseshoe-shaped staircase to the Chapelle des Pénitents (now home to the Town Hall). Finally, follow the pleasant path up to the **Chapelle Ste-Anne**, where you'll discover a fine view.

Château

⚓️Guided tours (1hr30min) Easter–Oct Sun–Fri 4pm (and 11.30am in Aug). ⏱Closed 1 Jan, 1 and 11 Nov, 25 Dec. ⊜8€. ✆04 94 04 43 95.

This austere 17C building dominating the valley of the Bresque has a high façade topped by a double row of tiles and wrought-iron balustrades. The château was the stronghold of the Castellane clan, followed by the Grignans

- ▶ **Population:** 1,016.
- ♿ **Michelin Map:** 340 M4.
- ℹ **Info:** 21 Cours Gabriel-Péri. ✆04 94 59 95 64. http://tourisme.entrecasteaux.fr
- ◐ **Location:** The town sits 11mi/18km south of Aups on D 31. There is a tourist map on the square next to the garden.

before passing to the Bruni family. After a long period of neglect, the château was restored by the British painter Ian McGarvie-Munn, who turned part of it into a museum before his death in 1981. The tour includes the castle kitchen, outbuildings, guard-rooms and salons.

ADDRESSES

🛏 STAY

⊜🍴🛏 **Chambre d'hôte Bastide Notre-Dame** – *L'Adrech de Ste-Anne.* ✆04 94 04 45 63. http://bastidenotredame.free.fr. *4 rooms. Closed 1 month in winter.* 🚫🏊. This hillside B&B has four simple rooms, a pool and veranda.

🍴 EAT

⊜🍴 **La Fourchette** – *Le Courtil, near the château.* ✆04 94 04 42 78. *Closed Dec–Feb, Sun eve–Mon.* Light and refined cuisine made from fresh market produce. The tiny, tiled dining room with a fresco of the village provides an intimate place for winter meals.

SPORT AND LEISURE

Provence Canoë – *New Évasion, on the D 562 between Lorgues and Carcès.* ✆04 94 29 52 48. *www.new-evasion.fr. Closed mid-Oct–Mar.* Canoe or kayak the Argens River. Half-day excursions.

CALENDAR

Local patron saints – Ste-Anne is celebrated on 26 July and St-Sauveur during the first weekend in August.
Pesto soup banquet – One Sunday in August.

Château, Entrecasteaux
© Var Tourisme

Cotignac★

Var

This peaceful Provençal village clings to the side of an imposing cliff (262ft/80m) shaped over the millennia by the course of the Cassole River.

VISIT
Old Village

A detailed walking tour map is available at the tourist office.

Shaded by plane trees, the **cours centrale** (main square) is lined with 16C–18C houses clustered around a **fountain** depicting the four seasons. Admire the three caryatids at 7 Grande Rue before heading to the 18C hôtel de ville and 15C belfry on place de la Mairie. The grassy **amphitheatre** *(opposite)* hosts summer arts events.

Follow the path to the clifftop dominated by two 14C towers, vestiges of a castle once belonging to the lords of Castellane, then to a two-storey **cave** (*guided tours Tue–Sat Jul–Aug 10am–noon, 3pm–7pm; 15 Apr–Sept 2pm–5pm; Mon morning only; 2€*), where the villagers once hid their food from pillagers. Return to place de la Mairie via the ancient **olive oil mill**.

30min round trip. South of the village, after the bridge. A walk through the Vallon Gué follows a pathway along the Cassole to a **waterfall**.

Chapelle Notre-Dame-des-Grâces

0.6mi/1km south on D 13 via a road to the right. Open daily 8am–7pm. 04 94 69 64 92.

This chapel, visited in 1660 by the young Louis XIV and his mother Anne of Austria, affords a pleasant **panorama** of the Argens Valley and Brignoles region.

50min round trip. A wooded path from the chapel leads to the **St-Joseph Monastery**. Only the chapel is open to the public.

▶ **Population:** 2,146

Michelin Map: 340 L4.

Info: 475 rte. de Carcès, 04 94 04 61 87. http://ot-cotignac.provenceverte.fr

Location: 9mi/15km south of Aups on the D 22.

Parking: Parking near the main square and the outskirts of the village.

ADDRESSES

STAY

Chambre d'Hôte Domaine de Nestuby – *3mi/5km south of Cotignac towards Brignoles. 04 94 04 60 02. www.nestuby-provence.com. Closed mid-Dec–mid-Feb. 5 rooms.* *Restaurant* . At the heart of a vineyard, this cottage contains comfortable rooms furnished with antiques. Wine tasting sessions are held in the dining room. Small fitness centre with sauna, spa, sports facilities.

EAT

Restaurant Le Clos des Vignes – *route de Montfort, 3mi/5km south of Cotignac. 04 94 04 72 19. www.restaurant-le-clos-des-vignes.fr. Closed Sun evening and Tue Oct–Jun, and Mon.* This former sheep barn surrounded by vineyards has been restored with a dining room-conservatory and a summer terrace. Cuisine made with fresh regional produce.

SHOPPING

Local Specialities – Wine, oil, honey and pine nuts *(pignons)*. The bakeries make delicious *croissants aux pignons*.

Markets – *cours Gambetta and pl. Joseph-Sigaud*– Provençal market Tue morning; country market Friday morning *(mid-Jun–mid-Sept)*.

Les Ruchers du Bessillon – *cours Gambetta. 04 94 04 60 39. www.les ruchersdubessillon.com.* This boutique sells a large selection of organic honey.

Abbaye du Thoronet★★

Var

Le Thoronet is the oldest of the three Cistercian abbeys (along with Sénanque and Silvacane) in Provence. It is surrounded by wooded hills in an isolated spot, in keeping with the strict rules of the Cistercian Order.

A BIT OF HISTORY

Granted land by Raymond Bérenger, Marquis of Provence, a group of monks from the abbey of Mazan (Ardèche) moved to Le Thoronet in 1136 and built the church, cloisters and monastic buildings between 1160 and 1190.

Weakened by internal wrangling, like many other Cistercian abbeys, Le Thoronet declined in the 14C.

Abandoned during the Revolution, it was bought by the French State in 1854.

ABBEY

Allow 1hr to visit.

Open Apr–Sept Mon–Sat 10am–6.30pm, Sun 10am–noon, 2pm–6.30pm; Oct–Mar Mon–Sat 10am–1pm, 2pm–5pm, Sun 10am–noon, 2pm–5pm. Closed 1 Jan, 1 May, 1 and 11 Nov, 25 Dec 7€. Guided tours (1hr) available on request. 04 94 60 43 90. http://thoronet. monuments-nationaux.fr.

- **Michelin Map:** 340 M5; (*see BRIGNOLES*)
- **Info:** 04 94 60 10 94. http://tourisme-lethoronet.com.
- **Location:** The abbey is situated between Lorgues and the Lac de Carcès (*see Driving Tour in BRIGNOLES*). From the A 8, exit Le Cannet.

The Poet Abbot

The abbey's most famous resident was **Folquet de Marseille**. His family came from Genoa, but he gave up a career in trade to devote himself to poetry. He became a famous troubadour, quoted by Dante, and then in 1196 decided to become a Cistercian monk. In 1201 he was appointed Abbot of Le Thoronet and then Bishop of Toulouse in 1205.

Church★

Squat, austere and geometric with stonework blocks accurately cut and assembled without mortar, the church is an example of the Provençal-Romanesque style. Built to withstand violent winds and the risk of fire, the square stone bell tower is an exception to the Order's preference for simple wooden structures. The **nave** is covered with

Abbaye du Thoronet

© Wadey James/Apa Publications

Monastic Austerity

There is hardly any sculpture or carved decoration in the church to detract from its majestic proportions and purity of line. There is, however, a gentle curve on the imposts on the pillars and the half-columns supporting the transverse arches rise to only 9.5ft/2.9m above the ground according to Cistercian tradition.

barrel vaulting, slightly pointed, supported on transverse arches. It consists of three bays, prolonged by a fourth of the same height at right angles to the transept: only the raised arches indicate the presence of two arms of the transept, which are vaulted like the nave. The **chancel** ends in a cul-de-four vaulted apse and is lit through three windows. It is preceded by a shallow bay, featuring a triumphal arch surmounted by an oculus. The aisles are lower than the nave and covered with rampant pointed vaulting.

Cloisters★

The cloisters on the north side of the church are austere and solidly built in the form of a trapezium. The south gallery is at the same level as the church, but the west (exhibition of manuscripts and illuminated texts) and the north and east (which once supported another storey beneath a pitched roof) are lower because of the uneven ground. The galleries have transverse arches and barrel vaulting. The solid, round-headed arches which open onto the cloisters' garth (now a garden) are each divided in two by a stout column. Opposite the refectory door, projecting into the garth, is the **lavabo**, where the monks washed their hands before meals.

Conventual Buildings

These structures stand on the north side of the church near the cloisters. The door of the **library** (*armarium*), which is on the ground floor, is surmounted by a triangular lintel. The **chapter house★**

dates from the early Gothic period. The ogival vaulting, in which the ribs fan out like palm trees, is supported by two columns with roughly sculpted capitals, ornamented with leaves, pine cones, palm fronds and a hand gripping a staff. These are the only carvings in the abbey. Next to the chapter house, the **parlour** also serves as a passage between the cloisters and the outer garden. The **dormitory** over the chapter house is reached by a vaulted stairway and roofed with pointed vaulting supported on transverse arches. At the southern end, jutting out above the cloisters, is the Abbot's chamber. The doors in the north gallery opened into the monks' room, the warming room, the refectory and the kitchen, which have all disappeared. The **store room**, on the west side of the cloisters, has pointed vaulting and contains 18C vats for wine and olive oil, as well as the remains of a press. The **lay-brother building**, at the northwest corner of the store room, provided separate housing for the lay-brothers, who carried out manual labour for the monks and lived a less restrained life.

Outbuildings

Beside the stream, the foundations of the **guesthouse** have been excavated. The tithe barn on the south side of the church was later converted into an oil mill and contains some mill stones.

ADDRESSES

♉/ EAT

🖙 **Le Tournesol** – *9 rue des Trois-Ormeaux, Le Thoronet, 2.5mi/4km from the Abbey.* ✆*04 94 73 89 81. Closed Jan, Tue, Wed. Open for lunch (dinner by reservation only).* 🍴. This tiny 17C house in a village alley with colourful walls and furniture serves homely food. Its charming terrace gives onto the street.

CALENDAR

Rencontres de Musique Médiévale – A medieval music festival in the abbey and nearby churches mid-Jul–Aug. *www.musique-medievale.fr.*

Le Luc

Var

Dotted with mossy fountains, impossibly narrow streets, uneven cobblestones and lazy cats in flowered courtyards, Le Luc oozes the romantic scruffiness of a typical Provençal village. Despite its sleepy atmosphere, it is also an important farming centre, serving as the collection point for regional harvests of grapes and olives in the Var plain.

▸ **Population:** 8, 711.
�I **Michelin Map:** 340 M5; region map: pp170–171.
🖹 **Info:** Château des Vintimille, Pl. de la Liberté. ✆04 94 60 74 51. www.mairie-leluc.com.
◐ **Location:** Le Luc lies at the crossroads between the A 8 (viaduct high above the village), RN 7, Brignoles and Draguignan.

OLD VILLAGE

Information panels on the main buildings provide a handy way of exploring the village.

Belfry

Le Luc lies in the shade of a 16C hexagonal bell tower (89ft/27m high) built in the style of Italian campaniles.

Oppidum de Fouirette Viewpoint★

🏃 *1.5hr round trip. Walk towards Le Vergeiras, then follow the signposted path (information available from the tourist office).*

From the top of the hill (984ft/300m high), there is a wonderful **view★** over the Maures hills, from Gonfaron to Rocher de Roquebrune.

SIGHTS

Musée du Centre-Var

24 rue Victor-Hugo. ◐*Open Jul–mid-Oct Mon–Sat 3–6pm.* ◐*Closed public holidays.* ✆*No charge.* ✆*04 94 60 70 12. www.coeurduvar.com.*

This local history museum housed in the 17C Chapelle Ste-Anne features collections of historical artefacts uncovered during local excavations, including fossils (dinosaur eggs), a carved Roman sarcophagus, medieval sculptures, minerals from the Maures Massif and ancient weapons. Historical displays treat Le Luc and the life of local marine engineer Jean-Baptiste Lebas (1797–1873), who transported the famous obelisk from Luxor to Place de la Concorde in Paris.

Musée régional du Timbre

Pl. de la Convention. ◐*Open Wed–Thu 2.30pm–5.30pm, Fri–Sun 10am–noon, 2.30pm–5.30pm.* ◐*Closed 1 Jan, 1 May, all of Sept, 25 Dec.* ✆*2€.* ✆*04 94 47 96 16. www.lemuseedutimbre.com.*

This regional museum devoted to the history of postage stamps and philately is housed in the Château de Vintimille, a striking 18C building.

Displays include philatelic counterfeiting and the different stages in the traditional manufacture of postage stamps.

16C hexagonal bell tower

© Var Tourisme

Campaniles in the Var

Les Arcs	Clock Tower (18C)
Aups	Clock Tower
Carcès	Campanile atop a fortified gate (18C)
Carnoules	Belfry (17C)
Cotignac	Campanile (16C)
Draguignan	Tower (17C)
Flassans	Atop the belfry (18C)
Le Luc	Tower (16C)
St-Tropez	Campanile (19C)
Salernes	Belfry (18C)
Tavernes	Campanile (18C)
Toulon	Arsenal tower (18C)

ADDRESSES

STAY

⊜⊜**Chambre d'hôte La Haute Verrerie** – *rte. de St-Tropez, Le Cannet-des-Maures, 3.7mi/6km east of Le Luc by D 558.* ℘*04 94 47 95 51. 3 rooms.* 🍴 ♿ 🅿 ⛲. A lively brook flows at the foot of this charming 1839 Provençal house, once used as a glass-making workshop. The rooms, housed in several outbuildings, are each decorated in their own style. The prettiest has a solarium.

⊜⊜⊜ **Chambre d'hôte Le Hameau de Charles-Auguste** – *rte. de Baraouque.* ℘*04 94 60 79 45. 4 rooms.* 🍴 🅿 ⛲. Set within outbuildings constructed around the original 18C farmhouse, this B&B has been lovingly decorated with flea-market finds and antiques.

🍽 EAT

⊜⊜⊜ **Le Gourmandin** – *pl. Louis-Brunet.* ℘*04 94 60 85 92. www.legourmandin.com. Closed late-Aug–mid-Sept, late-Feb–early Mar, Sun and Thu evenings, Mon.* This *auberge* in the heart of the village has a convivial atmosphere and a rustic dining room. Traditional cuisine.

SHOPPING

Provençal Market – Friday mornings.
Domaine de Lauzade – *D3423 rte. de Toulon D97.* ℘*04 94 60 72 51. www.lauzade.com. Closed Sat, Sun, public holidays.* Guided tours, tastings and direct sales of Côtes-de-Provence at this small vineyard. Regular art exhibits.
Domaine de la Pardiguière – *rte. des Mayons, Fontaines aux Grives. Open by appointment.* ℘*04 94 60 75 37.* Fine views extend over the countryside from this family-run organic vineyard and olive orchard. Olives, olive oil and wine sold on-site.

Lorgues

Var

Lorgues is a small medieval town with a beautiful market square shaded by plane trees. Beyond the village are wooded hilltops, cultivated with vines and olive trees. It exudes a sense of contentment.

OLD QUARTER
A Touch of Medieval Charm

⏱*The tourist office provides a map of the village walking tour. Plaques identify principal monuments.*
The streets of Lorgues radiate from a central square. Dotted with fountains and fortified 14C gateways, these narrow alleyways are lined with attractive houses decorated with lintels and wrought-iron work.

▶ **Population:** 8,550.
⚙ **Michelin Map:** 340 N5.
ℹ **Info:** Pl. Trussy. ℘04 94 73 92 37. http://lorgues-tourisme.fr.
▶ **Location:** Lorgues is 8mi/13km southwest of Draguignan on the D 557 and D 562. The medieval town stretches along the main shopping street. The more modern, 20C buildings lie to the west.
🕐 **Timing:** Allow half a day to discover Lorgues, 1hr for the old town, and 2–3hrs for the chapels in the vicinity.

Start your tour at the 18C **Collégiale St-Martin** (rue de l'église; ⏰open 9am–6pm; ☎04 94 73 92 37). This collegiate church was built by Bishop Fleury of Fréjus, who served as Louis XV's chief minister. It is unusually large, with a dressed stone façade and a Virgin and Child attributed to Pierre Puget. Don't miss the organ and carved pulpit.

Continue along rue de la Bourgade to the 13C **Font-Couverte**, one of only two covered fountains in Europe.

EXCURSIONS
Ermitage de St-Ferréol
▶ 0.6mi/1km. Follow the signs to the northeast of the town.

This chapel stands on a low wooded hill surrounded by traces of a Roman settlement.

Chapelle Notre-Dame-de-Benva
▶ 2mi/3km northwest, rte de St-Antonin. ⏰Open Jul–Sept Thu 10am–noon, 3.30pm–5pm. ☎04 94 73 92 37.

Designed to attract those passing by, the chapel of Our Lady of Benva (a corruption of the Provençal ben vai "good journey") stands on a hillside with its porch astride the old Entrecasteaux road. It is decorated inside and outside with 15C frescoes.

Monastère Orthodoxe St-Michel
▶ 8km/5mi north by D 10 or 6mi/10km by D 77. ✎Guided tours (40min) only 10am, 2pm, 3pm, 4pm. Closed Wed afternoon, Fri morning. ☎04 94 73 75 75.

These stone buildings are home to a French Orthodox community. The crypt, refectory and church are all adorned with Romanesque and Byzantine-like frescoes.

Taradeau
▶ 5.6mi/9km – southeast on D 10. On arriving in the village, take the D 73 towards Flayosc.

A Saracen tower and a ruined Romanesque chapel crown the bluff dominating the village of Taradeau.

▶ Take D 73 north. After 0.5 mi/1km, turn right onto a stony path marked "Table d'Orientation 800m".

🔼 From the top a vast **panorama**★ unfolds over Lorgues, Les Arcs, the Provençal plain and the Grasse Pre-Alps, the Esterel and the Maures.

Abbaye du Thoronet ★★
8mi/13km southwest. From Lorgues take D 562 towards Carcès. Turn left onto D 17 and turn right onto D 79.
👓See ABBAYE du THORONET.

ADDRESSES

🛏 STAY

🍴 **Chambre d'hôte La Bergerie du Moulin** – 55 rte de la Passerelle. ☎04 94 99 91 51. www.bergeriedumoulin.com. Closed 2 weeks in Jan. 5 rooms. 🅿🚭🛏. This rustic stone residence offers air-conditioned rooms with a Provençal feel. Pool and spa-jacuzzi.

🍴 **Villa Les Pins** – 3630 rte. de St-Antonin. ☎04 94 73 91 97. www.les-pins-lorgues.fr. Closed mid-Nov–mid-Mar. 5 rooms. 🅿🚭🛏. Restaurant 🍴. This grand villa under the pines is surrounded by vineyards. Three suites with a terrace next to the pool are located in an annexe. Two other rooms, in the main building, are decorated in the same Provençal style.

🍴 EAT

🍴 **Le Chrissandier** – 18 cours de la République. ☎04 94 67 67 15. www.lechrissandier.com. Closed Tue and Wed out of season. Nestled in the old medieval quarter, this rustic-style restaurant attracts a regular clientele at lunchtime and caters for tourists in the evening. The market-fresh menu changes every day.

SHOPPING
Marché – Tuesday.

Wine – A dozen vineyards can be found around Lorgues, many offering tastings and sales of their Côtes-de-Provence and Vins de Pays du Var and d'Argens. Ask for a list at the tourist office.

Les Arcs

Var

A major staging post on the Provence Wine Route, Les Arcs sits amid leafy vineyards under the shadow of a medieval keep.

OLD TOWN

▶ From pl. de l'Église take rue de la Paix up to the keep.

The historic quarter of **Le Parage** is named after an Occitan word for the upper reaches of a village next to a keep. Admire the side chapels of the **church** in place Ferré, with their frescoes of *(left)* the miracle of St Roseline's roses *(right)* and a **polyptych**★ in 16 sections by Louis Bréa (1501).

EXCURSION
Chapelle Ste-Roseline★

▶ 2.5mi/4km east of Les Arcs by the D 91. ◷Open Feb–Dec Tue–Sun 2pm–5pm. ⊜No charge. ℘04 94 73 37 30. This rural Provençal-style Romanesque chapel outside Les Arcs was once part of the 11C Abbaye de la Celle-Roubaud. The **interior**★ features a Baroque high altar (1635) framed by a wooden altarpiece (1514). A rare Provençal rood screen surmounted by a statue of St Catherine of Alexandria closes the

---

> **Population:** 6,108.
> **Michelin Map:** 340 N5.
> **Info:** Pl. du Général-de-Gaulle. ℘04 94 73 37 30. www.mairie-les-arcs-sur-agens.fr
> **Location:** The town is located in the Var, 15.5mi/25km west of Fréjus on the R N 7 and D 57. The modern town sits below the historic quarter.

---

choir, which is furnished with finely carved stalls (17C). **Marguerite Maeght** commissioned contemporary works of art for the church, including a mosaic by **Chagall** *(right side aisle)* and a bronze low relief and lectern by **Giacometti**.

ADDRESSES

☜ STAY

⊜⊜⊜ **Le Logis du Guetteur** – *pl. du Château.* ℘04 94 99 51 10. www.logisdu guetteur.com. Closed mid-Feb–mid-Mar. 13 rooms. Restaurant ⊜⊜⊜. This hotel-restaurant is housed in a renovated medieval castle on a promontory above the village. Rooms are classically decorated; four-poster beds evoke the building's history. Gastronomic restaurant. Pool.

☖ EAT

⊜⊜⊜ **Le Relais des Moines** – *Rte. de Ste-Roseline.* ℘04 94 47 40 93. www.lerelaisdesmoines.com. Closed 1 week Jan, 3rd week Nov, Sun evening and Mon Sept–Jun. This former sheep stable built against the hillside was used by monks as a refectory. The interior features fine 16C stone arcades. Shady terrace in the grounds.

SHOPPING
Maison des Vins Côtes-de-Provence – *rte nationale 7.* ℘04 94 99 50 20. www.caveaucp.fr. This country estate along the Argens River is the headquarters of Côtes-de-Provence appellation wines, with 700 different winemakers, a modern tasting area *(free)* and a gourmet restaurant.

The Legend of Sainte Roseline

The young Ste Roseline (1263–1329) of Château de Villeneuve, daughter of Lord Arnaud de Villeneuve, would hide food in her apron to distribute to the poor. One day a palace guard stopped her and asked what she was carrying. "Roses," she replied, and when she opened her apron the roses miraculously appeared. Her body is buried in a shrine in the church. Pilgrimages take place five times a year, including Trinity Sunday and the first Sunday in August.

Draguignan
Var

Situated between the Haut Var and the Haute Provence plateau, Draguignan built its wealth on the production of honey, olive oil, cork and silk. This prosperous market town is still the hub of agricultural life in the region today.

A BIT OF HISTORY
From the Middle Ages

Draguignan grew rapidly throughout the Middle Ages. By the 15C it was the fourth-largest town in Provence. Only two of the original gates that once pierced its 13C walls, now remain (porte des Portaiguières and porte Romaine). Louis XIV ordered the keep to be razed in retribution for a conflict between local factions in 1649.

The town became the administrative centre (*préfecture*) of the Var region by order of Napoleon in 1797, a position it lost to Toulon only in 1974. Azémar and Haussmann, both prefects of Var, laid out its shady tree-lined walks and straight boulevards in the 19C.

An American cemetery to the east of the town and a memorial to the Liberation on the corner of avenue Lazare-Carnot and avenue Patrick-Rosso recall the fighting that took place here in August 1944.

The town has been home to an artillery school since 1976.

St Hermentaire and the Dragon

The name Draguignan is derived from the Latin root *draco,* meaning dragon. Legend has it that, in the 5C, pilgrims on their way from Ampus to the renowned Lérins Abbey via Lentier encountered a dragon roaming the surrounding marshes. The terrified pilgrims appealed for help from the hermit Hermentaire, who lived in the area. He slayed the dragon and built a chapel dedicated to St Michael the Archangel.

The existing church of **St-Michel**, north of place du Marché, contains an 18C statue of St Hermentaire in gilded wood.

> ▶ **Population:** 37,088.
> ⚫ **Michelin Map:** 340 N 4.
> **Info:** 2 ave. Carnot. ℘04 98 10 51 05. www. tourisme-dracenie.com. For a guided tour of the town, call Musée des Arts et Traditions populaires ℘04 94 47 05 72.
> ⚫ **Location:** Off the N 555, 18.6mi/30km northwest of Fréjus, in Var.
> 🅿 **Parking:** Allées d'Azémar car park *(first hour free)*, between the tourist office and the old town.

☜ WALKING TOUR

OLD TOWN

▷ Begin at pl. du Marché.

The rue des Marchands opens onto Old Draguignan (pedestrian district), where the 14C gates, **Porte Romaine** and **Porte des Portaiguières**, frame an intricate maze of streets lined with ornate doorways and lop-sided houses. Continue along rue de l'Observance, one of the town's oldest streets and home to the nobility and bourgeoisie in the 15C and 16C.

▷ Turn left up montée de l'Horloge.

The **clock tower** replaced the keep demolished in 1660. It has four flanking turrets and an ornate wrought-iron campanile. The **view** from the top encompasses the town and the Nartuby Valley. The tower of the grassy **amphitheatre** affords a closer view over the roofs of the old town (⚫*open Jul–Sept Tue–Sat 10am–noon, 3pm–6pm;* ⚫*closed 14 Jul, 15 Aug;* ⚫*no charge*).

▷ Double back to the rue des Tanneurs, to the porte de Portaiguières, which pierces a 15C square tower.

DRAGUIGNAN

0 — 200 m
0 — 200 yds

WHERE TO STAY	
Moulin de la Foux (Hostellerie du)	(1)
Oliviers (Les)	(2)
St-Amour (Chambre d'hôte)	(3)

WHERE TO EAT	
L'Accomedia	(1)
Musée des Arts et Traditions populaires de moyenne Provence	**M**

Don't miss the façade of the 13C synagogue in rue de la Juiverie.

◐ At the end of the street turn right to the church and the pl. du Marché.

SIGHTS
Cimetière Américain et Mémorial du Rhône

553 blvd. J.F.-Kennedy. &. ◑*Open daily 9am–5pm.* ◑*Closed 1 Jan, 25 Dec.* ✆*No charge.* ✆*04 94 68 03 62.*

The Draguignan area was the scene of fierce fighting in 1944, particularly around the village of Muy. Laid out over 12 acres/5ha of lawns are the graves of 861 American soldiers from General Patch's 7th Army. A bronze map at the foot of the memorial retraces the campaign launched on 15 August 1944 in support of the Normandy landings.
The inside of the chapel is decorated with mosaics by the American Austin Purves.

Église Notre-Dame-du-Peuple

Southwest of the old town; see map.
This chapel was originally built in the 16C in Flamboyant Gothic style and enlarged in the 19C. It contains votive offerings to the Virgin who, according to local legend, saved the town from the plague *(pilgrimage 8 Sept)*. On the north wall is the central panel of a 16C altarpiece from the Brea school.

Musée Municipal

9 rue de la République. ♿ⓄOpen Mon–Sat 9am–noon, 2pm–6pm. ⓄClosed public holidays. ⬤No charge. ℘04 98 10 26 85.

Housed in a former 17C Ursuline convent remodelled as the summer residence of the Bishop of Fréjus in the 18C, this museum is one of the oldest in France. It boasts a collection of antique furniture, sculpture, ceramics from France (Vallauris, Moustiers, Sèvres) and the Far East, and Dutch and French paintings by Rembrandt, Rubens and Van Loo. Don't miss *Rêve au coin du feu*, a sculpture by Camille Claudel (1903), the *Enfant au béguin* by Renoir and Gallo-Roman items discovered during local digs.

👥 Musée des Arts et Traditions Populaires★

15 rue Joseph-Roumanille. ⓄOpen Tue–Sat 9am–noon, 2pm–6pm, Sun and public holidays 2pm–6pm. ⓄClosed Sun, Mon and public holidays Oct–Mar. ⬤3.50€, under 18 years no charge. ℘04 94 47 05 72.

This museum has a large exposition space as well as three gardens. On display are everyday objects from the region's farming, wine growing, olive and cork, bee-keeping, sheep-rearing, and silkworm-breeding activities, as well as hunting, and arts and crafts. One gallery exhibits agricultural machinery.

Exhibitions, workshops and events are organised for children several times a year.

Musée de l'Artillerie

Ave. de la Grande-Armée, 2mi/3km east of Draguignan by blvd. J.F.-Kennedy and D 59; at the artillery school's main entrance. ⓄOpen mid-Jan–mid-Dec Sun–Wed 9am–noon, 1.30pm–5.30pm. ⓄClosed public holidays. ⬤No charge. ℘04 83 08 13 86. http://musee.artillerie.asso.fr.

The artillery school (founded in 1791) was transferred to Draguignan in 1976 and merged with the Nîmes anti-aircraft school in 1983. The museum presents the evolution of weaponry and military strategy from ancient times to the contemporary period. The ground floor holds displays of heavy arms and modern artillery, including field weapons and trench equipment.

EXCURSIONS
Pays Dracénois
Malmont Viewpoint★

◗ 3.7mi/6km – about 45min. From Draguignan take blvd. Joseph-Collomp north 4mi/6km to a pass. Turn left onto a narrow road for 330yd/300m.

The **view★** takes in large swathes of Provence, including Mont Vinaigre in the Esterel, Agay harbour, the Argens Valley, the Maures Massif and Toulon.

Musée de l'Artillerie

Trans-en-Provence

◐ *3mi/5km south of Draguignan by D 1555.*

Up to the Second World War, this lively village was known for silk spinning. The town hall, built in 1779, with its **façade** decorated in *trompe-l'œil*, is an example of 18C civilian architecture. A fine altarpiece graces the 14C St-Victor church. A path leads from place de la Mairie in front of the town hall to the **Nartuby gorge**. This outstanding **site★** is best viewed from between Pont Vieux and Pont Bertrand.

On the Chemin du Cassivet, a Puit Aérien *(look for signs on left when entering the village; the path passes under the D 555)*, or "aerial well", was designed by the Belgian engineer Knapen in 1930. The well was intended to recover moisture from the night air to water crops during the day. Designed for use in Africa, it never worked here in Trans.

Flayosc

◐ *4.3mi/7km. About 45min. From Draguignan take D 557 southwest.*

This charming Var village overlooking vineyards, olive groves and orchards has retained its 14C fortified gates. The typically Provençal **place de la Reinesse** has plane trees, a mossy fountain and a small wash house; the Romanesque **church** has a massive square bell tower.

🚗 DRIVING TOUR

GORGES DE CHÂTEAUDOUBLE★
25.4mi/41km. Allow about 1hr.

◐ Leave Draguignan on ave. de Montferrat and follow D 955.

Pierre de la Fée

This 'fairy's stone' is a fine dolmen, with a table 19.7ft/6m long, 14.7ft/4.5m wide and weighing 40t resting on three standing stones more than 6.5ft/2m high.

View of Châteaudouble

© Olivier Simon/Var Tourisme

Gorges de Châteaudouble★

This serpentine gorge was carved by the Nartuby, a tributary of the Argens.

◐ Return to Le Plan and turn right onto D 51 to the village of Châteaudouble.

Châteaudouble

This village occupies a cliff overhanging the gorge of the Nartuby by 330ft/100m. Its medieval passages are interspersed with little squares and fountains.

The Saracen Tower offers a superb **view★** over the whole village. Steep paths lead from the gorge to the prehistoric caves of Mouret, Chèvres and Chauves-Souris.

◐ From Châteaudouble drive north towards Ampus. D 51 crosses a plateau through the Bois des Prannes.

Ampus

The village church is a well-restored Romanesque building. Just behind it, a path marked by modern Stations of the Cross (1968) leads to a rocky outcrop.

◐ Return to Draguignan on D 49 for a good view of the town.

ADDRESSES

🏠 STAY

Chambre d'Hôte St-Amour – *986 rte. de la Motte, Trans-en-Provence, 3mi/5km S of Draguignan. ℰ06 81 33 43 80. www.domainedesaintamour.com. 3 rooms.* 🅿. Large, rambling grounds and an unusual swimming pool are the setting for this 18C stone house offering a self-contained flat and several rooms, each of them decorated in a distinctive style.

Hostellerie du Moulin de la Foux – *941 chemin St-Jean-de-la-Foux. 2mi/3km south on D 1555, rte de Fréjus. ℰ04 98 10 14 14. www.hotel-du-moulin-de-la-foux.com.* 🅿 ♿. *23 rooms.* ☐7€. *Restaurant* ☐. This charming hotel in an ancient olive mill has a large leafy terrace overlooking the river. Rooms are simple yet comfortable.

Hôtel Les Oliviers – *2.5mi/4km West of Draguignan by D 557 (route de Flayosc). ℰ04 94 68 25 74. www.hotel-les-oliviers.com. Closed 10-20 Jan. 12 rooms.* 🅿. ☐7€. This roadside family hotel is conveniently situated on the way to Flayosc. The rooms, all on the ground floor, are light and neatly arranged.

🍽 EAT

L'Accomedia – *13 rue des Endronnes. ℰ04 94 50 72 72. Closed last 2 wks in Aug. Booking advisable.* This Italian restaurant is located opposite the local theatre embellished with a fresco evoking the Carnival. Typical Mediterranean specialities are served in a light, modern setting.

SHOPPING

Markets – Place du Marché hosts a lively, colourful market on Wednesday and Saturday mornings; there's also a market along Allée d'Azemar.

Moulin Traditionnel "Lou Calen" – *1 rue de l'Observance. ℰ04 94 47 21 87. Open Wed and Sat, 9am–noon or by reservation by calling ℰ06 19 69 09 77.* This early 20C mill located in the hills above Draguignan presses olives from local producers using traditional stone parts. Oil can be bought directly from the owners.

Oil mill

E. Barer/ MICHELIN

Moulin du Flayosquet – *Rte. d'Ampus, Le Bastidon, Flayosc. ℰ04 94 70 41 45. Open 9am–12.30pm, 2pm–7pm. Closed Sun Jun–Aug, enquire for rest of year. Closed public holidays.* This superb 13C mill has preserved its original equipment and still uses its old water-driven mill wheel. The boutique sells a selection of regional products in addition to olive oils.

Domaine Rabiega – *516 chemin du Cros d'Aimar. ℰ04 94 68 44 22. www.rabiega. com. Closed Sun.* A beautiful property situated among the olive trees and vineyards, the domain produces 20,000 bottles of organic wines (mostly reds) per year.

GETTING AROUND

Buses – *ℰ04 94 50 94 05.* Buses serve Draguignan and the surrounding districts. Single tickets are available from bus drivers, books of tickets from the bus Point Info' at 60 boulevard Rue des Martyrs-de-la-Résistance *(closed Sat and Sun).*

Coaches will take you to Fréjus *(50min)*, St-Raphaël *(60min)*, Toulon *(120min)* and to the SNCF train station Les Arcs-Draguignan *(25min). ℰ04 94 68 15 34.*

Roquebrune-sur-Argens

Var

A labyrinth of arches and alleyways, Roquebrune-sur-Argens is perched on a rocky peak at the foot of the Rocher de Roquebrune, a popular spot for hiking and canoeing.

SIGHTS
The Village
Originally a stronghold, this *castrum* was once surrounded by a curtain wall. The wall was mostly destroyed in 1592, during the Wars of Religion, but traces of it are still visible, particularly in boulevard de la Liberté. Across from the **clock tower**, the picturesque rue des Portiques is lined with some 16C arcaded houses. The fortifications and narrow, winding streets recall Roquebrune's medieval legacy.

Église St-Pierre-St-Paul
The 16C Gothic church features an unusual 18C façade and 12C remnants *(left)* of two chapels with thick quadripartite vaulting of rectangular-shaped diagonal and transverse arches. The first chapel contains a wooden altarpiece (1557) of John the Baptist; the second houses an altarpiece from the same period depicting the Last Judgement. In the nave is a 16C altarpiece composed of carved panels depicting the Passion.

Chapelle St-Pierre

© Olivier Simon/Var Tourisme

▶ **Population:** 11,405.
🚲 **Michelin Map:** 340 O5.
ℹ️ **Information:** 12 ave. Gabriel Péri. ℘04 94 19 89 89. www.paysmeresterel.com.
◗ **Location:** The town lies 7.5mi/12km west of Fréjus on the D 8, then the D 7. From the A 8, Puget-sur-Argens exit and take the N 7 west, then left on D 7.
🅿️ **Parking:** At the foot of the village.

Maison du Patrimoine
Impasse Barbacane, off rue des Portiques. 🚹🕑*Open May–Sept daily 9am–noon, 2pm–6pm; Oct–Apr Tue–Sat 8am–noon, 1.30pm–5pm. Closed public holidays except 14 Jul, 15 Aug.* 🎫*No charge.* ℘04 98 11 36 85.
The museum houses prehistoric and Roman finds excavated in the nearby Bouverie caves, which were inhabited from 30,000 to 8,000 BC by the **Bouverian** culture unique to southeastern France. Also displayed are fine objects from the Neolithic era and a remarkable reconstruction of a roofed Roman tomb.

Chapelle St-Pierre
From Roquebrune take D 7 southeast. 🕑*Open during exhibitions.*
The chapel has a Carolingian apse but was rebuilt in the Romanesque style in the 11C, with a recessed Renaissance *enfeu* (where bodies awaiting burial were left) on the façade. A rock tomb cemetery lies to the east.

Le Muy
◗ *5mi/8km west of Roquebrune by D 7, then D N7.*
Muy's popular Sunday morning market *(smaller one Thu)* offers a wide selection of regional products. The market is held around the **church** (16C) surmounted by an elegant wrought-iron campanile. Next to the **Charles-Quint tower** *(entrance to the village from D N7),*

which hosts temporary exhibits, the **Musée de la Libération** (*9 allée Victor Hugo;* ◔*open Jul–Aug Tue–Sat 9.30am– 12.30pm, 3pm–6pm, Sun 10am–12.30pm; Apr–Jun Sun 10am–noon;* ∞*no charge*) is housed in a cramped room charged with emotion; its collection of artefacts and documents explores the airborne operation mounted on the night of 14 to 15 August around Le Muy in support of the Allied landings in Provence.

🚗 DRIVING TOUR

ROCHER DE ROQUEBRUNE
8.5mi/14km round trip. Allow 1hr. Privately owned, the Rocher is accessible only on tours organised by Le Muy tourist office. 📞*04 94 45 12 79.* ∞*6€.*

The proud silhouette of Roquebrune's rock (red sandstone) forms a small, solitary massif between the Maures and the Esterel. Its jagged silhouette dominates the lower Argens Valley.

▶ From Roquebrune-sur-Argens, take the small road to the south opposite the cemetery.

Chapelle Notre-Dame-de-Pitié
The chapel stands on rising ground amid pine and eucalyptus trees. Next to the chapel, there is a **view★** of the Argens Plain, Fréjus, St-Raphaël and the Esterel.

▶ Return to Roquebrune and turn left onto D 7. After 547yd/500m turn left; 0.6mi/1km farther on, turn left again onto a forest road.

Roquebrune Summit★
🚶 *2hr on foot round trip; a difficult walk; keep to the path.*
From the summit (alt. 1,073ft/372m), there is an extended **view★** of the Maures, Fréjus Bay and the Esterel.
At the rock's summit stand three crosses by Vernet in memory of Crucifixions painted by Giotto, Grünewald and El Greco.

▶ Drive down the southern face of Roquebrune rock and turn right onto D 25. After 0.6mi/1km, turn right along the northern face. Drive through the hamlet of La Roquette.

Chapelle Notre-Dame-de-la-Roquette
🚶 *30min on foot round trip. Park in the car park by the road and take the path on the right.*
The ruined chapel, a meeting point for local hikers, is located in an attractive **setting★** of European hackberry, chestnut and holly trees beside a rocky outcrop of red sandstone. From the terrace (alt. 470ft/143m) the **view** includes the lower Argens Valley and the Provençal tableland.

ADDRESSES

🛏 STAY

⊖⊖🛏 **Chambre d'hôte Au Bois Fleuri** – *rte de Marchandise, La Commande quarter, 5mi/8.3km north of Roquebrune-sur-Argens, towards La Bouverie.* 📞*04 94 45 42 28. www.auboisfleuri.com. 3 rooms, 2 studios.* Surrounded by dense woodland, this house decorated with larchwood furniture has two ground-floor studios with private terraces and three air-conditioned rooms upstairs.

SHOPPING

L'Amie Ailée – *19 rue Jean Aicard.* 📞*04 94 45 30 20. www.lamieailee.fr. Closed Sun.* Sale of honey, pollen, nougat and Royal Jelly.

Local markets – Mon morning on place San Peïre, Les Issambres; Fri morning on place Alfred-Perrin, in Roquebrune-Village. The Honey Fair is held at place G. Ollier first weekend Oct.

SPORT AND LEISURE

Activities – Quad-bikes, canoeing, kayaking, diving, fishing, guided nature walks, leisure parks, Zen Océane, a health outfit/spa and much more.

FRÉJUS AND THE ESTEREL MASSIF

Tucked away in the farthest corner of Provence, on the eastern edge of the Var *département*, Fréjus and the Esterel Massif may not have the "flash and cash" of Cannes to the east or St-Tropez to the west, but nevertheless impress visitors with their perched villages, natural beauty, unspoiled forests and red rock mountains framing the cobalt-blue sea. Many come to this part of the Riviera to escape the summer crowds, yet lively towns like Fréjus and St-Raphaël, as well as the convenient proximity to Nice, keep the area from feeling overly secluded. For those who enjoy sweeping panoramic views, coastal hikes, Provençal meals overlooking deep gorges, ancient history and sandy beaches, this area is ideal to explore.

Highlights

1 Attend a musical concert in Fréjus' **2C Roman arena** (p200)

2 Take a guided tour of the ancient cloisters and baptistery of Fréjus' **Groupe Episcopal** (p203)

3 Explore underwater wrecks with the diving club at the **Port-Fréjus** (p208)

4 Drive along the Corniche d'Or to the **Pic de l'Ours** (p217)

5 See the works of Dada artist Max Ernst in **Seillans** (p222)

History

Like much of the French Riviera, Fréjus and the Esterel Massif were inhabited by the Romans, invaded by Saracen pirates, cultivated by monks, discovered by 19C travellers and liberated in the Second World War when the Allies landed on its beaches. What makes this area remarkable is how many historic sites still survive.

As one of the most important settlements of the Gallo-Roman era, Fréjus is home to some of the oldest buildings in France, including the 2C Roman amphitheatre and the 5C baptistery at the Groupe Episcopal. France's colonial troops from Africa and Asia acclimatised to French weather in Fréjus in the early 20C, leaving behind colourful examples of their religious devotion, including a Buddhist pagoda and a Sudanese mosque.

Other historic treasures dating back to pre-historic times can be found at the archaeological museum in St-Raphaël.

View of the Massif de l'Esterel from the coast

J. Malburet/MICHELIN

View from the Pic du Cap-Roux

Fréjus–St-Raphäel Hub

The dynamic centre of this area is found in the twinned cities of Fréjus, known for its prestigious history dating back to the Romans, and St-Raphäel, a modern resort town that became popular during the Belle Époque. Here, approximately 85,000 residents (and visitors) benefit from the cities' combined municipal services, coordinated environmental preservation policies and complementary cultural development.

Natural Beauty

The red porphyry rocks that define the Massif de l'Esterel make this one of the most aesthetically outstanding sites on the French Riviera. It remained relatively unspoiled throughout the 19C due to the late construction of a scenic road, the Corniche d'Or, in 1903, connecting the coastline to the peaks that afford panoramic **views** over the region.

The rocky inlets, interspersed with natural sand beaches, are framed by the gently sloping mountains covered in pine, oak, heather and arbousiers (wild strawberry trees). The inland areas are crossed by rivers and lakes such as Lac de St-Cassien in Fayence and the Villepey marshes outside Fréjus. Nature lovers will find a range of outdoor activities in the region, from windsurfing and snorkeling to hiking and mountain biking.

Resort Living

Sun-seekers have a variety of sandy beaches, secluded inlets and picturesque pleasure ports to explore, particularly around Fréjus Plage and St-Raphäel's historic riverfront walk. Watersports, underwater sightseeing and boat rentals can all be arranged through the local tourist offices.

For more peace and quiet, several high-end resorts such as the Terre Blanche Resort near Tourrettes have opened inland.

Local Economy

The main economic activity of the Fréjus and Massif de l'Esterel area is tourism, like most of the French Riviera.

Fishing and the production of wine, honey, olive oil, and fruits and vegetables has continued throughout the centuries, although agriculture in general is not very significant. Visitors will also find many local artisan crafts such as the clay *santon* figurines.

FRÉJUS AND THE MASSIF DE L'ESTEREL

0 — 5 km
0 — 3 mi

Legend:
- ★★★ Highly recommended
- ★★ Recommended
- ★ Interesting
- Worth seeing

PIC DU CAP-ROUX
Mont Vinaigre
Fréjus
Seillans

ALPES – MARITIMES

NICE
ANTIBES
CANNES

Pont de Pré-Claou
Montauroux
D 37
D 562
D 562
D 56
Lac de St-Cassien
Callian
D 56
D 4
Pays de Fayence
Tourrettes
D 563
Fayence
D 19
N.-D.-des-Cyprès
Forêt St-Paul

Gorges
Roche Taillée (Roman Aqueduct)
Source
Mons
D 56
D 656
Siagnole
D 53
Seillans
D 19

Siagne
Déous

D 25
D 915
D 562

198

N

Bagnols-en-Forêt

VAR

Barrage
de Malpasset

Roquebrune-
s-Argens

N.-D.-de-
Jérusalem

Auberge
des Adrets

Mont Vinaigre
614

MASSIF DE L'ESTEREL

Ravin du
Perthus

Mal
Infernet

Col des
Lentisques
492

LA SAINTE-
BAUME

Col Belle-
Barbe

46

261

La Napoule
Théoule-s-Mer
La Galère
Pte de l'Esquillon

LESTEREL

Miramar

PIC DE L'OURS

324
Col Notre-Dame
Le Trayas
159
Col de L'Évêque
PIC DU CAP-ROUX
453

Pte de l'Observatoire

DE

Anthéor

Sémaphore du Dramont

CORNICHE

Agay

Plage
du Dramont

St-Raphaël

Fréjus

Fréjus-Plage
Golfe
de
Fréjus

St-Aygulf

Étangs
de Villepey

Les Issambres

DN 7

DN 7

D 37

D 559

D 100

D 4

D 7

D 25

D 47

Reyran

Argens

Nartuby

BRIGNOLES

2

Driving tour with departure town

Corniche de l'Esterel

Voie Aurélienne

Route du Pic de l'Ours

Pays de Fayence

Vers le Lac de St-Cassien

199

Fréjus★

Var

Lying between the Maures and Esterel massifs in the alluvial plain of the Lower Argens, this former Roman port, Saracen stronghold, medieval bourg and exotic military base stands at the historic crossroads of Provence.

▶ **Population:** 51,537.
◔ **Michelin Map:** S 340 P5.
▉ **Info:** 249 rue Jean-Jaurès.
  ✆04 94 51 83 8.
  www.frejus.fr
◖ **Location:** 3mi/5km from St-Raphaël and 12mi/19km from Ste-Maxime, between the Esterel and the Maures.
▲▲ **Kids:** Aqualand, the Capitou zoo.
◕ **Timing:** Allow 2hr for the Roman remains, 1 day for the town as a whole.

A BIT OF HISTORY
Birth and Heyday (1C BC)

Fréjus takes its name from **Forum Julii**, a trading and staging post on the **Via Aurelia** founded by Julius Caesar in 49 BC. Octavian, the future Emperor Augustus, turned the market town into an important naval base (39 BC), where he established a colony of his veteran soldiers. The prosperous city expanded until it numbered 40,000 inhabitants.

Fréjus 2,000 Years Ago
◔*See map p201.*

Fréjus was once surrounded by ramparts pierced by four gateways corresponding to two broad streets, which quartered the town in the tradition of Roman settlements. An aqueduct 25mi/40km long brought a supply of fresh water.

Roman Fréjus was, first and foremost, a port. An existing lagoon was deepened to create the port basin, which measures 54 acres/22ha (more than half the surface area of the town). Bordered by 1.2mi/2km of wharves, it was linked to the sea by a canal 32yd/30m wide and 546yd/500m long, protected from the mistral by a wall. The entrance was marked by two large symmetrical towers. At night, a chain barred access to the port.

Decline

During the long years of Roman peace, the military aspect of the port declined, and in the late 2C AD the fleet was moved away, although the port remained a lively commercial centre until the 4C. The port and canal were neglected and began to silt up. At the beginning of the 10C the town was destroyed, then occupied by the Saracens.

Amphithéâtre

© Charlier-Intartaglia/Var Tourisme

ROMAN FRÉJUS

| 0 | 200 m |
| 0 | 200 yds |

— Extant structures
······ Non-extant structures
▨ Existing streets and buildings

In 990, under Bishop Riculphe, the city rose again on a much smaller scale. The medieval town walls followed the line of rue Jean-Jaurès and rue Grisolle. Henri II turned Fréjus into a large naval base, and during the French Revolution the port was sold as a national estate.

🐾 WALKING TOURS

AN EARLY ROMAN SETTLEMENT★

▶ The Roman ruins are scattered over a large area. Allow 1.5–2hr.
🅿 Park at pl. Agricola.

From place Agricola you can see one of the two remaining towers of the **Porte des Gaules**, the old gateway through the Roman ramparts.

▶ Go down rue H. Vadon.

Amphithéâtre (Arènes)★

Rue Henri-Vadon ◷*Open Tue–Sun 9.30am–12.30pm, 2pm–6pm (until 5pm Oct–Mar).* ◷*Closed public holidays.* ⊜*phone for admission fee.* ☏*04 94 51 34 31. www.ville-frejus.fr.*
Built outside the city in the 2C, the amphitheatre could accommodate approximately 10,000 spectators. Destined primarily for the pleasure of soldiers and veterans, it was clearly built with an eye to austerity and economy. In this respect it differs from the larger amphitheatres erected in Arles and Nîmes. On the esplanade *Le Gisant* is a sculpture commemorating the Malpasset disaster, which claimed more than 420 lives (◷*see EXCURSIONS*).

▶ Take rue Joseph-Aubenas, then ave. du Théâtre Romain. A detour via rue Gustave-Bret leads to the medieval ramparts.

PRACTICAL INFORMATION

Guided tours – The Fréjus tourist office and Ministry of Culture organise **8 itineraries** *(2hr ⌖5€)* covering the old city and the Roman ruins, as well as a **special tour** of a different site or monument each month *(1hr ⌖3€)*. In partnership with the ONF (National Forests Office), the tourist office also organises **forest hikes** in the Esterel.

Fréjus'Pass – *On sale at each site.* ⌖*4.60€ (12–18 years 3.10€).* This pass allows access to the Amphithéâtre, Archaeology Museum, Notre-Dame-de-Jérusalem, Jean Cocteau Chapel and Roman Théâtre with one ticket.
Buses – *Information and tickets on Pl. Paul-Vernet.* ℘*04 94 53 78 46.* The 11 Esterel Bus lines serve Fréjus, St-Raphaël, Draguignan, and Roquebrune.

"Philippe Léotard" Roman theatre

Ave. du Théâtre-Romain. ○*Same hours as the Arènes.*
This theatre is far smaller than the amphitheatre; it consists of only the radial walls on which the arches supporting the tiers of seats once rested. It measures 92yd/84m by 66yd/60m. Inside, the orchestra pit is clearly visible, together with the stage foundations and the slot into which the curtain panel slid.

▷ Return to the top of the street, taking a right and then a left to the Aqueduct on ave. Quinzième-Corps-d'Armée.

Aqueduct

Only the pillars and ruined arcades remain of the aqueduct that channelled water 25mi/40km from Mons to Fréjus. Rising level with the ramparts, the aqueduct ran beneath the northern parapet as far as the water tower *(castellum)*, from where it was channelled into distribution conduits.
Nearby are traces of a Roman **platform**, which served as the military headquarters *(praetorium)*: offices, storerooms, lodgings and baths. To the south lay the naval dockyard.

▷ Go down ave. du Quinzième-Corps-d'Armée to pl. Paul-Vernet; turn right on rue Raynaude, then left on pl. Castelli. Across the square, take the vaulted rue du Portalet to porte d'Orée, down rue des Moulins.

The Port

The **porte d'Orée** consists of a fine archway, most likely the remains of a chamber formerly attached to the port baths. Follow the path skirting the **Butte St-Antoine** to the southern quay, where a tower known as **Augustus' Lantern** was built in the Middle Ages atop Roman ruins as a landmark for sailors entering the port. The wall marking the sea canal stretches away to the southeast.

OLD CITY

45min from place Formigé.
Walk down the rue du Beausset to the former **Episcopal Palace** (now the town hall), with its original 14C façade in pink Esterel sandstone.

▷ Return to pl. Formigé and head north along rue de Fleury.

At no. 58, the Maison du Prévôt (also called Capitou) has an interesting façade and doorway pierced into a fortified tower, now the entrance to the Groupe Episcopal (◔*see Sights opposite).* At the end of the street *(no. 92, right),* there is a doorway in green serpentine from the Maures.

▷ Turn left onto rue Jean-Jaurès, following the medieval rampart ruins.

The former 18C **town hall** *(no. 112)* features an unusual façade embellished with a curved balcony and a loggia.

▷ Take a right on rue Sleyès.

At no. 53, the doorway framed by two 17C stone atlantes is all that remains of the former mansion of Abbé Sieyès.

▶ Continue past pl. Liberté to rue Grisolle on the right.

This street follows the line of the **medieval ramparts**, with a handsome round tower *(no. 71)* and a medieval façade *(no. 84, right)*. The picturesque **passage du Portalet** connects a string of little squares leading to place Formigé.

GROUPE ÉPISCOPAL

SIGHTS
Groupe Épiscopal★★
Allow 1hr. Pl. Formigé. At the bottom of the steps, the baptistery is to the left, the cathedral to the right and the cloisters straight ahead. ◯*Open Jun–Sept daily 9am–6.30pm; Oct–May Tue–Sun 9am–noon, 2pm–5pm.* ◯*Closed public holidays.* ✆*phone for admission fee.* ✆*04 94 51 26 30. www.fréjus.fr.*

Portal
◣*Guided tours only.*
Under an ogee arch, two **door panels★** are carved in the 16C to illustrate scenes from the life of the Virgin, St Peter and St Paul, portraits and coats of arms.

Baptistery★★
◣*Guided tours only.*
This baptistery, one of the oldest baptisteries in France, is thought to date back to the 5C. Separated from the cathedral by the porch, it has an octagonal-shaped interior featuring alternate curved and rectangular niches separated by black granite columns. The columns are topped by marble capitals taken from the ancient forum.

Cathedral★
The cathedral, an early example of Provençal Gothic art, is dedicated to Our Lady and St Stephen. Some parts of the building may date back to an earlier

Cloisters of the cathedral

© Var Tourisme

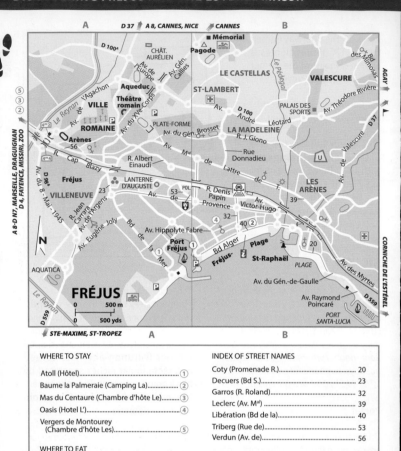

basilica. Over the apse rises the crenellated tower, which once protected the Episcopal Palace. The **choir stalls** date from the 15C and the white marble high altar from the 18C. There are also two 14C tombs; at the end of the aisle, near the tombs of the bishops of Camelin (17C), is a remarkable Renaissance crucifix in wood.

Cloisters★

The 12C–13C cloisters were intended for the chapter canons and comprised two storeys; only one upper gallery remains. The groined vaults once covering the galleries were replaced by a pinewood ceiling with exposed beams, decorated in the 14C with curious little **painted panels★** of animals, chimerae, grotesques and characters from the Apocalypse. Of the original 1,200, 400 are still visible (8min film).

Archaeological museum – (on first floor of the Cloisters; ◷open Tue–Sun 9.30am–12.30pm, 2pm–6pm, until 5pm Oct–Mar; closed public holidays; ⊜2€; ℘04 94 53 82 47). This museum presents a fine collection of Gallo-Roman antiquities recovered from local excavations. Finds include a rare Roman floor mosaic (one of the few to have survived whole), a two-headed marble bust of a faun and Hermes or Bacchus (now the city's symbol), uncovered in 1970, a head of Jupiter (1C BC) and several bronze statuettes.

Aerial view of the port

© Olivier Simon/Var Tourisme

ON THE WATER
Port-Fréjus
In 1989, after 10 years' work, Fréjus paid tribute to its long-standing maritime traditions by opening a yachting marina whose style recalls the city's Roman origins. The different areas are joined by gangways, which in summer are the scene of much colourful and lively activity.

Plages
Fréjus-Plage is a magnificent beach of fine sand running several miles from Port-Fréjus to the Pont du Pédégal. Another fine sand beach, **Plage de l'Aviation**, lies slightly farther west. Beside the sea (at blvd. de la Libération) stands a memorial recalling the sacrifice of Senegalese infantrymen (L'Armée Noire).

MILITARY HISTORY
In 1910 Fréjus resumed an active military role with the creation of the first air and sea base in France.
At the beginning of the First World War this base became a centre for colonial troops from Africa and Asia, who established a rest and recreation base here as a gentle acclimatization to the European climate. Their different cultures left a legacy of exotic buildings.

Mosquée Missiri

▷ Leave Fréjus by ave. de Verdun, then proceed towards Fayence on D 4. After 2mi/3km turn left (⊶closed to the public).

In a pine wood stands a large, dark pink Sudanese mosque, a concrete replica of the celebrated Great Mosque in the town of Djenné in Mali, built in the 1920s for **Senegalese soldiers**.

▷ Continue in the same direction, 0.6mi/1km after the bridge over the A 8 motorway.

Musée des Troupes de Marine
Route de Bagnols. ⊙*Open Jun–Sept Sun–Fri 10am–noon, 2pm–6pm; Oct–May Wed–Fri and Sun–Mon 2pm–6pm.* ⊙*Closed 24 Dec–2 Jan.* ⊸*No charge.* ℘*04 94 40 81 75. www.aamtdm.net.* This museum retraces the history of the Marine Corps since 1622. The expeditions during the great colonial period from the Second Empire (1852–70) to 1914 (Africa, Indochina, Madagascar) are re-created with arms, uniforms, pennants, dioramas, drawings and photographs. In the crypt are buried unknown marines from the Infantry Division who fell when fighting the Bavarians at Bazeilles (Ardennes) in 1870.

▷ Take ave. du Quinzième-Corps and then ave. du Général-Callies towards Nice. Turn right after the roundabout. Park in the car park between the two monuments and continue on foot.

Mémorial des Guerres en Indochine

862 ave. du Gén.-d'Armée-Jean-Calliès, via the ave. du Quinzième-Corps-d'Armée, ⊙*Open 10am–5.30pm.* ⊙*Closed 1 Jan, 1 May, 25 Dec.* ⊛*No charge.* ℘*04 94 44 42 90. www.memorial-indochine.org.*

At the foot of a hill, this imposing circular necropolis symbolically faces the sea. Since 1987, the remains of 24,000 soldiers and civilians who died in active service in former Indochina have been repatriated here. Illuminated maps and models are used to describe the historic events and battles.

Pagode Bouddhique Hông Hiên

Near the Memorial. ⊙*Open daily 10am–noon, 2pm–5pm (Apr–Oct 10am–7pm).* ⊛*2€.* ℘*04 94 53 25 29.*

Traditional Vietnamese architecture was the inspiration for this Buddhist Pagoda, built in 1917 by Vietnamese soldiers who had come to fight for France. The grounds surrounding the pagoda are planted with exotic flowers.

EXCURSIONS
Chapelle Notre-Dame-de-Jérusalem★

▷ *Ave. Nicolaï, 3mi/5km north of Fréjus by the R N 7. Park, then 5min on foot.* ⊙*Open Wed–Mon 9.30am–12.30pm, 2pm–5pm (until 6pm mid-Apr–mid-Oct). Last admission 15min before closing.* ⊙*Closed public holidays.*

This tiny chapel, situated in the Tour de Mare district, was the last building to be designed by **Jean Cocteau**. He had finalised the layout and the interior decor as early as 1961, but the chapel remained unfinished until two years after the poet's death, in 1965. The exterior mosaics were added in 1992. *The frescoes are fragile: please do not touch the walls.*

Parc Zoologique

▷ *In Capitou, 3mi/5km north of Fréjus on Ave. de Verdun (N 7), then right onto D 4 towards Fayence.* ♿⊙*Open daily Mar–May Sep–Oct 10am–5pm (until 6pm Jun–Aug); Nov–Feb 10.30am–4.30pm. Times given are last admissions, closes 1hr later.* ⊛*15.50€ (child 3–9 years 11€).* ℘*04 94 40 70 65. www.zoo-frejus.com.*

The Zoological Park covers about 49 acres/20ha in the foothills of the Esterel Massif. Walk or drive beneath the pines, oaks and olive trees and observe a variety of birds (pink flamingos, vultures and parrots) and wild animals (African elephants, zebras and lemurs). Animal shows are regularly scheduled.

Étangs de Villepey

▷ *3mi/5km. South from Fréjus take D 559 towards St-Tropez. Parking on the premises (fee charged at the entrance).*

Fed by both sea-water and fresh-water streams, these 360 acres/255ha of protected wetland, one of the rare lagoons between Marseille and Nice, include reed-beds, umbrella pine groves and brackish stretches along the N 98. More than 200 species of bird thrive here. Spring is the best time to see pink flamingos, herons and egrets.

Remains of Malpasset Dam

▷ *From Fréjus follow signs to "Nice par l'autoroute A 8". At the last roundabout before the motorway sliproad, take D 7 signposted "Barrage de Malpasset" for 3mi/5km.* 🚶 *1hr round trip.*

This arch dam was built in 1954 with a capacity of 1,730 million cubic ft/49 million cubic metres. It was intended to relieve the scarce water supplies in the Var coastal region. On the evening of 2 December 1959, torrential rains of previous weeks caused the abutments of the arch to collapse. Within 20 minutes, a 180ft/55m high wave surged through Fréjus, claiming 400 victims. A footpath goes up the Reyran Valley through sparse *garrigue* vegetation scattered with vast blocks of concrete torn off the dam.

ADDRESSES

🛏 STAY

Camping La Baume la Palmeraie – 3775 *rue des Combattants-d'Afrique du Nord. 2mi/4.5km north on D 4, rte. de Bagnols-en-Forêt.* ☏04 94 19 88 88. *www.labaume-lapalmeraie.com. Closed Oct–Mar.* This spacious camping resort features campsites set in lush surroundings with a swimming pool and 👫 playground equipment. Bungalow rentals are possible, and there is food service on-site.

Chambre d'hôte les Vergers de Montourey – *Vallée du Reyran.* ☏04 94 40 85 76. *vergers.montourey.pagesperso-orange.fr. 6 rooms.* 🅿 🍳 ⛱. This beautiful 18C farmhouse offers six good-size rooms, each named after a fruit.

Hôtel Atoll – *923 blvd. de la Mer.* ☏04 94 51 53 77. *www.atollhotel.fr. 30 rooms.* ⛱6€. Just 109yd/100m from the beach and near the marina stands this renovated hotel. Rooms are simply decorated.

Hôtel L'Oasis – *77 impasse J.-B. Charcot.* ☏04 94 51 50 44. *www.hotel-oasis.net. Closed mid-Nov–Jan. 27 rooms.* ⛱6.90€. Built in the 1950s, this hotel stands back from the promenade nestling in a quiet street in a nice neighbourhood. Family atmosphere. Pergola beneath the trees.

Hôtel L'Aréna – *139 rue du Général-de-Gaulle.* ☏04 94 17 09 40. *www.arena-hotel.com. Closed Nov. 36 rooms.* 🅿 ⛱14€. *Restaurant* ⛱⛱. This former coaching inn provides pleasant accommodation in carefully-kept rooms decorated in the Provençal style. Relax sipping your cocktail on the terrace or reclining by the pool. In the restaurant, enjoy sunny Southern food.

Chambre d'hôte Le Mas du Centaure – *1821 chemin du Gabron, Puget Sur Argens, 4.3mi/7km northwest of Fréjus.* ☏04 94 81 58 25. *4 rooms (reduced rates for children).* ⛱. *Closed 2 weeks in Sept or Oct, and mid-Dec–Jan.* Set in stunning natural surroundings, this lodging features rooms that are elegantly decorated and well equipped. Separate room for children. Swimming pool and private terrace.

🍴 EAT

Grand Café de l'Estérel – *14 pl. Agricola.* ☏04 94 51 50 50. *www.grand-cafe-esterel.com. Closed Sun.* A convivial and popular brasserie with a single menu offered at rock-bottom prices, renewed every day for lunchtime diners.

Les Micocouliers – *34 pl. Paul-Albert Février.* ☏04 94 52 16 52. *Closed Mon Nov–Mar.* This restaurant set up on the square opposite the Groupe Episcopal has a summer terrace. Inside, the brightly coloured tablecloths and rustic-style decoration blend in well with the owner's Provençal cooking.

Autres Ray'Son – *37 quai Marc Antoine.* ☏04 94 17 11 21. *www.autresrayson.com. Closed Mon except Jul–Aug. Reservations required.* Traditional yet creative French cuisine is served at this restaurant situated right on the quay.

L'Amandier – *19 rue Marc-Antoine Desaugiers.* ☏04 94 53 48 77. *Closed Mon lunch, Wed lunch, Sun.* This restaurant is located along a pedestrianised street, close to the town hall. Charming welcome and tasty and carefully prepared cuisine are the draws.

Le Mérou Ardent – *157 blvd. de la Libération.* ☏04 94 17 30 58. *Closed Sat, Mon, Thu lunches in season, Wed–Thu off season. Restaurant* ⛱–⛱⛱. This small restaurant with a nautical decor is located on the beachfront boulevard. Here, you'll find good service, as well as fish specialities.

Le Poivrier – *52 pl. Paul-Albert Février.* ☏04 94 52 28 50. *Closed Nov, Sun, Mon.* The tasty homemade cuisine at Le Poivrier is a mix of Mediterranean tradition and a pinch of exotica, served in a small, vaulted cellar going back to Roman times. There's also a summer terrace.

SHOPPING

Fréjus Markets – Held on Wednesday and Saturday in the old quarter; Sunday on blvd. d'Alger and blvd. de la Libération; Tuesday and Friday on pl. de la République (Fréjus-Plage), pl. de la Poste (St-Aygulf); Thursday at the Tour de Marre; and Saturday at Les Arènes.

LEISURE ACTIVITIES

CIP Port Fréjus – *Aire de Carénage, Port Fréjus Est.* ℘04 94 52 34 99. *www.cip-frejus.com.* This deep-sea diving centre for both beginners and experienced swimmers will take you round the shipwrecks of the Var coastline.

♣♣ Aqualand – *559 RN 98, Le Capou.* ℘04 94 51 82 51. *www.aqualand.fr. Closed Sept–mid-Jun.* ⊚25€ *(child 3–12 years, 18.50€).* Watersports enthusiasts will love this theme park, with its amazing waterslides, *Rapid Rafting* and *White Hole*, and its swimming pool with waves (the biggest in Europe). There's a miniature golf course, too.

Marina – *Capitainerie/Harbour Authority.* ℘04 94 82 63 00. *www.port-frejus.fr.* The 722ft/220m pier can accommodate more than 750 boats.

♣♣ Base Nature – *1196 blvd. de la Mer.* ℘04 94 51 91 10. *www.base.nature.free.fr. Open 6am–11pm.* This nature park welcomes hikers, cyclists (198 acres/80ha) as well as swimmers and sun-bathers to more than a 1mi/2km stretch of beach. Additional activities include sand-yachting, flying kites, playing boules and roller-skating.

CALENDAR

Bravade Saint-François – The third Sunday after Easter, a traditional religious procession winds through the historic centre of town.

Fête du Raisin – This festival is a celebration of the first wine grapes, harvested the first week in August. Enjoy wine tasting from the local producers on Pl. Formigé.

St-Raphaël★

Var

Situated on one of the last slopes of the Esterel, St-Raphaël lies on the eastern fringes of Fréjus Bay. Its sheltered beach and lively seafront make it a popular choice for sun-seekers. A former Roman trading post, it boasts a collection of ancient artefacts among the finest on the Riviera.

A BIT OF HISTORY
Origins

St-Raphaël, like Fréjus, is a daughter of Rome. A Gallo-Roman holiday resort stood on the site now occupied by the large **casino**, built on terraces with mosaics, thermal baths and a *vivarium* (fish reserve), where rich Romans came to enjoy the sea air.

In the Middle Ages the villas were plundered by Saracen pirates. After their expulsion by the Count of Provence at end of the 10C, the land was given to the monks of Lérins. The village that grew up around their monastery was subsequently handed to the Knights Templar in the 12C.

During the 18C, the old town was occupied by fishermen and peasants.

▶ **Population:** 33,084.

⬡ **Michelin Map:** 340 P5; region map: pp198–199.

🈂 **Info:** quai Albert 1er. ℘04 94 19 52 52. www.saint-raphael.com

▶ **Location:** St-Raphaël stretches along the Esterel coast for 21mi/35km.

♣♣ **Kids:** École de Cirque in Cap Esterel Village.

🕓 **Timing:** One day for the town and coastline.

Malaria made the town's inhabitants anemic, earning them the nickname *visages pâles* or "pale faces". After Corsica became part of France in 1768, the port became the terminus for a short-lived sealink with the island.

Bonaparte in St-Raphaël

On 9 October 1799, the small village was suddenly thrust into the limelight when Bonaparte, returning from Egypt, landed there after a voyage of 48 days (a pyramid standing in Avenue Commandant-Guilbaud commemorates this event). In 1814 St-Raphaël received

D 98ᶜ — FRÉJUS — VALESCURE D 37

ST-RAPHAËL

WHERE TO STAY	
Bellevue (Hôtel)	①
Douce Quiétude (Camping)	②
Les Roches Rouges	③
Provençal (Hôtel)	④
Santa Lucia (Hôtel)	⑤

WHERE TO EAT	
Sirocco (Le)	①
Sud (Le)	②

Napoleon once again, this time as a defeated man leaving for exile on the island of Elba.

Popular Resort

Alphonse Karr (1808-90) was an extravagant personality, who used his talents as a journalist and pamphleteer to oppose Napoleon III from Nice, where he was in exile. He settled in St-Raphaël in 1864, in a villa saucily named "Maison Close". Writing to a Parisian friend, he said: "Leave Paris and plant your stick in my garden: the next morning, when you awake, you will see that it has grown roses." Writers and artists responded to his invitation, including Alexandre Dumas, Maupassant, Berlioz and Gounod.

The local mayor and civil engineer **Félix Martin** followed Karr's lead and transformed the village into a smart resort, encouraging building, and linking St-Raphaël with Hyères by means of a small railway along the coast. Illustrious guests marked their stay in St-Raphaël with works of art: Gounod composed *Roméo et Juliette* in 1869, Scott Fitzgerald wrote *Tender is the Night* and Félix Ziem painted here.

St-Raphaël harbour

© Wadey James/Apa Publications

THE TOWN CENTRE

The original town centre consists of an important and somewhat rare collection of seaside architecture dating from the beginning of the Third Republic (in the late 19C).

Seafront

The bustling waterfront by the old harbour is lined with cafés and shops along the cours Jean-Bart and quai Albert-Ier. From beneath the palms and plane trees of promenade René-Coty and avenue du Général-de-Gaulle is a fine **view** of the sea and the twin rocks known as the "Land Lion" and the "Sea Lion".

Jardin Bonaparte

Above the car park, a landscaped **belvedere★** garden overlooks the bay. Accessed via a concrete gangway, the garden feels like a firmly anchored liner. It is also accessible via steps from the car park. Admire the azur blue of the Mediterranean and the fishing port below.

Villas

The rehabilitation of the residential district between the promenade René-Coty and the rue Alphonse Karr led to the demolition of a number of villas and Normandy-style houses.
Among the exotically decorated historic villa façades to survive are the **Villa Roquerousse** (1900) on the promenade René-Coty with its lavish ornamentation. Along Boulevard Félix-Martin are the charming oriental **Villa Sémiramis**, **Villa Pâquerettes** decorated with ceramic and a little farther, on avenue du Touring-Club, the shadow of Gounod still haunts the **Oustelet dou Capelan** ("The Priest's House" in Provençal). Both Plateau Notre-Dame and St-Sébastien hill are filled with remarkable villas.

Notre-Dame-de-la-Victoire-de-Lépante

This **church**, in neo-Byzantine style, was designed in 1883 by **Pierre Aublé**, the architect of many of St-Raphaël's villas. Built from pink Esterel sandstone, it is topped by a Byzantine-style dome, raising the height of the interior to 115ft/35m. The vault of the choir is decorated with Eastern-style paintings recalling the frescoes of St Sophia basilica in Istanbul.

QUARTIER DE VALESCURE

This district was once much patronised by international visitors. With advice from Charles Garnier, Carvalho, director of the Paris Opera in 1880, laid out a park adorned with vestiges from the Palais des Tuileries in Paris, including a fountain at the crossroads of rue Allongue and rue Maréchal-Leclerc.

Musée archéologique-Église St-Rafèu★

ⓒ*Open Tue–Sat 9am–12pm, 2pm–6pm.* ⓒ*Closed public holidays.* ⊜*No charge. www.saint-raphael.com.*
Situated at the crossroads between major land (Via Aurelia) and sea routes between Massalia (modern–day Marseille) and the trading posts of the Western Mediterranean, St-Raphaël enjoys an incredibly rich archaeological history. This museum houses an extensive collection of **amphorae★** uncovered from Roman ships wrecked in the bay 5C BC to 5C AD, completed by a display on the evolution of scuba diving equipment, maritime archaeology and underwater photography.

The collection also includes finds from local Prehistoric sites, from the Palaeolithic era to the Bronze Age, and an introduction to Var's many dolmens and menhirs. The museum garden (and stretches of rue Allongue) feature vestiges of the town's former ramparts.

Standing within the museum grounds, the **medieval church★** is built on a site occupied for over 2000 years. A visit to its crypts reveal, to spectacular effect, how archaeologists have unearthed each progressive layer. Many of the funeral and architectural artefacts found during **excavations** on this site are on display in the sacristy, including religious objects and low-reliefs. Built in the 12C in the Romanesque-Provençal style, the church, which has a single nave, served as a fortress and a refuge for the population during pirate attacks. In one of the side chapels, a red sandstone pagan monolith supports the altar table. The gilded wooden bust of St Peter is carried by the fishermen in procession to the Sea Lion in August.

From the 14C fortified tower, there is a wonderful **view★** over the sea, the Fréjus St-Raphaël bay, the Esterel massif and its rocky red rhyolite spurs.

The resort is dominated by the marvellous red porphyry slopes of the **Rastel d'Agay**, bordering by far the finest natural harbour of the Esterel. The main beach with its seasports centre stretches

Trips and Tours

Guided Tours – Discover St-Raphaël's heritage, every Thursday 10am. ⊜*2.30€.* For information contact the tourist office, ☎*04 94 19 52 52.*

Nature Walks – The tourist office can also organise nature walks along the coastal footpaths or in the Esterel hills, in partnership with the Office National des Forêts.

Boat Trips – ☎*04 94 95 17 46. www.tmr-saintraphael.com.* Departures from the old port (gare maritime) to St-Tropez Jul–Aug 9.30am, 11.30am, 2.30pm, 5pm (and 7pm mid-Jul–late Aug); mid-Apr–early Jun 9.30am (except Sun), 2.30pm; mid-Jun early Oct 9.30am, 2.30pm. 15€ round trip (2–9 yrs 10€). Excursions also available in the Esterel and Îles de Lérins. The Agay boat offers underwater views.

out to the left to a small jetty, beyond which lies the town's most popular beach, appreciated for its shade.

Anthéor

This smart little resort nestles beneath the peaks of Cap Roux. Anthéor-Plage lies along the western approaches to the town, while rocky inlets dot the eastern coastline.

Le Trayas

The coastline that runs along the foot of the Esterel massif is fringed with creeks and rocky inlets at the foot of which lie the occasional sand beach. Le Trayas was a major tuna fishing port in the 17C, when nets were cast into the open sea and left in place for four months. A tower was built on the shoreline to watch over them.

🚶*20min round trip.* Part of the village sits on a steep slope. Walk along the street bordered with villas and follow the signs for "Gare SNCF" to access the belvedere with a stunning **panorama★**.

ADDRESSES

🛏 STAY

🏕 **Camping Douce Quiétude** – *3435 Blvd J.-Baudino. 2mi/3km via northeast exit towards Valescure.* ♿ *℘04 94 44 30 00. www.douce-quietude.com. Closed mid-Oct–late Mar. Reservations required. 400 pitches.* Take a siesta under the shady pine trees before heading to the beach just minutes from this campsite reserved for caravans. Joint activities for children and parents; mini-club for children 6 years and older. Chalet and mobile home rental.

🏨 **Hôtel Bellevue** – *22 blvd Félix-Martin. ℘04 94 19 90 10. ⌁6€* 🅿. This modest hotel enjoys a central location close to the casino and the beach. Simply decorated rooms come with air-conditioning and double-glazing. Affordable rates for the resort.

🏨 **Hôtel Provençal** – *197 Rue de la Garonne. ℘04 98 11 80 00. www.hotel-provencal.com. Apartments with 3 beds. ⌁8€.* Located slightly away from the busy port, this entirely renovated building contains modern, functional rooms with good soundproofing.

🏨 **Hôtel Santa Lucia** – *418 Route de la Corniche. ℘04 94 95 23 00. www.hotelsantalucia.fr. Closed 21 Dec–mid-Feb. 12 rooms. ⌁. 🅿.* In this beautiful, recently renovated hotel, each guestroom re-creates the atmosphere of a different country (England, Morocco, Italy, Japan and others). Choose one at the back, overlooking the sea. There's a heated Jacuzzi on-site.

🏨 **Hôtel Les Roches Rouges** – *90 blvd. de la 36e Division-Texas, 83530 Agay, 3.7mi/6km east along D 559. ℘04 94 95 25 60. www.roches-rouges.fr. 🅿 (10€/night). 50 rooms. ⌁11€. Closed mid-Nov–mid-Feb.* At this authentic seaside hotel, most rooms look out towards the Îles d'Or. There's an outdoor swimming pool with a solarium and an edgeless sea-water pool set into the rocks on the shore. Access to the beach.

🍽 EAT

🍴 **Le Sirocco** – *35 quai Albert-1er. ℘04 94 95 39 99. www.lesirocco.fr. Closed mid-Dec–mid-Jan. Reservations recommended.* The hot dry Sahara wind may guide you towards this restaurant. Located for the past 20 years opposite the old harbour, it has consistently served tasty cuisine with a seaside flavour. Carefully laid tables, small summer terrace in front. Seaside atmosphere.

🍴 **Le Sud** – *16 Blvd. Darby. ℘04 94 44 67 86. Closed 22 Dec–5 Jan, Tue–Wed except Jul–Aug, Sat–Tue lunches.* 🅿. Located in an open-air shopping centre, this sunny restaurant is decorated with paintings and old photographs. The terrace is surrounded by a garden. Appetising, trendy Provençal menu.

ON THE TOWN

Casino de St-Raphaël – *Sq. Gand. ℘04 98 11 17 77. www.lucienbarriere.com/fr/casino/st-raphael/accueil.html. Open summer daily 10am–3am (Sat 4am).* ♿ 🅿. This casino was built in 1881 on the site of a Roman villa. It contains more than 150 slot machines and traditional games.

SPORT AND LEISURE

Golf de Valesscure – *765 ave. des Golfs. ℘04 94 82 40 46. Open Jul–Aug 8am–8pm; May–Jun, Sept–Oct 8am–7pm; Nov–Apr 8am–6pm.* This beautiful 18-hole golf course also boasts a restaurant located in a charming house, a hotel and a bar.

École de Cirque – *Cap Esterel Village. ℘04 94 82 50 11. Open Mon–Fri 9am–noon, 4pm–6pm. Closed early Jan–early Feb and early Nov–mid-Dec.* Circus training (trapeze, juggling, large or small trampoline, acrobatics, etc.) for children ages 6-12. Flying trapeze for adults and teenagers over 13 years of age. Individual classes or courses.

EVENTS

Les fêtes de la Lumière – In December there's a street theatre, skating rink and Christmas market.

Viva Mimosa – Second week in Feb. Procession of floral floats Sun afternoon.

Compétition de Jazz – Three days in July.

Massif de l'Esterel★★★

Var

Carpeted with pines and holm oaks, the slopes of the Esterel between St-Raphaël and La Napoule plunge steeply down to the sea. The contrast between the hustle and bustle of coastline and the seclusion of the inland roads will come as a welcome respite for nature lovers.

A BIT OF HISTORY
The Massif

Separated from its neighbour the Maures by the Argens Valley, the Esterel has been worn down by erosion. Its highest point, Mont Vinaigre, stands at an altitude of just 2,027ft/618m. However, the deep ravines and broken skyline of this mountain range dispel any impression of a mere succession of hills.

The Esterel is made up of volcanic rocks (porphyry), which give the range its characteristic profile, harsh relief and vivid red tints. Agay is the place where the Romans found the blue porphyry particular to their Provençal monuments.

Via Aurelia

The Esterel was bordered to the north by the Via Aurelia (Aurelian Way), one of the most important routes of the Roman empire, connecting Rome and Arles via Genoa, Cimiez, Antibes, Fréjus and Aix. Paved, cambered and more than 8ft/2.5m wide, the road made use of many bridges and other civil engineering structures to create the shortest route possible.

RESORTS

Stretching more than 18.6mi/30km between St-Raphaël and La Napoule, the striking landscape of the Corniche de l'Esterel is punctuated by several pleasant seaside resorts such as Boulouris and Agay.

- **Michelin Map:** 340 P/Q5.
- **Info:** Théoule-sur-Mer Tourist Office, 1 corniche d'Or, Théoule-sur-Mer. 04 93 49 28 28. www.theoule-sur-mer.org.
- **Location:** The Esterel stretches along the coastline of Var between Cannes and Fréjus, and encompasses several small villages and resorts such as St-Raphaël.
- **Parking:** Except in high season around the major towns, free parking is relatively easy to find near hiking trailheads. It is advisable to remove all valuables from your car when hiking.
- **Don't Miss:** The panoramic view from the Pointe de l'Esquillon, the scenic port in Agay, and for experienced hikers, the views from the Pic de l'Ours.
- **Timing:** You could easily drive through the Esterel along N 98 coastal road from Cannes to Fréjus in less than an hour, with a pause for a short hike at Dramont or the Point d'Esquillon. For the longer hikes, plan for at least a half day and be prepared by taking enough drinking water, food and appropriate footwear.

Boulouris

This small resort, where villas are scattered among pines in beautiful gardens, has several modest beaches and a harbour.

Agay

This resort borders a deep port, the finest in the Esterel, which was once used by the Ligurians, the Greeks and the

213

Agay Viaduct

S. Sauvignier / MICHELIN

Romans. The scenic bay of the **Rastel d'Agay** is lined by a large, sunny beach.

Anthéor
&see St-Raphaël.

Le Trayas
&see St-Raphaël.

Miramar
This elegant resort, with its private harbour, lies in **Figueirette Bay**. In January 1942, the British Special Operations Executive landed its first officer, Peter Churchill, at Miramar to make contact with the *Carte* Maquis network and the French Resistance.

La Galère
Built on the wooded slopes of the Esterel, this resort forms the western limit of La Napoule Bay. Below the road, the seaside development of **Port-la-Galère** *(private port)*, an astonishing design by the architect Jacques Couelle, seems to merge with its rocky environment.

Théoule-sur-Mer
Sheltered by the Théoule promontory, this resort has three small public beaches popular with line fishermen and accessible from the pedestrianised **promenade André-Pradeyrol**. The town's villas blend perfectly with their surroundings, which include a crenel-

Antoine de St-Exupéry

Born in Lyon in 1900, Antoine de St-Exupéry attended the Jesuits College and completed his education in Fribourg, Switzerland. Interested in flying from an early age, he joined the French Army Air Force in 1921, but resigned five years later to become a civilian pilot. He began writing in 1928.

His second novel, *Vol de Nuit,* was awarded a prize by the French Academy in 1931. However, the book for which he will always be fondly remembered is *Le Petit Prince* (1943), a charming fable for children. In the Second World War, he served as an instructor and carried out reconnaissance flights. On 31 July 1944, he set out for the Alps on one of these assignments but never returned.

A few days later, he was officially reported missing. His body was never recovered from the ocean waters, but the remains of his Lockheed Lightning P-38 were discovered off the coast of Marseille in 2004.

The Kingdom of Auguste I

The **Île d'Or** is a small red porphyry island off Dramont beach, marked by a strange tower that appears to grow out of the rock. This Medieval-style tower was built in 1897 by an eccentric Parisian doctor, Auguste Lutaud, who transformed the island into his own private kingdom, proclaiming himself King Auguste I of the Île d'Or.

He became the darling of fashionable Riviera society and organised lavish receptions during the Belle Époque. The monarch died in 1925. His island remains private property.

lated building flanked by two turrets. A soap factory in the 18C, it has now been transformed into a private château.

The **pointe de l'Aiguille** *départemental* park offers 17 acres/7ha of creeks and rocky inlets, with stunning **views** for hikers from its highest reaches.

🚗 DRIVING TOURS

1 CORNICHE DE L'ESTEREL★★★
25mi/40km. Allow about 4hr.

▶ From St-Raphaël (*see ST-RAPHAËL*), take D 559 south.

The road skirts the St-Raphaël marina. On the seafront is a memorial to the French Army campaigns in Africa.

▶ Drive through Boulouris to the D 559.

Plage du Dramont
See ST-RAPHAËL.

A **stele** erected to the right of the road commemorates the landing of the US Army, 36th Division, on 15 August 1944. Running alongside the Camp-Long beach and Dramont Forest, the road leads to the resorts of Agay and Anthéor. Shortly before reaching the Pointe de l'Observatoire, admire the **view** to the left, encompassing the red rocks of St-Barthélemy and Cap Roux.

Pointe de l'Observatoire★
The ruins of a blockhouse command a stunning **view**★ of the blood-red porphyry rocks against the cobalt

blue of the sea, and **views** of Anthéor, Cap Roux and Esquillon Points and La Napoule Bay.

▶ Drive through Le Trayas. On a bend near the Hôtel Tour de L'Esquillon in Miramar, pull off the road into the car park. A path (signed) leads up to Pointe de l'Esquillon.

Pointe de l'Esquillon★★
🚶 *15min round trip.*

A beautiful **panorama**★★ *(viewing table)* of the Esterel heights, the coast, Cap Roux, the Îles de Lérins and Cap d'Antibes is afforded. After La Galère, the road skirts Pointe de l'Aiguille, opening up a **view**★ of La Napoule Bay, Cannes, the Îles de Lérins and Cap d'Antibes.

Théoule-sur-mer
see RESORTS above.

2 VIA AURELIA★
20.5mi/33km from Théoule-sur-Mer to St-Raphaël. Allow about 5hr. Most of this route runs through woodland.

The ancient Via Aurelia *(camin aurélian in Provençal)*, one of the most important roads in the Roman Empire, skirted the Esterel to the north. At the end of each Roman mile (1,617yd/1,478m), distances would be indicated by a tall milestone, one of which is on display in St-Raphaël (Musée Archéologique).

Riders used the milestones as steps to mount their horses. Imperial messengers benefited from a string of posthouses along the road to catch up on their sleep, change horses and make repairs.

Théoule-sur-mer
see RESORTS above.

▶ Leave Théoule-sur-mer by the D 6098 then turn left at the Balcon d'Azur roundabout, left again at the San Peyre roundabout, then left on entering the D 6007 (number changes to N7 once in Var).

Auberge des Adrets
Dating from 1653, this coaching inn was the favourite haunt of the notorious 18C highwayman **Gaspard de Besse**. He also spent time in a cave on Mont Vinaigre, which the road hugs after the Logis-de-Paris crossroads.

This smart highwayman, dressed in red with silver buttons, robbed stage-coaches and postriders, helped by his loyal band of accomplices. He ended his career by being broken on the wheel on place d'Aix in 1781, at the age of 24. His head was nailed to a tree on the Via Aurelia, the scene of many of his exploits.

▶ At carrefour du Testannier, turn left onto a road marked "Forêt Domaniale de l'Esterel". At the Maison Forestière du Malpey, follow signs to Mont Vinaigre.

Mont Vinaigre★★
🚶 *30min round trip.*

A path leads to the top of the mountain (2,027ft/618m) which offers a splendid **panorama★★** on all sides: along the coast to Cap d'Antibes, Pointe de la Croisette, Cannes and La Napoule Bay, Pic de l'Ours with its tower and TV mast, Pic du Cap-Roux and Fréjus Bay, and inland across to the Massif des Maures, the Argens Valley, the limestone hills of Inland Provence and the southern tip of the St-Cassien lake. The Italian Alps and on the other side, Ste-Baume, are visible on a clear day.

This imposing setting would have been even more awe-inspiring in previous centuries when it was teeming with highwaymen such as Gaspard de Besse, who haunted the route de l'Esterel towards Italy. For many years, the phrase "to pass the Esterel pass" was used to describe any action involving a high degree of risk. The most dangerous spot was near Mont Vinaigre. Starting out from the D N7 to the Logis-de-Paris crossroads, the road passes in front of the Maison Forestière du Malpey (Provençal for "bad mountain").

Taking this route on foot, as the naturalist de Saussure did in 1787, took a lot of courage. Until the end of the 19C, the Esterel was still a perfect hideout for galley slaves escaping from the penal colony in Toulon.

Visiting the Massif

- Roads marked as "RF" on the map are open to traffic under certain conditions: speed limited to 25mph/40kph, no vehicles weighing over 3.5t and no traffic between 9pm and 6am. The roads marked with a red dotted line are closed to public traffic, but pedestrian access is possible.
- During periods of high fire risk, the ALARME plan is put into action and some roads may be closed to vehicles. Hikers are advised to avoid such areas.
- Camping is prohibited throughout the massif.
- When walking in the massif, respect plants and wild animals, do not litter the grounds, stay on the paths and keep dogs under control. Mountain bikers must not stray from the signposted paths and tracks laid out in the forests.
- For up-to-date information concerning the massif, call ☎04 98 10 55 41.

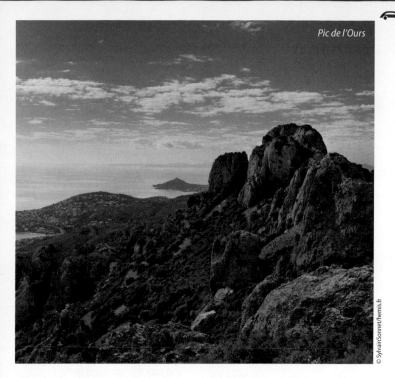

Pic de l'Ours

© SylvainSonnet/hemis.fr

▷ Return to the N 7.

At a bend, there is a **view** on the right towards the limestone plateau of Inland Provence as it passes into the Fayence region; the road then follows the Moure Valley. The original Via Aurelia followed the line of the forest road on the opposite bank.

Fréjus★
See FRÉJUS.

▷ Return to St-Raphaël by blvd. S.-Decuers.

③ PIC DE L'OURS★★
35.4mi/57km along steep, narrow roads that are not always surfaced. Allow one day.

▷ From St-Raphaël take D 559 southeast. Leaving Agay, take the Valesscure road and bear right towards Pic de l'Ours. Pass over the ford after the Maison Forestière du Gratadis, leave the Anthéor plateau on

the right and take the route du Pic de l'Ours (Moutrefrey crossroads).

The road climbs to the summit past holm oaks, barren land and red rocks, with the Mal Infernet ravine in the distance. It winds around the northern peaks of St-Pilon and Cap-Roux to reach the Col de l'Évêque and then Col des Lentisques *(one-way traffic between the two passes: take the road to the east of the peak on the outward journey, and the interior road on the way back),* with glimpses of the sea.

Pic d'Aurelle★★
1hr round trip by a marked path starting from Col des Lentisques.
The Aurelle is one of the major peaks in the Esterel coastal chain. From the top (1,060ft/323m) a fine **panorama★★** takes in the area running from Cap d'Antibes to the Pointe de l'Observatoire. *(You can take the car again before continuing.)*
The stretch between Col des Lentisques and Col Notre-Dame is one of the most beautiful drives in the Esterel, with

bird's-eye views★ of the Corniche de l'Esterel. From Col Notre-Dame (1,060ft/ 323m), a remarkable **panorama** extends over Cannes and La Napoule Bay.

Pic de l'Ours★★★

🚶 *1.5hr round trip.* 🅿 *Car park at Col Notre-Dame.*

The series of hairpin bends *(forbidden to private vehicles)* by which the path reaches the summit affords constantly changing **views** of the wooded ranges of the Esterel and coastline. The remarkable **panorama**★★★ from the summit (1,614ft/492m), where there is a television transmitting station, includes the coast and the Var countryside.

Beyond Col Notre-Dame, the road to the Col des Trois-Termes is forbidden to vehicles, but it is possible to continue to the Col de la Cadière on foot, where the **view**★ opens to the north and northeast towards La Napoule and the Massif du Tanneron.

▶ Return to St-Raphaël on D 559.

④ **ROUTE DU PERTHUS**★

12.4mi/20km. Allow 3hr. ♿ *See map below.*

▶ Leave St-Raphaël by D 559 south, as far as the Maison Forestière de Gratadis, then turn left towards the Col de Belle-Barbe. Parking at the pass. Vehicles are forbidden beyond this point.

Ravin du Mal Infernet★

🚶 *2hr round trip.*

Follow the footpath leading into the wooded ravine of Mal Infernet, a majestic setting overlooked by many jagged rocks. The path goes as far as the Lac de l'Écureuil. Seasoned hikers can continue on foot as far as Col Notre-Dame (an additional 1.8mi/3km) by skirting around the Pic and Dent de l'Ours to the north.

▶ Return to Col de Belle-Barbe. Take the road heading northwest. Leave the car in the Col du Mistral car park and take the left-hand path.

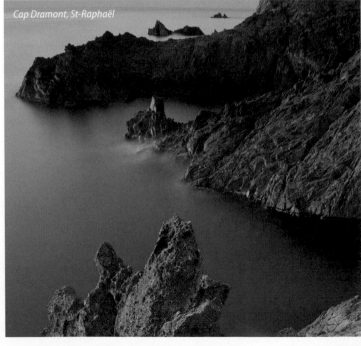
Cap Dramont, St-Raphaël

© M. Cavalier / hemis.fr

Ravin du Perthus★
🚶 *1.5hr.*

The road skirts the Perthus summits to the south. At Pont du Perthus an unmarked footpath leads into the Perthus ravine to the north. It offers a pretty setting for some easy hikes before the foothills of Mont Vinaigre. To the right stands the western **Pic du Perthus** (887ft/266m), with its scarlet porphyry rocks towering above the forest.

◐ Return to the car park at Col du Mistral by the same path and head towards Valescure and St-Raphaël by the Col de Belle-Barbe on D 100 and D 37.

⑤ SÉMAPHORE DU DRAMONT★★
🚶 *1hr round trip; the path is paved and signposted. Heading out of Dramont on the D 559, turn right immediately after the Dramont campsite. 110yd/100m farther, leave the car and take the path to the signal station.*

From below the signal station there is a **panorama★★** to the southwest of the Maures, the two porphyry rocks guarding the entrance to the Gulf of Fréjus *(Lion de Mer and Lion de Terre)*, and Île d'Or with its tower. To the north lies Mont Vinaigre; slightly to the right, behind the Rastel d'Agay, the rocks of the Cap-Roux massif and the Pic de l'Ours; to the right, the Agay natural harbour. Go back down via the signposted path *(on right)* leading to the port.

⑥ PIC DU CAP-ROUX ★★★
🚶 *2hr round trip from the Ste-Baume car park. You can reach the car park from St-Raphaël by taking tour ③ by D 559 and the forest road.*

The footpath leads to the Cap-Roux pass. From the summit (1,486ft/453m), there is a superb **panorama★★★**. Continue straight on with views of the Col de l'Evêque and out to sea to the Lérins Islands. The path descends to the refreshing **Sainte-Baume spring**.

🍃 Hiking Map 🍃

The ONF (National Forests Office) has a trail guide and hiking map available for sale at local tourist offices. 🔖 *www.onf.fr.*

⑦ LA SAINTE-BAUME★★★
🚶 *5.5hr round trip from the Ste-Baume car park.*

This longer, steeper version of the previous walk leads to the **Col du Saint-Pilon**. As you hike amid wild rosemary bushes, the view from the clifftop path unfolds: on the right the Cabrier rock and below, St-Barthélemy rock. The path follows the coastline on a deceptively sloping trail, crossing the railway line and road *(RN 98)* at the **pointe Maubois**. After the railway tunnel, continue to the Col de la Baisse-Martin and **Col du Cardinal**. Then it's all downhill. At the bottom is the delightful spring.

ADDRESSES

🏨 STAY

🍃🍃🍃 **France-Soleil** – *206 ave. des Pléiades, Agay. ☎04 94 82 01 93. Closed Nov–Easter. 18 rooms.* 🅿. This modest, family-run hotel has basic rooms spread out over three buildings, most overlooking the sea.

🍃🍃🍃🍃 **Miramar Beach** – *47 ave. Miramar. ☎04 93 75 05 05. www.tiara-hotels.com. 55 rooms.* 🅿. ⊇*19€.* This charming hotel is nestled in a red rock cove. Refined Provençal-style rooms and Oriental spa. Panoramic restaurant with summer terrace service.

OUTDOOR ACTIVITIES

Découverte de l'Esterel – *281 r. du 11-Novembre-1943. ☎06 09 09 73 90. www.decouvertedelesterel.com.* Original tours of the Esterel forest in an open-top vehicle. Visits end with a tasting session of regional products. Advance reservation by phone advised.

Fayence

Var

Surrounded by perched villages, Fayence enjoys a privileged setting between the mountains and the sea. Potters, stone and wood carvers, weavers, painters and coppersmiths still ply their trade in its warren of sloping cobbled streets.

☜ WALKING TOUR

OLD TOWN

The town's steep streets play host to a 17C gateway, fountains and wash houses, and the Porte Sarrasine, still crowned with machicolations.

The **18C church** has a Classical interior and a Baroque high altar, the work of the Provençal marble mason Dominique Fossatti (1757). From the terrace to the right of the church, the **view** ★ extends beyond the hang-gliding field to the Maures and Esterel heights.

From the top of the hill, where the ancient château used to be, is a **view** of the Pre-Alps of Castellane and Grasse *(viewing table)*.

Four du Mitan

Rue du Four-du-Mitan. ⏰*Open high season daily 10.30am–7.30pm; low season daily 10.30am–7pm.* ✎*2€ with slide show (15min).*

On the upper reaches of town, this 16C communal bakery has been turned into a small **bread museum**.

EXCURSION
Bagnols-en-Forêt

▶ *14km/8.7mi south by D 563 then D 4.* Beyond the Pic de la Gardette lies this charming hilltop village of sloping streets shaded by plane trees. Abandoned in the 14C, it was repopulated in 1447, when a group of Italian immigrants from Liguria settled here and manufactured millstones for making oil *(examples are on display in the* **Musée Archéologique** *in the tourist office on place de la Mairie,* ☏*04 94 40 64 68).* The town is a departure point for

▶ **Population:** 4,790.
◔ **Michelin Map:** 340 P4.
▯ **Info:** Pl. Léon-Roux, Fayence. ☏04 94 76 20 08. www.ville-fayence.fr. Pl. du Thouron, Seillans. ☏04 94 76 85 91. www.seillans.fr
▶ **Location:** Fayence lies on the edge of the Provençal tableland in the Var region, opposite its twin village Tourrettes, on the road from Draguignan to Grasse. Seillans lies in the foothills of the Canjuers plain *(◔see FAYENCE Driving Tours).*
▮▮ **Kids:** St-Cassien lake.
◔ **Timing:** Allow half a day for each driving tour through the Fayence countryside.

walks through the **forêt domaniale de Saint-Paul★**.

🚗 DRIVING TOURS

COL DU BEL-HOMME
56mi/91km. Allow about 4hr.

▶ From Fayence take D 563 south. Immediately on the right, then on the left, the road plunges deep into the vineyards (signposted tour).

Notre-Dame-des-Cyprès

1.8mi/3km from the village, chemin Notre-Dame-des-Cyprès. In a setting of tall cypress trees, this **Romanesque chapel** (12C) looks out over Fayence, Tourrettes and Montauroux.

▶ Go back to D 563, then turn right onto D 562. At 4-Chemins head towards Callas on D 25.

At 0.9mi/1.5km before Callas, take a small trail to the St-Auxile Romanesque chapel (7–12C), which crowns a rocky promontory on a Gallo-Roman site. It was fully restored in 1998.

Callas

Grouped around the castle ruins against a hillside, Callas is still a typical village of the Haut Var with its 17C belfry, porches and dovecote. The Romanesque **church** displays a 17C altarpiece above nine hooded penitents.

◖ Continue along D 25 over Col de Boussague.

Bargemon

The narrow alleyways, ramparts and 12C gateways of this former stronghold nestled amid olive and orange trees are guarded by a stately seigniorial castle. The 15C **church** near the town gateway was incorporated into the town's fortifications, with a 17C square bell tower and a Flamboyant doorway. The angel heads on the high alter are by Pierre Puget. Note the 16C triptych portraying St Antoine, St Raphaël and St Honorat. The village is dominated by the spire of the **Chapelle Notre-Dame-de-Montaigu** containing a miraculous statue of the Virgin Mary.

Housed in the Chapelle St-Etienne, the **Musée-Galerie Honoré-Camos** (◷ *open Jul–Sept Wed–Mon 10am–12.30pm, 3.30pm–7pm; Oct–Jun Wed–Sun 10am–12.30pm, 2.30pm–6.30pm, Mon 2pm–5pm;* ⊛ *no charge;* ✆ *04 94 76 72 88*) explores the town's history, traditional activities and the work of the painter **Honoré Camos** (1906–91).

The **Musée des fossiles et minéraux** (*8 rue de la Résistance;* ◷ *open Jul–Aug Wed, Fri–Sat 3pm–6.30pm, Thu–Sun 10am–noon, 3pm–6.30pm; Sept–Jun Wed–Sun 2pm–5.30pm;* ⊛ *no charge;* ✆ *04 94 67 61 44*) features a collection of 3,000 items from across the region. One of the three rooms is dedicated to ammonites.

◖ Leave Bargemon and take D 25 west.

The road rises sharply, offering **views** over Bargemon and its surroundings. This road was once used to transfer livestock to the fertile pastureland above the village.

View from Fayence

© webpicture/Fotolia.com

Col du Bel-Homme★

A path on the left leads to the top *(alt. 3,210ft/951m)*. From the viewing table, a **panorama★** extends south to the coast, northeast to Grasse, and north to the Canjuers plateau and the Castellane mountains. Canjuers is the largest military camp in Europe (87,000 acres/35,000 ha).

◑ Return to Bargemon and take D 19 towards Fayence.

After skirting the heights of Bargemon, the road winds through forests of pine and holm oaks with the Maures and Esterel on the horizon.

Seillans

In the foothills of the Canjuers plain, the ivory and pink houses of Seillans cascade down the slope of the Canjuers Plateau at an even steeper angle than the average perched village. Dadaist illustrator **Max Ernst** (1891–1976) chose to live here towards the end of his life. Quaint cobbled lanes lead up to the **church**, which was rebuilt in 1477 and incorporates 11C elements.

The Romanesque **Chapelle Notre-Dame-de-l'Ormeau** *(1.2mi/2km southeast on the Fayence road;* ◷*visit by reservation at Seillans tourist office;* ⌁*guided tours with commentary available year round;* ℘ *04 94 76 85 91)* is

Seillans

© Nico Gomez / Var Tourisme

flanked by a bell tower of dressed stone. The interior contains a remarkable 16C **altarpiece★★**. In the centre, a crowd of people climb the tree of Jesse. The left-hand part of the altarpiece illustrates the Adoration of the Shepherds, and the right-hand, the Adoration of the Magi.

◑ On leaving the village, turn left on D 53, then left again on D 563.

Mons★

At an altitude of 2,625ft/800m.

🛈 *Pl. St-Sébastien.* ℘*04 94 76 39 54.*

This **old village** is perched between earth and sky on a wild and sunny mountain plateau flourishing with every single type of sub-Alpine Provençal plant. Mons was repopulated after several plagues in the Middle Ages by Genoan families, who rebuilt the village and cultivated the land with olives and wheat.

Place St-Sébastien

Offset by an 18C fountain, the square has a terrace (505ft/814m) that looks out over the Siagne and Siagnole Valleys. It also provides an exceptional **view★★**, which on a clear day, extends from the Coudon (north of Toulon) to the Lérins islands and to as far as the Italian Alps *(viewing table).*

Church

⌁*Guided tours 2.30pm and 4pm by request. Apply at the tourist office.* ℘*04 94 76 39 54.*

The edifice, which was started in the Upper Provençal Romanesque style, was greatly altered in the 15C and 17C. It is fitted with unusually uniform furnishings: five Baroque altarpieces, including a huge triptych dating from 1680 on the high altar. To the right stands a beautiful 15C silver processional cross. The oldest of the three bells in the belfry was cast in 1438.

Dolmens

There are 11 dolmens dating from the late Neolithic period around Mons, three of which are listed historic monuments. Only the **dolmen de**

Riens, with its ogival pillars, is open to the public.

🐾 Walk to the dolmen by following rue Jean-Vadon across Mons. Take the D 56 for 33yds/30m on your right, then take the first road on the left to the chapelle St-Pierre. Continue about 77yds/70m and take the pathway on the left *(signed)*.

Return to the chapel road and climb towards Louquiers for views of the dolmen de la Colle (1.8mi/3km), then head for Escragnolles and the dolmen de la Brainée (4.3mi/7km).

▶ Take D 56 towards St-Cézaire-sur-Siagne, then continue right along D 56

Aqueduc de la Roche Taillée
Park on the embankment 218yds/ 200m beyond the site.

To supply Fréjus with drinking water, the Romans tapped into the Neissou springs at the foot of the Mons promontory and channelled their waters through a canal 8ft/2.5m wide, 164ft/50m long and 32ft/10m deep. A section of the canal is still in service today.

▶ Return along D 56, then straight ahead on D 656 towards St-Cézaire-sur-Siagne, then right on D 96 towards Montauroux.

The Dada Master

Max Ernst settled in Seillans with his wife, the painter Dorothea Tanning, in 1964. A small **museum** *(Collection Max Ernst – Dorothea Tanning; open Jul–Aug Mon–Sat 2.30pm–6pm; Sept–Jun Tue–Sat 2.30pm–5.30pm; closed public holidays; ✆2€; ☎04 94 50 45 54)* displays more than 70 of his lithographs and engravings, remarkable for their sense of humour.

The road overlooks the wooded **Siagne gorge** and the village of St-Cézaire-sur-Siagne, scattered along its deep green ridges.

▶ Turn left onto D 37, then right onto D 56.

Callian
The ancient streets of this village spiral towards a castle. **Views** from the main square look southwest over the Lac de St-Cassien beneath the Tanneron heights. French designer Christian Dior and Nadia, wife of Fernand Léger, are buried in the local cemetery.

Terraced café in Mons

S. Sauvignier/ MICHELIN

Callian
© Nico Gomez / Var Tourisme

▶ Continue along D 56, then turn right on D 256, right at the D 562 roundabout, then right on D19 to Fayence.

AROUND LAC DE ST-CASSIEN

18mi/29km. Allow about 2hr.

▶ Leave Fayence on the Tourettes road heading SE.

Tourrettes

0.8mi/1.3km east by D 563.
This quiet village affords **views** of the Maures and Esterel massifs from **place de l'Horloge** *(viewing table)*. Modelled on the St Petersburg Cadet School, the **castle** (⚭ *closed to the public*) was built in 1830.

▶ Continue on D 19, then take D 562 and D 56 towards Callian.

Callian

See Caillan (above).

▶ To the east of the village, take D 37 to Montauroux.

Montauroux

13mi/21km east by D 19.
This pretty village, known for its 13 fountains and 16C and 17C houses *(rue Eugène-Segond)*, was once home to the French designer **Christian Dior**. He paid for the latest restoration of the Chapelle St-Barthélemy, built in the 12C and initially restored in the 17C.

Les Bambous du Mandarin

Pont de Siagne. ✆ *04 93 66 12 94.* ⏱*Open Easter–Nov Sat and first Sun of month 8am–6pm.* ●●*Guided tour (1hr) 10.30am, 3pm, 4.30pm.* ✎*5€ (7yrs and older 2.50€).*
Explore more than 80 varieties of bamboo in lush green surroundings.

▶ Take D 37, and cross D 562 towards Lac de St-Cassien.

Lac de St-Cassien

⚲ *The Montauroux tourist office organises walks led by nature guides.*
This scenic lake nestled at the foot of the Tanneron (⚲*see MASSIF DU TANNERON*) was filled with water in 1965 following

Lac de St-Cassien
© Nico Gomez / Var Tourisme

the destruction of the Malpasset dam (&see FRÉJUS). It is fringed by wooded shores and a network of walking trails. The **pont de Pré-Claou** affords **views** of the entire lake (2.1 billion cubic ft/60 million cubic m), which is used for various sporting activities (swimming, canoeing and pedal boats). It is the largest stretch of water (1,062 acres/430 ha) on the Esterel.

To the west, a reedy marsh is home to 150 species of migratory waterfowl in the Fondurane nature reserve.

▶ Return to Fayence via the D 37, then left onto the D 562 and right onto the D 19.

ADDRESSES

🏠 STAY

⊜⊜🛏 **Auberge des Pins** – *Domaine Le Chevalier, Tourrettes. 1mi/2km south on D 19.* ℘*04 94 76 06 36. www.aubergedes pins.com. 16 rooms.* ⧉*10€. Restaurant* ⊜🛏. Surrounded by an estate offering a range of leisure facilities, this lodging offers modern rooms and studios in three pavilions. Local cuisine and grilled meats (evenings only).

⊜⊜🛏 **Combes Longues** *Les Hautes Combes Longues, Seillans, 2.4mi/4km north by D 53, rte de Mons and lane on right.* ℘*04 94 47 65 27. www.combeslongues.com. 3 rooms. Restaurant* ⊜🛏🛏(⧉). A peaceful 18C stone farm hidden amid woodland. Ask for a room in the converted stables with valley views. The restaurant serves homely fare made with organic produce.

⊜⊜🛏🛏 **Les Deux Rocs** – *1 pl. Font-d'Amont, Seillans.* ℘*04 94 76 87 32. www.hoteldeuxrocs.com. Closed Jan, first 2 weeks Nov. 14 rooms.* ⧉*13€. Restaurant* ⊜🛏. Imposing hotel housed in an old village building. The original staircase leads to rooms appointed with antique furniture. Enjoy your meal on the summer terrace.

⊜⊜🛏 **Moulin de la Camandoule** – *Chemin de Notre-Dame des Cyprès, 1mi/2km west of Fayence by rte. de Seillans (D 19), turn left into lane.* ℘*04 94 76 00 84. www.camandoule.com. 11 rooms.* ▣. ⧉*14€. Restaurant*⊜🛏🛏. An old olive mill at the foot of the village converted into a quaint Provençal hotel decorated in warm, southern colours. The grounds are home to a pool, a Gallo-Roman aqueduct and a terrace.

⍬ EAT

⊜🛏 **Au Bec Fin Chez Alain** – *51 pl. de l'Église, St-Paul-en-Forêt.* ℘*04 94 76 30 71. Closed Tue and Wed lunch.* Both the decor and menu are heavily influenced by the colours of Provence. Rabbit stew, fresh vegetables and homemade desserts top the list.

⊜🛏🛏 **La Farigoulette** – *pl. du Château, Fayence.* ℘*04 94 84 10 49. Closed Tue and Wed.* This former sheepfold offers the perfect rustic setting (exposed beams and stone walls, farmhouse furniture) to enjoy traditional cuisine with a modern twist.

⊜🛏🛏🛏 **Le Temp des Cerises** – *1 Pl. République.* ℘*04 94 76 01 19. Closed Tue, Wed, 1–27 Dec.* A typical Fayence restaurant serving regional specialities in the dining room or on the shady terrace.

SHOPPING

LOCAL MARKETS

Fayence – Pl. de l'Église, Tue, Thu and Sat 9am–1pm.

Bargemon – ℘*04 94 47 81 73.* Pl. St-Étienne, Thu. Car boot and bric-a-brac 1st Sun in May.

Callas – Sat mornings.

SPORT AND LEISURE

Aviron St-Cassien-Club Intercommunal du Pays de Fayence – *In Biançon, by D 37. 250 imp. Base Nautique, Montauroux.* ℘*04 94 39 88 64. www.avironstcassien.com.* Introductory rowing courses on the lake.

CANNES & THE GRASSE REGION

For centuries, Cannes and the Grasse region have been enchanting visitors from around the world. Encompassing the legendary perfume-making town of Grasse and its surrounding perched villages, the region includes three of the most dynamic resort towns in France. Travellers can take advantage of the lively nightlife and window shopping in Cannes, Juan-les-Pins and Antibes, or enjoy the quiet Provençal atmosphere of the Îles de Lérins and inland villages like Biot and Gourdon. Here prestigious museums and chic art galleries easily coexist with ancient fortified ramparts and centuries-old ruins. The proximity to Nice International Airport, easy access to major coastal and inland routes, and regional train service also make this region an ideal base from which to explore the rest of the French Riviera.

Highlights

1 Dine in the monks' seaside restaurant on **Île St-Honorat** (p240)

2 Visit the newly restored Musée Picasso in **Antibes** (p273)

3 Watch the sunset from the fortified ramparts in **St-Paul-de-Vence** (p284)

4 See **panoramic views** from the **Baou de St-Jeannet** (p291)

5 Rent a chaise-longue on one of the private beaches in **Cagnes-sur-Mer** (p292)

Lively Year Round

While many people think of the French Riviera first and foremost as a summer vacation destination, Cannes and the Grasse region are bustling throughout the year. A large population of "locals"

from around the world work in its various technology parks, in the greenhouses producing the region's flowers and fruits, on the superyachts requiring constant upkeep, and in the conference centres that attract international visitors. Cannes, Antibes, Villeneuve-Loubet and Grasse are the liveliest towns, with most hotels and restaurants remaining open year-round.

Illustrious Cultural History

Almost every town in this part of the French Riviera has attracted a loyal following of artists, writers and musicians. Antibes was home to the writer Nikos Kazantzakis, the cartoonist Peynet and artist Picasso during one of his more prolific periods. Renoir lived in Cagnes-sur-Mer until his death, Fernand Léger left his mark forever on the tiny village of Biot, while Modigliani and Soutine made St-Paul-de-Vence a trendy place for artists. Many of these towns have

Boulevard de la Croisette, Cannes

©Davide_69/Fotolia.com

Musée Picasso, Antibes

©Nicolas Thibaut/Photononstop/Tips Images

museums dedicated to their artists. Juan-les-Pins, on the other hand, holds an event – the Jazz Festival – to commemorate the great jazz artists who once lived there, such as Cole Porter and Sydney Bechet. Today the stars of the silver screen continue to visit the region during the Cannes Film Festival, making their temporary homes in the luxury hotels on the Croisette and the Cap d'Antibes.

Military Reminders

The forts in Antibes and on the Île Ste-Marguerite are no longer active military sites, although the greatest French general of them all, Napoleon Bonaparte, has left an indelible mark on the region with the Route Napoléon, which traces his triumphant journey from Juan-les-Pins to Grenoble following his escape from the island of Elba. Museums throughout the region attest to the military importance of this coastline throughout the centuries, from Greek and Roman times through to the Middle Ages and the 17C, when Antibes still protected the eastern border of France. The only invasion today comes in the form of summer sun-seekers.

Nautical Fans

Visitors with a nautical interest will find their heart's delight in the ports of Cannes and Antibes, where sleek private superyachts as big as cruise ships line up at the quays alongside more humble fishing boats and stunning sailing yachts. Watersport enthusiasts can pay homage to the man who invented water-skiing in Juan-les-Pins, while divers can head to Antibes to discover more about France's greatest marine explorer, Jacques Cousteau.

Sailing events take place throughout the year, and the local museums provide a detailed history of every aspect of shipping, sailing and boating on the Mediterranean back to Roman times.

Natural Wonders

This part of the Riviera has no shortage of natural beauty and sights of interest to nature lovers, including the stalactites of the Baume Obscure and the observatory in Saint-Vallier-de-Thiey, where you can spend an evening gazing at the stars.

Alternatively, hop along to Marineland to admire the sharks and performing dolphins, discover rare plants in the botanical gardens of Antibes or cool off in the waterfalls at the Gorges du Loup. Hiking trails offer stunning cliff views around Gourdon and an opportunity for peaceful contemplation on the Îles des Lérins.

Tourist offices in the region can provide special maps for those interested in the local flora and fauna.

CANNES AND THE GRASSE REGION

0   4 km
0   2 mi

Pas de la Faye   ★★   Recommended

Grasse   ★   Interesting

Gréolières   Worth seeing

Driving tour with departure town

Le massif du Tanneron

Préalpes de Grasse

Le plateau de Caussols

Les gorges du Loup

La haute vallée du Loup

La Route des Crêtes

ALPES-MARITIMES

Le Plan-du-Peyron

Clue

H^{te} vallée du Loup

Escragnolles

Pas de la Faye

Belv^{re} de Baou Mourine

1114

981

St-Vallier-de-Thiey

Baume Obscure

780

Col du Pilon

VAR

St-Cézaire

Cabris

Gorges de la Siagne

St-Cézaire-s-Siagne

4

Lac de St-Cassien

N.-D.-de-Peygros

Massif du Tanneron

N

MARSEILLE   B   BRIGNOLES

Cannes★★

Alpes-Maritimes

Framed to the west by the red rocks of the Esterel and the forested Îles de Lérins across the bay, Cannes is popular for its stunning setting and mild winter climate. It's a regular port of call for film stars during the Cannes Film Festival. Its English castle, Italianate villas and Russian church reveal the town's long love affair with the rich and famous.

A BIT OF HISTORY
Cannes, the coastal watchtower

Established as a trading post by the Ligurians and Romans (42BC), the small village of Canoïs, named after the reeds *(cannes)* that once grew in the surrounding marshes, sprang up at the foot of Mont Chevalier (also known as Le Suquet) in the early 10C. In 1131 the Comte de Provence granted Cannes to the abbots of Lérins, who fortified the town against the Saracens. Its defence was entrusted to the Knights Templar in the 12C, followed by the Knights of Malta.

Lord Brougham and the birth of the resort (1834)

Cannes was just a small fishing village of 4,000 inhabitants when the Lord Chancellor of England (1830–34), Lord Brougham, wintered here in 1834 after an outbreak of cholera prevented him from staying in Nice.

The wealthy traveller fell in love with the village and built himself a house here, soon followed by the English aristocracy, who exchanged the damp winters of London for the Mediterranean sunshine. The **château Eléonore**, named after Lord Brougham's daughter, has survived on avenue du Dr-Picaud, at the Croix des Gardes (private property). Cannes has inspired countless French writers, including the Provençal poet **Frédéric Mistral**, Prosper Mérimée (who died there in 1870) and Guy de Maupassant, who anchored his yacht in the bay between 1884 and 1888 while writing *Sur l'Eau (On the Water)*.

▶ **Population:** 70,610.

♿ **Michelin Map:** 341 D6; local maps: pp232–233 and p234

ℹ **Info:** Palais des Festivals, 1 blvd. de la Croisette. ℘04 92 99 84 22. www.cannes-destination.fr. Le Cannet: Pl. Benidorm, 73 Ave. du Campon. ℘04 93 45 34 27. www.lecannet.fr.

◖ **Location:** The most interesting areas of Cannes lie between the RN 7 and the sea, including the historic port and the district around the Palais des Festivals. The Old Town extends up the hillside of Le Suquet; upscale shops, hotels and beaches extend east along boulevard de la Croisette. A tourist train covers the main sights.

🅿 **Parking:** Street parking is metered with a maximum two-hour limit. Large indoor car parks *(charge)* may be found around the port, market and the train station.

⊛ **Don't Miss:** The colourful Marché Forville, the fortified monastery ruins on the Île St-Honorat, yachts in the Old Port, or the sandy beaches of La Croisette.

🕑 **Timing:** You'll need a full day to enjoy the sights of Cannes. Visit the Marché Forville and Îles de Lérins in the morning, then shop or head for the beach.

👫 **Kids:** The car-free Île Ste-Marguerite and Cannes' beaches are the perfect places to let the kids run free.

Cannes Festivals

Cannes hosts several world famous festivals. The **International Film Festival** is one of the highlights of the Riviera's artistic calendar. Other popular events include prestigious regattas, the International Record and Music Market (MIDEM) and the World Entertainment Content Market (MIPCOM).

 WALKING TOURS

① EXPLORING CANNES: SEAFRONT★

Follow the route marked on map pp232–233. Allow 2hr.

Boulevard de la Croisette★

This elegant seaside promenade bordered by palms and gardens is popular with winter strollers. Luxury hotels and chic boutiques line the seafront and side streets as far as rue d'Antibes.

At the top end of La Croisette, east of the port, stands the ultramodern **Palais des Festivals et des Congrès** and casino. Known as "The Bunker", the building comprises a 2,300-seat auditorium, theatre, broadcasting studios and the tourist office.

Between the conference centre and the gardens lies the **Allée des Stars**, an avenue of 200 slabs bearing handprints of movie stars who have attended the Film Festival. Farther east on the opposite side of the road, beyond the Majestic Hotel is a private 19C mansion, **La Malmaison** (*open Jul–Sept Sat–Thu 11am–8pm, Fri 11am–10pm; Oct–Mar Tue–Sun 10am–1pm, 2pm–6pm; closed public holidays; 3.40€; 04 97 06 44 90). Once part of the Grand Hotel, it now houses the municipal culture depart-ment and art exhibitions.

Nearby the former Noga Hilton (now a Marriott hotel) incorporates the façade of the Palais des Festivals, pulled down in 1988 after serving as the venue for the Cannes Film Festival for 40 years. Farther on is the Belle Époch **Carlton Hotel** (now an InterContinental hotel) and the Art Deco **Martinez Hotel**.

PRACTICAL INFORMATION

Tours and Transport

Bus – *Gare routière, pl. de l'Hôtel-de-Ville. 04 93 39 11 39. www.rca.tm.fr.* TAM buses operate between Cannes and Nice, with direct airport service.

Train Station – *SNCF Gare de Cannes. 0 892 35 35 35. www.ter-sncf.com/paca.* This train station is served by SNCF trains, the TGV and the local TER trains (service between Mandelieu-La-Napoule and Vintimille).

Trans Côte d'Azur – *3 quai des Îles 04 92 98 71 30. Closed Nov–Jan. www.trans-cote-azur.com.* Regular service to Île Ste-Marguerite *(15min; 12.50€ children, 5.50€)*, plus seasonal tours to l'Île de Porquerolles, Monaco, St-Tropez, etc.

▷ Proceed east along blvd. de la Croisette to pointe de la Croisette.

Pointe de la Croisette★

This point owes its name to a small cross that used to stand here. It offers splendid **views** of Cannes, the Îles de Lérins and the Esterel. Modern tourist developments include artificial beaches and the Palm Beach Casino complex, built in 1929. Beyond Palm Beach is a splendid **view★** of Golfe-Juan and Cap d'Antibes.

▷ Follow the avenue Maréchal-Juin and rue d'Antibes back into town.

② OLD CANNES AND THE PORT

Follow the route marked on map pp232–233. Allow 1.5hr.

The Harbour

Between the Palais des Festivals and Le Suquet lies the Old Port, teeming with fishing boats and luxury yachts.

The west side of the harbour is lined with shops and restaurants. To the southwest lies the embarkation point for trips to the Îles de Lérins.

Allées de la Liberté

Beneath the plane trees, overlooking the port, a large square features a statue of Lord Brougham, where an early morning flower market gives way to *pétanque* matches in the afternoon.

▶ Take rue Félix-Faure and rue Rouguière to rue Meynadier.

Rue Meynadier

Formerly the main street linking the new town to Le Suquet, rue Meynadier is bordered by a variety of local speciality shops and some fine 18C doorways.

▶ Head for Le Suquet via rue Louis-Blanc, rue Félix-Faure and rue Mont-Chevalier.

Le Suquet

The old town is built on the site of the former Canoïs *castrum* or "citadel" on the slopes of Mont Chevalier. Rue Perrissol leads to Place de la Castre surrounded by a defensive wall and dominated by **Notre-Dame-d'Espérance**, built in the 16–17C in Provençal Gothic style. The old bell tower leads to a long tree-lined terrace, offering a fine **view** of the town, port and Île Ste-Marguerite.

BELLE ÉPOQUE CANNES★

Discover 19C Cannes and its aristocratic past on this tour of the town's luxurious villas and gardens.

Quartier de la Croix des Gardes

To the west of Cannes, this hill offers a wonderful **panorama** over the bay, both day and night. Begin your tour at the early 20C **château de la Croix des Gardes**, which has an interesting Florentine façade. Continue towards Lord Brougham's villa (**Château Eleonore**) and its neighbour, the **villa Marie-Thé-**

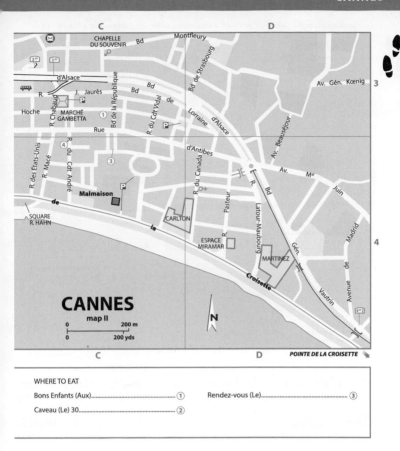

CANNES
map II

0 — 200 m
0 — 200 yds

N

POINTE DE LA CROISETTE

WHERE TO EAT

Bons Enfants (Aux)..①   Rendez-vous (Le)..③

Caveau (Le) 30..②

rèse, at no 2 ave. J.-de-Noailles. Once the residence of the dowager baroness de Rothschild and now home to the town's media library, it is set in pleasant parkland. The **palais Vallombrosa** and its park and the **villa Victoria**, once belonging to Victorian property developer and botany enthusiast Sir Thomas Robinson Woolfield, continue this prestigious promenade.

Quartier de la Californie

To the east of the town lie several residences that have marked the history of Cannes: on avenue du Roi-Albert-Ier, the **villa Kazbeck** was the scene of sumptuous parties given by the Russian Grand Duke Mikhail Mikhaïlovitch; the **villa Champfleuri** remains famous for its exotic gardens (which form the backdrop for the film *Gambling Hell* by J. Delannoy). *The Mystery of the Yellow*

Room (1930) by Marcel L'Herbier was shot in the **château Scott**, a Flamboyant Neo-Gothic pile on avenue du Mar.-Juin.

SIGHTS
Musée de la Castre★★

Le Suquet. ◷*Open Jul–Aug daily 10am–7pm (Wed til 9pm); Apr–Jun and Sept Tue–Sun 10am–1pm, 2pm–6pm (Wed til 9pm); Oct–Mar Tue–Sun 10am–1pm, 2pm–5pm (Wed til 9pm).* ◷*Closed public holidays.* ⊜*6€, free first Sun/month Nov–Mar.* ℘*04 93 38 55 26.* This 11C castle, built by the Lérins monks to guard the harbour, houses archaeological and ethnographic collections, mainly from the Mediterranean Basin. The small Cistercian Chapelle Ste-Anne at the entrance has **musical instruments★** from around the world. Room 4 looks out onto the 12C square watchtower (72ft/22m), Tour du Suquet. The top floor

Map of Cannes showing locations including CANNES, MOUGINS D 6185, MARSEILLE NICE A8, D 6185 GRASSE DIGNE, MUSÉE DE L'AUTOMOBILISTE D 135 A 8, Pl. Bellevue, Musée Bonnard, St-Sauveur, Château-Musée, Jardins de Tivoli, LE CANNET, Musée de la Poterie, VALLAURIS, LE PEZOU, ROCHEVILLE, SALLE LA PALESTRE, La Croix des Gardes, Chapelle Bellini, COL ST-ANTOINE, Palais Vallombrosa, Villa marie-thérèse, SUPER CANNES, Champfleuri, LA CALIFORNIE, St-Michel-Archange, see map II, GOLFE DE LA NAPOULE, PORT CANTO, PORT CANNES, Croisette, PORT DU MOURÉ ROUGE, Pointe de la Croisette, CASINO PALM-BEACH, ÎLES DE LÉRINS

WHERE TO STAY
Villa L'Églantier
(Chambre d'hôte)...... (1)

WHERE TO EAT
Bistrot des Artisans.......... (1)
Fred L'Écailler...................... (2)
Pézou.................................. (3)

affords a **panorama★** of La Croisette, Îles de Lérins and the Esterel hills.

Chapelle Bellini

61 bis ave. de Vallauris; from ave. Poralto, turn left onto the chemin du Parc-Fiorentina.

Once part of a sumptuous Tuscan palace the "Villa Fiorentina", this chapel was built in elaborate Baroque style in the late 19C for a Balkan noble family. The interior is decorated with works by Cannes painter Bellini (1904–89).

Église Orthodoxe Russe St-Michel-Archange

40 blvd. Alexandre-III.

Since Empress Maria Alexandrovna, wife of Tsar Alexander III, had taken to spending the winter months in Cannes, it was necessary to build a church large enough to accommodate her court. Inaugurated in 1894, this edifice holds a richly ornamented interior that contains remarkable icons and banners from the Russian imperial family.

The crypt (*closed to the public*) contains the bodies of members of the imperial family who died in exile. Opposite the church, and slightly to its right, in Alexandra Square, is the first Russian Orthodox edifice in Cannes, **Chapelle Tripet-Skryptine**.

DRIVING TOURS

3 LE CANNET

See map of Cannes above.

▷ Leave Cannes by blvd. Carnot.

Sheltered from the wind by a circle of wooded hills, Le Cannet, at an altitude of 361ft/110m, offers breathtaking **views**.

Musée Bonnard

16 blvd. Sadi Carnot. ○*Open Apr–Oct Tue–Sun 10am–8pm (Thu 9pm); rest of the year 10am–6pm. 5€. 04 93 94 06 06. www.museebonnard.fr.*
Set in a Belle Époque mansion to which a contemporary wing has been added, this museum is dedicated to French art-

ist **Pierre Bonnard** (1867–1947), who spent the last years of his life painting views of Le Cannet from the Villa Le Bosquet *(ave. Victoria)*. The collection features works he completed here, including *Paysage du Midi* (1942) and *Bathers at the End of the Day* (1946).

Le Vieux Cannet

The old town is reached by rue St-Sauveur, lined with 18C houses and pleasant shady squares. At no 19 is a mural by the artist Peynet representing *Les Amoureux (The Lovers)*. Farther on the left, the 15C **Chapelle St-Sauveur** *(108 rue St-Sauveur)* houses mosaics and stained-glass windows by **Théo Tobiasse** (b. 1927). Place Bellevue offers a superb **view** of Cannes and the Îles de Lérins. The old Calvys Tower (12C) still stands nearby, as well as the taller Danys Tower (14C). Both have fine façades topped with machicolations. The **Jardins de Tivoli** can be reached from the Hôtel de Ville via the pedestrian rue Cavasse, passing luxurious 1900 villas.

Chemin des Collines★

This road above Cannes offers fine **views** over La Napoule bay and the Îles de Lérins.

▷ Continue east to Col St-Antoine.

On the left in avenue Victoria sits the **Villa Yakimour** *(⚬━private property)*, an Oriental residence given by the Aga Khan to his wife Yvette Labrousse.

▷ Continue to Vallauris over Col de St-Antoine, then left onto D 803.

Vallauris *See VALLAURIS.*

Golfe-Juan★

1mi/2km southeast of Vallauris by D 135 (⚓see GOLFE-JUAN).
On returning towards Cannes on D 6007, the road skirts the hills of Super-Cannes revealing the Îles de Lérins and the red Massif de l'Esterel on the horizon; the **view★** is at its best at sunset.

▷ Return to Cannes along the seafront.

③ LA CROIX DES GARDES★

15min round trip, 5mi/8km (steep climb).

▷ Leave Cannes on ave. du Dr Picaud. Turn right on blvd. Leader. 110yd/100m beyond the entrance to the Pavillon de la Croix des Gardes, turn right onto ave. J-de-Noailles and continue 110yd/100m.

🗻 Take the footpath to the top of the hill (alt 538ft/164m) and a strategically placed 39ft/12m-high cross, which gave the area its name in the 16C. From the foot of the cross extends a marvellous **panorama★** over Cannes, the Îles de Lérins and the Esterel.

▷ Continue along avenue J.-de-Noailles to return to Cannes.

Lunch in Le Cannet

© Sylvaine Poitau/Apa Publications

ADDRESSES

🛏 STAY

Hotel Le Chanteclair – *12 rue Forville.* ℘*04 93 39 68 88. www.hotelchanteclair. com. Closed Dec–mid-Jan. 15 rooms.* ⊟ ⊒*6€.* This friendly hotel offers a selection of variously priced rooms depending on the level of comfort. Breakfast is served in a pleasant inner courtyard.

Hôtel Lutetia – *6 rue Michel-Ange.* ℘*04 93 39 35 74. www.hotel-lutetia-cannes.com. 8 rooms.* ⊒*7€.* A simple and comfortable hotel on a quiet side street, with air-conditioning and Provençal decor. Close to the train station.

Hôtel Appia – *6 rue Marceau.* ℘*04 93 06 59 59. www.appia-hotel.com. Closed mid-Nov–Dec. 32 rooms.* ⊒*7€.* Practicality takes precedence over comfort in this downtown hotel, where the well-kept, small rooms are air-conditioned and the windows double-glazed.

Hôtel Le Florian – *8 rue du Cdt-André.* ℘*04 93 39 24 82. www.hotel-leflorian.com. Closed Dec–mid-Jan. 20 rooms.* ⊒*6€.* This family-run hotel sits between the train station and the Palais des Festivals, on a semi-pedestrian street in the old town.

Chambre d'hôte Villa L'Églantier – *14 rue Campestra.* ℘*04 93 68 22 43. www.maison-eglantier.com. 3 rooms.* ⊟. ⊒. This impressive white villa dating from 1920 is surrounded by palm trees and other exotic species. The large, peaceful rooms are extended by a terrace or a balcony.

Hôtel Festival – *3 rue Molière.* ℘*04 97 06 64 40. www.hotel-festival.com. Closed early–mid Jan. 14 rooms.* ⊒*8.50€.* This family-run hotel lies within walking distance of the Croisette and the rue d'Antibes shopping area. Rooms have air-conditioning, soundproofing, WiFi, and marble bathrooms. Jacuzzi and sauna are available for guests.

Hôtel Le Mistral – *13 rue des Belges.* ℘*04 93 39 91 46. www.mistral-hotel.com. Closed mid–late Dec. 10 rooms.* ⊒*8€.* This boutique hotel with modern decor is situated just behind the Palais des Festivals. Rooms have air-conditioning, WiFi and a safe.

Hôtel Martinez – *73 blvd. de la Croisette.* ℘*04 93 90 12 34. http:// cannesmartinez.grand.hyatt.com. 409 rooms.* This seven-floor beachfront hotel, now a Hyatt property, has been a Cannes landmark since 1929. Spacious rooms come with a balcony and such amenities as bathrobe and slippers. Spa, fitness center, pool, three restaurants.

🍽 EAT

Aux Bons Enfants – *80 rue Meynadier.* ℘*No phone.* ⊟ *Closed 22 Nov–4 Jan and Sun and Mon.* This old-fashioned cantina near the Forville market serves ratatouille, grilled anchovies, aïoli, stuffed sardines, etc. Wine comes by the pitcher and there's a friendly family atmosphere.

Le Caveau 30 – *45 rue F.-Faure.* ℘*04 93 39 06 33. www.lecaveau30.com.* This large restaurant comprises two dining rooms decorated in the style of a 1930s brasserie. The terrace overlooks a shaded square. Fish and seafood are the house specialities.

Pézou – *346 rue St-Sauveur* ℘*04 93 69 32 50. www.lepezou.fr. Closed Nov, Wed, Sun eve Sept–Jun.* Far from the hustle and bustle of the Croisette, this pleasant restaurant is situated on a small square and has a summer terrace. Provençal cuisine is the fare.

Le Rendez-Vous – *35 rue F.-Faure.* ℘*04 93 68 55 10. Closed 5–20 Jan.* This chic bistro with an Art Deco-style ceiling, serves fish, seafood and other Mediterranean-flavoured dishes.

L'Affable – *5 rue Lafontaine -* ℘*04 93 68 02 09. www.restaurant-laffable.fr. Closed Sat lunch, Sun and Aug.* This excellent restaurant is recommended by locals, who love its sophisticated decor, its well-prepared bistro-style food and its fine selection of wines. Start with the octopus salad and move on to the roasted lamb.

Fred L'Écailler – *7 pl. de l'Étang.* ℘*04 93 43 15 85. www.fredlecailler.com.* A large neon sign marks the entrance to this rustic-style restaurant, the walls of which are draped with fishing nets. You'll find a fine selection of freshly-caught fish and seafood.

⊜⊜⊜ **Bistrot des Artisans** – *67 blvd. de la République.* ✆*04 93 68 33 88. Closed Sun.* Presenting a surprising decor of vintage craft tools, helmets, naïve-style mural frescoes and basic furniture, this restaurant serves generous portions of lovingly prepared Mediterranean food.

SHOPPING

Marché de Forville – *Closed Mon.* The colourful stalls overflow with fresh regional produce.

Allées de la Liberté – Held every day, this **market** brims with fresh flowers in the morning. On Saturdays, there's a flea market.

Shopping Streets – In the lively pedestrian area of **Rue Meynadier**, window displays of food and crafts are tempting. **Rue d'Antibes** is the place to shop for luxury clothes and luggage.

Cannolive – *16-20 rue Vénizelos.* ✆*04 93 39 08 19. Closed Sun, Mon morning and two weeks in Jan.* This shop boasts an incredible choice of Provençal products to take back home: household linens, tapenade, crockery, santons, soap and even Lérina liqueur from the nearby islands are just some of the merchandise on offer.

La Boutique du Festival – *blvd. de la Croisette.* ✆*09 61 56 56 82. www.festival-cannes.fr.* 🕐*Open daily 9am–7pm (Jul–Aug til 8pm).* Located on the ground floor of the tourist office in the Palais des Festivals, this store is a paradise for movie buffs, filled as it is, with souvenirs of the famous festival.

NIGHTLIFE

Palais des Festivals et des Congrès – *Espl. Georges-Pompidou, blvd. de la Croisette.* ✆*04 93 39 01 01. www.palaisdesfestivals.com.* Opened in 1982, the palais includes the Grand Auditorium (seating 2,300) and the Théâtre Debussy (seating 1,000).

L'Amiral – *73 blvd. de la Croisette.* ✆*04 92 98 73 00. www.hotel-martinez.com.* Attached to the Martinez Hotel, this bar is by far the most popular meeting place along the coast. It owes its reputation to the head barman and Jimmy, the American pianist *(every evening from 8pm).*

Le Bâoli – *Port Pierre Canto, blvd. de la Croisette.* ✆*04 93 43 03 43. www.lebaoli.com. Closed Sun–Tue, Mon–Fri off-season.* The hottest night spot in Cannes with beachfront **views** over the bay, this bar-restaurant-nightclub with an exotic decor can host up to 1,500 jetsetting partygoers in high season.

Pavillon Croisette – Havana Room – *42 blvd. de la Croisette.* ✆*04 92 59 06 90.* 🕐*Open daily noon–3pm, 7pm–10.30pm (summer 11pm). Closed Nov–Feb.* Worthy of the best London private members clubs, this bar offers a seemingly infinite drinks list.

LEISURE ACTIVITIES

For sailing, deep-sea diving or water-skiing, contact the tourist office or visit www.station-nautique.com.

Beaches – Some beaches on La Croisette charge a fee *(prices are listed at the top of the steps)*; some belong to a hotel. There are three **free beaches**, one of them behind the Palais des Festivals. Other public beaches lie west of the old port, on boulevard Jean-Hibert and boulevard du Midi, at Port Canto, and on boulevard Gazagnaire beyond La Pointe.

Ponton Majestic Ski Nautique – *blvd. de la Croisette.* ✆*04 92 98 77 47. http://majesticskisclub.online.fr. Closed Nov–Mar.* Water-skiing or parascending for the adventurous.

Air Odyssey – *Aéroport de Cannes-Mandelieu. Reservations:* ✆*06 09 56 06 54. www.air-odyssey.com. Departures hourly from 9am. 145 €/person. 45min.* The company organises flights with a commentary offering **panoramic views** above the Riviera over 80ml/130km at 1,300ft/400m altitude. The "Sea and volcanoes" tour takes you over Cannes Bay and the Massif de l'Esterel in a tourist aircraft.

CALENDAR

Cannes Film Festival – Lasting ten days in May, the festival includes free open-air cinema retrospectives on the beach (official screenings open to accredited professionals only). *www.festival-cannes.org.*

Nuits Musicales du Suquet – Held the last two weeks of July, these classical concerts are performed on the esplanade in front of the Église du Suquet. ✆*04 92 99 33 83.*

Îles de Lérins★★

Alpes-Maritimes

Surprisingly peaceful despite their proximity to the hustle and bustle of Cannes, these wooded islands afford a fine panorama of the coast from Cap Roux to Cap d'Antibes. Famous as the island prison of the Man in the Iron Mask, Ste-Marguerite and its fortified monastic neighbour, St-Honorat, were not always havens of tranquillity.

- **Michelin Map:** 341 D6.
- **Info:** Palais des Festivals, 1 blvd. de la Croisette. ✆04 92 99 84 22. www.cannes-destination.fr.
- **Location:** The islands can be reached by Cannes (*see Practical Information opposite*), or on your own boat (just drop anchor in one of the coves).
- **Timing:** Allow at least half a day to visit both islands.

A BIT OF HISTORY
The Island in Antiquity

In ancient times the Île Ste-Marguerite was a Roman port called **Lero** after a Ligurian hero. Excavations near Fort Royal have uncovered houses, wall paintings, mosaics and ceramics dating from 3C BC to 1C AD, while various shipwrecks and port substructures have been found off the coast.

VISITING THE ISLANDS
ÎLE STE-MARGUERITE★★

The closest and largest of the two islands, Ste-Marguerite measures 2mi/3km long and 1,000yd/900m wide. It is separated from the mainland by a shallow channel. The island belongs to the State except for the privately owned Domaine du Grand Jardin in the south.

Botanical Nature Trail

Many broad paths flanked by explanatory panels on Mediterranean flora cut through the **forest**.

Starting from the landing pier, follow the marked trail around the side of the fort, then join the Eucalyptus Walk, which leads to the Domaine du Grand Jardin, crossing the length of the island from north to south. En route, you'll enjoy views of the bell tower and abbey on Île St-Honorat. The Allée Ste-Marguerite leads back to the landing pier.

The cliffs are fairly steep, making it difficult to reach the shore, but there is a path that skirts the edge of the entire island *(2hr walk)*.

Coastline of Île Ste-Marguerite

J. Malburet/MICHELIN

PRACTICAL INFORMATION

Reaching the Islands (from Cannes)

To the Île Ste-Marguerite – *Cie Trans Côte d'Azur, Quai Laubeuf, Cannes.* ℘*04 92 98 71 30. www.trans-cote-azur.com.* Regular shuttle service, 4–8 depart-ures daily depending on the season. Excursions to Monaco, St-Tropez, etc.

To the Île St-Honorat – *Société Planaria, Quai Laubeuf, Cannes.* ℘*04 92 98 71 38. www.cannes-ilesdelerins.com.* ⊜*11€ round trip (5.50€ children).*

Regular shuttle service throughout the year.

ON THE ISLANDS

On the Île Ste-Marguerite – No hotels, only restaurants and cafés. Visitors are advised to bring food and water supplies for the day.

On the Île St-Honorat – The whole island is occupied by the monastery. A restaurant and boutique are run by the monks. Bicycles are forbidden and tourists are expected to dress appropriately.

Fort Royal

🕐*Open Apr–May Tue–Sun 10.30am–1.15pm, 2.15pm–5.45pm; Jun–Sept daily 10am–5.45pm; Oct–Mar Tue–Sun 10.30am–1.15pm, 2.15pm–4.45pm.* 🕐*Closed public holidays. Guided tours available Jun–Sept.* ⊜*3.50€.* ℘*04 93 38 55 26.*

This fortress was built by Richelieu and overhauled by **Vauban** in 1712, with a monumental entrance on the west side. The disgraced Maréchal Bazaine, blamed for France's humiliating defeat at the hands of the Prussian army in 1871, was imprisoned here (1873–74) until his escape to Spain.

From the terrace there is an extensive **view★** of the coast.

Prisons

The entrance hall gives access to the museum *(right)* and the prisons *(left)*. On the right is the cell of the **Man in the Iron Mask** (👁*see box*). The adjacent cells were occupied by six Protestant pastors, imprisoned after the Revocation of the Edict of Nantes (1685).

Musée de la Mer

The Marine Museum houses a display of archaeological finds excavated in the fort and offshore from a 1C BC Roman galley and a 10C Saracen ship. The

The Riddle of the "Iron Mask"

In 1687 the fortress of Ste-Marguerite, then a state prison, received the famous "Man in the Iron Mask", who, according to Voltaire, wore a leather mask with steel springs. Theories as to the identity of this prisoner abound. He is said to have been an illegitimate brother of Louis XIV, a secretary who had tricked the "Sun King", an accomplice of Madame Brinvilliers the poisoner, and even the son-in-law of a doctor whose autopsy of Louis XIII revealed the king's inability to father a child. An even wilder theory maintains that a lady companion to the Man in the Iron Mask gave birth to a son, who was taken away to Corsica. Entrusted (*remis de bonne part*) to foster parents, this child is said to have been "Buonaparte", the great-grandfather of Napoleon. The most likely explanation is, however, a little less romantic. Since prison governors were paid more for keeping high-ranking prisoners, the new governor of Ste-Marguerite, running low on condemned aristocrats, appears to have masked one of his prisoners and paraded him through Provence on his way to the island. This generated a buzz of excitement in far-off Paris, where rumours of an important prisoner whose identity was so sensitive it could bring down the kingdom spread like wildfire.

Brotherly Love

According to local legend, St Honoratus settled on Lérina, the smaller of the two islands, in the 4C and founded a monastery which was to become one of the most famous in all Christendom. Women were banned from the island, so his sister Marguerite set up a convent on the neighbouring island, where Honorat could come to see her regularly.

St Aigulf founded the Benedictine Order in this monastery in 660. Raids by pirates and the arrival of military garrisons were not favourable to monastic life, so by 1788 the monastery was closed. In 1859 the monastery once more became a place of worship, and in 1869 it was taken over by Cistercians from Sénanque Abbey.

collection features amphorae and Roman glass and pottery that are surprisingly well preserved and includes a bowl of 2,000-year old hazelnuts.

ÎLE ST-HONORAT★★

St-Honorat (1mi/1.5km long, 437yd/ 400m wide) is the private property of the monastery, but walking and swimming are permitted. Some of the land is used by the monks, who make a liqueur called Lérina, along with a small selection of wines, but the rest is covered by a fine forest of umbrella and sea pines, eucalyptus and cypress trees.

Island Walking Tour★★

🚶2hr.

Starting from the landing pier, an attractive shaded path skirts the coastline. Occasionally veering inland, it offers **views** of the island, its cultivated fields and forested paths, as well as Île Ste-Marguerite and the mainland.

Ancien Monastère Fortifié★

🕐*Open daily May–Sept 9.30am–6pm; Oct–Apr 9.30am–5pm. www.abbaye delerins.com.*

The remarkably high "keep" of this old fortified monastery on the southern coastline was built in 1073 by the Abbot of Lérins to protect the monks from Saracen pirates.

The **cloisters** with pointed arches and the 14C and 17C vaulting (one of the columns is a Roman milestone) enclose a square courtyard covering a rainwater tank paved with marble.

The upper gallery houses the chapel of the Ste-Croix. From the platform with

its 15C battlements and crenellations is a **view★★** extending over the coastline.

Monastère Moderne

Only the church is open to the public.
🕐*Open daily 8.30am–6pm.*
🎟*No charge.* ✆*04 92 99 54 00.*
www.abbayedelerins.com.

The early buildings (11C–12C) occupied by the monks have been incorporated into the "new" 19C monastery.

Two of the original seven ancient **chapels** scattered about the island have retained their former appearance: **La Trinité** (5–11C) to the east and the 17C **St-Sauveur** to the northwest.

ADDRESSES

🍴 EAT

🍽 **Le Guérite** – *Ste-Marguerite (Island). ✆04 93 43 49 25. www.laguerite.fr. Open for lunch and dinner Jul–Aug; rest of the year, lunch only.* Views of Cannes Bay complement the grilled fish and meats served at this no-frills restaurant. Wine made by island monks is on the menu.

🍽🍽 **La Tonnelle** – *St-Honorat (Island). ✆04 92 99 54 08. www.tonnelle-abbaye delerins.com.* Views of Île Ste-Marguerite from the large terrace *(heated in winter)* of this restaurant are wonderful. Gourmet French cuisine and snacks.

SHOPPING

CISTERCIAN SOUVENIRS
Boutique de l'Abbaye de Lérins – *Île St-Honorat. ✆04 92 99 54 00. www.abbayedelerins.com. Closed Dec.* This shop attached to the Cistercian abbey sells wine, honey and *Lérina* liqueur.

Mandelieu-la-Napoule

Alpes-Maritimes

Refreshed by the River Siagne and bordered by lush plains, this small town begins inland at the foot of the Tanneron massif in Mandelieu and stretches down to a pretty bay at La Napoule, popular for its small, family beaches.

THE SEASIDE

Three scenic beaches (two of which are private) run along the bay, offering impressive **views** of the area.

The **Port de la Napoule** can accommodate 1,140 pleasure craft, while the smaller Port de la Rague has 688 moorings. A coastal path *(0.6mi/1km)* connects the two.

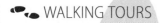 WALKING TOURS

Panoramic Tour★

🚶 *Leave from the post office by rue des Hautes-Roches. 45min round trip.*

This pleasant walk wends its way up the **Colline de San Peyré** and affords fantastic **views★** over the Tanneron, La Napoule Bay, Cannes and Cap d'Antibes.

Along the Siagne

🚶 A trail follows the River Siagne from the centre of Mandelieu *(behind the Salle Olympie)* all the way to the sea.

▶ **Population:** 20,200.

🚗 **Michelin Map:** 341 C6; region map: pp228–229.

ℹ **Info:** 806, ave. de Cannes. ℘04 93 93 64 64. www.ot-mandelieu.fr.

▶ **Location:** Lying at the foot of the Esterel and Tanneron massifs, Mandelieu sits on the coast 5mi/8km west of Cannes on the N 98.

🅿 **Parking:** There are several free parking areas near the casino and along the coastline in La Napoule.

PRACTICAL INFORMATION

Guided Tours – The **Mandelieu** tourist office runs guided **mimosa tours** of the Esterel and Tanneron massifs *(late Jan–early Mar)*. Guided tours of **La Napoule**, the castle and coastline are available from the La Napoule tourist office *(reserve 48 hours in advance)*.

SIGHT
Château-Musée

Ave. Henry Clews, La Napoule. ⏱*Open Feb–Oct daily 10am–6pm; Nov–Jan Mon–Fri 2pm–5pm, Sat–Sun and public holidays 10am–5pm.*👣*Guided tours (45min)* ⊛*6€.* ℘*04 93 49 95 05. www.chateau-lanapoule.com.*

Château-Musée garden

D. Pazery/MICHELIN

241

Only two towers remain of the original 14C stronghold converted by the American sculptor **Henry Clews** and his architect wife, Marie. Located on an outstanding **site★** at the foot of the Esterel corniche, the château is a curious blend of Romanesque and Gothic styles with an Oriental twist. Fantastical animals and human figures sculpted by the artist embellish the architecture. The salon, Gothic dining room, painting studio and crypt are open to the public. The tearoom terrace *(Apr–Dec)* offers an impressive **panorama** of the sea *(arrive early to secure a table)*. The beautiful **gardens**, with fountains and ponds, were designed by Mrs. Clews.

ADDRESSES

⌂ STAY

⊜⊜ **Corniche d'Or** – *pl. de la Fontaine, La Napoule.* ℘*04 93 49 92 51. www.cornichedor.com. Closed late Nov – mid-Dec. 12 rooms.* ⊆*3.50/8€.* Situated on a tiny square near the station, this modest hotel has simple rooms. Many have a small balcony, and two have a large terrace.

⊜⊜ **Hôtel Villa Parisiana** – *5 rue Argentière.* ℘*04 93 49 93 02. www.villa parisiana.com. 13 rooms.* ⊆*7€.* This Edwardian villa is located in a residential area. It houses a congenial, family-style hotel with a trellised terrace for a pleasant stay, despite the proximity of the noisy railway.

⟡ EAT

⊜⊜⊜ **Le Marco Polo** – *ave. de Lérins, Théoule-sur-Mer.* ℘*04 93 49 96 59. Closed mid-Nov to mid-Dec.* Casual restaurant ideally situated on the beach, with rattan furniture and a terrace overlooking the Bay of Cannes. Salads at lunch, hearty dinner menus.

⊜⊜⊜ **La Pomme d'Amour** – *209 ave. du 23 août.* ℘*04 93 49 95 19. Closed mid-Nov–early Dec, Tue lunch, Mon.* This small restaurant with a big reputation in La Napoule is located close to the station. Pleasantly cosy, artfully furnished dining room. Traditional and regional cuisine.

SHOPPING

MARKETS
Mandelieu – Place du Mail, Wednesday and Friday mornings.

La Napoule – Place St-Fainéant Thursday morning, and Place Jeanne-d'Arc on Saturday morning.

SPORT AND LEISURE

⚲⚲ Domaine de Barbossi – *3300 ave. du Fréjus.* ℘*04 86 11 91 99. www.ddeb.fr.* This upscale resort makes a perfect outing for the whole family. Besides a hotel and restaurant, there are facilities for tennis, mountain biking, trampolining, miniature golf, horseback riding and playing areas for children. Wines produced on the estate are for sale.

Golf de Cannes-Mandelieu Riviera – *ave. des Amazones.* ℘*04 92 97 49 49. www.ddeb.fr.* An 18-hole golf course at the foot of the Esterel, with putting green and driving range. Club house restaurant.

⚲⚲ Guy-Durante Organisation – *ave. du Gén.-de-Gaulle at plage de Robinson.* ℘*04 93 49 44 19. http://mandelieufunspot. over-blog.com.* ⏱*Jul–Aug daily 7.30am–7pm, May–mid-Oct 8am–6pm.* A popular spot with surfers and wake-boarders.

CASINO

Pullman Cannes Mandelieu Royal Casino – *605 ave. du Général-de-Gaulle.* ℘*04 92 97 70 00. www.pullmanhotels. com. Bar Royal Baie: 9am–2am.* This luxury establishment with two tennis courts, terrace and pool overlooks Cannes Bay; and a private beach features a casino, two restaurants, a nightclub and a piano bar with live music.

CALENDAR

La Fête du Mimosa – Held in early February, this ten-day festival celebrating the mimosa blossoms includes a parade.

Les Nuits du Château – In July and August, the Cour d'Honneur hosts a summer festival of dance, concerts and theatre at the Château-Musée.

Massif du Tanneron ★

Alpes-Maritimes

Far from the beaten path and yet easily accessible from Cannes, the rounded contours and rock formations of the Massif du Tanneron lie to the north of the Esterel. From mid-January to March, the countryside is covered in brilliant displays of yellow mimosa.

- **Michelin Map:** 341 C6.
- **Info:** Pl. de la Mairie, Tanneron. ℘04 93 60 71 73. www.ot-mandelieu.fr
- **Location:** Situated halfway between the Lac de St-Cassien and La Siagne, the Massif du Tanneron is separated from the Esterel to the north by a valley, through which the N 7 and Provençal motorway run.
- **Timing:** Time your visit to coincide with the blossoming of the area's mimosa trees between January and March.

DRIVING TOUR

FROM CANNES TO MANDELIEU
40mi/65km. Allow half a day.

From Cannes take D 6007 west towards Fréjus. For a description of the route as far as the Logis-de-Paris crossroads (see 2) Massif de l'ESTEREL p213.

Then turn right onto D 237, which offers **views** of La Napoule Bay and Mont Vinaigre. Beyond Les Adrets de l'Esterel the view extends to the Pre-Alps of Grasse. The road crosses the Provençal motorway before skirting St-Cassien lake.

Turn right onto D 38.

Lac de St-Cassien
See FAYENCE.

The road rises through a pine wood, offering glimpses of the lake, the dam and the mountain peaks on the horizon. Near the hamlet of Les Marjoris, it winds over mimosa-clad slopes down to the River Verrerie.

Before reaching Tanneron village, turn right onto a steep narrow road.

Chapelle Notre-Dame-de-Peygros ★
Alt. 1,352ft/412m.
From the terrace of the small Romanesque chapel, there is a fine **panorama★** of the Lac de St-Cassien, the Vallée de la Siagne and Grasse; to the east, Mont Agel and the Franco-Italian Alps; to the south, the Esterel and Maures.

Turn left after passing through Tanneron.

Mellow Yellow

The Mimosa tree was introduced into the Mediterranean region from Australia in 1839. Sweeping down the slopes of the Tanneron Massif, it has brought financial success to the region. There are three main varieties. Silver wattle *(Mimosa argenté)* has bluish-green bushes that blossom in winter and thrive on the terraces west of Cannes; blue-leaved wattle *(Mimosa glauque)* is characterised by its greyish pendant twigs and used for decorative purposes; the third and most common variety in Provence is four-seasons wattle *(Mimosa des quatre saisons)*, which grows in huge swathes and flowers all year round. The leaves are light green and its delicately fragrant pale yellow balls are a familiar sight in many parks and gardens on the Riviera.

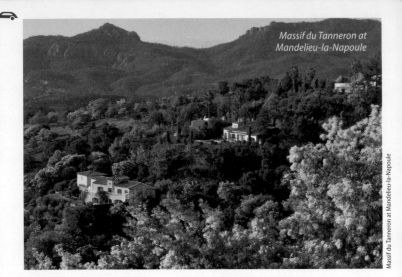

Massif du Tanneron at Mandelieu-la-Napoule

Massif du Tanneron at Mandelieu-la-Napoule

The descent affords **views** of Auribeau and its surroundings, Grasse and the vast hollow of the Siagne valley.

Auribeau-sur-Siagne★

◐ 4.3mi/7km – leaving from the Val-Cros crossroads (alt. 971ft/296m).

A twisting road between banks of mimosa leads up to the charming 12C village. Pass under the 16C Porte Soubran gateway and stroll through the stepped, narrow streets. The old houses huddle around the **church**, which contains a 15C silver-gilt and enamelled reliquary, and a 16C chalice. From the church square the **view** encompasses the Siagne Valley, Grasse and its ring of mountains. Take the stepped streets (Degrés de l'Église and Degrés Soubran) leading to Porte Soutran, the fortified gateway.

🚶Walk along the left bank of the Siagne to the north of Auribeau, along the D 38, and head for the gorges.

◐ Return to the D 9 (towards Pegomas), then the D 109 towards Mandelieu-la-Napoule. Take the D 309 towards Tanneron, and turn left onto the D 138.

Road to Mandelieu★★

The drive through the mimosa down the steep hill to Mandelieu-la-Napoule affords **views★★** of the Esterel, La Napoule Bay, Cannes and the Îles de Lérins, the Siagne Valley, Grasse and the Pre-Alps.

◐ Return to Cannes by D 92 and D 6098 along the seafront.

ADDRESSES

👉*See also addresses for CANNES and MANDELIEU.*

SHOPPING

Vial Bernard – *Les Carreiros, Tanneron.* ✆*04 93 60 66 32. www.vial-tanneron. com.* This honey producer's domain, surrounded by 25 acres/10ha of mimosa, eucalyptus and citrus trees, has hives on-site, in the Mercantour and in the Alps. Honey can be tasted and purchased on the premises. Other honey/wax products are also for sale.

HIKING

🚶 The Grand Duc forest has three hiking trails beginning at the picnic area. *Information available from the tourist office in Mandelieu.*

Grasse and the Grasse Region★

Alpes-Maritimes

The perfume capital of France sits at the foot of a high plateau overlooking fragrant plains. The modern town affords views of the cobalt-blue sea off the coast of Cannes, while boutiques and perfumeries line the narrow alleyways of the old town below.

A BIT OF HISTORY

In the Middle Ages, Grasse was a tiny republic, administered by a council whose members called themselves "Consuls by the Grace of God". Raymond Bérenger, comte de Provence, put an end to this independent existence in 1227. Thanks to its mild climate, the town later became a popular winter resort, hosting the estranged Princess Pauline Bonaparte in 1807–08 (her brother, the Emperor, would pass through the town on 2 March 1815 on the way to Paris following his escape from Elba Island). Queen Victoria spent several winters in Grasse at the Grand Hotel.

THE PERFUME INDUSTRY

Grasse had long specialised in leather work when perfumed gloves came into fashion in the 16C, marking the beginning of the perfume industry. The town's great *parfumeries* emerged in the 18C and 19C. The essences produced in Grasse, which are the base material of the perfume industry, are used locally or sent to Paris, where the great perfume houses blend them according to secret formula. The Grasse perfume industry has now diversified into the production of food flavourings.

Parfumeries – ☐*Visitor parking.* ⬥*See ADDRESSES for location and admission times.* Several perfume manufacturers in Grasse (also known as *parfumeries* or *usines*) such as Fragonard, Molinard and

▶ **Population:** 48,801.
⬥ **Michelin Map:** 341 C6.
▯ **Info:** Palais des Congrès, Pl. du cours Honoré-Cresp. ✆04 93 36 66 66. www.grasse.fr.
▶ **Location:** Grasse is located 10.5mi/17km northwest of Cannes on the N 85, leading past industrial and residential zones into the heart of the old town *(vieille ville)*. The most interesting part of Grasse is in the pedestrian streets between cours Honoré-Cresp, boulevard du Jeu-de-Ballon and place du 24 Août.
▯ **Parking:** Five indoor car parks in the centre include place du Cours Honoré Cresp, place de la Foux and at the Hôtel de Ville.
⬥ **Don't Miss:** The Musée International de la Parfumerie brings to light the town's main industry.
⬥ **Timing:** Plan on half a day for the old town, starting off with a visit to the perfume museum before taking a free tour of one of the perfume-makers. Then explore the streets of the old town, or a hike around the surrounding countryside for some excellent **panoramic views**.
⬥ **Kids:** The Grottes de St-Cézaire are popular with children.

Galimard give free **guided tours** of their perfume-making process. Try to visit on weekdays when workers can be seen making the *eau de toilette* and scented soaps on sale in the boutiques.

Flower Fields – ▯ *Information from the tourist office and from the parfumeries.*

PRACTICAL INFORMATION

Guided Tours – Themed guided tours of the town, its history, perfumeries and artists are offered in English from July to September. 🛈 *Enquire at the tourist office or visit www.vpah.culture.fr. Must be booked three weeks in advance.*

Transport – **Buses** – *Bus station at the Notre-Dame-des-Fleurs car park, pl. de la Buanderie.* 𝄞*04 93 36 37 37.* The city is served by 17 lines, which also go to Nice and Cannes.

♣♣ Petit Train Touristique – *Runs Apr–Oct and during Carnaval daily 10am–5pm.* 𝄞*06 07 75 63 60.* ⊜*6€ (3€ children 3–12).* Guided tours with a commentary *(40min)* depart from Cours Honoré-Cresp for the heights of Grasse and the Parc de la Princesse-Pauline on a small tourist train.

SNCF Train – There is train service between Grasse and Nice via Cannes. 🛈 *www.regionpaca.fr or www.grasse-riviera.com.*

In spring and summer, Fragonard and Molinard organise tours of their flower fields. The **Domaine de Manon** *(36 Chemin de Servan, Plascassier village, 4.3mi/7km southeast of Grasse; 𝄞06 12 18 02 69; www.le-domaine-de-manon.com)* allows access to its rose garden *(May–early Jun, Tue 10am)* and jasmine fields *(Aug–mid-Oct Tue 9am).*

🐾 WALKING TOURS

OLD TOWN★
Allow 1hr.
The houses of old Grasse are the colour of the sunset: red ochre, orange, yellow, pink and sometimes grey, since many of the villagers have abandoned the historic centre for more modern housing in the valley.

▷ Leave the car in the car park on cours Honoré-Cresp and take rue Jean-Ossola, then rue Marcel-Journet. Turn right on rue Gazan and walk to pl. du Puy.

Notre-Dame-du-Puy
Pl. du Petit-Puy.
This 10C cathedral was restored in the 17C. The double staircase at the entrance and two crypts were added in the 18C. The high narrow nave with heavy pointed rib-vaulting marks the beginning of the Gothic style in Provence. In the south aisle there are three **paintings★** by **Rubens** (*The Crown of Thorns, Crucifixion* and *St Helen in Exaltation of*

the Holy Cross). The cathedral also sports a fine **triptych** attributed to Louis Bréa depicting St Honoratus and a rare religious painting by Fragonard, *The Washing of the Feet.*

Place du 24-Août
From the far side of the square admire the chevet and bell tower of the cathedral. A fine **view** extends eastwards over the Grasse countryside. Close at hand rises the **clock tower** (Tour de l'Horloge).

▷ Turn left onto rue de l'Évêché.

Cour de l'Évêché
In the centre of cour de l'Evêché stands an elegant three-tiered **fountain**. At the tiny place de la Poissonnerie, follow the street of the same name to place aux Herbes and the town's market.

▷ Walk along rue Courte, turn left on rue Droite, then right onto rue Amiral-de-Grasse to pl. aux Aires.

Place aux Aires
This square was once used by local tanners. At no. 33, the **Hôtel Isnard** is an attractive town house built in 1781.

▷ Leave the square on your left and exit the old town via blvd. du Jeu-de-Ballon down to pl. du Cours.

Place du Cours★
This fine terraced promenade offers a charming **view★** over the countryside.

View of Grasse

J. Malburet/MICHELIN

GARDENS OF GRASSE
Jardin de la Princesse Pauline
Access via ave. Thiers, blvd. Alice-de-Rothschild and blvd. de la Reine-Jeanne. Keep to the left and look for the signs.
This grove of oaks that Napoleon's sister adored during her winter stay here is now a large ornamental garden with **panoramic views★** of Grasse, the Massif du Tanneron, the Esterel and the coast.

Parc Communal de la Corniche
Access as above, then turn a sharp left on blvd. Bellevue and then right on blvd. du Président-Kennedy.
⏰ *30min round trip.* At the bend, a path to the right *(sign)* leads to the edge of the steep Pre-Alps of Grasse. From the lookout point, the **view★★** extends from the Baou of St-Jeannet to the coast and from the Tanneron mountains to the peaks of the Esterel.

SIGHTS
Musée International de la Parfumerie★★
2 blvd. du Jeu-de-Ballon. ⏰*Open May–Sept daily 10am–7pm (Thu 9pm); Oct–Apr Wed–Mon 11am–6pm.* ⬅*3€.* ✆*04 97 05 58 00. www.museesdegrasse.com.*
Fresh from a four-year renovation, this modern museum, topped by a glass atrium, covers more than 3,000 years of perfume-making history. Among the **50,000 artefacts** on show are items from Guerlain, Patou, Lanvin and Chanel, including perfume flasks, vessels, scent bottles, boxes, chests, and even travel accessories belonging to Marie Antoinette.

Musée d'Art et d'Histoire de Provence
2 rue Mirabeau. ⏰*Open May–Sept daily 10am–7pm (Sat 9pm); Oct–Mar Wed–Mon 11am–6pm; Apr daily 11am–6pm.* ⏰*Closed public holidays.* ⬅*No charge. www.museesdegrasse.com.*
Set in an 18C mansion called "Petit Trianon", this museum explores the art and history of eastern Provence. The ground floor displays pottery (18C–19C) from Apt and Le Castellet and paintings by 19C Provençal artists (Chabaud, Camoin). In the basement are the mansion's reconstructed kitchens, and an archaeological display evoking the daily life of local people, from Prehistoric times to the late Middle Ages.

Villa-Musée Fragonard
23 blvd. Fragonard. ⏰*Same times and charges as the Musée d'Art et d'Histoire de Provence.*
The famous 18C painter **Jean-Honoré Fragonard** (⚓*see box opposite*),

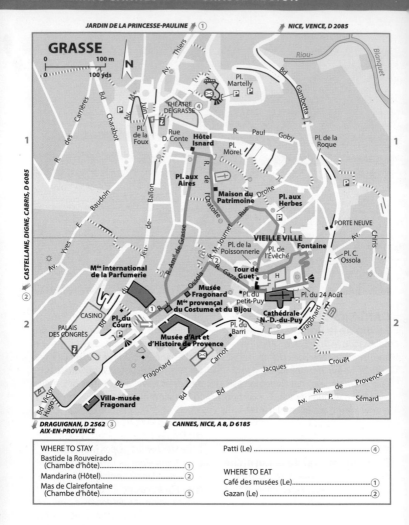

WHERE TO STAY		
Bastide la Rouveirado (Chambre d'hôte)		①
Mandarina (Hôtel)		②
Mas de Clairefontaine (Chambre d'hôte)		③

Patti (Le)	④

WHERE TO EAT

Café des musées (Le)	①
Gazan (Le)	②

who was born in Grasse, offered the Comtesse du Barry, the favourite of Louis XV, four paintings depicting each stage of a love affair: *The Meeting, The Pursuit, The Letters* and *The Lover Crowned*.

During the Revolution, he took refuge in this elegant country house, which now displays a selection of his original drawings and etchings, sketches and paintings.

Musée Provençal du Costume et du Bijou

2 rue Jean-Ossola. ⏰*Open daily 10am–1pm, 2pm–6.30pm.* ⏏*No charge.* ☏*04 93 36 44 65. www.fragonard.com.*

These private collections are housed in an annexe of the Fragonard perfumery. They focus on women's clothing in the 18C. Peasants' robes, weavers' skirts and middle-class finery are on show alongside curious ornaments made out of sea fossils *(étoiles de Digne)*. All the exhibits are genuine, except for the aprons.

🚗 DRIVING TOURS

PRÉALPES DE GRASSE★★
Round trip of 56mi/90km. Allow 5hr.

▶ From Grasse take blvd. Georges Clemenceau and turn left onto D 11.

Following a winding mountain road with **views** of the countryside between Grasse and St-Cézaire, the tour leads through the majestic route Napoléon and down to Grasse.

Cabris★
🏠 *9 rue Frédéric Mistral.* 🖉*04 93 60 55 63. http://cabris.chez-alice.fr.*
This charming village occupies a magnificent site on the edge of the Provençal plateau, looking out over the Grasse countryside to Lac de St-Cassien and the sea *(12mi/20km)*. The village has long been a favourite haunt of writers and artists. **Saint-Exupéry** wrote part of *Wind, Sand and Stars* there.
The village has several small **chapels**, including the 16C chapelle St-Sébastien *(10am–6pm)* and the primitive chapelle St-Jean-Baptiste (5C), restored in the 16C. From the defensive wall and terrace of the château, there is a superb **view★★** southeast to Mougins and the hills running down to Le Cannet, out to sea over La Napoule Bay to the Îles de Lérins, south beyond Peymeinade to the Esterel and west to the Lac de St-Cassien *(orientation table)*.

▶ Towards St-Cézaire, a small twisting route (on the right) passes close to the "9 Puits de la Vierge", nine wells of Roman origin.

👥 Grottes de St-Cézaire★
Outside the village de Saint-Cézaire.
🕐*Guided tours (40min) Jun–Aug 10.30am–6.30pm; Feb–May and Sept–Nov 10.30am–noon, 2pm–5.30pm.* 🎫*7.50€ (5€ children 6–12).* 🖉*04 93 60 22 35. www.lesgrottes desaintcezaire.com.*
Discovered accidentally in 1888, the caves emerged from the sea 6 mil-

lion years ago and descend 131ft/40m underground. They remain at a constant temperature of 57°F/14°C. Both the stalactites and the stalagmites are remarkable for the variety of their shapes – toadstools, flowers, animals – and their reddish colour, ascribed to the presence of iron oxide in the rock.

St-Cézaire-sur-Siagne
From its site dominating the steep Siagne Valley, this interesting village retains walls and towers that testify to its feudal past. A marked path from the church leads to a **viewpoint** *(viewing table)*.

▶ Leaving St-Cézaire, take a left onto the narrow D 105, direction Mons.

Gorges de la Siagne
The road runs up through rich vegetation in the deep gorge cut into the limestone by the waters of the Siagne.
After crossing the river (from the bridge, there is a **view** up and down the gorge), turn right onto the D 656, which is a very steep and narrow road. After meandering steeply above the gorge, the road broadens into an area of dry stone walls, fig and olive trees and holm oaks.

▶ At the crossroads turn left onto D 56.

St Vallier-de-Thiey

The name St. Vallier derives from St Valerio or Valerius, the first bishop of Antibes, martyred in the 4C. Thiey probably came from Theodosius, the emperor at the same time, who made Christianity the official religion of the Roman Empire. These origins certify that St-Vallier was, indeed, a Roman stronghold.

Sources de la Siagnole
🚶 *30min round trip.*

On the right beyond the bridge, a path leads to a pleasant spot, where several Vauclusian springs rise to form the River Siagnole. Farther on, a sign indicates the remains of a Roman aqueduct at **Roche Taillée**, still in use. There is a **view★** eastwards towards Grasse.

▶ At the pont de la Siagne, turn around and return to the D 105, then left towards St-Vallier-de-Thiey.

St-Vallier-de-Thiey
ℹ️ *10 pl. de la Tour.* 𝄢*04 93 42 78 00.*
🅿️ *Park at place du Grand-Pré (except on market day on Fri in summer) or pl. St-Roch (Fri market autumn–spring).*

Dominated by a seigniorial château with loopholes, this medieval village (once a Roman stronghold) is situated in the middle of a plateau of grassy "lunar" scrubland at the foot of the Pre-Alps. The 12C Romanesque **church**, restored in the 17C, has a 13C nave with pointed barrel vaulting and two Baroque altarpieces.

▶ Exit the village south and head towards St-Cézaire, then down the road to the cemetery and the "Grotte Baume Obscure". Continue beyond the cemetery for 1mi/2km to a large car park opposite a shelter over the ticket office.

👥 Souterroscope de la Baume Obscure
🕐*Open Jun–Aug daily 10am–6pm; Feb–May and Sept–mid-Nov Tue–Sun 10am–4pm.* 💰*8€ (4€ children).* 𝄢*06 80 90 70 59. www.baumeobscure.com.*
👁️*A warm sweater and shoes with non-slip soles is advised. Narrow passages.*

The cave consists of an underground network of galleries. The tour covers 547yd/500m, and takes visitors down 164ft/50m to the **Galerie du Pas de Course** and its stalactites.

Pas de la Faye★★
At an altitude of 3,228ft/984m, there is a **view★★** west towards Grasse, the Lac de St-Cassien, south towards the Esterel and Maures massifs, La Napoule bay and the Îles de Lérins.

Belvédère de Baou Mourine★
Park at La Colette car park. Signed pathway (red arrows).
👣 *30min round trip.* The path leads to a terrace with a **viewing point★** over the Vallée de la Siagne, La Napoule golf course, the Esterel and Maures.

▶ Return to D 6085. Turn around and head back to St-Vallier-de-Thiey, cross the village and turn right on D 4.

▶ Return on D 6085 and turn right.

Col du Pilon
This hill offers an exquisite **view★★** over Grasse and the sea.

LE PLATEAU DE GRASSE
24mi/38km. Allow 2.5hrs.

▶ Leave Grasse on the D 2085, heading northeast.

Magagnosc
On ave. Auguste Renoir, heading towards Nice, turn right on the road leading to St-Laurent's church.
This church and St-Michel's chapel both feature works by contemporary painter **R. Savary**. From the cemetery behind St-Laurent church, don't miss the

view★ over the sea towards Cannes and the Esterel.

◔ At the D 3 crossroads, turn left to Pré-du-La, then continue on D 2210 to Le Bar-sur-Loup.

Le Bar-sur-Loup★
See VALLÉE DU LOUP.

◔ At the crossroads with D 2085, turn left and take D 3 right towards Châteauneuf-Grasse.

Châteauneuf-Grasse
Built on a hill planted with centuries-old olive trees overlooking the Opio plain, this village is a typical perched Provençal village with ancient houses clustered along narrow alleyways leading to a church topped by a campanile. Don't miss the **view** from the cemetery.

◔ Drive towards Valbonne south on D 3. After the village of Opio, head towards the golf course, drive round it and turn left before the entrance.

Notre-Dame-du-Brusc
This charming restored chapel is all that remains of a basilica (11C), once the size of the Abbaye de Lérins (*guided tours by reservation at the tourist office; 04 92 60 36 03*).

◔ Return via Opio and the Moulin de la Brague, then by D 7 to Grasse.

FROM ST-VALLIER-DE-THIEY TO GOURDON
19mi/30km. Allow 2hr.

◔ Leave St-Valliers-de-Thiey and head north on D 6085 towards Pas de la Faye, then D 5 to the right. After going through a pass, Col de Ferrier, the road overlooks the valley of Nans. Leave the main road, taking D 12 leading off to the right (sign "Caussols").

The **Plateau de Caussols★**, sitting at an average altitude of 3,281ft/1,000m, is itself enclosed by higher land. It is one of the rare examples of karst relief in France. The plateau features dolines, swallow-holes and chasms, where the limestone has been eroded by rainwater. *Walkers should take care when near these pits and chasms, especially in rainy weather.*

Leave the centre of the sprawling village of **Caussols** to the east. The narrow road crosses the plateau diagonally to reach **Les Claps★** (Provençal for "rocks"), a remarkably rugged rock formation. Some stone dwellings *(bories)* indicate human habitation. Face the plateau for a view of the domes of the CERGA Observatory.

◔ Return to D 12 for 1mi/2km towards Gourdon. 1mi/2km after Caussols on D 12, a road leads off to the left signposted "St-Maurice – Observatoire du CERGA". After passing the houses, continue past the sign "Route Privée", which indicates the entrance to the CERGA property.

Observatoire de Calern
2130 rte. de l'Observatoire. Call for information on guided tours. 04 93 40 54 54. www.oca.eu.
The **Plateau de Calern** (4,265ft/1,300m) is home to the various installations and equipment of the CERGA Observatory, specialising in geodynamic and astronomical research. Teams work with interferometers (for measuring diameters of stars), the Schmidt telescope and astrolabes.

◔ Return to D 12 towards Gourdon.

The road continues to the eastern edge of the plateau and then descends into Gourdon.

Gourdon★
See GOURDON.
The first major bend in the road on the way to Gourdon reveals a magnificent **view★** of the Vallée du Loup (*see VALLÉE DU LOUP*).

ADDRESSES

🛏 STAY

GRASSE

🍴🛏 **Chambre d'hôte Le Mas des Anges** – *1377 chemin des Moulins, Le Tignet. ☎06 65 14 16 44. www.lemas desanges.info.* 📠 *Reservation required Nov–Easter. 5 rooms.* 🍽. *Dinner* 🍴🛏. Located at the end of a winding path on the edge of a forest, this Bed & Breakfast dominates the San Peyre valley, offering **views** of the Tanneron massif. Rooms are simple and well-maintained. Swimming pool with woodland views.

🍴🛏 **Chambre d'hôte L'Ousteau de l'Agachon** – *14 rue de l'Agachon, 8km/5mi east of Grasse on D 11. ☎ 04 93 60 52 36 or 06 03 44 16 84. www.cabris-chambres-hotes.com. Closed mid-Oct–Mar. 5 rooms.* 🍽. This yellow-fronted building holds simple, quiet rooms done in white. Some have pleasant **views** of the Esterel massif and the Lac de St-Cassien.

🍴🛏🏨 **Chambre d'hôte Bastide La Rouveirado** – *22 chemin des Colles, Chateauneuf-Grasse. ☎04 93 77 78 49. www.larouveirado.com. Closed Jan. 5 rooms.* 🍽. This modern B&B is hidden among evergreen oaks near Opio. Rooms have direct access outside to the pool and gardens through French doors. Simple decor, yet comfortably appointed.

🍴🛏🏨 **Hôtel Mandarina** – *39 ave. Y.-E.-Baudoin. ☎04 93 36 10 29. www. mandarinahotel.com. 36 rooms.* 🅿. 🍽*9€. Restaurant*🍴🛏. Overlooking the city of Grasse, this hotel is sure to be peaceful and quiet. Brightly decorated rooms offer pretty **views** of the coastline. Provençal fabric adds a lively touch to the dining room.

🍴🛏🏨 **Hôtel Le Patti** – *pl. Patti. ☎04 93 36 01 00. www.hotelpatti.com. 73 rooms.* 🍽*9€. Restaurant*🍴🛏. This 18C hotel in the old town is decorated in charming Provençal style with wrought-iron beds and walls of patina. Rooms have air-conditioning, WiFi and a stereo. Provençal products are for sale in the boutique. Mediterranean cuisine is served in the restaurant.

🍴🛏🏨🏨 **Chambre d'Hôte Mas de Clairefontaine** – *3196 route de Draguignan, Val du Tignet, 6mi/10km southeast of Grasse on Route de Draguignan/RD 562. ☎04 93 66 39 69.*

www.masdeclairefontaine.fr. 3 rooms. 📠. 🍽. This stone cottage is surrounded by a terraced garden dotted with umbrella pines and reeds. The rooms of this Bed and Breakfast are tastefully appointed. The service is excellent. Grounds include a terrace shaded by a century-old oak tree and a swimming pool.

CABRIS

🍴🛏🏨 **L'Auberge du Vieux Château** – *Pl. du Panorama. ☎04 93 60 50 12. www. aubergeduvieuxchateau.com. 4 rooms.* 🍽*9€. Restaurant*🍴🛏. Perched on a hill above the village church, this hotel offers a quiet retreat. Simply decorated rooms, awash in white, afford views of the sea or the mountains. The **restaurant** *(open Wed–Sun; no dinner Sept–Jun)* serves hearty dishes such as roasted quail, lamb and fish.

ST-VALLIER-DE-THIEY

🍴🛏 **La Relais Impérial** – *Rte. Napoléon, off the N 85. ☎04 92 60 36 36. www.relais imperial.com. 29 rooms, half board available.* 🍽. *Restaurant*🍴🛏. The main advantages of this hotel are its large, umbrella-shaded terrace for sunny summer breakfasts *(included in the rate)* and a bright, spacious restaurant with floor-to-ceiling windows. The cheery guests rooms are simply furnished.

🍴 EAT

CABRIS

🍴🛏 **Le Petit Prince** – *15 rue Frédéric Mistral. ☎ 04 93 60 63 14. www.lepetit prince-cabris.com. Closed Thu Nov–May.* Hidden behind plane trees opposite a large meadow, this restaurant has a pleasant rustic dining room, maintaining a high standard of Provençal cuisine. Large shady terrace in summer.

GRASSE

🍴 **Café des Musées** – *1 rue Jean Ossola. Closed evenings. ☎04 92 60 99 00.* This chic tearoom and café, across from the Musée Provençal, serves light dishes for lunch, such as beef carpaccio, smoked salmon, goats' cheese salad and homemade tarts. There's also a fine selection of local wines.

🍴🛏🏨 **Le Gazan** – *3 rue Gazan. Closed Dec–Jan, and Sun. ☎04 93 36 22 88.* Two delightful dining rooms with rustic furniture, linked by a spiral staircase, provide the setting for a succulent meal

Perfume Jars, Grasse

© Travel Pix Collection / age fotostock

seasoned with local olive oil and aromatic herbs. Located in the old quarter of Grasse.

SHOPPING

FOODS

Boulangerie La Floriette – *40 bis blvd. Victor-Hugo.* ℘*04 93 36 68 30. Closed Thu.* You can be confident that the focaccia and other specialty breads baked here are of the highest quality.

Espace Terroirs – *45 chemin des Castors (quartier St-Antoine quarter, near the exit of the Cannes-Grasse motorway).* ℘*04 93 77 83 23. www.espaceterroirs.com. By reservation only Tue–Sat 9am–6.30pm (Jul–Aug closed Sun).* Dedicated to educating the public about the flavours and food traditions of the French Riviera, this company offers presentations, cooking classes and demonstrations open to groups. The shop sells such items as locally produced honey, jams, olive oils, wines, syrups, candies and flowers.

PARFUMERIES

Usine Fragonard – *20 blvd. Fragonard.* ℘*04 93 36 44 65. www.fragonard.com.* Perfume has been made here since 1782. Introductory course on "The Essence of Aromas" *(Absolus Aromatiques)* by request.

Fragonard-La Fabrique des Fleurs v– *carrefour des Quatre-Chemins, rte. de Cannes.* ℘*04 93 77 94 30.* A modern perfume factory on the edge of Grasse, with tours and an aromatic flower and herb garden.

Parfumerie Molinard – *60 blvd. Victor-Hugo.* ℘*04 92 42 33 11. www.molinard.com. Closed Oct–Mar.* **No charge.** Traditional Provençal perfume house founded in 1849. Visitors are guided through each stage of the perfume-making process. There are also courses on how to create perfumes *(fee).*

Usine Galimard – *73 rte. de Cannes (going towards Mouans-Sartoux).* ℘*04 93 09 20 00. www.galimard.com.* **Guided tours year round.** **No charge.** Created in 1747, Galimard organises free tours of the perfume museum, labs, workshops and boutique.

Galimard-Studio des Fragrances – *5 rte. de Pégomas, rond point des 4 Chemins.* ℘*04 93 09 20 00. www.galimard.com. Course (2hr) on perfume-making. Open by appointment Mon–Sat.* Make your own fragrance with the help of a real "nose" from Grasse (they keep the "formula" you create on file in case you want to order more).

CALENDAR

Rallye de Grasse – Held annually in early April. *www.rallygo.com.*

Exposition Internationale de la Rose – More than 30,000 cut roses on display in bouquets mid-May, along with exhibits on the use of roses in perfume. *www.ville-grasse.fr.*

Fête du Jasmin – First weekend in August. Don't miss the famous "flower battle". *www.grasse.fr/Jasmine-festival* Local festivities in honour of **Our Lady** usually held on 15 August.

Vallée du Loup★★

Alpes-Maritimes

Emerging from Mount Audibergue and running down to the sea, the Loup is one of the best preserved gorges in Haute-Provence, framed by orchards, pine forests, high solitary plateaus and picturesque perched villages.

🚗 DRIVING TOURS

GORGES DU LOUP★★
56km/35mi. Allow one day.

▶ From Vence take D 2210 northwest. After 1.2mi/2km turn right. *See map pp228–229.*

Tourrettes-sur-Loup★
🅿 *Park outside the village and follow the pavement to the central square.*
The road offers surprising **views** of the village of Tourrettes on its rocky plateau above a sheer drop, then follows the cliff road that clings to the split limestone face of the Vallée du Loup.
Views are possible of the perched village of **Bar-sur-Loup★** (*see opposite*) and the hamlet of **Gourdon★** (*see GOURDON*) .

Old Village★
Enter this medieval village through the belfry gate in the south corner of the main square. Restored and inhabited by craftsmen and women, artists and restaurant owners, this village is crossed by cobbled streets, vaulted alleys and narrow stairways.
The **Grande Rue**, lined with artisans' shops, curves through the village to the other side of the square. Follow the line of the ramparts, fringed with Barbary fig trees, where the 16C fortifications are still visible, and admire the **panorama★**. The **church** on place de la Libération has a 15C nave and a Gallo-Roman altar.

♿ **Michelin Map:** 341 C/D5/6.

ℹ **Info:** Office de tourisme de Tourrettes-sur-Loup, 2 pl. de la Libération. ℘04 93 24 18 93. www.tourrettessur loup.com. Office de tourisme du Bar-sur-Loup, pl. F.-Paulet. ℘04 93 42 72 21. www.lebarsurloup.fr.

▶ **Location:** Countryside with olive orchards and snow-capped peaks. These driving tours, starting from Vence (*see VENCE*), lead you through both the high and low valleys of the scenic river.

😊 **Don't Miss:** The road through the gorges with **views** over the Loup.

👪 **Kids:** The Florian sweet shop at Pont-du-Loup.

🕐 **Timing:** One day for the gorge or 2hr for the upper Loup valley.

Cross the route de Grasse, the village's main road, for a refreshing stop at the **wash house**, fed by a spring since 1900.

Chapelle St-Jean
Rte. de St-Jean. 🕐*Open Apr–Sept.* ℘*04 93 24 28 93.*
This chapel was decorated in 1959 with naïve frescoes depicting the inhabitants of Tourrettes going about their daily business.

Pont-du-Loup
The Draguignan–Nice railway line, which crossed the entrance to the Gorges du Loup, was blown up by the Germans in 1944; the viaduct ruins are still visible.

▶ At the entrance to the village, turn right onto D 6.

The road runs through the splendid **Gorges du Loup★★**, which cuts vertically through the Grasse mountains, with huge, gaping holes, smooth and round,

Tourrettes-sur-Loup

© Christian Goupi/age fotostock

hollowed out of its sides. Just before the second tunnel, in a semicircular hollow, the **Cascade de Courmes★** spills down onto a mossy bed (130ft/40m).

▷ Park your car after the third tunnel.

Saut du Loup
🕐*Open May–Sept daily 10am–7pm.*
💶*1€.* 📞*04 93 09 68 88. www.cascade-sautduloup.com. Restaurant, snack bar.*
Amid lush vegetation, a huge megalith marks the entrance to the Saut du Loup, an enormous cauldron shaped by prehistoric marine and glacial erosion. The **Cascades des Demoiselles** waterfall gushes down through a strange setting of petrified vegetation.

▷ Just before the bridge, Pont de Bramafan, take a sharp left onto D 3.

As the road rises to Caussols Plateau, there are **views★** down into the gorge and the village of Courmes. An overhang has been built out from a sharp right-hand turn *(signposted)* with a fine **view★★** of the gorge to the sea.

Gourdon★
👣*See GOURDON.*
Drive down the slopes of the Caussols plateau on the D 3 towards **Le Pré-du-Lac**, with **views** of the Mediterranean

in the background. The road (D 2210) winds sharply, offering stunning **views** at each turn of the Gorges du Loup and the steep flanks of the mountains.

Le Bar-sur-Loup★
🅿 *Park at place des Carteyrades, near the tourist office.*
Nestled between the River Loup and its tributaries, Le Bar enjoys a privileged hillside site surrounded by terraced orange trees, jasmine and violets. The medieval village features a well-preserved castle dungeon. The narrow streets of the old town wind around the imposing 16C **castle** of the comtes de Grasse, with its four-corner towers and ruined keep. The **Amiral de Grasse** was born here in 1722. He went on to become a leading figure in the American War of Independence, winning the famous naval battle of Chesapeake Bay in 1781.

Église St-Jacques le Majeur
A Roman tombstone is embedded in the stonework at the foot of the bell tower. Upon entering the Gothic-style church, note the magnificent **panels** on the main door, believed to be carved by Jacotin Bellot (👣*see VENCE*). There is a large **altarpiece★** by Italian artist Louis Brea, and a **painting★** on wood titled *Dance Macabre*.

The Land of Violets

Violets have been grown in the fertile soil of Tourrettes-sur-Loup since 1880, although the "Parme" variety has long since given way to "Victoria", the only species grown here today. For an unforgettable walk along these colourful, fragrant fields, time your visit between October and March. Violets are grown in the open fields or under greenhouses on a dozen farms, covering a total area of 15 acres/6ha. From 15 October to 15 March, the flowers are picked in bouquets of 25 stems. At the end of the season, when the violets are in full bloom, the flower is picked without the stem for the region's confectioners (7,600 flowers per kilogramme). In early May and late July, the leaves of the violet are cut and the same day sent to the factories in Grasse to be processed and turned into perfume.

Take the D 6 on the right. Clinging to the hillside at an altitude of 217ft/350m overlooking the middle Vallée du Loup, the road follows the lower banks of the river. From the Vallon de la Siagne, there are **views** of the Loup and the Pre-Alps of Grasse in the distance. The road then descends along the valley floor.

La Colle-sur-Loup

This picturesque village sits in the plain where fruit and flowers are cultivated at the foot of the St-Paul hills. The name of the village comes from the Latin *collis* or "hill". It was populated by villagers from St-Paul, whose houses were stranded outside the walls erected by François I in 1537. Don't miss the **view** over St-Paul from avenue de l'ancienne gare.

🕭 *1.5hr round trip. Map from tourist office.* This hike along the banks of the Loup through the Berges du Loup nature park offers a **panorama** over the steep, dramatic Canyon de St-Donat gorge.

▷ Return to Vence by D 2 and D 236.

St-Paul-de-Vence★★

🕭 *See ST-PAUL-DE-VENCE.*
Beyond St-Paul the **view** extends to the foothills of the Pre-Alps of Grasse.

HAUTE VALLÉE DU LOUP★

22mi/35km. Allow about 2hr. This tour carries on from the gorge described above. From the pont de Bramafan, the D 3 emerges into the **upper Loup Valley★**, a stretch of country with **views** both before and after Gréolières *(D 2 on the left)*.

Gréolières

This perched village sits at the southern foot of the Cheiron ridges; to the north are the extensive ruins of Haut-Gréolières. To the south are the remains of an important stronghold. The alleys are very narrow, especially "L'Androne", which is no more than 27in/70cm wide. The **church**, which has only one aisle, has a Romanesque façade and a squat bell tower. It contains an **altarpiece★** of St Stephen by an unknown artist (15C).

West of Gréolières the road climbs 1,312ft/400m above the River Loup and snakes westward along the gorge through tunnels and beneath huge rock spurs of fantastic shapes and sizes. The **Clue de Gréolières★** was formed by a tributary of the Loup, its bare slopes pitted with giant holes and spiked with curious dolomitic rocks. The road emerges from the rift onto a broad plateau, Plan-du-Peyron.

▷ In Plan-du-Peyron turn right onto D 802, a road flanking Mont Cheiron.

Gréolières-les-Neiges

Alt. 4,757ft/1,450m. 🚡 *Ski-lift* 🕿*04 93 59 70 02.*
Located on the north face of Mont Cheiron, this resort is the most southerly of the alpine ski stations. It is well-equipped (14 lifts, 25 runs, 18.6mi/30km of cross-country trails), attracting locals.

▷ Drive back via Col de Vence.

ADDRESSES

🛏 STAY

🍽 **Auberge de Courmes** – *3 rue des Platanes, Courmes.* ✆*04 93 77 64 70. www.aubergedecourmes.com. 5 rooms.* 🍽 *5.50€. Restaurant*🍽. This local inn on the square of a tiny hamlet dominating the Loup Gorges offers five small rooms and a welcoming dining area. Outstanding **views** of the mountains, facilities for hiking and rambling and a peaceful atmosphere.

🍽 **Chambre d'Hôte La Cascade** – *635 Chemin de la Cascade, Courmes.* ✆*04 93 09 65 85. www.gitedelacascade.com. 5 rooms.* 🛏*. Meal* 🍽. Guest house with swimming pool near the waterfall of Courmes. The original building, now enlarged and restored, has tidy rooms particularly suitable for nature lovers, plus WiFi.

🍽 **Chambre d'hôte Le Clos de St Paul** – *71 chemin de la Rouguière, La Colle-sur-Loup.* ✆ *04 93 32 56 81. www.leclosstpaul.com.* 🛏*. 3 rooms and 1 apartment.* 🛏*.* Situated in a residential area at the foot of the village of St-Paul, this villa has classic ground-floor rooms. Generous breakfasts are served under the veranda, opposite the swimming pool.

🍽 **Chambre d'Hôte Mas des Cigales** – *1673 rte. des Quenières, 1mi/2km from Tourrettes, rte. de St-Jean.* ✆*04 93 59 25 73. www.lemasdescigales.com. 5 rooms.* ♿🛏*.* Handsome villa surrounded by a leafy garden. From the terrace running alongside the pool, you can look down onto a small waterfall, a tennis court and in the far distance, the sea. Air-conditioned rooms are charmingly decorated.

🍷 EAT

🍽 **Crêperie l'Hirondelle** – *14 ave. Georges-Clemenceau, La Colle-sur-Loup.* ✆*04 92 11 05 27. Closed Sun eve except Jul–Aug and Mon.* 🛏 Ideally located at the centre of the village, this relaxed, young restaurant stays open all afternoon. Ask for a seat in the brighter, more lively dining room.

🍽 **Auberge des Gorges du Loup** – *Le Pont-du-Loup.* ✆*04 93 59 38 01. www. auberge-gorgesduloup.com. Closed mid-Nov–mid-Dec, mid-Jan–mid-Feb, Sun eve and Mon.* 🅿 Flanked by palms and lemon trees, this inn boasts a traditional dining room serving local cuisine around a large fireplace. Simple, affordable food. Pleasant summer terrace.

🍽 **Le Médiéval** – *6 Grand Rue, Tourettes-sur-Loup.* ✆*04 93 59 31 63. Closed Dec, Wed–Thu.* While you are strolling the charming village streets, stop off at this family-run restaurant with its rustic dining room. Traditional, hearty French cooking without surprises or big prices.

🍽 **La Jarrerie** – *8 ave. Amiral-de-Grasse, Le Bar-sur-Loup.* ✆*04 93 42 92 92. www.restaurant-la-jarrerie.com. Closed Jan, Wed lunch, Tue.* Housed in a wing of a former 17C monastery, this restaurant provides first-rate cuisine in a majestic setting: exposed beams, huge fireplace and stonework. Large reception hall and a pleasantly shaded summer terrace.

SHOPPING

Confiserie des Gorges du Loup (Florian) – *Pont-du-Loup.* ✆*04 93 59 32 91. www.confiserieflorian.com. Free guided visit of production process 9am–noon, 2pm–6.30pm. Store open noon–2pm. Closed Dec 25.* Candied fruits, citrus jams, sugared flowers and preserves made with rose, jasmine, violet and chocolate, all made on-site.

Le Travail du Bois d'Olivier, Dubosq & Fils – *4 and 8 Grand-Rue, Tourrettes-sur-Loup.* ✆*06 24 34 29 35. www.boisdolivier.eu.* Son Guillaume Dubosq continues the family business, started in 1958. Traditional wooden bowls and vases are crafted with a contemporary look. The array of wooden products includes eating utensils, cutting boards and salad bowls of all shapes and sizes.

CALENDAR

Fête de l'Oranger – Every Easter Monday the villagers celebrate the annual orange blossom harvest, with plenty of *vin d'orange.*

Fête des Violettes, Tourettes – Every first or second week in March (according to the flowering season), a two-day festival is held with a Provençal market, tours of the flower fields and a huge parade of violets through the village.

Gourdon★

Alpes-Maritimes

Nicknamed "the eagle's nest", Gourdon is perched on a rocky spur more than 1,640ft/500m above the River Loup. Lined with craft workshops and art galleries, its medieval streets spring to life in summer.

A BIT OF HISTORY

Settled by the Romans, who built a double enclosure around the site, Gourdon was a feudal dependency of the comtes de Provence during the Middle Ages. Protected by a long rampart on the northern side of the village – the only vulnerable point in the fortifications, it was entered through a single gateway (on the site of the current place du Portail). Due to its isolated location, the village was largely spared the ravages of war and revolution, and remained in the hands of the Lombard family from 1598 to 1905.

◂◦◦ WALKING TOUR

GOURDON VILLAGE★

Allow 1hr. Park at the "Parking de la Rougière" at the entrance to the village and walk to the end of the car park.
Situated on the edge of the village, the modest 12C **Chapelle Saint-**

▸ **Population:** 437.
& **Michelin Map:** 341 C5.
▪ **Info:** Pl. Victoria.
  ℘04 93 09 68 25.
  www.gourdon06.fr.
◖ **Location:** The secluded Alpes-Maritimes village is found 8.7mi/14km northeast of Grasse on D 2085, then D 3. Gourdon can also be reached by a scenic route through the Gorges du Loup, leaving from Vence.
▣ **Parking:** All roads lead to a parking area just below the village. The village is accessible only by foot.

Pons stands in a **medieval garden.** Formerly used for threshing wheat, it now contains several species of Mediterranean plant.

◖ Continue east towards the village. At place du Portail, turn right onto pl. de la Fontaine.

The Classical **fontaine de Gourdon** was erected in 1859. Surmounted by a tall column and supported by a pedestal, it was installed upon the request of a local benefactor, who bequeathed 20,000

View of Gourdon

© Serge Villa/iStockphoto.com

francs for the purpose, a very large sum at the time. Forming a backdrop to the fountain is a restored **washing place** (1871). It has the singularity of being located on the ground floor of a house and is accessible through a dressed stone arcade of semi-circular arches.

▶ Continue to pl. du Château.

Château★

⚊ *Closed to the public.*

Built in the 12C on the foundations of an old Saracen fortress, the castle was remodelled in the 17C. The trapezium-shaped courtyard forms an impluvium sporting rivulets to channel rainwater into a well. It is skirted by an arcade similar (though on a much smaller scale) to Place des Vosges in Paris.

Château Gardens

Guided tours (45min) Jul–Aug Sun–Fri 3pm and 5pm. ⚊5€ *(3€children under 10).* 04 93 09 68 02. www.chateau-gourdon.com.

The **terraced gardens** were designed by Le Nôtre in the 17C and laid out on three levels. They are now part of a botanical garden centre, preserving typical Pre-Alpine flora.

▶ Continue along rue du Verger, pl. de la Citerne and into rue de l'Ecole.

Stop to admire the Chapelle Sainte-Catherine and the **oldest house** in Gourdon *(la maison du Chevalier),* whose wooden door carved with foliage is surmounted by a beautiful sundial.

▶ Retrace your steps and enter place de l'Eglise.

Built directly onto its rock base, the 12C **Eglise Saint-Vincent** contains the tombs of several lords of Gourdon, along with the relics of St Vincent, St Luce and St Just. Don't miss the small Romanesque font.

▶ Exit the church and turn right onto place Victoria.

Named after Queen Victoria, who visited Gourdon in April 1891, this small square offers a magnificent **panorama** over the Loup River, which emerges from the upper gorge and wends its way to the distant coast.

ADDRESSES

☕ EAT

⊜⊜ **Au Vieux Four** – *rue Basse (in the village).* 04 93 09 68 60. *Open lunchtimes Tue–Sun and eves by reservation.* The perfect place to round off your visit to the village. The owners prepare delicious Provençal food and grilled meat in an open fireplace before your eyes. Simple, refreshing decoration and reasonable prices.

SHOPPING

Sainte-Catherine – *rue de l'École.* 04 93 09 68 89. www.sainte-catherine. com. *Closed Jul–mid-Sept.* Gourmet food lovers will be at home in this deliciously-smelling boutique stocked with herbs and spices, jams, jellied fruits and plenty of regional mustards, vinegars, honey and olive oils.

La Source Parfumée – *rue Principale.* 04 93 09 68 23. www.galimard.com. A boutique of scented candles and perfumes blended on request in the old distillery, sold at wholesale prices. Also free tours of the flower fields.

Mougins★

Alpes-Maritimes

The old village of Mougins dominates the summit of a hilltop crowned by ancient ramparts and a 12C fortified gateway (known as the "Saracen Gate"). Restored houses and cobblestone streets corkscrew up the hill amid lush greenery.

SIGHTS

Begin at Place du Commandant-Lamy *(map with commentary available at the tourist office)*, a lively square with restaurants and an ancient fountain shaded by a giant elm. Wander northwest and turn left towards place des Patriotes, which offers a **panorama★** of the coast.

Espace Culturel

Pl. du Commandant-Lamy. ○*Open May–Aug Mon–Fri 10am–1pm, 2pm–7pm, Sat–Sun 11am–7pm; Sept–Oct and mid-Dec–Apr Mon–Fri 10am–1pm, 2pm–6pm, Sat–Sun 11am–6pm.* ○*Closed Nov–mid-Dec and public holidays.* ◎*No charge.* ℘*04 92 92 50 42.*

The former St-Bernardin chapel now houses the town hall, the Salle des Mariages and the **Musée Maurice Gottlob** (1885–1970), an artist who lived in Mougins from 1924–60. An interesting retrospective of the history of Mougins includes a section on the African explorer **Commandant Lamy**, born here in 1858.

▶ **Population:** 19,361.
& **Michelin Map:** 341 C6.
⊞ **Info:** 15 Ave. Ch-Malet. ℘04 93 75 87 67. www.mougins.fr.
◖ **Location:** Mougins lies between Cannes (3.7mi/6km) and Grasse (7mi/11km) on the N 85. The vestiges of the old ramparts, which date back to the town's fiefdom under the Lérins Abbots, mark the limits of the pedestrian-only Old Town.
P **Parking:** Several parking areas can be found at the foot of the Old Town.

Musée de la Photographie André Villers

Porte Sarrazine. ○*Open Feb–Dec Mon–Fri 10am–12.30pm, 2pm–6pm (7pm Jun–Sept), Sat–Sun 11am–6pm (7pm Jun–Sept).* ◎*No charge.* ℘*04 93 75 85 67.*

Located behind the church bell tower, adjoining the 12C Saracen gate, this three-level museum features numerous photographs by **André Villers** (b.1930) of his friend Picasso, as well as works by famous photographers Clergue, Doisneau, Duncan, Lartigue, Roth, Otero, Denise Colomb and Ralph Gatti. A collection of old cameras includes a **cidoscope**.

Village of Mougins

S. Sauvignier/MICHELIN

Gallery in Mougins

© Damian Davies/age fotostock

Musée d'Art Classique de Mougins

32 rue Commandeur. Open daily *9.30am–7.30pm.* 12€. 04 93 12 34 50. www.mouginsmusee.com.

Displayed over four floors, this collection of some 600 artefacts harmoniously combines objects from a diverse range of cultures, including Roman, Greek and Egyptian sculptures in marble and bronze, sarcophagi, vases, coins, jewellery and glassware.

From the Egyptian crypt on the lower ground floor to the collection of antique weapons on the fourth floor, the collection is rife with paintings, drawings and sculptures by artists inspired by the south, including Chagall, Matisse, Dufy, Cézanne, Yves Klein and Jean Cocteau, along with two Mougins residents, Picasso and Picabia. The display is worthy of a national museum.

EXCURSIONS
Ermitage Notre-Dame-de-Vie

◗ *3.7mi/6km. Leave Mougins to the north west by D 235, then right onto D 35; after 1mi/2km turn right.* Open *during Mass Sun mornings, 9am.*

The **site**★ is strikingly beautiful: the hermitage of Notre-Dame-de-Vie stands at the top of a long meadow bordered by two rows of giant cypresses (on the right beneath the trees stands a 15C stone cross). The **view**★ towards Mougins is reminiscent of a Tuscan landscape. Pablo Picasso chose to spend his last years here (1961-73), in the house just opposite, with his wife Jacqueline. The 17C **chapel**, roofed in colourful tiles, has three Gallo-Roman funeral inscriptions and a collection of votive offerings.

◗ A road suitable for motor vehicles leads to the D 3, which takes you back to Mougins.

The Minotaur's Lair

As early as 1935 **Pablo Picasso** discovered Mougins in the company of painter and photographer Dora Maar and the American-born avant-garde photographer Man Ray. He and his wife Jacqueline Roque settled in Mougins in 1961 and remained there until his death in 1973. They lived in the Notre-Dame-de-Vie district in the *mas* called L'Antre du Minotaure (The Minotaur's Lair), which became a creative workshop for artists – Picasso painted Jacqueline an astonishing 160 times in 1963 alone. In 1986, Jacqueline killed herself here with a gun.

▶ 2mi/3km by the D 35 towards the golf course. At the roundabout take avenue de Grasse and then turn right on promenade de l'Étang.

Étang de Fontmerle

This 15acre/5ha pond was neglected for many years until it became a protected site for the cultivation of lotus flowers (*Nelumbo nucifera*). It is now the largest in Europe. Visit July to mid-September to see the flowers in full bloom. The pond is also popular with migratory birds (egrets, grey herons and ducks).

Mouans-Sartoux

▶ 2mi/3km northwest on the D 6185. This town is made up of the medieval village of Sartoux, ruined by the Saracens, and the ancient fortress of Mouans that once protected the route de Grasse. In 1588, Suzanne de Villeneuve, widow of a Huguenot, defended her village against the troops of the duc de Savoie. After he razed the château despite a pact signed between them, Suzanne had him chased all the way to Cagnes, where he was forced to pay heavy compensation.

Espace de l'Art Concret★

Château de Mouans. ⏱*Open Jul–Aug daily 11am–7pm; Sept–Jun Wed–Sun noon–6pm.* ⌂*5€.* ☎*04 93 75 71 50. www.espacedelartconcret.fr.*
This lush green park is home to the 19C Château de Mouans. A delightful setting for contemporary art exhibits, it also hosts the **Albers-Honegger Collection**, housed in a green-yellow concrete cube building on the site. This exceptional collection of over 500 works by Abstract, Cubist and Minimalist artists includes pieces by Swiss designers and artists Max Bill, Richard Paul Lohse and Camille Graeser, as well as Gottfried Honegger, Antonio Calderara and François Morelle.
Contemporary artists, such as Daniel Buren, Olivier Mosset and Niele Toroni are also featured in the collection.

Jardins du Musée International de la Parfumerie

979 chemin des Gourettes. ⏱*Open May–Sept daily 11am–8pm (Oct–Apr until 6pm). Free guided tour Sat 2pm. Closed Tue (except in Apr), Jan, 1 May, 8-28 Nov and 25 Dec.* ⌂*3€ (free 18 years and under).*
Take an olfactory walk in this 6acre/2.5ha botanical garden and fields. Every day in May about 5pm, visitors are welcome to pick the famous centifolia roses (*pick only the flower, not the stem*).

ADDRESSES

🛏 STAY

⊜⊜⊜ **Hôtel du Val de Mougins** – *95 ave. du Maréchal-Juin.* ☎*04 92 28 37 77. www.val-de-mougins.com. 8 rooms.* ⌂*7.50€.* This family-run establishment on the route Napoléon has air-conditioned rooms with pretty linens, many with balconies. The quietest rooms face the mountain behind the hotel.

🍽 EAT

⊜⊜ **La Ferme de Mougins** – *10 ave. St-Basile.* ☎*04 97 21 95 76. www.la-ferme-de-mougins.com. Closed Sun eve. and Mon.* This restaurant offers several terraces, including one bordering a small stream, plus an artfully decorated dining room. All-you-can-eat buffet with 50 starters, several hot main courses and 20 desserts.

⊜⊜⊜ **L'Amandier de Mougins** – *48 ave. Jean-Charles Mallet.* ☎*04 93 90 00 91. www.amandier.fr.* A 14C press has been converted into a lovely inn with a vaulted dining area and a tiny terrace that is invariably booked for both lunch and dinner. It has earned a well-deserved reputation, thanks to its attractive setting, home cooking and warm, congenial welcome.

⊜⊜⊜ **La Méditerranée Brasserie** – *32 pl. du Commandant Lamy.* ☎*04 93 90 03 47. www.brasseriemediterranee.fr.* This bistro on the village square has a fine terrace overlooking the main street. The menu presents Provençal specialities made with fresh local produce. At least half a dozen wines by the glass are available.

Valbonne
Alpes-Maritimes

Valbonne's tidy grid of picturesque, lovingly restored streets lined with art galleries and chic boutiques stands in stark contrast to its high-tech neighbour Sophia-Antipolis, Europe's answer to Silicon Valley.

SIGHTS
The Village
Map available from the tourist office.
A haven of calm, light years from the technology park next door, this village was rebuilt by the monks of Lérins on a grid pattern in the 16C, with the houses doubling as ramparts. The **place des Arcades**, with its 15C–17C arcading and old elm trees, provides an attractive backdrop to its lively cafés and restaurants. The 19C drinking troughs and fountains, rings for tethering horses and donkeys, and *chasses-roues* wheelblockers placed at the corner of buildings to slow down speeding carriages hint at the village's car-free past.

Church
South of the village on the Brague River.
An abbey founded in 1199 by the Chalais Order now serves as the parish church.

- ▶ **Population:** 12,114.
- **Michelin Map:** 341 D6.
- **Info:** 1 pl. de l'Hôtel-de-Ville. ☎ 04 93 12 34 50. www.tourisme-valbonne.com.
- **Location:** Valbonne is situated between Grasse (7mi/11.5km) and Biot (5.6mi/9km) on the D 4.
- **Parking:** The village itself is a pedestrian zone, with several large free-parking areas to the west and south of the town.
- **Don't Miss:** The parc de Valmasque for a short hike.
- **Timing:** Allow 2hr to visit the historic village and the musée du Patrimoine.
- **Kids:** Nature discovery walks and play areas in the parc de Valmasque.

Its Latin cross layout with a square chevet is typical of austere Chalais buildings. The abbey houses an interesting **Musée du Patrimoine** (◷ *open Tue–Sat Jun–Sept 3pm–7pm, public holidays 2pm–6pm; Oct–mid-Dec and mid-Jan–*

Place des Arcades

© ARCO/Lenz, G/age fotostock

May 2pm–6pm; ⊚2€; ℘04 93 12 96 54; www.abbyvalb.org) that explores the area's heritage through 2,000 items of furniture, tools, utensils and costumes displayed in authentic settings. The highlight of the museum, a vast room on the upper floor, presents the ancient crafts of Valbonne, traditional domestic life in the village and the leisure pursuits of yesteryear.

Guided tour of the village – ℘04 93 12 96 54. ⊚8€. The "Amis de l'Abbaye" organises tours *(1.5hr)* of the Romanesque Chalais abbey church, the heritage museum and the town's glass-blowing and pottery workshops.

🚶 *5.6mi/9km.* A scenic, wooded path runs along the Brague River between Valbonne and Biot village, accessible from the bridge by the church.

Parc de Valmasque

🍃 Stretching between the districts of Valbonne Sophia-Antipolis and Mougins, this 1,386 acre/561ha park offers 12.4mi/20km of paths shaded by pines and oak trees, 300 picnic tables, bird-spotting platforms and play areas. Nature walks, workshops, introductions to ecosystems and climbing for adults and children are regularly organised by local organisations (visit www.cg06.fr for more details).

Sophia Antipolis

Covering an area of 5,930 acres/2,400ha and dotted with buildings that blend perfectly into its vast green spaces, this site has been designed on the model of an American campus. Sophia Antipolis was founded by an association of the same name in 1969, under the auspices of the director of the École des Mines, Pierre Laffitte. Its proximity to the motorway and Nice-Côte d'Azur international airport make Sophia Antipolis an ideal location for 1,200 French and international businesses specialising in five main sectors: information technology; electronics and telecommunications; health sciences and biotechnology; teaching and research; and environmental sciences. A total of 26,000 people work on the site.

Europe's leading technology park, Sophia Antipolis marks the end of the **high-tech route** that links a number of hubs between Aix-en-Provence and Valbonne.

Exhibitions are held at the Fondation Sophia Antipolis on-site.

ADDRESSES

🛏 STAY

⊚⊜🍴 **Chambre d'hôte Le Cheneau** – *205 rte d'Antibes.* ℘04 93 12 13 94. *http://riviera-bandb.vadif.com.* 🚭. *3 rooms.* 🚲 Located between Valbonne and Mougins, this spacious Provençal villa set in parkland has comfortable, well-appointed rooms with large bathrooms. A fully-equipped kitchen is available for the use of guests. Shady terrace.

⊚⊜🍴🍴 **Château de la Bégude** – *Opio, 2km/1mi northeast of Valbonne by rte de Biot.* ℘04 93 12 37 00. *www. opengolfclub.com/begude. Closed mid-Nov–mid-Dec. 34 rooms.* 🅿. 🚲20€. *Restaurant* ⊚⊜🍴🍴. This luxurious 17C manor with a pool on the site of the Opio-Valbonne golf course combines the sensuality of old stone with modern conveniences. The restaurant is also used as a clubhouse and bar for golfers.

🍴 EAT

⊚⊜🍴 **Auberge Fleurie** – *1016 rte. de Cannes, 0.6mi/1.5km by the D 3.* ℘04 93 12 02 80. *Closed early Dec–mid-Jan, Mon–Tue.* Choose between the dining room or the outdoor veranda to enjoy the generous helpings of imaginative and carefully prepared cuisine, with dishes such as duck pâté with aubergines (eggplant).

CALENDAR

Village market – Every Friday.

Antiques fair – First Sunday of every month in Valbonne village.

Fête de la Saint-Blaise – On or near the feast of St-Blaise (3 Feb), discover local wines, honey, olives and olive oil and herbs at this late-Jan-early Feb festival.

Christmas market – 22–24 December in Valbonne.

Vallauris
Alpes-Maritimes

Pablo Picasso chose to spend his final years in this small village on a gently sloping hill, where he indulged his passion for ceramics and revived the village's ancient pottery-making traditions.

SIGHTS
Château-Museum★
Pl. de la Libération. ○*Open Jul–Aug daily 10am–7pm; Sept–Jun Wed–Mon 10am–12.15pm, 2pm–5pm.* ∞*3.25€.* ℘*04 93 64 71 83. www.vallauris-golfe-juan.fr.*

A rare example of Renaissance architecture in Provence, this former Lérins priory with pepperpot towers houses three museums.

Musée national "War and Peace" – Produced by **Picasso** in 1952 and gifted to the French state in 1956, this huge narrative painting housed in the vestibule of a former 12C Romanesque chapel consists of two panels: the first, dominated by black, depicts invaders attacking the symbols of civilisation, justice and peace; the second is an explosion of bright colours representing the innocent joys of peace and prosperity.

Musée Magnelli – A major collection of works donated by **Alberto Magnelli** (born in Florence 1888, died 1971), retraces the development of his style from pure colours to abstraction (*Explosion lyrique*), which he abandoned in 1920 and returned to in 1931 (*Attention naissante, Rien d'autre, Volontaire no 3*).

Musée de la Céramique – One of the rare French museums dedicated to contemporary ceramics, this museum showcases award-winning pieces donated by renowned ceramists (vaulted rooms). On the first floor, grouped around a major display of works by Declein, the collection explores traditional designs from Vallauris, including superb pieces by Massier featuring naturalist and symbolist forms. The surprising collection of **pre-Colombian ceramics** reveals the ingenuity of their creators.

▶ **Population:** 30,561.
○ **Michelin Map:** 341 D6.
 Info: Sq. 8-Mai-1945. ℘04 93 63 82 58. Golfe-Juan annexe: Vieux-Port, ℘04 93 63 73 12. www.vallauris-golfe-juan.fr.
▶ **Location:** Attached to the same municipality as the seaside resort of Golfe-Juan *(0.9mi/2km on the D 135)*, the modern town of Vallauris stretches eastward of the Old Town and its château.
 Parking: Park above the château or next to the tourist office.
○ **Timing:** Allow half a day to visit the village, museum and workshops.

A beautiful balustraded staircase then leads to a collection of **ceramics by Picasso**, who developed a passion for this artform while living in Golfe-Juan in 1946. Among the 4,000 works he created over the next 20 years, some are on display here. Superb and fantastical, they combine the genius of his painting and sculpture in human and animal forms.

Musée de la Céramique Kitsch
rue de la Fontaine. ○*Open Wed–Mon 10am–12.15pm, 2pm–5pm.* ∞*No charge on presentation of entry ticket to the Chateau-Museum.* ℘*04 93 64 71 83. www.vallauris-golfe-juan.fr.*

This museum houses the collection of Gil Camatte who spent years collecting items sold to tourists in Vallauris from the 1960s to the 1980s.

Musée de la Poterie et de la Céramique
21 rue Sicard. ○*Open daily 2pm–7pm.* ∞*2€.*

Located in a working pottery studio, this museum shows how clay was worked in the first half of the 20C. The neighbouring streets are lined with pottery shops and workshops.

La Route Napoléon

After landing at Golfe-Juan on 1 March 1815, Napoleon and 700 loyal troops, preceded by an advance guard, made a brief overnight stop at Cannes. Wishing to avoid the Rhône area, which he knew to be hostile, Napoleon headed towards Grasse in order to reach the Durance Valley by way of the Alps. Beyond Grasse the small column had a difficult time proceeding along the mule tracks. They halted at St-Vallier, Escragnolles and Séranon, from whence, after a night's rest, they reached Castellane on 3 March. The next day, the party lunched at Digne and halted that evening at Château de Malijai.

Napoleon lunched in Sisteron on 5 March and left the town in an atmosphere of growing support for his cause. Once more on a coach road, he arrived that night at Gap, where he was given an enthusiastic welcome. On 7 March he reached La Mure, only to find royalist troops from Grenoble facing him at Laffrey. They ended up joining the Emperor en masse, and that same evening he entered Grenoble with thousands at his side to shouts of: "Long live the Emperor!"

Espace Jean-Marais

3 ave. des Martyrs-de-la-Résistance.
&⊙*Open Jul–Aug Tue–Sat 10am–1pm, 3pm–7pm; Sept–Jun Tue–Sat l0am–12.30pm, 2pm–6pm.*
⊘*No charge.* ✆*04 93 63 46 11.*
www.vallauris-golfe-juan.fr.

Housed in the former gallery of the artist-actor Jean Marais are sculptures, paintings and ceramics inspired by the Jean Cocteau films in which he acted *(Beauty and the Beast, Orphée).*

🚗 DRIVING TOUR

35mi/57km. Allow one day.

ROUTE NAPOLÉON

The Route Napoléon – Napoleon's Road – follows the route taken by the Emperor on his return from exile in Elba, from the point where he landed in Golfe-Juan to his arrival in Grenoble. The new road was opened in 1932.

▶ Leave from Golfe-Juan

Golfe-Juan

It was on the beach of Golfe-Juan that Napoleon and his army of 1,100 men landed from the island of Elba on 1 March 1815 (⚓*see Route NAPOLÉON above).* This fishing port developed in the second half of the 19C by exporting local ceramics. With its 1.8mi/3km of fine

sand and large choice of watersports, Golfe-Juan is now a popular summer resort. The natural harbour is sheltered by the hills of Vallauris, the Cap d'Antibes (⚓*see ANTIBES)* and the Îles de Lérins (⚓*see ILES DE LERINS).*

The road winds round the west face of Super-Cannes hill, facing the Îles de Lérins and the Esterel Massif.

Cannes★★
⚓*See CANNES.*

▶ From Cannes take N 85 to Mougins.

The road rises above the town and the sea past the perched village of **Mougins★** (⚓*see MOUGINS).*

Mouans-Sartoux
⚓*See MOUGINS.*
On leaving Mouans-Sartoux, the road reveals Grasse spread out across the mountain slope ahead.

Grasse★
⚓*See GRASSE.*

▶ From Grasse take N 85 northwest.

The road skirts "Napoleon's Plateau" where he halted on 2 March outside the town. Pass through the Provence Plateau and then the Pre-Alps of Grasse. The route crosses three passes in succession: **Col du Pilon** (2,566ft/782m), **Pas de la Faye** (3,218ft/981m) and **Col de Valferrière** (3,805ft/1,169m), where the **view south** is magnificent.

Col du Pilon
From the southern slope there is a **view★★** of La Napoule Bay.

St-Vallier-de-Thiey
See ST-VALLIER-DE-THIEY.
As the road climbs to Pas de la Faye, there are some very fine **views★**.

Pas de la Faye★★
Similar **view** to that seen from Col du Pilon. Those travelling south over the pass suddenly discover the Mediterranean and the Riviera coastline below.

▶ 0.6mi/1km before Escragnolles, near a petrol station, a road to the Belvédère de Baou Mourine branches off left.

Belvédère de Baou Mourine★
0.6mi/1km, plus 30min on foot round trip. ⛰ *Path marked with red arrows.*
Walk to the terrace **viewpoint★** over the Siagne Valley. After Escragnolles, where Napoleon made a brief stop, there are fine **views** to the south.

▶ For an alternative route to Cannes via Grasse described in reverse order *see GRASSE: Driving Tours p249.*

ADDRESSES

🛏 STAY

⊜⊜ **Hôtel Val d'Aurea** – *11 bis blvd. du Docteur Jacques Ugo, Vallauris.* ☏*04 93 64 64 29. 26 rooms. Closed late Aug–mid-May.* Although the hotel is fairly unimpressive outside, once you go inside, a warm, family welcome awaits you. The rooms are standard and functional. Request one at the back of the hotel. The bathrooms are decorated with colourful tiles.

⊜⊜ **Hôtel de la Mer** – *226 ave. Liberté, Golfe-Juan.* ☏*04 93 63 80 83. www.hotelmer.com. 35 rooms. Closed early Nov–early Dec.* 🚭. Although this hotel is close to the road, its simple rooms, crisp and clean in appearance, are double-glazed and located to the rear; some have balconies. Swimming pool, with breakfast served on the pool deck in summer.

🍴 EAT

⊜⊜ **Le Clos Cosette** – *1 ave. du Tapis-Vert.* ☏*04 93 64 30 64. Closed Mon eve.* Ordinary from the outside, this city centre restaurant has a spacious reception room and a dining room with a dry stone wall decorated with drawings and paintings. Traditional, market-fresh cuisine of a consistently high standard is served.

⊜⊜⊜⊜ **Nounou** – *On the beach at Golfe-Juan.* ☏*04 93 63 71 73. www. nounou.fr. Closed mid-Nov–Dec, Sun eve and Mon (except in Jul–Aug).* Regional cuisine and seafood specialities are on the menu at this landmark seaside restaurant that has been open for business since 1928.

CERAMICS
Tour of traditional pottery workshops – *Apr–Sept Mon–Fri 9am–6pm; rest of the year Mon–Fri 9am–4pm. Possibility of guided tour (30min) depending on demand. Closed Sat–Sun and public holidays.* ✆*No charge.* ☏*04 93 64 82 07. www.bleudargile.com.*

CALENDAR
Fête de la Poterie – This pottery festival takes place on the second Sun in Aug.

Biennial International Festival of Ceramic Art – ☏*04 93 64 34 67, http://biennale.vallauris.free.fr.* Even years, late Jun to mid-Nov.

Festival Jean Marais – Theatre and variety festival every summer, Jul– Aug.

Reenactment of Napoleon's landing – First weekend of every Mar on Golfe-Juan beach.

Juan-les-Pins★

Alpes-Maritimes

Renowned for its jazz festival, trendy nightclubs and endless stretch of sandy beaches, Juan-les-Pins is one of the Riviera's most lively summer resorts. Protected by the Cap d'Antibes and Pointe de la Croisette, the bay enjoys a mild climate and easy access to Cannes and Antibes.

THE SWING ERA

The thriving musical nightlife of Juan-les-Pins began in the 1920s with the arrival of the first American tourists, who revolutionised the atmosphere: they sunbathed on the beaches, waterskied and listened to an unfamiliar music called jazz. **Frank Jay Gould** founded the first summer casino, frequented by the likes of Douglas Fairbanks, Mary Pickford and actress Mistinguett.

After the Liberation, **Sydney Bechet** restored music to the town and the first jazz festival took place in 1959, a year after his death, attracting legends such as Louis Armstrong, Count Basie, Duke Ellington, Dizzy Gillespie and Miles Davis. Today, the festival's music embraces rock (Chuck Berry), Brazilian (Gilberto Gil) and Afro-Cuban (Buena Vista Social Club).

- ⑥ **Michelin Map:** 341 D6.
- ⓘ **Info:** 55 blvd. Charles-Guillaumont, Juan-les-Pins ℘04 97 23 11 10. www.antibesjuanlespins.com.
- ◐ **Location:** Technically part of the same municipality, Juan-les-Pins is connected to Antibes on the east by the Cap d'Antibes (◐*see ANTIBES*) and to the west by Golfe-Juan, along the RN 7 or the coastal N 98. The train station lies only a few blocks from the beaches.
- Ⓟ **Parking:** Parking spots are difficult to locate in summer, but typically can be found by the station *(gare)* or along the beach *(fee)*.

RESORT LIFE

Down by the shore, the **Promenade au Soleil**, running between the landing-stage and the **casino**, is teeming with restaurants, open-air cafés and night-clubs. The **port Gallice**, to the east, is home to dozens of luxury yachts. During the day, admire the architecture of many hotels and private homes built in the 1920s and 1930s *(request a map at the tourist office)*.

Beach at Juan-les-Pins

©Musat Christian/Dreamstime.com

Beaches

The pines (La Pinède is Juan-les-Pin's famous pine garden) grow right down to the gently sloping beach, a superb stretch of fine sand some 1.8mi/3km long and sheltered from the winds. There are several private and public beaches all around, dotted between the ports of Golfe-Juan and La Gallice.

Parc Exflora

Off D 6007 towards Golfe-Juan. ⏱*Open daily Sept and Mar–May 9.30am–7pm; Jun–Aug 9.30am–9.30pm; Oct–Feb 9.30am–5pm.* ☎*04 97 23 11 10 (tourist office).*
Set within a vast orchard of olive trees are many different incarnations of Mediterranean gardens, from antiquity to the 19C. Included are a Roman garden, a palm tree garden, a labyrinth, a winter garden and an oasis overlooking the sea.

ADDRESSES

🛏 STAY

🍴🍴🍴 **Hôtel Cécil** – *8 rue Jonnard.* ☎*04 93 61 05 12. www.hotelcecil-france.com. Closed Nov–Jan. 21 rooms.* ⌷*6.80€* This traditional residence converted into a hotel in 1920 is situated in the town centre, not far from the beach. The impeccably kept rooms are laid out over three floors. Dinner is served on the terrace in summer.

🍴🍴🍴 **Éden Hôtel** – *16 ave. L. Gallet.* ☎*04 93 61 05 20. www.edenhoteljuan.com. Closed Nov–Feb. 17 rooms.* ⌷*€7.* Built in 1930, this hotel offers guests breakfast on the terrace and a welcoming atmosphere, just minutes from the beach. Simple rooms; some have **sea views**.

🍴🍴🍴🍴 **Hôtel Sainte Valérie** – *rue de l'Oratoire.* ☎*04 93 61 07 15. www.hotel-sainte-valerie.fr. Closed mid-Oct–Easter. 24 rooms.* ♿🅿. ⌷*23€.* Just off a quiet street, this hotel has carefully maintained, air-conditioned rooms. All have terraces or balconies overlooking pretty gardens, where breakfast is served on warm days. Outdoor pool.

🍽 EAT

🍴🍴 **Le Capitole** – *26 ave. Amiral-Courbet.* ☎*04 93 61 22 44. Closed Tue.* Only the shelves remain in this former grocery shop, converted to a smart restaurant serving traditional fare.

🍴🍴🍴 **L'Amiral** – *7 ave. de l' Amiral-Courbet.* ☎*04 93 67 34 61. www.lamiral-restaurant06.com. Closed Mon.* Small, family-run business providing tasty local cuisine on nicely decorated tables in a modern, friendly setting. If you like couscous, go on Thursday, but book first.

🍴🍴🍴 **Bijou Plage** – *blvd. du Littoral.* ☎*04 93 61 39 07. www.bijouplage.com.* Locals and tourists alike flock to this beach restaurant on the road to Golfe-Juan. The menu pays tribute to bouillabaisse and other fish dishes. Private beach and watersports facilities.

NIGHTLIFE

Eden Casino – *blvd. Édouard-Baudoin.* ☎*04 92 93 71 71. www.casinojuanlespins.com.* Seaside casino with traditional table games and 180 slot machines, restaurant and themed bars.

Le Crystal – *ave. Gallice, carrefour de la Joie.* ☎*04 93 61 02 51. Closed mid-Nov–mid-Dec.* First opened in 1936, this family brasserie was housed in a small hut surrounded by grazing sheep. Today it is a popular club hemmed in between the casino and a host of other bars.

LEISURE ACTIVITIES

Watersports – Ask at the tourist office about beaches offering water skiing, wind surfing, scuba diving and paragliding.

👥 **Visiobulle** – *Leaves from the Embarcadère Courbet, opposite the Maison du Tourisme.* ☎*04 93 74 85 42. www.visiobulle.com. Closed Oct–Mar. Booking recommended in Jul and Aug.* 🎫*13€ (6.50€ children).* This glass-bottomed boat offers **views** of the sea depths up to Cap d'Antibes, which cannot be reached by land.

CALENDAR

Jazz à Juan Festival – July. La Pinede and other venues. ☎*04 97 23 11 11. www.jazzajuan.com.*

Antibes★★

Alpes-Maritimes

Situated on the western shores of the Baie des Anges, Antibes hugs the coastline between two coves, Salis and St-Roch. The marina, the old town with its covered market, and the Cap d'Antibes deserve a place on everyone's Riviera must-do list.

A BIT OF HISTORY
Greek Antipolis

From the 4C BC the Greeks of Massalia, modern day Marseille, set up a chain of coastal trading posts with the Ligurian tribes.

Antipolis, the new Greek city that grew opposite Nice, was contained between the Cours Masséna and the sea. The Greeks were succeeded by the Romans and then by pirates and Barbarians, whose invasions gradually undermined the city's prosperity.

Antibes, frontier outpost

The kings of France realised the key military role that Antibes could play from the 14C, when the town stood on the Franco-Savoyard frontier. It became the property of the Grimaldis in 1386, and was later purchased by King Henri IV. Each reign improved or enlarged the fortifications until the work was completed by Vauban with the Fort Carré in the 17C.

Bonaparte at Antibes

In 1794, Napolean Bonaparte, charged with defending the coast, settled his family in Antibes. Although he was a general, his pay seldom arrived on the appointed day, so his mother did the household laundry herself in a nearby stream. Bonaparte was imprisoned for a time in Fort Carré after the fall of Robespierre during the French Revolution.

Notable Residents

Nikos Kazantzakis (1885–1957) wrote *Zorba the Greek* and the *Last Temptation of Christ* while living in Antibes. **Nicolas de Staël** (1914–55) painted his last canvasses in Antibes, before taking his own life. A young, glamorous American

▶ **Population:** 75,820.

Michelin Map: 341 D6

Info: 11 Pl. du Général-de-Gaulle. ℘04 97 23 11 11. www.antibesjuanlespins.com.

▶ **Location:** Antibes has four major areas: the Port Vauban and Fort Carré to the north, and Old Town *(vieil Antibes)*, La Salis beaches and Cap d'Antibes to the south. The narrow streets of the Old Town should be explored on foot, but there is also a sightseeing train *(Le Petit Train d'Antibes; Aprr–Oct daily departures; ℘06 15 77 67 47; http://capdantibestour.com)*.

P Parking: There are a few underground car parks in the Old Town, but it's easier to park in one of the large car parks along the Port Vauban *(fee in high season)*.

Don't Miss: The Picasso Museum in the Château Grimaldi, the Provençal market at the Cours Masséna, the immense yachts on the Quai de la Grande Plaisance, the **panoramic views** of the coastline from La Garoupe lighthouse, and the scenic beach and walking trail at the Plage de la Garoupe.

Timing: Antibes deserves a full day. The sights of the Old Town and port should be visited first, then any museums or the Fort Carré. Then drive around the Cap d'Antibes and hike along the coastal path *(sentier)* or the sandy beaches.

Kids: At the northeast end of Antibes is the popular Marineland waterpark, La Petite Ferme du Far West and Adventure Golf.

Port Vauban and Fort Carré

J. Malburet/MICHELIN

couple, **Sara** and **Gerald Murphy**, fell in love with Antibes in the mid-1920s and their villa became a favourite holiday haunt for their many American friends, including the **Fitzgeralds** and the **Hemingways**.

WALKING TOUR

OLD ANTIBES★
Allow 3hr (☞see map I next page).
To reach the old town follow the signs for "Palais-vielle-ville" and park in the "Chemin des pêcheurs" car park.

▶ Begin at avenue de Verdun.

Port Vauban
Avenue de Verdun commands a good **view** of the marina and the 16C **Fort Carré** (☞ *see ADDITIONAL SIGHT*), with the heights of Nice in the background. The Port Vauban, one of the largest in the Mediterranean, is lined with luxury cruise yachts, the largest of which can be found along the Quai de la Grande Plaisance (also known as *Quai des Millionaires*).

▶ Enter the old town by the sea gate and follow the montée des Saleurs around the ramparts to the promenade Amiral-de-Grasse.

Promenade Amiral-de-Grasse
This former seafront promenade runs along the vestiges of the 17C ramparts below the old cathedral and the

---

PRACTICAL INFORMATION
MUSEUM PASS – A 7-day pass (⊜10€) is available at these participating museums: Peynet, Picasso, de la Tour, Archéologie, Napoléonien and Fort Carré.
TOURS – The tourist office provides a fold-out map with four walking itineraries called "Balades au Coeur d'Azur". The office can also help arrange mini-bus excursions.
TOURS & PUBLIC TRANSPORT
Buses: *EnviBus – Gare Routière, Pl. Guynemer.* ℘04 89 87 72 00. *www.*

envibus.fr. ⊜1€ *(3hr),* 8€ *(10 tickets).*
The most convenient lines are 1 and 3 (going to Juan-les-Pins), 2 (around the Cap d'Antibes), 10 (to Biot and Valbonne) and 5 (to Vallauris). Most buses run between 7am and 9pm.

Train: The **TER line 4** connects Antibes and Juan-les-Pins.

Boat Trips: Small **powerboats** can be rented by the hour from Port Vauban's Quai des Pêcheurs, just outside the Porte Marine (☞*see JUAN-LES-PINS for glass-bottomed boat tours of the CAP d'ANTIBES*).

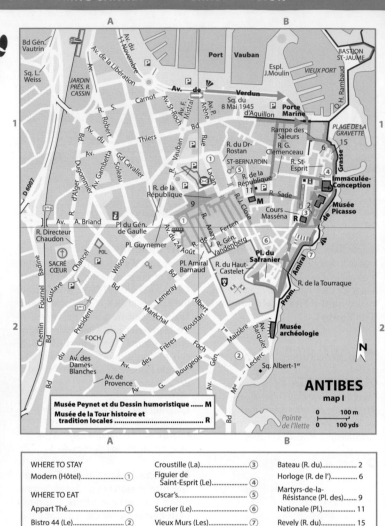

ANTIBES
map I

Musée Peynet et du Dessin humoristique ...... M
Musée de la Tour histoire et
    tradition locales .... R

Château Grimaldi. The original 12C castle overlooking the sea was built on the foundations of a Roman camp situated on the Antipolis acropolis. It was reconstructed in the 16C but the square Roman tower, battlement walk and pairs of windows remain from the original structure. The castle was home to the Grimaldi family until the 17C. It provides a magnificent **panoramic view★★** of the coastline stretching towards Nice and the Alps.

▶ Return along the promenade to the Musée archéologique.

Musée d'archéologie★

1 ave. Maizière (Bastion Saint-André). ♿◷*Open Tue–Sun mid-Jun–mid-Sept 10am–noon, 2pm–6pm (until 8pm and Fri Jul–Aug); late Sept–early Jun 10am–1pm, 2pm–5pm.* ◷*Closed 1 Jan, 1 May, 1 Nov, 25 Dec.* ⊚*3€.* ℘*04 92 90 53 36. www.antibesjuanlespins.com.*
The 17C Bastion St-André contains an **archaeological collection** illustrating 4,000 years of local history, including the reconstruction of a Roman ship used for transporting amphorae and an ornamented lead sarcophagus. The back of a large vaulted room, built on a reser-

voir, houses a bread oven and objects salvaged from shipwrecks from the Middle Ages to the 18C. Recent acquisitions include a marble statuette of Dionysus (1–2C).

▶ Retrace your steps to the promenade and take the first street on the left.

Place du Safranier

This square lies at the heart of the free commune known as "Le Safranier", set up in the wake of the Second World War. The writer Nikos Kazantzakis lived at 8 rue du Bas-Castellet. The plaque on the façade encapsulates his philosophy: "I fear nothing. I expect nothing. I am a free man".

▶ Return to rue de la Tourraque and take rue de l'Orme on the right.

Musée de la Tour, Histoire et Traditions locales

1 rue de l'Orme. Reservation required (minimum 8 people). ℰ04 92 90 54 28. www.antibesjuanlespins.com.
Housed in the Tour de l'Orme, this museum displays everyday folk objects from the 18C and 19C, along with a pair of water skis belonging to **Léo Roman**, who invented the sport in 1921 in Juan-les-Pins.

▶ Turn left down rue du Bateau.

Musée Picasso★★

Pl. Mariejol. ♿○Open Tue–Sun mid-Sept–mid-Jun 10am–noon, 2pm–6pm; late Jun–early Sept 10am–6pm (Jul–Aug Wed and Fri until 8pm). ○Closed 1 Jan, 1 May, 1 Nov, 25 Dec. ⊗6€. ℰ04 92 90 54 28. www.antibesjuanlespins.com.
The museum's wood and concrete design provides a spacious setting for the works on display and easy circulation for visitors.
The vaulted ground-floor rooms host the **Donation Hartung-Bergamn**. A large staircase leads to the first floor, devoted to temporary exhibits and the works of **Nicolas de Staël**, who spent his last

winter in Antibes. Note in particular *Still Life with Chandelier*, *Fort Carré* and the gigantic canvas entitled *Grand Concert*. The **Picasso collection** is displayed on the second floor, which was once the artist's studio.

Donation Picasso★ – Soon after his arrival on the Riviera in the autumn of 1946, **Pablo Picasso** (1881–1973), who had part of the castle at his disposal, began work on some large-scale paintings. Over the course of one season, he produced the majority of the 23 paintings, lithographs and 44 drawings in the collection. Due to post-war canvas shortages, he painted on fibro-cement and plywood.

His **paintings** are joyful works bursting with imagination, inspired by the marine and mythological life of the Mediterranean: *Ulysses and the Sirens*, *Fish*, *La Joie de Vivre*, *Watermelon*, *The Oak Tree* and an imposing triptych, *Satyr, Faun* and *Centaur with Trident*.

An impressive collection of Picasso's **ceramics**, created at Vallauris between 1948 and 1949, are displayed in showcases around the museum.

In the **courtyard** is a composition by the sculptor Arman depicting guitars inspired by Picasso's *À ma Jolie*. In the **terrace garden** are statues by Germaine Richier and works by Miró, Pagès, Amado Spoerri and Poirier.

▶ Take the steps leading to the church.

Église de l'Immaculée-Conception

Only the east end of the original Romanesque church, which served as a cathedral in the Middle Ages, remains. The belfry is a converted 12C watchtower. Art treasures include a wooden crucifix (1447) in the choir, a former pagan stone altar in the south apsidal chapel, a 16C **Recumbent Christ** carved in limewood and a 1515 altarpiece by in the south transept.

▶ Return to the cours Masséna (morning market) and take rue Sade to place Nationale.

Eden-Roc, an Edwardian Paradise

This majestic palace surrounded by an estate (20acres/8ha) is set on a promontory of Cap d'Antibes. Famous for its quaint huts *(cabanes)* and its private beach, it has become an essential port of call for film stars visiting the Riviera. A party given by Russian princes in spring 1870 launched the Grand Hôtel du Cap. After a slack period, the Grand Hôtel was resuscitated at the instigation of the American Gordon Bennett. In 1914 an annexe – the Eden Roc – together with its private beach was built. Since then it has known unflagging success, with a varied and cosmopolitain clientele featuring such eminent figures as General Eisenhower (who used it as his winter quarters), the painters Picasso and Chagall who worked here, and rich eccentrics like the oil magnate Calouste Gulbenkian (Mister 5%).

Musée Peynet et du Dessin humoristique★

Pl. Nationale. &○*Open Tue–Sun 10am–noon, 2pm–6pm (Jul–Aug Wed and Fri until 8pm).* ○*Closed public holidays.* ☞*3€.* ✆*04 92 90 54 29. www.antibesjuanlespins.com.*

Housed in a 19C school, the museum has a collection of lithographs, ink drawings, watercolours, sculptures and greeting cards by the cartoonist **Raymond Peynet** (1908–99), who moved to Antibes in 1950. He is best known for his two young lovers, "Les Amoureux", whose adventures were published in *Paris Match*, *Marie-Claire* and *Elle*.

ADDITIONAL SIGHT
Fort Carré

Ave. du 11 Novembre (north of Port Vauban). ○*Open Tue–Fri 12.30pm–4pm, Sat–Sun 10am–4pm.* ☞*Guided tours every 30min.* ○*Closed 1 Jan, 1 May, 1 Nov, 25 Dec.* ☞*3€.* ✆*04 92 90 52 13. www.antibesjuanlespins.com.*

Built atop an isolated outcrop in 1550, the central St-Laurent tower was consolidated by four surrounding citadels 15 years later. Thanks to the fortification work carried out by **Vauban**, this stronghold braved many an assault during its existence, yielding only to the duc d'Epernay and Napoleon's enemies.

EXCURSIONS
▲▲ Marineland★

▶ *2.5mi/4km north towards Nice.* &○*Open daily Jul–Aug 10am–11pm; mid-Apr–Jun and Sept 10am–7pm; Oct–Dec and mid-Feb–early Apr 10am–6pm.* ☞*35€ (27€ children 3–12). Combined one- and two-day tickets available.* P ✆*04 93 33 49 49. www.marineland.fr.*

The largest marine zoo in Europe (4,000 animals), Marineland has many large pools with **killer whales**, dolphins, elephant seals and sea lions. There are regular acrobatic shows. A spectacular **"Sharks"** exhibit takes visitors down a 98ft/30m tunnel with a **view** of a dozen grey sharks and tiger sharks. Marineland also houses a small museum of models and marine instruments.

▲▲ Parc Aqua-Splash

Entrance via Marineland. ○*Open mid-Jun–early Sept daily 10am–7pm.* ☞*26€ (20€ children 3–12), combined entrance for Marineland available.* ✆*04 93 33 49 49. www.marineland.fr.*

The largest water leisure park on the French Riviera features a swimming pool with waves, water slides (2,187yd/2,000m), a giant pool, space boat, kiddie pool and a pirate island.

▲▲ La Petite Ferme du Far West

Entrance via the Marineland car park. &○*Open Feb–Dec daily 10am–dusk. Opening days change every month, check website for details.* ☞*13€ (10€ children 3–12).* ✆*04 93 33 49 49. www.marineland.fr.*

ANTIBES
map II

```
0        500 m
0        500 yds
```

WHERE TO STAY

Bastide du Bosquet
(Chambre d'hôte La)...①

Bleu Marine (Hôtel)......②

Jabotte (Hôtel La).........③

INDEX OF STREET NAMES

Phare (Route du)...........13

This Wild West town re-creates the spirit of the frontier with a fort, Mississippi riverboats, train raids, friendly horses and a farmyard for younger children.

👥ᴸ Adventure Golf

Entrance via the Marineland car park.
&.◔*Open Jul–Aug daily noon–
midnight. Rest of year, enquire for
details.* ⊗*11€ (9€ children 3–12).*
🖉*04 93 33 49 49. www.marineland.fr.*
Enjoy miniature golf here featuring three different 18-hole courses with a Jules Verne theme.

🚗 DRIVING TOURS

CAP D'ANTIBES★
6mi/10km. Allow 2hr (◔see map II).

The garden-like peninsula, which stretches from the south of Antibes to Juan-les-Pins, is dotted with sumptuous hotels and villas catering to both summer and winter visitors. They include the **Hôtel du Cap-Eden-Roc**, a Belle Époque luxury resort popular with stars in town for the Cannes Film Festival.
👣◔1hr. The **coastal path** extends from the plage de la Garoupe to Villa Eilenroc, passing Pointe Bacon (◔*see below*).

▷ Begin at Pointe Bacon, just past La Salis beach on blvd. de Bacon.

Pointe Bacon
This point permits a **view★** of Antibes and Fort Carré that sweeps across the Baie des Anges opposite Nice and the surrounding countryside to Cap Ferrat.

▶ Continue on blvd. de La Garoupe and right on to blvd. Francis Meilland. Follow the signs for Phare de La Garoupe.

Sanctuaire de la Garoupe

635 rte. du Phare. ♿🕐*Open daily 10am–noon, 2.30pm–7pm.* ✆*04 93 67 36 01.*

Two 17C wrought-iron gates form the entrance to this small church and its two chapels. Inside is an interesting collection of **votive offerings**; the oldest dates back to 1779. Over the high altar is the Sebastopol icon, a magnificent Russo-Byzantine work believed to date from the 14C. There are 60 naval votive offerings, maritime souvenirs and a gilded wood statue of **Notre-Dame de Bon-Port** (Our Lady of Safe Homecoming), patron saint of sailors. Every year in July the statue of Our Lady, taken to the old cathedral in Antibes on the previous week, is brought back in procession to La Garoupe by the seamen.

Beside the sanctuary stands the curious Oratoire de Ste-Hélène, first patron of Antibes, who has been worshipped here since the 5C AD in the original pagan shrine.

Phare de la Garoupe

This **lighthouse**, one of the most powerful on the Mediterranean coast, has a beam that carries 32mi/52km out to sea and 62mi/100km for aircraft.

▶ Double back and turn right on blvd. Meilland. Follow blvd. du Cap to the INRA - VIlla Thuret.

Jardin Thuret

90 chemin Raymond. 🕐*Open Mon–Fri Apr–Oct 8am–6pm; Nov–Mar 8am–5.30pm.* 🕐*Closed public holidays.* 👓*No charge.* ✆*04 97 21 25 00. http://jardin-thuret.antibes.inra.fr.*

Covering 8.5acres/3.5ha, these botanical gardens were created in 1857 by the scientist Gustave Thuret, who used them to acclimatise plants and trees from hot countries, including the first eucalyptus trees from Australia.

Bequeathed to the state, the gardens are currently administered by the National Institute of Agronomic Research. They contain a magnificent collection of some 3,000 rare plant and tree species. Villa Thuret, the gardens' botanical centre, contains offices and research labs.

▶ Return to blvd. Meilland and continue along ave. L.H. Beaumont.

Villa Eilenroc

♿*Ave. L.-H.-Beaumont.* **Villa:** 🕐*Open Sept–Jun Tue–Wed 9am–5pm;* **Gardens and Eco-Museum:** *Open Tue–Wed and Sat 9am–5pm.* 🕐*Closed public holidays.* 👓*No charge.* ✆*04 93 67 74 33.*

Built in 1867, this seaside estate was designed by **Charles Garnier**, architect of the Paris Opera. It was left to the city of Antibes, which uses it for receptions and the annual "Musiques au Cœur d'Antibes" lyrical arts festival *(early Jul).* The interior retains its 1930s decor. The villa grounds include a rose garden and olive tree conservatory.

🚶 *1hr.* Follow the street around the back of the gardens to join the "Sentier Littoral" walking path that leads back to La Garoupe beach.

▶ Return to avenue Beaumont and turn left onto blvd. J F. Kennedy.

Espace du Littoral et du Milieu Marin

⚿*Closed temporarily.* ✆*04 93 61 45 32.*

Part of the Naval Museum, the former Le Grillon battery has been converted into a coastal and marine museum. The displays include a number of ingenious inventions, such as the shark cage in which the great French marine explorer **Jacques Cousteau** was lowered into the sea, surrounded by swirls of deadly sharks, an underwater jet ski used to travel along the ocean currents, and one of the first ever deep-sea cameras. From the roof, there is a fine **view★** over the wooded headland to the Îles de Lérins and to the distant Alps.

ADDRESSES

🛏 STAY

Hôtel Bleu Marine – *614 chemin des 4-Chemins (north Antibes, near hospital).* ☏*04 93 74 84 84. www.bleumarineantibes.com. 18 rooms.* ▣. ⊐*7€.* A contemporary hotel near Marineland and the pebble beaches, with easy access to the A 8 and N 7. Top-floor rooms have **sea views**.

Hotel La Jabotte – *13 ave. Max-Maurey, Cap d'Antibes.* ☏*04 93 61 45 89. www.jabotte.com. Closed Nov–10 Feb. 10 rooms.* ▣. ⊐*10€. Restaurant*. On a street perpendicular to La Salis beach, this hotel features individually decorated rooms overlooking a sunny patio.

Modern Hôtel – *1 rue Fourmilière.* ☏*04 92 90 59 05. www.modernhotel06.com. 17 rooms.* ⊐*7€.* At the entrance of a pedestrian zone, this small hotel features simple, minimalist decor.

Chambre d'Hôte La Bastide du Bosquet – *14 chemin des Sables, (Domaine des Mûrlers), Cap-Antibes.* ☏*04 93 67 32 29. www.lebosquet06.com. Closed mid-Nov–20 Dec. 4 rooms.* ⊐. This attractive 18C country house sits in the heart of a residential area. Provençal furnishings. Leafy garden and terrace.

🍴 EAT

Appart Thé – *24 rue Lacan.* ☏*09 54 04 08 24. Closed Sun, Mon.* This small and stylish tearoom just off the pedestrian square serves salads, quiches and ice cream, in addition to 15 types of tea. Small summer terrace.

La Croustille – *4 cours Masséna.* ☏*04 93 34 84 83. Closed Mon.* Settle on the charming terrace of this creperie-salad bar in old Antibes and soak up the lively, colourful atmosphere of the local market. The cosy interior is decorated with family photographs. The prices are reasonable.

Le Brasserie – *L'Ilette, 24 blvd. Maréchal Leclerc.* ☏*04 93 63 00 00. http://provencal-brasserie.com.* This sleek and modern restaurant serves beautifully presented Provençal-style dishes with fish, veal or other meats. But the desserts are absolutely astonishing.

Bistro 44 – *44 blvd. Albert-1er. t04 93 34 43 08.* ⴵ *Closed Nov and Mon.* This family restaurant, just off the seafront, serves traditional French dishes.

Oscar's – *8 rue Rostan.* ☏*04 93 34 90 14. www.oscars-antibes.com. Closed 1–15 Jun, 20 Dec–15 Jan, Sun–Mon.* Italian-inspired Provençal cuisine is served in an elegant dining room.

Le Figuier de St-Esprit – *14 rue St-Esprit.* ☏*04 93 34 50 12. www.christianmorisset.fr. Closed Mon and Wed lunch,and Tue.* A modern, stylish restaurant on the ramparts recently taken over by chef Christian Morriset. Contemporary French cuisine. Shady terrace.

Les Vieux Murs – *25 promenade Amiral-de-Grasse.* ☏*04 93 34 06 73. www.lesvieuxmurs.com. Closed 12 Nov–3 Dec, Tue lunch, and Mon mid-Sept–mid-Apr.* Red stone walls, Murano chandeliers and silk fabrics adorn the dining room of this seafront restaurant. The Mediterranean cuisine emphasises fish and fresh market produce.

SHOPPING

Marché Provençal – *Cours Masséna. Closed afternoons, Mon in low season.* This colourful, covered market features typical regional produce.

Rue Sade – The picturesque street stretching from the Cours Masséna to Place Nationale is full of charming boutiques and gourmet food shops.

SPORT AND LEISURE

Beaches – The long pebble beach of Antibes extends way beyond Fort Carré. Four other public beaches are covered in fine sand: La Gravette (south of the old port), the Îlette, La Salis and La Garoupe.

Watersports – Antibes has a wide variety of watersports on offer, from water-skiing and scuba diving to sailing and windsurfing. *Contact the tourist office or visit www.station-nautique.com.*

AMC Croisères – *1228 blvd de la Garoup, Cap-d'Antibes.* ☏*09 75 39 89 71. www.am-catamaran.com.* ⌖*From 40€.* Catamaran cruises leave from Antibes, St-Raphael or St-Tropez, with diving and sea-kayaking equipment on board.

Biot★

Alpes-Maritimes

Biot is a picturesque hillside village famous for its pottery, blown glass, and museum dedicated to the artist Fernand Léger.

SIGHTS
Old Village

To appreciate the authentic charm of the picturesque streets, start from the tourist office and head for porte des Migraniers (Grenadiers) and porte des Tines (both 16C), leading to the beautiful **place des Arcades** with its rounded and pointed arches.

Church

Set back from place des Arcades with a mosaic stone pavement, the church is actually below street level, with stairs leading down from the entrance. Rebuilt in the 15C, it was decorated with murals, which the bishop of Grasse considered crude and had painted over in 1699. On the west wall is an **altarpiece★** of the Virgin of the Rosary attributed to **Louis Bréa**. At the far end of the

> ### 2,500 Years of History
>
> Built on a bed of clay, sand, manganese and tuff deposit (oven stone), Biot was already known for its earthernware jars under the Phocaeans, Celto-Ligurians, Greeks and Romans. The tradition was continued during the Middle Ages under the Templars, who took possession of the village in 1209, and survived war and the Black Death in the 14C. Famous until 18C for its varnished jars, which were used for storing oil shipped from the ports of Antibes and Marseille, Biot is still home to a number of potters specialising in decorative ware. Since 1956, the town's reputation has been built on its glass-blowing workshops, which produce brightly coloured bubble-flecked glass.

▶ **Population:** 8,791.

⚙ **Michelin Map:** 341 D6.

🚩 **Info:** 46 rue St-Sébastien. ☎04 93 65 78 00. www.biot.fr.

◗ **Location:** Biot is 2.5mi/4km inland, about 4.6mi/7.5km northwest of Antibes on the N 7, then the D 4.

🅿 **Parking:** Only residents can drive into the village, but there are several free parking areas around the town, with regular shuttles to the village centre.

🕐 **Timing:** Allow half a day for the town and museums.

👪 **Kids:** Glass-blowing demonstrations at the Verrerie de Biot.

church is another altarpiece, attributed to **Canavesio**, in the form of an **Ecce Homo** with two cherubs and the instruments of the Passion. The panel above shows the Flagellation, Christ Reviled and the Resurrection.

Musée National Fernand Léger★★

Southeast of the village, just off D 4 (signposted). ♿🅿🕐*Open Wed–Mon May–Oct 10am–6pm; Nov–Apr 10am–5pm.* 🕐*Closed 1 Jan, 1 May, and 25 Dec.*🎫*5.50€.* ☎04 92 91 50 30.

Built in 1960 by local architect **Andreï Svetchine**, this museum houses 348 works by **Fernand Léger** (1881–1955). The gardens were donated to the State by Nadia Léger and Georges Bauquier.

The **façade** is decorated by a vast **mosaic** (5,382sq ft/500sq m) celebrating sports, designed for the Hanover Stadium.

The **interior** was redesigned in 2008 by the architect Marc Barani. On the ground floor, the large stained-glass windows are inspired by one of Léger's drawings. On the first floor the **permanent collection** features 450 works displayed chronologically in two large areas separated by a biographical

Success Story

The architect Andreï Svetchine was the son of a Russian general. Born and raised in Nice, he attended the Academy of Decorative Arts there. He soon demonstrated remarkable skills as an architect and was to design some of the most prestigious private residences and museums on the Riviera, notably the Fernand Léger Museum in Biot (&see Sights opposite). In the early 1960s, the artist Marc Chagall asked him to build a house and adjoining studio. The result, "La Colline", was a splendid construction in white Provençal stone arranged in rectangular shapes. Svetchine also refurbished La Colombe d'Or, the famous hotel in St-Paul-de-Vence catering to an exclusive international clientele. In 1984, towards the end of his life, he supervised the challenging task of restoring St-Nicolas, the superb Russian Orthodox Cathedral in Nice.

room. After Leger's early Impressionist works, such as *Portrait of the Uncle* (1905) and *My Mother's Garden*, Cézanne's influence becomes increasingly evident in Leger's *Study of a Woman in Blue* (1912–13) and *14 July*.

After 1945 the artist painted large canvases praising the virtues of hard work, industrial civilisation (*Builders*, 1950), marks a significant achievement in style and inspiration), relaxation and *joie de vivre* (*Campers*). *The Great Parade* (1954) pays homage to the circus.

Musée d'Histoire Locale et des Céramiques Biotoises

9 rue Saint-Sébastien. ◷*Open Jul–Sept Wed–Sun 11am–7pm; Oct–Jun Wed, Sat, Sun and public holidays 2pm–6pm, Thu–Fri 10am–6pm.* ⊗*4€.* ℘*04 93 65 54 54.*

This museum of local history and ceramics is situated in the restored **Chapelle des Pénitents-Blancs**, topped by a three-sided pinnacle. The displays feature ancient ceramics, a reconstruction of a local kitchen, photographs and artefacts exploring life in Biot.

👥 Bonsai Arboretum

Chemin du Val de Pôme, just south of Musée Fernand Léger. ◷*Open Feb–Dec Wed–Mon 10am–noon, 2pm–6pm.* ⊗*4€ (2€ children).* ℘*04 93 65 63 99. www.museedubonsai-biot.fr.*

This sloping garden (10 763sq ft/ 1000sq m) displays a large collection of bonsai trees against the backdrop of a reconstructed Japanese garden.

Group and individual bonsai courses are available. A small store sells trees, pots and tools.

ADDRESSES

🍴 EAT

⊜⊜ **Le Café de la Poste** – *24 rue St-Sébastien.* ℘*04 93 65 19 32. Closed Mon.* One of the oldest cafés on the Riviera, this bistro-type restaurant includes a pretty wooden counter and a huge fresco on painted ceramics. Traditional cuisine.

SHOPPING

Verrerie de Biot – *chemin des Combes, at the foot of the village, along D 4.* ℘*04 93 65 03 00. www.verreriebiot.com. Closed 1 Jan and 25 Dec.* This small factory, founded in Biot in 1956, features several workshops that demonstrate the successive stages of the art of glass blowing, characterised by a bubbly texture peculiar to the Biot production. The different shops sell all kinds of glassware: vases, glasses, etc. Discover the history of glass-blowing in the **ecomuseum**.

TOURS

Self-guide maps of the village are available at the tourist office. Their Vallée de la Brague hiking map has 11 trails along the Brague River (&see VALBONNE).

Electric car tours depart from rue St-Sébastien 1pm–7pm. Village *(20min)* 3.50€; village + country *(40min)* 7.50€. ℘*06 78 37 94 25.*

Vence★

Alpes-Maritimes

Perched on a rock at the foot of the Baous mountain range, Vence is surrounded by rivers, ravines and pine forests. Famous for its modern and contemporary art galleries, the old town also plays host to a regular Provençal market.

A BIT OF HISTORY
An Episcopal Town

A major Roman town, Vence became a powerful episcopal seat under bishops St Veranus (5C) and St Lambert (12C), and the Italian prince Alessandro Farnese, the future Pope Paul II (16C). During the Wars of Religion, Vence survived a siege by the Huguenot Lesdiguières in 1592. The victory is celebrated each year at Easter.

Bishop Godeau (17C)

The memory of Antoine Godeau has remained vivid throughout the region. He began as the oracle of the House of Rambouillet, in great demand among cultured society ladies *(les précieuses)* because of his wit, fluency and rich-and-ready poet-ical vein.

Richelieu made him the first member of the French Academy. At the age of 30, Godeau took holy orders and became Bishop of Vence. He took the new role seriously, repairing his cathedral and

▶ **Population:** 18,931.

♿ **Michelin Map:** 341 D5.

ℹ **Info:** 8 pl. du Grand-Jardin. ℘04 93 58 06 38. www.vence.fr.

◐ **Location:** Vence sits on a hillside 6mi/10km inland, between Nice and Antibes.

🅿 **Parking:** Three indoor car parks are located to the west of the village.

🕐 **Timing:** Allow 2hr to explore the medieval vtown centre.

👥 **Kids:** Contact the tourist office for children's events.

introducing various industries (perfumery, tanning and pottery).

🐾 WALKING TOUR

◐ Start from pl. du Grand-Jardin.

Before entering the old town, admire the large ash tree at **place du Frêne**, supposedly planted for the visit of François I and Pope Paul III in 1538.

OLD TOWN

The old town was enclosed within elliptical walls pierced by five gateways. Skirt the 15C square tower adjoining

Fountain at the Place du Peyra, Vence

S. Sauvignier/MICHELIN

the château to reach the Peyra Gateway (1441), one of five that enclosed the old town. Today the village bustles with artists, craftsmen and boutiques.

▶ Walk through the gate and onto pl. du Peyra.

Château de Villeneuve – Fondation Émile-Hugues

2 pl. du Frêne. ○Open Tue–Sun 10am– 12.30pm, 2pm–6pm. ⊜5€. ℘04 93 58 15 78. www.museedevence.com.

The 17C castle of the barons de Villeneuve incorporates a 13C watchtower. The castle organises regular themed exhibits of contemporary and 20C works inspired by Vence, including paintings by Matisse, Dubuffet, Dufy and Chagall.

▶ Exit the château and return to pl. du Peyra.

Place du Peyra★

The striking square with its gushing fountain in the form of an urn (1822) was the forum of the Roman town.

▶ From the south side of the square take rue du Marché and turn left onto pl. Clemenceau, site of the cathedral.

Cathédrale Notre-Dame-de-la-Nativité

Pl. Clémenceau.

The Roman temple of Mars and a 5C Merovingian church originally occupied this site. The present church was begun in the Romanesque style, with Roman inscriptions on the Baroque façade dedicated to the emperors Elagabalus and Gordian.

The tomb of St Lambert is located in the second chapel *(right)*. A 5C Roman sarcophagus of Veranus is in the third chapel *(right)*.

The north aisle contains a handsome carved doorway with Flamboyant Gothic rose windows and a 16C altarpiece of angels.

The baptistery features a mosaic by Chagall.

The **gallery** has a lectern and **stalls★** from the choir with risers, elbow rests and misericords by Jacques Bellot, a sculptor from Grasse (15C).

Chapelle du Rosaire (Chapelle Matisse)★

466 ave. Henri-Matisse. ○Open Mon, Wed and Sat 2pm–5.30pm; Tue and Thu 10am–11.30am, 2pm–5.30pm. Closed public holidays. ⊜3€. ℘04 93 58 03 26.

"Despite its imperfections I think it is my masterpiece... the result of a lifetime devoted to the quest for truth." This was Henri Matisse's opinion of the chapel, which he designed and decorated between 1947 and 1951. From the outside it resembles an ordinary Provençal house. Inside, everything is white except for the stained-glass windows and the mural compositions, a play of black lines on a white background. The gallery contains studies made by Matisse for his finished designs.

Ramparts

Leave the cathedral through the east door onto **place Godeau**, overlooked by the square tower with its parapet. At the centre stands a Roman column erected to the god Mars.

▶ Take rue St-Lambert and rue de l'Hôtel-de-Ville to the 13C Signadour Gateway. Turn left.

The **porte de l'Orient** was opened in the 18C (the date 1592 carved on a stone refers to the siege during the Wars of Religion). Boulevard Paul-André follows the line of the ramparts, where several narrow stepped streets branch off to fine **views** of the foothills of the Alps. Re-enter the old town through the Gothic Lévis Gateway (13C) and walk up rue du Portail-Lévis between handsome old houses to place du Peyra.

🚗 DRIVING TOUR

ROUTES DES CRÊTES★★
Round trip 37mi/59km. Allow half a day.

▶ Leave Vence by D 2210, going northeast towards St-Jeannet.

WHERE TO STAY	WHERE TO EAT	INDEX OF STREET NAMES
Diana.......................................①	Armoise (L')..............................①	Alsace-Lorraine (R.)..................... 2
Mas de Vence (Hôtel)..............②	Pêcheur de Soleil (Le)............②	Hôtel-de-ville (R. de).....................4
Miramar (Hôtel).........................③	Seigneurs (Auberge des)......③	Place-Vieille (R.)........................... 6
Tour de Vence (Chambre d'hôte La)................④	Vieux Couvent (Le).................④	Résistance (Av. de la)....................7
Villa Roseraie (Hôtel).................⑤		

The road skirts three peaks – Baou des Blancs, Baou des Noirs and Baou de St-Jeannet – and provides a long, leisurely **view**★ of St-Jeannet (&see Driving Tour, Cagnes-sur-Mer).

Gattières

This perched village looks out over vineyards and olive groves to the Var Valley. The charming Romanesque-Gothic **church** contains a naïve painted sculpture of St Nicholas and the three children he revived (right of chancel).

▷ Leave Gattières by D 2209.

Carros

The old village occupies a remarkable position huddled around the castle (13C–16C). Just below the village a rock bearing traces of an old mill has been made into a terrace: **panorama**★★. The road from Carros to Le Broc provides magnificent **views**★ of numerous hill villages and of the Var.

▷ Follow the D 1.

Le Broc

This hill village has a fountain (1812) in the arcaded square and a 16C **church** decorated by the modern painter Guillonet. From the village there is a fine **view** of the Var Valley. The road overlooks the confluence of the Esteron and the Var before turning west into the Bouyon ravine.

Bouyon

Every part of the village offers a **view**★ of Mont Cheiron (alt. 5,833ft/1,778m), the Var and Esteron valleys and the Alps.

▷ South of Bouyon the road (D 8) skirts Mount Chiers.

Coursegoules

Perched on a rocky spit at the foot of Mont Cheiron, the tall houses rise above the ravine of the River Cagne.
The Jaboulet workshops established in this tiny village are famous for their santons.

▷ Take D 2 southeast to Vence.

The road runs through barren countryside above the River Cagne.

Col de Vence★★

Alt. 3,182ft/970m.

Just south of the pass, a fine **panorama★★** opens up to the peaks east of the Var as far as Mont Agel, along the coast from Cap Ferrat, past the Baie des Anges, Cap d'Antibes and the Iles de Lérins to the Esterel. To the north, the white slopes of Mont Cheiron stand out dramatically.

🥾 **Hike** *From the pass to St-Jeannet. 4hr.* After the Col de Vence, a trail to the left leads to St-Jeannet via the GR 51 footpath, stretching alongside the Cagne.

ADDRESSES

🛏 STAY

⊝⊜🖥 **Auberge des Seigneurs** – *1 rue du Dr Binet.* ℰ*04 93 58 04 24. www. auberge-seigneurs.com. Closed mid-Dec–mid-Jan. 6 rooms.* �린*9€.* This handsome 17C mansion sits at the entrance to the medieval district. It has been a family-operated hotel since 1916. Here, the rustic setting, with its thick wooden tables, is alleviated by the refined silverware in its **restaurant** (⊝⊜🖥).

⊝⊜🖥 **Hôtel Mas de Vence** – *539 Ave. E.-Hugues.* ℰ*04 93 58 06 16. www.azurline. com/mas. 41 rooms.* ⅋🅿. ⊡*10€.* This modern Provençal-style hotel with ochre walls overlooks the main route into town. Covered terrace and swimming pool. Air-conditioned rooms have free WiFi.

⊝⊜🖥 **Hôtel Miramar** – *167 ave. Bougearel.* ℰ*04 93 58 01 32. www.hotel-miramar-vence.com. Closed 17 Nov–12 Dec. 18 rooms.* 🅿. ⊡*12€.* In a pretty, 1920s house with a pink façade overlooking the valley, this hotel has charming, flower-themed rooms.

⊝⊜🖥🖥 **Hôtel Diana** – *79 Ave. des Poilus.* ℰ*04 93 58 28 56. www.hotel-diana.fr. 28 rooms.* 🅿. ⊡*12€.* In the heart of Vence, with an open-air Jacuzzi, solarium and fitness room, this stylish hotel has **panoramic views**. Some rooms are equipped with a kitchenette.

⊝⊜🖥🖥 **La Tour de Vence** – *310 Chemin du Baou-des-Noirs, on the road to St-Jeannet.* ℰ*04 93 24 59 00. www.la tourdevence.com. Closed Nov–Dec.* 🍴. *5 rooms.* 🅿. ⊡. **Restaurant** ⊝⊜🖥.

Constructed entirely of stones from a Burgundian monastary, this luxurious B&B overlooking the valley is equipped with a swimming pool, pétanque court, tennis, and spacious guest suites, all tastefully decorated.

⊝⊜🖥🖥 **Villa Roseraie** – *128 ave. Henri Giraud.* ℰ*04 93 58 02 20. www. villaroseraie.com. Closed 8 Nov–14 Dec, and 5 Jan–15 Feb. 12 rooms.* 🅿. ⊡*12€.* A 1900 villa is the setting for this tastefully appointed hotel, in which the small rooms are cool and attractive. Tempting outdoor pool; pretty terrace adorned with sculptures.

🍴 EAT

⊝ **Le Pêcheur de Soleil** – *1 pl. Godeau.* ℰ*04 93 58 32 56. www.pecheurdesoleil.com. Closed mid-Dec–mid-Feb.* This restaurant in the medieval quarter of Vence has an astounding choice of homemade pizzas, freshly baked in an open oven and served in the rustic dining room.

⊝⊜🖥 **L'Armoise** – *9 pl. du Peyra.* ℰ*04 93 58 19 29. www.larmoise.com. Closed Sun eve, Mon, Tue lunch, and lunch Jul–Aug.* This tiny seafood restaurant overlooks the pretty square. Try the house bouillabaisse.

⊝⊜🖥 **Le Vieux Couvent** – *37 Ave. Alphonse-Toreille.* ℰ*04 93 58 78 58. www.restaurant-levieuxcouvent.com. Closed Thu lunch and Wed; see website for Nuits Festival closures.* The stone-vaulted ceilings of this former 17C chapel provide a unique setting for this restaurant serving regional specialities.

SHOPPING

MARKETS

Flowers and regional produce – This market takes place Tuesday to Sunday mornings on Place du Grand-Jardin and Place Surian.

CALENDAR

Fête de Pâques – Coinciding with Easter celebrations, this festival honours the village's victory over the Hugenot siege in the Wars of Religion1(592). Parades, music, dancing.

"Les Nuits du Sud" – Music Festival, mid-July to mid-August.

St-Paul-de-Vence★★

Alpes-Maritimes

Saint-Paul's slender silhouette rises up from the peaceful hills and fertile valleys of the Pays de Vence. Part of a chain of fortified towns guarding the Var frontier until 1860, St-Paul has been a leading centre for modern art since the arrival of the Fondation Maeght in 1964.

WALKING TOUR

Place des Jeux de boules

Officially known as place du Général-de-Gaulle, this small square at the entrance to the village hosts a modest market after daybreak before reverting to its primary role as the village boules court. Yves Montand and Lino Ventura were both regular *tireurs* here, as many of the older players will confirm.

Rue Grande

Rue Grande is the main street *(closed to traffic)* running the full length of the village. Many of the arcaded 16C and 17C houses bearing coats of arms are now artists' studios, antique shops and art galleries. Don't miss the urn-shaped **fountain**(1850), supplied with water

Narrow street of St-Paul-de-Vence
© Sergio Piramitz/age fotostock

▸ **Population:** 3,336.
  Michelin Map: 341 D5.
  Info: Maison de la Tour, 2 rue Grande. ℘04 93 32 86 95. www.saint-paul devence.com.
▸ **Location:** The village is 2.5mi/4km south of Vence on the D 2. Enter through the north gate. A square machicolated tower houses the tourist office *(Syndicat d'Initiative),* together with a permanent exhibition of modern paintings. In high season the narrow streets of the village are packed with tourists.
P **Parking:** Park your car in one of the car parks provided at the entrance to the village, before passing through the north gate.
  Timing: Allow one day for the town and the Fondation Maeght.

from the Malvan and Font Renaude springs, and the vaulted washing place.

▸ Climb up the stepped street above the fountain. Take the first right and then the first left to the church.

Church

Perched at the highest point of the village, this 14C Gothic building with 17C vaulting and an 18C bell tower has three naves and four chapels, 17C choir stalls in carved walnut, and a chapel adorned with a Madonna of the Rosary (1588), with Catherine de' Medici in the crowd. The **treasury** is rich in 12C to 15C pieces: statuettes, a processional cross, reliquaries, a 13C enamel Virgin and Child, and a parchment signed by King Henri III.

Musée d'Histoire Locale

Pl. de l'Eglise. ◐*Open daily Apr–Sept 11am–1pm, 3pm–6pm; Oct–Mar 2pm–5pm.* ◐3€. ℘04 93 32 41 13.

Illustrious Visitors

After a period of prosperity in the Middle Ages, the village declined in the 19C to the benefit of Vence and Cagnes. It was "rediscovered" in the 1920s by painters such as Signac, Modigliani, Bonnard and Soutine, who used to meet in a café that has since become the sumptuous **La Colombe d'Or** (*℘04 93 32 80 02; www. la-colombe-dor.com*), whose walls are covered in paintings by famous artists. Other artists came – sculptors, illustrators, writers and entertainers – making St-Paul a famous Riviera landmark. The village was once a favourite among celebrities from the silver screen, such as Simone Signoret and Yves Montand.

Eight illustrated scenes with life-size figures depict stages in the village's history, which often mirror those of Provence itself, starting with the arrival of the comte de Provence, Raimond Bérenger V, in St-Paul in 1224. An exhibition of photographs of famous people who have stayed in St-Paul adds a contemporary note to this historical display.

Chapelle des Pénitents Blancs

Pl. de l'Eglise. ⓒ*Open daily Apr–Oct 10am–noon, 3pm–6pm; Nov–Mar 2pm–5pm.* ⬡*3€.* ℘*06 24 97 42 25.* Surmounted by a three-sided clock tower, this 17C chapel was converted into an artistic site in 2008. Decorated by the artist Jean-Michel Folon, it features stained-glass windows, a mosaic, eight canvases and two sculptures.

Donjon

The only surviving element of the former castle of St-Paul, the **keep** opposite the church currently houses the town hall and a bell founded in 1443.

▶ Return to rue Grande and continue down to the south gate.

Ramparts★

From the bastion of the south gate, overlooking the cemetery, there is a superb **view** of the Alps and the coastline. The ramparts remain much as they were when built (1537–47) by François I to rival the citadelle in Nice. Follow them round anti-clockwise using the parapet walk, where possible.

SIGHTS
Fondation Maeght★

Chemin des Fumerates. Reduced permanent collection during temporary exhibits. ⓒ*Open daily Oct–Jun 10am–6pm; Jul–Sept 10am–7pm.* ⬡*15€.* ℘*04 93 32 81 63. www.fondation-maeght.com.*

This modern art museum located northwest of St-Paul on the colline des Gardettes was designed by **Josep Lluís Sert** in true Mediterranean style using white concrete and rose-coloured

View of St-Paul-de-Vence

© yanc/Bigstockphoto.com

bricks. Surrounded by a sculpture park, its two buildings, divided by a courtyard adorned with sculptures by Giacometti, house a collection of modern art exhibited in rotation, including works by Braque, Chagall, Léger, Kandinsky, Miró, Giacometti, Bonnard, Hartung, and Alechinsky, as well as artists of a younger generation (Adami, Garache, Messagier, Viallat).

ADDRESSES

🏠 STAY

😋🍽🛏🛏 **Les Bastides de St-Paul** – *880 chemin Blanquières, D 336. ℰ04 92 02 08 07. www.hotelbastides.fr.* 🅿. *20 rooms.* 🍴*10€.* Set just off a main road, this colourful farmhouse inn has spacious, soundproofed rooms. In the garden is a shamrock-shaped swimming pool.

😋🍽🛏🛏 **Hostellerie des Messugues** – *Quartier des Gardettes, by route de la Fondation Maeght 1mi/2km. ℰ04 93 32 53 32. www.hotel-messugues-saintpaul.com. Closed Nov–Mar.* 🅿. *16 rooms.* 🍴*14€.* Just below the Fondation Maeght, in a lush and peaceful garden, lies this big Provençal villa surrounded by vines. The upstairs rooms are larger and slightly more comfortable. Don't miss the heated pool and its small island.

🍴 EAT

😋🍽 **Café de la Place** – *pl. du Général-de-Gaulle. ℰ04 93 32 80 03. Closed Nov–Dec.* This café, set up on the main square where villagers like to congregate and play pétanque, is at the heart of life in St-Paul. It belongs to the legendary Colombe d'Or Hotel *(located opposite)*, once the property of the actor Yves Montand.

😋🍽 **Chez Andréas** – *Western ramparts. ℰ04 93 32 98 32.* Settle on the delightful terrace of this restaurant and sip a *pastis* as you admire the setting rays of the sun. A tastefully decorated dining room, with salads, the day's special and a choice of local wines.

😋🍽🛏 **La Cocarde de Saint Paul** – *23 rue Grande. ℰ04 93 32 86 17.* In the main street at the heart of St-Paul, this combination restaurant-tea shop offers an artful blend of Mediterranean dishes. Excellent cuisine and homemade pastries.

😋🍽🛏🛏 **La Colombe d'Or** – *pl. de Gaulle. ℰ04 93 32 80 02. www.la-colombe-dor.com. 25 rooms.* 😋🍽🛏🛏. 🍴. *Closed late Jan, Oct–mid-Dec.* Enjoy a delicious meal accompanied by artwork by Picasso, Chagall, Leger and other famous artists at this celebrated hostelry, in business here since 1920. Over the years, artists and movie stars have supped in the sunny garden terrace or in the wood-rich dining room.

SHOPPING

MARKETS

Marché d'Yvette – Fruit and vegetable market every Tuesday, Thursday, Saturday and Sunday beneath the wash house at the village entrance.

Flower Market – Fresh flowers beneath the wash house at the village entrance, every Saturday morning.

Regional Products – Provençal market every Wednesday morning near the boules court. Fruits and vegetables, nougats, brioches and other breads, olives, cheeses, flowers and more.

LEISURE

Walking itineraries – The tourist office has a map of four self-guided walking and hiking itineraries of the old town and nearby historical sites.

CALENDAR

Les Nuits de la Courtine – *ℰ04 93 32 86 95. www.saintpauldevence.com.* Place de la Courtine is transformed into a giant stage for concerts and theatrical performances in July and August.

Fête de la Ste-Claire – This three-day festival honouring the town's patron saint includes a procession on Friday evening and fireworks on Sunday, followed by a dance.

Cagnes-sur-Mer★

Alpes-Maritimes

Surrounded by rolling hills carpeted with olive, cypress and citrus trees, Cagnes-sur-Mer has always been a magnet for artists. Its long stretch of pebble beach is popular with fans of windsurfing, water skiing, diving and fishing.

A BIT OF HISTORY
The Grimaldis of Cagnes

Originally a fortress built by Rainier Grimaldi in 1309, Cagnes castle was converted by Henri Grimaldi in 1620 into a sumptuous palace. Loyal to the king of France, he persuaded his cousin, Honoré II of Monaco (*see MONACO*), to place himself under French protection (Treaty of Péronne, 1641). The Grimaldi family was finally driven out during the Revolution.

THE VILLAGE
Haut-de-Cagnes★

▷ Take the free daily shuttle from the central bus station or walk up to Haut-de-Cagnes along montée de la Bourgade (steep climb).

This quaint **bourg★**, circled by ramparts and dominated by a medieval castle, has steep, cobbled streets and

- ▷ **Population:** 48,313.
- **Michelin Map:** 341 D6.
- **Info:** 6 blvd. Maréchal-Juin. ✆04 93 20 61 64. www.cagnes-tourisme.com.
- ▷ **Location:** Cagnes lies on the coast between Nice and Antibes. It comprises Haut-de-Cagnes, crowned by a medieval castle; Cagnes-Ville, the modern quarter, and Cros-de-Cagnes, a fishing village and beach.
- **P** **Parking:** The largest car park *(fee)* is at Place St-Luce (*see map p289*) in Cagnes-Ville near the bus station. There are also some spaces in Haut-de-Cagnes at the *Boule de Château* car park.
- **Don't Miss:** The ancient streets of Haut-de-Cagnes, the **views** from the Château Museum, and jet-skiing at the beach.

vaulted passageways lined with 15C and 17C houses. The **Porte de Nice** near the church tower dates back to the 13C.

Église St-Pierre

The entrance to the church is through the gallery. The early-Gothic nave contains the Grimaldi tombs, while a larger nave added in the 18C houses a statue

Haut-de-Cagnes

© mirko albini/Fotolia.com

PRACTICAL INFORMATION

Guided Tours of the City – The tourist office organises tours of the small fishing village in Cros-de-Cagnes *(Tue 10am in front of the Cros-de-Cagnes tourist office)* and the picturesque cobbled district of Haut-de-Cagnes *(Tue 2pm at the Haut-de-Cagnes tourist office). Contact the tourist office for rates.*

Museum Pass – Available at the tourist office. ∞6€ double ticket for the Renoir Museum and Château Museum.

of the Virgin and Child and an altarpiece of the 18C Spanish School.

SIGHTS
Château-Musée Grimaldi★

Pl. Grimaldi. ◐*Open Wed–Sun 10am–noon (Jul–Aug until 1pm) and 2pm–5pm (May–Oct until 6pm).* ◐*Closed public holidays.* ∞*4€.* ✆*04 92 02 47 30.*
A double staircase and a Louis XIII doorway give access to this imposing castle crowned with machicolations. The elegant Renaissance **patio★★** contrasts with the feudal castle's austere façades. Eight low-vaulted medieval rooms open onto the patio galleries, featuring exhibits of medieval artefacts, 2C Roman sculptures discovered in Cagnes, and an **Olive Museum**. The former boudoir of the marquise de Grimaldi on the first floor houses the **Suzy Solidor Donation★**, 40 paintings donated by the famous singer. The ceiling of the

banqueting hall features the **Fall of Phaeton★**, a 17C *trompe-l'œil* painted by the Genoese artist Carlone. On the second floor, the **Musée d'Art Moderne Méditerranéen** explores contemporary Mediterranean art, with a rich collection of works by 20C painters, such as Dufy and Vasarely. From the top of the tower a fine **view★** extends over the roofs of Old Cagnes from the Ailps to the sea.

Musée Renoir

Chemin de Collettes. ◐*Same hours as Musée Grimaldi.* ∞*4€.* 🅿*Free.* ✆*04 92 02 47 30. www.cagnessurmer.fr.*
Pierre-Auguste Renoir (1841–1919) spent the last 12 years of his life at Les Collettes amid a peaceful olive grove. Ten of the **canvasses** belonging to his last, particularly sensual period (**Bathers, 1901–02**) are exhibited on the ground floor. The museum garden planted with olive, orange and lemon trees is dotted with sculptures by the artist, including his large bronze **Venus Victrix★**.

Chapelle Notre-Dame-de-Protection

🚶 *Access via montée du Château.* ◐*Open for group tours. Reservation required.* ∞*Enquire for details.* ✆*04 93 20 61 64. www.cagnes-tourisme.com.*
The Italianate porch and bell tower of this chapel inspired Renoir. The apse is decorated with 16C frescoes attributed to Andrea de Cella. A 17C altarpiece of the Virgin of the Rosary is displayed in the north chapel.

Renoir at Les Collettes

Pierre-Auguste Renoir was born in Limoges and moved to Paris as a young man, where his talents blossomed under the Impressionists. From 1882, he made several visits to Provence with Cézanne and in 1900, with his wife and son Jean, who later became a film director. In 1907, his reputation universally established, Renoir settled permanently at Les Collettes in Cagnes-sur-Mer. His last years were saddened by the death of his wife, the wounding of his sons in the First World War and the inexorable progress of his illness, which confined him to a wheelchair and paralysed his right hand. During his life he received many honours and exhibitions in the major museums of the world; in August 1919, his work was officially accepted by the Louvre in Paris. On 2 December 1919, just before his death, Renoir was still at work painting a bouquet of anemones.

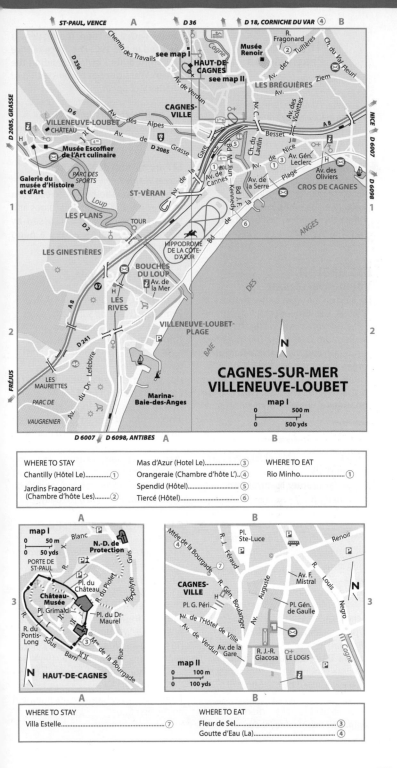

CAGNES-SUR-MER VILLENEUVE-LOUBET

map I

0 — 500 m
0 — 500 yds

WHERE TO STAY		WHERE TO EAT
Chantilly (Hôtel Le)............①	Mas d'Azur (Hotel Le)......................③	Rio Minho..........................①
Jardins Fragonard (Chambre d'hôte Les)..........②	Orangeraie (Chambre d'hôte L')......④	
	Spendid (Hôtel).......................⑤	
	Tiercé (Hôtel)..............................⑥	

map I

HAUT-DE-CAGNES

map II

CAGNES-VILLE

WHERE TO STAY	WHERE TO EAT
Villa Estelle...⑦	Fleur de Sel...③
	Goutte d'Eau (La)...................................④

The Birth of Peach Melba

A native of Villeneuve, the "chef of kings and king of chefs" Auguste Escoffier (1846–1935) made his name in Nice before moving to the Petit Moulin-Rouge in Paris. In 1898, César Ritz persuaded him to set up the kitchens of his new luxury hotel, where Escoffier delighted guests by creating dishes tailored to their tastes. Peach Melba, made in honour of the Australian soprano Nellie Melba, is perhaps the most famous example.

EXCURSION
Villeneuve-Loubet

Located on the coast between Nice and Antibes, this Provençal village dominated by a medieval castle sits on the banks of the Loup River, bordered by a vast beach and the **Marina-Baie-des-Anges**.

Follow the charming sloping alleys to the foot of the 13C **château de Villeneuve**. Property of the Villeneuve

PRACTICAL INFORMATION
Nature Walk

The **Vaugrenier Natural Park** (access by the RN 7) stretches more than 247 acres/100ha, encompassing both prairie and forest areas. There are 3.7mi/6km of trails and a small wetland marsh for observing waterfowl.

Tours

Balade Gourmande combines a tour of Villeneuve-Loubet village, a visit to the Musée Escoffier and a special surprise tasting. *Contact the tourist office (above).*

Marina-Baie-des-Anges, called the Concrete Mountains by some, has been recognised by the Ministry of Culture as a 20C heritage site. It's up to you to decide. Take a guided tour. *Contact the tourist office (above).*

family, with a 9C keep, the castle was restored in the 19C. The Truce of Nice was signed here in 1538, ending the Italian Wars between François I and Charles V of Spain.

The Riverbanks *1mi/2km*

This hike leads from the village along the banks of the Loup River.

Parc naturel de Vaugrenier
Access via RN 7.

The park covers some 247 acres/100ha of meadow and woodland (pines and several species of oak) crossed by 3.7mi/6km of pathway and a pond that's ideal for birdwatching.

Musée Escoffier de l'Art Culinaire★

3 rue Escoffier. Open daily Jul–Aug 2pm–7pm (Wed and Sat 10am–noon, 2pm–7pm); Sept–Oct and Dec–Jun 2pm–6pm. *Closed public holidays.* 5€ *(child 2.50€).* 04 93 20 80 51. www.fondation-escoffier.org.

Housed in the villa where Auguste Escoffier was born in 1846, this collection of items once belonging to the ambassador of French cuisine reveals his unique approach to the culinary arts. Included is a display of contemporary utensils, a Provençal kitchen and a collection of miniature cars (used as part of the dining room service), alongside 1,500 menus from 1820 to today.

Galerie du Musée d'Histoire et d'Art

137 rue de l'Hôtel-de-Ville. Open daily 2pm–7pm (Wed and Sat 10am–7pm). *Closed public holidays.* No charge. 04 92 02 60 39.

This museum is devoted to major 20C conflicts fought by France, including WWI and WWII, the wars of Indo-China (1945–54) and Algeria (1954–62), interventions in Chad and Zaire (1969–84), and Lebanon (1982–87), ending with the Gulf War (1991).

Temporary art exhibitions are mounted on the first floor.

🚗 DRIVING TOURS

THE BAOUS AND THE CORNICHE DU VAR★

Round trip of 20mi/32km. Allow about 1hr15min (excluding the ascent of the Baou of St-Jeannet).

▷ From Cagnes take avenue Auguste-Renoir and D 18 north to La Gaude.

La Gaude

From the ridge above the River Cagne, La Gaude – which owes its prosperity to vineyards and flower cultivation – now houses research centres in the fields of data processing and horticulture. The 14C castle in the St-Jeannet district is attributed to the Templars.

▷ At Peyron take the D 18 north through orchards and vineyards.

St-Jeannet

This charming village occupies a remarkable **position**★ on a terrace at the foot of the Baou of St-Jeannet. Behind the church on the left a "Panorama" sign points to a terrace offering a **view**★ of the peaks *(baous)* and the coastline.

Baou de St-Jeannet

The signposted path starts from pl. Ste-Barbe by Auberge St-Jeannet.
🚶 *2hr round trip.*

This sheer cliff 2,657ft/810m high, dominates the village. From the top *(orientation table)* a vast **panorama ★★** extends from the Esterel to the Alps.

▷ Return to D 18 towards La Gaude. Turn left onto D 118.

Centre d'Études et de Recherches IBM

The huge buildings on the left of this Research Centre, consisting of two opposing Y-shapes raised on concrete pillars, provide a good example of architecture harmonising with its natural surroundings.

Corniche du Var★

This scenic road clings to the hillside on the west bank of the Var, with a clear **view** of the river valley and Nice's hinterland. The steep slopes of the valley are covered in flowers and olive groves.

St-Laurent-du-Var

Until the County of Nice passed to France in 1860, the Var formed the frontier with the Kingdom of Sardinia. Locals usually forded the river, often on a man's back. The first permanent bridge was built downstream in 1864. Near the mouth of the River Var, a large lake protected by a dyke has been developed into a yachting harbour.

▷ Return to Cagnes by D 6007.

Castle and village, Villeneuve-Loubet

© AGE/Photononstop

ADDRESSES

🛏 STAY

🛏🛏 **Hôtel Le Mas d'Azur** – *42 avenue de Nice.* ℘*04 93 20 19 19.* 🅿 *15 rooms.* ⊐*7.50€.* Just off a main road, in an 18C building, this hotel has small, tidy rooms. Lush, flowery setting and breakfast terrace.

🛏🛏 **Hôtel Chantilly** – *31 chemin Minoterie.* ℘*04 93 20 25 50. www.hotel-lechantilly.fr. 18 rooms.* 🅿. ⊐*8€.* This hotel, housed in a villa behind the racecourse, offers modest comfort at reasonable prices. Clean rooms in a verdant setting and a relaxed, family atmosphere.

🛏🛏🛏 **Chambre d'hôte L'Orangeraie de la Baronne** – *66 chemin du Maoupas, La Gaude.* ℘*04 92 12 13 69. www.orange raie.fr. Closed Jan, Feb and Dec.* 🅿 *4 rooms.* ⊐. *Restaurant* 🛏🛏🛏. Located in the heart of a fruit and citrus orchard, this bed & breakfast has spacious, simply decorated rooms with air-conditioning. There is also an organic restaurant serving dinner nightly, a swimming pool and bike rental.

🛏🛏🛏 **Chambre d'hôte Les Jardins Fragonard** – *12 rue Fragonard.* ℘*04 93 20 07 72. 5 rooms.* ⊐🍴. Peaceful grounds planted out with Mediterranean species form the heavenly backdrop to this 1925 bed and breakfast. The large rooms are decorated in the Provençal spirit with rattan furniture; modern bathrooms.

🛏🛏🛏 **Hôtel Splendid** – *41 blvd. du Maréchal-Juin.* ℘*04 93 22 02 00. www. hotel-splendid-riviera.com.* 🅿. *26 rooms.* ⊐*9€.* A quiet, modern hotel in the centre of town. Although somewhat dated, the rooms are comfortable and most face the inner courtyard.

🛏🛏🛏🛏 **Tiercé Beach Hotel** – *33 blvd. Kennedy.* ℘*04 93 20 02 09. www.hoteltiercebeach.com. 23 rooms.* 🅿. ⊐*10€. Closed Nov.* The bright and tidy rooms in this modern hotel face the sea or the hippodrome next door. Air-conditioning, WiFi.

🛏🛏🛏🛏 **Villa Estelle** – *5 montée de la Bourgade.* ℘*04 92 02 89 83. www.villa-estelle.com.* 🍴. *5 rooms.* ⊐. This tastefully renovated inn offers individually decorated rooms (some with **sea views**), a cosy lounge, a pleasant courtyard terrace and a charming garden.

🍴 EAT

🍴 **Rio Minho** – *34 ave. de Nice.* ℘*04 92 02 86 05. Closed Aug and Mon.* Once the haunt of General de Gaulle, this charmingly decorated inn 🛏🛏 *(10 rooms; ⊐5€)* is known for its couscous dishes and Oriental tearoom.

🍴 **L'Olivier** – *4 pl. Verdun, Villeneuve-Loubet.* ℘*04 93 20 85 11.* Pleasant restaurant serving traditional cuisine.

🍴🍴 **La Goutte d'Eau** – *108 montée de la Bourgade, Le Haut-de-Cagnes.* ℘*04 93 20 81 23.* After climbing the steep, cobbled alleys, you reach this small restaurant serving simple fare. The sun-blessed terrace welcomes you in fine weather.

🍴🍴 **Fleur de Sel** – *85 montée de la Bourgade.* ℘*04 93 20 33 33. www.restaurant-fleurdesel.com. Closed 6–20 Jan, 10–17 Jun, 25 Oct –7 Nov.* This rustic little restaurant next to the church has Provençal decor and an open kitchen, where you can watch the chef whip up seasonal specialities.

SPORT AND LEISURE

Watersports – Cagnes-sur-Mer has 2.2mi/3.5km of pebble beaches, including several private beaches, where you can dine or rent *chaise longues.* It's possible to waterski, wakeboard, jet-ski and parasail in season at Tampa Beach *(between the Madrague and Neptune restaurants;* ℘*04 93 20 17 46).*

Hippodrome de la Côte d'Azur – ℘*04 92 02 44 44. www.hippodrome-cotedazur.com.* ⊛*4.50€.* This famous racecourse is the backdrop to many equestrian events between December and March, as well as in July and August.

EVENTS

Promenade en Fête – A festival along the seafront promenade mid-Jul–mid-Aug.

Fête de la Châtaigne – Craft market, events and a countryside picnic celebrating the chestnut. Mid-Nov.

Fête de l'Olivier –In Mar, at the Musée Renoir. Chef demonstrations.

NICE, THE RIVIERA AND MONACO

Nice and Monaco are the uncontested stars of the French Riviera, the headliners who never fail to impress or draw a crowd. Nice's seaside Promenade des Anglais and Monte Carlo's majestic casino have been the stuff of legend since the late 19C when the arrival of the railway brought throngs of tourists eager to see this millionaires' playground of sumptuous villas, private yachts and palace hotels. Of course, you don't have to break the bank to enjoy this part of the French Riviera, where the roads winding between coastal resorts and precariously perched villages offer panoramic views and scenes of stunning natural beauty. Important vestiges of Roman, Greek and medieval structures enrich this area's architectural heritage and a vibrant arts and music scene continue to enhance the cultural character of this dynamic region for the millions of visitors who still flock to its sunny shores.

Almost Not French

This part of the French Riviera is, historically speaking, hardly French at all. Although much of the southeast of France was controlled by the comtes de Provence, Nice and its surrounding villages were mainly governed by the ducs de Savoie and the kings of Sardinia, from their secession from Provence in 1388 until their purchase by Napoleon III in 1860. Monaco's Grimaldi lords purchased their own principality from the Genoese in 1308 and, although ruled independently, have been under French "protection" since 1861, when they sold Menton and Rocquebrune to France. Not only has the architecture, cuisine and even language of the Niçois, Monacans and their neighbours been strongly influenced by their colourful and diverse Italian roots, they have also contributed

Highlights

1 Taste traditional Niçoise socca at the **Cours Saleya market** (p301)

2 Enjoy the scenic drive along the famous **Grande Corniche** (p317)

3 Tour the villa and gardens of the **Villa Ephrussi de Rothschild** (p327)

4 Hike the breathtaking coastal path around the **Cap Ferrat** (p328)

5 Place your bets at the Belle Époque **casino in Monte Carlo** (p339)

to the fiercely independent and highly distinctive character of the region's inhabitants.

View of Monaco Port

© Sylvaine Poitau/Apa Publications

A Haven for Artists

"When I realised that every morning I would wake up to this light, I couldn't believe my luck...." When Matisse moved to Nice in 1917, at the age of 48, it was a revelation. He found the quality of the light so intense, the colours so vivid, that he spent the next 27 years on the Riviera, channelling this new landscape into the airy flowing lines of his paintings and the vivid blues of his later gouache cut-outs, many of which are on display at the Musée Matisse in Nice. Matisse often drew inspiration from the coast, travelling everywhere "from the hills of Éze to Cagnes-sur-Mer". It was here, in 1917, that he met one of the founders of Impressionism, Pierre-Auguste Renoir, at the Villa des Collettes, now the Musée Renoir, where the artist spent the last 12 years of his life. Matisse himself received regular visits from another artist, Raoul

Street in the Old Nice

Dufy, who fell in love with the Riviera's *joie de vivre* on the first of his many visits to the region in 1919. His paintings of the Baie des Anges and its palm trees have come to define his work, much of which is now on display in the Musée des Beaux Art in Nice.

As well as its light and landscape, the Riviera's artistic traditions have also worked their charm on many other artists. Arriving in Vence in 1950, Marc Chagall swapped his paintbrush for the potter's wheel when the Ramié family, owners of the Madoura ceramics factory in Vallauris, lent him a studio. The result was a series of haunting and colourful pieces reflecting the biblical themes now explored in the Chagall Museum in Nice. The Madoura studio was also the regular haunt of another major artist. After moving to the Riviera in 1947, Picasso transformed the manufacturer's everyday jugs into sinuous women and its plates into bullrings, marking the start of a new chapter in his career, which you can now explore at the Musée Picasso in Antibes.

Picasso's presence in the south inevitably attracted a host of other artists, including his friend, Jean Cocteau. Influenced by the mythology of the Mediterranean, Cocteau has left his mark along the coast, from the Villa Santo Sospir in Cap Ferrat to Le Bastide in Menton, where a major new museum was opened in 2011 in his memory. Unsurprisingly, Nice continued to attract artists throughout the 20C, becoming a hotbed for France's abstract, Fluxus, figurative and conceptual movements, which can all be explored at the MAMAC (see p307).

Not Just for Tourists

Nice and Monaco may owe their international prominence to the lucrative tourism industry, but today the region is also an important centre for scientific research and high-tech development. Given the encouragement of local governments, an enviable setting and a pool of qualified graduates from local universities, many international companies have opened offices here. The region's hotels, international airport, and top-notch restaurants make it the ideal place for business conferences, which take place throughout the year. While some corners of the French Riviera are virtually closed down in winter, Nice and Monaco never stop moving.

Time to Celebrate

The month of February is the best time to join in the festivities on the Riviera, when the 16-day carnival takes over the streets of Nice, and mountains of lemons and oranges decorate the processions for Menton's Fête du Citron. In May, Monaco's Grand Prix attracts the biggest crowds, who come from around the world to watch the Formula 1 cars race through the centre of Monte Carlo.

Nice★★★

Alpes-Maritimes

Overlooking the vast sweep of the Baie des Anges, the capital of the French Riviera is a city of contrasts. A medley of medieval red and ochre façades, Belle Époque villas, Art-Deco apartments, fishermen's cottages and luxury hotels, the architecture is rivalled only by the cuisine, which fuses French, Italian and Provençal flavours. A muse for generations of artists, Nice boasts the richest modern and contemporary art collections outside Paris.

A BIT OF HISTORY
Greeks to the House of Savoie

Excavations along the eastern reaches of Nice, at a site called Terra Amata (*see MUSÉE TERRA AMATA p311*), have revealed evidence of a human presence in Nice 400,000 years ago. The first Greek settlement in the Ligurian trading post of Nikaia (from the Greek niké, "victory") was founded in 4C BC on the rock that currently dominates the port to the east of the quai des Etats Unis. It was eclipsed three centuries later by the Romans, who shifted the settlement north to Cimiez (Cemenelum), where they built a thriving town, complete with baths, an amphitheatre and a temple complex. Following the Barbarian and Saracen invasions, which left Cimiez in ruins, ancient Nikaia returned to prominence under the comtes de Provence in the 10C. At the end of a long civil war, in 1388 Nice switched its allegiance from Louis d'Anjou, comte de Provence, to Amédée VII, comte de Savoie. Nice now formed part of a vast transalpine territory with its capital in Turin and stretching as far as Sicily and Sardinia to the south.

Catherine Ségurane

In 1543 the King of France François I and his Turkish allies besieged Nice, an ally of the Holy Roman Emperor, Charles V. According to local tradition, Catherine Ségurane was bringing food to a soldier on the ramparts when the Turkish assault

▶ **Population:** 347,060.

◔ **Michelin Map:** 341 E5.

🛈 **Info:** 5 promenade des Anglais. ✆0 892 707 407 (0.34€/min). Train Station Annex: Ave. Thiers. www.nicetourisme.com.

◑ **Location:** The Old Town is wedged between the Château Hill (east), the seaside Promenade des Anglais and the Promenade du Paillon. West of this promenade is Place Masséna, surrounded by shopping streets. To the east of the Château Hill is the old port and Cap de Nice. On the hills to the north are the museums and gardens of Cimiez district. **Getting around** on foot is not difficult, but for Cimiez or the port consider using the city bus or take a double-decker bus sightseeing tour (*see Practical Information opposite*).

🅿 **Parking:** Car parks can be found all over town, at the market and near the port. There are no free spaces, even on the streets.

◉ **Don't Miss:** The winding streets and market of the Old Town; sunset **views** from Château Hill; Cimiez's Gallo-Roman ruins.

◔ **Timing:** You could easily spend a week in Nice, but if you have just one full day, start on the seafront and the Old Town, then visit Cimiez and one or two of the major museums.

👥 **Kids:** Children will enjoy the merry-go-round at the Jardin Albert I or the playground in the park at the top of the Château Hill.

PRACTICAL INFORMATION
SIGHTSEEING AND TOURS

Admission to Nice's municipal museums and galleries is free.

Guided tours – *Centre du Patrimoine, 75 quai des Etats-Unis. ℘04 92 00 41 90.* Tours of the Old Town *(2hr).* ≈*3€.*

Nice Riviera Pass – A 1-, 2- or 3-day sightseeing pass with free entry to many sights, tours and shopping and dining advantages, from 24€ to 54€. Available at the tourist office or online at www.frenchrivierapass.com.

♣♣ Petits Trains Touristiques – ♿*Tours (40min) Apr–Sept 10am–6pm (Jun–Aug until 7pm); Oct–Mar 10am–5pm. Closed mid-Nov–23 Dec, and end of Christmas holidays until first weekend in Jan.* ≈*7€ (3€ under 9). ℘06 16 39 53 51. www.petittrainnice.com.* Departures from the seafront at the Jardin Albert I. Tours of the Old Town, port and château.

Nice le Grand Tour – *Departs every 30 min from Jardins Albert I.* ≈*21€. ℘04 92 29 17 00. www.nicelegrandtour.com.* Double-decker, open-top bus tours with commentary in English *(90min).* Hop-on, hop-off the 14 different stops from the Promenade des Anglais, Cimiez and the Port.

Trans Côte d'Azur – *quai Lunel. Operates Mar–Apr Tue–Wed, Fri and Sun 11am, 3pm; May–Oct Tue–Sun 11am, 3pm. ℘04 92 00 42 30. www.trans-cote-azur. com.* ≈*15€.* Guided tours *(1hr)* of the coast of Nice, Bay of Villefranche and Baie des Anges. *Reservations a must.*

PUBLIC TRANSPORT

Bus/Tram – The Ligne d'Azur network *(10 ave. Félix-Faure; ℘0 810 061 006; www.lignedazur.com)* includes buses for the city of Nice and its suburbs, and a new tram line in central Nice. Individual tickets, 10-journey cards and unlimited travel passes (1- and 7-day) available. The TAM coach network *(various departure points across the city; ℘800 06 01 06; www.rca.tm.fr)* has services to towns such as Antibes, Cannes and Grasse.

TER Train – *SNCF Gare, Avenue Thiers. ℘0 891 70 30 00. www.ter-sncf.com/paca.* Local train services to Draguignan, Fréjus, St-Raphaël, Cannes, Grasse, Antibes, Menton, Vintimille (Vintimiglia in Italy), Monaco. The Nice-Cuneo line crosses the Bévéra and Roya valleys.

Rental Bikes and Cars – Nice has set up dozens of self-service **bicycle rental** docking stations **(vélos bleues)** across the city. Guidelines and rates (per hour, day, week or month) are available at www.velobleu.org.

A similar scheme for electric cars, **Auto Bleue**, was launched in 2011 with a slightly more complicated registration process. For details visit www.auto-bleu.org.

Promenade des Anglais, Nice

© Sylvaine Poitau/Apa Publications

© haak78/Bigstockphoto.com

Nice Carnival

King of the Carnival

The **Nice Carnival★★★** is one of the biggest celebrations in the region, with two weeks of parades, confetti battles, fireworks and masked balls *(veglioni)*. The **floral parades**, or *batailles de fleurs,* offer a picturesque spectacle and attract huge and excited crowds, drawn by the colourful fruit and flowers.

The tradition dates back a long way in Nice, with references as long ago as 1294, on the occasion of the visit of the comte de Provence, Charles II. Nice Carnival has always been a welcome diversion from social tensions and conflicts, which were constantly breaking out as a result of Nice's geographical location and disputed ownership. Until the end of the 18C, the carnival took place after the Lenten fast in the form of local festivities in the old part of the city.

After a break of several years, caused by the Revolutionary and Napoleonic wars, the first parade of carnival floats took place in 1830 in honour of the royal visit of King Charles Félix to Nice and the return to Sardinian sovereignty. The modern form of carnival dates back to 1873, with the establishment of the various stages of the festivities and the setting of a different official theme every year.

Carnival-going families from Nice belong to long lines of tradition verging on outright dynasties. Each "stable" of carnival floats has its own characteristics. Before the advent of synthetic materials, about one tonne of papier-mâché was used in the making of each float. Famous painters from this area have also played their part in enriching the carnival decorations.

The festivities begin with the triumphal entry of "Sa Majesté Carnaval" about three weeks before Shrove Tuesday, or Mardi Gras. An effigy of the King of the Carnival is later ceremoniously burned to mark the end of the carnival season. During the intervening period, celebrations are in full swing, with parades of carnival floats accompanied by people in costumes sporting huge comical heads made of papier-mâché.

began. Knife in hand, she flung herself at the Turks, who appeared at the top of the wall, and hurled several attackers into the moat below. As a final insult to the enemy, she gathered her skirts and bared her behind. Their morale boosted, the men of Nice contained the attack and a statue was erected to Catherine by her fellow citizens.

Bonaparte in Nice

Overrun by French revolutionary troops in 1792, the comté de Nice became the Département des Alpes-Maritimes the following year. In 1794 Bonaparte, then general of artillery in the army, lived at no. 6 in the street which now bears his name, where he was arrested after the fall of Robespierre. In 1796 he stayed in Nice again, on rue St-François-de-Paule, as commander-in-chief of the French armies in Italy. He had married Josephine only a few days earlier, and it was from Nice that he wrote his famous letter: "My darling, anguish at our parting runs through my veins as swiftly as the waters flow down the Rhône...." At the fall of the Empire in 1814, Nice was handed back to the Kingdom of Piedmont-Sardinia under the Treaty of Paris.

Two local heroes

André Masséna (born in Nice, 1758; died in Paris 1817), son of a wine merchant, became one of Napoleon's most successful generals, beating the Austrians and Russians at the Battle of Zurich, and helping Napoleon to clinch the Battle of Marengo over the Italians. He conquered the Kingdom of Naples in 1806. **Giuseppe Garibaldi** (born in Nice, 1807; died in Caprera, 1882) fought alongside Mazzini to unify Italy during the 1848 and 1859 revolutions. Exiled to South America, he rallied to the cause of republicans in Uruguay and Brazil. The "Che Guevara" of Nice earned himself the nickname "hero of the Two Worlds".

Plebiscite

As a result of the 1858 alliance between France and the King of Sardinia, Napoleon III helped the Sardinians drive the Austrians out of the provinces of north-

ern Italy. As his reward, the 1860 Treaty of Turin between France and Sardinia stipulated that Nice be returned to France "without any constraint on the will of the people". The plebiscite was an overwhelming victory for France: 25,743 in favour, 260 against. The regions of Tende and La Brigue were to remain Italian territory for 87 years until the treaty of 10 February 1947 allowed France to extend its natural frontiers to the Alps.

Nice Today

Now the fifth-largest city in France, Nice is home to the Sophia-Antipolis technology park. A major administrative centre, Nice boasts dozens of prestigious museums, a music conservatoire, a national contemporary art centre and a world-class university.

 WALKING TOURS

THE SEAFRONT★★
Allow 2hr.

▷ Begin from the intersection of Blvd. Gambetta and Promenade des Anglais.

Promenade des Anglais★★

This wide promenade, facing south and flanking the sea along its entire length, provides wonderful **views** of the Baie des Anges and is a popular place for a lengthy stroll.

Until 1820 access to the shore was difficult, so the town's rich English residents, present in large numbers since the 18C, paid for the construction of a coastal promenade. Although now edged by six lanes of traffic, it has retained its mythical aura, and many legendary buildings still overlook the sea.

Begin at the **Palais de l'Agriculture** (1900) and continue to the **Hôtel Negresco** (c. 1900), both striking Belle Époque structures. Pass the imposing Classical façade of the **Musée Masséna** to reach the **Palais de la Méditerranée**, designed in 1928 by Frank Jay Gould. Narrowly escaping demolition in the 1980s, it has now been turned into a

Cours Saleya

© Sylvaine Poitau/Apa Publications

luxury casino and hotel. Pass in front of the rather incongruous glass-and-steel Ruhl Casino and Hotel Méridien (1973), then take avenue de Verdun around the **Jardin Albert I**, an oasis of greenery surrounding a fountain, The Three Graces by Volti.

Place Masséna

Stradling the **promenade du Paillon**, which follows the course of the covered mountain torrent of the same name, this harmonious square built in Turin style is lined with restored, red-ochre buildings with arcades at street level. The north side of the square opens into **avenue Jean-Médecin**, the main

shopping street. To the west is the area the English called "Newborough" in the 18C, running along **rue Masséna** and **rue de France**, a pedestrian area filled with smart shops, cinemas, cafés and restaurants.

Continue along the promenade, which is currently being transformed into a 123 acres/50ha "green corridor" (set for completion in 2014) to the marble cubes of the national theatre and modern art gallery, and down to the corner of the jardin Maréchal-Juin and the **Tête Carrée** (Square Head) by Sacha Sosno, housing the Louis-Nucéra Library.

The Port

For 2,000 years ships were simply moored at the foot of the Château Hill. The deep-water port was created only as recently as 1750 under the duc de Savoie, who ordered the excavation of an area of marshland called the Lympia. It was further extended in the 19C. **Place Île de Beauté**, a square facing the port, is lined with porticoed houses with pleasing 19C façades.

Today Nice harbour is a busy maritime centre frequented by fishing boats, yachts, Corsican ferries, luxury liners and merchant ships. Stroll through the flea markets at quai Lunel, then return along the **quai Rauba Capeu**, which links the port to the Promenade des Anglais.

Midday Cannon

Each day at noon a short cannon shot can be heard. This custom was introduced by a visiting Englishman, Sir Thomas Coventry, who grew tired of irregular meal times. He offered to buy and maintain a cannon for the town so that each day a shot could be fired at noon from the castle hill. The tradition continues, but the cannon has been replaced by a harmless explosive charge.

OLD NICE★

After soaking up the dazzling Riviera sunshine, head for the Baroque district of Nice, tucked between the Château Hill and rue des Ponchettes.

Cours Saleya

Lined with shops and restaurants, this elegant Baroque square is home to the famous **flower and vegetable market** (antiques on Monday). Note the yellow façade of the **Caïs de Pierla Palace**, where Matisse lived between 1921 and 1938, first on the third floor, then on the fourth floor facing the sea.

Chapelle de la Miséricorde★

2 Pl. Pierre-Gautier. ○Open Sept–Jul Tue 2.30pm–5.30pm.

Halfway along the market, this fine example of Niçois Baroque belongs to the brotherhood of the Black Penitents. It was built in 1740 by Vittone according to the plans of the famous 17C Italian priest-architect Guarini.

Inside, angels circle the gilded beams and faux-marble columns. Two primitive Niçois **altarpieces★** in the sacristy represent the Virgin of Mercy: one painted in hieratic Byzantine style by Jean Miralhet (1429) and the other by **Louis Bréa** (1515), whose graceful work, typical of the Italian Renaissance, features probably the earliest depiction of Nice.

▷ Move back towards the east end of the square and turn left onto rue de la Poissonnerie.

Chapelle de l'Annonciation

○Open 8am–noon, 2.30pm–6pm. ✆04 93 62 13 62.

Built in the 13C and remodelled in the 17C, this chapel, known locally as the **Chapelle Ste-Rita**, has a stern exterior typical of Nice Baroque and a lavish Baroque **interior★** with altars and rails inlaid with marble, sumptuous altarpieces, painted and coffered vaults and fine panelling. Ordered according to a typical Baroque hierarchy, it is plain and austere at eye-level and rises in an increasingly complex swirl of decoration as it mounts towards the sky.

▷ Continue straight ahead then take a right on rue de la Place-Vieille, then take a left.

Église St-Jacques or Gésu★

3 pl. Rossetti. ○Open Thu 2pm–4pm, Sat 9am–noon, Sun 7am–8pm (2nd Sun in month 9am–noon).

Built as a chapel in the 17C (the façade dates from 1825), this church is typical of the Counter Reformation style with its single, wide, fairly low nave and strict, straight lines mitigated by its highly ornate, gilded decorations, including 164 painted and 48 carved cherubs. The ceiling is painted with scenes from the life of St James. The **sacristy**, formerly the chapter house, contains 14 huge walnut cupboards (1696), displaying the church treasures.

▷ Rue du Jésus (across from the church) leads to rue Ste-Réparate and the cathedral on the right.

Cathédrale Ste-Réparate

Pl. Rossetti. ○Open Mon–Sat 9am–noon, 2pm–6pm. ✆04 93 92 01 35.

Designed in 1650 by local architect J.-A. Guiberto in honour of Nice's patron saint, the cathedral is topped by an 18C bell tower and a magnificent dome of 14,000 glazed tiles that stands out on the Nice skyline.

The **interior★** is a riot of Baroque plasterwork and marble. Note above the high altar, to the right of the painting *La Gloire de Sainte-Réparate*, a view of Nice and its castle in the 17C. The frieze, emblazoned with the arms of the ducs de Savoie, is particularly vivid.

▷ Proceed along rue Rossetti opposite and take the third left into Rue Droite.

Palais Lascaris

15 rue Droite. ○Open Wed–Mon 10am–6pm. ∞No charge. ✆04 93 62 72 40.

This Genoese-style palace, influenced by local tradition, was built in 1648 by J.B. Lascaris, a descendant of the counts of Ventimiglia.

On the ground floor a **pharmacy** from Besançon (1738) has been reconstructed to display a fine collection of flasks and tripods. A grandiose balustraded and vaulted **staircase★** decorated with 17C paintings and 18C statues of Mars and Venus in rockwork niches leads to the "noble floor" *(second floor)*. These rooms reveal how a noble family would have lived in Nice before the Revolution. Flemish tapestries based on sketches by Rubens hang in the antichamber to the grand salon decorated with 18C trompe-l'oeil ceiling frescoes attributed to the Genoese painter Carlone. Superb atlantes and caryatides hold up the stucco partition leading through to the ceremonial room. On the other side of the staircase is a private apartment with 18C ceilings and painted medallions framed in stuccowork and Louis XV woodwork inlaid with silver-plated copper. Don't miss the bed in its glazed alcove, where the head of the household

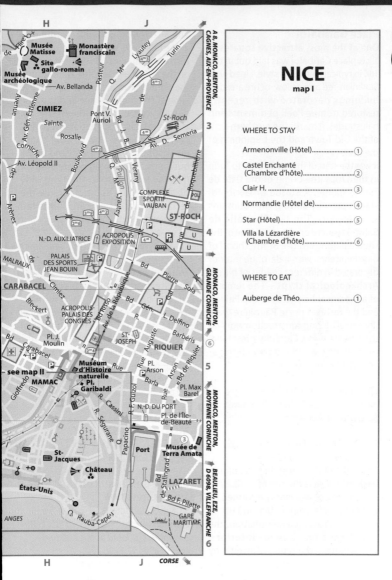

would receive visitors to discuss local administrative affairs. A collection of 18C musical instruments, acquired in 2009, trace a good portion of music's history.

◗ Turn left along rue Droite and rue St François. Note the cannon ball on the corner of rue Droite and rue de la Loge, which dates from the siege of Nice by the Turks in 1543.

Place St-François

This square, home to the morning fish market, is overlooked by a fine 18C building, the former labour exchange, behind which is the **St-François clock tower**, once part of the Franciscan monastery transferred to Cimiez.
Continue along lively rue Pairolière, where several eateries serve **socca**, a local speciality *(♨ see p306)* that you will want to try.

Place Garibaldi

One of the most attractive squares in Nice, place Garibaldi was laid out in the 18C in typical Piedmont style. Lined with Sardinian-red and yellow-ochre arcaded buildings decorated with recently restored trompe l'oeil pediments and balustrades, it marks the northern limit of the Old Town and the beginning of the new.

It was the start of the royal route to Turin in the 1700s (the origin of the Café de Turin's name). A statue of Garibaldi stands proudly among the fountains and greenery. The 18C **Chapelle de Saint-Sépulcre** on the south side of the square belongs to the Brotherhood of Blue Penitents, with a Baroque interior decorated in different shades of blue.

Archaeological crypt – The remains of a medieval bridge over the Paillon and the fortified porte Pairolière were uncovered during construction work on the new tramway. Carefully preserved, they can now be visited upon reservation at the tourist office.

▷ From Pl. Garibaldi, take rue Neuve past the Café de Turin to the church of St-Martin-St-Augustin.

Église St-Martin-St-Augustin

1 pl. Sincaire. ℘*04 93 92 60 45.*
This is the oldest parish in Nice, dating back to 1510. It is the site of Garibaldi's baptism as well as a mass performed by the Augustinian monk, Martin Luther, before the Protestant Reformation. The church has a fine Baroque **interior★** with a **pietà** at the centre of an altar by **Brea**. Outside the entrance a low-relief sculpture pays tribute to the local heroine Catherine Ségurane.

▷ Turn right out of the church and along rue St-Augustin to rue de la Providence, then climb the steep steps up to the château.

Château Hill

Access via château lift. rue des Ponchettes. ◷*Open Jun–Aug 9am–8pm; Apr–May and Sept 9am–7pm; Oct–Mar 10am–6pm.* ℘*04 93 85 62 33.* ◒*1€.*

The 302ft/92m high hill, arranged as a garden walk, was the site of Nice's fortress until it was destroyed in 1706 on the orders of Louis XIV. Walk around the cemetery boundary for a bird's-eye view of the roofs of Nice and the Baie des Anges. On the southeastern side are the exposed foundations of an **11C cathedral** (apse and apsidal chapels), built on top of Roman and Greek buildings. A sweeping **panorama★★** *(viewing table)* unfolds from the wide platform on the summit. Below the terrace an artificial waterfall is fed by waters from the Vésubie River.

▷ Steps lead down to Tour Bellanda.

Tour Bellanda

Despite its appearance, this imposing circular bastion dates only from the 19C, when it was built as an identical replacement for one of the towers of the medieval citadel destroyed in 1706. The famed composer **Hector Berlioz** (1803–69), who lived in Nice for a time, wrote his Grand Ouverture for *King Lear* here in 1831.

THEMED VISITS MODERN AND CONTEMPORARY ART

See Maps I and II for locations.

Musée des Beaux-Arts Jules-Chéret★★

33 Ave. des Baumettes. ◷*Open Tue– Sun 10am–6pm.* ☛*Guided tours (1hr) available.* ◷*Closed public holidays.* ◒*5€.* ℘*04 92 15 28 28. www.musee-beaux-arts-nice.org.*
This 1878 residence, built in the style of a 17C Genoese Renaissance palace for the Russian princess Kotschoubey, houses a rich collection of works sent to Nice by Napoleon III in 1860, along with a number of donations.

Ground Floor

European masterpieces of the 17C, 18C and 19C are displayed on the ground floor, including a rare work by A. Tassi, *Paysage avec Jésus guérissant l'aveugle.* One room is devoted to the **Van Loo**

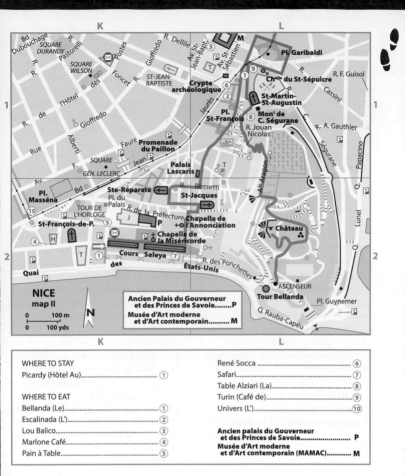

dynasty, including works by **Carle Van Loo** (born in Nice, 1705). The main gallery is lined with female portraits and *Thamar* by Cabanel. The patio is home to *Bronze Age* by Rodin and *Triumph of Flora* by Carpeaux.

First Floor

The main staircase, once used for concerts, leads to displays of late 19C and early 20C artists, starting with **Jules Chéret**, the inventor of the modern poster, who died in Nice in 1932. Works by Orientalists and Romantics include several sculptures by Carpeaux. A room devoted to **Raoul Dufy**, which features his work *Bois de Bologne*, leads to a series of paintings by the pre-Impressionist Félix Ziem, ceramics by

Picasso, and a **Van Dongen** gallery housing the Fauvist's major works.

Musée Matisse★★

164 ave. Arènes des Cimiez. ⟨⟩ ⟨⟩*Open Wed–Mon 10am–6pm.* ⟨⟩*Guided tours available.* ⟨⟩*Closed public holidays.* ⟨⟩*No charge.* ⟨⟩*04 93 81 08 08. www.musee-matisse-nice.org.* Built on the site of a cabin *(cabanoun)* surrounded by the ancient remains of Cimiez, this 17C Genoese villa with a pebble-dash façade and trompe-l'oeil decoration extended by balustraded terraces was once owned by the consul of Nice. After the villa fell into ruin, the city of Nice bought it in 1950. Since its redevelopment in 1993, it has housed the Musée Matisse.

The collection includes some 30 paintings and provides an overview of the career of **Henri Matisse** (1869–1954), exploring the transition from his sober, northern palette to the dazzling hues of the Mediterranean. Taking his cue from Cézanne, then Signac in St-Tropez, by the time he reaches Collioure in 1905, his solid colours propel him to the vanguard of the **Fauvist** movement. After a short stay in Morocco, on arrival in Nice (1916), he makes increasingly masterful use of simple, evocative colours edged in black (*Portrait of Laurette*), while his gouches, oil paintings and drawings begin to reveal a heightened sensuality, nourished by his travels and the **view** over the sea from his studio in Nice (1921–38): *Odalisque with a Red Box* (1926), *Window in Tahiti* (1935), *Nude in an Armchair* (1937), *Woman Reading at a Yellow Table* (1944) and *Still Life with Pomegranate* (1947). His favourite subjects – light, women and the sea – are now approached with a joyful abandon, as expressed through the pure lines of his paper cut-outs of "absolute blue" gouache (*Blue Nude IV, Bather in the Reeds*).

A number of Matisse's **bronze sculptures** are also on display, including *The Serf* (c.1900), and *The Serpentine* (1909), along with the progressively abstract *Jeanette* series (1910-1913).

Lastly, two major series are presented in rotation: his sketches and drawings for the **chapelle du Rosaire** in Vence (◔ *see VENCE*), regarded by the artist himself as his "master-piece", and 41 preparatory studies (drawings, gouache cut-outs, engravings and oil paintings) for the Merion Dance.

Musée Marc-Chagall★★

Ave. du Docteur-Ménard, Cimiez. ♿ ◔ *Open Wed–Mon May–Oct 10am–6pm; Nov–Apr 10am–5pm.* ☞ *4.50€ (free first Sun of the month).* ☎ *04 93 53 87 20. www.musee-chagall.fr.*

This museum, built in 1972, houses the most important permanent collection of the painter's works, including all 17 canvasses that make up the **Biblical Message**, an uninterrupted endeavour lasting 13 years (1954–67) and donated to the museum by the artist himself.

Designed to resemble a "house" in fulfilment of the artist's wishes, this simple building by architect A. Hermant (a colleague of Le Corbusier) is surrounded by a garden featuring a **mosaic** (1970) of the prophet Elijah.

Chagall's poetical lyricism is visible in 12 paintings based on the **Jewish Bible**, while 5 paintings depicting the Song of Songs illustrate his fantastical imagination.

Socca

The day started early in those days in the Nice bar where my uncle and I enjoyed our *socca*. The ingredients include chick-pea flour, olive oil and salt beaten into a smooth mixture in a large copper pan. It is baked in a wood fire oven, a cooking time based on exact calculation or long experience and a speedy hand in cutting the cake into pieces when it is served. Socca will not wait; it must be eaten piping hot and seasoned with pepper.

The recipe has never changed. This is the same *socca* that used to be delivered all over the town. It was put in a box with a zinc lid and the trays in the delivery vans were kept warm with charcoal heaters. Nothing was more satisfying to labourers, office workers, women shopping or anyone else overcome by the desire for a little something in the morning. It is the same socca which the dockers, who had knocked back a laced coffee at 5 o'clock, used to consume in the bars of Nice at half past six. It was their breakfast.

Louis Nucera
Chemin de la Lanterne (1981)
Published by Éditions Grasset

Ruins of the baths, Site Archéologique Gallo-Romain and Musée Matisse in the background

Don't miss the 105 etchings and engravings for the Bible edited by Tériade in 1956.

The museum has a fairly new bookshop and store, while the café (*℘04 93 53 87 32; no admission charge required*) is a popular lunch spot in fine weather.

Musée d'Art Moderne et d'Art Contemporain★★

Promenade des Arts. ○*Open Wed–Mon 10am–6pm.* ○*Closed public holidays.* ⊛*No charge.* ℘*04 97 13 42 01.* *www.mamac-nice.org.*

Designed by Yves Bayard and Henri Vidal, the striking Museum of Modern and Contemporary Art (MAMAC) consists of four square towers with roof-top terraces linked by glass passageways.

The collections present works by the **Nice School** and the French and American avant-garde art movements from the 1960s to the present day. The permanent collection is displayed on the two upper floors, with temporary exhibits housed on the first floor.

In the early 1960s Nice became a hot-house for **French Nouveau Réalisme** (*☞see Klein below*), an artistic movement that attempted to express the reality of daily life in a modern society of consumerism and popular culture. While Pop artists Andy Warhol, Roy Lichtenstein and others appropriated objects belonging to mass culture, the New Realists more derisively sought inspiration from those same objects as symbols of modern life, by collecting or breaking them (Arman), compressing them (César), capturing them under glass (Spoerri), or wrapping them (Christo). A section of the museum is devoted to the French painter **Yves Klein** (1928–62), the movement's founding father, whose happenings reflected the idea of total art, while his monochrome works explore the concept of pure abstract art. Total art was also the inspiration of the neo-Dada **Fluxus** movement, whose principle representative, Ben, enjoys a strong presence in the museum.

The development of abstract ideas in France is illustrated by the **Supports/Surfaces** galleries, which extend the work of American Abstract Expressionists such as Morris Louis and Frank Stella by reducing painting to its material reality. Influenced by American Minimalism (Sol Le Witt, Richard Serra), the **BMPT** (Buren, Mosset, Parmentier and Toroni) reduced art to its simpler expression – medium, colour and material.

The 1980s saw the return of figurative works by artists such as **Niki de Saint Phalle** and the classical beauty of murals in Naples by **Ernest Pignon-Ernest**.

Villa Arson

20 Ave. Stephen Liégeard. Bus 4, 7 (Deux Avenues). ○*Open Jul–Aug daily 2pm–7pm; Sept–Jun Wed–Mon 2pm–6pm.* ○*Closed between exhibitions.* ◎*No charge.* ℘*04 92 07 73 73. www.villa-arson.org.*

The Villa Arson is situated to the north of the city in a Mediterranean garden on St-Barthélemy hill affording a **panoramic view** of the Baie des Anges. The 18C villa, influenced by the Bauhaus architectural movement, houses the École Nationale Supérieure d'Art, an artists' residence and a national centre of contemporary art showcasing international artists.

CIMIEZ

♿*See the city map p303. Served by bus 15 (stop at Arènes).*

Long before Cimiez was occupied by the French and visited by Queen Victoria (who is commemorated by a statue at the top of Boulevard de Cimiez), this was the site of the Roman city Cemelenum. In 2C there were at least 20,000 Romans living here. Many vestiges of their city remain.

▶ Starting from pl. Jean-Moulin, behind the Acropolis, drive west along blvd. Carabacel and follow the map.

Arènes

The ellipse-shaped amphitheatre, which is only 220ft/67m by 184ft/56m, could hold 4,000 spectators. Traces remain of the gangways and of the sockets on the external façade, which held the posts supporting a huge adjustable awning *(velum).* The amphitheatre was designed for spear contests and gladiatorial bouts, but not for animal fights. Traditional festivals take place here all year round *(♿see CALENDAR p316).*

Musée Archéologique

160 ave. Arènes. ♿○*Open Wed–Mon 10am–6pm (last entrance 1hr before closure).* ◎*5€.* ℘*04 93 81 59 57. www.musee-archeologique-nice.org.*

The collections include finds excavated at Cimiez and around Nice, along with a number of donations. There are ceramics and bronzes from the great Mediterranean civilisations (Greece, Etruria and Roman Africa) and artefacts such as the superb **mask of Silenus★**, many salvaged from shipwrecks. Ligurian and Roman items include the Bronze Age statue of a warrior from Mont Bégo, Iron-Age finds from perched strongholds or oppida) and milestones (1C) from the Via Julia Augusta.

Roman civilisation is represented through examples of every-day artefacts, a display of imperial coins, as well as representations of Cimiez.

Site Archéologique Gallo-Romain★

○*Same as the Musée Archéologique.*

Steps lead down into the *decumanus maximus* (the main east–west street of a Roman town) with its central drain and shops. To the left are the **northern baths** for high-ranking Romans containing a **frigidarium** (cold room), the dimensions of which (33ft/10m high by 30ft/9m wide) give an idea of their huge scale. The warm room and the hot rooms are built above a **hypocaust** (a system of channels through which hot air passed). Still visible today, it is one of the best-preserved examples anywhere in the former Roman Empire. On the eastern side are the latrines. On the other side of the main street are the less elaborate but fully equipped **eastern baths** for the general public, which can be viewed from a walkway.

The western end opens into the *cardo maximus* (main street running north–south). To the left of this street are the remains of the more recent **western baths**. Turned into a Paleo-Christian baptistery in the 5C, some parts of an early cathedral are still visible and the choir, in the former frigidarium, contains traces of an altar.

▶ Cross the public olive tree gardens to pl. du Monastère.

Studios de la Victorine

With the dawn of cinema, Nice provided film-makers with the ideal ingredients for their future success: almost constant light and sunshine, the sea and the presence of magnificent hotels as natural backdrops.

Louis Feuillade, who made *Fantômas*, was one of the first to spot the potential of the area; the roofs of the Hôtel Négresco passed into cinematic posterity in the Fantômas-Judex chase.

"Azure cinema" really took off in 1920, when a large unoccupied estate west of the town centre, La Victorine, was acquired by the fabulously rich Hollywood producer Rex Ingram, who had launched Rudolf Valentino and Roman Navarro. He produced the epic *Mare Nostrum* to promote his new studios. For the following 10 years the Victorine studios were an essential part of the prosperous French and European film industry before changes in public tastes brought about a decade of inactivity. The Armistice of 1940 caused French cinema to seek refuge in Nice (Abel Gance, Prévert, Carné), and in 1943 the filming of *Les Visiteurs du Soir* revived the production of large-scale films. In 1944 came *Les Enfants du Paradis,* the greatest production at La Victorine, co-produced by Marcel Carné and Jacques Prévert, with Arletty and Jean-Louis Barrault. The reconstruction of *Boulevard du Crime* in the middle of the Second World War required more than 30t of scaffolding and nearly 4,186sq yd/3,500sq m of fencing for the sets, as well as 2,000 extras, who were recruited in Nice. A worsening economic situation temporarily brought a halt to Nice's creativity. The post-war years were good, but were followed by a lull. A revival now seems to be underway.

Place du Monastère

A twisted column of white marble, rising in the square in front of the church, bears a Calvary dating from 1477. The Fauvist painters Raoul Dufy and Henri Matisse are buried in the nearby **Notre Dame cemetery**. Matisse's tomb lies in an olive grove to the north of the wall.

Monastère Franciscain★

The Franciscans, who in the 16C took over the buildings of a former Benedictine monastery founded in the 9C, have restored and considerably enlarged the abbey church.

Église Sainte-Marie-des-Anges

pl. du Monastère. ⊙*Open Mon–Thu, Sat 9am–6pm, Fri 9am–noon, 3pm–6pm, Sun 12.30pm–6pm* ℘*04 93 81 00 04.*
The church possesses three **masterpieces★★** by the local artist Louis Bréa, illustrating the Nice School. To the right of the entrance stands a **Pietà** (1475), one of his best works. The arms of the cross and the stiff body of Christ emphasise the horizontal perspective.

The **Crucifixion** to the left of the choirs is remarkable for the total absence of a Gothic aesthetic. The **Deposition** in the third chapel complements the Crucifixion and adheres to Renaissance principles: the figures aligned obliquely on the body of Christ are counterbalanced by the vertical lines of the landscape.

Musée Franciscain

⊙*Open Mon–Sat 10am–noon, 3pm–6.30pm.* ⊙*Closed public holidays.* ⊛*No charge.* ℘*04 93 81 00 04.*
The museum recalls the work of the Franciscans in Nice from the 13C to the present day.

Monastery Gardens★

On the south side of the monastery there are terraced gardens with flower beds and a **viewpoint** looking down on the Paillon Valley, the castle hill and the sea, Mont Boron and the observatory. A copse of cypress and holm oak marks the site of the former Ligurian *oppidum*.

NICE'S RUSSIAN HERITAGE

Around the middle of the 19C, after Empress Alexandra Fedorovna, widow of Tsar Nicolas I, settled in Nice, many wealthy Russian aristocrats chose the city as their winter residence. These "eccentrics", as the locals called them, recreated the atmosphere of their native land on the Riviera. Baron Von Dewies, who designed the Russian railway system, commissioned the Gothic **Château de Valrose** (Nice University) and set up an *izba*, shipped especially from Kiev. To the west of Nice, the **Château des Ollières** features an impressive keep flanked by four turrets. The nearby **Palais Kotschoubey** houses the Musée des Beaux-Arts. Two other notable examples of Russian architecture are the **Palais Impérial** and the **Résidence Palladium** on blvd. Tsarévitch.

Cathédrale Orthodoxe Russe St-Nicolas★

ave. Nicholas-II. ○*Open daily May–Sept 9am–noon, 2pm–6pm; Oct–Apr 9.30am–noon, 2pm–5pm.* ○*Closed Sun morning.* ☞*3€.* ☎*04 93 96 88 02. www.acor-nice.com.*

Inaugurated in December 1912, the **Russian Orthodox cathedral** is the largest Russian religious building outside Russia. It has six gilded onion domes and an ochre brick façade; the cathedral's domes are coated with gold leaf. Inside, the choir is decorated with an **iconostasis★** featuring religious artworks from Moscow.

At the end of the park on the left is a **Byzantine chapel** dedicated to Tsarevich Nicolas, the son of Tsar Alexander II, who died here in 1866.

SIGHTS
Parc Phœnix★

405 Promenade des Anglais. From the promenade, head toward Nice airport, then turn right into the park. ♿○*Open daily Apr–Sept 9.30am–7.30pm; Oct–Mar 9.30am–6pm. Last entry 1hr before closing.* ☞*No charge.* ☎*04 92 29 77 00. www.nice.fr.*

This vast botanical garden (some 17 acres/7ha), inaugurated in 1991, is organised by theme and contains more than 1,500 plant species from all over the world. The "Île des Temps Révolus" (Island of Bygone Times) features a display of living plant fossils: cycads, ginkgo biloba, tree ferns, etc.

An **aviary** houses a collection of colourful parrots and other tropical birds, while the **giant greenhouse★**, a tropical hothouse covering 75,300sq ft/7,000sq m beneath a 82ft/25m high roof, contains 7 different climates.

Next door are the carnivorous plants and the butterfly house.

Musée des Arts Asiatiques★★

405 promenade des Anglais. ♿○*Open Wed–Mon May–mid-Oct 10am–6pm; late Oct–Apr 10am–5pm.* ☞*No charge.* 🅿*(fee).* ☎*04 92 29 37 00. www.arts-asiatiques.com.*

Delicately poised on the lake in Phœnix Park, this white marble construction (1998) by the Japanese architect **Kenzo Tange** presents sacred and traditional objects from Asia.

The ground-floor galleries are devoted to China, Japan, India and Southeast Asia, while the rotunda explores the history of Buddhism. Temporary exhibitions are held on the lower ground floor. Tea ceremonies are organised in

© Sylvaine Poitau/Apa Publications

Cathédrale Orthodoxe Russe St-Nicolas

the Japanese **tea room** *(Sun 3pm, by reservation; ℘04 92 29 37 02).*

Musée International d'Art Naïf Anatole Jakovsky★

Château Sainte-Hélène, ave. de Fabron. Leave the town centre by promenade des Anglais. ○*Open Wed–Mon 10am–6pm.* ⊚*No charge.* ℘*04 93 71 78 33.*

Housed in an elegant château, the Anatole Jakovsky Bequest comprises 600 canvasses by naïve artists from around the world, including Croatian artists Generalic and Rabuzin, French artists Bauchant and Vieillard, and works from Italy, Belgium and the Americas.

Musée Masséna★

65 rue de France. Museum: ○*open Wed–Mon 10am–6pm; Gardens: open Jun–mid-Sept 9am–8pm; Apr–May and rest of Sept 9am–7pm; Oct–Mar 9am–6pm.* ⊚*No charge.* ℘*04 93 91 19 10.*

This museum explores the history of Nice from the 19C to the 1930s. It was built in 1898 for Victor Masséna, great-grandson of Napoléon's famous general; his son André gave it to the town in 1919. Presented on two floors, the exhibits retrace the life of André Masséna and explore the history of Nice during the Revolution and Empire, the Sardinian restoration, and its rise as a fashionable seaside resort. A restored library on the top floor houses more than 30,000 photos and 3,000 maps *(reservation required).*

Acropolis-Palais des Congrès★

1 Esplanade Kennedy. ○*Closed Jul–Aug* ℘*04 93 92 82 35. www.nice-acropolis.com.*

This enormous convention centre resembles a majestic vessel anchored to five robust vaults spanning the River Paillon. Designed by a group of local architects, it features works by contemporary artists including Volti *(Nikaia),* Vasarely, Arman *(Music Power),* César *(Thumb),* Paul Belmondo and Cyril de la Patellière *(Mediterranean Tribute).*

Théâtre de la Photographie et de l'Image

27 Blvd. Dubouchage. ○*Open Tue–Sunn 10am–6pm.* ⊚*No charge.* ℘*04 97 13 42 20. www.tpi-nice.org.*

This exhibition space dedicated to photographic images benefits from an original architectural setting.

▲♣ Muséum d'Histoire Naturelle

60 Blvd. Risso. ○*Open Tue–Sun 10am–6pm.* ○*Closed public holidays.* ⊚*No charge.* ℘*04 97 13 46 80. www.mhnnice.org.*

Nice's first museum has a large collection of zoological, geological and botanical specimens.

▲♣ Musée de Terra Amata

25 Blvd. Carnot. ○*Open Tue–Sun 10am–6pm.* ⊚*No charge.* ℘*04 93 55 59 93. www.musee-terra-amata.org.*

Situated on the site of one of the earliest human settlements known in Europe, dating back 400,000 years, this museum features tools, animal bones and traces of a hunter's hearth.

Prieuré du Vieux-Logis

59 Ave. St-Barthélémy. ◆*Guided tours 1.50€, by reservation Jun–Sept Sat 5pm; Oct–May Sat 3pm.* ℘*04 93 84 44 74.*

A medieval home has been reconstructed within a 16C farm and richly decorated with works of art, 14C to 17C furniture and items from everyday life (note the outstanding kitchen). There are numerous statues, including a 15C Pietà from Franche-Comté.

Église St-Barthélémy

13 montée Claire-Virenque.

This church houses a triptych *(right side aisle)* by François Bréa of the *Virgin in Majesty* flanked by *Saint John the Baptist* and *Saint Sebastian.*

Église Ste-Jeanne-d'Arc

11 rue Gramont.

This is a modern concrete church designed by Jacques Droz with an ellipsoidal porch as its main doorway.

The belfry wreathed in flames rises to 215ft/65m. Inside, the soaring vaulting is striking. *The Stations of the Cross* frescoes are by Klementief (1934).

🚘 DRIVING TOURS

INLAND FROM NICE

The hinterlands of Nice are dotted with cliff-top villages and **panoramic** peaks accessible by narrow winding roads.
🛈 Tourist offices at Gilette Val d'Esteron, *℘04 92 08 98 08, www.esteron.fr*; at L'Escarène, *℘04 93 79 62 93, www.escarene.fr;* or at Contes, *℘04 93 79 13 99, www.ville-contes.fr.*

1 LES DEUX MONTS★★
Round trip of 7mi/11km. Allow 1hr15min.

▶ Leave Nice from pl. Max-Barel on D 6007, Moyenne Corniche, going east. After 1.5mi/2.5km, turn a sharp right onto a forest road. After 0.6mi/1km turn left onto a signposted path to the fort.

16C fort of Mont Alban

©Guy Thouvenir/Robert Harding

Mont Alban★★
Alt. 728ft/222m. A footpath circles up to a splendid **view★★** of the coastline: to the east lie Cap Ferrat, Cap d'Ail, the Bordighera Point and the Tête de Chien. To the west lies the Baie des Anges.
A small pathway leads to the massive 16C fort bastions and watchtowers *(private).*

▶ Return to the fork and proceed straight ahead to Mont Boron.

Mont Boron★
Alt. 584ft/178m. **Views★** from this mountain extend over Villefranche harbour, along the coast to Cap d'Antibes and the mountains around Grasse. Bones, stone tools and a hearth used by Acheulian hunters were found on the western slope *(♿see Musée Terra Amata p311).*
🚶 Walk along the 710yd/650m botanic **woodland trail** featuring dozens of species of aromatic and medicinal plants with a **view★** over the Baie des Anges.

▶ Return to Nice along the Corniche Inférieure (N 98).

2 PLATEAU ST-MICHEL★★
Round trip of 12mi/19km. Allow 1hr.

▶ Leave Nice going E along ave. des Diables-Bleus and the Grande Corniche (D 2564).

Observatoire du Mont-Gros
Turn right off the Grande Corniche onto a private road. ⏳Guided tours (1.5hr) daily 2.45pm. ⬤6€. ℘04 93 85 85 58. www.astrorama.net.
This international centre for astronomical research was founded in 1881. The shell was designed by **Charles Garnier**; the metal frame for the dome (85ft/26m in diameter) housing the astronomical telescope was built by **Gustave Eiffe**l. At 59ft/18m long, with an optical diameter of 30in/76cm. it was once the largest instrument of its kind.

▶ Take the D 2524 towards Eze for 1mi/1.5km, then E 34 right; after 547yd/500m, park in the car park.

Plateau St-Michel Viewpoint★★

From here, you can see the coast as far as Cap de St-Hospice in Nice and Cap Ferrat.

◗ Continue along D 34 and then bear left onto the Moyenne Corniche (D 6007).

After a tunnel there is a **view★** of Beaulieu, Cap Ferrat, Villefranche-sur-Mer, Nice and Cap d'Antibes. The road winds round above Villefranche harbour.

◗ Return to Nice via Pl. Max-Barel.

③ TOUR OF MONT CHAUVE★
Round trip of 33mi/53km. Allow half a day.

◗ From Nice take blvd. Cessole, ave. St-Sylvestre and ave. du Ray north; turn sharp left onto ave. de Gairaut (D 14). Pass under the motorway (0.6mi/1km), bear right on D 14 and then left (follow signs).

Cascade de Gairaut

The waters of the Vésubie Canal tumble down into a basin over two great rock shelves. From the chapel terrace there is a beautiful **view★** of the town.

◗ Return to D 14.

The road then rises towards Aspremont, the *baous* and the Var valley.

Aspremont

The village, built to a concentric plan, is perched on a hilltop site (1,800ft/550m). The **church** has a Gothic nave decorated with frescoes. The terrace above the town permits a **panorama★** of several hill villages, Cap d'Antibes, the hills beyond Nice and Mont Chauve. As you leave the village, a small road on the left signposted "Mona Cima" leads to a sheepfold *(park at pl. des Selettes and continue on foot)* with **views** of Aspremont and the Var.

◗ On leaving the village, take D 719 over Col d'Aspremont between Mont Chauve and Mont Cima.

Tourrette-Levens

Circled by mountains, this village on the Salt Route clings to a knife-edged rock. The **18C church** has a carved wooden altarpiece. Walk through the village to the partially restored château and the **Musée des Métiers Traditionnels** *(◖open Tue–Sun 2pm–6pm; ℰ04 97 20 54 60)* exhibiting some 6,000 tools. The walk ends at the **Musée d'Histoire Naturelle**, with a collection of exotic butterflies *(◖open Tue–Sun Apr–Oct 2pm–6.30pm; Nov–Mar 2pm–5.30pm; ℰ04 93 91 03 20).*

◗ Return to D 19, turning left into the Gabre Valley, then right on D 114.

Falicon

This typical Niçois village huddles on a rocky outcrop among olive groves. Illustrious guests have included Queen Victoria. The **church**, founded by the Benedictines of St-Pons, has a square belfry and *trompe-l'oeil* façade. Climb the stairway, then turn right to the terrace **views★** of Nice and Mont Angel.

◗ Return to D 114 on the left. At the chapel of St-Sébastien turn right onto D 214, a narrow road, to Mont Chauve. Leave the car at the end of the road.

Mont Chauve d'Aspremont
Alt. 2,802ft/854m.
🚶 *30min on foot round trip.*
"Chauve" means bald and the mountain lives up to its name. A disused fort stands on the summit offering a magnificent **panorama★★** of the snow-clad Alps and the coast from Menton to Cap Ferrat.

◗ Return to D 114 left; then right on D 19 after 1mi/2km. After 0.6mi/1km turn right to St-Pons.

Église St-Pons★

The Benedictine abbey of St Pontius was founded during the reign of Charlemagne. The church, rebuilt in the 18C, stands on a headland above the Paillon Valley, its Genoese campanile visible from all sides.

ADDRESSES

🏨 STAY

◉ **Au Picardy Hôtel** – *10 blvd. Jean-Jaurès.* ✆*04 93 85 75 51.* 🍴 *11 rooms.* ⊑*4€.* Between the train station and Old Town, this friendly, family-run hotel has basic rooms: small, yet soundproofed.

◉◉ **Clair Hotel** – *23 blvd. Carnot, Impasse Victor Lavagna.* ✆*04 93 89 69 89. http://clair-hotel-nice.com. 10 rooms.* ⊑*8€.* This converted schoolhouse near the Terra Amata museum has rooms all on one floor (in old classrooms) and a Mediterranean garden terrace, where breakfast is served in summer. Quiet neighbourhood; friendly atmosphere.

◉◉ **Hôtel Armenonville** – *20 ave. des Fleurs.* ✆*04 93 96 86 00. www.hotel-armenonville.com. 12 rooms.* 🅿. ⊑*11€.* At the end of a passage in the old Russian district of Nice, this retro hotel built in 1900 has charming rooms decorated with antiques. WiFi, garden, air-conditioning and free parking.

◉◉ **Hôtel de Normandie** – *18 rue Paganini.* ✆*04 93 88 48 83. www.hotel-normandie.com. 44 rooms.* ⊑*7€.* Practical location a few steps from the train station with a typical Niçoise decor. Rooms are simple, yet well-equipped, and there's free WiFi and a hot meal distributor in the lobby.

◉◉ **Star Hôtel** – *14 rue Biscarra.* ✆*04 93 85 19 03. www.hotel-star.com. Closed mid-Nov–23 Dec. 24 rooms.* ⊑*8€.* Small hotel close to the Nice Étoile shopping centre, offering simple accommodation with air-conditioning and free Internet access.

◉◉◉ **Chambre d'hôte Castel Enchanté** – *61 route St-Pierre-de-Féric.* ✆*04 93 97 02 08. www.castel-enchante.com.* 🍴. *4 rooms.* ⊑. A 19C villa on the hills above Nice, with a huge terrace surrounded by orchards. Rooms are cosy and comfortable. Swimming pool amid palm trees and bougainvillea.

◉◉◉ **Chambre d'hôte Villa la Lézardière** – *87 blvd. de l'Observatoire.* ✆*04 93 56 22 86. www.villa-nice.com. 5 rooms.* 🅿. ⊑. Perched on the Grande Corniche, this Provençal-style villa has great **views** over the Alps. Personalised bedrooms, some with kitchenettes. Also a large pool and enclosed garden.

🍽 EAT

To experience the best in local cuisine (*salade niçoise, socca, pan bagnat, poutine, tourte aux blettes, beignets de fleurs de courgettes*), look for restaurants displaying the "Cuisine Nissarde" label. A guide to these restaurants is available free of charge at the tourist office.

◉ **Le Pain à Table** – *3 rue St-François-de-Paul (cours Saleya).* ✆*04 93 62 94 32. www.lepainatable.com.* Sit at one of the communal wooden tables and order fresh breads with spreads, salads and open sandwiches. Brunch is served on weekends.

◉ **Réné Socca** – *2 rue Miralhéti.* ✆*04 93 92 05 73 .* 🍴 *Closed Mon.* The most popular "Nissart" restaurant in town. Follow the line, order your food and sit at one of the long tables with your meal. Don't miss the *socca*, cooked fresh in the wood-fired oven, the *pissaladière* and stuffed courgette blossoms.

◉◉ **Auberge de Théo** – *52 Ave. du Cap-de-Croix, colline de Cimiez.* ✆*04 93 81 26 19. www.auberge-de-theo.com. Closed Sun, Mon.* This eatery in Cimiez, where good restaurants are a rarity, specialises in the cooking of Southern Italy. The Neopolitan owner and his son prepare antipasti, pizza, charcuterie, fish, beef and other dishes of high quality. Rustic decor and pleasant patio.

◉◉ **Café de Turin** – *5 pl. Garibaldi.* ✆*04 93 62 29 52. www.cafedeturin.fr.* ♿. This brasserie, which is over 100 years old, has become an institution in Nice. It serves seafood dishes à la carte at reasonable prices throughout the day. Pleasant, welcoming setting, although a bit noisy on the terrace.

◉◉ **L'Escalinada** – *22 rue Pairolière.* ✆*04 93 62 11 71. www.escalinada.fr.* 🍴. ♿. *Closed mid-Jan–mid-Feb, and 1 week in Mar.* Nestled in the old quarter, this charming restaurant offers attractively presented regional cuisine in a spruced-up dining room with rustic overtones. Friendly service.

◉◉ **Lou Balico** – *20-22 ave. St-Jean-Baptiste.* ✆*04 93 85 93 71. www.loubalico.com. Closed Jul–Aug and Sun lunch.* Three generations of the same family have been serving classic Niçois dishes in this cosy dining room, equipped with a piano and guest book with signatures from around the world.

Marlone Café – *4 rue de l'Opéra.* *04 93 85 96 15 . www.marlonecafe.com. Closed Sun, Mon.* This gourmet refuge just off Place Masséna serves traditional meals in a comfortable, thoughtfully decorated dining room.

La Table d'Alziari – *4 rue François-Zannin.* *04 93 80 34 03. Closed Sun, Mon and 12–23 Jan, 1–5 Jun, 5–16 Oct, 7–18 Dec.* This family restaurant sits in a small alley in the old town. Typical dishes from Nice and the Provence area, chalked up on a slate, are served without fuss with wines recommended by the owner. The *poche de veau* (veal) is a house classic. Outdoor seating too.

Le Bellanda– *85 quai des États-Unis.* *04 93 76 65 28. www. lebellanda.com.* Don't be fooled by the high-design decor of this new brasserie facing the Promenade: it serves Niçois-style tapas and other regional specialities, including courgette fritters, *daube à la niçoise* (Niçois beef stew), *tourte de blettes* (sweet chard pie) and fig tart. Outdoor terrace.

Safari – *1 cours Saleya.* *04 93 80 18 44. www.restaurantsafari.com.* A trendy address overlooking the market at Cours Saleya, this restaurant has a beautiful terrace and prepares local specialities, including a large selection of fish and seafood. Great for people watching.

L'Univers-Christian Plumail – *54 blvd. J. Jaurès.* *04 93 62 32 22. www.christian-plumail.com. Closed Sat lunch, Mon lunch and Sun.* Decorated with modern paintings and sculptures, this prestigious Niçois restaurant serves regional cuisine with a twist. Set menus available.

NIGHTLIFE

Casino Ruhl – *1 promenade des Anglais.* *04 97 03 12 22. www.lucienbarriere.com.* The casino boasts 300 slot machines and has facilities for French and English roulette, blackjack, stud poker, etc. American bar. Live cabaret performances on Fridays and Saturdays (except July–August). Bring photo ID.

Le Relais – *Hôtel Negresco, 37 promenade des Anglais.* *04 93 16 64 00. www.hotel-negresco-nice.com.* The sumptuous decoration of this bar belonging to the legendary Negresco Hotel has remained the same since 1913: Brussels tapestry

(1683), 18C paintings, replicas of the wall lamps adorning the ballroom in Fontainebleau. Piano bar every evening.

La Trappa – *rue de la Préfecture and rue Gilly.* *04 93 80 33 69. Closed Sun–Mon.* A lively tapas bar with deep, comfortable settees and red walls awaits you at La Trappa, open since 1886. Sip a Cuban cocktail while you listen to Latin American music (DJ weekends). Friendly atmosphere and local wine list.

SHOPPING

Many shops in Old Nice are closed on Mondays.

SHOPPING STREETS

The streets surrounding the Cathédrale Ste-Réparate are lined with shops selling typical Provençal articles: fabrics *(rue Paradis and rue du Marché)*, arts and crafts *(rue du Pont-Vieux and rue de la Boucherie)*, olive oil and *santons* (clay figures) *(rue St-François-de-Paul)*.

SHOPS

Alziari – *14 rue St-François-de-Paule.* *04 93 85 76 92. www.alziari.com.fr. Closed Sun–Mon.* One of the best addresses in town for olive oil and regional specialities.

À l'Olivier – *7 rue St-François-de-Paule.* *04 93 13 44 97. www.alolivier.com.* Every brand of French olive oil with the AOC label is sold in this boutique, originally opened in 1822, in Nice since 2004. Also, a fine selection of elegant glassware, dishes, tablecloths.

Confiserie Auer – *7 rue St-François-de-Paule.* *04 93 85 77 98. www.maison-auer.com. Closed Sun, Mon.* A gorgeous vintage boutique selling sugared fruit and crystallised flowers from the Nice region, as well as chocolates and *calissons* from Aix (iced, candied fruit with almond paste).

Florian – *14 quai Papacino.* *04 93 55 43 50. www.confiserieflorian.com.* *Guided tours of the factory 9am–noon, 2pm–6.30pm.* Sugared fruit, lemon, orange and grapefruit preserve, chocolates and sweets, crystallised petals and delicious jams made with rose, violet and jasmine blossom.

Maison Poilpot – Aux Parfums de Grasse – *10 rue St-Gaétan.* *04 89 00 41 49. Closed Sun afternoon and Mon.* This traditional perfumery produces more than 80 different fragrances, including popular Mediterranean scents such as mimosa, rose, violet and lemon.

L'Art Gourmand – *21 rue du Marché.* ℘*04 93 62 51 79.* This Old Nice boutique has many treats available to go or eat in: nougats, *calisson*, sugared fruit, cookies, pastries, ice cream and northern French specialities. There's a tea room on the mezzanine decorated with murals.

MARKETS

Marché aux Poissons – The fish market occurs on pl. St-François Tue–Sun 6am–1pm.

Marché aux Fleurs – The flower market is held on the cours Saleya Tues–Sun 6am–5.30pm.

Marché aux Fruits et Légumes – The colourful food market on the cours Saleya takes place Tue–Sun 6am–1.30pm.

Marché de la Liberation – Locals' food market on the avenue Malausséna and place Charles de Gaulle.

Marché aux Puces – Flea market on place Robilante Tue–Sat 10am–6pm.

Marché de la Brocante –Antique market on cours Saleya on Mon 7.30am–6pm.

LEISURE ACTIVITIES

Beaches – The Baie des Anges covers a 3mi/5km stretch of coastline with smooth pebbles *(galets)*. There are many public beaches placed under close surveillance and 15 private beaches hosting sporting activities.

Hiking – *Club Alpin Francaise de Nice-Mercantour. 14 ave. Mirabeau.* ℘*04 93 62 59 99. www.cafnice.org. Office open Mon, Tue, Thu, Fri 4–8pm.* CAF (Club Alpin Français) organises one-day hiking tours across the Nice hinterland and Mercantour Park leaving from Nice.

Skiing – *www.cotedazur-tourisme.com.* The nearby ski resorts of Auron (℘*04 93 23 02 66)* and Valberg (℘*04 93 02 52 27)*, which are only a 2hr drive away, are undoubtedly among the main attractions of the Nice area.

CALENDAR

There are many traditional festivals throughout the year in Nice. Ask at the tourist office for a complete schedule.

Nice Carnival – This colourful, extravagant event invariably attracts large crowds every year. Festivities take place around Shrove Tuesday *(Mardi Gras)* and last for a fortnight. They include processions, floats, firework displays, costume balls and battles where showers of flowers and confetti are thrown. *www.nicecarnaval.com.*

Fête de la Mer et de la St-Pierre – A festival celebrating the sea and St-Peter on the port and quai des Etats-Unis the last weekend in June.

Nice Jazz Festival – The jazz festival is held in Nice the last two weeks of July on pl. Massena, attended by leading performers from all over the world. *www.nicejazzfestival.fr.*

Fête de la San Bertoumiéu – A festival of traditional arts and crafts, regional foods and entertainment in the Old Town the first weekend in September.

Crèche Vivante Lou Presèpi – A living Nativity scene with people and animals on place Rossetti the week of Christmas.

Prom' Party – Held 14 Jul–5 Aug. The promenade des Anglais is closed to traffic in the evenings for one week. from the Hôtel Négresco to the grassy amphitheatre *(www.tdv-nice.org)*. At 9pm begin the concerts, street spectacles, fireworks and other fanfare. *No charge.*

Village de Noël – From late Nov to the beginning of Dec at la place Masséna. Outdoor ice-skating rink, festive lighting displays, and a Christmas village selling crafts and seasonal treats.

Corniches de la Riviera★★★

Alpes-Maritimes

Between Nice and Menton the mountains plunge sharply down to the sea. Running along these heights are three famous routes: the Grande Corniche, the Moyenne Corniche and the Basse Corniche. The first affords the most stunning views, climbing to 1,476ft/450m. The second offers beautiful vistas along the shore; while the third provides access to the coastal resorts.

- 🖏 **Michelin Map:** 341 F/G5.
- 🗐 **Info:** Cap d'Ail tourist office: 87bis Ave. du 3-Septembre. ℘04 93 78 02 33. www.cap-dail.com
- 🕭 **Don't Miss:** The Grande Corniche has the best **panoramic views**.
- 👪 **Kids:** Check out the stars from Astrorama.
- 🕐 **Timing:** If time is short, take a 3-hr drive along the Grande Corniche.

🚗 DRIVING TOUR

1 GRANDE CORNICHE★★★

MENTON TO NICE
19mi/31km. Allow 3hr.

The Grande Corniche, built by Napoleon along the route of the ancient **Via Julia Augusta**, passes through La Turbie 1,470ft/450m above Monaco.

◐ From Menton take ave. Carnot and ave. de la Madone (D 6007). Leaving the Moyenne Corniche on the left, the road (D 2564) runs above the town and Cap Martin. 437yd/400m after entering Roquebrune-Cap-Martin, take a sharp right onto a small road leading to the village.

Roquebrune-Cap-Martin★
See ROQUEBRUNE-CAP-MARTIN.

◐ Return to D 2564.

Le Vistaëro★★
From nearly 1,000ft/300m above the sea, a marvellous **view★★** extends out over Bordighera Point, Menton and, immediately below, Monte Carlo Beach. Farther inland is the Alpine Trophy.

La Turbie★
The hilltop village of La Turbie *(alt. 1,575ft/480m; population 3,155),* built in

a pass on the Grande Corniche, is most famous for its **Alpine Trophy** *(🖏 see below),* a masterpiece of Roman art. When Caesar died, the Alps were occupied by unconquered tribes who posed a constant threat to communications between Rome and its possessions in Gaul and Spain. **Augustus** ended this threat by extending Roman rule into the region. In 6 BC the Senate and the Roman people commemorated the victory with the erection of the trophy on the **Via Julia Augusta**. (Only one other Roman trophy is still standing, in Romania). On Avenue Charles-de-Gaulle is a 19C **fountain**, built at the end of a Roman aqueduct. Below, from the southwest corner of **place Neuve**, a fine **view★** of the coast is obtained. **Rue Comte-de-Cessole** was once part of the Via Julia Augusta. Pass through the West Gate, climbing past medieval houses to the Trophy. A house on the right bears a plaque with verses Dante dedicated to La Turbie.

Église St-Michel-Archange – The 18C church *(🕐 open daily 9am–6.30pm; ℘04 93 41 21 15)* is a fine example of the Nice Baroque style, with paintings attributed to J-B Van Loo and Veronese *(light switch in the chapel on the right).*

Return to the rue de Cessole and climb to the top of the hill to take a look at the Trophy, then return towards **rue Droite** (also once part of the Via Julia), passing under the East Gate. Bring your camera to capture the great **panorama★★★** of Monaco, the Italian Riviera, Èze and the heights of Mont Agel from the **terraces** here.

Trophée des Alpes★

&⏺ *Open Tue–Sun mid-May–mid-Sept 9.30am–1pm, 2.30pm–6.30pm; late Sept–early May 10am–1.30pm, 2.30pm–5pm.* ◎*5€.* ☎*04 93 41 20 84. www.ville-la-turbie.fr.*

The Alpine Trophy consisted of a circular Doric colonnade with niches for statues of the Roman generals who took part in the campaign to conquer the Alps. The base featured a long dedication to Augustus, whose statue probably stood on a small dome over the monument. In the Middle Ages it was converted into a fort, then served as a

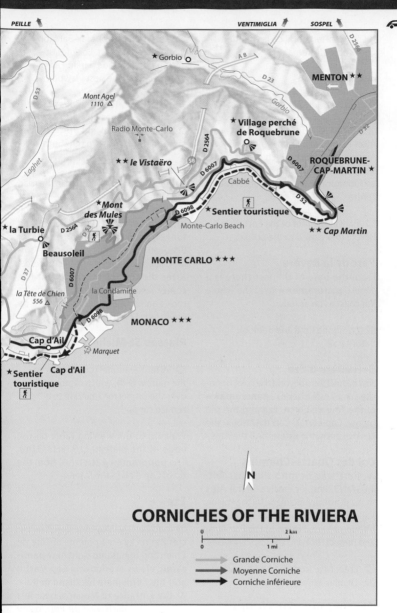

CORNICHES OF THE RIVIERA

N

0	2 km
0	1 mi

Grande Corniche
Moyenne Corniche
Corniche inférieure

source of building stone, before being mined by Louis XIV. It has been partially restored to a height of 115ft/35m. The **museum** recounts the story of the Trophy and its restoration.

The Grande Corniche reveals distant **views** of Cap Ferrat, then of Èze village as the road reaches its highest point at 1,804ft/550m.

Col d'Èze

Alt. 1,680ft/512m. There is an extended **view** to the north over the mountains and valleys. Mont Bastide, on the left, was a Celto-Ligurian *oppidum* and a Roman camp.

▷ On leaving Col d'Èze towards Nice, turn right up the road signed

319

"Parc Départemental de la Grande Corniche-Astrorama".

🧍🧍 Astrorama

La Trinité. 🕐*Open Jul–Aug Tue–Sat 7pm–11pm; Mar–Jun and Sept–Oct Fri–Sat 7pm–11pm.* 👓*9€ (6–25 years 7€).* 📞*04 93 85 85 58. www.astrorama.net.* After a series of hairpin bends, the road reaches a plateau, which is home to a former **Feuillerins** gun battery, now an astronomical research and observation centre.

▶ Park at the foot of the Fort de la Revère (⛔ closed to the public).

Parc de la Revère

From the base of the fort there is a superb **panorama★★** over the whole Var coast as far as Italy.

🚶 *1hr.* Signed flora and geology nature trail.

Belvédère d'Èze

Just 0.7mi/1.2km beyond the pass, opposite a small café extends a **panorama★★** of the Tête de Chien, Èze and the sea below, Cap Ferrat, Cap d'Antibes, the Iles de Lérins, the Esterel and the Alps.

Col des Quatre-Chemins

A short way beyond the pass (alt. 1,037ft/327m), one can see the Alps through an opening made by the Paillon Valley. Soon the road descends steeply, offering a wide **view★** of the Pre-Alps, and then of Nice and the Cap d'Antibes.

▶ Enter Nice from the east by ave. des Diables-Bleus.

② MOYENNE CORNICHE★★

NICE TO MENTON

19mi/31km. Allow 2hr.
Shorter and less winding than the Grande Corniche, the Moyenne Corniche is a modern road built between 1910 and 1928. It tunnels through the larger mountain chains and provides the only access by road to the village of Èze.

▶ Leave Nice by pl. Max-Barel on D 6007 heading east. Look for the designated roadside parking areas provided at all the best viewpoints.

Views of Nice, the château, port and the Baie des Anges give way to **views** of the Esterel chain and the limestone mountains of Grasse to the southwest.

Col de Villefranche

Alt. 489ft/149m. From a bend in the road soon after the pass, Villefranche-sur-Mer harbour and Cap Ferrat come into sight. Just before entering a 200yd/180m-long tunnel, an extraordinary **view★★** of Beaulieu, Cap Ferrat, Villefranche-sur-Mer, Nice and Cap d'Antibes unfolds. After the tunnel, the village of Èze comes into view, perched high on its rock against the backdrop of Tête de Chien (alt. 1,880ft/556m).

Plateau St-Michel★★

▶ After the tunnel turn right onto the narrow D 34, which climbs back over the tunnel for 1mi/2km to a terrace car park.

Walk up to the viewing table on the edge of the plateau (2,339ft/731m). The **panorama★★** stretches from the tip of Cap d'Ail to the Esterel.

Èze★★

👜*See ÈZE.*
Beyond Èze, the Moyenne Corniche circles the rocky escarpments of Tête de Chien and brings into sight new **panoramic views** overlooking Cap Martin and the Bordighera headland in Italy. At the entrance to Monaco, bear left onto D 6007, which skirts the Principality and offers remarkable **views★** of Monte Carlo, Cap Martin and the Italian coast.

Beausoleil

This resort forms part of the Monaco conurbation, although it is officially on French territory. Its houses, reached by stepped streets, project from the slopes of Mont des Mules like balconies.

▶ Bear left onto D 53.

Mont des Mules★

🚶 *0.6mi/1km, plus 30min round trip along a marked path.*
From the top there is a fine **panorama**★ *(viewing table).*

▶ Passing below the Vistaëro belvedere, the road joins the Basse Corniche at Cabbé.

Cap Martin★★
🕭*See ROQUEBRUNE-CAP-MARTIN.*

③ CORNICHE INFÉRIEURE★★

NICE TO MENTON
21mi/33km. Allow about 6hr.
First floated in the 18C by the princes of Monaco, the idea of constructing the Basse Corniche finally took shape in 1857 when it was inaugurated by the empress of Russia. It was completed in 1881. The road, running at the foot of the mountain slopes and following the contours of the coast, serves all the Riviera resorts.

▶ From Nice take blvd. Carnot, D 6098, heading southeast.

The road skirts the base of Mont Boron with **views**★ of the Baie des Anges, Cap Ferrat, Villefranche-sur-Mer port, Èze and Tête de Chien in succession.

Villefranche-sur-Mer★
🕭*See VILLEFRANCHE-SUR-MER.*

Cap Ferrat★★
🕭*See CAP FERRAT.*

Beaulieu-sur-Mer★
🕭*See BEAULIEU-SUR-MER.*
As the road skirts **Cap Roux**, there is a view across the water to Cap d'Ail.

Èze-Bord-de-Mer
The resort lies beneath the cliffs on which Èze Village is perched. Views over Cap d'Ail are possible.

Cap d'Ail
Controversial stock market magnate **baron de Pauville**, founder of the "Petit niçois" regional weekly paper, was very attached to this small resort and built his first speculative properties here in 1879. The arrival of the railway and the main road at the end of the 19C further boosted its development. In 1908, the resort was finally opened.
Dominated by the Tête de Chien (1,640ft/500m) escarpment, which occupies the last slopes, the resort runs down to the sea, surrounded by palm trees, cypresses and pines; it includes some 70 early 20C villas. Countless celebrities have made their homes here, including Sacha Guitry (villa Les Funambules), Greta Garbo (villa Le Rock), the Caritta sisters (villa Le Chien Bleu aka "the bamboo cabin"), and one of the Lumière brothers.
Six parks and gardens fill the village streets with Mediterranean scents (parc Sacha-Guitry and the jardin des Oliviers) and afford stunning **views** over the sea and the small port (the Balcon des Salines). **Pointe des douaniers**, which resembles a wild volcanic landscape, offers exception flora and sea **views**.
For sun-seekers the **plage Marquet**, close to the port, is open to everyone. The wild **plage Mala**, niched in the rock, and **Les Pissarelles**, fringed by rocks, are difficult to access but offer **views**.

Coastal Path of Cap d'Ail★
🚶 *1hr round trip. On the east side of the station, descend the steps into a tunnel that comes out on a road. Turn left and at Restaurant La Pinède, take another flight of steps on the right down to the sea.*
A coastal footpath running eastwards skirts the rocks at the foot of Cap d'Ail. To the west lie Beaulieu, Cap Ferrat and Monaco Rock. The footpath ends on Marquet beach. You can take the road into Monaco.

Monaco★★★
🕭*See MONACO.*
The road joins the Moyenne Corniche close to Cabbé beach.

Notre-Dame-de-Laghet

S. Sauvignier/ MICHELIN

Cap Martin★★
See ROQUEBRUNE-CAP-MARTIN.

④ BASSE CORNICHE

AROUND MONT-AGEL★★
80km/50mi. Allow half a day.
See map p294.

▷ Leave Nice on the Turin road (D 2204) heading NE. At La Trinité turn right on to the D 2204A towards Laghet.

Notre-Dame-de-Laghet
Surrounded by woods, this Italianesque church was the setting for a series of miracles said to have been worked by the Virgin Mary in 1652; it has attracted pilgrims from Nice and Italy ever since. An example of High Baroque, the church is decorated with a carved wooden Madone de Laghet on the high altar. The cloister and church are filled with **ex-votos**. The most beautiful examples are displayed in a **museum** on place du Sanctuaire (&Ⓞopen Jul–Aug Sat–Sun 3.30pm–5.30pm; winter Tue–Sun 3pm–5pm; ⬤no charge; ℘04 93 41 50 50; www.sanctuaire-laghet.cef.fr).

▷ Continue on D 2204A and D 2564 to La Turbie.

La Turbie
See LA TURBIE.

▷ Turn left out of the village onto the D 53 towards Peille.

St-Martin-de-Peille
This isolated **church** rises out of olive groves planted up the mountain slopes. Modern and strikingly simple, it has plastic stained-glass windows and an altar made from a length of olive wood.

▷ Continue beyond St-Martin-de-Peille on D 53 for several kilometres and turn right onto D 22 towards Ste-Agnès.

The small road winds around the foot of **Mont Agel** with **views** of the Peille below and Berre-les-Alpes in the distance.
The **Col de la Madone** (3,041ft/927m) lies at a high altitude, just miles from the sea as the crow flies, which can be seen in the distance.
☛ *3hr round trip.* From Col de la Madone, a trail leads to the **Cîme de Baudon** (4,153ft/1,266m) affording a breathtaking **panorama**.

Ste-Agnès★
8mi/13km.
The road is uphill all the way with **views** of the Gorbio Valley. Bear right at **Col St-Sébastien** (alt. 1,969ft/600m), which

has a particularly fine **view**★ of Ste-Agnès. Located barely 2mi/3km from the sea, yet at an altitude of 2,559ft/780m, this community is the highest coastal village in Europe.

The picturesque cobblestone streets of the village, lined with craft shops, include rue Longue and the vaulted rue des Comtes-Léotardi. A rocky path leads from behind the graveyard to the ruins of the castle and a marvellous **panorama**★★.

Fort Maginot de Ste-Agnès

At the village entrance, turn towards the parking Sud and park the car on the left, near the fort. The interior is chilly. Guided tours (1hr) Jun–Sept daily 10.30am–noon, 3pm–7pm, Oct–May Sat–Sun 2.30pm–5.30pm. 5€. 04 93 51 62 31. www.sainteagnes.fr.

This imposing building, camouflaged by overhanging rocks, was completed in 1938 as part of the Alpine **Maginot Line**. Its firing slots are equipped with 81mm mortars and 75/135mm guns facing southeast over Menton Bay.

The barracks, deep in the cliff, still house an electric generator, a neutralisation room and kitchens. The tour gives an insight into life in a fort in WWII.

Outside, set slightly downhill, a platform overlooking the Provençal motorway offers a **view**★★ of the coast from Bordighera in Italy to Cap Martin.

▶ Head towards Menton on D 22, right onto C17 towards Gorbio, then right again onto D 23.

Gorbio★

5.6mi/9km.

The Gorbio Valley, with its flowers, olives, pines and luxury residences, contrasts with the stark appearance of the village, perched on its rocky **site**★. For the feast of Corpus Christi, the villagers organise a parade, known as the Procession des Limaces.

Behind the church is a fine **viewpoint** across to Bordighera Point.

▶ Take the D 50 to the Grande Corniche (D 2564) and return to Nice.

ADDRESSES

🍴 EAT

Le St-Yves – *St-Agnes.* 04 93 35 91 45. Closed Fri. 7 rooms. €5.50. This restaurant serving regional fare enjoys a warm, rustic atmosphere and breathtaking countryside views. Homemade antipasti, rabbit with herbs, and boar stew. Vast panoramic terrace. Simple guest rooms with open views.

Le Relais St-Martin Chez Cotton – *St-Martin-de-Peille – 12.5mi/4km from La Turbie, north of Peille.* 04 93 41 16 03. www.chezcotton.com. Closed Nov, Sun eve and Mon. A refreshing spot to escape the summer heat. Regional dishes and grilled meat served in a bright dining room (fireplace on winter evenings) or on the shady terrace. View over the valley and mountains.

Le Réserve de la Mala – *Plage de la Mala, down ave. Combattants Afrique-du-Nord.* 04 93 78 21 56. www.capresort.com. Closed Nov–late Mar. A small corner of paradise located right on the beach and accessible on foot from the Cap d'Ail tourist trail or the town centre. Mediterranean fish and world flavours.

CALENDAR

LA TURBIE

Soupe au pistou and retraite aux flambeaux – Local pistou soup festival and evening torch-lit parade, held 13 July on pl. Neuve, 8.30pm.

Les Musicales du Trophée – *www.musicalesdutrophee.fr. Second half of July.* Classical music concerts are performed at Saint-Michel church and Le Trophée.

GORBIO

Snail procession – Early to mid-June. Snail shells filled with oil are lit with a wick and placed on window sills.

LEISURE ACTIVITIES

Discovery hikes – Five-day hikes around the perched villages of the Corniches with Destination Merveilles. *www.voyages-randonnees.com.*

Villefranche-sur-Mer★

Alpes-Maritimes

Villefranche is a fishing port and holiday resort overlooking one of the most beautiful harbours in the Mediterranean, with a deep bay where cruise liners lie at anchor. The town has preserved its 17C character, with a picturesque port, citadel and streets lined with sherbet-coloured houses.

A BIT OF HISTORY
The Origins of Villefranche

The town was founded in the 14C by the comte de Provence, Charles II of Anjou, nephew of St Louis. Between its cession to Savoie in the late 17C and the excavation of the harbour in Nice in the mid-18C, Villefranche was a major port, popular for its tax privileges and free port rights (Villefranche literally means "Free Port"), granted by its Savoyard and Sardinian rulers.

The Congress of Nice

In 1538 the Congress of Nice was convened by Pope Paul III to bring peace between François I and Charles V. The Queen of France, sister of Charles V,

▶ **Population:** 6,610.
🕭 **Michelin Map:** 341 E5; local map: *see CORNICHES de la RIVIERA*.
🄸 **Info:** Jardin François-Binon. ℘04 93 01 73 68. www.ville franche-sur-mer.com.
▶ **Location:** Located 3.7mi/6km east of Nice on the Basse Corniche. Rue du Poilu is the main street in a network of narrow alleys, some of which are stepped or vaulted.
🄿 **Parking:** There is parking (absolutely packed in summer) around the citadel and the old port.

went to see her brother, whose ship was moored at Villefranche. Charles, giving his hand to the Queen and followed by the duc de Savoie and the lords and ladies of his suite, advanced majestically to the jetty from the ship, when the gangway collapsed.
The Emperor, Queen and Duke, soaked and dishevelled, were pulled ashore by onlookers. The peace of Nice lasted barely five years.

Villefranche-sur-Mer

S. Sauvignier/ MICHELIN

VILLEFRANCHE-SUR-MER

WHERE TO STAY

Patricia (Hôtel)........................①
Riviera (Hôtel Le)...................②
St-Michel (Hôtel)...................③

WHERE TO EAT

Grignotière (La)......................①
Oursin Bleu (L')......................②

From Naval Base to Zoological Station

In 1856, after the Crimean War, the Russian military fleet, deprived of access to the Mediterranean via the Bosphorus, used Villefranche harbour. In 1893 the sailors were replaced by a team of Russian scientists from Kiev who conducted oceanographic research until the 1930s, when the premises were reclaimed by the Université de Paris as the site of a marine zoology station.

SIGHTS
Old Town★

The old town opens onto a charming port whose quaysides are lined with brightly coloured houses. The **rue du Poilu** is the main thoroughfare through this labyrinth of alleyways, often stepped or vaulted. The curious **rue Obscure**, whose foundations date back to the 13C, once followed the medieval ramparts. Covered to a length of 142yd/130m, it provided the inhabitants with shelter during bombardments.

Église St-Michel

6 rue Baron-de-Brès.

This Italian Baroque church contains 18C altarpieces and in the north transept, a 17C crucifix carved with impressive realism from the trunk of a fig tree by an unknown convict.

Harbour (Darse)

Once a military port where galleys were built and manned, the harbour is now a marina for yachts and pleasure boats. *To admire the harbour from above, climb the wooded Mont Alban and Mont Boron (see p312).*

Chapelle St-Pierre★

Open Tue–Sun mid-Mar–mid-Sept 10am–noon, 3pm–7pm; late Sept–mid-Nov and mid-Dec–early Mar 10am–noon, 2pm–6pm. 2.50€. 04 93 76 90 70.

In 1957 this chapel was decorated with frescoes by **Jean Cocteau** (1889–1963) His theme, the life of St Peter, is illustrated by simple realistic scenes. There are also some secular scenes celebrating the young women of Villefranche.

Citadelle

🕐*Open daily Jun–Sept 10am–noon, 3pm–6.30pm (closed Sun morning); Oct–May 10am–noon, 2pm–5.30pm (closed Sun morning).* 👁*5€.* 🌿*04 93 76 33 27.*

This stronghold was constructed in 1554 by the Duc de Savoie to guard the port. Admired by Vauban, Louis XIV spared it, along with the fort on Mont Alban, when he ordered the destruction of Nice's defences. Restored in 1981, it now comprises the town hall, the former **chapel of St Elme** used for temporary exhibitions and an open-air theatre. The citadel is also home to three museums (🕐*same hours as the Citadelle*).

Musée Volti★

Housed in the main courtyard of the citadel, this collection features sculptures by **Antoniucci Volti** (1915–89), a citizen of Villefranche of Italian origin.

Musée Goetz-Boumeester

This museum displays more than 100 works by Picasso, Miró, Hartung and Picabia gifted to Villefranche by the painterengraver **Henri Goetz** (1909–89).

Collection Roux

This exhibition of ceramic figurines displayed in small tableaux evokes everyday life in the Middle Ages and during the Renaissance.

ADDRESSES

🛏 STAY

🍽🍽 **Hôtel Patricia** – *ave. de l'Ange-Gardien via the Corniche Inférieur.* 🌿*04 93 01 06 70. www.hotel-patricia. riviera.fr. Closed Jan.* 🅿. *13 rooms.* 🛏*7.50€.* Despite the close proximity of the train tracks, this hotel is well-placed just a few steps from the beach. The rooms are tastefully decorated; the ones on the upper floors have views of the sea.

🍽🍽 **Hôtel St-Michel** – *2000 ave. Olivula.* 🌿*04 93 01 80 42. www.hotel-saint-michel.com. 30 rooms.* 🛏*9€.* Located in the peaceful residential hills above the town, this hotel has recently renovated its rooms in the main building. Larger rooms are in the annexe, some with kitchenettes. WiFi available.

🍽🍽🍽 **Le Riviera** – *2 ave. Albert-1.* 🌿*04 93 76 62 76. www. hotelriviera villefranche.com. Closed mid-Dec.–Jan. 23 rooms.* 🛏*10€.* This unpretentious, prettily restored hotel is located on the Basse Corniche. Some rooms afford views of the sea. The agreeable rooftop terrace is great for summer breakfasts.

🍴 EAT

🍽🍽 **La Grignotière** – *3 rue du Poilu.* 🌿*04 93 76 79 83. Closed for lunch Nov–Mar.* This restaurant makes a point of serving hearty meals made with fresh ingredients. Follow the locals and tuck into a gargantuan dinner of Mediterranean dishes.

🍽🍽🍽🍽 **L'Oursin Bleu** – *11 quai de l'amiral Courbet.* 🌿*04 93 01 90 12. www. restaurant-oursin-bleu.com.* The charming nautical decor and centrepiece aquarium complement this popular port-side seafood restaurant. Elegant white tablecloths and wicker high-back chairs set the stage for entrées such as smoked salmon, duck foie grasse, bouillabaisse, prawns and turbot.

TOURS

Guided tours – Guided themed tours of the old town and citadel *(1hr45min)* Fridays 10am. Tour Apr–Sept Friday includes breakfast in the museum gardens and a tour of the citadel and the old town. 👁*5€. Reserve at the tourist office.* 🌿*04 93 01 73 68.*

👥 **Tourist Train** – *Apr–Oct.* 👁*6€ (child 3€).* 🌿*04 89 00 47 76. www.train-touristique-de-villefranche-sur-mer.com.* Departures from Wilson car park for round-trip tour *(45min)* of the town with commentary.

Cap Ferrat★★
Alpes-Maritimes

Tucked between Villefranche and Beaulieu, the prestigious Cap Ferrat peninsula is known for its lush vegetation, rugged cliffs and luxurious villas, including the spectacular Villa Ephrussi. Some of the best views of the coast can be had from the Sentier Littoral and St-Hospice Point.

SIGHTS
Villa Ephrussi-de-Rothschild★★
○ *Open Feb–Oct daily 10am–6pm (7pm Jul–Aug); Nov–Jan Mon–Fri 2pm–6pm, Sat–Sun 10am–6pm.* ⌬*12€.* ℘*04 93 01 33 09.* *www.villa-ephrussi.com.*

The villa was built in 1905 by baroness Béatrice Ephrussi de Rothschild to house her collection of more than 5,000 works of art. The villa's **setting★★★** offers sea **views** to Villefranche and Beaulieu. The tour begins with a covered patio, surrounded by columns of pink marble from Verona and decorated with furniture and paintings from the Middle Ages to the Renaissance, including a 15C altarpiece and a painting by Carpaccio. The patio gives onto two period rooms: the grand salon lined with panelling from the Hôtel de Crillon in Paris and decorated with Louis XVI furniture displayed on a carpet from a chapel in the Château

▶ **Population:** 2,172.
Ⓖ **Michelin Map:** 341 E5.
🅱 **Info:** 59 Ave. Denis-Semeria. ℘04 93 76 08 90. www.saintjeancapferrat.fr.
▶ **Location:** Also known as St-Jean-Cap-Ferrat (St-Jean being the name of the actual town), the peninsula is accessible by the narrow Bas Corniche, along the coastline.
👤 **Kids:** The shell museum.
○ **Timing:** At least half a day: 2hr at the Villa Ephrussi and 3hr on the coastal path.

de Versailles. The small salon is decorated with late-18C Gobelin tapestries. The fireguard bears the monogram of Marie Antoinette. The private apartments include a bedroom, bathroom, dressing room and boudoir.

Musée Île-de-France★★
🗣 *Guided tours only daily 11.30am, 2.30pm, 3.30pm and 4.30pm (and 5.30pm Jul–Aug)* ⌬*3€ extra.*

Housed in the Villa Ephrussi, the first floor of this museum displays an exceptional collection of Vincennes, Sèvres and Saxe porcelain. The curious "monkey room" features an orchestra of Meissen porcelain monkeys.

©Mgvuvan/Dreamstime.com
Cap Ferrat

ST-JEAN-CAP-FERRAT

WHERE TO STAY

Belle Aurore
Hôtel.............................①

Brise Marine
(Hôtel)..........................②

WHERE TO EAT

Capitaine Cook...........①

Plage
de Passable................②

Gardens★★

The villa is surrounded by beautiful grounds (17 acres/7ha). The central **French garden**, shaped like a ship's deck decorated with waterfalls and a rock garden with the sea on either side, was designed so the baroness could imagine herself on the steamship "Ile de France", on which she had enjoyed an unforgettable voyage. Below the steps, the **Spanish garden** is shaded with arum lilies, pomegranate trees and daturas. Farther on, the **Florentine garden** is graced with an ephebe surrounded by cypress trees. Fountains, capitals, gargoyles and low-reliefs (medieval and Renaissance) decorate the more romantic **stone garden**. After the delightful **Japanese garden**, an **exotic garden** filled with surprising plants leads to the **rose garden**.

≗♿Musée des Coquillages★★

Quai du Vieux-Port. ⏱*Open Mon–Fri 10am–noon, 2pm–6pm, Sat–Sun 2pm–6pm.* ⊚*2€ (1€ children under 15).*

℘04 93 76 17 61. www.musee-coquillages.com.
Discover more than 4,000 shells from the Mediterranean Sea as well as some from distant waters on view at this museum. There are microscopic specimens that can be seen only through binoculars. The collection includes notable specimens from the Villefranche-sur-Mer marine zoology station gathered around Cap Ferrat between 1930 and 1960.

CAP-FERRAT PENINSULA★★

6mi/10km. Allow about 1hr.
🚶 *3.7mi/6km from the port.*
For those who prefer to walk, this footpath winds along the steep cliffs and creeks of the peninsula, skirted with typical Mediterranean vegetation.

St-Jean-Cap-Ferrat★

Once a fishing village, St-Jean is now an exclusive winter resort. A few historic houses overlook the **port** and its luxury yachts. The stepped street south of boulevard de la Libération leads to a **viewpoint★** over the Tête de Chien mountain, Èze, Mont Agel and the Italian Alps in the distance.

1hr round trip from the port of St-Jean. The **Promenade Maurice-Rouvier★** runs along the coast to Beaulieu bay with **views** of Èze and the Tête de Chien.

Pointe St-Hospice

A pleasant stroll between private houses, past an 18C prison tower, leads to a 19C chapel affording a good **view★** of the coast and inland from Beaulieu to Cap Martin.

2mi/3.5km. A **path★** winds around the pointe St-Hospice from **plage Paloma** to the baie des Fossettes.

ADDRESSES

STAY

Belle Aurore Hôtel – *49 ave. Denis Séméria, St-Jean-Cap-Ferrat. ℘04 93 76 24 24. Closed Oct–Apr.* 24 rooms. This hotel overlooks the sea. Nicely decorated rooms are air-conditioned, each with a private bath. Daily breakfast buffet, on-site spa and swimming pool.

Hôtel Brise Marine – *58 ave. Jean-Mermoz. ℘04 93 76 04 36. www. hotel-brisemarine.com. Closed Nov–Jan. 16 rooms.* 14.50€. Located in a quiet street, this charming house is reached through lush grounds. It offers superb views of the bay and Cap Ferrat. Book the rooms in the villa, rather than in the annexe.

EAT

Capitaine Cook – *ave. Jean-Mermoz. ℘04 93 76 02 66. Closed early Nov–late Dec, Thu lunch and Wed.* Halfway between Paloma beach and the marina, this family-style restaurant serves classic Mediterranean cuisine.

Plage de Passable – *chemin de Passable. ℘04 93 76 06 17. www.plage-de-passable.com. Closed mid-Oct–Mar.* This beach restaurant is located in Villefranche port on the way to Cap Ferrat. Salads, pizza, pasta and seafood are served. Enchanting spot sheltered by pines and palms.

LEISURE ACTIVITIES

Beaches – There are several "galet" (smooth stone) beaches in Cap Ferrat: **Plage de Passable** facing Villefranche, **Plage Paloma** facing Beaulieu, **Plage du Cro des Pins** near the port and a beach at the **Pointe St-Hospice**.

Plage de Passable

Beaulieu-sur-Mer★

Alpes-Maritimes

This fashionable resort, sheltered by a belt of wooded hills, has been renowned since Antiquity as one of the warmest spots on the Riviera. This haven of peace is clustered around the Baie des Fourmis and the exotic gardens of the *Petite Afrique* neighbourhood along boulevard d'Alsace-Lorraine.

- ▶ **Population:** 3,714.
- **Michelin Map:** 341 F5.
- **Info:** Pl. Georges-Clemenceau. ☎04 93 01 02 21. www.beaulieusurmer.fr
- ▷ **Location:** Hugging the coastline between Nice and Monaco, Beaulieu sits right next to Villefranche. The best way to get here is via the Basse Corniche (*see CORNICHES de la RIVIERA*).
- **P Parking:** The best places are around the port, behind the Hôtel de Ville. For walking along Promenade Maurice-Rouvier, leave the car on Avenue Blundell-Maple.

 WALKING TOURS

SENTIER DU PLATEAU St-Michel★★

2hr round trip – steep climb.
Starting north of Boulevard Édouard-VII, the path leads up the Riviera escarpment to the plateau, affording wonderful **views** from Cap d'Ail to the Esterel.

Promenade Maurice-Rouvier★

1hr round trip. 1.4mi/2.3km.
This remarkable promenade runs para-llel to the Mediterranean shore from Beaulieu to **St-Jean-Cap-Ferrat**, passing fine white villas set in beautiful gardens, including La Fleur du Cap, once home to both Charlie Chaplin and David Niven. Amazing **views** of the Riviera coastline to pointe St-Hospice.

SIGHT
Villa Grecque Kérylos★★

Free audio guide. Open Feb–Oct daily 10am–6pm (Jul–Aug until 7pm); Nov–Feb Mon–Fri 2pm–6pm, Sat–Sun 10am–6pm. ⊕8.50€. Combined ticket with Ephrussi-de-Rothschild 15€. ☎04 93 01 45 90. www.villa-kerylos.com.
On a **site★** reminiscent of the Aegean, this faithful reconstruction of an ancient Greek villa was the brainchild of archaeologist **Théodore Reinach** and

Promenade Maurice-Rouvier

D. Chapuis/MICHELIN

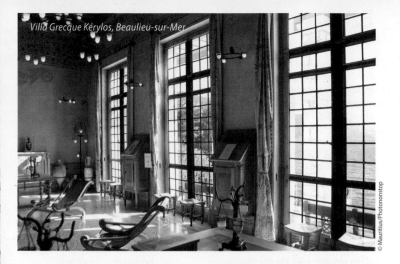

Villa Grecque Kérylos, Beaulieu-sur-Mer

© Mauritius/Photononstop

designed by the architect Pontremoli in 1902. It was bequeathed to the Institut de France in 1928. Built from precious materials (Carrara marble, alabaster and exotic woods, such as Australian plum and Cylon lemon), the villa is furnished with authentic objects from ancient Greece, including mosaics, lamps, amphorae, and replicas of chests, desks and tables incrusted with ivory, bronze and leather. The windows give directly onto the sea. The lower floor **gallery** has reproductions of classical statues.

A Love Story

In 1891 this small harbour was discovered by the American press tycoon **Gordon Bennett**, who immediately fell in love with it. He offered to finance the building of a pier but the proud local fishermen declined his offer. However, the winding corniche road linking Beaulieu to Villefranche was his doing and it still bears his name.

ADDRESSES

STAY

⊜🖬🖬 **Le Sélect** – *1 rue André-Cane and Pl. Général-de-Gaulle.* ℘04 93 01 05 42. www.hotelselect-beaulieu.com. *Closed Jan. 19 rooms.* ⊐7€. Housed in a multistorey building, this hotel with a Provençal decor offers air-conditioned rooms with large beds and well-equipped bathrooms.

⊜🖬🖬🖬 **La Réserve de Beaulieu** – *5 blvd. du Mar.-Leclerc.* ℘04 93 01 00 01. www.reservedebeaulieu.com. *Closed 21 Oct–21 Dec. 39 rooms.* This ultra-luxurious hotel sits right on the sea. Spacious rooms are richly appointed. Its very pricey **Restaurant des Rois** (⊜🖬🖬🖬) serves Provencal fare in a long, elegant room. Spa and large pool.

⊉/ EAT

⊜🖬🖬 **Les Agaves** – *4 ave. Mar.-Foch.* ℘ 04 93 01 13 12. www.lesagaves.com. *Closed late Nov–mid-Dec and Sun.* Decorated in Provençal tones of blue and yellow, complete with original stucco and panelling, this restaurant serves inventive cuisine.

⊜🖬🖬 **La Maison Beaulieu** – *port de Plaisance.* ℘04 93 01 06 50. Tasty Mediterranean dishes are served in the Baroque-style dining room or on the terrace overlooking the marina.

LEISURE ACTIVITIES

Beaches – The small, sheltered pebble beaches with a southern exposure are located on either side of the marina: Baie des Fourmis beach and Petite Afrique at Nord beach.

Èze★★

Alpes-Maritimes

A quaint, isolated hamlet dominating the coast, Èze clings to its rocky outcrop 1,410ft/427m above the sea. This stunning site★★ never fails to impress.

SIGHTS
Medieval Village★

A 14C double gateway with crenellations and a sentry walk leads into the steep, narrow streets of the village. Stepped and vaulted, these alleyways are lined with boutiques, artists' studios and tastefully restored houses fronted by flower pots. Most streets afford **views** of the mountains or the Mediterranean. The **church** was rebuilt in the 18C with a Classical façade and a two-storey tower. The Baroque interior contains a fine statue of the Assumption (18C), attributed to Muerto and a 15C font.

Chapelle des Pénitents-Blancs
Carriera Plana.

This simple 14C chapel is decorated with enamelled panels illustrating the life and death of Christ and the Virgin. To the left is a Crucifixion, an early example of the Nice School attributed to Ludovic Bréa; on the high altar is an unusual Catalan crucifix (1258) with a smiling Christ.

▶ **Population:** 2,932.
⌖ **Michelin Map:** 341 F5.
🛈 **Info:** pl. du Général-de-Gaulle. ℘04 93 41 26 00. www.eze-riviera.com.
▷ **Location:** Between Nice and Monaco, Èze is accessible by RN 7 – Moyenne Corniche (⌖*see CORNICHES de la RIVIERA*).
🅿 **Parking:** There are two parking areas *(next to the tourist office)* where you'll need to leave your car before climbing up to the village. Parking is also available at the perfume houses, for clients only (⌖*see ADDRESSES opposite*).
🕓 **Timing:** Allow 1hr to stroll through the old village. The gardens merit half a day.

Jardin d'Èze

Rue du Château. 🕓*Open Jul–Aug 9am–8pm, Jun and Sept 9am–7.30pm; rest of the year, closes earlier.* ⬱*5€.* ℘*04 93 41 010 30.*

Many varieties of succulents and cacti flourish in these gardens crossed by a maze of pathways and crowned by the

View from Jardin d'Èze

© Arthurr/Dreamstime.com

① 🚌 🅿 **GRANDE CORNICHE** 🚶 **D 6007, MONACO**

PARFUMERIE GALIMARD
CORNICHE
MOYENNE D 6007
Pl. Gén. de Gaulle
Pl. de la Colette
PARFUMERIE FRAGONARD
N
NICE
D 46
Av. du Jardin Exotique
Pl. A. Fighiera
Sentier Friedrich-Nietzsche
ÈZE-BORD-DE-MER
Pl. du Centenaire
Pl. de l'Église
Église
R. de l'Église
PORTE FORTIFIÉE
ANCIEN CHÂTEAU
R. de la Paix
R. du Brec
Jardin exotique
R. du Château
Chapelle des Pénitents-Blancs
R. Principale
R. du Barri
PORTE DES MAURES
R. de la Pise
CHÂTEAU DES RIQUIERS
Pl. du Planet
R. du Burnou
ÈZE
0   50 m
0   50 yds

WHERE TO STAY
Èze Hermitage Hôtel......................................①

Philosopher's muse

The philospher Friedrich Nietzsche first visited the Riviera between December 1883 and April 1884 to complete his masterpiece, *Thus Spoke Zarathustra*. Although his morale was low when he arrived – his books were selling badly and he had fallen out with his close friend Wagner – the light and landscape of Èze transformed his mood. A keen walker, he notably recalls composing a chapter of the book:

"...as I climbed the steepest rocks from the station to the wonderful Moorish village built in the middle of the rocks."

---

remains of a 14C château. The terrace has a splendid **panorama★★★** over the sea and coastline.

EXCURSIONS
Astrorama
▶ *Take D 46 to the Col d'Èze (ℂsee CORNICHES de la RIVIERA, circuit ①).*

Sentier Frédéric-Nietzsche★
🚶 *About 2hr round trip.*
Nietzsche thought out the third part of his masterpiece *Thus Spoke Zarathustra* on the picturesque mule path, which leads through pines and olive groves to the seaside resort of **Èze-Bord-de-Mer.**

ADDRESSES

⌂ STAY
⊖⊜⊜ **Eze Hôtel Hermitage** – *1951 ave. des Diables Bleus. 1.5mi/2.5km by D 46 and Grande Corniche. ℘04 93 41 00 68. www.ezehermitage.com. 16 rooms.* ♿🅿. � 12.50€. Restaurant ⊖⊜⊜. A rustic and peaceful hotel with splendid terraces, overflow pool and sea views. Rooms are pleasantly decorated, with air conditioning and free WiFi. The airy, cheerful dining room is the stage for chef-prepared dishes such as lamb and sea bass. In summer, patrons may dine outdoors around the pool.

FRAGRANCES
Parfumerie Fragonard – *Èze.* ♿🔊Guided tours (30min) daily Feb–Oct 9am–6.30pm; Nov–Jan 8.30am–noon, 2pm–6pm. 🔊No charge. ℘04 93 36 44 65. www.fragonard.com. This annexe of the Grasse perfumery displays the various stages in the manufacturing of essential oils, perfumes and soaps. Boutique on-site.

Parfumerie Galimard – *pl. du Général-de-Gaulle. ℘04 93 41 10 70. www.galimard.com. 🔊No charge.* Founded in 1747, this perfume house gives free tours of its manufacturing and small museum. Products are on sale in the boutique.

Monaco★★★

The Principality of Monaco, a sovereign state overlooking the Mediterranean between Nice and the Italian border, perfectly captures the essence of the Côte d'Azur with its Rococo palaces, lush gardens, world-famous casino and glamorous royal family. Luxury hotels, exclusive shopping boutiques and the annual Formula 1 Grand Prix make this a popular jet-set destination.

A BIT OF HISTORY
The Grimaldi Family

Although Monaco was a Greek settlement and a Roman port, its place in history begins with the Grimaldi dynasty. Expelled from Genoa during a family feud, **François Grimaldi** captured Monaco disguised as a monk, with a small band of armed men in 1297. François was soon forced from the town and it was another Grimaldi, **Charles I,** (1331–57) who secured Monaco in 1331.

A Turbulent History

The history of Monaco has been fraught with family and political dramas. In the 16C Jean II was killed by his brother Lucien, who in turn was assassinated by his nephew; in 1604, Honoré I was thrown into the sea by his subjects. Monaco has also been subjected to foreign occupation on several occasions: by the Spanish from 1524 to 1641; by the French from 1641 to 1814; and by the kingdom of Sardinia from 1815 to 1861. Menton and Roquebrune, which originally belonged to the Principality, were bought in 1861 by Napoleon III, following the annexation of Nice.

The Monégasques

There are just over 7,000 native Monacan citizens in the Principality, all exempt from taxes and military service. They are not, however, permitted to gamble in Monaco's casinos.

▶ **Population:** 32,020.

Michelin Map: 341 F5; local map: *see CORNICHES de la RIVIERA.*

Info: 2A blvd. des Moulins. ℰ00 377 92 16 61 66. www.visitmonaco.com.

▷ **Location:** The 487 acres/ 197ha making up the Principality are divided into five districts: Monaco-Ville, the old town on The Rock (*La Rocher*); Monte Carlo, with its luxury shops and casino; the busy La Condamine port; the new district of Fontvieille to the east; and the beaches of Larvotto to the west.

P **Parking:** Parking garages (free for the first hour) can be found at Place du Casino and the Parking des Pêcheurs in Monaco-Ville. Access to the Rock (Le Rocher) is permitted only to vehicles with local (06) licence plates.

Don't Miss: The interior of the Monte Carlo Casino and Opéra, the winding streets of old Monaco-Ville leading to the Prince's Palace and the **panoramic views** from the hillside Jardin Exotique.

Timing: Count on at least a half day to see the best of Monaco, or a full day if you plan on shopping or going to the beach. Start in Monaco-Ville, which has the most attractions and souvenir shops in one area. The casino tables don't open until 5pm.

Kids: Child-friendly museums include the Collection des Voitures Anciennes and the aquariums of the Musée Océanographique.

PRACTICAL INFORMATION

TELEPHONE
To telephone Monaco from France, dial 00 followed by 377 (code for Monaco) and then the 8-digit telephone number.

CURRENCY AND POSTAGE
Monaco uses euros just like France, but it has an independent postal system. All letters mailed from within the Principality must have Monacan stamps.

PUBLIC LIFTS
Large-capacity lifts are available to make it easier to move around certain neighbourhoods. The main roads and attractions served are pl. Ste-Dévote to blvd. de Belgique (the longest route), plages du Larvotto (and Musée national) to pl. des Moulins, ave. Hector-Otto to blvd. de Belgique, auditorium Rainier-III (blvd. Louis-II) to the casino terraces, the Pêcheurs car park to the Musée océanographique, ave. de Grande-Bretagne to ave. des Citronniers, Centre Commercial de Fontvieille to pl. d'Armes, port de Monaco to ave. de la Costa.

TOURS AND PUBLIC TRANSPORT

Bus: C.A.M. – ☏*00 377 97 70 22 22. www.cam.mc. Service every 10min daily 7.30am–8.30pm.* ✆*Tickets 1€ each or 3€ for day pass.* Six regular bus lines loop around the Principality. Maps available at the tourist office.

Taxi: Two main **taxi** stands are located near the casino and at the train station. ☏*00 377 93 50 56 28 or 00 377 93 15 01 01.*

Tourist Bus: Le Grand Tour – *Twelve stops around the Principality, include the Palais Princier and the Casino.* ☏*00 377 97 70 26 36. www.visitmonaco.com.* ✆*17€.* This small hop-on, hop-off tourist bus makes 1hr round trip journeys around the Principality.

Boat Trips: Aquavision – *Compagnie de Navigation et de Tourisme de Monaco, Quai des Etats-Unis.* ☏*00 377 92 16 15 15. www.aquavision-monaco.com. Daily departures Apr–Oct.* ✆*11€ (child 8€).* Glass-bottom boat trips affording views of the sea depths, and marine fauna and flora (55min).

Helicopter: Héli Air Monaco – *Héliport de Monaco, Fontvieille.* ☏*00 377 92 05 00 50. www.heliairmonaco.com. Prices start at 107P.* Regular daily service (6min) every 15min between Monaco and the Aéroport de Nice-Côte d'Azur. Also 10min sightseeing tours of Monaco and daily flights between Monaco and Fréjus.

Sport: Monaco is home to a number of exclusive sporting facilities. For tennis fans, the **Monte Carlo Country Club** has 23 courts (☏*04 93 41 30 15. www.mccc.mc*). Golfers will enjoy the prestigious **Monte Carlo Golf Club**, which boasts an 18-hole course at an altitude of 2,650ft/810m (☏*04 92 41 50 70*).

Le Rocher

© Alex Trefilov/Bigstockphoto.com

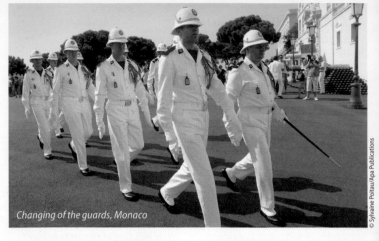

Changing of the guards, Monaco

© Sylvaine Poitau/Apa Publications

Changing of the Guard

The tightly choreographed Changing of the Guard takes place daily on place du Palais at 11.55am.

Birth of Monte Carlo

The first casino was an unremarkable establishment in Monaco-Ville itself, set up in 1856 by the Prince, who was short of funds. Only in 1862 did the casino move to its own premises in Monte Carlo, where it remained in humble isolation for several years. The arrival of **François Blanc**, director of the casino and spa in Bad Hamburg, transformed its fortunes. Within a few years the casino became fashionable and the surrounding land was covered with luxurious residences, mostly owned by the Société des Bains de Mer (SBM), directed by Blanc himself. Profiting from the presence of the rich and famous, Monaco organised its first Rallye Monte Carlo rally in 1911, followed by the Grand Prix de Monaco in 1929, one of the most famous Formula 1 championships in the world.

A Thriving Economy

To accommodate the influx of visitors attracted by its gambling tables and tax concessions, Monaco began to erect buildings at a furious pace. Once all the available space had been occupied, the shoreline was extended into the sea (the 55acre/22ha Fontvieille district), expanding its territory by 25 percent. Tourism remains its main activity, along with conference facilities (such as the **Grimaldi Forum** on the Larvotto shore), which rival those of Cannes and Nice. Home to about 40 international banking institutions, Monaco is a player in the financial world.

Town-planning

Following the construction of a dozen high-rise buildings in the late 1970s, the 1980s saw the emergence of a new urban strategy designed to satisfy the growing demand for residential and service facilities: underground buildings. All new access roads are now linked to the French network by deep tunnels, the train station is below ground level, and connections between neighbourhoods are made via groups of lifts or escalators. Behind the façade of some of Monaco's luxury hotels are access ramps to large public car parks hollowed out of the rock.

WALKING TOURS

THE ROCK★★

Tour: allow 3hr. Park in Parking des Pêcheurs and take the elevator.
Crowned by the old town of Monaco-Ville and its **ramparts**, the Rocher de Monaco juts 875yd/800m out to sea over the bay. Resembling a studio set, its neat

little 18C houses with their salmon-pink façades are squeezed along quaint alleyways. This is the medieval heart of the Principality, home to some of its most popular sights.

♦♦ Musée Océanographique de Monaco★★

Ave. Saint-Martin. &⊙*Open daily Jul–Aug 9.30am–7.30pm; Apr–Jun and Sept 9.30am–7pm; Oct–Mar 10am–6pm.* ∞*14€ (6–18 years 7€). Combined ticket with Palais Princier 19€.* ✆*00 377 93 15 36 00. www.oceano.mc.*

The Oceanographic Museum and Research Institute overlooks the Mediterranean from an impressive cliff (280ft/85m). Founded in 1910 by marine research enthusiast Prince Albert I to house his scientific collections dating back to 1885, it has a most remarkable **aquarium★★**, with some 6,000 specimens representing 350 species of tropical fish, shark, turtle, and live coral reef from the Red Sea. The lower ground floor is divided into a Mediterranean section and 90 tanks teeming with tropical species, including clown fish, moray eels and leopard sharks.

The **Salle d'Océanographie Zoologique★**, also known as Salle de la Baleine, contains the skeletons of large marine mammals, including a 66ft/20m-long whale beached on the Italian coast in 1896. The "Marine inspirations" exhibit of objects inspired by the sea from the 4C to the present, includes carved shells and ceramics. The second-floor terrace *(lift)* permits a magnificent **view★★** along the coast, including the Tête de Chien and the Mont Agel beyond. The restaurant is also located on this floor.

Monte Carlo Story

Near the Musée Océanographique. ✆*00 377 93 25 32 33.* &⊙*Open daily Jul–Aug 2pm–6pm; rest of the year until 5pm. Closed Nov–25 Dec.* ∞*8€.*

On a giant screen is shown the history *(35min)* of the Grimaldi family and the evolution of the Principality up to Prince Albert II's enthronement.

▷ Take ave. St-Martin towards the cathedral.

Jardins St-Martin★

The shaded pathways of this Mediterranean garden afford delightful **views** over the sea. A bronze statue of Albert I by François Cogné (1951) stands in the centre.

Cathédrale

The cathedral was built between 1875 and 1903 in Romanesque Byzantine style with white stone from La Turbie on the ruins of the church of St-Nicolas. A series of royal family tombs in the ambulatory include that of Princess Grace. It has a collection of **early paintings from the Nice School★★** along with two altarpieces by Louis Bréa.

Musée Océanographique de Monaco

© Sylvaine Poitau/Apa Publications

The Grimaldi Family Today

In July 2005, the 47-year-old Prince Albert II of Monaco succeeded his father, Prince Rainier III, who died in April 2005 after ruling the Principality for 56 years. Albert and his sisters (Princesses Caroline and Stéphanie) lost their mother, the Hollywood actress Grace Kelly, in a car accident in 1982. For many years the Prince's single status and his sisters' rocky relationships were closely followed in the European tabloids. At the age of 53, the Prince married former South African Olympic swimmer Charlene Wittstock on 1 July 2011.

▶ Follow rue Comte Félix Gastaldi (featuring fine Renaissance doorways) to rue Princesse-Marie-de-Lorraine.

Chapelle de la Miséricorde

This chapel's classic pink and white Baroque façade was completed in 1646 by the brotherhood of the Black Penitents. The **Recumbent Christ** by the Monacan sculptor Bosio is carried through the old town on Good Friday.

▶ On leaving turn right onto picturesque rue Basse to pl. du Palais.

Place du Palais★

◷*Open Apr–Oct daily 10am–6pm.* ⊛*8€.*

This vast square, ornamented with cannons given to the Prince of Monaco by Louis XIV, is bordered to the northeast by a crenellated parapet from which there is a **view** of the port de la Condamine, Monte Carlo and the coast as far as the Bordighera headland. To the southwest is the **Promenade Ste-Barbe**, which gives onto Cap d'Ail.

▲▲ Don't miss the **Changing of the Guard**. The soldiers are dressed in black in winter and white in summer.

Palais Princier★

◷*Open Apr 10.30am–6pm; May–Oct 10am–6pm.* ⊛*8€. Combined ticket with Musée Océanographique 19€.* ℘*00 377 93 25 18 31. www.palais.mc.*

The palatial home of the Grimaldi family was built in the 17C on the site of the original 13C Genoese fortress. The formidable perimeter is built into the vertical rock, with battlemented towers.

A monumental doorway with the Grimaldi arms adorns this robust-looking ensemble. The tour leads visitors through the Hercules Gallery decorated with 16C and 17C frescoes, past the **main courtyard** paved with 3 million stones, through to the Throne Room with a ceiling attributed to Orazio Ferrari (17C), then onto the state apartments where official receptions are held.

▶ Follow the Rampe Major to the right of the palace through 16C, 17C and 18C gates down to pl. d'Armes. Turn right onto ave. du Port.

LA CONDAMINE

Allow 30min.

In the Middle Ages this term applied to land owned by a lord and cultivated exclusively for him at the foot of a village or castle. Nowadays La Condamine is the **commercial district** and port stretching between the Rock and Monte Carlo.

Port

Prince Albert I commissioned this harbour, with its luxury yachts and terraced promenade. From the northwest corner of the harbour a valley separating La Condamine from Monte Carlo runs under a viaduct to the church.

▶ Follow the blvd. Albert I to the passage leading to pl. Ste-Dévote.

Église Ste-Dévote

Ste-Dévote was martyred in Corsica in the 3C when, according to tradition, the skiff carrying her body to Africa was guided by a dove to the shores of Monaco. In the Middle Ages relics of the saint were stolen by sailors. But the thieves were caught and their ship razed, a legend commemorated every 26 January when a ship is burned in the church square.

▶ Turn right down rue Grimaldi, a popular shopping street, to rue Princesse Caroline and finish at pl. d'Armes.

MONTE CARLO★★★
Allow 1.5hr.
Monte Carlo is a name famous throughout the world, bringing to mind high-stakes gambling as well as the majestic setting of its palaces, casinos, luxurious shops and exotic gardens.

Place du Casino
Place du Casino lies at the centre of the action, where the Café de Paris and the Hôtel de Paris flank the **casino**, surrounded by beautiful gardens. Around the back of the casino is a fine **terrace★★** with **views** towards Italy.

Casino
Forbidden to anyone under 18 years of age. ◷*Slots and European gaming rooms open from 2pm (noon on weekends); blackjack tables open from 8pm.* ◷*Closed when the last person leaves.* ◉*10€ public rooms, 20€ private rooms. ID/Passport required.* ℘*00 377 98 06 21 21. www.casinomontecarlo.com.*
The façade facing the sea and the theatre/opera house opposite the vast central hall were built by Charles Garnier in 1878. Once home to Diaghilev's **Ballets Russes**, the casino rose to fame under Nijinsky. Before entering, admire the *Olive Gatherers* fresco by Jundt and in the public gaming rooms on the left, the sumptuous late 19C Renaissance Room. An oasis of palms, the casino **terrace★★** affords **views** from Monaco to Bordighera.

Avenue Princesse-Grace
Beyond the sleek Grimaldi Forum are the luxurious beaches of **Larvotto Plage**. Here you'll find shops, cafés and restaurants overlooking the beach. Two diving platforms are anchored offshore.

Musée des Souvenirs Napoléoniens et des Archives du Palais★
Pl. du Palais. ◷*Open daily Apr–Oct 10am–6pm; rest of the year 10.30am–5pm. Closed 1 Jan, Nov, 25 Dec.* ◉*4€.* ℘*00 377 93 25 18 31. www.palais.mc.*
One wing of the Palace is devoted to a museum dedicated to Napoleon, including geneological charts showing how the Bonapartes are related to the Grimaldi princes. Many of the Emperor's personal souvenirs are on display. The upper floor explores the history of Monaco, including the charter recognising its independence granted by Louis XII.

Nouveau Musée National de Monaco
Villa Sauber, 17 ave. Princesse-Grace ℘*00 377 98 98 91 26 and VIlla Paloma, 56 blvd. du Jardin Exotique* ℘*00 377 98 98 48 60.* ◷*Open daily 10am–6pm.* ◉*6€ (under 26 free). www.nmnm.mc.*
Split between two sites, the New National Museum of Monaco (NNMM) is dedicated to the preservation and communication of Monaco's extensive cultural and natural heritage, including many artworks rarely displayed in public. The Villa Sauber, housed in a **Charles Garnier** villa fronted by a rose garden, and the Villa Paloma, a stark white residence built for an American millionaire at the beginning of the 20C, will both invite artists, curators and other personalities to explore a contemporary subject, such as fashion, the environment or the ocean using objects as varied as diving equipment from the oceanographic museum, or the Principality's extensive collection of early-19C dolls and automata.

♣♦ Collection des Voitures Anciennes★
Terrasses de Fontvieille. ♿◷*Open daily 10am–6pm.* ◷*Closed 25 Dec.* ◉*6€ (8-14 years 3€).* ℘*00 377 92 05 28 56. www.palais.mc.*
Housed in a sumptuous exhibition hall, some 100 vintage vehicles and carriages

MONACO
MONTE CARLO

0   200 m
0   200 yds

WHERE TO STAY

WHERE TO EAT

INDEX OF STREET NAMES

Princess Grace

Grace Kelly was born in Philadelphia on 12 November 1929, the third of four children. After studying at the New York Academy of Dramatic Arts, she began work as an actress for television and the theatre. She got her first break in *High Noon* (1952), in which she played a young bride married to Gary Cooper. Many films were to follow, but her name has remained closely associated with that of British director Alfred Hitchcock, for whom she starred in *Dial M for Murder* (1954), *Rear Window* (1954) and *To Catch a Thief* (1955), shot entirely on location in the South of France. Grace Kelly was introduced to Prince Rainier of Monaco at the Cannes Film Festival and they were married in April 1956. She gave birth to three children, Caroline, Albert and Stéphanie. The new princess soon won the affections of the Principality's residents. She spent much of her time supporting charitable causes such as the Red Cross and AMADE, an organisation set up to help developing countries. Her life was to end tragically in 1982 when her car crashed off the Grande Corniche.

from the royal collection are displayed over five levels. On the first level are the barouches used by Prince Charles III. Next is the De Dion Bouton (1903), the first car owned by Prince Albert I, and a 1952 Austin London taxi converted for Princess Grace. The 1929 Bugatti (winner of the 1st Grand Prix) and a 1989 Ferrari F1 (600hp) have pride of place in the Formula 1 hall.

Musée Naval

Terrasse de Fontvieille. ♿ⓒ*Open daily 10am–6pm.* ⊚*4€.* ℘*00 377 92 05 28 48. www.musee-naval.mc.*
A showcase for more than 250 objects, this museum features the cream of the royal collection of model ships, including models built by Prince Albert I in 1874, and a **gondole impériale** made in 15 days for the inspection of Napoleon I at Antwerps.

Musée des Timbres et des Monnaies

11 terrasse de Fontvieille. ♿ⓒ*Open daily 9.30am–5pm; Jul–Sept until 6pm.* ⊚*3€.* ℘*00 377 93 15 41 50.*
Housed in a very modern setting, this museum contains stamps issued by the Principality, together with rare stamps collected by the Grimaldis. A collection of coins and bank notes illustrates the history of numismatics in Monaco.

Musée de la Chapelle de la Visitation

Pl. de la Visitation. ♿ⓒ*Open Tue–Sun 10am–4pm.* ⊚*3€.* ℘*00 377 93 50 07 00.*
This 17C Baroque chapel houses the extensive Barbara Piasecka-Johnson collection of **sacred artworks**. Of particular interest are masterpieces by **Zurbarán**, Rubens and **Ribera**.

FAUNA AND FLORA
Jardin Exotique★★

52 blvd. du Jardin-Exotique. ⓒ*Open daily mid-May–mid-Sept 9am–7pm; rest of the year until 6pm.* Ⓧ*Closed 19 Nov, 25 Dec.* ⊚*7€.* ℘*00 377 93 15 29 80. www.jardin-exotique.mc.*
This exceptional collection, grouping several thousand species of succulent, including huge candelabra-like euphorbia, giant aloe and Barbary figs, some more than a century old, clings dramatically to the cliffs above Monaco. Down 279 steps, the **Grotte de l'Observatoire★** *(guided tour 30min)* is adorned with stalactites and stalagmites. Tools and Prehistoric animal bones dating back 200,000 years excavated at the site are on display in the **Musée d'Anthropologie Préhistorique★** *(access through the Jardin Exotique; same hours).* This display reveals how the region was once home to reindeer, mammoths, cave bears and even hippos. Don't miss the impressive group of early *homo sapien* skeletons.

Jardin Exotique

©Photononstop/Tips Images

Jardin Japonais★

Ave. Princesse Grace. ♿ ⏰*Open daily Apr–Oct 9am–7pm; rest of the year until 6pm.* 🎫*No charge.* ☎*00 377 98 98 83 36. www.visitmonaco.com.*
Designed by the Japanese landscape artist **Yasuo Beppu**, this garden (17 acres/7ha) in the luxurious **Larvotto district** is a green oasis beside the sea. A miniature representation of Shintoist philosophy, it includes symbols of longevity and a **Zen garden** for meditation.

👫 Jardin Animalier

Terrasse de Fontvieille. ⏰*Open daily Jun–Sept 9am–noon, 2pm–7pm; Mar–May 10am–noon, 2pm–6pm; Oct–Feb 10am–noon, 2pm–5pm.* 🎫*4€ (8-14 years 2€).* ☎*00 3// 93 50 40 30.*
The zoo terraces, on the southwest face of the Rock, present 50 species of mammal, reptile, exotic bird and numerous monkeys.

Parc Paysager

Terre-plein de Fontvieille.
Plant species from across the world cluster around a charming lake. Nearby lies the **Princess Grace Rose Garden,** with more than 4,000 bushes belonging to 150 different rose varieties.

Before Laying a Bet

Stroking the knee of the equestrian statue of Louis XV in the entrance of the Hôtel de Paris before heading into the casino is said to bring the gambler good luck. Admission is free to the slot machine rooms in the casino, in the Café de Paris (also on Place du Casino), and at the Sun Casino (in the Fairmont Hotel, 12 avenue des Spélugues). During the summer season (July–mid-Sept) gambling takes place in the Salles des Palmiers of the Sporting-Club de Monte Carlo. Gaming tables usually require a fee of 10€–20€ to play.

Coastal Path to Cap Martin★★

🚶 *3hr round trip* ⏱*see MENTON and CORNICHES de la RIVIERA. Take the steps to left of Monte Carlo Beach hotel, between the two villas.*
Tourists wishing to take a shorter route can drive to the train station of Roquebrune-Cap-Martin and join up with the path running below.

ADDRESSES

🏨 STAY

Hôtel de France – *6 rue de la Turbie. Near the train station.* ✆*00 377 93 30 24 64. www.Monte Carlo.mc/france. 26 rooms.* ☎*10€.* Charming, soundproofed rooms are decorated in Provençal hues and a modern breakfast lounge is enhanced with metal and wood furniture.

Hôtel Miramar – *126 ave. du 3-Septembre, Cap d'Ail.* ✆*04 93 78 06 60. www.Monte Carlo.mc/hotel-miramar-capdail. 25 rooms. Closed Feb.* 🅿. ☎*7.50€.* Miramar is a good-value, family-run hotel in the neighbouring village of Cap d'Ail. Rooms have WiFi; some face the sea.

Novotel Monte Carlo – *16 blvd. de la Princesse Charlotte.* ✆*00 377 99 99 83 00. www.novotel.com. 218 rooms.* 🅿. ☎*17€.* This stylish, modern hotel in the heart of Monaco with all the latest amenities, includes a heated pool, fitness centre, bar and restaurant.

🍴 EAT

Le Bistroquet – *Galerie Charles III, ave. des Spéluges.* ✆*00 377 93 50 65 03. www.mcpam.com. Closed 24–25 Dec.* This lively restaurant and bar with a heated terrace faces the casino gardens. Serves a combination of bistro fare and French classics; wines by the glass. Live music Fri–Sat evenings.

Castelroc – *pl. du Palais.* ✆*00 377 93 30 36 68. www.restaurant-castelroc.com. Closed mid-Dec–mid-Jan, Sat.* The terrace under the trees with a view of the palace makes a lovely setting for a meal of Mediterranean specialities.

Polpetta – *2 rue Paradis.* ✆*00 377 93 50 67 84.* This small Italian restaurant offers three different settings: the veranda close to the road; the rustic dining room; and a more intimate cosy space to the rear. Don't miss the family specialities.

Maison du Caviar Petrossian – *1 ave. St-Charles.* ✆*00 377 93 30 80 06. Closed Sat lunch, Sun.* This prestigious house has been serving choice caviar to Monaco's residents for the past 50 years. In an unusual setting made up of bottle racks and wooden panelling, you can also order salmon and foie gras.

Café de Paris – *pl. du Casino.* ✆*00-377 98 06 76 23. www.monte carloresort.com.* An elegant and chic brasserie with terraces overlooking the casino square and the sea. Seafood and traditional French dishes, as well as light salads and sandwiches.

Loga – *25 blvd. des Moulins.* ✆*00-377 93 30 87 72. www.leloga.com. Closed mid–late Aug, Wed evening, and Sun.* A friendly family-run establishment popular with the locals, serving traditional regional cuisine and daily specials on the slate board.

Zelo's – *10 ave. Princesse-Grace, 98000 Monaco.* ✆*00 377 99 99 25 50. www. zelosworld.com.* This trendy prototypical Monacan restaurant is the place to see and be seen. Mediterranean cuisine with a modern twist, with the bonus of a terrace overlooking the sea.

NIGHTLIFE

Casino de Monte Carlo – *pl. du Casino.* ✆*00 377 98 06 21 21. www.casino-Monte Carlo.com.* Europe's leading casino. The gambling salons and lavish dining hall Le Train Bleu, decorated in the style of the Orient-Express, are truly impressive.

Crystal Bar (Hôtel Hermitage) – *Sq. Beaumarchais .* ✆*00 377 98 06 40 00. www.montecarloresort.com.* This superb Belle-Époque palace offers, among other pleasures, a stylish bar with a terrace providing views of the harbour and The Rock. A fine selection of cocktails, champagnes and wines.

Sass Café – *11 ave. Princesse-Grace.* ✆*00 377 93 25 52 00. www.sasscafe.com.* Exclusive bar-restaurant with a cosy atmosphere, where members of the local jet set drop in for a fancy vodka or champagne cocktail before meeting up at Jimmy'z.

Le Jimmy'z – *26 ave. Princesse-Grace.* ✆*00 377 98 06 73 73 . fr.jimmyzmonte carlocom.* It would be unthinkable to leave Monte Carlo without having paid a visit to the legendary Jimmy'z. Formal eveningwear is expected in this small, but select club, where the rich and famous love to congregate, whether they come from the banking, advertising, fashion or entertainment world.

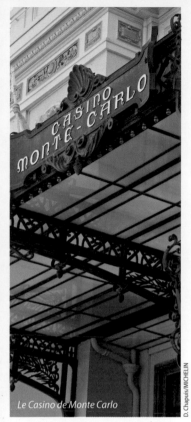

Le Casino de Monte Carlo

D. Chapuis/MICHELIN

Stars'N'Bars – *6 quai Antoine-1.*
℘00 377 97 97 95 95. www.starsnbars.com.
This is a popular American bar, where the ambience is slightly more relaxed than in the Principality's other establishments. Stars'N'Bars caters for a younger clientele eager to drink beer, eat a hamburger or two, play billiards, surf on the Internet and dance the night away.

ENTERTAINMENT

Le Cabaret – *pl. du Casino. ℘00 377 92 16 36 36. www.montecarloresort.com. Shows mid-Sept–mid-Jun Wed–Sat from 10.30pm; bar/restaurant open from 8.30pm.* This cabaret, run by the Monte Carlo Casino, presents nightly flamenco, jazz or pop concerts.

SHOPPING

All the famous fashion brands have boutiques in Monte Carlo. Shops specialising in traditional goods are to be found in the narrow streets of the Rock *(Le Rocher)* opposite the palace. Hunt out **Boutique du Rocher** on ave. de la Madonne for traditional Monacan handicrafts, made in the on-site workshops.

If exclusive brands such as Dior and Chanel on **ave. des Beaux Art** are beyond your reach, head for the **Fontevielle shopping centre**, where you'll find dozens of ready-to-wear chain stores, a hypermarket and fast-food outlets. Most of the Principality's high-street stores (music, books, electronic equipment, furniture and cosmetics) are situated in Monte Carlo along **ave. Saint-Charles** (which is where you'll also find the **Marché de Monte Carlo**, selling fresh fruit and vegetables) and farther south around **ave. des Spélugues**. For traditional open-air markets, hop over to the port in the **Espace Commercial de la Condamine**, where you'll also find a host of specialist delicatessens and other food stores.

CALENDAR

Monte Carlo Rally – Held every year since 1911 at the end of January.

Feast of Ste-Dévote – Monaco's Patron Saint feast on 27 January.

Spring Arts Festival – Art, music, theatre and dance festival from the end of Mar to early April.

International Tennis Masters Series – Held every April.

Monaco Grand Prix – Every May in the streets of the Principality on a winding circuit (2mi/3,145km).

Monte Carlo Golf Open – Held in the hills of Mont Agel every June.

National Day of Monaco – Picturesque procession around the Rocher, plus a range of other cultural events and shows: 19 November.

Roquebrune-Cap-Martin★

Alpes-Maritimes

This pretty resort extends along the coast below the perched medieval village of Roquebrune and its Carolingian-era castle keep.

A BIT OF HISTORY

The castle was built at the end of the 10C by the Conrad I, comte de Ventimiglia, to hold back the Saracen invaders. For several centuries it belonged to the Grimaldis (*see MONACO*). The fortress enclosed the keep and the village within its battlements, with six gateways. In the 15C the keep (donjon) became known as the castle (château) and the fortress became the village.

▸ **Population:** 11,692.
▸ **Michelin Map:** 341 F5; local maps: *see MENTON: DRIVING TOURS p355 and Corniches de la RIVIERA.*
▸ **Info:** 218 ave. Aristide-Briand. ℘04 93 35 62 87. www.roquebrune-cap-martin.com.
▸ **Location:** Roquebrune village sits on the Grande Corniche above Menton and the resort of Roquebrune-Cap-Martin.
▸ **Parking:** Available at the village entrance.
▸ **Don't Miss:** Nature lovers should hike the coastal path on the Cap Martin.

👣 WALKING TOUR

THE PERCHED VILLAGE★

Allow 1hr. This maze of steep covered alleys and stairways has preserved its medieval appearance despite the influx of art galleries and souvenir shops.

▸ Start on pl. de la République (the former barbican), then cross the pl. des Deux-Frères (two rocks) to rue Grimaldi, then turn left.

Rue Moncollet★

This street, long and narrow, has many covered and stepped passageways. Medieval houses with barred windows, in which those invited to join the seigneurial court once lived, face the road in front, while at the back they lie against or are cut right into the rockface.

▸ Rue Moncollet leads into rue du Château. Turn left towards the keep.

View of Roquebrune-Cap-Martin

Sylvaine Poiteau/Apa Publications

Église Ste-Marguerite

© Sylvaine Poitau/Apa Publications

Donjon★

Pl. William–Ingram. ⏱*Open daily
Jul–Aug 10am–12.30pm, 3pm–7.30pm;
Apr–Jun and Sept 10am–12.30pm,
2pm–6.30pm; Feb–Mar and Oct
10am–12.30pm, 2pm–6pm; Nov–Jan
10am–12.30pm, 2pm–5pm.* ⬠*3.70€.*
☎*04 93 35 62 87.*

The keep (80ft/26m) has 6-12ft/2-4m
thick walls complete with remarkable
defensive features, including cannon
embrasures, machicolations, battlements and loopholes. Steps lead up to
the Hall of Feudal Ceremonies, a small
guard-room, a prison and the archers'
dormitory. On the third floor are furnished baronial apartments, a dining
room, a primitive kitchen and a bedroom containing ancient weapons. The
fourth floor includes the upper artillery
platform, with a sweeping **panorama★★**
of the picturesque roofs of the village, the
sea, Monaco and Mont Agel.

▶ Return to rue du Château, turn
right then turn left onto rue de la
Fontaine.

Olivier Millénaire

On the Chemin de Menton (219yd/200m)
beyond the end of the village), you'll find
a 1,000-year-old **olive tree**, said to be
one of the oldest trees in the world.

▶ Return to rue du Château (left).

Église Ste-Marguerite

The fairly plain Baroque façade masks
the original 12C church, which has
undergone many alterations over the
years. Inside are two paintings by a local
painter, **Marc-Antoine Otto** (17C).

Protected Marine Areas

The coastline around Vallauris-Golfe-Juan, Beaulieu-sur-Mer and Roquebrune-
Cap-Martin is subject to a number of restrictions (no mooring, diving or fishing
of any kind) in order to protect and nurture its biodiversity. Posidonia seagrass
and gorgonia are closely monitored in these areas, and artificial reefs have been
placed along the sea bed.

Marine pollution is taken very seriously by these coastal towns. Checks are
performed and protective measures put in place to optimise the quality of
swimming water and fishing grounds, including the taking of water samples in
high season, improving the quality of the water channelled into the sea via
purification plants, aerial surveillance of the coast and the fining of polluters.
A *Ports Propres* or Clean Ports scheme has been set up to eliminate land and sea
pollution in the region.

▶ Return to rue de la Fontaine and turn right into the cemetery, where you'll find the tomb (square J, no. 3) of Le Corbusier, designed by the architect himself.

TOURING THE RESORT
Cap Martin★★

With its magnificent estates, Cap Martin is the wealthy residential suburb of Menton. A massive tower of feudal appearance rises at the centre, formerly the old beacon, now converted to a telecommunications relay station. At its foot lie the ruins of the 11C basilica of St-Martin, built by the monks of the Iles de Lérins and destroyed by pirates in 1400. From the road along the eastern shore, a marvellous **view**★★ of Menton in its mountain setting and the Italian coast is gained. There are several beaches below the old village at Cabbé and Carnolès to the east.

Le Cabanon de Le Corbusier

📞 *Guided tours (2hr) Tue and Fri 9.30am by reservation at the tourist office.* ⬤*8€.* 📞*04 93 35 62 87.*
Built in 1952, this "cabin" is located below the promenade Le Corbusier, which stretches along the coast between Cap-Martin and Cabbé. The architect lived in this deceptively plain

---

Traditional Processions

For the past 500 years a procession, representing the principal scenes of Christ's Passion in six tableaux, has been held on 5 August for two hours. The **Procession of the Entombment of Christ** takes place at 9pm on Good Friday with a train of some 60 people walking through the village streets repre-senting Roman centurions and legionnaires, disciples carrying the statue of Christ and holy women. The town is decorated with lighted motifs recalling the symbols of the Passion and illuminated by countless tiny lights formed by snail- and seashells filled with olive oil.

---

construction every summer until his death in 1965. Measuring 12ft by 12ft/3.6m by 3.6m, it consists of a simple 107sq ft/10sq m room and a corridor decorated with a fresco. This unique design applies Le Corbusier's **modulor** system to a traditional Marseille cabin. Calculated to suit the proportions of the human body, modulor was a measuring tool invented by the architect for use in the design of the "Cité Radieuse" apartment block in Marseille.

Coastal Path★

🅿 *Ave. Winston-Churchill car park at the end of Cap Martin. A sign "Promenade Le Corbusier" marks the start of the footpath.* 🚶 *4hr round trip.* This coastal footpath runs from Cap Martin to Monte Carlo beach and skirts the grounds of private early 20C villas with **views** of Cap Ferrat, the Tête de Chien and Mont Agel.

▶ A flight of steps on the right crossing the railway line provides a shortcut back to Carnolès beach via the town hall.

ADDRESSES

🛏 STAY

⬤⬤⬤ **Hôtel Alexandra** – *93 avenue Winston Churchill.* 📞*04 93 35 65 45. www.alexandrahotel.fr. 40 rooms.* 🅿. 🍽*10€.* A beachside hotel typical of the 1960s/1970s. Make sure to request upper floor rooms facing the sea.

🍴 EAT

⬤⬤ **La Roquebrunoise** – *12 ave. Raymond-Poincaré.* 📞*04 93 35 02 19. www.laroquebrunoise.com. Closed Nov–Dec, Mon except Jul–Aug, Tue–Fri lunch.* This pretty pink house on the edge of the village has a country-style dining room. The food is unpretentious and tasty; a terrace overlooks the sea.

⬤⬤⬤ **L'Hippocampe** – *44 ave. W. Churchill* 📞 *04 93 35 81 91. www.hippocampe-restaurant.com. Closed Nov–Dec, evenings Jan–May and Mon.* Family-run place specialising in fillets of sole and, if you order in advance, bouillabaisse and coq au vin.

Menton★★

Alpes-Maritimes

Menton is a coastal resort famous for its annual lemon festival and mild climate. The picturesque old town is framed by mountain cliffs and terraced citrus and olive groves.

A BIT OF HISTORY

Although there is evidence of a human settlement in the **Palaeolithic Era** on this site, the name Menton was mentioned in an official document for the first time in 1261. Purchased by the **Grimaldis of Monaco** in 1346, it occupied a strategic position on the border between France and the Kingdom of Sardinia, and swapped hands several times before being permanently attached to France in 1860. In the late 19C and early 20C, Menton was highly popular with the European aristocracy, who flocked here to nurse their health or simply enjoy the mild winters. Today, Menton is a lively, cosmopolitan resort town.

 WALKING TOUR

OLD TOWN★★
Allow 2hr.

Rue St-Michel

This pedestrian street linking the old and new towns is bordered by boutiques and orange trees. **Place aux Herbes**, with its coloured paving stones, decorative colonnade and a fountain, gives onto the market. Note the splendid Belle Époch façades of the former Hôtel d'Orient *(1 rue de la République)*, Winter Palace *(20 ave. Riviera)*, Riviera Palace *(28 ave. Riviera)* and covered market *(quai de Monléon)*.

▶ At pl. du Cap, walk up rue des Logettes to rue Longue.

Rue Longue

This street was once the main street of Menton and formerly part of the Via Julia Augusta.

▶ **Population:** 27,655.

Michelin Map: 341 F5; local maps: *see p294 and CORNICHES de la RIVIERA.*

Info: Palais de l'Europe, 8 Ave. Boyer. ℘04 92 41 76 76. www.menton.fr.

▶ **Location:** Menton is the last coastal town before the Italian border, about 18.6mi/30km east of Nice on the Corniches *(see CORNICHES de la RIVIERA).* For those interested in getting there faster on a less scenic route, take the A 8.

Parking: Most of the public parking places are around the port; all require payment, whether parking garages or metered street parking.

Don't Miss: The colourful parades during the annual Lemon Festival *(Fête du Citron)* in February, the picturesque streets of the old town *(vieille ville)* and the scenic **views** from the Cap Martin.

Kids: A visit to the Serre-de-la-Madone gardens and the Koaland park.

Timing: Allow at least a half day to walk around the pedestrian streets of the old town and the Promenade du Soleil, and visit one of the sights, such as the Musée Jean Cocteau or the Musée des Beaux-Arts. A full day would include a trip to the beach, a hike along the Cap Martin or a driving excursion inland to Castillon, with a walk in the Forêt de Menton.

Menton with Basilique St-Michel Archange

© Taylor Richard/Sime/Photononstop

Parvis St-Michel★★

Access by the Chanoine-Gouget ramps.
At the top of the steps is a charming square in the Italian style framed by Baroque façades, overlooking the sea. The square is paved with a mosaic depicting the Grimaldi arms.

Façade of the Chapelle de la Conception★

The façade of this chapel of the White Penitents (1685, restored in the 19C) has statues of the theological virtues.

Basilique St-Michel-Archange

This is the largest and finest Baroque church in the region. Its two-tier **façade** in yellow and pale green reflects a variety of architectural influences. The tower (15C) on the left, which belonged to an earlier building, was topped with an octagonal campanile with a glazed tile roof in the 17C. The great Genoese-style campanile (174ft/53m) was added in the 18C. Local artists such as Puppo and Vento contributed to the decora-

tion of the side chapels. Above the handsome 18C choir stalls is the **altarpiece of St Michael** (1569) by Manchello. The exuberant Baroque high altar is crowned by St Michael slaying the Devil.

▶ Climb the steps to the rue du Vieux-Château, leading to the cemetery.

Cimetière du Vieux-Château

○*Open daily May–Sept 7am–8pm; Oct–Apr 7am–6pm.* ℘*04 93 57 95 99.*
This international cemetery, laid out in the 19C on the site of the former medieval castle, has terraces with tombs arranged by religion or nationality. The cemetery recalls a time when Menton welcomed rich residents from all over the world, including Russian princes (Volkonsky and Ouroussov), the uncle and aunt (Delano) of Franklin D. Roosevelt, and rugby founder Revd. William Webb Ellis. From the southern corner of the English graveyard there is a beautiful **view★** of the old town and the sea.

SEAFRONT AND BEACHES

▶ Start from the Casino Municipal.

Promenade du Soleil★★

1.2mi/2km. The wide promenade faces the sea and a gray pebble beach, following the shore beneath the old town and the Alps. Its edge is lined with the terraces of cafés that overlook the water.

😊 A Bit of Advice 😊

Many pedestrian streets in Menton are decorated with traditional mosaics made with smooth *galets*, or river stones, which are colourful yet a bit uncomfortable to walk on. Be sure to have thick-soled shoes if you plan on doing a lot of walking.

Old Port

The harbour, used by local fishermen and tourists alike, is flanked by the **jetée Impératrice-Eugénie** and **quai Napoléon-III** and its lighthouse. The far end of the port, home to Volti's sculpture of St Michael, commands pleasant **views★** of old Menton. In the distance you can admire the Italian coastline.

Plage des Sablettes

Windsurfing and jet-skiing forbidden. The gravel beach is dominated by the promenade de la Mer and **quai Bonaparte**. From the top, there is a nice **view** of the old quarter. A long flight of steps leads up to the church of St-Michel.

Garavan

This luxurious residential suburb, running between promenade de la Mer and boulevard de Garavan, has many examples of the eclectic architecture of the Belle Époch (like the Fondation

"Artium Civitas"

This inscription on the front of the town hall declares Menton's ambition to be a city of the arts. Art exhibitions are held throughout the year at the Palais de l'Europe. The **Classical Music Festival** enjoys an international reputation and features world-famous guest artists. There are flower carnivals throughout the summer, but the most famous festival is the **Fête du Citron**, held in the Biovès Gardens since 1929. The event calls for more than 100 tonnes of citrus fruit – oranges, lemons, grapefruit and kumquats – used to cover decorative metal frames erected in the gardens to illustrate a different theme each year. The festival closes with a procession of floats decorated with citrus fruit.

Katherine Mansfield (1888–1923)

This writer from New Zealand spent a year in Menton from spring 1920. Her delicate health caused her to choose Garavan, and she moved into the Villa Isola-Bella *(now on avenue Katherine-Mansfield)*.

In this peaceful haven she wrote five of her best works, including *The Stranger, The Chambermaid* and *The Girl*. Writing in her diary, she said: "The house faces the sea; on the right is the old town with its little port and pepper plants growing on a tiny quay. This old town is the loveliest place I have ever set eyes on."

Barriquand-Alphand, d'Abel Gléna on Boulevard de Garavan). The marina can accommodate boats up to 132ft/40m long. The pretty 17C Baroque **Chapelle St-Jacques** houses a municipal gallery of contemporary art.

GARDENS OF MENTON★

At the end of the 18C, Menton, where orange trees flourish, resembled a large greenhouse open to the sky. The English, who flocked there in winter, imported their legendary love of botany and talent for harmonious planting. The choice of tropical species and the unusual layout of these gardens reflects the fertile imagination of the town's international residents over the past century.

♟♙ Serre-de-la-Madone★

74 rte. de Gorbio. ⏰*Open Tue–Sun Apr–Oct 10am–6pm; Dec–Mar 10am–5pm.* ⏰*Closed Nov.* ∞*8€ (8-12 years 4€, under 12 no charge).* ✆*04 93 57 73 90. www.serredelamadone.com.*

This private garden, created between 1924 and 1939, survived war and neglect before being purchased by the Conservatoire du Littoral in 1999. Its *palazzo* and restored terraces feature rare plants from around the world, including a Moorish garden, a rock garden, and antique garden statues.

Jardin du Val Rameh★

Chemin de St-Jacques. ⏰*Open Wed–Mon Apr–Sept 10am–12.30pm, 3.30pm–6.30pm; Oct–Mar 10am–12.30pm, 2pm–5pm.* ∞*6€.* ✆*04 93 35 86 72. www.jardins-menton.fr.*

These grounds arranged around the English Val Rameh Villa in the 1930s are now part of the Musée d'Histoire Naturelle de Paris. The terraced garden features 700 species of Mediterranean, tropical and sub-tropical flora, with magnificent views of the town and the sea.

Jardin Fontana-Rosa

Ave. Blasco Ibañez. ☜*Guided tours (1.5hr) only with the Maison du Patrimoine, Mon and Fri 10am.* ∞*6€.* ✆*04 92 41 76 76. www.jardins-menton.fr.*

This unusual residence, built in 1921 by the Spanish novelist **Vicente Blasco Ibañez**, features a porch adorned with

Serre-de-la-Madone, Menton

© Sylvaine Poitau/Apa Publications

Musée des Beaux-Arts, Menton

D. Chapuis/MICHELIN

ceramics that pay homage to leading names in Spanish literature.

Jardin de Maria Serena

21 promenade Reine-Astrid. Guided tours (1hr 30min) only with the Maison du Patrimoine, Tue 10am. 5€. 04 92 41 76 76. www.jardins-menton.fr.
Supposedly built by Charles Garnier (architect of the Paris Opera House), this garden is known for its extensive collection of palm trees and **views** over Menton.

Jardin Biovès

Next to the tourist office.
These beautiful gardens in the town centre are bordered by palms and lemon trees, planted with flowers and ornamented by fountains and statues (*Goddess of the Golden Fruit* by Volti).

Oliveraie du Pian

Blvd. de Garavan. Also accessible from a staircase in the Val Rameh gardens.
This olive grove is planted with more than 530 olive trees, many of them over 100 years old.

SIGHTS
Musée des Beaux-Arts (Palais Carnolès)★

Access by ave. Carnot, 3 ave. de la Madone. Open Wed–Mon 10am–noon, 2pm–6pm. 5€. 04 93 35 49 71.

This former summer residence of the princes of Monaco was built in the 17C in the spirit of the Grand Trianon in Versailles. After heavy remodelling in the 19C, it was restored by the Danish architect Georg Tersling and decorated with frescoes on antique themes. The original stuccowork and gilding have survived in the Grand Salon de Musique and the Salon Bleu.

The first floor is dedicated to a collection of **early religious art** by French, Italian and Flemish masters, including Bréa, da Vinci, Luini and Orsi. There are also modern works by Suzanne Valadon, Kisling and Camoin. A collection of **contemporary and modern art** is housed on the ground floor, including pieces from the Wakefield Mori Collection (Picabia, Forain, Dufy) and contributions from various Biennales de Peinture (up to 1980).

The garden features more than 50 species of citrus tree.

Musée JeanCocteau Collection Séverin Wunderman

2 quai Monléon. Open Wed–Mon 10am–6pm. Closed public holidays. 6€ (includes entry to Musée du Bastion). 04 89 81 52 50. www.museecocteaumenton.fr.

Designed by Rudi Ricciotti, this resolutely 21C semi-transparent maze is fringed by wave-like structures on the seafront. Some 1,700 drawings, paintings, books, jewellery, ceramics, stained glass, photographs and tapestries by Jean Cocteau include illustrations from his novel, studies for the film *Orphée*, and a portrait of Picasso (1917).

Musée du Bastion

Quai Napoléon III, Bastion du Vieux Port. ○Open Wed–Sun 10am–noon, 2pm–6pm. Closed public holidays. ✆6€ (includes entry to Musée Jean Cocteau Collection Séverin Wunderman). ✆04 93 57 72 30.

This 17C bastion, built by Honoré II of Monaco, was restored and converted into a museum by Cocteau in 1957. Its pebble mosaics in traditional Menton style explore several themes close to his heart. Le Bastion now houses temporary exhibitions of work by artists from around the world.

Hôtel de Ville

Pl. Ardoïno. ○The hall decorated by Jean Cocteau is open Mon–Fri 8.30am–noon, 2pm–4.30pm. ✆2€. ✆04 92 10 50 00. www.menton.fr.

The **salle des mariages★**, where marriages are celebrated, is decorated with paintings by **Jean Cocteau** depicting the story of Orpheus and Eurydice. The furniture, which includes a palm tree-shaped candelabra, was also chosen by Cocteau, who drew Mariannes (the symbol of the French Republic) on the room's two large mirrors.

▲▲ Musée de Préhistoire Régionale

Rue Lorédan-Larchey. ○Open Wed–Mon 10am–noon, 2pm–6pm. ○Closed public holidays. ✆No charge. ✆04 93 35 84 64.

This museum was opened in 1909 in a building specially designed by the architect Adrien Rey.

The ground floor features items discovered in the Grottes de Grimaldi and other local prehistoric sites, from 1 million years ago to 1,500 BC. Reconstructions of the interiors of Menton houses during the 19C and a poster gallery commemorating the golden age of Menton, from 1870 to 1914, are also on display.

Église Orthodoxe Russe

Rue Paul-Morillot, access by ave. Carnot. ☞Guided tours fourth Sat of each month Sept–Jun at 2.30pm. ✆5€. ✆04 92 10 97 10.

The Russian Orthodox Church (1892) was designed by Georg Tersling, a Danish architect. Although its small size would be more suited to a chapel, the interior is lavishly decorated with murals by Prince Gagarin and many icons.

🚗 DRIVING TOURS

MENTON TO ROQUEBRUNNE-CAP-MARTIN

▶ From Menton take ave. de Verdun, then ave. de Sospel, following the signs to the left up a steep, narrow road.

L'Annonciade★

3.7mi/6km.

The 17C **chapel** has been a centre for pilgrimages to the Virgin since the 11C. From the terrace (738ft/225m) there is a **panorama★** of the coastline.

▶ Take rte. de Castellar north.

Castellar

4.3mi/7km.

Castellar is an attractive hilltop village and a popular place for hiking (it lies at the crossroads of the GR 51 and 52 trails). Fine **view** from pl. Clémenceau.

▶ Return to the road. After 2.5km/1.5mi, turn right on the "Chemin du Mont-Gros".

Roquebrune-Cap-Martin★

See ROQUEBRUNE-CAP-MARTIN.

COL DE CASTILLON ROAD

8mi/13km, 1.5hr; route marked in red.

▶ Leave Menton by ave. de Verdun and ave. de Sospel.

The road over Col de Castillon – also called "route de la Garde" – makes its

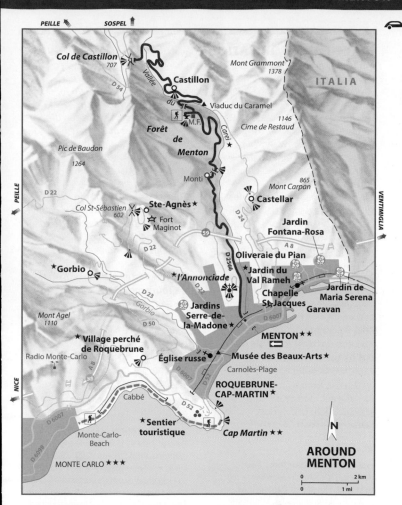

Col de Castillon
707
Castillon
Mont Grammont
1378
ITALIA
Viaduc du Caramel
Forêt
de
Menton
1146
Cime de Restaud
Pic de Baudon
1264
Monti
PEILLE
D 22
Mont Carpan
865
Col St-Sébastien
602
Ste-Agnès ★
Castellar
Fort
Maginot
Jardin
Fontana-Rosa
VENTIMIGLIA
D 22
Oliveraie du Pian
★ Gorbio
l'Annonciade
★ Jardin du
Val Rameh
Chapelle
St-Jacques
Jardin de
Maria Serena
Mont Agel
1110
Jardins
Serre-de-
la-Madone ★
Garavan
MENTON ★ ★
Village perché
de Roquebrune
Radio Monte-Carlo
Église russe
Musée des Beaux-Arts ★
Carnolès-Plage
NICE
Cabbé
ROQUEBRUNE-
CAP-MARTIN ★
★ Sentier
touristique
Cap Martin ★ ★
Monte-Carlo-
Beach
N
MONTE CARLO ★ ★ ★
AROUND
MENTON

0   2 km
0   1 mi

way through a break in the ridge of hills running parallel to the coast.

The D 2566 climbs up the beautiful **Vallée du Careï★** beneath the ridges of the Franco-Italian border. After leaving the hamlet of Monti, the road skirts Menton Forest, with fine **views**.

Forêt de Menton

1hr round trip. To the left of the forest refuge a marked path leads to a **view★** *(viewing table)* of the coast. The road passes the **Caramel Viaduct**, part of the former Menton-Sospel tramway.

Castillon

The village was reconstructed twice: after the earthquake of 1887 and after the bombardments of 1944. Its main district overlooks the village, occupied by artisans, painters and sculptors.

◗ After the village, turn left toward the vallée de Sospel; follow the old tramway tracks. Road on right leads to the pass.

Col de Castillon

Alt. 2,320ft/707m. The **view** to the north takes in the Bévera Valley with the Peïra-Cava and Aution peaks in the distance. To the left D 54 takes a picturesque route to Col St-Jean.

PRACTICAL INFORMATION

Train: *pl. de la gare –* ℮*08 92 35 35 35, www.ter-sncf.com/paca.* Regional TER Nice/Vintimille line serving Monaco and Menton.

Bus: *ave. de Sospel –* ℮ *04 93 35 93 60.* SIngle tickets and packets of 10 tickets on sale from drivers. Monthly pass from coach station. Ten routes serving Menton and the surrounding area.

TOURS

The mosaics made from **pebbles** turned sideways are a traditional form of decoration in Menton. Make sure you wear a good pair of shoes if you are planning to walk around the old town.

Guided tours – *Contact the Maison du Patrimoine, Palais d'Adhémar de Lantagnac, 24 r. St-Michel. Programme on www.menton.fr.* ℮ *04 92 10 97 10. www.vpah.culture.fr.* Menton has been classified as a **Ville d'art et d'histoire**; guided tours given by professional guides registered with the Ministry for Culture and Communication are organised regularly by the tourist office - *reservations:* ℮ *04 92 41 76 76, www.tourisme-menton.fr.*

Garden tours – The Maison du Patrimoine *(see above)* organises tours of the town's gardens throughout the year. Highlight: Garden Month *(Jun)*, Mediterranean Garden Days and Heritage Days *(Sept)*.

Tourist train – *Departs from the promenade du Soleil (near the Bastion).* ℮*04 93 41 31 09. Guided tour (30min) 10am–noon, 2pm–5pm. Jul–Aug, evening tours to admire the town's lights.*

Compagnie de Navigation et de Tourisme *–3 bis Traverse du Bastion, quai Napoléon-III, Vieux Port.* ℮ *04 93 35 51 72. Contact for times and charges. Closed mid-Oct–mid-Apr.* This company organises sea trips with a commentary in French, leaving from Menton.

ADDRESSES

🍽 STAY

⊜⊜⊜⊜ **Hôtel L'Aiglon** – *7 ave. Madone.* ℮*04 93 57 55 55. www.hotel aiglon.net. Closed Dec. 29 rooms.* ▣. ⌐*9.50€. Restaurant*⊜⊜. This hotel is housed within a beautiful villa with a garden terrace and swimming pool. Elegantly appointed rooms have WiFi. Fine dining restaurant ⊜⊜.

⊜⊜⊜⊜ **Hôtel Chambord** – *6 ave. Boyer.* ℮*04 93 35 94 19. www.hotel-chambord.com. 40 rooms.* ⅄▣. ⌐*11.50€.* Modern, sound-proof hotel near the Palais de l'Europe and casino. Breakfast served exclusively in the rooms.

⊜⊜⊜⊜ **Hôtel de Londres** – *15 ave. Carnot.* ℮*04 93 35 74 62. www.hotel-de-londres.com. Closed Nov–mid-Jan. 24 rooms.* ⅄▣. ⌐*10€.* This hotel near the coast features soundproofed rooms of varying sizes, appointed with either rustic or modern furniture and WiFi. Pleasant terrace.

⊜⊜⊜⊜ **Hôtel Napoléon** – *29 porte de France.* ℮*04 93 35 89 50. www.napoleon-menton.com. 44 rooms.* ⅄▣. ⌐*12€.* Elegant, contemporary hotel right on the beach. Air-conditioned rooms; ones facing the sea have pretty teak balconies. The beachside restaurant serves grilled fish, barbecue meats and ice-cream desserts.

⊜⊜⊜⊜ **Hôtel Paris Rome** – *79 porte de France.* ℮*04 93 35 70 35. www.paris-rome.com. Closed Nov–Dec. 22 rooms.* ⌐. *Restaurant* ⊜. Run by the same family for a century, this rustic Provençal hotel and restaurant offers themed package stays and a friendly welcome.

⊜⊜⊜⊜ **Hôtel Prince de Galles** – *4 ave. General de Gaulle.* ℮*04 93 28 21 21. www.princedegalles.com. 64 rooms.* ▣ ⌐*11.50€. Restaurant*⊜⊜⊜. Formerly the headquarters for the Monaco palace guards, this hotel offers all modern comforts and views over the sea. The Petit Prince restaurant has a large garden terrace.

🛏🛏🛏🛏 **Hôtel Princess et Richmond** – *617 promenade du Soleil.* 📞*04 93 35 80 20. www.princess-richmond.com. Closed Nov–mid-Dec. 46 rooms.* 🅿. 🍽*11€. Restaurant🛏🛏.* This seaside hotel boasts a smooth pebble beach and rooftop solarium and Jacuzzi. Some rooms face the sea, all have air-conditioning, WiFi and classic contemporary decor.

🍴 EAT

🛏🛏🛏 **A Braijade Méridiounale** – *66 rue Longue.* 📞*04 93 35 65 65. www.abraijade.fr.* Hidden in an alley of the old quarter, this comfortable restaurant provides Provençal dishes and grilled meats at reasonable rates. Pretty dining room with visible stonework, beams and a fireplace.

🛏🛏🛏 **La Cantinella** *8 rue Trenca.* 📞*04 93 41 34 20. Closed Jan, lunch in Aug, Tue and Wed lunch.* The Sicilian owner delights in sharing his Mediterranean-influenced cuisine in a friendly, laid-back atmosphere.

ENTERTAINMENT

Palais de l'Europe de Menton – *8 ave. Boyer.* 📞*04 93 41 76 50. Exhibition gallery: Wed–Mon 10am–noon, 2pm–6pm; tourist office ticket office: Mon–Fri 10am–noon, 2pm–5pm.* An attractive 730-seater events centre featuring ballets, opera and operetta, theatre and classical music concerts. It also houses a free contemporary art gallery showcasing current artists.

Casino Barrière de Menton – *2 bis ave. Félix-Faure.* 📞*04 92 10 16 16. www.lucien barriere.com. Open from 10am.* Traditional games and slot machines, restaurant, disco, amphitheatre and bar-lounge.

SHOPPING

Lemons – Many shops in Menton pay tribute to this sunny fruit by selling a wide range of produce made or flavoured with lemons: tarts and pies, gingerbread, wine, jam, soaps, etc.

Marchés – *Open every morning.* Covered market on quai de Monléon. Careï market at the top of the Biovès Gardens, beneath the railway bridge.

Confitures Herbin – *2 rue du Vieux-Collège.* 📞*04 93 57 20 29. www.confitures-herbin.com. Kitchen tours Mon, Wed, Fri 10.30am. Shop closed Sun.* An impressive range of mouthwatering jams made on the premises of this family business. There are also different types of honey, vinegar, confit and mustard.

SPORT AND LEISURE

Sports – La Promenade de la Mer is the place where most of the sports and recreation companies are found, including scuba diving, sailing, tennis and windsurfing clubs.

👥 **Koaland** – *ave. de la Madone.* 📞*04 92 10 00 40. www.parckoaland.fr.* Leisure park for children and the younger generation, with a miniature golf course.

CALENDAR

Fête du Citron (Lemon Festival) – Three weeks in February–March *(around Mardi Gras).* Book at least two months in advance for this popular event. 📞*04 92 41 76 95. www.feteducitron.com.*

Salon des Orchidées – Held during the lemon festival, this orchid exhibition includes flower parades and fireworks.

Menton Chamber Music Festival – Held the first two weeks of August on the esplanade of the Église St-Michel. This prestigious event is attended by talented soloists and conductors from around the world.

Ma Ville est Tango – Mid-July. Courses, competitions, shows and gastronomic events based around this passionate South American dance. 📞*04 92 41 76 76. www.tango-menton.fr.*

Christmas Fair – First weekend in Dec to first week in January. Ice-skating, Christmas market, concerts and walks.

THE PRE-ALPS OF NICE

Although officially part of the Alpes-Maritimes, and therefore grouped with the French Riviera, the mountains and valleys north of Nice have their own distinctive character. There are no fancy casinos or palace hotels, no beaches or yachts and few examples of the conspicuous wealth found along the coast. This is a region of modest inns and humble perched villages, where nature-loving visitors come to admire the flora and fauna, try their hand at forest skiing, discover religious art treasures and ancient churches, or simply get away from the crowds and heat of the Riviera. While the deep ravines and vertiginous peaks make for impressive panoramic views, the narrow, winding roads require attentive driving as they hairpin up and down the mountains and cut through the often icy or even snow-covered forestland.

Highlights

1 Stunning **views** from the **Madone d'Utelle Panorama** (p373)
2 Drive the Authion or Col de Braus Road in the **forest of Turini** (p380)
3 Rafting or canyoning on the **Bévéra River in Sospel** (p382)
4 15C frescoes in the **Chapelle Notre-Dame-des-Fontaines** (p389)
5 Prehistoric engravings in the **Vallée des Merveilles** (p393)

Nature Close-Up

These hinterlands running along the Italian border at the foot of the Alps don't quite meet the sea, but their proximity contributes to the unique mix of Mediterranean and Alpine landscapes. Olive groves and Maritime pines give way at higher altitudes to oaks, firs, spruces, and Swiss pines, as well as flowering plants such as edelweiss and saxifrage. The rivers, notably the Roya and Bévéra, have cut deep into the valleys on their way to the sea, creating fascinating rock formations and waterfalls as the snow melts on the pre-Alpine peaks. Much of this natural beauty is protected as part of the Parc National du Mercantour, which, partnered with the bordering Parco Naturale Alpi Marittime in Italy, is home to the prehistoric engravings of the Vallée des Merveilles, over 200 rare plant species including wild orchids, and many endangered or rare animals, including grey wolves, golden eagles, ibexes and bearded vultures.

Sporting Activities

The uniquely rugged character of this landscape provides ample opportunity for sports enthusiasts of all abilities. There is a variety of trails for hikers, some of which follow sections of the national GR (Grand Randonnée) trails,

Chapelle Notre-Dame-des-Fontaines, near La Brigue

© Christian Goupi/age fotostock

Village of Utelle

with several refuges providing food and shelter. Rock climbing is also popular, particularly teamed with the *via ferrata* routes, which traverse some of the deeper canyons. For watersports fans, Sospel and Tende host many river-rafting and canyoning companies, which provide proper equipment and seasoned guides in the summer months. Of course, the hinterlands of Nice also attract visitors in the winter season to a handful of slopes in La Colmiane-Valdeblore, Camp d'Argent in the forest of Turini, and Peira-Cava near Lucéram. Regardless of the season, anyone setting out into the wild should check the local weather reports and be sure to dress and pack accordingly for inclement weather.

Religious Heritage

There are no large monasteries in this part of the French Riviera, but the mountain passes and perched villages house a surprising number of Gothic chapels, with 14C frescoes, Italian-style churches with their distinctive bell towers, and many rare artworks by artists such as Louis Bréa and Giovanni Baleisoni (aka Jean Baleison), as well as altarpieces and organ decorations from the Nice School. Many of these churches and chapels are open only during religious services or upon request, so be sure to call ahead to avoid disappointment before making a long journey to see them.

Unique Biodiversity

A succession of lakes, passes, peaks and gorges, the pre-Alpine landscape passes from meadows of Mediterranean orchids to rocky glaciers within the space of just a few miles. Home to 25 species of reptile and amphibian, it's a good place to spot sun-loving green grass snakes sharing the slopes with cold-blooded sand lizards, which are found at altitudes as high as 7,545ft/2,300m. It also numbers more than 10,000 species of insect, many endemic to these valleys. Fortunate hikers might catch a glimpse of the rare red-and-black spotted Petit Apollon butterfly, for example, which is found only in Boréon and Gordolasque. The Massif de Mercantour alone is crossed by 12 rivers, each flowing into its own basin, giving rise to an extremely original range of indigenous fish species, including the arctic char and the white-clawed crayfish. Of the 101 species of land mammals found in France, at least 60 are present in the pre-Alps region, including chamois, ibexes and wolves, along with both Arctic and Mediterranean bat species. Its 155 species of migratory, occasional and nesting birds include the rare Alpine ptarmigan, a species of grouse with a remarkable talent for mimicry.

THE PRE-ALPS OF NICE

ITALIA

Lac de
Terre Rouge

Parc

national

Le Boréon   *Parc Alpha*

D 89

Madone
de Fenêstre

du

Baus de la
Frema △ 2250

D 94

Rimplas   La
Bolline

GR 5

D 66

D
2565

St-Martin-Vésubie

St-Sauveur-
sur-Tinée

La Colmiane

Berthemont-
les-Bains

**Vallon de la
Gordolasque**

St-Dalmas-
de-Valdeblore

Venanson

D 2565

D 72

C^{ade}
du Ray

**Pic de La
Colmiane**
1795

Vésubie

D 171

Forêt de

Mont Tournairet
2085

Roquebillière

Belvédère

La Bollène-Vésubie

St-Honorat

Lantosque

D 70

D 2205

**Vallon de
Ste-Élisabeth**

Tinée

Peïra-Cava

DIGNE-LES-BAINS

VAR

Pierre Plate
1481

D 21

Utelle

D 2565

D 2566

D 6202

Pont de la Mescla

**MADONE
D'UTELLE**
1174

D 32

Mont Vial 1549

Défilé du
Chaudan

Saut des
Français

Vieux-
Pierrefeu

**GORGES DE
LA VÉSUBIE**

Duranus

Lucéram

Touët-de-
l'Escarène

Bonson

Coaraze

L'Escarène

D 17

Gilette

Plan-
du-Var

Levens

Paillon de Contes

D 615

D 215

Berre-les-Alpes

Esteron

D 2209

Basse

D 19

D 2209

Vallée

Châteauneuf-
Villevieille

D 815

Contes

D 15

D 5202

VAR

np

Gabre

Ruines de
Châteauneuf

D 21

D 2209

Paillon

A 8

np

D 6098

D 6007

NICE

D 19

MARSEILLE, GRASSE ⬇

➡️ Driving tour with departure town

→ Les deux Paillon

→ Vallées du Var et de l'Esteron

→ De Plan-du-Var à St-Martin-Vésubie

→ Route de Valdeblore

→ L'Authion

→ Vallon de Ste-Élisabeth

→ Route du col de Braus

→ Route du col de Brouis

→ Gorges de Saorge et de Bergue

5

Col de Tende/
Colle di Tenda

ᶜⁱme du Gélas
³059

Cᵃᵈᵉ del'Estrech

Fontanalbe

Vallée des
Merveilles

St-Dalmas-
de-Tende

Tende

La
Brigue

D 143

N.-D.-des-Fontaines

D 91

Roya

Levense

Granile

Mercantour

L'Authion

Pⁿᵗᵉ des
3-Communes

889

2082

Gorges de Bergue

D 6204

Gorges
de Saorge

Saorge

Monᵗ aux morts

Col de Turini
1607

Vallée
de

Turini

La Giandola

Roya

N.-D.-de-
la-Menour

D 2566

Moulinet

879

la

Bévéra

D 2204

Breil-s-Roya

Col de Brouis

ITALIA

Col du
Perus

Piène-Haute

654

Nervia

rges du
Piaon

ᵖl de
aus

St-Roch

Bévéra

D 6204

GENOVA

002

Sospel

847

Fort Suchet

642

Braus

Col de
Castillon

Col St-Jean
Clue de Braus

S 20

Col des
Banquettes

orges du
aillon

744

D 2566

Roya

GENOVA

Peille

A 10

S 1

MENTON

Peillon

6

THE PRE-ALPS OF NICE

MONACO

0 ___ 5 km
0 ___ 3 mi

MEDITERRANEAN SEA

MADONE D'UTELLE	★★★	Highly recommended
Pierre Plate	★★	Recommended
Sospel	★	Interesting
Lantosque		Worth seeing

N

Arrière-Pays Niçois★★

The cradle of *nissard* culture and the gateway to the metropolis, the back country of Nice is light years away from the hustle and bustle of its urban neighbour. The irresistible mountain landcape holds valleys that rise and fall through myriad vales, and bare summits that reach giddily above steep slopes carpeted with pine forests. As you wind along its hairpin bends, you'll glimpse perched villages nestled among olive trees and copses of cypresses. Their ancient churches are filled with religious treasures created by the comté de Nice's finest artists and craftsmen, such as the organ-building Grinda brothers, the architect Guibert, and the painters of the Nice *primitif* school.

🚗 DRIVING TOURS

① THE TWO PAILLONS★
Round trip of 56mi/90km. Allow 1 day.

The Paillon de l'Escarène emerges from the northeast of Col St-Roch, whereas the Paillon de Contes springs from the slopes of Rocca Seira to the northwest. These two rivers meet at Pont de Peille and flow into the sea at Nice. The suggested route goes up one valley and

🛈 **Info:** Tourist offices at: Gilette Val d'Esteron, ✆04 92 08 98 08, www.esteron.fr; l'Escarène, ✆04 93 79 62 93, www.escarene.fr; Contes, ✆04 93 79 13 99, www.ville-contes.fr; Peille Mairie (Pl. Carnot), ✆04 93 91 71 71, www.peille.fr.

🠺 **Location:** The Arrière Pays lies in the mountains and valleys north of Nice, towards the Alps, along the Italian border.

🠺 **Don't Miss:** Views from the Plateau St Michel or Mont Alban.

🚹 **Kids:** Lou Ferouil museum at Gilette.

🕙 **Timing:** Allow one day for the perched villages of the vallée du Paillon and half a day for the vallée de l'Estéron.

down the other, with detours at Peille and La Turbie.

🠺 Leave Nice by boulevard J.-B.-Vérany northwards and the route de Turin (D 2204).

Hugging the left bank of the Paillon, pass along the village of Drap, with its glazed-tile bell tower and trompe-l'oeil façades.

View of Peillon

Rock climbing in Peille

© Kaliste A/Fotolia.com

▶ After crossing the bridge over the Paillon, take D 21 right, then a few miles farther, right again onto D 121, which leads to Peillon village.

Peillon★

Set back on a narrow spur overlooking the vallée du Paillon, this spectacular **village** has strict architectural unity, a layout imposed both by its site and defences. Virtually untouched since the Middle Ages, it has a few, narrow streets linked by steep steps and covered alleyways lined with flower-decked houses. The 18C **Eglise St-Sauveur**, with its octagonal lantern, crowns the village. Inside are 17C and 18C paintings and an 18C wooden statue of Christ. A lovely **panorama★** from the Plaça dei Gleia (place de l'Église), the Esterel and St-Martin valley (orientation table) can be seen.

Chapelle des Pénitents-Blancs

🕐 20min guided tour by advance request. ⌖1€. ℘06 24 97 42 25.
The chapel's most interesting feature are the **frescoes★** by Giovanni Canavesio. At the far end is the Crucifixion with St Antony and Ste Petronella. On the walls and ceiling are scenes from the Passion, in particular the *Flagellation* and *Judas' Kiss*, vividly portrayed. On the altar stands a Pietà in painted wood.

🚶 You can still walk along the old Roman road from Peillon to Peille (2hr).

Standing at the confluence of the Launa and Paillon rivers, the aptly named hamlet of Moulins ("mills" in French) is home to two 19C mills, both perfectly preserved and in good working order. The **oil mill** and **flour mill** (the only grain mill in the vallée du Paillon) operate using the same original cannon wheel.

▶ Take D 21 on the right and up the vallée du Paillon. After passing the cement works, turn right after the bridge onto D 53 to Peille village.

Peille★

Peille's Ligurian name, Pilia, which means "on the naked and grassy heights", is a perfect fit for this medieval village, perched dramatically above olive groves and rocky ravines.
From the 13C **tower**, at the edge of the D 53, follow the steps down the rocky rue de la Sauterie, with its intersecting staircases and arched passages, until you arrive at place A. Laugier.
On the right, rue Centrale leads to the Town Hall, housed under the dome of the 13C **Chapelle Saint-Sébastien**. You can also admire the former **Hôtel des Consuls** with its coupled windows and archways.
Behind the **Gothic fountain**, under a house, two half-arches lean against a Roman pillar. The right leads to the rue Lascaris and towards the war memorial, where you'll find a superb **view**. The left

Pelhasque: a Local Dialect

Some of the older inhabitants of this quiet village still speak *Pelhasque*, a local variation of the *Nissart* dialect of Nice.

opens onto **L'Arma**, the oldest part of the village.

The **Musée du Terroir** explores local customs through objects, furniture, tools and clothing donated by the village's inhabitants *(town hall, ⏰open Sat–Sun 2pm–5pm; ⊜no charge; ℘04 93 91 71 71).*

Flanked by an elegant pyramid-shaped Lombard bell tower, the 12C **church** is made up of two coupled chapels. On the left upon entering is a retable, with 15 compartments made by Honoré Bertone in 1579. On the right is a representation of Peille as it looked in the Middle Ages. Ste-Anne is featured on a 14C fresco.

Via ferrata L'Escale – *Park in the public car park at the entrance to the village and follow the signposts.*

🥾 *0.5mi/800m. Allow 3.5hr. Admission ⊜3€. Equipment hired on-site. Contact the Absinthe bar, ℘ 04 93 79 95 75. To hire a guide, contact a professional mountain guide ("guide de haute montagne").*

This energetic hiking trail above the village of Peille crosses a series of secure footbridges and rope bridges.

▷ Take CV 7 "route des Banquettes" to Col des Banquettes.

This pretty, shaded panoramic route leading to the **Col des Banquettes** (2,440ft/744m) offers fine **views** over the Baie de Menton and the Mediterranean. 🥾 *4hr round trip.* From the pass, there are a number of hiking trails leading to the Pointe Siricocca, a former watch tower perched above Ste-Agnès, offering breathtaking **views** over the Menton coast and back country.

▷ Return to Peille and back along the vallée du Paillon, then right on D 21.

Gorges du Paillon★

The route crosses a lush, wooded ravine.

L'Escarène

Built from 1591 to the 19C at the junction of the road to the resort of Peïra-Cava and the beginning of hairpin turns leading up to Col de Braus, this large town stretches along the bottom of the Paillon Valley. It was an important staging post on the Salt Road from Nice to Turin *(Route du Sel – 🔊see SOSPEL).*

Église St-Pierre★

Flanked by two chapels of the Black and White Penitents, this 17C church is the work of the Niçois architect Guibert.

On the road to Col de Turini, the imposing **mausoleum** dedicated to the 1st Division France Libre, inaugurated in 1964 by General de Gaulle, commemorates the sacrifices and battles of the Liberation at the end of the Second World War.

▷ Take D 2204 south to Col de Nice and turn right onto D 215.

Berre-les-Alpes

This village is built on a charming site at an altitude of 2,215ft/675m. From the cemetery there is a **panorama★** of the Pre-Alps of Nice and the sea.

▷ Return downhill on the same road, bearing right onto D 615.

The road wends its way through chestnut and olive groves.

Contes

Originally a Roman settlement, the village is built on a rocky promontory that dominates the vallée du Paillon de Contes like a ship's prow.

The south chapel of the **church** contains a remarkable altarpiece by an artist belonging to the Nice School (1525). The central panel representing Ste-Madeleine has disappeared, but the **predella★** illustrates her life.

Bordering Paillon *(on D 15, in the direction of Coaraze)* is the **site of two mills**: a 13C oil press still in use by the village *(Dec–Mar)*, and a 14C iron forge, where large farming tools were made until 1958. You can visit the forge and a reconstruction of a 19C country kitchen *(○open Wed–Sun 10am–noon, 2pm–6pm; 1st Fri/month 8pm–10pm; ∞2€; ℘04 93 79 19 17; www.musee-contes.fr).*

○ Take D 715 to La Grave; cross the Paillon and take D 815.

The road winds uphill through pines and olives above the Paillon, giving way to the rocky outcrop of Contes and Berre-des-Alpes.

Châteauneuf-Villevieille
This village on the site of a Ligurian settlement, later a Roman camp, overlooks the vallée du Paillon de Contes. The 11C Romanesque church, **Madone de Villevieille**, is decorated with festoons and Lombard bands. The interior was restored in the 17C with ceiling frescoes. Behind the high altar, a fine plaster altarpiece frames a 15C wooden statue of the Virgin and Child.
The deserted ruins of the medieval walls and towers (⚡ *1mi/2km, 30min round trip)* contrast starkly with the rocky landscape. In the Middle Ages, the villagers hid here during attacks. From the top of the bluff there is a sweeping **panorama★**.

○ Go back to D 15, which leads to Nice via the vallé du Paillon.

② VALLÉE DU VAR AND VALLÉE DE L'ESTERON
41mi/66km. Allow half a day.

○ Leave Nice by the promenade des Anglais, which becomes promenade Corniglion-Molinier. Join the D 6007, then turn right towards Plan-du-Var.

The D 6202, which hugs the east bank of the Var, allows quick access to Nice's hinterland. In a landscape composed of flower beds and vegetable plots, vineyards and olive groves, the hill vil-

lages loom into view, one by one: on the west bank Gattières, Carros and Le Broc; on the east bank Aspremont and Castagniers at the foot of Mont Chauve, followed by St-Martin-du-Var and La Roquette-sur-Var. The **view★** includes the snow-capped Alps on the horizon.

○ Cross the river over pont Charles-Albert and take D 17 to Gilette.

The site of the village of Bonson, on an impressive rocky spur high above the river on the west bank, comes into view followed by Gilette, nestling in a cleft.

Gilette
🚶 2.4mi/4km before Gilette, stop at the **Musée Lou Ferouil★** to explore the tools and crafts of yesteryear *(○open Tue–Sun 10am–5.30pm; ∞4€, under 12 years 1.50€; ℘04 92 08 96 04; www.louferouil.fr).*
From place de la Mairie follow the arrows up to the castle ruins for an impressive **view★** of the *corniche* roads, the Var valley and the Pre-Alps of Nice.
There is a pleasant walk, bordered by acacias and plane trees, below the castle with fine **views** of the hill villages – Bonson and Tourette-du-Château – and of the Alps to the north.

○ From Gilette take D 17 north up the Esteron valley; 1mi/2km beyond Vescous turn right onto a narrow road, which climbs to Vieux-Pierrefeu.

Vieux-Pierrefeu
Alt. 2,028ft/618m. The village is reserved for pedestrians.
Austere and proud, this handsome perched village has beautifully restored stonework throughout. High above the Esteron Valley, the former Roman signalling post *(Petra Igniaria)* was a link in the chain that ran from Hadrian's Wall on the border between England and Scotland to Rome.
The church just down the road in Pierrefeu has been converted into a picture gallery called the **Musée "Hors du Temps"** *(○open Jul–Aug; ∞2€; ℘04 93 08 58 18).* This small museum houses

N

TORINO

△ Mᵗ Clapier
3045

★ Cᵃᵈᵉ de
l'Estrech   Fontanalbe   ○ Casterino

✓ Baisse de Valmasque

2935 △   △ 2872
    ✓ Mᵗ Bégo

★★ Vallée des
Merveilles

2685 △
Cime du Diable

MERCANTOUR

★ Tende ○

○ ★ La
    Brigue

St-Dalmas-   D 143
de-Tende ○   ○
    D 43   N.-D.-des-
D 91   Levense   Fontaines ★★

Mᵗ Saccarel
2200

Granile ○

HAUTE VALLÉE DE LA ROYA

Gorges de Bergue ★

L'Authion ★★

Monᵗ aux
Morts
1889   ★★ 2082 pⁿᵗᵉ des
    3-Communes ★★

Fontan ○

D 6204

★ ★ **Gorges
de Saorge** ★★

Saorge ★★ ○

Col de Turini
607

Cabanes
Vieilles

La Giandola ○

Turini   Mᵗ Mangiabo
△1801

Breil-s-Roya

Moulinet

D 2566

**N.-D.-de-
la-Menour** ○   **Col de Brouis** ★
    879   D 6204

★ **Col du
Perus** ○
Mᵗ   654
Agaisen   Piène-
745   Haute ★

orges du   Col de
Piaon ★   Vescavo
ol de   477
raus ★   ★ St-Roch
2002
2204   847   **Sospel** ★   Olivetta

Braus   642   **Fort Suchet**
Col St-Jean   Col de Castillon
lue de Braus 🚶   707   ○ **Castillon**

**Col des
Banquettes**   Viaduc du Caramel

u Paillon   744   ○ **Monti**
Peille ★   59
    ○ **Castellar**
★ Ste-Agnès   D 53

○ Gorbio
Peillon ★   Mont Agel
    1110 △   Roquebrune
★ ✕ **St-Martin-de-Peille**
N.-D.-de-
Laghet

57   ★ La Turbie

MONTE CARLO ★★★

Èze ★★ ○   ○ **MONACO** ★★★
    Cap-d'Ail

ITALIA

GENOVA

GENOVA

○ SAN
    REMO

○ Ventimiglia

MENTON ★★
Roquebrune-Cap-Martin ★

Cap Martin ★★

M E D I T E R R A N E A N

S E A

0 ____ 5 km
0 ____ 3 mi

View of Bonson

© Valery Trillaud/age fotostock

a unique collection of paintings on the theme of Genesis, with the work of 40 contemporary artists including Brayer, Carzou, Folon, Erni, Vicari, Villemont and Moretti.

The drive down D 17 affords **views** of the Var valley, Bonson and La Roquette, perched on its rock.

Bonson★

Bonson was built on a remarkable **site★** high on a rocky spur above the Var valley. It offers an exceptional **view★★** from the church terrace of the Vésubie springing from its gorges and meeting with the waters of the Var, the Défilé de Chaudan. This famous, wooded area was razed by a fire in 1994 that destroyed everything up to the edge of the village. The **church** contains three beautiful *primitif* paintings from the Nice School. On the back wall there is an **altarpiece of St Antony**, where the figure of Ste Gertrude, who was invoked against the plague, is identified by the great rats climbing up her shoulders. In the south aisle is an **altarpiece of John the Baptist**, attributed to Antoine Bréa (the centre panel has been spoiled by overpainting). At the high altar, in a Renaissance frame, an **altarpiece of St Benedict★** includes the figure of Ste Agatha clutching her wounded breasts. Ask for the key at the town hall (☉open Mon–Fri 9am–noon, 3pm–5pm, closed Thu afternoon; ℘04 93 08 58 39; www. bonson.org).

Mont Vial★

12.4mi/20km north of Bonson.

▷ Take D 27 west towards Puget-Théniers.

The picturesque road twists and turns along the flank of the hill with attractive glimpses of Gilette. After Tourette-du-Château, take the road going sharply down to the right that winds to Le Vial ridge before reaching the summit (5,082ft/1,549m, *U-turns possible*). Those who have made the effort to climb up will be rewarded by an impressive **panorama★★**.

▷ Return to Bonson by the same route.

The road loops down to pont Charles-Albert, permitting beautiful **views★** of the Var valley. Cross the bridge and turn left onto D 6102. North of Plan-du-Var cross the River Vésubie where it joins the Var. The road to the right climbs up the Gorges de la Vésubie (☝see VALLÉE de la VÉSUBIE).

Défilé du Chaudan★★

The defile, named after the little village of Chaudan at its southern end, has been created by the Var, which has worn a deep, narrow and winding channel through the rocks. The road follows the course of the river in and out of every bend and through four tunnels.

At the northern end, at **pont de la Mescla**, the River Tinée flows into the Var.

▷ Go back to Nice on D 6102.

EXCURSIONS
Coaraze★
▷ *6mi/10km north of Contes on D 15.*
Heading up towards the Col St-Roch (3,248ft/990m), the stunning "route du soleil" skirts around a hill covered with olive trees. A small, tastefully restored village, home to the artist Jean Cocteau in the 1950s, dominates the scene.
The **historic streets★** and long, vaulted passageways of this charming medieval bourg end in a series of small squares and fountains. Surrounded by cypress trees, the terrace garden affords **views** down the valley and over the Rocca Seira peak.
Walk through the old cemetery to the **St-Jean-Baptiste** church. The Baroque interior contrasts starkly with its plain bell tower and façade. The church has no fewer than 118 stuccowork angels and cherubs.
Notre-Dame-de-la-Pitié – *Return to the D 15 northwards, then take the small road on the left – Route de la Chapelle-bleue.* A former oratory dedicated to the Virgin Mary, it is also known as the "blue chapel" because the life of Christ is painted on the walls in monochrome blue (Ponce de Léon, 1962). There's a fine **view** of the village from the terrace.
Chapelle St-Sébastien – *Take D 15 south. After 1.2mi/2km turn right towards La Gardiola, route des Jouncas.* Nestled in the landscape, on the route de Nice, this chapel is dedicated to St Sebastian, invoked to protect against the plague. It is decorated with elegant frescoes dating from 1530, repainted in the 19C.

Levens
Perched at an altitude of 1,968ft/600m, the medieval village streets of Levens, are lined with ancient houses and fountains, are a pleasant place to stroll.
The place de la République opens onto an attractive public garden whose shaded terraces overlook the valley

Sundials of the Rich and Famous
The alleyways of Coaraze are filled with sundials, many designed by celebrities. Jean Cocteau created *Les Lézards (The Lizards)*, Mona Cristi designed *La Chevauchée du Temps (Riding Time)*, while *Blue Time* is the work of Goetz. *Le Piton et sa Couronne en Vert et en or* (The Peak and its Green and Gold Crown) on place de l'église is by Spanish explorer Ponce de Léon.

and the curved façade of the Baroque **Chapelle des Pénitents-Blancs**. In rue du Docteur-Faraud, the Chapelle des Pénitents-Noirs presents a fine collection of artworks, many displayed in the crypt. At the summit of the village, you'll find an open-air **swimming pool**.

▷ Go up rue Masséna.

Past the Masséna family home (1722), explore the surviving ramparts and the **Maison du Portal** (◷ *open Jul daily 2.30pm–6.30pm; Aug daily 10am–noon, 2.30pm–6.30pm; Sept–Jun Sat–Sun 2.30pm–5.30pm; ⬪no charge; ℰ04 93 79 85 84; www.lamaisonduportal.fr)*, which houses the sculptures of **Jean-Pierre Augier** and temporary exhibitions.
At place de la Liberté a vaulted passageway leads to the heavily restored church.

▷ Take the path on the left.

The **view★** extends over the confluence of the Var and the Vésubie, and the Cheiron and Mercantour massifs.

Duranus
▷ *5.2mi/8.5km from Levens on D 19 north.*
The road overlooks the deep Gorges de la Vésubie (ℰsee VALLÉE de la VÉSUBIE) from a great height, with a glimpse of the chapel of Madone d'Utelle *(left)* high in the mountains. Duranus, a pretty village surrounded by orchards and vineyards, was founded in 17C by the people

Celebrating Liberty

In 1621 the people of Levens were tired of paying heavy taxes to their feudal Lord Grimaldi, so they destroyed the château. Ever since, on the Festival of St-Antonin (early September), everyone in the village jumps off a symbolic stone in place de la Liberté to celebrate their escape from tyranny.

of Rocca-Sparviero, a ruined village at Col St-Michel.

🔺 *3hr round trip.* Discover the remains of an ancient village deserted after an earthquake in the 17C, before returning to Duranus to explore the 19C **aqueduct**.

Saut des Français★

Accessed shortly after leaving Duranus. Information point selling guides and craft products (◷ open Jul–Aug 10.30am–6.30pm).

At the northern end of Duranus is Frenchmen's Leap, commemorating the Republican soldiers who were hurled over the edge in 1793 by guerrillas from the Vésubie valley. Utelle and its chapel overlook the dizzying vertical drop.

ADDRESSES

🛏 STAY

🛏 **Annexe Lou Pourtail** – *Entrance at l'Auberge de la Madone, Peillon.* ✆*04 93 79 91 17. Closed Nov–Jan and Wed. 5 rooms.* �^13€. *Restaurant* 🛏🛏🛏*by group request only.* At the foot of the village, this old cottage inn is full of charm. Regional cooking is served in the rustic dining room and on the garden terrace.

🛏 **Hotel La Vigneraie** – *rte. St-Blaise, Levens.* ✆*04 93 79 77 60. Closed mid-Oct–mid-Feb. 18 rooms.* 🅿. ☐6€. *Restaurant* 🛏🛏. This family-run, country-style inn and restaurant is known for its generous home cooking and comfortable, if basic, guest rooms.

🛏🛏🛏 **Chambre d'hôte les Cyprès** – *289 rte de Châteauneuf, Contes.* ✆*04 93 62 58 77. www.lescypres.fr.* 🖂 *3 rooms.* ☐. This 1920s Niçois house has bedrooms on the ground floor. The decor is sombre yet refined. Breakfast is served under a pergola or vine arbour.

🛏🛏🛏 **Chambre d'hôte Les Lys** – *288 chemin des Meingarde, access via D 215 towards L'Escarène, Berre-les-Alpes.* ✆*04 93 91 81 09. www.les-lys.com.* 🖂 *3 rooms.* ☐. Situated in an annexe to a large property, the rooms afford a panorama of the surrounding mountains. There's a vast garden where BBQ is sometimes served.

🛏🛏🛏 **Chambre d'hôte La Maison aux Oliviers** – *360 rte des Mortissons, Pierrefeu.* ✆*04 97 02 12 81. www.maison-aux-oliviers.com.*🖂 *3 rooms.* ☐ La Maison aux Oliviers offers fully equipped, and individually decorated rooms and suites surrounded by an olive garden.

🍴EAT

🍽 **La Voûte** – *42 r. centrale, Peille.* ✆*04 93 04 56 85. Closed evenings from 8.30 pm and Wed.* 🖂. This central restaurant features a small, rustic dining room that opens onto the Hôtel du Consul. The house speciality is pizza pancakes.

🍽🍽🍽 **La Capeline** – *5.5mi/9km from Gilette by D 17, Toudon.* ✆ *04 93 08 58 06. Closed Mon–Thu Nov–Feb. Reservation required.* This small house in the vallée de l'Esteron serves a fresh menu of regional dishes seasoned with homemade olive oil. Simple, rustic decor and shady terrace.

🍽🍽🍽 **La Fleur du Thym** – *3 blvd. Charles Alunni, Contes.* ✆ *04 93 79 47 33. www.lafleurdethym.fr. Closed mid- to late Aug, early Jan, Tue eve and Wed.* Decorated in yellow hues, this rustic Provence restaurant serves generous portions of regional cuisine.

🍽🍽🍽 **Le Mas Fleuri** – *RD 19, Le Grand-Pré, Levens, close to the stadium.* ✆*04 93 79 70 35. www.masfleuri.com. Closed late Oct–mid-Nov. 7 rooms* 🛏🛏. ☐7€. This refreshing and recently restored restaurant features a simple white dining room as well as a shady terrace. The chef, a "champion de France du dessert", serves a traditional menu of Niçois dishes. Plain, rustic bedrooms are available to overnight guests on the upper floor.

Lucéram★

Alpes-Maritimes

The pretty village of Lucéram, perched dramatically on a steep rock below the Cime du Gros Braus, is known for its colourful roof tiles and an exceptionally rich collection of religious art.

VISIT
Medieval Village★

▶ On pl. Adrien-Barralis, follow the arrows to the church (église).

A maze of stepped streets, Gothic houses and vaulted alleyways make up the medieval town. The church terrace affords **views** over Lucéram and beyond the hills to the sea.

Église Ste-Marguerite

Guided tour on request at the tourist office (2.50€) or included in village tour (5€). 04 93 91 60 51.
The interior of this simple 15C church was remodelled in the 18C with elaborate plasterwork. The 15C **altarpieces★★** are the most complete group attributed to the Nice School. In the south transept is the altarpiece of St-Antoine framed in Flamboyant Gothic panelling. Behind the high altar, the altarpiece of Ste Margaret, divided into 10 panels, was done by **Louis Bréa**: around the central figure are Mary Magdalene *(bottom left)* and St Michael *(top left)*. Three fine altarpieces by the Bréa School are in the nave.

▶ **Population:** 1,228.
◔ **Michelin Map:** 341 F4.
⊞ **Info:** Maison de Pays de Lucéram, pl. Adrien-Barralis. 04 93 91 60 51. www.luceram.com
◖ **Location:** 13mi/21km northeast from Nice.
ℙ **Parking:** Near the fire station and close to the post office.

The **treasury★** comprises some remarkable pieces: a silver statuette of Ste Margaret (1500), a finely engraved 14C reliquary, a statue-reliquary of Ste Rosalie from Sicily, two candlesticks and an alabaster Virgin (16C). On the left of the entrance stands an unusual Baroque Pietà in painted wood, and to the left of the chancel another one in plaster on cloth dating from the 13C.

▶ Exit the church, go down to the right and walk up montée du Terron.

This path leads to the **ramparts** (15C), of which a corner and a defensive tower remain.

Musée des Vieux Outils★

Guided tour on request at the tourist office. €2, or included in the village tour (€5). 04 93 78 46 50. www.musee-de-luceram.com.
Opened in 1998, this museum retraces the history of the village and its sur-

Lucéram

© Xavière Belon/Fotolia.com

Noël des Bergers★

Each year shepherds from the neighbouring mountains make their offering of lambs and fruit to the church to the strains of fife and tambourine music.

rounding area. Set in the sumptuous St-Jean chapel, the collection includes tools for working the land, turning wood, mining arsenic, forging iron, and growing vines and olives. The walls are lined with black and white photographs of the village and its inhabitants, offering a glimpse of rural life before the arrival of mechanised tools. Don't miss the anti-wolf collar.

Musée de la Crèche★

◷Same opening times as the Musée des Vieux Outils. During the Circuit des Crèches (below), open Tue–Sun.

Unique in the region, this museum on the village square contains crèches from around the world, the oldest dating from 1948. Between 150 and 200 items were designed and donated by the village's inhabitants. The most impressive was made using 33,000 matchsticks. The santons (clay figures) are made from a range of local materials: clay, porcelain, matchsticks, glass, wood, wool, fabric, wire and even chocolate.

Chapelle St-Grat

0.6mi/1km to the south on D 2566, turn left on leaving the village before the tunnel. Walk down the path.

This chapel is decorated with frescoes attributed to **Jean Baleison**. Beneath a triple Gothic canopy are the *Virgin and Child*, who is holding a dove, St Grat bearing the head of John the Baptist and St Sebastian in elegant attire with an arrow in his hand.

Chapelle Notre-Dame-de-Bon-Cœur

1.3mi/2km northwest on D 2566, park on the left, then 15min on foot. Interior visible through the bars.

The frescoes, attributed to Jean Baleison, are interesting despite some shoddy repainting. In the porch are *Good and Bad Prayer* and the martyred St Sebastian. In the chapel is the *Adoration of the Shepherds*, the *Adoration of the Magi* and scenes illustrating the life of the Virgin.

ADDRESSES

EVENT

Circuit des Crèches – *Ask for information at the tourist office.* In December–January, more than 400 Nativity scenes (crèches) are displayed in the cellars and streets of Lucéram and Peïra Cava. A shepherd's procession and mass in Provençal take place on Christmas Eve.

Lucéram's Medieval History

Lucéram was divided into two distinct parts: the upper village, built on a steep rocky slope between ravines, and the lower village, a former passage on the **Salt Road**. Due to its exceptional defensive advantages, Lucéram has been home to a staggering range of inhabitants over the last 3,000 years, starting with the Ligurians, Celts and the Romans followed by the Franks, who each built residences and strongholds on the site. The comtes d'Anjou later built a **château** (13C), of which there are extensive remains to the south of the village. Another particular feature of Lucéram is its multitude of chapels belonging to brotherhoods. A stronghold of the Order of Malta and the Templars, Lucéram had seven such chapels outside the village. Just two remain today: the Chapelle St-Grat and the Chapelle Notre-Dame-de-Bon-Cœur.

Utelle★

Alpes-Maritimes

This isolated village, lying at an altitude of 2,625ft/800m, projects like a balcony over the Vallée de Vésubie. Once the most important village between Tinée and Vésubie, Utelle has preserved much of its original medieval character.

SIGHTS
Église St-Véran★

This 14C church, altered in the 17C, has a surprising interior combining mountain austerity (groin vaulting and rounded arches resting on archaistic Romanesque columns and capitals) with elaborate Baroque details (stuccowork around and on the arches). It has an elegant Gothic porch with carved panels illustrating the legend of St Veranus in 12 tableaux.

A carved wooden **altarpiece★** depicts scenes from the Passion. There is an altarpiece of the Annunciation (Nice School) above the first altar in the north aisle and a 13C Recumbent Christ below the altar in the south aisle.

Chapelle des Pénitents-Blancs

The chapel near the church contains a carved wooden altarpiece of the Descent from the Cross by Rubens and six 18C paintings.

EXCURSION
Madone d'Utelle
Panorama★★★

3.7mi/6km southwest.

The sanctuary of the Madonna of Utelle, founded in 850 by Spanish sailors who had survived a storm, was rebuilt in 1806. Pilgrimages take place on 15 August and 8 September.

The interior contains a large number of ex-votos. A short distance from the chapel stands a viewing table (alt. 3,852ft/1,174m) covered by a dome. Take in a breathtaking **panorama★★★** over a wide expanse of the Alpes-Maritimes *département* and the Mediterranean.

Population: 660.

Michelin Map: 341 E4; region map: p366–367.

Info: pl. du village ℰ04 93 03 17 07. www.vesubian.com.

Location: Utelle sits outside the gorges of the Vésubie valley (left at St-Jean-la-Rivière). Hairpin bends lead to the village.

Madone d'Utelle

© Nicolas Thibaut/Photononstop

ADDRESSES

☐/EAT

☐☐ **Le Bellevue** – *Rte. de la Madone.* ℰ*04 93 03 17 19. Closed early Jan–early Feb and Wed.* On the outskirts of the village, perched on a ledge, this family restaurant is perfect for mountain enthusiasts. Clean rooms (☐☐) and swimming pool with views over the valleys. Simple cuisine prepared with vegetables from the garden.

☐☐☐ **L'Aubergerie Del Campo** – *Rte. d'Utelle, St-Jean-la-Rivière, 3mi/5km east of Utelle on D 132. ℰ04 93 03 13 12. ⊨. Reservation recommended eves.* This small inn with a bohemian atmosphere is built on the remains of a former sheepfold. Small dining with a terrace overlooking the Vésubie gorges. Provençal cuisine.

Vallée de la Vésubie★★

Alpes-Maritimes

The pines of the upper Vésubie valley merge into a patchwork of terraced vines, olive trees and perched villages before sweeping down the slopes to the deep gorges and mountain torrents below.

🚗 DRIVING TOUR

PLAN-DU-VAR TO ST-MARTIN-VÉSUBIE
75mi/122km. About 5hr.

📷 If you wish to stop and take a photograph, use one of the rare roadside parking areas. Stopping on these narrow passes can be very dangerous.

▷ D 2565 follows the narrow, winding **Gorges de la Vésubie★★★**. In St-Jean-la-Rivière turn left onto D 32, which climbs towards Utelle.

La Madone d'Utelle★★★
👁*See UTELLE.*

▷ Make a U-turn at St-Jean-la-Rivière and turn left onto D 2565.

Beyond St-Jean-la-Rivière, the valley squeezes between bluffs of rock, skirting the foothills of the Brec d'Utelle.

Lantosque
This tiny perched village has a canyoning **via ferrata** course *(2hr)*, which crosses the Gorges of Lantosque *(contact the Mairie for information, 📞04 93 03 00 02).*

Roquebillière
This little town has been rebuilt six times since the 6C due to rock falls and floods. After the last landslide in 1926, most of the villagers left their austere old houses and moved to the west bank, where the **Église St-Michel-du-Gast**, a church combining Romanesque and Gothic styles, has stood since the 15C.

♿ **Michelin Map:** 341 E4; local map: pp366–367.
ℹ️ **Info:** Pl. du Gén.-de-Gaulle, la Bollène-Vésubie. 📞04 93 03 60 54. www.vesubian.com. Syndicat d'initiative de Belvédère, rue Victor-Maurel. 📞04 93 03 51 66. www. mairie-belvedere.fr.
▷ **Location:** The Vésubie, an eastern tributary of the Var, is formed by two torrents: the Madone de Fenestre and the Boréon.
🕐 **Timing:** Allow one day to discover the valley.

▷ On leaving Roquebillière-Vieux, turn right onto the road to Belvédère (D 171).

The picturesque road winds up the **Vallon de la Gordolasque★★** between Cime du Diable (Devil's Peak) and Cime de la Valette.

Belvédère
The **site★** of this charming village overlooks both the Gordolasque and the Vésubie. From the terrace behind the mairie (town hall), there is a **view★** over the downstream waters of the Vésubie, with Mont Férion and the forêt de Turini on the left , Mont Tournairet on the right and Roquebillière-Vieux below. The road (D 171) continues up the valley past massive rocks and tumbling waterfalls, including the **Cascade du Ray★**, where the river divides into two branches.

Cascade de l'Estrech★
The road ends near a path (🥾 *0.6mi/1km of mountain track)* that leads to the beautiful Estrech waterfall flowing down from a **cirque★★** of snow-capped mountains. The surrounding area is teeming with mountain orchids, passerines, golden eagles and ibexes.

▷ Return to D 2565; turn right on D 72.

© Wolfgang Staib/iStockphoto.com

Reintroduction of Bearded Vultures

Driving through the gorges, you may be fortunate enough to catch a glimpse of a **bearded vulture**. An endangered species in Europe, this majestic bird has a wingspan of 9ft/2.8m. The biggest of all the Alpine birds, it has some very curious habits: alternating between gliding and steep dives, it surveys the sloping pastureland for the carcases of chamois or ewes before swooping down and lifting their bones (which can weigh up to 7lb/3kg) into the air. They then drop the bones onto the rocks below, shattering them into pieces. The vulture was once considered as useful to shepherds as sheepdogs are now.

Decimated in the 19C in the Alps, it survived in the Pyrenees and in Corsica. As part of a vast national programme to reintroduce them to the area, conservationists have been releasing the vultures into the Alps and the **Parc national du Mercantour** for the past 20 years.

Berthemont-les-Bains

This therapeutic spa has naturally sulphurous waters of 86°F/30°C used as long ago as Roman times. As the road climbs, the valley changes to a landscape of chestnuts, pines and green pastures that has earned the region around St-Martin-Vésubie the title of "Suisse Niçoise" (Nice's Switzerland).

ADDRESSES

STAY

▱▱▱ **Auberge du Bon Puits** – *Le Suquet, 3.4mi/5.5km south of Lantosque towards Nice.* ℘04 93 03 17 65. *Closed Dec–Easter, Tue except Jul–Aug.* ⌷. This roadside inn, with a small number of modest rooms, is built from local stone and stands on the banks of the Vésubie. The dining hall features an open fireplace and exposed beams. There is an ornamental park with ponies and a play area for children.

CALENDAR

Polenta festival –In early March, Belvédère plays host to a major festival devoted to polenta served with a generous helping of *daube*, a local beef or boar stew.

St-Martin-Vésubie★

Alpes-Maritimes

St-Martin-Vésubie stretches out along a rocky cliff between the Boréon and Madone-de-Fenestre rivers. Surrounded by peaks and Alpine greenery, this popular summer mountaineering destination is known as the "Switzerland of Nice".

> ▶ **Population:** 1,331.
> ⓘ **Michelin Map:** 341 E3; region map: pp366–367.
> ▤ **Info:** pl. Félix-Faure. ℘04 93 03 21 28. www.saintmartinvesubie.fr.
> ◖ **Location:** Located 44mi/71km north of Nice on the D 2565.
> ▣ **Parking:** Park to the northwest of the entrance to the old town.

WALKING TOUR

◉ Start under the plane trees on pl. Félix-Faure.

Rue du Docteur-Cagnoli

A narrow street bordered by Gothic houses with handsome porches and lintels runs north–south through the town. Several 14C houses survived the fire of 1487 (Maison du Coiffeur).

Chapelle des Pénitents-Blancs

The chapel has a carved façade, a bulb-shaped bell tower and, below the altar, a recumbent Christ with cherubs holding instruments of the Passion.

◉ From rue Dr-Cagnoli turn left into rue du Plan to pl. de la Frairie.

Place de la Frairie

From the terrace overlooking Madone de Fenestre Torrent is a **view** of the gushing river and nearby mountains, Cime de la Palu and Cime du Piagu. The church rises behind the square.

Church

This Roman building, beautifully decorated in the 17C, features a richly dressed 12C statue of the Madone de Fenestre. On the last Saturday in June, it is carried in procession to a mountain sanctuary (ⓘ*see Excursions*), where it remains until September.

The second chapel's left-hand aisle houses two panels from an altarpiece attributed to Louis Bréa.

From the terrace is a partial **view** of the Boréon valley and Venanson village.

EXCURSIONS

Venanson★

◉ *3mi/4.5km.* Leave St-Martin-Vésubie by the Boréon bridge and take D 31 south.

The village square, standing on a triangular rocky outcrop 3,819ft/1,164m high, commands a good **view★** of St-Martin and the Vésubie valley.

Chapelle St-Sébastien

◷*Open on request at the restaurant La Bella Vista.* ℘*04 93 03 25 11.*

This 15C chapel is considered one of the most complete examples of Niçois art, with the interior covered in **frescoes★** by Jean Baleison. At the far end, beneath a Crucifixion, St Sebastian is pierced by arrows; on the side walls and the ceiling are scenes from the saint's life.

Parish church

Pl. de l'Eglise.

On the left of the entrance is a triptych of the *Virgin and Child*, flanked by *St John* and *St Petronella*. At the high altar a Baroque altarpiece (1645) of the Coronation of the Virgin features the donor.

Le Boréon★★

◉ From St-Martin-Vésubie take D 2565 5mi/8km north up Le Boréon's west bank.

The resort stands on a superb site (4,201ft/1,500m) on the southern edge

A Mountaineering Pioneer on the Riviera

The Chevalier Victor de Cessole (1859–1940), a member of an old Nice family, took to climbing late in life when his doctor recommended exercise and fresh air. He enrolled in the new Club Alpin Français when already in his thirties and became a compulsive mountaineer, successively climbing the highest peaks in the Alpes-Maritimes (Mont Clapier and Mont Gélas) and setting several records in the Massif de l'Argentera.

De Cessole's recommended walks, described in illustrated brochures, are forerunners of the guidebooks of today. His activities earned him the presidency of the Club Alpin Français, a position which he held for 40 years, and enabled him to inaugurate and organise a chain of mountain refuges. In 1901 he opened the Nice refuge above Madone de Fenestre. He initiated the first skiing competitions and is considered to be the founder – in spirit at least – of Beuil, the oldest resort in the area. His interest in nature led him to establish the first measures for the protection of wildlife in the region – the banning of the picking of *Saxifraga florulenta*, now the emblem of the Parc du Mercantour.

of the **Parc National du Mercantour** by the **Cascade du Boréon★**, where the river drops 130ft/40m down a narrow gorge. Le Boréon is the starting place for forest walks, up to the high peaks and mountain lakes.

👥 Parc Alpha★

🕐Open daily Jul–Aug 10am–6pm (last admission 4.30pm); late Apr–Jun and Sept–mid-Nov and Christmas holidays 10am–5pm (last admission 3.30pm); Jan–mid-Apr Sat–Sun 10am–5pm (last admission 3.30pm). 🕐Closed late Nov–mid-Feb (except school and Christmas holidays). 💶12€ (4-12 years 10€), online discount 2€. 📞 04 93 02 33 69. www.alpha-loup.com.

At 4,900ft/1,500m altitude, this unique site has been created to help visitors learn more about the **Parc national du Mercantour**. The Parc Alpha, named after the dominant couple in wolf packs, aims to reconcile man with the environment and the wolf.

After crossing a nature preserve (Le Pas du Loup, a grandiose and refreshing pass surrounded by larches, pines and spruces), cross the Boréon to the Temps des Hommes to watch a short audiovisual show presented by mountain professionals in the former cowshed.

View around Le Boréon

© Nicolas Thibaut/Photononstop

The Return of the Wolf

In 1995 the presence of a pack of eight wolves *(Canis lupus)* was confirmed in the Parc du Mercantour. Constantly in search of new territory, these wolves had crossed from the Abruzzi in Central Italy, where the wolf population is estimated at more than 500. There were 19 in the Parc National du Mercantour in 2000 and 12 in 2002. The wolves suffer a bad reputation, so the Parc du Mercantour conducts a campaign of awareness and education with shepherds, who now pen flocks at night and use sheepdogs (the Pyrenean Patou) to prevent wolf attacks. It also teaches them more about this animal at the root of so many legends and stories. The wolf centre at Boréon will, perhaps, help to change the way these creatures are regarded and so help conserve them in their natural habitat.

After learning about the reintroduction of the wolf to the valley, return to the 29 acre/12ha park, half of which is reserved for three packs of wolves living in semi-liberty in vast enclosures (36 wolves in 2009). The large number of wolf cubs born here every year (between 6 and 7 per litter) is seen as evidence of the successful integration of these mammals into their new environment. Their health is monitored by a team of carers, while a group of scientists studies their behaviour.

Observation cabins in the Le Temps du Loup area allow you to observe these creatures in the wild. Visitors never have to wait long before the spell-binding show begins. Arrive at **feeding time** *(check website for schedule and place)* to watch them circle their food, before wolfing down huge pieces of beef, chicken, fish and rodents.

It is possible to drive east to **Vacherie du Boréon** *(1.5mi/2.5km)* and admire the strange outline of the Cougourde. To the west, skirting the park, a 2.4mi/4km road crosses the **vallon de Salèse**.

Vallon de la Madone de Fenestre

▶ *7.4mi/12km east – about 30min. From St-Martin, take avenue de Saravalle.*

The road climbs rapidly up the Madone valley between Cime du Piagu and Cime de la Palu, crossing and re-crossing the river. It ends in a rugged rock **cirque★★** much appreciated by mountaineers. Caïre de la Madone, huge and pointed,

rises nearby, and the slopes of Cime du Gélas (10,312ft/3,143m), covered with frozen snow, dominate the northern horizon on the Italian border. The **Madone de Fenestre** chapel is a place of pilgrimage, which houses the statue of Our Lady of Fenestre in summer. In September it is returned to St-Martin-Vésubie in solemn procession.

🚶 HIKE
Via Ferrata du Baus de la Frema★

At the Col St-Martin, turn right opposite the mini-golf (sign "Via Ferrata"). Parking possible on the access slope. The Via Ferrata begins at the end of the car park. ◷*Open Jun–Sept daily.* ⊘*4.50€.* ℘*04 93 23 25 90. www.colmiane.com.* Via Ferrata offers ideal facilities for anyone wishing to learn rock-climbing. The full course to the Baus de la Frema peak takes 4hr and includes a footbridge (115ft/35m long; 164ft/50m above ground level) and rope bridges.

🚗 DRIVING TOUR

ROUTE DE VALDEBLORE★★
18mi/29km. Allow 2.5hr.

▶ North from St-Martin by D 256.

The road linking the valleys of the Tinée and the upper Vésubie passes through the Valdeblore district, a mountainous region of pastures and wooded slopes. Before the tunnel, a fine **view★** extends over Vésubie valley and St-Martin.

La Colmiane

This ski resort in the Col St-Martin (alt. 4,921ft/1,500m) consists of chalets and hotels dotted among the pines.

▶ At Col St-Martin turn left onto a narrow road leading to the ski-lift.

Pic de La Colmiane★★

Ski-lift to the summit. Open Jul–Aug daily 10am–6pm; Jun and Sept Sat–Sun 10am–5.45pm); mid-Dec–Feb 9am–5pm. Closed Mar–May, Oct–mid-Dec. round trip 3.50€ (summer), 4.50€ (winter). 04 93 23 25 90.
From the top, an immense **panorama★★** is possible south over the Vésubie valley and Turini forest; east over the Mercantour; north and west over the Baus de la Frema to Mont Mounier and Valdeblore.

St-Dalmas-de-Valdeblore

Stroll through the winding alleyways of this village before visiting the Romanesque **Ste-Croix church**, which features a pyramidal Alpine-style bell tower, stout buttresses and Lombard bands on the chevet. Above the high altar there is a polyptych by Guillaume Planeta of **St Dalmas**, St Roch and the Evangelists. In the north aisle, an altarpiece of St Francis is attributed to André de Cella. Behind an altarpiece of the Rosary (17C) in the south apsidal chapel are the partial remains of some very old frescoes.

La Bolline

This pleasant summer resort sits at the heart of a light chestnut grove that contrasts sharply with the dark wood on the opposite slope.

▶ West of La Bolline turn right on D 66.

Rimplas

The curious **site★** of this village on the edge of a cliff (3,281ft/1,000m high) is striking. From the chapel, an extensive **view★** of the Tinée valley, Bramafan valley and Valdeblore is obtained.
2hr round trip. A nice, easy trail leads down into **St-Sauveur-sur-Tinée** by the GR 5, northwest of the village.

By road towards Valdeblore on D 2565, then La Tinée on D 2205, right for St-Saveur, left for Nice.

ADDRESSES

🏨 STAY

La Châtaigneraie – 04 93 03 21 22. www.raiberti.com. Closed Oct–mid-May. 37 rooms. 6€. Restaurant. Pleasant accommodation nestling in a peaceful park with a pool and WiFi. Ideal for those who wish to go climbing or hiking in the Parc du Mercantour.

🍴 EAT

Le Pic Assiette – La Colmiane, at the summit of Pic de La Colmiane. 06 21 01 63 68. Closed Nov. Reservation required. 1 room. At 5,900ft/1,800m altitude, this restaurant has astounding mountain views. Ride up by chairlift in summer, and come down by mountain bike.

La Trappa – 7 pl. du Marché, St-Martin Vésubie. 04 93 03 29 23. Closed late Oct–late Nov, Wed in Jul–Aug, Sun evening and Mon. This Niçois restaurant offers a summer terrace overlooking a quiet pedestrian street.

SHOPPING

Markets – Tue, Sat and Sun on pl. du Marché (summer season).

SPORT AND LEISURE

Ski – Le Boréon has 18.6mi/30km of cross-country ski trails.

Escapade – Pl. du Marché. 04 93 03 31 32. www.guidescapade.com. This company of mountaineering guides has been in business in the St-Martin-Vésubie area for 20 years. Summer activities for customers include hiking, canyoning and mountain climbing; winter choices include cross-country skiing, heli-skiing, snowshoeing and off-piste skiing.

Forêt de Turini★★

Alpes-Maritimes

Bristling along the slopes between the Vésubie and Bévéra valleys, the Forêt de Turini is carpeted with fresh young maritime pines and oaks, rising to a dense thatch of maple, beech and spruce topped by a crown of bright green larches.

- **Michelin Map:** 341 F4; local map: pp366–367.
- **Location:** Situated in the Nice hinterland 9.6mi/15.5km from Menton, the forest covers 1,350 acres/3,500ha between the Vésubie and Bévéra valleys.
- **Timing:** Allow one day for the Col de Braus tour.

🚗 DRIVING TOUR

L'AUTHION★★
Round trip 11mi/18km from Col de Turini. Allow 45min.

The Authion road passes through magnificent mountain scenery. *Roads blocked in winter.*

Monument aux Morts
The Authion Massif has twice been a backdrop to military action. In 1793 the Convention's troops fought here against the Austrians and Sardinians, and in April 1945 the DFL (Free French Forces) pushed back the German army. There's a panoramic **view**★ from the memorial. Continue along D 68, then right at the fork to Cabanes Vieilles military camp. The road runs through Alpine pastures with **views**★ of the Roya Valley.

▶ Turn right by another monument onto a track and continue 547yd/500m.

Pointe des Trois-Communes★★
This altitude (6,830ft/2,082m) offers a **panorama**★★ of the peaks in the Mercantour and Nice Pre-Alps.

▶ Return to D 68; at the war memorial take the road back to Col de Turini.

VALLON DE STE-ÉLISABETH★
Round trip 11mi/18km from Col de Turini. Allow 1hr.

The road (D 70) winds northwest, cutting its way between the peaks of Calmette and Scoubayoun overlooking the Vésubie tributary.

Gorges de Ste-Élisabeth
This rugged gorge cuts a savage gash in the concertina-like folds in the rock.

▶ Soon after the tunnel, stop at the Chapelle St-Honorat.

St-Honorat Viewpoint★
The **view** extends from the terrace by the chapel over the perched village of Bollène, the Vésubie and the Mercantour peaks.

La Bollène-Vésubie
From this village at the foot of the Cime des Vallières, the road winds down the Vésubie Valley on D 2565 *(towards Nice)*. The **Turini Camp-d'Argent** ski resort (5,577ft/1,700m) offers forest skiing. Return to Nice along the valley and D 2565.

COL DE BRAUS ROAD★★
Round trip 47mi/76km, leaving from Col de Turini. Allow one day.

The drive to Peïra-Cava passes through the thickest part of Turini forest.

Peïra-Cava★ *Alt. 4,757ft/1,450m.*
This summer resort and winter sports centre is perched on a ridge between the Vésubie and Bévéra valleys.

▶ Beyond the village turn right into a car park, then walk 55yd/50m to a stairway on the left.

La Bollène-Vésubie

J. Malburet/MICHELIN

Pierre Plate★★

This peak provides a **panoramic view★★**. Return downhill to D 2566 and in La Cabanette turn left onto D 21. The road descends through steep bends with magnificent **views★**.

▶ D 21 continues to Lucéram.

Lucéram★

See LUCÉRAM.

▶ South of Lucéram D 2566 slopes into the Paillon valley to L'Escarène.

L'Escarène

See NICE 1: The Two Paillons.
From L'Escarène D 2204 climbs north-east up the Braus Valley to Sospel.

Touët-de-l'Escarène

The road passes through this charming little village with a Baroque church.

Clue de Braus

The rift that opens up beyond Touët village is short, but impressive. From St-Laurent (hamlet), one can reach the Braus waterfall (⬅ *15min*). The D 2204 winds around 16 hairpin bends before climbing to **views★** of the Nice observatory and Cap d'Antibes.

Col de Braus

Alt. 3,287ft/1,002m.
Beyond the pass the road descends through 18 bends, offering extensive **views★★** of the Bévéra valley. The road skirts **Mont Barbonnet**.

Col St-Jean

At Col St-Jean, between the dwellings on the left, an old army road leads to **Fort Suchet** (◷*open Jul–Aug; contact Sospel tourist office ℘04 93 04 15 80*), built from 1883 to 86.

Sospel★

See SOSPEL.
The D 2566 climbs northwest through the forest up the **Bévéra valley★**. There is a beautiful waterfall on the right.

Gorges du Piaon★★

The *corniche* road runs beneath an over-hang of rock high above the bed of the stream, strewn with huge boulders.

Chapelle Notre-Dame-de-la-Menour

An oratory marks the beginning of a path that provides views of the valley. The route passes through the charming village of Moulinet before returning through the forest to the Col de Turini.

ADDRESSES

🏠 STAY

Les Chamois – *Turini (Col de). ℘04 93 91 58 31. www.hotel-les-chamois.com. 15 rooms.* This mountain-style restaurant has an inviting terrace. Les Chamois also offers pleasant accommodation; some guest rooms come with balconies.

Sospel★

Alpes-Maritimes

Once the capital of the comté de Ventimiglia, this mountain village straddling the Bévéra river was a staging post on the Salt Road linking Turin, capital of the Kingdom of Sardinia, to the coast. Today its historic houses and olive groves, surrounded by high mountains, create a picturesque backdrop for hiking, canyoning and river rafting.

 WALKING TOUR

OLD TOWN★

A map of the village is available from the tourist office.

Right Bank

Place St-Michel is framed by a church and a run of arcaded houses. The oldest (Palais Ricci), to the right of the church, bears a plaque recording the stay of Pope Pius VII, exiled by Napoleon in 1809.

Église St-Michel

At the time of the Great Schism this church was a cathedral. The Romanesque bell tower with Lombard bands flanks an imposing Baroque façade. The interior decor is pure Baroque: huge altarpieces, *trompe-l'oeil* frescoes and

▶ **Population:** 3,440.

Michelin Map: 341 F4; region map: pp366–367.

Info: 19 ave. Jean-Médecin, Sospel. ℘04 93 04 15 80. www.sospel-tourisme.com. Vallées Roya-Bévéra. ℘04 93 04 92 05. www.sospel-tourisme.com.

Location: Sospel lies 12mi/19km north of Menton on narrow, winding roads.

Timing: Allow half a day, with 1hr for Fort St-Roch.

gilding. In the north apsidal chapel the **Immaculate Virgin★** is one of François Bréa's most accomplished works.

Old Streets

To the right of the parvis, large stairways lead to the ruins of a Carmelite convent, now almost hidden by vegetation. Continue on to reach the remains of some fortifications, including a huge 15C corner tower and farther on, a semicircular arched gateway.

Go through this gateway and follow a stairway to **rue St-Pierre**, which runs on from the cathedral parvis. Note **no. 30**, which has two ornate Renaissance

Old bridge of Sospel

© Rémy Masseglia/Fotolia.com

Village of Piène-Haute

S. Sauvignier/MICHELIN

windows and a Gothic ground floor with an ogival door. The road, lined by arcades, leads to the square behind the *mairie* (town hall).

Old Bridge★

The toll tower on the 11C bridge, rebuilt after the Second World War, now houses the *Syndicat d'Initiative* (tourist office) and in season, an information centre about the Mercantour National Park.

Left Bank

Cross the old cobblestone bridge to **place St-Nicolas**, with its old houses and 15C fountain, the oldest in the village. Rue de la République to the right once housed a host of small businesses and enormous cellars used by passing merchants as warehouses before they settled their toll at the bridge. The houses along this road feature beautifully carved stone lintels *(nos. 14, 15, 23 and 51)*. The picturesque and narrow rue des Tisserands leads to the 17C Ste-Croix Chapel.

EXCURSIONS
Fort St-Roch★

◗ *0.6mi/1km south of the village, on D 2204 to Nice; turn right after the cemetery (signed).* ◷*Open Jul–Aug daily 2pm–6pm; Apr–Jun and Sept Sat–Sun and public holidays 2pm–6pm.* ◌*5€.* ℰ*04 93 04 00 70.*

This fort was part of the Alpine **Maginot Line** of fortifications built in the region during the 1930s. An underground town 164ft/50m deep, it could survive for up to three months without contact with the outside world.

The tour covers the underground galleries, the kitchens, an electricity generating station, an operating block, the firing stations, a small cinema and artillery rooms, as well as the periscopes that enabled the inhabitants to view their surroundings.

Piène-Haute via Col de Vescavo★

5.6mi/9km. Allow half a day.
◗ *From Sospel take D 2204 east. After 1mi/2km turn right onto a road signed "Piène-Olivetta". After 2.5mi/4km D 93 reaches Col de Vescavo (alt. 1,568ft/478m). The road then crosses the border to the Italian village of Olivetta. Follow D 193 to the left.*

The road continues to climb up to the charming little village of **Piène-Haute**, in solitary splendour on an outcrop 2,011ft/613m in altitude. *(The best place to park is on the esplanade at the entrance to the village.)*
Before setting off downhill on foot, admire the **view★** of the old houses huddled side by side below the castle ruins. The church, on a rise, has a beauti-

Water over the bridge

Sospel toll bridge is one of the last fortified bridges in Europe. Originally lined with shops and homes, it was also used as an aqueduct to supply water to the left bank.

ful carved bell tower and an unusual red marble altarpiece.

Above the village, by the castle ruins, are splendid **views** of the Roya valley.

🥾 HIKING TOURS

▷ *The path is below D 93 to the right towards the Olivetta frontier post. Go down the slope from the road towards the railway, then turn left under the bridge. A signpost near a ruin marks the start of the botanical footpath.*

Botanical Trail

🥾 *1.5hr on foot round trip.* This delightful footpath, marked with boards detailing the plants to be seen, goes through a wood of young oak trees, scrubland (which was once cultivated in terraces) and a holm oak wood.

▷ 4.3mi/7km by car. From Sospel take the road beside the post office that climbs up the north bank of the Bévéra. After 1mi/1.5km, turn right and follow a road uphill towards Serres des Bérins.

Mont Agaisen

🥾 *1hr on foot round trip.* On entering the Bérins district, take the surfaced road on the right, heading south. After a short stretch through some woods, the old army road reaches the first small forts of

the fortified complex of Mont-Agaisen (⊶*closed to the public*). Leave the car in any free space along the road.

On the path that leads to the summit (alt. 2,444ft/745m) is the occasional casemate or firing turret. To the south at the edge of the summit is a large metal cross with a good **view** of the village, the Bévéra valley and Mont Barbonnet. There are other **viewpoints** on the summit, towards Col de Brouis and north towards the valley dominated by the bare peak of Mont Mangiabo (alt. 5,909ft/1,801m).

🥾 *3hr.* More experienced ramblers can opt for a variation on this excursion, leaving from the village and undertaking it entirely on foot. In this case, they should leave from the Groupe Scolaire overlooking the village and follow the path leading off to the right, marked *"GR 52 – Mont Agaisen"*.

The track merges with the GR 52 (red and white blazes) for about 0.6mi/1km. Turn left onto a surfaced road at the junction and follow it uphill for another half a mile or so until you reach the first military ruins and rejoin the itinerary described above.

🚗 DRIVING TOUR

9 COL DE BROUIS ROAD

21km/13mi. Allow about 1hr.
🕰 *See region map pp 360–61.*

This road is an extension of the Col de Braus Road (🕰 *see FORÊT de TURINI*) towards Turin, formerly known as the **Salt Road**.

▷ From Sospel take D 2204 east.

The Salt Road

Owing to its essential role in the preservation of meat and the tanning of hides, salt has always been of considerable interest to tradesmen. Provençal salt-works have supplied Piedmont since the Middle Ages. The salt was unloaded from sailing barges in Nice and transported by mule to Turin through the Col de Braus, Col de Brouis and Col de Tende via Sospel and Saorge. This strategic highway became known as the Salt Road (Route du Sel). Now embellished with works of modern art, it is still the main highway between the Riviera and Piedmont.

There is a **view** to the rear over Sospel guarded by the Fort du Barbonnet.

Col du Pérus

Alt. 2,146ft/654m. The road runs just above the deep Bassera ravine.

Col de Brouis★

Alt. 2,884ft/879m. This pass takes its name from the heather-like shrub that thrives in the area, known as brouis. The monument above the car park on the right commemorates the last French attack of April 1945 against the German forces, who had been driven back into the valleys. A broad **view ★** opens up of the peaks on the far bank of the Roya. The road descends to La Giandola.

La Giandola

This attractive mountain hamlet has a Renaissance church tower.

▶ Return by the same itinerary; it is also possible to take a detour via Breil-sur-Roya (*see BREIL-SUR-ROYA overleaf*) or to return through the Vallée de la Roya to Saorge, 3mi/5km away (*see SAORGE*).

ADDRESSES

⌂ STAY

Chambre d'hôte Le Domaine du Paraîs – *La Vasta Supérieure.* ℰ04 93 04 15 78. domainedupurais.monsite-orange.fr.⌿. 2 rooms. ⌑. This large mansion has retained many of its charms, including the original Tende stone sink and drainer in the kitchen.

Chambre d'hôte Villa Amiel – *ave. des Martyrs de la Résistance.* ℰ04 93 04 12 69. www.villaamiel.com. By reservation mid-Nov–Feb. ⌿. ⊡.4 rooms. ⌑ 5.50€. Owned by an English couple passionate about hiking, this residence bordering a small stream has two upper bedrooms and two smaller, as well as charming rooms in an annexe building. Organic breakfasts.

Hôtel des Étrangers – *7 blvd. de Verdun.* ℰ04 93 04 00 09. www.sospel. net. Closed Nov–Mar. 27 rooms. ⌑8€.

Restaurant. This unpretentious hotel-restaurant makes a great base for exploring the area. Swimming pool. Dishes prepared with fresh produce.

⌖ EAT

Le St-Donat – *quartier La Vasta. 1.8mi/3km NW via rte du Col de Turini.* ℰ04 93 04 14 94. Closed Oct–May and Mon–Tue lunch except Jul–Aug. Reservation required in low season. Situated in the Mas Fleuri campsite, this restaurant is open year round. The chef prepares all the dishes himself, including the pasta.

Le Restaurant Le Bel-Aqua – *Hôtel des Étrangers.* Regional cuisine prepared with market-fresh produce. Opt for the terrace overlooking the Bévéra in summer.

Côté Cuisine – *5 blvd. Jean-Médecin.* ℰ 04 93 79 81 37. www. restaurant-cotecuisine.com. Closed Mon–Wed. Reservation recommended. A former grocery opposite the bridge, this restaurant is run by a farming couple. Local cuisine prepared with organic or regional produce: homemade bread, pasta and farm olives.

SHOPPING

The village is known for its honey and its handcrafted objects made from olive wood.

Markets – Pl. Gianotti on Thu and pl. de la Cabraïa on Sun mornings (especially honey, olive oil and goat's cheese).

LEISURE ACTIVITIES

Canyoning – ℰ04 93 04 15 80. www.sospel-tourisme.com Contact the tourist office for details. Canyoning is authorised between April and October on Monday, Wednesday, Friday and Sunday from 9am–5pm.

Hiking – A list of all the hiking paths starting from the village is available from the tourist office. There are also facilities for exploring the neighbouring countryside on horseback.

CALENDAR

Les Baroquiales festival d'art baroque – www.lesbaroquiales.com. First weekend in July. Baroque music concerts, street events, tastings.

Breil-sur-Roya
Alpes-Maritimes

A popular spot for fishing, hiking and watersports, Breil lies below the summit of Mont Arpette (5,282ft/1,610m), astride the Roya river, just a few miles from the Italian border.

VISIT

The old village consists of picturesque streets shored up by ramparts and ancient gateways. South of the parish church, the Renaissance **Chapelle Ste-Catherine** hosts regular art exhibits.

Église Sancta-Maria-in-Albis
Pl. Brancion.
The vast 18C church features carved doors (1719) and a Baroque interior. The ornate 17C **organ loft** is of gilded wood. An early **altarpiece** (1500) stands to the left of the chancel.

♣♦ Écomusée du Haut-Pays et des transports
Gare de Breil. ⏱*Open May–Sept daily 2pm–6.30pm.* ✆*04 93 04 42 75. www.ecomusee-breil.fr.* ⊛*2€.*
The old Breil train station has been transformed into a railway museum featuring an old steam train, a tramway trolley and working model trains.

PRACTICAL INFORMATION

Tours
Self-Guided Tours – The tourist office provides a detailed map for exploring the village, as well as three hiking itineraries promising "fascinating and panoramic views".

Transport
Access by train: The Italian and French rail links from Nice and Ventimiglia towards Cuneo and Turin pass by the stations of Breil (Roya-Bévéra), Sospel and Tende. A particularly scenic trip.
♣♦ In summer take the "Train des Merveilles", which has live commentary of the route ((☞*see Planning Your Trip p32*).

▶ **Population:** 2,092.
◔ **Michelin Map:** 341 G4; region map: pp366–367.
🛈 **Info:** Pl. Bianchéri. ✆04 93 04 99 76. www.breil-sur-roya.fr. Office du tourisme de la Vallée de la Roya. ✆04 93 04 92 05. www.royabevera.com.
◉ **Location:** Breil is situated on the main road from Ventimiglia to Turin, via the Col de Tende pass, 14mi/23km from Sospel.

ADDRESSES

🛏 STAY

🍽🛏🛏 **Hôtel Le Roya** – *3 pl. Biancheri.* ✆*04 93 04 48 10. www.hotleroya.com. 13 rooms.* ⊟*8€. Reservation essential in winter.* This hotel on the left bank of the Roya stands out because of its brightly coloured façade. Simple, unadorned rooms and spacious bathrooms. We recommend the rooms overlooking the mountain or the river.

LEISURE ACTIVITIES

AET Nature – *392 chemin du Foussa.* ✆*04 93 04 47 64. www.aetcanyoning.com. Open daily by reservation.* This company organises hikes, *via ferrata*, rafting and a camping refuge for up to 20 (*reservations required*).

Roya Évasion – *11 blvd Rouvrier.* ✆*04 93 04 91 46. www.royaevasion.com. Jul–Aug 9am–noon, 2pm–7pm; Apr–Jun and Sept–Oct Sat–Sun and public holidays 9am–noon, 2pm–7pm.* Canoeing, rafting, hiking and mountain biking excursions. Equipment for hire.

CALENDAR

La Vallée des santons et des crèches – *Mid-Dec–mid-Jan.* Village inhabitants proudly exhibit more than 300 crèches outdoors.

Festival international des orgues historiques de la Roya-Bévéra – ✆*04 93 04 92 05. www.royabevera.com.* Organ concerts held in August in area churches.

Saorge★★

Alpes-Maritimes

Situated at the mouth of a gorge, between two rocky cliffs, Saorge clings to the steep slopes of a natural amphitheatre. For centuries, this extraordinary site was an invincible stronghold, protecting the valley, with its fortified castles.

- **Population:** 431.
- **Michelin Map:** 341 G4; region map: pp366–367
- **Info:** Mairie (Town Hall), ave. Dr-Joseph-Davéo. ℘04 93 04 51 23. www.saorge.fr.
- **Location:** Saorge is located 7mi/11.5km north of Breil-sur-Roya.
- **Parking:** Park at the north entrance to the village.
- **Timing:** Allow 2hr for the village and one day for the gorges.

🐾 WALKING TOUR

OLD VILLAGE★

The stepped and vaulted streets lined with 15C houses fronted by sculpted lintels are spread over three levels, each with its own small square and fountain. Don't miss the terrace offering a good **view★** over the Gorges de la Roya.

Église St-Sauveur

The south nave of this 16C church has an 18C canvas depicting *Elijah with the Virgin and Child*, a fine Renaissance tabernacle, a 15C font beneath a painting by a local artist (1532), and a *Virgin* in gilded wood beneath a canopy (1708).

▶ Leave from the southern end of the village, bearing right at the road fork.

Madonna del Poggio

🔒*Private property.*
The early Romanesque building has a soaring **belfry** with six rows of Lombard bands. This is the oldest religious building in the Roya valley. The journey back to the village offers a fine **view** of Saorge and its terraced olive groves.

▶ Take a sharp right at the road fork towards the monastery.

Couvent des Franciscains

🕐*Open Wed–Mon May–Sept 10am–noon, 2pm–6pm; Feb–Apr and Oct 10am–noon, 2pm–5pm.* 🐾*Guided tours (1hr) 10.30am and 3pm.* ⊕5€. ℘04 93 04 55 55.
This 17C Franciscan convent, reinhabited by monks in 1969, is set among olive trees. The Italian Baroque-style church has a bell tower capped by a bulbous roof of coloured tiles. Small **cloisters** are decorated with paintings on pious themes. There is a splendid **view★★** of Saorge and Roya Valley.

Couvent des Franciscains

© Nicolas Thibaut/Photononstop

🚗 DRIVING TOUR

SAORGE GORGES AND BERGUE GORGES

24mi/39km. Allow 4hr. ♿See regional map pp360–61.

Breil-sur-Roya
♿*See BREIL-SUR-ROYA.*

▶ Leave Breil-sur-Roya to the north by D 6204.

The road to Col de Brouis (♿*see SOSPEL*) forks off to the left.

La Giandola
(♿*See SOSPEL*).

Gorges de Saorge★★

The narrow road hugs the river's every curve beneath overhanging rocks. At the end of the gorge, there is a **view** between two rock cliffs of the stunning **setting★★** of Saorge, built in curved tiers on a hillside clad in olive trees.

Gorges de Bergue★

Beyond Saorge and Fontan, the road ascends gorges cut through red schist where the rock appears deeply coloured and foliated. The hamlet of **Granile** (♿*see TENDE*) can be reached from here on a pleasant pathway. The valley widens out into the St-Dalmas-de-Tende Basin (♿*see TENDE*).

ADDRESSES

🛏 STAY

⊜⊜ **Berghe Chambre d'hôte Le Berghon** – *Hameau de Berghe Inférieur, 3.4mi/5.5km from Fontan on D 42.* ☎*04 93 04 54 65. www.leberghon.com. Reservation required in winter.* ⊟ *3 rooms.* ⊇*. Restaurant* ⊜⊜. This gîte in a tiny perched hamlet has three simple rooms. Pleasant hiking trails along the Céva mule track to the vallée des Merveille.

🍴 EAT

⊜⊜ **Le Bellevue** – *5 rue L.-Périssol.* ☎*04 93 04 51 37. Closed evenings except Jul–Aug and Mon evening in Jul–Aug, Tue.* Interrupt your tour of the covered alleys and settle in the yellow dining room. Panoramic views of the Roya Gorges.

La Brigue★

Alpes-Maritimes

Part of Italy until 1947, La Brigue is a charming mountain village set amid vineyards in the Levense Valley, with views over Mont Bégo. The former domain of the Lascaris family, the village played an influential role in the Niçois *art primitif* movement.

👣 WALKING TOUR

OLD VILLAGE

Topped with green schist roofs, the village's ancient houses cluster around the foot of the 14C chateau ruins. Some of the houses are built over arcades; others have carved lintels, often with a heraldic

- ▶ **Population:** 630.
- ♿ **Michelin Map:** 341 G3; region map: pp366–367
- ℹ **Info:** Pl. St-Martin. ☎04 93 79 09 34. www.labrigue.fr. Pôle touristique de Roya-Bévéra. ☎04 93 04 92 05. www.royabevera.com.
- ▶ **Location:** Located inland from Nice in the Roya valley. Arrive via St-Delmas-de-Tende, crossing the Roman bridge over the river, for the best **view** of Mont Bégo.
- 🕐 **Timing:** Allow 2–3hr to explore La Brigue and its sights.

Village of La Brigue

© Rémy Masseglia/Fotolia.com

detail (particularly rue de la République). Place Vieille commands a fine **view** over Mont Bégo.

To the right of the parish church stand two Penitents' chapels: the 18C **Chapelle de l'Assomption** with its Baroque façade and graceful Genoese bell tower; and to the left the **Chapelle de l'Annonciation**, also Baroque, on a hexagonal plan, with a collection of ecclesiastical ornaments.

Collégiale St-Martin★

This parish church has a fine late-15C square Romanesque bell tower and a doorway framed in the Antique style (1576), with an older (1501) green schist lintel. The 17C organ was repaired in the 19C. The white marble font is crowned by a painted and gilded baldaquin.

The church contains a remarkable collection of **Niçois** *primitif* **paintings★**. Chapels along the south aisle contain a Crucifixion with saints and donors comparable with Louis Bréa's in Cimiez, an altarpiece of St Martha recounting the legend of her arrival in Marseille on a boat, a rare realist painting by Bréa of the Sufferings of St Elmo, and a fine altarpiece of the **Adoration of the Child**, also by Bréa. On the north side, the first chapel contains a triptych by the

Italian Fuzeri of **Our Lady of the Snows** (1507) with its 18C Baroque frame.

Local Trails

Ask for the maps from the tourist office. The "Chemin des Oratoires" from La Brigue to St-Dalmas-de-Tende *(1hr).* Nature Interpretation Trail between La Brigue and Notre-Dame-des-Fontaines *(1.5hr).*

EXCURSION
Chapelle Notre-Dame-des-Fontaines★★

▷ *2.5mi/4km east on D 43.*
◔ *Open May–Nov 10am–12.30pm, 2pm–5.30pm. Rest of the year by request at tourist office. ∞2€.*

Set alone in the Mont Noir Valley near Mont Bégo and overlooking a mountain stream, the 14C chapel is built on the site of a former sanctuary dedicated to water, frequented as early as the 2C and 3C. It was succeeded by a small chapel, of which the 12C choir remains. Before the nave was raised in the 18C with seven clerestory windows, it was expanded to receive an extraordinary series of frescoes in 1492.

The frescoes★★★ – The chancel panels were discovered in 1950 under a coat of wash. They were painted in 1451 by

E. Baret/ MICHELIN

Jesus Questioned by Pilate by Giovanni Canavesio

Painted Chapels of the Nice Hinterland

Scattered in the valleys of the Roya, the Paillon and the Basse-Tinée, many medieval chapels contain superb frescoes designed to teach the Scriptures:

- Coaraze, St-Sébastien
- Lucéram, Notre-Dame-de-Bon-Cœur and St-Grat
- Peillon, Pénitent Chapel
- St-Dalmas-Valdeblore Church
- Venanson, St-Sébastien

There are also several modern successors worthy of note: Matisse in Vence, Cocteau in Villefranche and Tobiasse in Le Cannet.

Jean Baleison, master of the Gothic style. They depict the Four Evangelists (on the vault), the Resurrection of Christ and the Virgin's Assumption (on the walls), each painted in his light, delicate and graceful style. The nave (The Passion) and the inside of the façade (The Last Judgement) was decorated in the same period by the Renaissance Primitive **Giovanni Canavesio** (1420–early 16C), in a dramatic, realist and sombre Gothic-inspired style, revealing both a greater tension and a Renaissance sense of space and perspective. St. Peter is depicted brandishing a large knife and a scimitar during the arrest of Jesus; in the garden of olives, he sleeps lying down (not sitting) and during the denial, he is surprised in the process of warming the soles of his feet; when Jesus prepares to wash them, they remain strangely on the surface of the water. These anomalies may hide a secret pre-Reformation criticism of the papacy (represented by Peter), avid for political and temporal power (knife), attached to its physical comforts (warm feet) and unconcerned by the need for purification (symbolised by water).

ADDRESSES

🏠 STAY

🛏 **Chambre d'hôte Le Pra-Réound** – *On D 43 outside the village after the Maison Adapeï. ☎04 93 04 65 67. Closed late Nov–Feb. 6 rooms.* 🍴. ⌂*6€.* Hikers will appreciate this small refuge with motel-style rooms and terraces facing the peaks.

🛏🛏 **Hôtel Mirval** – *3 rue Ferrier, 4mi/ 6.5km southeast of Tende on D 6204 and D43. ☎04 93 04 63 71. www.lemirval.com. 18 rooms.* 🅿. ⌂*8.50€.* This late-19C mountain inn has functional rooms. The contemporary dining room and veranda overlooking the peaks serve simple regional cuisine.

Tende★

Alpes-Maritimes

Tende (alt. 2,677ft/816m) enjoys a breathtaking alpine setting on the banks of the Roya, beneath the steep rockface of the Riba de Bernou. Along with St-Dalmas, Tende is an ideal starting point for trips to the Vallée des Merveilles (&see Vallée des MERVEILLES overleaf).

SIGHTS
Old Town★

Set in a maze of narrow streets, Tende's houses, many dating from the 15C, are built from local green and purple schist stone. Note the Renaissance bell-towers on the chapels of the Black and White Penitents. A 66ft/20m length of wall is all that is left of the mighty **castle** built by the Lascaris family and dismantled by the French in 1692. The site now affords a **view★** over the village.

Collégiale Notre Dame-de-l'Assomption

This 15C collegiate church was built on the orders of Honoré Lascaris (comte de Tende) from green schist, except for the Lombard tower, which is capped with a small dome. The Renaissance-style **doorway** is flanked by two Doric columns resting on two lions. The inside is divided into three aisles by thick, green-schist columns; the Lascaris lords are buried here.

▶ **Population:** 2,025.

  Michelin Map: 341 G3; region map: pp366–367.

  Info: Ave. 16-Septembre-1947. &04 93 04 73 71. www.tendemerveilles.com. Pôle touristique de Roya-Bévéra. &04 93 04 92 05. www.royabevera.com.

▶ **Location:** The old town huddles below the | château ruins on the left bank of the Roya river. Tende, full of dizzying switchbacks all the way up to its peak, was once part of the Old Salt Road to Cuneo and Turin.

👥 Musée des Merveilles★

Ave. du 16-Septembre-1947, opposite the Customs Office. &🕐*Open Wed–Mon May–mid-Oct 10am–6.30pm; late Oct–Apr 10am–5pm.* 🕐*Closed 12–24 Mar, 13–25 Nov, public holidays.* ⊛*2€.* &*04 93 04 32 50. www.museedes merveilles.com.*

This museum explores the history of the Vallée des Merveilles and its inhabitants through a series of relief maps and models outlining the local geological landscape. An archaeology section, which addresses the beliefs and daily lives of people in the Copper and Bronze Ages, includes castings of the

Tende

© Christian Goupi/age fotostock

Changing Borders

When the comté de Nice became part of France, the Italian King Victor-Emmanuel II managed to keep the upper Roya Valley for his hunting excursions. At the end of the Second World War, the peace treaty with Italy – confirmed on 12 October 1947 by a plebiscite – finally ended this situation and the upper valleys of the Roya, Tinée and Vésubie became part of France, thus naturally aligning the border along the waterways.

famous *chef de tribus* stele, dioramas and displays of objects discovered during local excavations. A final section explores the economic life of the region over the centuries.

EXCURSIONS
St-Dalmas-de-Tende
▶ *3mi/5km south.*
This attractive resort, once the main frontier post on the road linking Nice to Cuneo, is a good jumping-off point for excursions into the **Vallée des Merveilles,** with facilities for cycling, riding, skiing and hiking.

La Brigue★
▶ *4mi/6.5km southeast.*
◉ *See La BRIGUE.*

Granile

▶ 6mi/10km to the south. Head towards Casterino (D 91), turning left after 0.6mi/1km. After 3mi/5km, park just outside the village at Granile.

This seemingly isolated village, surrounded by mountains, is lined with typical houses decorated with wooden balconies and stone slab roofs. There is an impressive **view** of the Gorges de la Roya.

▶ Return to St-Dalmas-de-Tende and continue up the valley.

The apple trees in the meadows contrast with the rock-strewn olive groves in the regions around Sospel and Breil.

ADDRESSES

🍽 STAY

⊜⊜⊜ **Auberge du Mouton Dort** – *28 ave. des Martyr-de-la-Résistance, St-Dalmas-de-Tende, 2.5mi/4km south of Tende on D6204, above the train station.* ☎*04 93 79 18 08. www.lemoutondort.com. 7 rooms.* ⌂ *10€.* This house, perched on a steep slope close to the Italian border, offers simple, well-appointed rooms with purpose-made wooden furniture. Meals are served in the small, simple restaurant attached to the inn.

⊜⊜⊜ **Hôtel Le Prieuré** – *31 rue Jean Médecin, St-Dalmas-de-Tende, 2.5mi/4km south of Tende by D 6204.* ☎*04 93 04 75 70. www.leprieure.org. 24 rooms.* 🅿. ⌂ *8€. Restaurant*⊜⊜. Tastefully restored former priory with large, well-kept rooms decorated with locally-made furniture. The vaulted dining hall opens out onto a pleasant patio. Menu offers Mediterranean cuisine. The terrace overlooks Mont Bego.

SPORT AND LEISURE

Lucien Bérenger – ☎*04 93 04 77 85. www.berengeraventures.com.* Professional mountain guides, abseiling, rock-climbing and canyoning.

Via Ferrata des Comtes de Lacaris – Rope bridges and vertiginous canyon crossings using special mountain-climbing equipment. A short course available *(2.5hr). Map of the course and tickets available at the tourist office.* 🎫*3.50€ (children 12–18 years 1€).*

Skiing – Fans of the slopes can find the nearest ski resorts across the Italian border at Limone *(accessible by train).* Cross-country skiing and snowshoeing can be found in Casterino. *For information, contact the tourist office.*

Vallée des Merveilles★★

Alpes-Maritimes

Lying at the foot of **Mont Bégo** (alt. 9,423ft/2,872m) in a region of glacial lakes, valleys, moraines and rocky cirques dating from the Quaternary period, the Vallée des Merveilles is famous for its thousands of Bronze Age rock engravings.

Access Routes

There are two different ways of getting to the Vallée des Merveilles, although both involve a long hike:

◐ Take the N 204 up the Roya Valley to St-Dalmas-de-Tende, then D 91 to Casterino and follow one of the footpaths:

🔼 *3hr.* Lac des Mesches to the Arpette area and the Refuge des Merveilles.

🔼 *2.5hr.* Casterino refuge to the Fontanalbe refuge and the Fontanalbe district.

◐ From Belvédère to St-Grat (◐ see Vallée de la VÉSUBIE) and the footpath to Pas de l'Arpette.

More than 373mi/600km of marked trails cover the area, including sections of the GR 5 and GR 52A trails, which circle the Mercantour National Park and cross through the Vallée des Merveilles. There are also trails that lead to Authion, Boréon and to the Madone de Fenestre (◐ see VALLÉE de la VÉSUBI and FORÊT de TURINI).
The engravings can be visited from June to September (◐ see Practical Information for guided tour information).

A BIT OF HISTORY

The name Bégo is derived from an Indo-European root, which means the sacred mountain *(Be)*, inhabited by the bull-god *(Go)*.
The region of Mont Bégo is an **open-air museum** comprising more than 40,000 engravings.

⚅ **Michelin Map:** 341 F3/4.

▯ **Info:** Maison du Parc National du Mercantour, àv. Du 16-Septembre-1947, Tende. ℘04 93 04 73 71. www.mercantour.eu. Point d'information estival du Parc national at Castérino. ℘04 93 04 89 79. www.mercantour.eu.

◐ **Location:** The site known as the Vallée des Merveilles consists of seven distinct regions around Mont Bégo: the Vallée des Merveilles itself, which is the largest area; the Vallée de Fontanalbe, which is narrower; the Valmasque, Valaurette, Lac Sainte-Marie, Col du Sabion and Lac Vei del Bouc areas, which contain only a few scattered carvings.

◈ **Don't Miss:** The Bronze Age engravings.

◔ **Timing:** An overnight stay in a refuge is preferable for the Vallée des Merveilles.

Although the engravings were discovered and identified at the end of the 17C, it was not until 1897 that they were studied systematically by the British amateur archaeologist **Clarence Bicknell.** When the region became part of France in 1947, more intensive research was carried out by a team working under Henry de Lumley, who spent 30 years recording every engraving within an area of 30 acres/12ha.
Cut into the rockface worn smooth by glacial erosion 15,000 years ago, the linear engravings date from the Gallo-Roman period through the Middle Ages to the present day. The most interesting ones date back to the early Bronze Age (c. 2,800 BC–1,500 BC).
A stippling technique was used by juxtaposing tiny dots punched into the rockface with flint or quartz tools.

Vallée des Merveilles★★

Finding Your Bearings

The site consists of seven separate sectors radiating out from **Mont Bégo**: the largest site, the **Vallée des Merveilles**, is tucked between the Grand Capelet and Mont Bégo, and contains more than half of the engravings; the smaller **Vallée de Fontanalbe** features around 40 percent of the engravings; lastly the Valmasque, Valaurette, Lac Ste-Marie, Col du Sabion and Lac Vei del Bouc sectors contain only rare, scattered engravings.

The Engravings

There are roughly 40,000 figurative engravings dispersed over 3,700 rocks in the Vallée des Merveilles, at an altitude of 5,500 to 8,500ft/1,700 to 2,600m. Most figures are corniform, consisting of at least a body and a pair of horns (74 percent); the remaining engravings are made up of geometric figures, many divided into sections (15.8 percent), weapons (daggers, halberds and axes) (8.1 percent), and anthropomorphic shapes, mainly divinities (2 percent). The corniform figures have a body (square, rectangular, round and triangular) and an appendage, such as a neck, head, eyes, tongue, hooves or tail. They are often linked by a yoke pulling a shaft attached to a swing plough guided by a small human form. The weapons have been important in dating the site to the Copper and Bronze Ages since many similar objects have been found at nearby archaeological sites, such as triangular daggers fitted to handles and halberds with blades in the form of long perpendicular shafts. The anthropomorphic shapes are often depicted in groups of corniform figures, headless men with zigzag arms, or networked figures. These petroglyphs may correspond to a symbolic language and, along with Sumerian cuneiform (3,300 BC) and the Egyptian hieroglyphics of the Nile Valley (3,200 BC), they are possibly one of man's oldest forms of writing. The consistency of the engraving techniques and the iconographic themes suggest these figures were not produced by chance, but correspond to a conception of the world that was handed down from generation to generation through a graphic code.

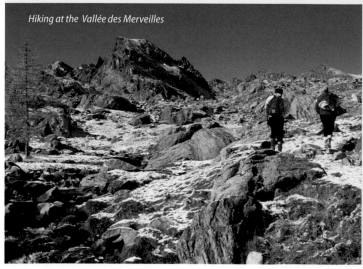

Hiking at the Vallée des Merveilles

© Dominique Lerault/Photononstop

The Magic Mountain

The engravings reveal the preoccupations of the Ligurian people living in the lower valleys 4,800 to 3,500 years ago. The Ligurians believed that Mont Bégo had divine powers and the mountain cult was devoted to the bull god, who symbolised the power of lightning and fertilising rain. Paying homage to the bull god would have been particularly important to these agricultural and pastoral people, who hoped to ensure the continuity of the rain, springs and rivers that watered their crops. The ploughs and harnessed animals suggest

Engravings at Vallée des Merveilles

© Valery Trillaud/age fotostock

agriculture was practiced, while the crisscross patterns may represent parcels of land. Although the more rare human figures have been given names (Christ, the Chieftain, the Dancer, etc.), their exact meaning is not clear. Others are more enigmatic, such as the Tree of Life at Fontanalbe. The most famous engraving, the Wizard, shows what looks like a bearded man with his hands above his head, his palms facing towards us and his fingers spread wide. Although he looks as if he is casting a spell, this is, in fact, the bull god brandishing lightning. Certain original engravings can be seen at the **Musée des Merveilles** in Tende *(see TENDE)*.

Symbol	Legend
▲	Rock engravings
◌	Protected area
····	Boundary of the Parc National du Mercantour

Wolf at Parc National du Mercantour

© Ataglier/Dreamstime.com

Mercantour National Park

Created in 1979, this 170,000 acre/ 68,500ha nature reserve spanning the Alpes-Maritimes and Haute-Provence regions was once part of the hunting grounds of the King of Italy. It is now twinned with the **Parco Naturale Alpi Marittime**, with which it shares a 20.5mi/33km border.

The Mercantour is the only European massif inhabited by three mountain ungulates, or hoofed animals, which thrive in the park's glacial valleys and deep gorges: chamois (some 9,000), mouflons (890) and Alpine ibexes (more than 520). The park's medium-altitude woodland is teeming with stags, deer, hares, stoats and marmots. It also provides an ideal habitat for black grouse, snow partridges and numerous birds of prey, including the short-toed eagle and golden eagle. The **bearded vulture** has been successfully reintroduced to the park and for the first time in France since 1942, wolves have begun breeding in the Massif du Mercantour after crossing from Italy, where they benefit from a protected environment (&see ST-MARTIN-VESUBIE).

 WALKS

VALLÉE DES MERVEILLES

▶ 6mi/10km north of St-Dalmas-de-Tende by D 91. Leave the car at Lac des Mesches.

⊀ *8hr round trip for strong walkers.*
Take the signed footpath *(3hr on foot)* to the Refuge des Merveilles and then to Lac Long, the starting point for a guided tour of the Arpette area *(2hr round trip).* It is possible to spend the night at the refuge *(reservation necessary),* and then the following morning, walk up the Vallée des Merveilles as far as the **Baisse de Valmasque** *(about 2.5hr).* Return by the same route to reach the car park in the late afternoon.

VALLÉE DE FONTANALBE

▶ 7.4mi/12km north of St-Dalmas-de-Tende by D 91. Park in Casterino.
⊀ *5hr round trip. Easier walking than the first hike; ideal for families.*

Start south of Casterino by the information panel *(sign: Fontanalbe),* taking the wooded path west and continuing to the refuge *(about 1hr).* Bear left of the refuge building and continue to **Lac Vert** *(about 45min),* the starting point for self-guided tours of the Sentier du Découverte *(1.5hr round trip).*
For a guided tour of the engravings, continue along the side of the lake to the guides' hut at **Lacs Jumeaux.** By staying overnight at the Fontanalbe refuge it is possible to climb the foothills of Mont Bégo as far as the **Baisse de Fontanalbe** (alt. 8,423ft/2,568m). Continue towards the Valmasque Refuge or return to Casterino by the outward route.

PRACTICAL INFORMATION

Hiking In The Vallée Des Merveilles

Important: these sites are situated at a high altitude (5,429-8,202ft/1,600-2,500m), so certain preparations are advisable: good physical stamina, mountain boots and warm clothing as protection against the cold and rain. Storms are frequent and sometimes violent, so it is wise to listen to the weather forecast. Study the route in advance on Map 1/25 000 – Vallée de la Roya – published by the Conseil Général des Alpes-Maritimes.

Regulations at the Sites

Basic Guidelines: The main regulations are symbolised by the signs shown below *(don't walk on or touch the engravings or use iron-tipped hiking poles)*. Violations of these regulations, if detected by the official park guides, are punishable by heavy fines.

Visiting the Engravings: Although the Bronze Age rock engravings are protected for most of the year by a covering of snow, in recent years they have suffered considerable damage, inflicted intentionally or unintentionally by human visitors. To prevent such defacement the trustees and the officers of the Parc National du Mercantour have limited public access to the Arpette and Fontanalbe sectors only. Visitors may only enter these areas accompanied by the guides, who are on daily duty at the sites throughout the summer season.

For the Vallée des Merveilles – *Depart from the Refuge CAF des Merveilles. Jul–Aug daily 8am, 11am, 1pm, 3pm; Jun and Sept Fri–Mon and public holidays 8am, 1pm.* ⬠*10€. www.vallee-merveilles.com.*

For the Vallée de Fontanalbe – *Open 8am from the Refuge de Fontanalbe, Jul–Aug daily 8am, 11am, 2pm; Jun and Sept Fri–Mon and public holidays 8am, 11am, 2pm.* ⬠*10€. www.vallee-merveilles.com.*

Within the National Park

No domestic animals, no fires, no camping within an hour of the park boundaries and no disposing of waste within the boundaries. Refreshments and accommodation are available from the two refuges. Advance reservation highly recommended.

Official Guides

Merveilles, Gravures & Découvertes – *Harneau de Castérino, St-Dalmas-de-Tende.* ☏*06 86 03 90 13. www.vallee-merveilles.com.* Registered mountain guides approved by the Mercantour National Park for hikes and tours of the engravings.

Destination Merveilles – *10 rue des Mesures, Villeneuve-Loubet.* ☏*04 93 73 09 07. www.destination-merveilles.com.* Organises various outings and hiking tours in the Vallée des Merveilles.

REFUGES

Refuge de Fontanalbe – ☏*04 93 04 89 19. By reservation mid-Jun–mid-Sept. Closed Oct–May.* Accommodation and snacks available on-site. Reserve well in advance in season.

Refuge des Merveilles – ☏*04 93 04 64 64. www.cafresa.org (online reservations). Open mid-Jun–Sept; off season* ☏*04 93 04 88 90 or 06 27 00 59 44.* Accommodation and half-board on-site. Advanced reservation required.

INDEX

INDEX

INDEX

INDEX

INDEX

INDEX

INDEX

Z

W

Walking Tours

INDEX

🏨 STAY

🍽 EAT

MAP LEGEND

	Sight	**Seaside resort**	**Winter sports resort**	**Spa**
Highly recommended ★★★		☆☆☆	✳✳✳	♯♯♯
Recommended ★★		☆☆	✳✳	♯♯
Interesting ★		☆	✳	♯

Additional symbols

🛈	Tourist information
═══ ═══	Motorway or other primary route
❶ ❶	Junction: complete, limited
▭═══ ═══	Pedestrian street
⊥≡≡≡≡⊥	Unsuitable for traffic, street subject to restrictions
▥▥▥ - - - -	Steps – Footpath
🚆 🚉	Train station – Auto-train station
🚌 S.N.C.F.	Coach (bus) station
─────┼────	Tram
⌂	Metro, underground
P R	Park-and-Ride
♿	Access for the disabled
✉	Post office
☎	Telephone
⊠	Covered market
⁕✕⁕	Barracks
⚠	Drawbridge
∪	Quarry
✕	Mine
B **F**	Car ferry (river or lake)
🚢	Ferry service: cars and passengers
🚤	Foot passengers only
③	Access route number common to Michelin maps and town plans
Bert (R.)...	Main shopping street
AZ B	Map co-ordinates

Selected monuments and sights

◉ ⟹	Tour - Departure point
⛪ ✝	Catholic church
⛪ ✝	Protestant church, other temple
✡ ⊡ 🕌	Synagogue - Mosque
▤	Building
▪	Statue, small building
✝	Calvary, wayside cross
◎	Fountain
●─●─■►	Rampart - Tower - Gate
⋈	Château, castle, historic house
∴	Ruins
⌣	Dam
✿	Factory, power plant
☆	Fort
∩	Cave
▣	Troglodyte dwelling
⋔	Prehistoric site
▼	Viewing table
Ⓦ	Viewpoint
▲	Other place of interest

Abbreviations

A Agricultural office
(Chambre d'agriculture)

C Chamber of Commerce
(Chambre de commerce)

H Town hall (Hôtel de ville)

J Law courts (Palais de justice)

M Museum (Musée)

P Local authority offices
(Préfecture, sous-préfecture)

POL. Police station (Police)

🛡 Police station (Gendarmerie)

T Theatre (Théâtre)

U University (Université)

Sports and recreation

🏇 Racecourse

⛸ Skating rink

🏊 🏊 Outdoor, indoor swimming pool

🎥 Multiplex Cinema

⛵ Marina, sailing centre

⛺ Trail refuge hut

▫━■━■━▫ Cable cars, gondolas

▫━┼┼┼┼┼━▫ Funicular, rack railway

🚂 Tourist train

◈ Recreation area, park

🎢 Theme, amusement park

🐂 Wildlife park, zoo

⊛ Gardens, park, arboretum

COMPANION PUBLICATIONS

REGIONAL AND LOCAL MAPS

To make the most of your journey, travel with Michelin maps at a scale of 1:200 000: **Regional maps nos. 513, 518 and 519** and the local maps, which are illustrated on the map of France opposite.

MAPS OF FRANCE

And remember to travel with the latest edition of the **map of France no. 721**, which gives an overall view of the region of the Châteaux of the Loire, and the main access roads that connect it to the rest of France. The entire country is mapped at a 1:1 000 000 scale and clearly shows the main road network. Convenient Atlas formats (spiral, hard cover and "mini") are also available.

INTERNET

Michelin is pleased to offer a route-planning service on the Internet: **www.travel.viamichelin.com www.viamichelin.com** Choose the shortest route, a route without tolls, or the Michelin recommended route to your destination; you can also access information about hotels and restaurants from *The Michelin Guide*, and tourists sights from *The Green Guide*. There are a number of useful maps and plans in the guide, listed in the Map Legend.

The Michelin Adventure

It all started with rubber balls! This was the product made by a small company based in Clermont-Ferrand that André and Edouard Michelin inherited, back in 1880. The brothers quickly saw the potential for a new means of transport and their first success was the invention of detachable pneumatic tires for bicycles. However, the automobile was to provide the greatest scope for their creative talents. Throughout the 20th century, Michelin never ceased developing and creating ever more reliable and high-performance tires, not only for vehicles ranging from trucks to F1 but also for underground transit systems and airplanes.

From early on, Michelin provided its customers with tools and services to facilitate mobility and make traveling a more pleasurable and more frequent experience. As early as 1900, the Michelin Guide supplied motorists with a host of useful information related to vehicle maintenance, accommodation and restaurants, and was to become a benchmark for good food. At the same time, the Travel Information Bureau offered travelers personalised tips and itineraries.

The publication of the first collection of roadmaps, in 1910, was an instant hit! In 1926, the first regional guide to France was published, devoted to the principal sites of Brittany, and before long each region of France had its own Green Guide. The collection was later extended to more far-flung destinations, including New York in 1968 and Taiwan in 2011.

In the 21st century, with the growth of digital technology, the challenge for Michelin maps and guides is to continue to develop alongside the company's tire activities. Now, as before, Michelin is committed to improving the mobility of travelers.

MICHELIN TODAY

WORLD NUMBER ONE TIRE MANUFACTURER
- 70 production sites in 18 countries
- 111,000 employees from all cultures and on every continent
- 6,000 people employed in research and development

Moving
for a world

Moving forward means developing tires with better road grip and shorter braking distances, whatever the state of the road.

CORRECT TIRE PRESSURE

RIGHT PRESSURE

- Safety
- Longevity
- Optimum fuel consumption

-0,5 bar

- Durability reduced by 20% (- 8,000 km)

-1 bar

- Risk of blowouts
- Increased fuel consumption
- Longer braking distances on wet surfaces

forward together
where mobility is safer

It also involves helping motorists take care of their safety and their tires. To do so, Michelin organises "Fill Up With Air" campaigns all over the world to remind us that correct tire pressure is vital.

WEAR

DETECTING TIRE WEAR

The legal minimum depth of tire tread is 1.6mm. Tire manufacturers equip their tires with tread wear indicators, which are small blocks of rubber moulded into the base of the main grooves at a depth of 1.6mm.

Tires are the only point of contact between the vehicle and road.

The photo below shows the actual contact zone.

NEW TIRE

WORN TIRE
(1,6 mm tread)

If the tread depth is less than 1.6mm, tires are considered to be worn and dangerous on wet surfaces.

Moving forward
means sustainable mobility

By 2050, Michelin aims to cut the quantity of raw materials used in its tire manufacturing process by half and to have developed renewable energy in its facilities. The design of MICHELIN tires has already saved billions of litres of fuel and, by extension, billions of tons of CO2.

Similarly, Michelin prints its maps and guides on paper produced from sustainably managed forests and is diversifying its publishing media by offering digital solutions to make traveling easier, more fuel efficient and more enjoyable!

The group's whole-hearted commitment to eco-design on a daily basis is demonstrated by ISO 14001 certification.

Like you, Michelin is committed to preserving our planet.